The Smartest Guys
in the Room

The Smartest Guys in the Room

THE AMAZING RISE AND SCANDALOUS FALL OF ENRON

Bethany McLean

AND

Peter Elkind

VIKING
an imprint of
PENGUIN BOOKS

VIKING

Published by the Penguin Group
Penguin Books Ltd, 80 Strand, London WC2R 0RL, England
Penguin Group (USA), Inc., 375 Hudson Street, New York, New York 10014, USA
Penguin Books Australia Ltd, 250 Camberwell Road, Camberwell, Victoria 3124, Australia
Penguin Books Canada Ltd, 10 Alcorn Avenue, Toronto, Ontario, Canada M4V 3B2
Penguin Books India (P) Ltd, 11 Community Centre, Panchsheel Park, New Delhi - 110 017, India
Penguin Books (NZ) Ltd, Cnr Rosedale and Airborne Roads, Albany, Auckland, New Zealand
Penguin Books (South Africa) (Pty) Ltd, 24 Sturdee Avenue, Rosebank 2196, South Africa

Penguin Books Ltd, Registered Offices: 80 Strand, London WC2R 0RL, England

www.penguin.com

First published in the United States of America by Portfolio 2003
First published in Great Britain by Viking 2003
1

Copyright © Fortune, a division of Time Inc., 2003

Photographs courtesy of *Fortune*

Grateful acknowledgement is made for permission to reprint the following copyrighted works:
 "Hotel Kenneth Layla" by James A. Hecker, © 1995 James A. Hecker.
Used with permission; "Perfect Day" by Tim James and Antonina Armato, © 2001 WB Music Corp.,
 Out of the Desert Music, and Tom Sturges Music o/b/o Antonina Songs.
All rights reserved. Used by permission of Warner Bros. Publications U.S. Inc. and Tom Sturges Music.

The moral rights of the authors have been asserted

All rights reserved.
Without limiting the rights under copyright
reserved above, no part of this publication may be
reproduced, stored in or introduced into a retrieval system,
or transmitted, in any form or by any means (electronic, mechanical,
photocopying, recording or otherwise), without the prior
written permission of both the copyright owner and
the above publisher of this book

Printed in Great Britain by Clays Ltd, St Ives plc

A CIP catalogue record for this book is available from the British Library

ISBN 0-670-913715

For Chris

—B.M.

For Laura

—P.E.

AUTHORS' NOTES AND ACKNOWLEDGMENTS

Enron is well on its way to becoming the most intensively dissected company in the history of American business. This book is published as that process continues, with investigations and litigation that will surely drag on for years. Because our aim has been to chronicle the company's rise and fall—amazing and scandalous indeed—we have deliberately ended our narrative with Enron's filing of the largest bankruptcy case in U.S. history. We leave it to others to describe the resulting investigations and trials, as well as the jockeying over Enron's spoiling remains.

Enron's story is a sprawling tale, and, during the 16 months of intensive reporting that produced this book, it has taken us down many trails. A good portion of our work involved poring through a mountain of public and private documents involving Enron and the colorful cast of players—executives, bankers, auditors, lawyers, investors, and analysts—who appear in these pages. We have reviewed divorce records, executive calendars, personnel files, court records, depositions, personal e-mails, letters, consultants' studies, internal memos and presentations, board minutes, SEC filings, congressional testimony, and dozens of reports from Wall Street analysts. This massive written record, much of it contemporaneous with what we describe, has provided an extraordinary window into events involving Enron.

Ultimately, though, this is a story about people. We believe we have gained considerable insight into the thinking and behavior of virtually every major character in this book. We have conducted hundreds of interviews with people who worked at every level of the company, from the fiftieth-floor executive suite to the board of directors to the secretarial pool, in addition to scores of others who worked outside Enron. Yet for an assortment of understandable reasons—in some cases, involving the continuing criminal investigations; in other cases, involving the stigma that results from any association with Enron—many of those who spoke to us insisted on talking on "background" only. Under this arrangement, the information provided was on the record—we could use it freely—but we could not identify the source by name. This allowed many sources who would otherwise have been constrained to speak openly to us. On occasion, with those who saw themselves as likely government targets, facing possible surveillance, our arrangements assumed a cloak-and-dagger quality, with clandestine meetings arranged through coded messages. A few other individuals discussed events in great detail but only through trusted personal surrogates. The result is a book that relies, in considerable part, on unnamed sources.

We are exceedingly grateful for the cooperation, trust, and patience of all those (both named and unnamed) who spoke with us—in more than a few cases, a dozen times or more. Their participation in this project was an act of faith, and their insight has been invaluable.

■   ■   ■

This book was made possible through the support of *Fortune* magazine. The idea for it took hold shortly after Enron filed for bankruptcy, when we realized that there was an extraordinary and compelling business narrative in the company's downfall and that we wanted to tell that story. We also realized something else: piecing together the fall of Enron was going to be an unusually challenging reporting task. For the reasons discussed above, many of the principals were hardly in a position to talk publicly about their experience; Enron's financial machinations were also complicated, requiring considerable time and effort to understand—and then to explain.

What made our work manageable was the active involvement of Joseph Nocera, editorial director for the magazine. He served as impresario for this project, guiding us as we did our reporting, then acting as editor extraordinaire once we started writing. He is a true partner in the creation of this book; we are grateful to his wife, Julie Rose, too, who lived through the challenging times of this endeavor along with the rest of us.

Rik Kirkland, *Fortune*'s managing editor, allowed us to dedicate a year and a half to this project and never wavered from his strong and vocal support. Jeff Birnbaum tapped into his wealth of Washington sources, landing key interviews and pulling together the Washington angles to the Enron story. Colleagues Carol Loomis, Carrie Welch, Laury Frieber, Pattie Sellers, Tim Smith, David Rynecki, David Kirkpatrick, and John Helyar were generous with their advice and wisdom. Brian O'Reilly shared the extensive interviews he conducted with Enron executives for his story, "The Power Merchants," published in *Fortune*'s April 17, 2000, issue. We received valuable reporting aid from former *Fortune* reporter Suzanne Koudsi. The Time Inc. Business Research Center, especially Doris Burke and Patricia Neering, provided fabulous research help. Arlene Lewis Bascom kept track of the book's finances. Alix Colow pulled together the photos. Former Assistant Managing Editor James Impoco edited the original Enron story in *Fortune* written by coauthor McLean and was there with an encouraging word when we most needed it. Time Inc. editor in chief Norman Pearlstine and editorial director John Huey gave their blessing to this project. We hope the result justifies so much faith in us from so many.

We are appreciative of our many colleagues in journalism who broke fresh ground in reporting on Enron, notably *Forbes*'s Toni Mack, who was asking tough questions back in 1993 and was generous with her friendship and counsel a decade later; freelance writer Harry Hurt; *Texas Monthly*'s Mimi Swartz; Delroy Alexander, Greg Burns, Robert Manor, Flynn McRoberts, and E. A. Torriero of the *Chicago Tribune*, for their excellent four-part series on the fall of Arthur Andersen; Peter Behr and April Witt, for their early five-part series on the demise of Enron in the *Washington Post*; and the *Houston Chronicle*'s Tom Fowler and Mary Flood, who overcame the hometown paper's coziness with Enron's hierarchy to dig into the story. University of San Diego law professor and author Frank Partnoy offered early insights into Enron that were very helpful. The work of *Wall Street Journal* reporters Rebecca Smith and John Emshwiller made them players in the Enron tale. In the postbankruptcy period, the *New York Times*, led by Kurt Eichenwald, blanketed the story, covering dozens of angles. We also want to acknowledge the work and generous encouragement of *Times* business writer David Barboza and Washington correspondent Rich Oppel.

Amid much finger pointing in the nation's capital, several congressional committees did yeoman work. The U.S. Senate's Permanent Subcommittee on Investigations, through its detailed reports and hearings on Enron's incestuous relationship with commercial and investment banks, shed considerable light on dark corners of the Enron tale. We are grateful for the assistance of the committee and its staff, including Elise Bean, Robert Roach, and Mary Robertson. The Senate Committee on Governmental Affairs produced enlightening work on the watchdogs that didn't bark—government regulators, Wall Street analysts, and credit agencies.

Our stalwart agent, Liz Darhansoff, served as a fierce negotiator, sage critic, and fervent advocate. Our editor, Adrian Zackheim, instantly understood how a complex business story could make a gripping tale and was with us all the way. We'd also like to thank Will Weisser, Mark Ippoliti, Alex Gigante, David Hawkins, and Bonnie Soodek.

Finally, we owe our greatest debt to our loved ones.

Bethany's parents, Helaine and Robert McLean, while far removed from the specifics of Enron, added their wisdom to the age-old human elements of the story. Her sister Claire McLean offered constant words of encouragement and perfect company for the occasional shoe-shopping break. Bethany's husband, Chris Wilford, kept a glass (or two) of wine waiting long into the night. And Barolo provided a constant reminder of what it really means to be a bulldog.

David Elkind, Ellen Duncan, and Mary Clare Ward aided this project in untold ways. Laura Elkind, Peter's wife, did double duty, offering insightful editorial suggestions and tending bravely to the home front (Stephen, Landon, George, Adele, and Sam) while enduring long absences and late nights of writing with remarkable patience, support, and grace.

To all of them, we are especially grateful.

—Bethany McLean and Peter Elkind
July 2003

CONTENTS

CAST OF CHARACTERS

Ken Lay—Founder, chairman, and CEO of Enron.
Jeff Skilling—President and chief operating officer. Served as CEO from February to August 2001.
Andrew Fastow—Chief financial officer.
Rebecca Mark—CEO of Enron International and later of Azurix.

Jim Alexander—CFO of Enron Global Power and Pipelines (EPP).
John Arnold—Enron's young trading superstar.
Ron Astin—Vinson & Elkins lawyer.
Cliff Baxter—Jeff Skilling's chief deal maker and trusted confidant. Briefly served as CEO of Enron North America.
Tim Belden—West Coast power trader who figured out how to game the California market.
Arthur and Robert Belfer—father-son Enron directors and New York–based investors.
Louis Borget—CEO of Enron Oil. Went to jail as a result of Enron Oil scandal.
Ray Bowen—Enron finance executive. Became treasurer after Ben Glisan was fired.
Ron Burns—Former CEO of Enron's pipeline division. Briefly co-CEO with Skilling of Enron Capital and Trade Resources (ECT).
Rick Buy—Head of Risk Assessment and Control division (RAC).
Rebecca Carter—Enron's corporate secretary and Skilling's second wife.
Rick Causey—Chief accounting officer.
Margaret Ceconi—Former GE manager who joined Enron Energy Services (EES). Later tried to blow the whistle.
David Cox—Enron Broadband Services' chief deal maker.
Wanda Curry—Enron accountant who dug up problems at EES.
Dave Delainey—Executive who took over EES from Lou Pai.
Jim Derrick—Enron's general counsel.
Joseph Dilg—Vinson & Elkins lawyer.

Bill Dodson—Michael Kopper's domestic partner.

John Duncan—Enron director and chairman of the board's executive committee. Gave Lay his first job as CEO.

Jim Fallon—Trading executive who took over Broadband after Ken Rice left.

Lea Fastow—Andy Fastow's wife and former assistant treasurer at Enron.

Mark Frevert—Longtime Enron executive. Became vice chairman in the last months.

Ben Glisan—Fastow's structured-finance accounting whiz. Became Enron treasurer.

Wendy Gramm—Enron director and former chairman of the Commodities Futures Trading Commission. Wife of U.S. Senator Phil Gramm of Texas.

Rod Gray—Rebecca Mark aide. Worked at both Enron International and Azurix.

Mark Haedicke—General counsel, Enron North America.

Gary Hamel—Management guru who touted Enron.

Kevin Hannon—Former Bankers Trust employee who became Ken Rice's deputy at Enron North America and Enron Broadband.

John Harding and Steve Sulentic—Louis Borget's direct superiors at Enron during Enron Oil scandal.

Joe Hirko—Former Portland General CFO who served as co-CEO of Enron Broadband with Rice.

Forrest Hoglund—CEO of Enron Oil and Gas.

Kevin Howard—Enron Broadband finance executive who worked on Project Braveheart.

Ron Hulme—Lead McKinsey & Company partner on the Enron account.

Robert Jaedicke—Enron director, and chairman of the audit committee. Former dean of the Stanford Graduate School of Business.

Vince Kaminski—Head of Enron's Research Group. In-house skeptic of Fastow's deals.

Bob Kelly—John Wing deputy.

Rich Kinder—President and chief operating officer before Skilling. Left to start Kinder Morgan.

Louise Kitchen—Trading executive who implemented idea for Enron Online.

Mark Koenig—Enron's head of investor relations.

Michael Kopper—Fastow's top deputy and investor in Chewco partnership. Later left Enron to run Fastow's LJM partnerships.

Mike Krautz—Enron Broadband finance executive who worked on Project Braveheart.

John Lavorato—Greg Whalley deputy. Later became head of trading in North America.

Judith Lay—Lay's first wife.

Linda Lay—Lay's former secretary and second wife.

Mark Lay—Lay's son, who worked for the company and later joined a company that did business with Enron.

Robyn Lay—Lay's stepdaughter, who once had an Enron jet deliver her bed to Monaco.

Sharon Lay—Lay's sister, whose Houston travel agency got most of its business from Enron.

Charles LeMaistre—Enron director and chairman of board compensation committee. Former president of the University of Texas M. D. Anderson Cancer Center.

Kathy Lynn—Worked for Fastow at Global Finance. Later employed by Fastow's LJM partnerships. Investor in Fastow deal.

Kevin McConville—Head of Enron's Industrial Group. Every deal his group made went sour.

William McLucas—Wilmer, Cutler & Pickering lawyer, special counsel to Enron.

Jeff McMahon—Enron's corporate treasurer until replaced by Glisan. Became CFO after Fastow was fired.

Nancy McNeil—Lay's secretary and Kinder's second wife.

Amanda Martin—Enron executive who later joined Azurix.

Thomas Mastroeni—Treasurer of Enron Oil under Borget. Pled guilty in the Enron Oil scandal.

R. Davis Maxey—Masterminded Enron tax-avoidance schemes.

Jordan Mintz—General counsel for Fastow's Global Finance division. Pressured Fastow to give up the partnerships.

Kristina Mordaunt—In-house lawyer, served as general counsel of Global Finance and Broadband division. Made $1 million on a $5,800 investment in one of Fastow's deals.

Mike Muckleroy—Executive who bailed out the company during the Enron Oil scandal.

Cindy Olson—Head of human resources.

Lou Pai—Skilling lieutenant who headed early trading operation. Later CEO of EES.

Mark Palmer—Enron's head of corporate communications.

Anne Yaeger Patel—Global Finance employee who left to work for the LJM partnerships. Investor in Fastow deal.

Ken Rice—Key member of Skilling's inner circle. CEO of Enron Wholesale and, later, Enron Broadband Services.

Richard Sanders—Head of litigation for Enron North America.

Mick Seidl—Enron president during Enron Oil scandal.

John Sherriff—Whalley deputy and head of Enron Europe.

Susan Skilling—Jeff Skilling's first wife.

Joe Sutton—Rebecca Mark's longtime deputy. Took over Enron International after she left.

Beth Tilney—Enron executive and Lay confidante. Married to Merrill Lynch investment banker Schuyler Tilney.

John Urquhart—Enron director. Former executive vice president at General Electric.

Lord John Wakeham—Enron director and former British secretary of state for energy. As government official, approved Teesside.

Pinkney Walker—economics professor at the University of Missouri. Lay's first mentor.

Charls Walker—Enron director and top Washington lobbyist. Pinkney Walker's brother.

Chris Wasden—Azurix executive.

Sherron Watkins—Global Finance executive. Wrote whistle-blowing letter to Ken Lay.

Greg Whalley—Head of the trading operation in late 1990s. Became president and COO after Skilling resigned.

General Tom White—Enron international executive. Later Pai's number two at EES. Became secretary of the army in the George W. Bush administration.

John Wing—Launched Enron's international business. Built Teesside.

Herbert (Pug) Winokur—Enron director, former Pentagon official.

David Woytek—Enron auditor during Enron Oil scandal.

THE ACCOUNTANTS

Carl Bass—member of Andersen's Professional Standards Group. Chief Enron skeptic in the firm.

Joseph Berardino—CEO of Arthur Andersen.

David Duncan—Lead Arthur Andersen partner on the Enron account.

James Hecker—Andersen partner who penned "Hotel Kenneth-Lay-a."

John Stewart—Head of Andersen's Professional Standards Group.

Nancy Temple—Andersen lawyer.

WALL STREET AND THE BANKS

Ron Barone—Analyst for PaineWebber and later UBS Warburg.

Dan Bayly—Merrill Lynch's global head of investment banking.

David Bermingham, Giles Darby, and Gary Mulgrew—NatWest bankers who allegedly conspired with Fastow to steal millions that belonged to the bank.

Jim Chanos—Short seller who runs the hedge fund Kynikos Associates. Early short seller of Enron stock.

Carol Coale—Prudential analyst. Viewed as authoritative voice on Enron.

Donato Eassey—Analyst with Merrill Lynch. Replaced John Olson after he was fired.

Anatol Feygin—J. P. Morgan Chase analyst.

David Fleischer—Goldman Sachs analyst.

Robert Furst—Merrill banker who worked with Schuyler Tilney.

Scott Gieselman—Goldman Sachs investment banker.

Rick Gordon—Head of Merrill Lynch's energy investment banking group.

Richard Gross—Analyst with Lehman Brothers.

Richard Grubman—Short seller who runs the hedge fund Highfields Capital Management. Early short seller of Enron stock.

Curt Launer—Enron-friendly analyst with Donaldson, Lufkin & Jenrette and, later, Credit Suisse First Boston.

James (Jimmy) Lee—Head of investment banking at Chase Manhattan Bank. Named vice chairman when Chase bought J. P. Morgan.

Andre Meade—Commerzbank analyst.

Ray Niles—Analyst with Schroder & Company and later Citigroup.

John Olson—Analyst with Sanders Morris Harris. Longtime Enron skeptic.

Mark Roberts—Short seller who operates a firm called Off Wall Street.

Robert Rubin—Member of the office of the chairman of Citigroup. Former treasury secretary in the Clinton adminstration.

Marc Shapiro—Vice chairman of finance and risk management at Chase Manhattan Bank. After the merger of J. P. Morgan and Chase, became a vice chairman of J. P. Morgan Chase. Longtime acquaintance of Lay's.

Schuyler Tilney—Merrill Lynch investment banker. Firm's primary contact with Enron and Andrew Fastow.

Rick Walker—Chase Manhattan (later J. P. Morgan Chase) banker, served as key contact with Enron.

THE JOURNALISTS

Peter Eavis—Reporter for Thestreet.com.

John Emshwiller and Rebecca Smith—*Wall Street Journal* reporters who exposed Fastow's partnerships in October 2001.

Harry Hurt III—Wrote skeptical 1996 story about Enron for *Fortune.*

Toni Mack—Wrote skeptical 1993 story about Enron for *Forbes.*

Jonathan Weil—*Wall Street Journal* reporter who raised question about mark-to-market accounting in September 2000.

THE ACQUIRERS

Chuck Watson—CEO of Dynegy, Enron's crosstown rival.

Steve Bergstrom—President of Dynegy.

RESPECT: We treat others as we would like to be treated ourselves. We do not tolerate abusive or disrespectful treatment. Ruthlessness, callousness, and arrogance don't belong here.

INTEGRITY: We work with customers and prospects openly, honestly, and sincerely. When we say we will do something, we will do it; when we say we cannot or will not do something, then we won't do it.

COMMUNICATION: We have an obligation to communicate. Here, we take the time to talk with one another . . . and to listen. We believe that information is meant to move and that information moves people.

EXCELLENCE: We are satisfied with nothing less than the very best in everything we do. We will continue to raise the bar for everyone. The great fun here will be for all of us to discover just how good we can really be.

—From Enron's 1998 Annual Report

On a cool Texas night in late January, Cliff Baxter slipped out of bed. He stuffed pillows under the covers so his sleeping wife wouldn't notice he was gone. Then he stepped quietly through his large suburban Houston home, taking care not to awaken his two children. The door alarm didn't make a sound as he entered the garage; he'd disabled the security system before turning in. Then, dressed in blue jogging slacks, a blue T-shirt, and moccasin slippers, he climbed into his new black Mercedes-Benz S500 and drove out into the night.

At 43, John Clifford Baxter, the son of a Long Island policeman, had made it big in Texas. Before quitting his job eight months earlier, he had served as vice chairman of a great American corporation, capping a decade-long career as the company's top deal maker. Baxter was rich, too—thanks to a generous helping of stock options, a millionaire many times over. But as he cruised the empty streets of Sugar Land, Texas, Baxter was drowning in dark thoughts. Always given to mood swings, he had become deeply depressed in recent days, consumed by the spectacular scandal that had engulfed his old company.

Everyone seemed to be after him. A congressional committee had already called; the FBI and SEC would surely be next. *Would he have to testify against his friends?* The plaintiffs' lawyers had named him as a defendant in a huge securities-fraud suit. Baxter was convinced they were having him tailed—and rummaging through his family's trash. Then there was the media, pestering him at home a dozen or more times a day: *Did he know what had gone wrong? How could America's seventh-biggest company just blow up? Where had the billions gone?* No one, at this early stage, viewed Baxter as a major player in the company's crash. Yet he took it all personally. In phone calls and visits with friends, he railed for hours about the scandal's taint. It's as if "they're calling us child molesters," he complained. "That will never wash off."

Desperate to get away, he'd spent part of the previous week sailing in the Florida Keys. Sailing was one of Baxter's passions. For years, he'd decompressed floating on Galveston Bay aboard his 72-foot yacht, *Tranquility Base*. But he'd sold the boat several months earlier. When Baxter returned from Florida, his doctor prescribed antidepressants and sleeping pills and told him to see a psychiatrist. He'd called the shrink's office that day to make an appointment.

But when the receptionist explained that the schedule was booked until February, Baxter hung up—he wasn't going to wait that long.

Less than 48 hours later, at about 2:20 A.M. on January 25, 2002, Baxter stopped his Mercedes on Palm Royale Boulevard, a mile and a half from his home. It was cloudy and a bit chilly that evening by Texas standards—about 48 degrees—but the sedan was tuned to an interior temperature of precisely 79. An open package of Newport Lights sat in the center console, a bottle of Evian water in the cup holder. Baxter's black leather wallet lay on the passenger seat. Baxter parked the car in the middle of the street, with the doors locked, the engine running, and the headlights burning. Then he lifted a silver .357 Magnum revolver to his right temple and fired a bullet into his head.

Seven days later, Cliff Baxter's friends from Enron gathered to mourn. The Houston energy giant's collapse into bankruptcy had already become the biggest scandal of the new century. Baxter's death had stoked the media bonfire and tossed a fresh element of tragedy into a bubbling stewpot of intrigue. Enron's influence ranged widely—from Wall Street to the White House. So feared was this company, so powerful were its connections, so much was at stake that there was open speculation Baxter had actually been murdered—the target of a carefully staged hit, aimed at silencing him from spilling Enron's darkest secrets. The rumblings had forced the Sugar Land police department to treat an open-and-shut case—Baxter had even left a suicide note in his wife's car—like a capital-murder investigation, requiring DNA testing, handwriting experts, ballistics studies, and blood-spatter tests.

The Texas memorial service took place after Baxter was buried in a private ceremony in his hometown on Long Island. He was laid to rest in a plot he had secretly purchased there just a few weeks earlier, in the throes of his deepening funk. An Enron corporate jet—a remaining vestige of the company's imperial ways—flew Cliff's family and a few others east for the funeral.

Now it was Houston's turn. The precise location of the service—the ballroom of the St. Regis, the city's swankiest hotel—remained a secret until noon that day, at the insistence of Carol Baxter. Cliff's widow was bent on avoiding the press. She blamed reporters' intrusions for pushing her husband over the edge. So the 100 hand-picked guests who pulled up to the valet-parking station on this Friday afternoon had been summoned by furtive phone calls just two hours earlier.

For 90 minutes, those who knew Baxter—family members, fellow "boat people" from his beloved yacht club, and Enron friends—heard warm stories about his gentler side. There were images of Cliff with his family, Cliff sailing, Cliff fronting his rock band. Baxter was a gifted musician. When police found his body, there were two guitar picks in his wallet. Everyone left the service with a compact disc of his favorite songs, prepared with the help of J. C. Baxter, Cliff's

16-year-old son. The opening track was perhaps Cliff's favorite: a bouncy pop tune called "Perfect Day."

> *On this perfect day*
> *Nothing's standing in my way*
> *On this perfect day*
> *Nothing can go wrong*
> *It's a perfect day*
> *Tomorrow's gonna come too soon*
> *I could stay*
> *Forever as I am*
> *On this perfect day*

It was a tragedy layered on tragedy, but there wasn't much talk about the company's Icarus-like fall among the former Enron executives thrust together again that afternoon. This wasn't the time for such grim shoptalk; what's more, their lawyers had pointedly instructed them to avoid such conversations. Ken Lay, Enron's founding father, was conspicuously absent. At the insistence of the company's creditors, he had finally yielded his job as CEO and chairman just two days before Baxter's death; Lay sent his wife, Linda, to attend the service instead. Enron's deposed chief financial officer, a onetime whiz kid named Andrew Fastow, was missing, too; he and Baxter had fought bitterly.

But former chief executive officer Jeffrey Skilling—once touted as a brilliant visionary and the man who shaped Enron in his own image—was very much in evidence. Baxter had been his closest confidant at Enron, the nearest thing Skilling, who kept his own counsel, had to a sounding board. Widely feared during his reign at Enron, known for his unflinchingly Darwinist view of the world, Skilling spent the service in tears.

In the months after Cliff Baxter's memorial service, Jeff Skilling could often be found in an otherwise empty hole-in-the-wall Houston bar called Muldoon's, downing glasses of white wine. A short, fit man of 48 with slicked-back hair and cool blue eyes, Skilling typically appeared in faded jeans, a white T-shirt, and a two-day growth of beard. This is where he came to brood over what had happened at Enron—often for hours at a time.

More than anyone else, Skilling had come to personify the Enron scandal. Part of it was his audacious refusal, in the face of a dozen separate investigations, to run for cover. Alone among Enron's top executives summoned before a circuslike series of congressional hearings, Skilling had ignored his lawyers' advice to take the Fifth and defiantly spoken his piece. The legislators were convinced that Skilling had abruptly resigned as CEO of the company—just four months before Enron went belly up—because he knew the game was over. But Skilling wouldn't have any of it. At the time he quit, he insisted, he believed Enron was "in great shape"; he had left for "personal reasons." The nationally televised testimony was vintage Skilling: articulate, unapologetic, and prickly. He didn't hesitate to lecture, even scold, U.S. senators.

"Enron was a great company," Skilling repeatedly declared. And indeed that's how it seemed almost until the moment it filed the largest bankruptcy claim in U.S. history. *Fortune* magazine named it "America's most innovative company" six years running. Washington luminaries like Henry Kissinger and James Baker were on its lobbying payroll. Nobel laureate Nelson Mandela came to Houston to receive the Enron Prize. The president of the United States called Enron chairman Lay "Kenny Boy." Enron had transformed the way gas and electricity flowed across the United States. And it had bankrolled audacious projects around the globe: state-of-the-art power plants in third world countries, a pipeline slicing through an endangered Brazilian forest, a steel mill on the coast of Thailand.

As Skilling saw it, Enron had fallen victim to a cabal of short sellers and scoop-hungry reporters that triggered a classic run on the bank. Privately, he would grudgingly acknowledge occasional business mistakes—including one, the failure of Enron's broadband venture, that cost the company more than $1 billion. Yet Skilling remained remarkably unwilling to accept any personal responsibility for the company's demise. "You're not going to find one memo where Skilling said, 'Fuck with the numbers,' " he told a friend. "It isn't there." He was reluctant even to pronounce judgment on Fastow, his handpicked finance chief, who—the U.S. Justice Department alleged—had not just done a lousy job as CFO but stolen millions and collected kickbacks right under Skilling's nose. What happened to Enron, Skilling insisted, was part of the brutal cycle of business life. "Shit happens," he liked to say. Enron was a *victim*.

Unfortunately for Skilling, no one else believed that. Enron, which once aspired to be known as "the world's greatest company," became a different kind of symbol—shorthand for all that was wrong with corporate America. Its bankruptcy marked not merely the death of a company but the end of an era. Enron's failure resonated powerfully because the entire company stood revealed as a sort of wonderland, where little was as it seemed. Rarely has there ever been such a chasm between corporate illusion and reality. The public scrutiny Enron triggered exposed more epic business scandals—tales of cooked books and excess at companies like Tyco, WorldCom, and Adelphia. Enron's wash swamped the entire U.S. energy industry, wiping out hundreds of billions in stock value. It destroyed the nation's most venerable accounting firm, Arthur Andersen. And it exposed holes in our patchwork system of business oversight—shocking lapses by government regulators, auditors, banks, lawyers, Wall Street analysts, and credit agencies—shaking faith in U.S. financial markets.

Yet Skilling continued to plead his case with a compelling arrogance. At different times, before different audiences, he could be self-righteous, self-pitying, sarcastic, profane, even naive. Sometimes, he was all of these things at once. Periodically, he'd launch into an extended rant: about the media, about politicians, about the aggressive tactics of government prosecutors ("Welcome to North Korea"). The investigation was "a travesty," Skilling declared. "It makes me ashamed to be an American."

Even after the bankruptcy filing, he continued to exult over the innovative ways in which Enron went about its business. In an industry built on brawn, Enron prided itself on being a company that ran on brains. And Enron *was* smart—in many ways, too smart as it turned out. Just as he had when Enron was riding high, Skilling labeled ExxonMobil a "dinosaur"—as though it didn't matter that the oil giant was thriving while Enron was nearly extinct. "We were doing something special. *Magical.*" The money wasn't what really mattered to him, insisted Skilling, who had banked $70 million from Enron stock. "It wasn't a job—it was a mission," he liked to say. "We were changing the world. We were doing God's work."

In the public eye, Enron's mission was nothing more than the cover story for a massive fraud. But what brought Enron down was something more complex—and more tragic—than simple thievery. The tale of Enron is a story of human weakness, of hubris and greed and rampant self-delusion; of ambition run amok; of a grand experiment in the deregulated world; of a business model that didn't work; and of smart people who believed their next gamble would cover their last disaster—and who couldn't admit they were wrong.

In less combative moods, Skilling reflected on his plight. "My life is fucked," he said. He would tear up as he spoke about what building Enron had cost him: he had destroyed his marriage, ignored his kids. "People didn't just go to work for Enron," Skilling would tell acquaintances. "It became a part of your life, just as important as your family. *More* important than your family. But at least I knew we had this company."

Skilling was seeing a psychiatrist and taking antidepressants. "I view my life as over," he said during an extended dark spell. Before his funk eased, in the months after Baxter took his own life, Skilling openly mulled over whether his friend had done the right thing. "Depending on how it plays out, it may reach a point where it's not worth sticking around," he said. "Cliff figured out how it was going to play out."

The Smartest Guys
in the Room

CHAPTER 1

Lunch on a Silver Platter

It is no accident that Ken Lay's career in the energy business began—and, most likely, ended—in the city of Houston, Texas.

Houston was the epicenter of that world, home to giants like Exxon, Conoco, and Pennzoil. Spindletop, the legendary field that triggered the first Texas oil boom, back in 1901, is just up the road. To the south and east, sprawled over thousands of acres, lie refineries, petrochemical plants, gas-processing facilities, and tank farms—the grimy monstrosities that feed the nation's hunger for plastics, fertilizer, heat, electricity, and gasoline.

For most of the twentieth century, Houston's economy rose and fell with the price of crude. In the 1970s, when an Arab oil embargo was strangling the rest of America, Houston boomed. By 1987, when lower energy prices were pumping fresh life into the country, the city was flat on its back.

Houston also perfectly reflected the culture of the energy business. It was sprawling and rough, lusty and bold, wide open to opportunity and worshipful of new money. A city built on a swamp, Houston was a place where a man with a wildcatting spirit could transform himself virtually overnight; a like-minded company could remake itself, too.

The romance and myth in the energy business, of course, had always been about oil. It was crude that built empires, inspired legends, and launched wars. It was oil that the Mideast sheiks used to hold America hostage. It was oil that created the towering fortunes of Rockefellers and Hunts.

But Ken Lay's destiny lay in a humbler hydrocarbon: natural gas. Transparent, odorless, lighter than air, natural gas, composed mostly of methane, lies trapped in underground pockets, often beside oil deposits. America has long had vast reserves of gas, and it burns far more cleanly than either coal or oil. Yet for the first half of the last century, America had little use for the stuff. It was a mere by-product in the quest for oil, priced so cheaply it wasn't worth laying new pipelines to move it across the country. Instead, natural gas was usually just burned off as waste or was pumped back into the ground to maintain pressure to extract more oil.

By the 1950s, however, the perception of natural gas had begun to change. Gas was never going to attain the mythic status of oil—not even after Enron arrived on the scene—but it gradually became useful and even important. A flurry of pipeline construction had linked gas supplies in Texas and Louisiana with the rest of the country. Dozens of new petrochemical plants—many along the gulf coast of Texas—relied on natural gas as their basic fuel. By the time Richard Nixon took office in 1969, gas heated a large percentage of the nation's homes and powered thousands of industrial sites year-round. Still, except for the occasional pipeline explosion, natural gas remained largely an afterthought, literally beneath notice, crawling silently about the country at ten miles per hour through a network of buried steel.

Back in those less complicated times, there were lots of industries that operated more or less by rote: the old banker's motto, for instance, was "3-6-3": take money in at 3 percent, lend it out at 6 percent, and be on the golf course by 3 P.M. But few industries were as downright sleepy as the gas-pipeline business. Yes, there was the occasional pipeline company that explored for gas, too; exploration has always been the most romantic part of the energy business. But mostly the pipeliners bought gas from oil giants and smaller independent exploration companies, then moved it across the country through their networks of underground pipes. Most of the gas went directly to industrial customers, while the rest was sold to regional gas utilities, which piped it to smaller businesses and consumers.

It was all very simple and straightforward—especially since every step of the process was under government control. The federal government regulated interstate pipelines, dictating the price they paid for gas and what they could charge their customers. (State agencies regulated intrastate pipelines in much the same fashion.) However much executives spent on operations, whether for moving gas or redecorating their offices, Washington let them recover their costs and tack on a tidy profit. "In the pipeline business, you'd have to make one or two decisions a year," says one former Enron executive. "Everyone who operated in it was pretty much brain dead."

It wasn't until the 1970s that things began to change—or at least to change enough to attract the interest of a bright, shrewd, and intensely ambitious young man like Ken Lay. Far from being afraid of the coming changes, Lay wanted to push things along, to accelerate the pace of change. In later years, colleagues joked about his penchant for taking rapid action—*any* action—describing Lay's management style as "Ready, fire, aim."

A Baptist preacher's son, Lay believed powerfully in the dogma of deregulation. He sermonized about the virtues of unshackling the gas industry, propelling it into a new, deregulated world, where the free market set prices. In this new world, surely, there would be winners and losers: those who had the skills to thrive in a deregulated universe and those who didn't. From the start, he saw himself as one of the winners. He could envision taking control of a lowly pipeline company and transforming it into the first "gas major," a company with the power, brains, resources, and global reach of the oil giants.

Lay usually expressed his preference for deregulation in ideological terms;

his training as an economist had taught him that free markets simply worked better than markets controlled by the government, he liked to say. But he also believed that deregulation would create opportunities to make money—lots of money. And making money was terribly important to Ken Lay.

In later years, when Enron was at the peak of its powers, Lay was viewed as he'd always wanted the world to see him—as a Great Man. He was acclaimed as a business sage, a man of transcendent ideas who had harnessed change in an industry instinctively opposed to it. In the public face he presented, Lay seemed to care deeply about bettering the world. He spent much of his time on philanthropy: in Houston, he was the go-to man for charitable works, raising and giving away millions. He spoke often about corporate values. And he was openly religious. "Everyone knows that I personally have a very strict code of personal conduct that I live by," he once told an interviewer for a religious magazine called *The Door*. "This code is based on Christian values."

Lay was a hard man not to like. His deliberately modest midwestern manner—Lay made a point of personally serving drinks to subordinates along for the ride on Enron's flagship jet—built a deep reservoir of goodwill among those who worked for him. A short, balding man with an endearing resemblance to Elmer Fudd, he remembered names, listened earnestly, and seemed to care about what you thought. He had a gift for calming tempers and defusing conflict.

But this style, soothing though it may have been, was not necessarily well suited to running a big corporation. Lay had the traits of a politician: he cared deeply about appearances, he wanted people to like him, and he avoided the sort of tough decisions that were certain to make others mad. His top executives—people like Jeff Skilling—understood this about him and viewed him with something akin to contempt. They knew that as long as they steered clear of a few sacred cows, they could do whatever they wanted and Lay would never say no. On the rare occasion when circumstances forced his hand, he'd let someone else take the heat or would throw money at a problem. For years, Lay seemed to float, statesmanlike, above the fray, removed from the tough day-to-day business of cracking heads in corporate America. Somehow, until Enron fell, Ken Lay never seemed to get his hands dirty.

A man of humble origins, Lay also became addicted to the trappings of corporate royalty. For years, he spent most of his time playing power broker. He traded personal notes with presidents, pulled strings in Washington, and hobnobbed with world leaders. Back in Houston, he was known as someone whose ring any aspiring politician needed to kiss. Indeed, there was talk he would someday run for mayor—if he didn't accept a president's call to serve in the cabinet instead. Some of that, unquestionably, came with the territory; some of it even benefited Enron. But it came at a big cost: over time, he lost touch with his company's business.

Though few people complained about it before Enron fell, Lay's behavior also betrayed a powerful sense of personal entitlement. Long after his annual compensation at Enron had climbed into the millions, Lay arranged to take out large personal loans from the company. He gave Enron jobs and contracts to his relatives. And Lay and his family used Enron's fleet of corporate jets as if they owned them. On one occasion, a secretary sought to arrange a flight for an executive on Enron business only to be told that members of the Lay family had reserved *three* of the company's planes.

At lunchtime, top Enron executives, who worked on the richly paneled fiftieth floor of the company's headquarters tower in downtown Houston, routinely dispatched their assistants to fetch lunch so they could eat at their desks. Most ate their sandwiches on deli paper. Not Ken Lay. When his meal arrived, his staff carefully unwrapped it, placed the food on fine china, and served him lunch on a covered silver platter.

There was no fine china in Kenneth Lee Lay's early life. He grew up dirt-poor. Indeed, the Enron chairman's history is a classic Horatio Alger story. He was born in 1942 in Tyrone, Missouri, an agricultural dot on the map in the Ozarks. Before Lay became a business celebrity, the region's most famous former resident was Emmett Kelly, the circus clown known as Weary Willie.

Lay portrays his childhood, spent largely in tiny farm towns with outhouses and dirt roads, in Norman Rockwellesque terms. But the Lays were always struggling—until he was 11 years old, Ken Lay had never lived in a house with indoor plumbing—and at a young age, he set his mind on finding his fortune.

His parents, Omer and Ruth Lay, had three children; he was the middle child, after Bonnie and before Sharon. For a time, the Lays owned a feed store. Then disaster wiped them out: the Lays' deliveryman crashed a truck, slaughtering a load of chickens. Omer had to take to the road as a traveling stove salesman; the family followed from town to town, until they were finally forced to move in with in-laws on a farm in central Missouri. Omer, a Baptist lay preacher who held a succession of day jobs to feed the family, started selling farm equipment. Acutely conscious of the family circumstances, young Ken always worked: running paper routes, raising chickens, baling hay. "It's hard for me not to think Ken was an adult when he was a child," his sister Sharon said years later. The hardship honed Lay's ambition. He later spoke of spending hours on a tractor, daydreaming about the world of commerce, "so different from the world in which I was living."

Lay's parents never made it past high school, but college transformed his life. The family eventually resettled in Columbia, Missouri, where all three children attended the University of Missouri. Omer worked as parts manager in a Buick dealership then as a security guard at the university library while preaching at a small Baptist church. Ken painted houses, earned scholarships, and took out loans to pay his way through school.

Lay was a devoted and stellar student, serious beyond his years, with a natural intellectual bent. He'd entered college planning to become a lawyer but became enraptured by the study of economics during an introductory class taught by a popular professor named Pinkney Walker. He discovered that theory and fresh ideas fascinated him. But his passion always had a pragmatic side. He cared about politics and public policy, how government could shape markets. "Ken was one of these 4.0 guys who had some street sense," says Phil Prather, a Missouri classmate and lifelong friend. "Most 4.0 guys I know are a bunch of savants."

Although Lay stood out for his brains, he was never the stereotypical egghead who spent every waking moment in the library. Though slight, low-key, and quiet—he struggled for years to overcome a mild stammer—he was popular as well. At Missouri he won election as president of Beta Theta Pi, the university's largest and most successful fraternity. (Among Lay's predecessors in the Missouri frat house: Wal-Mart founder Sam Walton.) Lay became an inveterate collector of relationships. At each major stop in his early life, he forged bonds that lasted for decades. These weren't only personal acquaintances. Time and again, he would tap his growing network: for a job, for a favor, or to surround himself with those he trusted. This skill propelled his climb.

The first key relationship, in fact, was with Pinkney Walker. Walker was drawn by Lay's brains and ambition and quickly became his mentor. "We just hit it off with each other from the first," remembers Walker. "It was always inevitable that he would be a man of wealth." After a lifetime of pinching pennies, Lay was eager to start making money. But after graduating Phi Beta Kappa in economics, he remained in school to get his master's degree after Walker convinced him that he would be better off in the long run with a master's on his résumé. Lay finished school in 1965.

For the next six years, Lay paid his dues: first in Houston, at Humble Oil (a forerunner to Exxon), where he worked as an economist and speechwriter while taking night classes toward his Ph.D., then in the navy, in which he enlisted in 1968, ahead of the Vietnam draft. Originally intended to become a shipboard supply officer, perhaps in the South China Sea, Lay was abruptly reassigned to the Pentagon. This assignment introduced him to Washington. Lay later attributed such critical turns in his life to divine intervention, but in this instance, there was no miracle involved: Pinkney Walker had pulled some strings for his protégé. Instead of putting in his tour of duty at sea, Lay spent it conducting studies on the military-procurement process. The work provided the basis for his doctoral thesis on how defense spending affects the economy. At night he taught graduate students in economics at George Washington University.

At each of these early stops, Lay received a taste of life at the top. At Humble, he wrote speeches for CEO Mike Wright; at the Pentagon, he recruited a high-level officer to provide support for his work as a lowly ensign.

By then Lay was a father of two. He was married to his college sweetheart, Judith Diane Ayers, the daughter of an FBI agent from Jefferson City, Missouri. They met in French class, and like so many others, Judie recalls being drawn by

Ken's "maturity and dependability." Ken and Judie wed in the summer of 1966, after she completed her journalism degree. Ken was 24, Judie 22. Their children, Mark and Elizabeth, arrived in 1968 and 1971.

Before joining the navy, Lay had promised Exxon (the name had been changed from Humble) that he would return to the company. But once again, Pinkney Walker had other ideas. President Richard Nixon had just named Walker to the Federal Power Commission—then the agency regulating the energy business—and Walker wanted Lay as his top aide. The new commissioner placed a call to Exxon's CEO, urging him to let Lay off the hook. "I made it clear to him he was making a friend," says Walker.

Though Walker wound up staying only 18 months in Washington, it was long enough for his young deputy to make an impression. In October 1972, the Nixon White House tapped Lay for a new post as deputy undersecretary of energy in the Interior Department. He became one of the administration's point men on energy policy. Lay's new government position paid him a higher salary than was typical for such rank, thus requiring a special exemption from the U.S. Civil Service Commission. Interior Secretary Rogers Morton made the request. "The potential of an energy crisis is of immense proportion," wrote Morton. Without the exemption, "the Department of the Interior cannot hope to attract a man of Dr. Lay's stature and unique talents." Lay was 30 years old.

What a time it was to be making energy policy for the United States! Or rather, what a time it should have been. In early 1973, shortly after Lay began his new job, the country suffered electrical brownouts and natural-gas shortages. Then came the Arab oil embargo. Pump prices soared, and people had to line up for blocks to get gasoline for their cars. Government officials warned Americans to curtail long vacation trips. After decades of consuming ever more energy, the country was in the midst of a full-fledged energy crisis. The president capped the year by announcing that because of the crisis, he wouldn't light the national Christmas tree.

But the Interior Department's new deputy undersecretary of energy wasn't around long enough to effect policy. Concluding that the energy crisis was bound to mean big changes for the staid old pipeline industry, Lay decided the time was ripe to exit the government and head into the world of business. In September 1973, less than a year after he arrived at the Interior Department, Lay put out a feeler to W. J. (Jack) Bowen, CEO of a midsize pipeline company called Florida Gas, whom he'd met at a public hearing in his capacity as deputy undersecretary. "As you know, I have been involved in energy policy making in Washington for the past two and one-half years," Lay wrote, using Interior Department stationery. "I feel it is now time I begin thinking about returning to the private sector and resuming my career in business. I would be most interested in being considered for possible job opportunities with Florida Gas Company. The natural-gas industry, obviously, faces some very difficult challenges in the months and years ahead, and I would like to be in a position in industry to help meet these challenges."

Bowen, a West Point graduate, met with Lay in Washington then brought him and Judie down for a visit to the company's headquarters in the Orlando suburb of Winter Park. Bowen also personally called his references: Lay's old boss at Exxon, a rear admiral in the Pentagon, and, of course, Pinkney Walker. Bowen took notes on their comments. "Never had a better man technically. Would like to have—tops!" declared the admiral. "Head's screwed on straight," said Walker. "Think a great deal of him. . . . Good worker. Very smart," added the Exxon man, who went on to offer the only cautionary note: "Maybe too ambitious." By year's end, Lay was in Winter Park as vice president for corporate planning, with a starting salary of $38,000 a year plus 2,500 stock options.

Bowen left the next year for Transco Energy, a much bigger pipeline company in Houston. That only accelerated Lay's rapid ascent. By 1976 he was president of the pipeline division at Florida Gas; by 1979, president of the entire company. For the first time in his life, Ken Lay was flush. He owned a $300,000 house, joined the Winter Park Racquet Club, and bought a beach condo on the Florida coast and a ski condo in Utah. In 1980 Lay made $268,000.

His marriage, however, was falling apart. The preacher's son was carrying on an affair with his secretary, a divorced mother of three named Linda Phillips Herrold, who would become his second wife. Newspaper profiles later described Lay's divorce as "amicable." And indeed, in the years after his split, Lay established a remarkably cordial relationship with his first wife. Over the years, Lay even paid for Judie and their two kids to accompany him, Linda, and Linda's children on family ski trips and cruises. When friends showed up for the Lays' Christmas parties in Aspen, they were startled to discover *both* of his wives there, mixing amiably. Says one friend: "I was expecting to see Judie in Ken's Christmas card."

But if the aftermath was friendly—a testament to Lay's ability to smooth over any conflict—the split itself was anything but. Lay began talking to Judie about separating in late 1980. About that time he called up his old boss, Transco chairman Jack Bowen, told him he had "domestic problems," and asked if Bowen had a job for him in Houston. Once again, a key relationship Lay had forged paid off. Bowen, then 57, hired the 39-year-old Lay as Transco's president—and his heir apparent. In late April 1981 Lay filed for divorce, requesting custody of his two children, just days before officially beginning his new job in Houston. About this time, Linda Herrold was also transferred to Florida Gas's Houston office.

Judie responded in court papers that Ken was unfit to have custody. A few weeks later, Judie suffered what doctors later called a "psychotic episode" resulting from "manic-depressive illness." She spent several months undergoing treatment at hospitals in Houston and North Carolina. At one point, at her doctors' urging, Ken had signed legal papers to have his estranged wife involuntarily committed. The psychiatrists treating Judie concluded that the episode was triggered by the couple's impending divorce. As one psychiatrist later testified in deposition: "The divorce or the thought of a divorce hit her very hard. 'It was like dying,' as she put it."

By the end of 1981, Judie had recovered, and the year-long courtroom sparring resumed. As a court date loomed, her lawyers deposed Lay, Jack Bowen, and Bill Morgan, a University of Missouri frat brother Lay hired to work for him as an attorney at Florida Gas. The two sides finally signed settlement papers in June 1982, with the trial just a week away. Under the agreement, Judie would get primary custody of the children. Lay would make a lump-sum payment of $30,000 plus $500 a month in child support, alimony of $72,000 a year for four years, and $36,000 a year thereafter. (Lay later voluntarily increased his payments to Judie on five occasions—most recently in 1999, to $120,000 a year.)

A Florida Gas executive named John Wing—who later played a big role at Enron—served as the legal witness for Lay at the three-minute hearing in which the divorce was finalized. When it was over, Lay headed straight to the Orlando airport, where a Transco jet was waiting to fly him to Texas. Lay and Linda Herrold were married one month later in Houston.

Judie Lay, who still lives in Winter Park, credits her ex-husband for extending an olive branch. About three years after the divorce, she says, their children told her that Ken and Linda had invited them all to go skiing together for Christmas— and that he would pay for her hotel room. "We didn't all sit down under the Christmas tree the first year," she says. "It kind of gradually became more togetherness. The bad times sort of flowed away. We're all good friends now. He's treated me very nicely."

It was at Transco that Ken Lay came to be widely regarded as a rising star. Unlike Florida Gas, Transco was a big-time company. It controlled a 10,000-mile pipeline system that provided almost all of New York City's natural gas and served large portions of New Jersey and much of the Southeast. But it wasn't just the size of the company that allowed Lay to shine; it was the condition of the pipeline industry. The business was in terrible shape.

One part of the nation's energy crisis was a persistent shortage of natural gas; in some regions, schools and factories had been forced to close because the gas needed to heat them was in such short supply. Gas producers, not surprisingly, argued that the problem was that the government-mandated price was simply too low to encourage new exploration efforts. So in 1978 Congress hiked the regulated price that would be paid to producers (as exploration companies are called) for some types of natural gas. At the same time, though, Congress passed legislation barring the use of natural gas for any new industrial boilers. Thus the first law was intended to increase supply, while the second was intended to depress demand. Although this was hardly full-scale deregulation, it was the government's first tentative step in that direction.

Unfortunately for the pipeline industry—and here was the great irony of the situation—the new rules worked far too well. Sure enough, the higher prices jump-started gas exploration and increased the nation's supply of natural gas. But at the same time, demand for gas began dropping precipitously, not only because of government action but because as natural gas prices rose, many industrial customers switched to coal or fuel oil, which were suddenly cheaper. Over time, this put the pipeline companies in an impossible position.

Why? Because the pipelines, eager to protect themselves against future shortages, had started cutting long-term deals with individual producers to take virtually all the gas they could provide at the very moment when demand was dropping. The contracts they'd signed were called "take or pay," meaning they were obliged to pay for the gas at the new higher rates *even if they didn't need it*. Then, in the mid-1980s, the government made a bad situation even worse when it took its next small step toward deregulation: it freed utilities and industrial customers from their contracts to buy from the pipelines, allowing them to shop for better prices on the open market or turn to cheaper fuels.

But the government refused to let the pipelines out of their expensive take-or-pay commitments. This put pipeline companies between a rock and a hard place: stuck with huge volumes of gas at prices they could no longer pass on to customers. As a result, many of the companies became technically insolvent, and a few went bankrupt. Some form of relief was obviously needed—from Washington, the gas producers, or the courts. Over time, the companies pursued all three avenues: lobbying, negotiating, and litigating. Orchestrating it all took years and proved expensive. It wasn't until the late 1980s and early 1990s that the crisis finally ended and the natural-gas business, including the pipeline industry, was largely deregulated.

But though the beginning of this crisis was bad for the industry, it was certainly good for Ken Lay. With his Ph.D. in economics, his Washington experience, and his long advocacy of deregulation, Lay seemed like just the right man for the new age. With the industry in paralysis, he began helping Transco work through its take-or-pay problem by setting up a fledgling spot market for natural gas, where producers who let Transco out of its take-or-pay obligation could sell directly to their customers, paying Transco just to move the gas. Thoughtful and articulate, Lay was in demand at industry conferences and Capitol Hill hearings. "Ken isn't bound by tradition," declared John Sawhill, head of the global energy practice for the consulting firm, McKinsey & Company. Even Wall Street viewed him as a major asset. The *Houston Chronicle* wrote in 1983, "Some analysts attribute the strength of Transco's stock price to Lay's credibility and his bold and unique accomplishments."

If Lay had stayed at Transco, he probably would have become CEO in 1989, when Bowen planned to retire. But as it turned out, he didn't have to wait nearly that long to become a chief executive. In the summer of 1984, opportunity came knocking, and he eagerly answered the call. It came in the form of a meeting with a man named John Duncan, who had helped put together the old conglomerate Gulf & Western, and was a key board member of a midsize pipeline company called Houston Natural Gas (HNG).

Lay and Duncan had gotten to know each other a few months earlier, when HNG had been trying to repel a takeover attempt by a corporate raider and Transco had offered to act as a white knight—a friendly alternative acquirer. Ultimately, Transco's help wasn't needed, but Lay had clearly made an impression. In their meeting, which took place over breakfast on a Saturday morning, Duncan popped the question: would Lay consider becoming CEO of HNG? He didn't require a lot of convincing. "By Sunday morning," Lay later recalled, "it was sounding kind of interesting."

Houston Natural Gas had a special place in the city. Though smaller than many local rivals—annual revenues were $3 billion—it had for years assumed the role of the "hometown oil company." Part of that was its heritage: the company dated back to 1926, and it had long been the prime gas supplier to the huge industrial plants on the Texas coast. Part of it was due to Robert Herring, its longtime chairman, who was active in every important civic project and charitable event in town. Herring's wife, Joanne, was an international socialite, and the couple's home in exclusive River Oaks—one of America's wealthiest neighborhoods—became Houston's preeminent salon, a place where oilmen mixed with international royalty. Herring had died of cancer in October 1981; HNG, though still profitable, hadn't been quite the same since. His successor, 60-year-old M. D. Matthews, was a nondescript caretaker type. Even after the takeover attempt was repulsed, HNG's modest debt made it a juicy target for corporate raiders. And the takeover battle had left the HNG board convinced that it needed stronger leadership.

On Monday, Lay won Jack Bowen's blessing for his departure, and in June 1984, at the age of 42, Ken Lay became chairman and chief executive officer of Houston Natural Gas. After her husband assumed his big new job, Linda Lay exulted to a friend: "It's fun to be the king." HNG would serve as the foundation for building Enron.

From the moment he walked in the door, Lay operated on one theory: get big fast. His core belief, as ever, was that deregulation—*real* deregulation—was coming soon. And when it did, he believed, the price of the commodity would reflect true market demand and the companies with the best pipeline networks would be the ones calling the shots. In just his first six months, Lay spent $1.2 billion on two pricey acquisitions that dramatically extended HNG's pipeline system into the growth markets of California and Florida. (The Florida pipeline had been owned by Lay's old company, Florida Gas.) He even talked to his old friend, Jack Bowen, about a deal with Transco. At the same time he unloaded $625 million in holdings outside the core pipeline business, including coal-mining properties and a fleet of barges.

Then came a bit of luck. In April 1985 Lay got a call out of the blue from a man named Sam Segnar, the CEO of InterNorth, a big Omaha pipeline company. Because Lay was in Europe at the time courting investors, John Wing, his old deputy from Florida Gas—who had just hired on as HNG's chief strategy officer—handled the call. Segnar wanted to pitch the idea of InterNorth's buying HNG. But it quickly became apparent that Segnar was too eager for his own good.

InterNorth, three times the size of HNG, had long been one of the most respected operators in the pipeline business. Among its 20,000 miles of pipeline was a genuine prize: Northern Natural, the major north-south line feeding gas from Texas into Iowa, Minnesota, and much of the rest of the Midwest. For decades, InterNorth had assumed a role in Omaha much like that of HNG in Houston. It was the caretaker of civic causes—the number one corporate citizen. Like HNG it had been run for years by a beloved figure, Bill Strauss. Under Strauss, InterNorth was a quiet, steady company with low debt and terrific cash flow that paid executives modest salaries and carefully watched expenses.

But in 1981 Strauss had turned the company over to Segnar, a charmless personality who upset many in frugal Omaha with a series of ham-handed moves. He purchased a company jet, bought a corporate ranch in Colorado, and closed the fifteenth-floor corporate dining room to all but a few top executives, who were served by white-gloved waiters. Worst of all, Segnar made a string of bad diversification investments. InterNorth was also powerfully motivated by the fact that Irwin Jacobs, a corporate raider, was buying up its shares. Jacobs's looming presence sent Segnar into a panic. He persuaded the board that the only way to make InterNorth "sharkproof" was to make the company bigger and dramatically increase its debt. Buying HNG would accomplish both goals.

Lay and Segnar turned over negotiations to Wing and Rocco LoChiano, Segnar's top deputy. They met at the St. Regis Hotel in Houston and quickly started talking price. At the time, HNG was trading at about $45 per share. LoChiano figured HNG was worth perhaps $60, $65 tops. But Wing, a canny negotiator, took advantage of InterNorth's desperation to strike a deal, and quickly brought the price up to $70 a share. And that wasn't all. Wing demanded that the smaller company's younger management team ultimately end up in charge. Amazingly, LoChiano and Segnar agreed: Lay would replace Segnar, then 57, as CEO and chairman of the combined company after just 18 months. "I think I get this," LoChiano told Wing over a cup of coffee. "We're the rich old ugly guy with all the money, and you're the good-looking blonde." Wing laughed. "Yeah, that's right," he replied.

Just 11 days after the first phone call, the two CEOs won approval for the $2.3-billion deal from their respective boards. From a business standpoint, HNG InterNorth, as it was called, seemed an elegant combination: with 37,500 miles of pipeline, the new $12 billion company would have the largest gas-distribution system in the country, running from border to border, coast to coast. It would have access to the three fastest growing gas markets: California, Texas, and

Florida. And it had some $5 billion in debt, surely more than enough to put it safely beyond the reach of raiders like Irwin Jacobs. As for Ken Lay, he wound up with a personal windfall: a $3 million profit from converting his stock and options in the wake of the merger.

Mergers that sound good on paper often wind up facing a far harsher reality. Such was the case with HNG InterNorth. There were two fundamental issues. The first was that almost immediately after the transaction closed, the InterNorth directors came down with a bad case of buyer's remorse. As the implications of the deal sunk in, they began to realize that even though their company was the acquirer, they had pretty much given away the store to the Texans. Why, they now wondered, did HNG come before InterNorth in the new name when Inter-North had been the acquirer? Why was Segnar so quick to agree to give the CEO job to Lay in 18 months? Did it have anything to do with promises of a fat severance package? (Segnar ended up walking away with $2 million.) Why did HNG have almost as many seats (8) on the new board as InterNorth (12)? The more they thought about how they'd been snookered, the madder they got, but they were far angrier at their man, Segnar, than at Ken Lay, whose company had done the snookering.

Among the old-line InterNorth directors, the biggest fear of all was that the Texans were planning to move the company's headquarters to Houston, even though everyone concerned, including Lay, had repeatedly promised that the company would remain in Omaha "for the forseeable future." This wasn't just a matter of jobs (though 2,200 were at stake); it was also a question of civic pride. It quickly became evident that the promises really weren't worth much. Houston, after all, was the center of the U.S. energy business. Once the merger went through, the issue became so heated that the board created a special committee to study the matter. The committee retained the management-consulting firm, McKinsey & Company, to make a recommendation.

The McKinsey consultants, who included Lay's old friend John Sawhill and a young partner named Jeff Skilling, were scheduled to unveil their recommendation to the board on November 11, 1985, a frosty day in Omaha, at the Marriott Hotel. They were indeed going to advise the company to move to Houston. But the meeting quickly took a different turn, and the consultants were told to wait outside. Hours later, Segnar stepped out of the board meeting with tears in his eyes. He shook Sawhill's hand. "I'm leaving InterNorth," he told the consultant.

Afterward, all parties claimed that Segnar had voluntarily resigned. In truth, the meeting had been a bloodbath, and he hadn't really had a choice. Convinced that Segnar had made a series of secret side deals with Lay to betray Omaha, the old InterNorth directors demanded his head. Of course, since the board didn't have another CEO candidate, it also meant that Ken Lay would become chief executive immediately, instead of having to wait the agreed-upon 18 months.

As a counterweight to Lay, the board brought back Bill Strauss as nonexecutive chairman and some even tried to mount a bid to reclaim the company for the

River City. But the effort quickly fizzled when Strauss refused to lead the charge and quit after just four months, giving Lay the chairman's title, too. It wouldn't have succeeded in any case, for Lay had quietly won control of the board. A father-son pair of old InterNorth directors, Arthur and Robert Belfer, had lined up behind Lay. Two new directors, appointed after the merger by agreement between both sides, also turned out to be Texas partisans.

Over the next three years, the Omaha bloc was purged, and Lay started packing the board with his own directors, including a powerful Washington lobbyist named Charls Walker—Pinkney Walker's brother—and an old Pentagon friend named Herbert (Pug) Winokur. John Duncan, the HNG director who had hired Lay, became head of the executive committee. And the corporate headquarters? The directors resolved to split the difference, maintaining an executive headquarters in Omaha and an operating headquarters in Houston. But that arrangement obviously couldn't last long, and it didn't. In July 1986 Lay announced that the company's corporate headquarters would relocate to Houston, to a silver-skinned downtown skyscraper at 1400 Smith Street.

In Omaha, this decision was bitterly resented for years to come.

There was a second issue looming, of far more consequence than the question of where to put the company's headquarters. It was this: all the good things Ken Lay assumed would happen once the HNG-InterNorth merger took place simply weren't happening. For the moment, Lay's get big fast strategy was only bringing bigger problems.

Irwin Jacobs? Even though the new company was now drowning in debt, the raider and an investor group allied with him still wouldn't go away. Lay wound up having to shell out about $350 million—a modest premium to the market price—to buy out the group's 16.5 percent stake. There wasn't enough cash in the corporate coffers to pay the greenmail, so Lay had to tap the company's pension plan for the money.

Deregulation? All of a sudden, there was a glut of gas on the market, prompting prices to plunge to levels no one had ever imagined. That only multiplied the company's take-or-pay problem. Lay's new business had more than $1 billion in take-or-pay liabilities.

Lay seemed unable to assemble a coherent management team amid bitter political infighting involving not just the old HNG and InterNorth executives but also the pipeline businesses he'd acquired the year before and a handful of well-paid friends that Lay had hired from outside.

Lay even ran into trouble coming up with a trendy new name for the company. After four months of research, the New York consulting firm Lay had hired had settled on Enteron in time for the merged business's first annual meeting, in the spring of 1986. But then the *Wall Street Journal* reported that Enteron was a term for the alimentary canal (the digestive tract), turning the name into a laughingstock. Though it meant reprinting 75,000 covers that had already been printed for the new annual report, the board convened an emergency meeting and went with a runner-up on the list: Enron.

Oh, and just for good measure, Lay had to battle the government of Peru, which nationalized the company's Peruvian production assets just a month after he'd become CEO. That alone produced a $218 million charge to earnings.

In early 1986 Enron reported a loss of $14 million for its first year. Lay announced a series of cost-cutting measures and job cuts. He froze pay for top executives and started selling off assets to cut debt, including 50 percent of the Florida pipeline he purchased just two years earlier.

Enron's financial situation had grown so dire that by January 1987 Moody's had downgraded its credit rating to junk status. One former executive recalls that during this period there was even worry about meeting payroll. "The company was in deep shit," Bruce Stram, then vice president of corporate planning, says.

What Ken Lay and Enron desperately needed was a fresh source of profits— while there was still time.

CHAPTER 2

"Please Keep Making Us Millions"

Not every part of the old InterNorth wound up being relocated to Houston; at least one small division stayed right where it was. That unit was InterNorth's oil-trading business, which had its offices in a suburb of New York City, in a small town called Valhalla, about an hour's drive from Wall Street. Enron Oil, as it was renamed, wasn't anything like the rest of the company's gritty industrial operations. It was "the flashy part" of the business, as one employee later put it.

After the merger, Enron tucked Enron Oil away in a division that was a hodgepodge of businesses with little in common other than that they all made some of their money outside the United States. In Enron's financial reports, earnings from the oil-trading operation weren't broken out separately, and Enron didn't talk up its oil trading to Wall Street analysts or investors. But that only heightened the importance of the operation internally. The traders were a kind of secret weapon in the ongoing struggle to improve Enron's financial appearance. For unlike most of the rest of Enron, oil trading actually made money. Internal financial reports often bragged about the profits the traders were producing.

In more than location, the oil traders were closer to the freewheeling world of Wall Street than to the slow-moving, capital-intensive, risk-averse world of natural gas pipelines. Oil trading was about *trading,* not about oil. It was pure speculation: the oil traders came to work every day and made bets on the direction of crude oil prices. Enron's top brass knew very little about how the trading operation worked, and, if truth be told, they didn't much care. Oil trading looked like fast easy money, and that's all that mattered.

Of course, easy money is rarely as easy as it looks; such was the case with Enron's oil trading division. By the time Ken Lay and his minions in Houston realized something was horribly wrong—more accurately, by the time they were willing to face up to what they should have seen all along—the oil traders had come within a whisker of bankrupting the company. And Wall Street had its first indication that Enron and its leader didn't always play by the rules that were supposed to apply to publicly held corporations. Although it took place a long time ago, it seems obvious now that the Enron Oil scandal was the canary in the coal mine.

• • •

The man who created Enron Oil was named Louis Borget. Within Enron, he was a shadowy figure who divulged as little as possible about the details of his operation and kept a wary distance from Houston. To most Enron employees— even most of the top executives—he was little more than a voice at the other end of the telephone line, cryptically telling them that everything was just fine.

Borget was born in 1938 in New York, the son of an abusive, alcoholic father. According to court documents, he shined shoes to make money for his family at the age of nine. A brilliant student, he graduated from high school by the time he was 16. From there, he joined the army, where he learned to speak fluent Russian, then put himself through night school at New York University. In 1964, he took a job with Texaco, where he slowly rose through the ranks, becoming special assistant to the chairman and later running a small division. But after 17 years with Texaco, he abruptly left the oil giant, signing on with a company called Gulf States Oil and Refining, which wanted him to set up an oil-trading division. Three years after that, in January 1984, InterNorth came calling, asking him to set up *its* oil-trading subsidiary and offering him a lucrative package, which included Wall Street–style bonuses based on whatever profits he brought in. By the time of the InterNorth-HNG merger, Borget's operation was about a year and a half old.

Back then, oil trading was the hot new thing, both on Wall Street and in the oil patch. The big oil companies had long traded contracts promising to deliver oil in the future. This was a way to lock in a profit and mitigate the risk that oil prices would rise or fall. But the business had been limited by a couple of factors. For one thing, there was no standard contract for oil, which meant that the details of every trade had to be hammered out separately. And second, these contracts, by definition, meant that a cargo of oil would be delivered (or received) at a certain time in the future. Because there was so little trading—so little liquidity, as they say in the business—there was little opportunity and a lot of risk for those who didn't actually want to take possession of the oil. These factors tended to keep most speculators away.

In 1983 the New York Mercantile Exchange began to trade crude oil futures, in effect, a standard version of these contracts. Yes, the contract still theoretically came with the obligation to deliver, or receive, oil in some future month. But now that there was a standard contract, it could be traded many times over before anyone had to receive any oil. (If, indeed, oil was received at all: many times, the contracts were settled financially.) Suddenly oil looked a lot like other commodities, such as soybeans or pork bellies, or a financial instrument, like a stock or a bond. Suddenly, you could speculate in the stuff.

As a general rule, trading begets more trading. As a market becomes liquid— meaning that it's easier to find a willing buyer or seller—it attracts more participants. That further increases the liquidity, which further attracts new participants. Fueled by this so-called virtuous circle, the oil-trading business exploded in the mid-1980s. Texaco and the other major oil companies were no longer content to trade merely as a price hedge. Now they hoped to make money purely on the act of trading. It wasn't long before they all had trading desks. And it wasn't just the energy industry that piled in. Wall Street firms like Drexel Burnham Lambert (whose most famous employee was Michael Milken) and Goldman Sachs jumped into the business. So did many less reputable players, sketchy fly-by-nighters who saw a chance to make quick profits. By some accounts, those early years in the oil-trading business were wild and woolly. There were all kinds of little scams being run, even by the reputable trading firms. Yet there was also a seemingly limitless opportunity to make money.

Borget, for his part, loved playing the role of a big-time oil trader. He kept Dom Pérignon and caviar in the office refrigerator for afternoon toasts. He and his traders dressed casually—Borget would even wear jeans—before the term business casual was widespread. They all drove company cars and ate daily catered lunches. A former trader named David Ralph Hogin recalls that Borget drove a Mercedes; when Hogin asked for a Mercedes, too, he was told that "Lou's the only one who has a Mercedes. Would you settle for a Cadillac?" Enron Oil's offices in Valhalla were sleek and modern and sheathed in glass, a far cry from the more modest quarters favored by energy industry executives. Borget himself could be charming, but he also could be intimidating; he had an odd combination of corporate polish and a trader's swagger. "He was very intelligent, very imposing, sophisticated, and slick," recalls someone who knew him then. Traders were loyal to him; they liked both his unflappability and his steadfastness in sticking by his trading decisions.

"We were the golden-haired boys in the Enron fold," recalls Hogin. In 1985, the year of the InterNorth-HNG merger, Borget's group made $10 million. The following year—a year when Enron's ongoing business lost money—the oil traders made $28 million for the company. That year their bonus pool was $9.4 million, to be split among just a handful of traders. (Borget kept the lion's share for himself.) And there was every expectation that Borget and his crew would keep pumping profits into the company. As Borget himself put it reassuringly, in a 1986 report he prepared for the Enron board: oil trading "as done by professionals in the industry today, using the sophisticated tools available, can generate substantial earnings with virtually no fixed investment and relatively low risk. . . ." In other words, it was the perfect modern business.

Or was it?

The first sign that Enron Oil might not be what it appeared came in early 1987. On the morning of January 23, David Woytek, the head of Enron's internal audit department, received a startling phone call from someone at the Apple Bank in New York. An Enron account had been opened by a man named Tom Mastroeni. Mastroeni was a nervous yes-man who served as the treasurer of Enron Oil. Wire transfers amounting to about $5 million had been flowing in from a bank in the Channel Islands, and over $2 million had flowed out to an account in Mastroeni's name. Alarmed, Woytek immediately called Enron's general counsel, Rich Kinder, who was rapidly becoming Ken Lay's most trusted lieutenant.

Kinder told Woytek to track down Borget's nominal superiors, John Harding and Steve Sulentic, who oversaw Enron Oil from Houston. While Woytek tried to track down the two men, his deputy, John Beard, made another frightening discovery: the Apple Bank account could not be found anywhere on Enron's books. To the auditors, this reeked of disaster. Beard jotted his worst fears in his notes: "misstatement of records, deliberate manipulation of records, impact on financials for the year ending 12/31/86."

But according to internal documents, court testimony, and notes detailing these events, Sulentic and Harding had an explanation for the whole thing. The Apple Bank account was part of a tactic Borget had used to "move some profits from 1986 into 1987 through legitimate transactions," Woytek noted in a memo; Borget had done so because "Enron management had requested" it. Nor was this the first time that Borget had shifted profits. Since 1985, the oil trader had been setting up prearranged deals with other entities—they had names like Ilsa, Southwest, and Petropol—that in essence allowed Enron Oil to generate a loss on one contract then have the loss cancelled out by a second contract that would generate a gain in the same amount. Using this technique, Borget had repeatedly moved income from one quarter to another. In his memo, which he sent to Lay and other Enron executives, Woytek described this as the creation of "fictitious losses."

Harding now insists that whatever happened was not profit shifting, just the "prepayment of expenses," and that he believed Borget's actions were perfectly legal. But in testimony given over a decade ago, Borget said that Harding asked him to shift profits, originally for tax reasons. He also said that Harding approved bonuses as if the shifted profits from Enron Oil had remained in the year in which they were earned. For his part, Sulentic later testified that Enron Oil and other subsidiaries were "routinely instructed by Enron senior management to shift profits from month to month and year to year."

It was easy enough to understand why Enron would want to do this: like every public company, it hoped to show Wall Street that it could produce steadily increasing earnings, which is what the stock market rewards. Indeed, lawyers later charged that Enron used the profit shifting for precisely that purpose. But it also had a more pressing reason: Enron's ability to get bank loans absolutely depended on its ability to show earnings. Under the terms of its long-term bank debt, Enron was required to produce a certain amount of income every quarter, at least 1.2 times the interest on its debt. What's more, because Enron was so strapped for cash, it constantly needed new loans to pay back maturing loans. In 1986, for instance, Enron had over $1 billion in commercial paper—short-term loans that mature quickly—that needed to be refinanced. With all its mid-1980s problems, Enron was constantly on the verge of being in violation of its loan

agreements. As Lay put it in an Enron annual report about that time: "The present business climate provides no margin for error."

Later, in court testimony, Borget described Enron Oil as "the swing entry to
meet objectives each month." Extra earnings in one quarter didn't do Enron
much good—unless the income could somehow be deferred to help the company
meet its targets in the next quarter. It was all very logical, really. Profit shifting
can be done legally—though even then it amounts to earnings manipulation.
What subsequent events showed was that no one wanted to dig deeply enough to
see if Borget and Mastroeni were staying on the right side of the law.

On February 2 Borget and Mastroeni were summoned to Houston. They met in
the office of a man named Mick Seidl, an old Ken Lay buddy who had followed
Lay from Florida Gas to Enron and served as his number two. Woytek and
Beard, the internal auditors, were there, as were a number of Enron's senior executives, including Kinder, Harding, and Sulentic. (Some people remember Lay
being present; Harding says he wasn't there.) Sulentic defended the transactions.
In a memo he wrote summarizing his views, he argued that Enron Oil's Apple
Bank account, and its transactions with Isla, Southwest, and Petropol "represents
a sincere effort on their [Borget and Mastroeni's] part to accomplish the objective of a transfer of profitability from 1986 to 1987." He did concede that the
methods Borget and Mastroeni had used were "not acceptable," but he didn't
recommend any sort of punishment, not even a public admission of what had
happened.

Next up was Mastroeni. While admitting that he had diverted funds to his
personal account, he insisted that it was merely part of the profit-shifting tactic
and that he had always intended to repay the money. He presented bank statements, however, that the auditors knew had been doctored, because they had
gotten the original documents from Apple Bank. What was Mastroeni's explanation? He and Borget had paid a bonus to a trader and didn't want to have to explain it to corporate executives. Stunningly, most of the Enron executives in the
room appeared to accept Mastroeni's explanation. Mastroeni wasn't even reprimanded. Neither was Borget. Says an Arthur Andersen accountant who was involved, "No one pounded the table and said these guys are crooks. They thought
they had the golden goose, and the golden goose just stole a little money out of
their petty cash."

Still, the internal auditors continued to dig. They discovered a $7,800 deposit
into the Apple Bank account from the sale of Borget's company car. There were
payments totalling $106,500 to an M. Yass. Was this a play on "My ass?" Not
at all! Borget said he was an English broker who had faciliated the bonus to the
Enron trader; Mastroeni claimed he was a Lebanese national. They searched
directories of trading organizations looking for the names Ilsa, Southwest, and
Petropol and came up empty-handed. They went to Valhalla but didn't get very

far. Finally, they got the word: they were to return to Texas and turn the investigation over to Enron's accountants at Arthur Andersen. "Fieldwork . . . not completed based on advise [*sic*] from Houston," jotted Beard at the time. There was no doubt by then what the auditors thought of the Enron Oil operation. "They were a bunch of scam artists," one of them said years later.

For the next few months, the Arthur Andersen team took up the investigation, but they didn't get much further than the internal auditors did. The Enron executives were terrified of offending Borget. Before the accountants went to Valhalla to interview Borget, Seidl sent the head oil trader a memo detailing Andersen's concerns so that he would be better prepared to address them. After one conference call among Arthur Andersen, Seidl, and Borget, Seidl sent a telex to Borget. "Lou," it read. "Thank you for your perservance [*sic*]. [Y]ou understand your business better than anyone alive. Your answers to Arthur Andersen were clear, straightforward, and rock solid—superb. I have complete confidence in your business judgment and ability and your personal integrity." Then he added, "Please keep making us millions. . . ."

In late April, Arthur Andersen discussed its findings with the audit committee of the board. The accountants told the board that they "were unable to verify ownership or any other details" regarding Enron Oil's supposed trading partners. They noted that the Apple Bank transactions had no purpose beyond shifting profits. And they'd found a few other troubling things. For instance, Enron Oil was supposed to have strict controls to prevent the possibility of large losses; its open position in the market was never supposed to exceed 8 million barrels, and if losses reached $4 million, the traders were required to liquidate the position. Yet when the Arthur Andersen auditors had tried to check whether Enron Oil was complying with the policy, they later reported, they discovered that Borget and Mastroeni had made a practice of "destroying daily position reports."

Still, Andersen refused to opine on the legality of what had come to be known internally as Borget and Mastroeni's "unusual transactions," claiming that it was beyond their professional competence. Nor were the auditors willing to say whether the profit shifting had a material effect on Enron's financial statements. Both things would require the company to disclose the transactions to the Securities and Exchange Commission, restate its earnings, and face possible sanctions from the IRS. Instead, the auditors said, they were relying on Enron itself to make those determinations. And Enron did. Arthur Andersen noted that the firm had received a letter from Rich Kinder and another Enron lawyer concluding that "the unusual transactions would not have a material effect on the financial statements . . . and that no disclosure of these transactions is necessary."

And that, stunningly enough, was that. According to the minutes of that same board meeting, "Dr. Jaedicke called upon management for a matter that involved Enron Oil Corporation that was investigated by the company and subsequently investigated by Arthur Andersen. . . . After a full discussion, management recommended the person involved be kept on the payroll but relieved of financial responsibility and a new chief financial officer of Enron Oil Corporation be appointed. The committee agreed with reservations. . . ."

"Management," says Woytek, was Lay—who openly said at the board meeting that the traders made too much money to let them go. And the new watchdog chief financial officer was none other than Steve Sulentic, who, once he moved to Valhalla, reported to Borget. "Dr. Jaedicke" referred to Dr. Robert Jaedicke, then the dean of the Graduate School of Business at Stanford and the head of Enron's audit committee.

Two months later, what lawyers later called a "whitewash" was completed when an Enron lawyer wrote a memo—which Kinder eventually sent to the board—concluding that the profit-shifting deals were "legitimate common transactions in the oil trading business" and that they did not "lack economic substance." In other words, there was no reason to report the transactions to the outside world. It was an absurd position to take, given that an in-house auditor had called the transactions "fictitious." But not terribly surprising. As one lawyer on the Enron side remarked many years later, "Enron knew they were crooks. But they thought they were profitable crooks."

As it turned out, Borget and Mastroeni weren't engaging in criminal acts just for the good of the company. They were stealing from Enron as well. They were keeping two sets of books, one that was sent to Houston and one that tracked the real activities of Enron Oil. They were paying exorbitant commissions to the brokers who handled their sham transactions and demanding kickbacks. The so-called counterparties—Isla and Southwest and Petropol—weren't legitimate trading entities. They were creations of Borget and Mastroeni, phony companies they set up in the Channel Islands. Mastroeni's Apple Bank account was indeed one of the places he and Borget were hiding money they had skimmed from the company. In total, the two men and the other brokers stole some $3.8 million from Enron. And with Ken Lay and the other Houston executives so willing to look the other way, they would have gotten away with it, too, except that they made the one mistake Enron couldn't abide. They stopped making money.

Back in Houston there had always been a few executives who were skeptical of the oil traders. One was Mike Muckleroy, the head of Enron's liquid-fuels division and a former naval officer. An experienced commodities trader, Muckleroy had begun to hear rumors in mid-1986 that Enron Oil was making massive bets on the direction of oil prices. One thing that had long seemed obvious to Muckleroy was that Enron Oil had to be ignoring the trading limits that were supposed to prevent the traders from huge losses. Nothing else made sense. After all, the limits didn't just keep losses under control; they also had the inevitable effect of limiting gains as well. To Muckleroy, it just didn't seem possible that the Enron's oil traders could be racking up their eye-popping profits without exceeding their trading limits. He took his worries to Seidl, who scoffed and replied that Muckleroy must be jealous of Borget's bonus.

The rumors wouldn't go away. At least a half dozen times, Muckleroy says, he pressed his concerns with Seidl. Finally, Seidl sent him to Lay. But the Enron CEO was no more interested in looking into it than Seidl had been; he told Muckleroy that he was being paranoid. "What do I have to do to get you to understand that this could do devastating damage to our company?" Muckleroy asked Lay. Then, in the summer of 1987, Muckleroy began to hear from friends in the business, as he later recalled, "that we were huge on the wrong side of a trade." But so unconcerned were the Enron brass that at the company's mid-August board meeting, the Enron board *increased* Borget's trading limits by 50 percent. One skeptical Enron executive who attended that meeting returned to his office and told a colleague: "The Enron board believes in alchemy."

It wasn't until October that the truth began to come out—and then only because there was simply no way to hide it any longer. On October 9, 1987, Seidl met Borget for lunch at the Pierre hotel in Manhattan. It was supposed to be a social lunch; Seidl's wife was upstairs in her room, waiting to join them. But as soon as Borget explained the situation to Seidl, he immediately called his wife and told her to stay put. He spent the rest of the lunch trying to absorb what Borget was telling him. For months, Borget had been betting that the price of oil was headed down, and for months, the market had stubbornly gone against him. As his losses had mounted, he had continually doubled down, ratcheting up the bet in the hope of recouping everything when prices ultimately turned in his direction. Finally, Borget had dug a hole so deep—and so potentially catastrophic—that there was virtually no hope of ever fully recovering. Borget was confessing because he had no choice.

This time, Seidl understood the gravity of the situation. He called Houston immediately after the lunch and, in a panicked tone, declared that as a result of Borget's trading losses, Enron was "less than worthless." Within two hours, he was on a plane to Newfoundland to meet Lay, who was returning from Europe and had to stop there to have his jet refueled. In Houston, Muckleroy was on his way back from lunch when he was confronted by an ashen Rich Kinder, who had just talked to Seidl. Muckleroy hopped on the next plane to New York to see if there was any way he could salvage the situation.

Muckleroy quickly discovered that things were far worse than anyone realized. Enron Oil was short over 84 million barrels. The position was so huge that it amounted to roughly three months' output of the gigantic North Sea oil field off the coast of England. If Enron were forced to cover its position, it would have been on the hook for well over $1 billion. "Less than worthless" was exactly the right description: when you added $1 billion-plus to Enron's $4 billion in debt, the company's total debts outstripped its net worth. And, of course, given how strapped the company was for cash, there was simply no way it could cover its trading losses without filing for bankruptcy.

But Enron got lucky. Exactly the right person had gone to Valhalla to take charge of the problem. Experienced commodities trader that he was, Muckleroy took one look at Enron Oil's books and sat Mastroeni down. "Unfortunately, I've had to kill people in my past," he told the terrified treasurer, "and I sleep like a baby." He demanded to see the real books. At eight the next morning, Mastroeni produced them. Muckleroy told Borget to leave the premises and asked Enron's security officer to change the locks on the doors. Then he went to work.

For the next three weeks, he and a small team of traders worked 18- to 20-hour days. His goal was to shrink the size of the position so that when the company finally had to settle up, the loss would at least be manageable. His only hope was to bluff his way out of his dilemma; if other traders knew what trouble Enron Oil was in, they were likely to bid the price of oil even higher, then demand payment. To fool them, Muckleroy pretended that Enron had crude oil in hand; he even bought some to sell into the market. The bluff bought him time. Within a few days, oil prices began to decline. Or at least they fell enough that Muckleroy and his team were able to close down Enron Oil's positions, reducing the damage to the company to around $140 million. That still hurt, but it was no longer life-threatening. "If the market moved up three more dollars Enron would have gone belly up," Muckleroy later said. "Lay and Seidl never understood that."

After almost a year of pretending in the face of overwhelming evidence that nothing was awry at Enron Oil, Ken Lay and the other Enron executives now had to pretend the opposite: that they were shocked—*shocked!*—by the actions of these rogue traders. The company announced that it would take an $85 million after-tax charge to 1987 earnings and blamed it on "losses from unauthorized trading activities by two employees in its international crude oil trading subsidiary." As rumors of the fiasco had trickled out, Enron's stock began to fall; by the time of the October announcement it was down 30 percent. But now Lay insisted to Wall Street analysts that this was a freak event that would have no long-term effect: "I would not want anyone to think at any time in the future this kind of activity would affect our other businesses," he said.

At an all-employee meeting in late October, Lay told the crowd that he had been blindsided by Borget. "If anyone could say that I knew, let them stand up," he said. Two people had to physically prevent Muckleroy from standing. At a board meeting held to discuss the loss, Lay again denied any responsibility, according to one person who was there. Lay also played dumb with Enron's bankers, who were infuriated when they learned of the trading losses. As well they should have been. For at the same time the scandal was unfolding internally, Enron was in the midst of raising money from its banks. The deal closed just before Enron announced the $85 million charge but well after the company knew about the problem. "Everyone went apeshit," recalls one banker. "They felt like they were lied to." Well, they *had* been lied to.

The most ironic part of the aftermath was a massive suit Enron filed against Borget, Mastroeni, and a handful of others alleging a conspiracy to "defraud" Enron through what it now called "sham trades" with entities like Ilsa, Southwest, and Petropol, among others. Nobody at Enron was calling trades with these entities "unusual transactions" anymore. Defense lawyers for other trading companies argued that Enron was merely playing the victim to cover up its own complicity. "Any honest competent management, confronted with the conduct of Borget and Mastroeni, as revealed to Enron's senior management in January 1987, would have fired these gentlemen without delay," wrote one lawyer. (The suits were eventually settled.)

There were also investigations by both the SEC and the U.S. attorney's office, but it seems that Enron got lucky once again. The investigations focused on the phony transactions Borget and Mastroeni had concocted to shift profits from quarter to quarter, transactions that several Enron executives had encouraged and that several others, including Ken Lay, had condoned after the fact. Yet for reasons that mystify many lawyers involved in the case, the government chose not to prosecute the company. In early 1988 Enron restated its financials for the previous three and a half years, blaming "unauthorized activities . . . designed to shift income."

In addition to charging both Borget and Mastroeni with fraud and personal income tax violations, the U.S. attorney charged Borget with "aiding and assisting the filing of a false corporate income tax return" by hiding income with "sham transactions." But, said the government, "there is no indication that Enron knew the information supplied by Borget and contained in the consolidated tax return was false." Of course, anyone who poked around could have found plenty of indications. In early 1990 Borget pled guilty to three felonies and was sentenced to a year in jail and five years' probation. (When reached by telephone, he said, "My memory is fading, and I don't have much to say about an episode that is painful.") A month later, Mastroeni pled guilty to two felonies. He received a suspended sentence and got two years' probation. But by then, the Enron Oil scandal had long been forgotten.

■   ■   ■

Inside Enron, there was a second, less public kind of aftermath: the scandal marked the rise of Rich Kinder as a force inside the company. Mick Seidl had become the company's number two man largely on the strength of his friendship with Lay. He had much in common with Lay: he was a former academic with a Ph.D. in economics and a former government policy maker who had worked with Lay at the Interior Department in the early 1970s. But Seidl also shared other tendencies with Lay. He had a terrible time making decisions that might anger somebody. And he was far more interested in the glamour of being a corporate executive than in the hard work of making the company profitable. He wanted to be Mr. Outside, but Enron already had a Mr. Outside: Ken Lay himself.

Kinder was the opposite. Where Seidl was weak, Kinder was tough. Where Seidl was forgiving, Kinder was demanding. Where Seidl was easily flustered,

Kinder was decisive. Even though his title was only general counsel, Kinder had a natural authority that other Enron executives lacked. Unlike Seidl, Kinder was the perfect complement to Lay. "Ken isn't the kind of guy to take people to the woodshed the way he needed to," says one former executive. Nobody ever said that about Kinder.

Like Seidl, Kinder had known Ken Lay a long time, since college, in fact, where their girlfriends (later their first wives) were sorority sisters and best friends at the University of Missouri. But after graduation, their paths diverged. Kinder earned a law degree, served a stint in the army, and returned to the small Missouri river town where he was raised, Cape Girardeau, to practice law (in a firm run by Rush Limbaugh's father). He also had an entrepreneurial streak. By the late 1970s he was a partner in a local racquet club and owned a bar called the Second Chance, as well as a Howard Johnson's Motor Lodge and some apartment buildings. But his real estate investments proved disastrous: in late 1980 Kinder was forced to file for Chapter 7 bankruptcy protection; he listed $2.14 million in debts and just $130,750 in assets. Kinder and his wife Anne claimed to have just $100 in cash.

Bill Morgan, a third University of Missouri buddy who had gone to work for Lay at Florida Gas, rescued his old college friend, hiring him as an in-house lawyer. When Lay bought Florida Gas's pipeline business shortly after becoming CEO of Houston Natural Gas, he also brought Kinder to Houston and soon named him Enron's general counsel.

There was no secret why Kinder stood out: he got things done. He had rough edges—one person who worked with him called him "smart, rough and tumble, and selfish"—but they worked to his advantage. People were afraid of him. "You didn't mess with Rich Kinder," recalls another former executive. "If you messed with Rich Kinder, he was going to cut you to shreds." Another adds, "Rich was a mean son of a bitch. You didn't want to cross him. But he imposed the kind of discipline we didn't have before, which we really needed." A Churchill fanatic and history buff, Kinder would walk around the office chomping on an unlit cigar, striking fear into the hearts of Enron executives.

In August 1987 Lay moved Kinder out of the general counsel's office and gave him the title chief of staff. In effect, he was designating him the company's chief problem solver. And though it was another three years before Kinder became chief operating officer, replacing Seidl, who'd left the company in 1989, he took unofficial charge of Enron well before then. There is one meeting in particular that everyone at Enron remembers as marking the moment Kinder became the boss. In the Enron mythology, it came to be known as the Come to Jesus meeting.

The meeting took place in 1988. The Enron Oil scandal was no longer on the front burner, but the company was still plagued with problems. After the Inter-North-HNG merger, Lay had hired lots of his old cronies. They had ill-defined jobs and a line straight to the man who had hired them. Morale was terrible.

Backbiting had become part of the Enron culture. Power plays were a daily occurrence. And it was nearly impossible for the company to act decisively, because executives felt they could always get Lay to reverse a management decision. All the politicking had practically paralyzed the company.

Lay was also at the Come to Jesus meeting. He made a few tepid remarks about how the company needed to embrace gas deregulation. But mostly this was Rich Kinder's show. *"Enough of this!"* he declared, and then he lit into the group. He was tired of the chaos, tired of people going behind his back to Lay, tired of the constant complaints and excuses about why the company wasn't doing better. And it was going to stop. The company's problems were like alligators, he growled. "There are alligators in the swamp," he said. "We're going to get in that fucking swamp, and we're going to kick out all the fucking alligators, one by one, and we're going to kill them, one by one." And on that note, the meeting ended.

CHAPTER 3

"We Were the Apostles"

In the aftermath of the Come to Jesus meeting, things did settle down at Enron, thanks largely to Rich Kinder. He took on the tough job of paring costs, he found ways to pay down some of the crushing debt, and he helped Enron negotiate its way out of the take-or-pay crisis with surprisingly little financial pain. By the end of 1988 Enron was even back in the black, earning $109 million.

But it wasn't a sustainable profit. In fact, without onetime gains from selling assets and stock it held in other companies, Enron would have declared another loss. The big problem still remained, and it wasn't going to go away no matter how many alligators Kinder killed. Enron was still a company in search of a future. Ken Lay had gotten into the pipeline business in the first place because he believed deregulation was inevitable and felt sure there was money to be made in a deregulated industry. He was right about the first; by the late 1980s, wholesale deregulation had largely arrived. But neither he nor Kinder nor anyone else at Enron had the foggiest idea how to create a brand-new business model, one that could make a big profit in this new world. What Enron needed—indeed, what the entire natural-gas industry needed—was someone who could show them the way.

And, lo and behold, there he was.

For better or worse—and over the years it would be both—Enron found its visionary in Jeffrey Skilling. When Skilling looked at the natural-gas industry, he didn't see natural gas. Instead, he saw the needs of customers on one side and the needs of suppliers on the other—and the gaps in between where, he believed, serious money could be made. To put it another way, he saw the ways in which the natural-gas industry resembled commodity businesses like wheat and pork bellies and especially financial services, where money itself is the commodity. That no natural-gas executives shared his vision didn't bother Skilling in the least; other energy executives, he believed, were hidebound, unimaginative, and hemmed in by the past. Never having worked in the industry before joining Enron—never having run *any* business before joining Enron—Skilling felt no such constraints. He fervently believed that he saw the way the industry should operate, and for him, "should" and "would" were pretty much the same. Over time, his way of thinking not only reshaped Enron, it helped revolutionize the entire natural-gas industry.

In part, Skilling's influence can be explained by his particular brand of intelligence. When people describe Skilling they don't just use the word "smart"; they use phrases like "incandescently brilliant" or "the smartest person I ever met." Skilling in the late 1980s wasn't a physically striking man—he was smallish, a little pudgy, and balding—but his mental agility was breathtaking. He could process information and conceptualize new ideas with blazing speed. He could instantly simplify highly complex issues into a sparkling, compelling image. And he presented his ideas with a certainty that bordered on arrogance and brooked no dissent. He used his brainpower not just to persuade but to intimidate.

Without question, Skilling's formidable intelligence had a lot to do with turning Enron into a company that was successful—at least for a while. But he also had qualities that were disastrous for someone running a big company. For all his brilliance, Skilling had dangerous blind spots. His management skills were appalling, in large part because he didn't really understand people. He expected people to behave according to the imperatives of pure intellectual logic, but of course nobody does that (including, it should be said, Skilling himself). One former top executive recalls arguing with him constantly, struggling to explain, "Jeff, people will do things just because they're people."

Skilling also had a tendency to oversimplify, and he largely disregarded—indeed, he had an active distaste for—the messy details involved in executing a plan. What thrilled Skilling, always, was the intellectual purity of an idea, not the translation of that idea into reality. "Jeff Skilling is a designer of ditches, not a digger of ditches," an Enron executive said years later. He was often too slow—even unwilling—to recognize when the reality didn't match the theory. Over time his arrogance hardened, and he became so sure that he was the smartest guy in the room that anyone who disagreed with him was summarily dismissed as just not bright enough to "get it."

And there was one other thing about Skilling. For all his analytical abilities, he was a gambler at heart and had been from an early age. He always assumed that he could beat the odds. In the end, that was Skilling's most dangerous blind spot of all.

Like many of the other major players in the Enron saga, Jeff Skilling made his way to the top of American business by sheer force of will. He wasn't poor the way Ken Lay was poor, but his family lived on the thin line that separates the working class from the middle class. He grew up feeling that he couldn't ask his parents for money, because they didn't have much. As a result, making his own way financially was always important to him.

Born in Pittsburgh in 1953, when that city was still the heart of America's industrial economy, Skilling was the second of Betty and Thomas Skilling's four children. His father was a salesman for a company that made large valves for heavy machinery. When Skilling was just a baby, the family moved to Westfield, New Jersey, where his father had been transferred and where he later bought a lovely house that was beyond his means. In 1965 his father changed jobs, and the family moved again, this time to Aurora, Illinois, a blue-collar town at the end of the Chicago commuter rail line. For the children, who had loved the woods behind their New Jersey home, the move was traumatic, all the more so because their father was already working in Aurora and couldn't come back to help them move. So the four children and Betty drove across the country. His younger sister, Sue, remembers Skilling sitting in front of the Rambler station wagon, helping his mother read the map, and filling water bottles at gas stations to keep the old car from overheating.

To a surprising degree, considering that he became a business celebrity, Skilling was a wallflower in high school. Aurora was a quintessentially midwestern football town, and he was a smart kid, not a jock. He has described himself as a "bit of a loner," and apart from brief stints on the school paper and the student council, Skilling wasn't actively involved in the life of the school. Today, former classmates remember his older brother, Tom, far more vividly; the older Skilling boy, who used to do weather updates over the PA system in grade school and by age 15 on local radio, is now a Chicago TV weatherman. Though Skilling made National Honor Society his junior and senior years and graduated sixteenth of a class of 600, he later told friends that school was "sheer boredom." His childhood was unhappy; one friend describes him as "a tortured soul."

He found his solace in work. Soon after moving to Aurora, he got a job at a start-up local TV station. His first duties were cleaning out 40-odd years of accumulated debris from the old Moose Lodge, where the new station was housed. He painted the walls. Then, as each piece of equipment arrived, Skilling learned to operate it. When the production director quit, Skilling took his job. He was 14 years old. After school, his mother would drive him to the TV station, where he would stay until midnight. Throughout his high school years, he worked upward of 50 hours a week.

When Skilling was applying to college, his father took him to see his alma mater, Lehigh University, in Bethlehem, Pennsylvania. From the school, Skilling could stare down into the valley upon acre after acre of aging, decrepit steel mills, many of them boarded up and abandoned. Skilling had an immediate visceral reaction to the sight: this, he thought, was what he was trying to get away from. Not long afterward, he visited Southern Methodist University in Dallas, which dangled the prospect of an engineering scholarship in front of the young midwesterner. The sun was shining, the campus was neat, and the girls were out in their bathing suits. Perhaps most important, there were no aging steel mills anywhere. "They're going to pay me to go here?" he thought. At a place like SMU, a person could start fresh. Though he was only 17, that's what Jeff Skilling wanted to do.

Even though he had a scholarship, Skilling still had to work in college;

despite all the money he'd made in high school, he was flat broke. The problem wasn't that he'd spent it; no, he'd lost it playing the stock market. Today, of course, that's hardly likely to raise eyebrows. Lots of people, including teenagers, got caught up in the market in the late 1990s and lost money as the bull market soured. But it was different in the 1960s and early 1970s. The stock market had not yet become part of daily life in America, and a teenager putting his money in the market was almost unheard of. Skilling, though, poured all the money he'd made at the TV station—more than $15,000—into shares of his father's employer, a company called Henry Pratt. He got in at $8 to $9 a share, and for a while, the stock was a winner, going as high as $25 a share. Convinced that the stock was headed even higher, Skilling borrowed thousands against his stake to buy a car. But then came the bear market of the 1970s, and before long Henry Pratt was at $2; and because he'd borrowed against the stock, Skilling had to liquidate his holdings to pay off the loan. He was soon wiped out.

Most kids would have been chastened by such an experience. Not Skilling. The summer between his freshman and sophomore years, he had a bad accident while working a summer job: a truckload of heavy equipment fell on him, crushing his back. He was in a full body cast for three months, but he came out of it with a $3,500 workers' compensation check. And once again, he plunged the money into the market, this time the bond market. But he didn't buy low-risk bonds. Instead, he leveraged his money almost three to one and bought $10,000 worth of deep-discount bonds. Interest rates were sky-high, and Skilling was betting that they'd soon drop. Instead, they kept going up. Skilling started getting margin calls and finally had to sell just two weeks before the rates began to fall. For the second time in less than a year, he was wiped out.

Despite the losses, Skilling's interest in the market did have one benefit: it led him to business classes. That's when the lightbulb switched on; once he discovered business, Skilling knew he'd found his intellectual passion. Though he'd dutifully taken his engineering classes, he found them "mind-numbing." By contrast, business was fun, engaging, even creative. He also thought his engineering background could help him: he could apply scientific logic to business and thereby gain an edge. His GPA in engineering was 2.6. In his senior year, he concentrated on business and got a 4.0. For his entrepreneurship class, he had to read a thesis written by a Ph.D. candidate at the University of Chicago on the subject of converting commodities contracts into tradable securities. To Skilling, it was a thrilling idea, and he never forgot the paper.

Skilling graduated in 1975 but skipped the ceremony to drive to Chicago to marry Susan Long, a fellow midwesterner who was his college sweetheart. Three days later, he returned to Texas and began a job at First City National Bank in Houston. Assigned to the bank's operations center, he was soon moved to corporate planning. His starting salary at the bank was $800 a month. By the time he left First City, he was making $22,000 a year and was the youngest officer at the bank.

What changed the course of his life—and Enron's history—was Skilling's next big gamble. He decided to apply to the country's most prestigious business finishing school: Harvard Business School. The gamble wasn't so much that he'd set his sights on Harvard but that he applied nowhere else. It was going to be Harvard or nothing; if he didn't get in, he thought, he'd just stay in his job and get his MBA at the University of Houston at night. Despite his middling college grades, though, he did get in—because he acted like Jeff Skilling. An interview at Houston's Hyatt Hotel with the dean, who was meeting candidates about whom the school was on the fence, was going nowhere fast. Then the dean asked, "Skilling, are you smart?" "I'm *fucking* smart," he replied. Skilling rented a U-Haul truck, drove to Cambridge, and entered the business school in the fall of 1977.

Here at last Skilling was in his element. At Harvard he became a star. He stood out in part because of his brilliance and in part because of his harshly libertarian view of business and markets. The markets, he believed, were the ultimate judge of right and wrong. Social policies designed to temper the market's Darwinian judgments were wrongheaded and counterproductive. And that wasn't all. John LeBoutillier, a Skilling classmate (and later a one-term congressman), remembers one class in which the students were discussing a product that might be—but wasn't definitively—harmful to consumers. The question for the class: what should the CEO do? "I'd keep making and selling the product," replied Skilling. "My job as a businessman is to be a profit center and to maximize return to the shareholders. It's the government's job to step in if a product is dangerous." (Skilling has always denied this story.)

Skilling graduated a Baker Scholar, a coveted honor bestowed upon the top 5 percent of the class. He decided that his talent was "pattern recognition," which meant that he thought he was good at seeing how the techniques used in one industry could be applied to another. Degree in hand, Skilling did one of the appropriately prestigious things that Baker Scholars often do, probably the one thing that best matched his mental proclivities. He joined the nation's bluest-chip consulting firm, McKinsey & Company.

McKinsey was founded in 1926 by a University of Chicago accounting professor named James McKinsey, and the firm has dominated the business of corporate strategic consulting ever since. McKinsey has always had a special aura about it, a sense that it employs only the best of the best, that its management advice is smarter and better than anyone else's, and that its theories are a little akin to tablets handed down from on high. It's a coveted place to work—overachievers who go to work at McKinsey can be comfortable that they will continue to overachieve—and it can also be a stepping stone to other enviable perches. Lou Gerstner, the recently retired CEO of IBM, is one of many former McKinseyites who went on to lead major corporations. The 1982 book *In Search of Excellence*, perhaps the best-selling management tome of all time, was written by two McKinsey partners.

Operating on the belief that intellectual brawn is more important than practical experience, McKinsey prefers to hire new consultants straight out of places like Harvard Business School rather than from industry itself. In fact, it's hard to think of a place that believes in the value of brainpower more than McKinsey. The firm spends a great deal of time sorting out stars from the merely superbright; perhaps not surprisingly, those who prosper there often develop a smug superiority. A McKinsey partner once told *Forbes*: "We don't learn from clients. Their standards aren't high enough. We learn from other McKinsey partners." A McKinsey alum described the firm to a new recruit as a place where "the smartest people in business tackle the most important and challenging issues of the world's leading corporations." Indeed, the firm likes to think of itself as bringing enlightenment to the business world. McKinsey ideas often sound incredibly compelling, even pure, in a way that makes it impossible to believe they could ever be corrupted. But like Skilling himself, McKinsey partners tend to be designers of ditches, not diggers of ditches. When it comes to executing their lofty theories, well, consultants lean toward leaving those messy realities to the companies themselves.

Even by McKinsey standards, Skilling was phenomenally successful, rising through the extremely competitive ranks with almost surreal speed. He started his career in Dallas. Six months later he moved to the Houston office, where he was the third employee. (The Houston office is now one of McKinsey's biggest.) It normally took a successful McKinsey consultant seven years to become a partner and another dozen or more to become a director. Skilling made partner in five years and director in ten; by 1989, he was overseeing the worldwide energy and North American chemical practices. He is still proud of the fact that only a handful of people (they include Lou Gerstner) rose through the ranks faster than he did.

It would be hard to imagine a place that suited Skilling more perfectly. The McKinsey thought process reduced a chaotic world to a series of coolly clinical, logical observations. That's precisely how Skilling thought. McKinsey valued sheer brainpower; he had it to spare. It favored people who were quick on their feet and who could "present well." That was Skilling through and through. He had a way of turning practical disagreements into abstract arguments and could outdebate just about anyone. "It was difficult to disagree with Jeff because he would elevate the disagreement to an intellectual disagreement, and it was hard to outsmart him," says a former partner who worked with him.

But McKinsey also played to his weaknesses. Working at McKinsey only heightened his natural arrogance. McKinsey could be a cold place, ruthless in sorting out the stars from the also-rans. Skilling embraced that ruthlessness. The culture rewarded individual achievement, as opposed to teamwork. Skilling was never much of a team player. If he thought he was smarter than someone—and he usually did—he would treat him harshly if he had the temerity to disagree with him. Other McKinsey partners began saying of Skilling, "Sometimes wrong, but never in doubt."

Ultimately, though, McKinsey was the formative experience of Jeff Skilling's business life. Though McKinsey has since sought to distance itself from Skilling and Enron, much of what he brought to Enron—not only ideas about how to re-shape the natural gas industry but ideas about what companies should value and how they should be run—came out of his experience at McKinsey.

His first goal, upon arriving in Houston as an up-and-coming consultant, was to start a financial services practice. But within a few years, the price of oil, which had skyrocketed during the energy crisis of the 1970s, began to decline, hurting not only the companies that drilled for oil but all the big Texas banks that had loaned them money. Clearly a financial services practice was not going to fly. So he did other kinds of consulting work. According to the *Houston Chronicle*, a study Skilling did of the Houston Fire Department so thoroughly impressed the fire chief that he told Skilling, "You could be the best fire chief in the nation if you ever need a job." And he did occasional consulting for InterNorth, work that continued after the company changed its name to Enron.

By the late 1980s Skilling was spending about half his time on Enron work. In the process, he was also learning about the natural-gas business; not surprisingly, he was appalled at what he saw. It was, he has said, "the screwiest business I'd ever seen in my life. All the rules were written in Washington. It was like *Alice in Wonderland*." All true, of course. But it was also true that the industry had to change, and Skilling reveled in that opportunity. "It was fabulous," he has said. "It was like starting from scratch." By the late 1980s Skilling was con-vinced that he had devised an answer—nay, *the* answer—to the industry's prob-lems. He saw one of those patterns he so liked to recognize. Put simply, he believed the natural-gas business could get out of its predicament by becoming more like the financial-services industry. He called his idea the Gas Bank, and it soon catapulted Skilling into Enron for good.

The biggest single issue facing the entire natural-gas industry was astound-ingly basic: the interaction between buyers and sellers. It wasn't all that long ago, you'll recall, that gas was sold under long-term contracts between produc-ers, pipelines, and local utilities, with the price set by the government. But by the late 1980s, with the onset of deregulation, some 75 percent of all the natural gas sold in the country changed hands on the spot market during a frantic few days of deal doing at the end of every month.

The problem with such a system was its inherent uncertainty. A sudden cold spell in the Northeast could cause prices to rise overnight, hurting consumers. A wave of warm weather could depress prices, causing the gas producers to lose money. Even though there was a glut of natural gas, big industrial customers couldn't be sure that they would always be able to lock up as much supply as they needed from one month to the next. And it was a risky bet for a pipeline company to guarantee a long-term supply at a fixed price to a customer because the pipeline couldn't count on being able to secure a steady supply of gas at a price that would ensure a profit. No wonder many industrial users of natural gas were switching to oil and coal. No wonder they no longer viewed natural gas as a reliable fuel. As for the pipelines, they were struggling to make profits, because the margins on spot-market deals were so low. Indeed, by the late 1980s, Enron was trying to convince the industry to move back to longer-term contracts—just like in the old days, except the price would be negotiated between the parties rather than set by the government.

Enron took the first steps in that direction by setting up a new division called Enron Gas Marketing, which tried to get customers to sign up for long-term deals. In March 1988, for example, Enron signed a 15-year contract with Brooklyn Union to supply 21 million cubic feet of gas a day to a plant being built in Bethpage, New York. The deal was a coup for several reasons. Brooklyn Union agreed to pay a hefty premium to the market price of gas because Enron was willing to guarantee the supply for so many years. Second, Brooklyn Union was not one of Enron's old-line natural-gas customers; in fact, it wasn't even connected to Enron's pipeline system. Enron would have to contract with another pipeline to get the gas to Brooklyn Union. Although deregulation had mandated such "open access" a few years earlier, this was one of the first deals that took advantage of the new rules. But while such a deal diminished the uncertainty for Brooklyn Union, it actually *increased* Enron's risk. If gas prices rose and the contract became unprofitable, that was Enron's problem, not Brooklyn Union's. And Enron was assuming the transportation risk as well; if, for some reason, the Houston company couldn't get the gas to the New York utility, Enron would be liable.

Enter Skilling's Gas Bank. It was nothing less than the first serious effort to diminish the level of risk for everybody involved in natural-gas transactions. The basic idea was this. Producers (acting as depositors) would contract to sell their gas to Enron. Gas customers (the borrowers) would contract to buy their gas from Enron. Enron (the bank) would capture the profits between the price at which it had acquired the gas and the price at which it had promised to sell the gas, just as a bank earns the spread between what it pays depositors and what it charges borrowers. Everybody would be happy. So long as Enron had a balanced portfolio of contracts—that is, contracts to sell gas at a specific price were matched by contracts to acquire gas at a specific price—the spot-market price of natural gas could go crazy and it wouldn't matter. Enron would already have locked in the profits. Just as important, for both sellers and buyers, the uncertainty of the spot market would be replaced by the contractual certainty that Skilling's Gas Bank offered. "The concept was pure intellectually," Skilling has said. "It made all the sense in the world."

In late 1987 Skilling pitched his idea to a meeting of 25 top Enron executives, including Lay and Kinder, in a conference room on the forty-ninth floor of Enron's headquarters in downtown Houston. In classic Skilling fashion, he used just one slide in his presentation—which shocked the Enron executives, who were expecting dozens—and he spoke for less than a half hour. When he had finished, an executive named Jim Rogers declared the idea dumb, and virtually all of the others agreed. In the elevator afterward, Skilling apologized to Kinder for not explaining his concept well. Kinder, chomping on his unlit cigar, replied that when he had heard Rogers call the idea stupid, he knew it was the right move.

Later, after Skilling had become a celebrity, the Gas Bank was described as his first great triumph at Enron. But that was just part of the Enron myth. In fact, however "intellectually pure" the Gas Bank was, it didn't work very well at first. Selling the gas wasn't a problem; local utilities and industrial customers were eager to sign long-term contracts that guaranteed them a steady supply of gas. And they were willing to pay a price that was higher than the spot-market price—sometimes twice as much—for that security. The problem was persuading the people who controlled the supply of natural gas—the producers—to get on board. Although there were daily fluctuations on the spot market, natural-gas prices remained deeply depressed. But natural-gas producers were wildcatters at heart, and they had the wildcatter's mentality: tomorrow will surely be better than today. And for that reason, they were reluctant to sign long-term contracts to deliver gas at a fixed price that they viewed as "too low." Thus Enron still had to buy gas on the spot market to fulfill the terms of its Gas Bank contracts with utilities. If prices shot up, the contracts would be wildly unprofitable; indeed, a McKinsey study was predicting just such a price hike. (As it turned out, McKinsey was wrong: prices stayed low, and those initial contracts turned out to be supremely profitable.)

Skilling had another rationale for why the Gas Bank was having trouble: he wasn't in charge of it. Rich Kinder seemed to think the same thing; before long, Kinder approached Skilling about joining Enron and running the Gas Bank himself. And so it was that in June 1990, after several months of negotiations, Jeff Skilling joined Enron. Though it's rare for a McKinsey partner to leave the storied firm, Skilling felt he couldn't pass up the opportunity to test his theory about how to fix the natural-gas business. His title was chairman and CEO of something called Enron Finance, a new division that was established so that he could run it. His mandate was to make the Gas Bank work. His salary was $275,000, a far cry from the $1 million or so that a McKinsey partner typically makes. But the real reward was not supposed to come from his salary. Instead, Skilling's contract gave him something called phantom equity in his division, which would allow him to share in whatever economic value he created. If Enron Finance was a success, he'd be far richer than any mere management consultant, even a McKinsey consultant, could ever hope to be.

• • •

Skilling had an idea about how to solve the problem of getting producers to supply gas, and he immediately went to work putting it into practice. Instead of paying producers for their gas over the life of a contract, he decided to give them cash up front in return for a long-term supply of the gas they got out of the ground. That changed everything. Problems in the oil patch had created a banking crisis in Texas. Saddled with huge portfolios of bad loans—not just to energy companies but to the real estate sector, which was suffering its own meltdown—banks weren't about to lend new money to the natural-gas industry. Yet without loans, producers couldn't drill for new gas. Presented with the option of cold, hard cash from Enron, producers were suddenly happy to sign long-term contracts. As Skilling has described it, "If you offered to buy gas at a fixed price for 20 years, they would throw you out. But if you offered to hand the producer $400 million to develop reserves, he saw you as a partner."

Although Enron was assuming the traditional role of the banker, it had major advantages over banks. In extending a loan, a bank would try to err on the conservative side, because it had no idea where the price of gas was going. If the price plummeted, the producer might go bankrupt. (In fact, this had happened quite often after the energy bubble of the 1980s burst, which is why so many banks were in trouble.) But Enron absolutely knew the price it could get for the gas: *it had already sold it.* And because of that knowledge, it was able to lend far more money than a bank typically would. What's more, Enron structured its deals so that it still had the right to the gas, even if the producer went under. After all, for Enron, getting the gas was what mattered.

Finally the Gas Bank began to work: producers as well as customers were signing contracts. Now that supply and price could be guaranteed, natural gas—which was far more environmentally friendly than coal—soon became an attractive fuel again for utilities. They began building new gas-fired plants. That, of course, increased the nation's reliance on natural gas. In one fell swoop, Skilling and Enron had finally figured out a way to make deregulation work and to profit from it.

Skilling had one more trick up his sleeve—in retrospect, the most important one of all. These new natural-gas contracts Enron was devising—these promises to buy and sell natural gas at a fixed price—could be *traded,* just the way oil-futures contracts were traded. Eventually, you needed the same essential elements: the contract had to be standardized and there needed to be a critical mass of participants to create liquidity, but it certainly could be done. If Skilling hadn't come up with the idea of creating a market for natural-gas contracts, somebody else surely would have; indeed, a number of banks had begun talking about it. But he had the idea first, and in implementing it, he put Enron at the very center of this new business. After which, Enron was never the same.

As Skilling envisioned it at first, trading was meant to be a tool to help natural-gas executives better manage the business. In this it mirrored the evolution of other commodities markets, which are not about speculation, at least at first. Trading natural gas, for instance, could allow for far greater flexibility than was possible when Enron had to buy up supply at one end and deliver gas at the other. Now Enron could sign a deal to supply gas to a utility on Long Island and use forward contracts to "hedge" the price risk on that transaction in order to help ensure that it was profitable.

Hedging itself is an old financial technique. It's exactly as the word sounds: it's a way to reduce risk. Suppose the price of oil is $20 a barrel and you've promised a customer that you'll sell it oil at that price for the next two years. In effect, you are now short oil. If prices fall, you're in great shape, because you're selling the oil for a higher price than it's costing you. But if prices rise, you'll have to sell the oil for less than it costs you to fulfill your promise. So if you don't want to take that risk, you can hedge by taking an offsetting long position, or agreement to buy oil, at the same price. Thus, it doesn't matter to you whether the price goes to $60 or to $10; either way, you're still paying and receiving $20 a barrel. But being fully hedged also means you're making no profit on any price move in oil; all the profit comes from the deal you've cut with the customer. If you think you know where prices are headed, you might not want to be fully hedged. The other issue is that commodities markets are complicated beasts, and it is often impossible to be truly fully hedged. And so terms sprung up like dirty hedge, meaning that your hedge doesn't precisely offset your risk, and stack and roll, meaning that you are hedged for the early years of the contract but not the later ones.

In a sense, Skilling's innovation had the effect of freeing natural gas from its physical qualities, from the constraints of molecules and movement. The Gas Bank had been a kind of physical hedge; now trading took the next step. It freed Enron from having to own assets involved in the production and transportation of natural gas. In theory, instead of owning a portfolio of assets—natural-gas reserves and pipelines—Enron could simply own a portfolio of contracts that would allow it to control the resources it needed. Instead of seeing a commitment to deliver natural gas as something that necessarily involved a pipeline, Enron saw it as a *financial* commitment. It was a whole new way of conceptualizing the business, one that in theory required less capital and therefore would enable better pricing and more flexibility for customers.

Along with the different way of thinking about the business came a different kind of financial obligation: a derivative. Derivatives were already common on Wall Street, but no one was using them in the natural-gas business. On Wall Street, a "call" gives the owner the right to buy a stock at a certain price. Enron created calls that gave, for instance, someone the right to buy gas under certain conditions. That was one kind of derivative. There were many others—with names like swaps, options, puts, and forwards—that revolved around the idea that natural gas could be reduced to its financial terms. It's almost impossible to overstate the radical change that this required in the gas industry. But if Enron could be at the center of all this—and wasn't that always the plan?—it stood to make a ton of money.

Without question, natural-gas trading was more complicated than other kinds of commodities trading. Unlike wheat or soybeans—or crude oil, for that matter—natural gas flowed continuously, 24 hours a day. Different hubs in North America, such as Chicago's City Gate or the Katy Interconnect near Houston, had their own pricing variations. There were transportation contracts, which were different from contracts guaranteeing price. There were capacity contracts, which reserved space on pipelines. And different users had different needs: power plants wanted long-term supplies; industrial users wanted more gas in good economic times and less in tougher times; utilities wanted seasonal gas, that is, they wanted more gas in the winter, when their customers had to heat their homes. Some customers were willing to pay a premium price to ensure the transportation of the gas; others might decide to pay less and contract with someone else for the transportation. There was an almost infinite number of moving pieces.

Skilling reveled in the complexity of the natural-gas market he was creating. He had one of his ready-made analogies so that everyone could see it the way he saw it. A natural gas contract was a little like a cow, he used to say. A cow doesn't just have one kind of meat; it has all sorts of different meats, from sirloin to hamburger. And people are willing to pay different prices for the part that they want. In the same way you could divide a gas contract into many different parts and sell them to people with different needs.

In fact, some of the people you traded with might not even be in the natural-gas business at all. To be a player in this new business, you just needed to understand the price of natural gas and the concept of risk. In the coming years, Wall Street firms piled into the business, but Enron always had a huge advantage. Its immense network of physical assets, its ability to tie all the moving pieces together and provide physical delivery of the gas itself, and its long history in the gas business gave it insights its Wall Street competitors could never match. These, alas, were lessons Enron would one day forget.

But that was still in the future. For now there was tremendous excitement in Skilling's group about what they were doing, and they brought to it a missionary zeal. Early employees in Skilling's division would always recall those days as pure magic—a time when anything seemed possible and much of what they did turned to gold. Skilling himself was down-to-earth, accessible, and open to argument in a way he wasn't later. "In the early days, we were printing money," Cliff Baxter later recalled. "We saw things no one else could see." Amanda Martin, another former executive, added, "In the beginning, it was brilliant, we were riding a train, we were proselytizing. We were the apostles. *We were right.*"

It wasn't long before a skeptical industry began to agree. In the spring of 1990, the New York Mercantile Exchange began trading natural-gas futures, though very limited ones, dealing only with gas delivered to a key hub in Louisiana. But

Enron's fast-growing trading desk was handling other, more complicated trades, and Skilling knew that he needed some of Wall Street's expertise in pricing and managing the risk associated with derivatives. To get that expertise, he cut a deal with Bankers Trust, which was one of the leaders on Wall Street in derivatives trading. It was a sweet deal for Bankers Trust: in return for sharing its smarts, it would get a third of the profits. Too sweet, in fact; it wasn't long before the Enron crowd and the Bankers Trust crowd began bickering.

Still, it was exhilarating to see natural-gas trading start to work, to see this intellectually pure idea take hold in the real world in much the way Skilling had envisioned it. "This was the most creative period. It fundamentally changed the industry," says one former executive. Then he adds sadly, "What happened later is where it all went wrong."

Even before joining Enron, Skilling had made a very strange demand. His new business, he told Lay, had to use a different type of accounting from the one ordinarily used by the natural-gas industry. Rather than using historical-cost accounting like everyone else, he wanted Enron Finance be able to use what's known as mark-to-market accounting. This was so important to him—"a lay-my-body-across-the-tracks issue," he later called it—that he actually told Lay he would not join Enron and build his new division unless he could use mark-to-market accounting.

Because much of what happened at Enron can be traced to the decision to use mark-to-market accounting, it's important to take a moment to understand it. Suppose you've booked an asset and a liability on your balance sheet, for instance, a ten-year contract to supply natural gas to a utility in Duluth. Under conventional accounting, the value on your books continues to reflect your initial assumptions over the life of the deal, even if the underlying economics change. Using the concept of marking-to-market, however, you're forced to adjust the values on your balance sheet on a regular basis, to reflect fluctuations in the marketplace or anything else that might change the values. That's the first big difference. Here's the second. When you use conventional accounting, you book the revenues and profits that flow from the contract as they come through the door. But under the mark-to-market method, *you can book the entire estimated value for all ten years on the day you sign the contract.* Changes in that value show up as additional income—or losses—in subsequent periods.

The question, of course, is why was Skilling so adamant about an accounting method, of all things? He could list several reasons. One rationale in particular spoke volumes about the way Skilling viewed business. He'd never let go of the consultant's conceit that the idea was all and the idea, therefore, should be the thing that was rewarded. He felt that a business should be able to declare profits at the moment of the creative act that would earn those profits. Otherwise businessmen were mere coupon clippers, reaping the benefit of innovation that had been devised in the past by other, greater men. Taken to its absurd extreme, this line of thinking suggests that General Motors should book all the future profits of a new model automobile at the moment the car is designed, long before a single vehicle rolls off the assembly line to be sold to customers. Over time this radical notion of value came to define the way Enron presented itself to the world, justifying the booking of millions in profits on a business before it had generated a penny in actual revenues. In Skilling's head, the idea, the *vision,* not the mundane reality, was always the critical thing.

Skilling also insisted that mark-to-market accounting gave a truer reading of a company's financial reality than the more common historical-cost accounting. "There's no way around it," he would tell people. "It reflects the true economic value." To him this wasn't even a debatable issue. His favorite example was the S&L crisis (which was still in full swoon at the time Skilling joined Enron). Historical-cost accounting allowed S&Ls to keep loans that had collapsed in value on their books at wildly inflated prices, which in turn allowed them to hide the true state of their finances. By contrast, Wall Street firms, which have to use mark-to-market accounting to value their portfolios, take hits when, say, the stock market collapses because they have to mark the value of their assets to the current market price. Mark-to-market accounting, in fact, is an important component in ensuring the "transparency" of portfolio values. Because portfolio managers are forced to mark their holdings to market every day, their investors know precisely how much they've made—or lost.

What's also true, though, as we now know from painful experience, is that any accounting method is susceptible to abuse. And the natural-gas business at this critical moment in its history was ripe for mark-to-market accounting abuse. Why? Because the value of a natural gas contract cannot be determined with the same precision that one can determine the price of a share of stock. Sure, you can gauge today's natural gas price precisely, and with the growth in NYMEX futures contracts, there is even a market price for gas, say, 12 months in the future. But natural-gas contracts might have durations of 10, even 20 years. And who could say with any certainty what the price of gas was going to be 10 years from now at a hub like the Chicago City Gate? Yet to book all that revenue and profit up front, as mark-to-market accounting required, somebody at Enron had to estimate the price of gas 20 years hence. Even well-intentioned estimates might turn out to be completely wrong.

And of course there would also be times when those estimates weren't so well-intentioned, times when somebody needed a little extra income to make the earnings Enron promised Wall Street or get paid a big bonus or stash earnings away for a rainy day. Indeed, over the years, Enron extended mark-to-market accounting well beyond natural gas to other areas where the "value" was even more subjective—and abuse even more tempting.

There are two other potential problems with mark-to-market accounting. The first is the mismatch between profits and cash. Just because a company can book twenty years' worth of revenues and profits in one fell swoop doesn't mean it actually has the money in hand. On the contrary: even if everything happens precisely as predicted, the money rolls in quarter after quarter, year after year, for the duration of the contract. And so with mark-to-market accounting, there is often a large discrepancy between the profits the company is reporting to its shareholders and the cash it has on hand to run the business. Sure enough, Enron's financial filings soon included this phrase: "recognized, but unrealized, income." In other words, Enron had booked the earnings, but it didn't yet have the cash. If the estimated value is correct, then over the life of the contract, the cash should equal the earnings, but the longer the term of the contract, the bigger the initial mismatch. And of course, you can't run a business on paper profits—at least, not forever.

The most dangerous problem of all is the very thing that makes mark-to-market accounting seem so seductive in the first place: growth. When the initial deals are cut and all the potential profits are immediately posted, a company using mark-to-market accounting appears to be growing rapidly. Wall Street analysts applaud, and the stock rockets upward. But how do you keep that growth rate up? True, you're still receiving the cash from past contracts. But you can't count it in your profits, because you've booked it already. It's as if you have to begin every quarter fresh. If you did one deal last quarter, in order to show growth you have do two the next and four the quarter after that and eight after that and on and on. And if you're promising Wall Street that your earnings will increase at a 15 percent annual clip, well, soon enough you're on a treadmill that becomes faster and steeper as the company gets bigger.

Despite the potential dangers Skilling had little difficulty convincing Kinder, Lay, and Enron's board to see things his way. On May 17, 1991, some 11 months after Skilling joined Enron, the audit committee of Enron's board approved the use of mark-to-market accounting for Skilling's new business. Now all he had to do was persuade the Securities and Exchange Commission. As it turns out, that wasn't much more difficult. In a letter dated June 11, 1991, Enron asked the SEC not to object to Enron's new choice of accounting methodology. Among Enron's arguments was that "as a trader" Skilling's new business "creates value and completes its earnings process when the transactions are finalized" and that "other commodity trading businesses which are analogous" used mark-to-market accounting. Enron included a missive from its accountants at Arthur Andersen stating that mark-to-market accounting was indeed preferable.

Over the next six months, at least eight letters were exchanged between the agency and the company, and two meetings between Skilling and other Enron representatives and the SEC staff took place. A review of the correspondence shows that the SEC was focused on a key issue: how would Enron estimate price? The agency even suggested that Enron consider some additional disclosure to investors in its financial filings until it got a better sense of the reliability of its estimates. Enron resisted, asserting that mark-to-market earnings would be calculated based on "known spreads and balanced positions" and that its numbers would not be "significantly dependent on subjective elements." At which point, the SEC essentially caved.

On January 30, 1992, the SEC told Enron that it would not object to the use of mark-to-market accounting beginning that year. On getting the word, Skilling was ecstatic. He quickly gathered his troops in the conference room of the thirty-first floor, where his group had its offices. To celebrate, he brought in champagne: champagne to toast an accounting change! By 2 P.M., most of Skilling's staff, which numbered around 50, were reveling in the celebration.

And then Enron did something quite telling. Less than two weeks later, on February 11, Enron sent the SEC a letter informing them that it had decided that the "most appropriate period" for the adoption of mark-to-market accounting was not 1992 after all. Rather, Enron wrote the agency that it planned to apply mark-to-market accounting to the year that had just ended: 1991. Since Enron had not yet filed its financial statements for 1991, it could now do so using the new accounting methodology. Enron said the impact on earnings was "not material." In the big picture, that was true: Enron reported $242 million in earnings that year. But earlier in the year Skilling's division had estimated that its mark-to-market earnings for 1991 transactions would be about $25 million. That number, assuming it held up, amounted to half the profits in Skilling's new division.

There was one last lingering issue: Bankers Trust. Practically from the moment Skilling brought Bankers Trust in, he regretted it. He hated the way the New York bankers treated the Texans like rubes. He hated even more the fact that he had agreed to give such a large percentage of Enron's trading profits to Bankers Trust, especially once he decided that his team didn't really need the bank's expertise in derivatives. He and his group could learn how to do it themselves—indeed, they *were* learning how to do it themselves.

Bankers Trust felt the same way about Enron: why did they need to be in partnership with these guys when they could run their own trading operation and keep *all* the profits? They were contemptuous of the Enron traders and too arrogant to hide it. They would openly complain that they were working with neophytes. Meetings soon deteriorated into pitched battles about who was assuming what risk and how much each of the partners should be compensated.

Finally, in June 1991, Bankers Trust decided to pull out of the deal. In retrospect, it was a foolish move, given the extent to which Enron soon dominated the natural-gas trading business—and the sweet deal Bankers Trust had extracted from Skilling. And the Bankers Trust executives only compounded their mistake by the way they went about their departure. They did it in the dead of night, without ever informing anyone at Enron, and as they walked out the door they pulled a dirty trick. Knowing the bank was going to walk away from Enron, one of its executives called in a junior employee named Kevin Hannon and ordered him to delete all the files containing the trading information. Over one summer weekend, Hannon did just that. He then jumped on a plane and flew back to New York.

On Monday morning an Enron executive named Lou Pai came running up to Skilling. "Those fuckers," he yelled. "They erased all the tapes!"

"Who?" asked a surprised Skilling.

"BT," replied Pai. "They're gone!" It was a crisis but not a protracted one. An Enron employee worked around the clock for the next month to rebuild the files, and the Enron trading desk was in the black by July. Never again did Jeff Skilling involve an outside party in his trading operation. "This is *our* business," he thought. And it was.

CHAPTER 4

The First Prima Donna

Even as Jeff Skilling was beginning to build one part of the new Enron, a second executive was etching out another new part of the company. He was every bit as aggressive as Skilling and every bit as arrogant. He also ran his division with every bit as much autonomy—more, actually. For years, he managed a billion-dollar portfolio of Enron projects from offices near his home in the Woodlands, 30 miles north of downtown Houston, and simply refused all entreaties that he move his operation to the company's headquarters. In his fiefdom, he demanded total loyalty—to himself, not Enron.

In other ways, though, he and Skilling could not have been more different. He had not the slightest interest in intellectually pure theories; he viewed himself as being a part of the rough-and-tumble, focused only on getting the job done, whether it was building a power plant or completing a deal. He had about him an aura of mystery, which he encouraged. He was loud and profane, and though he had it in him to kill with kindness, he had no qualms about browbeating people into submission. His personality was volcanic. His name was John Wing, and the division he helped create was eventually called Enron International. In time, the part of the company he started became one the linchpins of the modern Enron. Wing, though, was long gone by then.

To a large extent, John Wing is the forgotten man of the Enron saga. On one level, that's completely understandable: he left the company nearly a decade before Enron imploded, so one could hardly blame him for what happened. When Enron was flying high, Wing's contributions were also usually ignored; his eventual successor at Enron International was his former protégé and lover, a woman named Rebecca Mark, who, in the mid-1990s, was the single most glamorous figure at the company and hardly the type to deflect credit to her ornery predecessor.

But internally, the Enron old-timers never forgot John Wing. With his over-the-top personality, Wing was a mythic figure, by far the most memorable character of Enron's early days. He was also a genuine moneymaker. At a time when nothing else was working, Wing's early deals brought the company badly needed cash. His greatest triumph, a landmark power project in England called Teesside, pushed Enron onto the world stage and gave it credibility and profits—real profits, not the mark-to-market kind—that the company milked for the next decade. It was Enron's first international development deal, and while the company did dozens of such ventures in the years that followed, none earned nearly as much.

This is not to say that people at Enron *liked* John Wing. On the contrary: many of the company's executives loathed him. They viewed him as a master manipulator who took care of himself first. He was so divisive a figure yet so valuable that he was cut loose—and brought back—three separate times. After each parting, Wing somehow emerged with an even richer deal than he had before. His ultimate take from the company exceeded $25 million.

None of this was lost on other Enron executives, including Skilling and Mark. Wing was Enron's first true prima donna. He was the first Enron executive to get genuinely rich, the first to insist that he get a piece of the projects he developed, the first to bully Lay into letting him do whatever he wanted, and the first to see Enron not as a place for a long, happy career but rather as a place for mutual exploitation. He was hardly the last. Other executives saw what Wing got away with and realized they could do whatever they wanted, too.

"I can be your greatest friend or your worst enemy," John Wing liked to tell new acquaintances. At Enron, he was both.

John Wing is 57 now and semiretired, tending to his many investments and moving with the climate from his home base in suburban Houston to his cabin in Aspen to his winter residence in Hawaii to a sprawling farmhouse he owns in upstate New York. Even in semiretirement, though, he hasn't exactly mellowed. With his booming voice, craggy features, and bulldoglike build, he remains a physically intimidating man, even though he stands less than six feet tall. A West Point graduate, he laces his conversation with the kind of moral certainties one typically associates with military men: "Never, *ever* abandon your wingman." And: "Never, *ever* do the easy wrong instead of the harder right." His bluntness can be startling. His judgments are fierce and unyielding, and when it comes to much of Enron's old senior leadership, largely unflattering. And though he firmly believes that Lay made a huge mistake in finally letting him go in 1991, he also understands why his departure was inevitable. As he once put it in an interview, "I'm basically unemployable and a pain in the ass inside the corporate culture."

The son of a farmer and schoolteacher from upstate New York, Wing went to both West Point and Harvard Business School, where, like Skilling, he graduated a Baker Scholar. In the army, he flew intelligence missions in Vietnam, leaving active duty in 1973 with the rank of captain and a Bronze Star. One result of his military background was that he preferred hiring other military men at Enron: they thought the way he did and knew how to get things done. Wing's intelligence background also helped create a sense of danger and intrigue, which he reveled in. From time to time, he'd simply disappear from Enron's offices, stirring rumors that he was off on a secret mission for the CIA.

Wing hooked up with Lay at Florida Gas in 1980 at the age of 34, shortly after earning his MBA from Harvard. Though they were hardly kindred spirits, the two men became friends. They lived just a few houses apart from each other in Winter Park, their wives were close, and their children played together. When Lay got his divorce, Wing served as his court witness. After Lay left for Transco, Wing took a job at General Electric, developing power plants for the company's new CEO, Jack Welch. Lay hired him again, as senior vice president in charge of strategy, shortly after taking over at HNG. It was in that capacity that Wing negotiated the merger with InterNorth, essentially picking the larger company's pockets.

That negotiation was classic Wing and a good part of the reason Lay liked having him around. He could move fast and decisively. He fought for every inch of advantage. He was a cunning negotiator and hard-nosed adversary. And he was absolutely fearless. "John has balls of steel," says one former deputy. "If you were on the other side of the table, there was hell to pay." Wing was also relentless. No one was better at ramrodding a deal or a project through to completion; Wing blew through deadlocks like a load of TNT clearing a beaver dam.

Wing used his volcanic personality as a tactical weapon, especially in the middle of a deal. Lawyers drove him crazy. He once gave a speech advising anyone who wanted to complete a power project to "get all the lawyers in one room, then shoot 'em—in the *mouth,* because it's impossible to miss." In late April 1985, he was in New York, baby-sitting the legal teams rushing to tie up final details of the InterNorth merger so the deal could be publicly announced. When progress ground to a halt, Rich Kinder roused Wing from his hotel bed in the middle of the night. Dressed in his workout clothes, Wing stomped into the Wall Street offices where the 30 lawyers from the two sides filled a conference room. "Let's play a little game here," he began. "Let's all get up and stretch. Now everybody who is trying to get this deal done, go to this end of the room. Everyone who is trying to fuck this thing up, go to that end of the room."

Even apart from the HNG-InterNorth negotiations, Wing had more than proved his worth to Lay. Since the early 1980s, Lay had been eager to invest in cogeneration projects—plants that not only provided electric power but also captured the heat from the plant's turbines for sale as steam, typically to an industrial facility adjacent to the plant. A well-designed cogen project was clean and profitable and far more efficient than a conventional plant that ran on coal or fuel oil. It also, of course, provided a big new customer for natural gas.

Soon after Wing joined HNG, he'd gotten the company into the cogen business. Within a few years, Wing had brought Enron into three cogen projects: two in Texas, one in New Jersey. All were big moneymakers, not just for Enron but for Wing himself. He insisted on getting a small piece of each project. Lay, in a pattern that repeated itself over and over, acceded to his demand. Wing's payout amounted to $100,000 or more annually for each plant for up to 20 years. There was, however, one noteworthy difference between Wing's deal and the many deals Lay cut with other executives in later years. For Wing to get his maximum payout, the cogen plants first had to do well for the company: in this case, they needed to return at least 25 percent annually on Enron's investment. In fact, all three plants racked up much bigger returns. As Wing later put it, "If I didn't produce hugely for the shareholders, the compensation was extremely pedestrian. If I did produce hugely for the shareholders, there was something in it for me."

Just weeks after the HNG-InterNorth merger closed, Wing made the first of his many trips through Enron's revolving door. Citing Omaha-Houston corporate politics, Lay told Wing that he wasn't going to be able to give him the job of running the combined company's power business. That job, Lay said, had been promised to an InterNorth executive. Instead, Lay offered Wing the job of presiding over the company's pipelines. Wing said no; pipelines were too boring.

Part of Wing's canny genius was knowing when he was in a position to employ maximum leverage. "Always make it about the other guy, never about yourself," Wing liked to say. By that he meant that a good negotiator needs to create a set of possible outcomes that allow him to win no matter what the other side does. And so it was here. Wing told Lay that it was completely up to the CEO to decide who should get the power-business job. It didn't matter to him one way or the other. But since the choice Lay had made required him to break Wing's employment contract, the Enron CEO would have to pay him to go away. Wing negotiated a two-year consulting agreement that raised his guaranteed pay to $265,000 a year, included all the stock options and club memberships he'd been promised as a company executive, and maintained his payout on the existing projects. (Not that Enron was Wing's only source of income. By then, he had already made the first of many investments that produced a fortune, betting $15,000 on a friend who was launching the Boston Beer Company. After the brewery introduced Sam Adams beer and went public, Wing's stake was worth millions.)

Six months later, Lay called again. The company's fourth cogen investment, a new plant in Texas City launched by the former InterNorth executive, had stalled. Lay gave Wing a new consulting deal, including an additional $10,000 a month, a $250,000 bonus for arranging the plant's financing, up to $150,000 a year from its future profits, and more stock options. Wing completed the financing within a year.

In August 1987, Wing became an Enron employee again, this time as chairman and CEO of the company's new cogeneration division. Now he got a five-year deal at $300,000 annually plus a 5 percent stake in the business in addition to his continuing share in all the projects. This, too, didn't last long. By April 1988, Enron was reeling from the combined effects of the take-or-pay crisis, shrinking margins in its pipeline business, and the Enron Oil debacle. Desperate for cash, Lay decided to sell half the cogen company, whose value had soared in a matter of months. The deal with Virginia-based Dominion Energy generated

$90 million for Enron and triggered a $9 million buyout for Wing. And that wasn't all. Because Dominion didn't want Wing to run the business, Enron also paid him under a termination agreement, giving him $400,000 a year for five years plus a consulting agreement that gave him a stake in any new investments he brought in.

Enron's joint venture with Dominion was a bust. Part of the problem was that as cogeneration plants caught on, other companies raced to build them, so there was soon a glut of competition. Inevitably, the easy profits had dried up. The Enron-Dominion group didn't build a single power plant; within a year, the two companies parted ways.

Even before the Dominion deal went south, Wing had begun looking elsewhere for deals. One of his strengths as a businessman was his shrewd sense of where opportunity lay. He could see that the U.S. cogen business was getting tougher. To Wing, the next big opportunity—the place where Enron could make a spectacular amount of money—was not in the United States but abroad. Specifically, it was in an industrial region in northeast England known as Teesside. England: where coal was king, where power plants were built by state-owned British utilities, and where gas-fired plants were not only unheard of; they were *illegal.* But never mind all that. John Wing was convinced that the best prospects were in England, so that's where he headed. He was going to build a gas-fired cogeneration plant at Teesside, and not just any gas-fired cogeneration plant. He was going to build the biggest cogen project the world had ever seen: a 1,825-megawatt monster, big enough to supply 4 percent of the electricity needs for the entire United Kingdom. The estimated cost was $1.3 billion.

Had Wing lost his mind? Not at all. He was making a contrarian bet, to be sure, but one that was rooted in powerful logic and exquisite timing. What he realized was that England was poised to begin deregulating its energy industry, just as the United States had done a decade before. Ronald Reagan's great ally, Prime Minister Margaret Thatcher, was still in power, rapidly moving her country away from government monopolies and toward free-market economics. An American company that got in early—a company that was willing to work with the government—would serve as the poster child for the benefits of privatization. Wing thought Enron ought to be that company.

Sure enough, a deregulation measure passed Parliament in 1989, and the Teesside project quickly assumed the role of privatization showcase. Wing knew better than to try to go it alone on foreign soil, so he partnered with the British chemicals giant, ICI, which had a huge industrial complex in the region. That one relationship gave the project instant credibility. Realizing the importance of staying on the right side of government officials, many still leery of deregulation, Wing and Lay skillfully courted influential players in England, most notably John Wakeham, Thatcher's secretary of state for energy. (Lord Wakeham joined Enron's board after his retirement from public service.) Enron became a million-dollar supporter of Prince Charles's favorite charity, The Prince's Trust. Wing lunched in England with the Prince of Wales, who toured Teesside after it was built; Prince Charles later attended a fund-raising lunch at Ken Lay's home in Houston.

Even with these advantages, though, the project was a high-risk venture that could well have fallen apart at any number of junctures. Wing and his 20-member team would need to line up producers to provide the huge gas supply for the plant, some 300 million cubic feet a day. Since the nearest gas fields were beneath the North Sea, they had to arrange construction of a new 140-mile pipeline. They had to find customers for the steam and electricity Teesside would produce. They had to arrange the project's $1.3 billion in financing. *And* they had to construct a plant in a scant 29 months, a plant that was twice the size of anything Enron had ever been involved in before. Each of these factors brought its own set of complex negotiations, and any one of them could have brought the project down.

The gas-supply deal fell into place first, struck with the big oil companies that were drilling in the North Sea, which also agreed to build the pipeline. Finalizing agreements to sell Teesside's power proved a tougher sell. ICI would buy the steam and a little of the electricity. But well into 1990, most of Teesside's electrical capacity remained unsold. Frustrated at the lack of progress, the companies supplying the gas set a deadline: if Enron didn't finalize the electricity sale by then, they would pull the gas contract, which would finish off Teesside before it even got off the ground. Wing and his team met the deadline by exactly four minutes, completing a big signing ceremony at 11:56 P.M. on September 10, with Teesside's new customers, four regional electric companies that also became 50 percent partners in the plant. In a press release, Lay seemed almost palpably relieved that Enron had brought Teesside to "contractual reality." The first crisis had passed.

The next big hurdle was the financing. In any power-plant deal, the financial close is a major event. It means that the developer (in this case, Enron) will immediately be repaid the millions in expenses it has incurred to get the project off the ground. Teesside was supposed to be built largely with borrowed money: project financed, as they say in the business. Project financing allows developers to stretch their own capital by investing just a sliver of the cost of any project. Instead of looking to Enron for repayment of the debt, the lenders would instead rely on cash flows from the project, comforted by the presence of the long-term contracts for gas supply and purchase of the plant's power and steam. Because the financing was non-recourse, Enron would have no legal obligation to cover any default. The equity investment in such financing was often split with partners, which means Enron could build and control projects in which its own money represented as little as 10 percent of the total cost. At Teesside, Enron would have to lay out an equity investment of only $150 million to buy a 50 percent interest in the $1.3 billion project.

Or at least that was the theory. In reality, the Teesside financing—the biggest such private power deal ever—had proved difficult to close. In November 1990, with all the other elements in place but the financing still cloudy, Lord Wakeham granted official approval for Teesside to be built. Enron now faced a dilemma: the entire project depended on meeting a string of tight deadlines. But if Wing started construction right away, Enron would have to foot the bill. And what if the financing *never* closed? Wing urged Houston to roll the dice. With Houston's approval, he made a point of starting construction on the day Wakeham gave his approval. For six nerve-racking months, Enron used its own money to carry the project forward, ultimately laying out $300 million in cash toward getting Teesside built.

The financing eventually did close; Goldman Sachs took the lead in arranging the $1.3 billion loan from a syndicate of international banks. Along the way, there were plenty of ruffled feathers, hardly a surprise given who was running the show for Enron. At one point, Wing carried on an argument with a Goldman executive on the streets of London that became so animated that he finally yanked on the banker's necktie. Lay called the next day to pass on the dismay of the top brass at Goldman Sachs. When progress inevitably bogged down, Wing assumed his old role as jam-breaker. "The time for dancing is over!" he declared to a roomful of lawyers, pounding his fist on the table. "The time for killing has begun." In June 1991, the financing was completed.

With construction crews working round the clock, Teesside was up and running on March 27, 1993, on schedule and under budget. It proved a hefty profit center for Enron all through the 1990s. Even before Enron switched on the plant, the company was booking juicy construction and development fees to hit its quarterly earnings targets. The construction of Teesside alone generated profits of more than $100 million.

Few outside Enron knew how much risk the company had taken to build Teesside, and afterward, few cared. But long after Wing had departed, the Teesside team cut one final deal that Enron would come to regret.

To get the producers to build the new North Sea pipeline, Enron had agreed to reserve half its capacity, even though it needed only a quarter of the capacity for the gas it purchased to fuel Teesside. Wing had assumed that once the pipeline was in place, other gas buyers would crop up for the additional natural-gas production that was coming online in the North Sea, and that they would use the Enron capacity to move it from well to customer. The other possibility was that Enron itself would use the capacity, for a second gas-fired plant.

By early 1993, the buzz about Teesside had helped generate a near frenzy in Europe about gas's rosy prospects, setting in motion what was dubbed "the dash for gas." It was at that very moment, with prices near their peak, that Enron signed a long-term contract to take another 260 million cubic feet of gas per day, starting in 1996, from North Sea fields known as J-Block. That was enough gas to fill the rest of the pipeline capacity that Enron had reserved, giving the company twice as much as it needed for Teesside.

Here's the most astonishing part, though: the J-Block purchase, negotiated with a consortium led by Phillips Petroleum, was a take-or-pay agreement. Despite all the problems Enron had had with take-or-pay in the United States, it had agreed to do it again in England. The company's executives in Britain were betting, just as their U.S. colleagues had years before, that natural gas prices would continue to rise, allowing Enron to make money by either using the gas to supply a second plant or selling it to other customers.

Because the J-Block deal was negotiated by Wing's old deputies, there are those who believe Wing—who had by then left Enron yet again—offered his tacit support of the purchase. But Wing himself later insisted that he knew nothing about it and was horrified when he heard what had been done. And in fact the agreement had required the approval of Enron's top executives back in Houston.

As it turned out, the J-Block bet was horribly wrong and would trigger a major crisis at Enron. But that came later. In the immediate euphoria of the Teesside deal, nobody paid attention to the huge mistake the Teesside team had just made.

During the years he was putting together Teesside, Wing officially remained a consultant to Enron. But it was a very odd arrangement. Though he wasn't formally an Enron employee, he was unquestionably in charge, and almost everyone he hired was brought in as an Enron executive.

Most had backgrounds much like Wing's. His top lieutenant was his old West Point roommate, Bob Kelly, who held a doctorate in economics from Harvard. To supervise the plant's construction, he reached into the Pentagon for another West Point grad, Brigadier General Tom White, a former Vietnam tank commander who served as General Colin Powell's personal aide. White was assisted by a retired three-star general, Lincoln Jones.

Harvard Business School provided Wing's second major talent pool. Mark Russ, a navy veteran, signed on after Wing swooped into Boston's Logan Airport to recruit him during his second year. Russ recalls Wing's bounding out of an Enron jet, dressed in cowboy boots and a sweater emblazoned with a big American flag. They talked for hours. "Mark," Wing told him, "everyone I've ever hired is a millionaire."

Working for Wing was indeed lucrative, but it was also brutal, like fighting a war. "Everyone I've worked with, I've sledgehammered a bunch of times," he later said. "With each person, you try to find the right combination of cheerleading and ass kicking." Wing's team in London worked around the clock; he didn't hesitate to call anyone at 5 A.M. He held a staff meeting every morning at seven, and it wasn't unusual for staffers to show up at those meetings in the same clothes they'd worn the night before. Ever the master negotiator, Wing was also grandly manipulative with his own staff. He'd periodically tell even trusted subordinates they were failures, strip them of their titles, or make them report to someone junior. "We were all fired at least ten times," recalls one member of the team. Those who worked directly for Wing never quite knew where they stood. Which, of course, was the idea.

No one endured the Wing treatment, professionally and personally, quite like Rebecca Mark. Mark signed on to the development team in 1986, hired by Kelly to work in finance. She was in her early thirties at the time and married, with twin baby boys. She soon became Wing's protégé—and his lover. As a former Enron director later observed, "That's like putting two firecrackers together."

For years, the two were locked in a stormy personal relationship. But at work, Wing (who also was married) treated Mark even more harshly than other subordinates. In 1988, after Mark enrolled at Harvard Business School, her husband began divorce proceedings; the split was finalized a year later. Mark had made noises about hoping Harvard would provide some distance from Wing. Yet even in school, she continued to work for him, helping develop a small power plant outside Boston during the school year and spending the summer in London, working on Teesside. In the spring of 1990, she completed the last final exam for her MBA, then jumped on a plane for England that night. Although she held the title of president and CEO of Enron Power by then, Wing sometimes treated her like a secretary, ordering her to fetch his coffee or type his letters. A member of Wing's Teesside team says: "It was like some on-again, off-again relationship out of a novel: 'Fight, sleep together; fight, sleep together; fight, sleep together.' " After one particularly brutal day, Mark collapsed in tears in a colleague's arms. "Why does he treat me like this?" she sobbed.

Months later, after the relationship had finally ended, Mark was visiting Wing in Aspen when *another* woman with whom he was involved burst into the house to confront him. Ultimately, Wing confessed his infidelities in an extraordinary letter to his wife, Karen. In it, he listed a string of women he'd slept with during their marriage and professed shame at his indiscretions. Karen Wing and Rebecca Mark ended up commiserating with each other. Wing, meanwhile, vowed to make up for his actions. The Wings quietly divorced, and Karen received a large settlement.

But Wing and Mark's relationship reverberated for years. In the aftermath of their affair, Wing told friends that Mark continued to hope that he would marry her; he also openly derided Mark's contribution to Teesside. For her part, Mark confided that she felt Wing would rather see her fail than succeed without him. She also said, though, that she'd learned a great deal from Wing.

But during their future business encounters—and there were more—the bitterness between John Wing and Rebecca Mark was palpable. Their workplace affair soon entered into Enron legend and forever cast a shadow on her rapid rise.

In February 1990, as Teesside was becoming a reality, Ken Lay decided to tear up Wing's old consulting agreement and give him a new one that was even more lucrative. Under Wing's new five-year agreement, his fee rose to $600,000 a year (from $400,000), and he got a new title (chairman of Enron Power Corporation), and a new bonus: $1 million, which he would receive upon Teesside's financial close. Most important, in exchange for a modest equity contribution, Wing also received a 3.5 percent stake in the project.

It wasn't long, though, before Wing was dissatisfied with his new deal. By early 1991, people inside Enron were beginning to sense that Teesside was going to be a very big deal for the company's bottom line, surely the biggest win in the company's history. Wing returned to the United States, flush with success and determined to set fresh terms for any continuing association with Enron. "Wing got this air of invulnerability, the Midas touch," says an Enron executive who worked closely with him. "He used to tell me, 'I can hire anyone and turn them into a power developer.' "

He arranged an audience with the company's board to state his terms. In essence, Wing was ready to demand almost total autonomy. He wanted an affirmation of his right to continue to operate out of the office at the Woodlands. (His refusal to move into Enron's headquarters had long been a sore point.) He wanted the right to name a bloc of his own directors for Enron Power. And he wanted to take the power-development business public; one investment banker had already run numbers projecting that an Enron Power IPO would produce a public company with a market value of $1 billion or more.

This time, though, Wing's timing was less than perfect. For despite the Teesside triumph, there were forces at Enron strongly agitating to rein him in. Despite his record for making the company money, Wing had always been viewed by many at Enron headquarters with a mixture of jealousy, fear, and distrust. He always seemed to be out for himself. He was certainly no team player; he made little effort to disguise the contempt he harbored for most of the executives who worked at other Enron divisions. The consensus at headquarters—and this very much included Ken Lay—was that Wing's operation should move downtown so that the company could better control it. Certainly, Lay was not interested in making Wing *more* independent.

Wing and Enron were on a collision course, and the point of impact was a July 1991 board meeting, set for Old Baldy, an exclusive golf and fishing resort in Wyoming. On the afternoon the board members and select executives began arriving in Enron jets, Wing played a round of golf with a director named Jack Urquhart, an old friend from General Electric. Lay had already warned some directors what was up: Wing was talented, he told them, but he drank too much and was hard to control. Now, out on the course, Urquhart advised Wing to be conciliatory. "You've got to do what the CEO wants," Urquhart told him. "Not really," Wing responded. That evening, Wing advised his top lieutenents—Mark, Kelly, and White—that a showdown seemed imminent.

Late the next morning, Wing made his case. "I know this business better than anyone else," he told the directors. "This is the way Enron shareholders will benefit the most. And one of the reasons is that if you do it this way, I'll stay involved. And if you don't, I *won't*." As Wing saw it, he was the one indispensable person at Enron, and he wanted to be treated as such. "He wanted all or nothing, and he didn't want anybody to tell him anything," recalls one former Enron director who participated in the meeting. After 45 minutes, Wing was asked to step out of the room.

It didn't take long for the board to make a decision. "We were just sick of John Wing and his machinations," says this same board member. Lay walked out to speak to Wing. "We're terminating your contract," he said.

Wing was stunned—and furious. Because it was raining that day, the Enron executives who didn't serve on the board were gathered in the dining room after lunch instead of out playing golf. They all watched as Wing marched out through the dining room, snatched his bags, and hopped in a car for an Enron plane that would fly him home.

And *still* Lay and the board were unwilling to make a clean break. They needed Wing to finish Teesside, of course, and that meant paying him. Lay and Wing signed a new termination agreement, exchanging his equity stake in the project for almost 330,000 shares of Enron stock, about $18 million worth. And at the same time, Wing signed a new two-year consulting contract that gave him $600,000 a year and continued his right to the $1 million Teesside bonus.

Wing's latest firing triggered a tug-of-war for his staff. Would the team Wing had assembled stick with Enron or with Wing? Each would have to make a choice, Wing advised them; there was no middle ground. Virtually everyone—including Kelly and White, who were busy overseeing Teesside—opted to remain with Enron. Wing reestablished his own development team, called the Wing Group. And how did he fund it? Amazingly, with Enron's money. Despite everything that had happened, Lay had agreed to help bankroll Wing's firm.

By year's end, Enron had signed a deal to sink $3 million into the Wing Group. Under the terms of Wing's new contract, he was free to compete for projects with Enron's own development team—headed by Rebecca Mark.

CHAPTER 5

Guys with Spikes

He wasn't a consultant anymore. Jeff Skilling was now a hard-charging executive in control of a fast-growing division at a company in the midst of dramatic change. He was hiring people by the bushelful, negotiating their pay, overseeing their progress. He was expanding his empire and posting profits that were increasing every year (thanks, at least in part, to mark-to-market accounting). He was turning his ideas into reality.

Not all of Skilling's ideas were about transforming the natural-gas business, though. He also had very clear ideas about how to build an organization, what to look for in people, and how those people should be rewarded. At McKinsey, Skilling had always felt that he'd been part of a true intellectual meritocracy, and that's what he strove to instill at Enron Finance. He wanted to create a place where raw brains and creativity mattered more than management skills and real-world experience, where young MBAs were free to chase a pipe dream with company millions (even behind their boss's back), where generating profits was rewarded not just handsomely but *fabulously,* and where those who failed to measure up would be quickly cut from the herd. If it all sounded very Darwinian, well, that was the point. Skilling believed that greed was the greatest motivator, and he was only too happy to feed it. "I've thought about this a lot, and all that matters is money," Terry Thorn, an Enron managing director, recalls Skilling telling him. "You buy loyalty with money. This touchy-feely stuff isn't as important as cash. That's what drives performance."

Skilling had other ideas, too. He used to say that he liked to hire "guys with spikes." By this, he meant that if an executive had a singular narrow talent—a spike—Skilling was willing to bring him into Enron and lavish him with money, no matter what his other shortcomings. Egomaniacs, social misfits, backstabbers, devotees of strip clubs: Skilling didn't really care about their foibles so long as they had a skill he needed. Nor did it much matter to him whether they were team players. "Jeff could care less whether people got along with each other," says one of his early hires. "In many cases, he felt it was better if they *didn't* get along, since it created a level of tension that he believed was good for helping people come up with new ideas." A former trading executive adds: "Jeff always believed pitting three people against each other would be the quickest way to assure the best ideas bubbled to the top. He *wanted* them to fight."

They were all smart, of course; that went without saying. "Every person around Skilling was exceptional in one way or another," says a former longtime executive. "Did they have the skills to run a very complex business? Ha!"

Which offers up the problem: no company can prosper over the long term if every employee is a free agent, motivated solely by greed, no matter how smart he is. No company can function if it only hires brilliant MBAs—and sets them against each other. There is a reason companies value team players, just as there's a reason that people who get along with others tend to do well in corporate life. The reason is simple: you can't build a company on brilliance alone. You need people who can come up with ideas, and you also need people who can implement those ideas and are well compensated for doing so.

The pure meritocracy Skilling thought he was installing was, in fact, a deeply dysfunctional workplace. That was hard to see in the early days, when the place felt vibrant and heady and exciting and they all were working so hard that they didn't have time for anything else. But over the years, as the business became more established, the sense of excitement waned and the dysfunction became more evident. The very qualities Skilling prized—the opportunity for creativity to run wild, the mixture of brains and hubris, the absence of gray hair and structure—turned Enron Finance into a chaotic, destructive, free-for-all. Over time, as that culture infected the entire company, Enron began to rot from within. But that came later.

Jeff Skilling liked to say that he was presiding over a start-up, going so far as to declare that "other than Microsoft, we were the largest start-up company in the last 20 years." Never mind that Enron had roots that went back to the early days of the gas pipeline business; indeed, even Skilling's own division wasn't as much of a start-up as he liked to think.

In 1991, Lay and Kinder merged Skilling's Enron Finance with something called Enron Gas Marketing, the part of the company that sold natural gas to wholesale customers. The move made perfect sense, since much of the work done by Skilling's traders consisted of buying and selling natural-gas contracts that would allow the company to fulfill its obligations to those same customers. The merger gave Skilling a nice built-in profit stream as well as additional staff. Then, a year later, he was handed one of Enron's prized assets, the intrastate Houston Pipeline, which piped gas to the many industrial sites on the Gulf coast. This also gave Skilling access to ready profits while providing important competitive intelligence for his traders. The growing business was soon renamed Enron Capital and Trade Resources, ECT, as everyone at Enron took to calling it.

What *is* true is that Skilling acted as if he were operating a start-up, instituting rules and practices that were often at odds with the rest of Enron. On the thirty-ninth floor of the Enron building, where ECT was housed, Skilling's disciples—known internally as Skillingites—were remarkably disdainful of the company that employed them. "We had the authority to do anything and everything we wanted to do," recalls one early arrival. "We thumbed our nose at any personnel policies that the rest of Enron had." ECT had its own compensation system: it gave fat bonuses to employees at a time when that sort of thing just wasn't done in the energy business. Everyone got Wall Street–style titles, such as managing director. Traditional offices were torn out, replaced with cubicles and glass walls. Instead of pursuing engineers from the University of Nebraska and Texas A&M, Skilling recruited MBAs from Wharton, the University of Texas, and Harvard. Over time, people from less prestigious schools were made to feel as if they didn't measure up.

As a boss, Skilling was intensely loyal to his inner circle, and those who came through for him in the early 1990s could later do no wrong. He gave them mind-blowing piles of cash and stock options. As Skilling rose to the top of Enron, he took his chief lieutenants with him, and they assumed key roles as corporate officers. Thanks to Skilling, they left Enron with millions of dollars, in some cases, tens of millions. Yet Skilling never demanded the same kind of loyalty in return. He forgave those who strayed or screwed up, who manipulated or even betrayed him as long as they remained useful. In 1992, despite objections from some of his staff, Skilling even hired Kevin Hannon, the junior Bankers Trust executive who erased the trading desk's computer files.

The man who offers perhaps the starkest illustration of what Skilling valued in an employee was an executive named Lou Lung Pai, the key architect of Enron's trading operation who was later placed in charge of several other key Skilling initiatives. Pai, who carefully measured his words, was viewed as an enigma by his coworkers and as a terrible man to cross. More than anyone else, he became the instrument of Skilling's will. Publicly, Skilling touted him as "my ICBM." But Enron executives knew him for something else as well: his longtime infatuation with strippers. A married, middle-aged father of two, Pai maintained an ongoing secret relationship with an exotic dancer he'd met during one of his frequent visits to topless bars.

Few other American corporations would have tolerated Pai's antics, inside or outside the office. Indeed, several times Skilling contemplated firing Pai in his first years at the company. But once he proved himself on the trading desk, Pai became untouchable. Skilling gave him complete freedom to run trading as he saw fit, and no matter how much he abused his colleagues or underlings, he almost never reined him in.

Born in Nanjing, China, Pai came to America at the age of two, and grew up in College Park, Maryland, where his father was a math professor at the University of Maryland. Pai went to the same school, earning a master's degree in economics, and even worked for a few years as an economist at the Securities and Exchange Commission. He came to Enron in 1986 from Conoco, where he'd labored in obscurity. Pai was 44 when Skilling hired him in 1990, and he emerged as the top man on the tiny trading desk after the ugly split with Bankers Trust. Everyone at Enron agreed that Pai was smart; indeed, one former executive calls him "the most incisive businessman I've ever met." He also had a keen eye for trading talent.

But his real genius was a certain brutish political skill. Pai was Enron's fiercest corporate warlord. He made short work of the executives who had been placed over him. He took credit for others' achievements, ridiculed adversaries behind their backs, undermined them in front of colleagues, and simply ignored orders that he didn't like. "Lou was extremely good at eliminating everyone in his way," says one longtime ECT executive. Adds an early trader who worked for Pai: "It became apparent that you don't mess with Lou." And a third: "If you got in the way of Lou's agenda, he'd get rid of you." Once Ken Lay convened an off-site employee conference where the featured speaker was Stephen Covey, author of the management best-seller *The Seven Habits of Highly Effective People*. "Throw that away," Pai told a colleague whom he spotted with a copy of the book. "Buy Sun-tzu's *The Art of War*."

Pai served as the human template for the trading culture at Enron. He saw things in black and white. "Lou was the purest character I ever met because it was always about one thing: money," says a longtime Enron trader. Colleagues were struck by Pai's unerring instinct for pocketing the most personally from every financial opportunity. Years later, when Enron spun off a shaky new business that Pai chaired, one senior colleague made a point of buying shares merely because he figured that Pai, who owned a hefty stake, would figure out a way to reap a windfall.

Strip clubs were Pai's other passion. Topless bars had long been part of the old all-male oil-and-gas culture, and Houston was a breeding ground for their latest incarnation: upscale gentlemen's clubs with a veneer of polish and private VIP rooms, where a big spender could buy lap dances while sipping Dom Pérignon. In the early 1990s, some gas industry deal makers still entertained out-of-town customers at such places. But Pai wasn't there just with clients; he could be found there regularly after work, hanging out for hours at Rick's Cabaret, the Men's Club, or Lipstick. One early ECT colleague recalls jetting to Dallas with Pai for an industry conference then heading straight from the airport to a topless bar. "We didn't even go to the convention," he says. "The only thing Lou wanted to do was go to a strip joint." Pai dropped so much money on the strip-bar scene that there was gossip he owned a piece of one of the clubs. In truth, much of the entertainment was courtesy of Enron shareholders. A group of traders could easily run up a thousand-dollar tab at Rick's, and they routinely charged their outings to their Enron expense accounts.

One evening, Pai joined an Enron group for a bachelor party at Lipstick. At about 2 A.M., as everyone was preparing to clear out, an unmarried member of the group asked Pai his secret: how did he keep his wife from smelling the dancers' scent on his clothes?

"That's easy," Pai explained. "I go to a gas station, and rub some gasoline on my hands, and it kills the perfume."

"If you do that, Lou," someone shot back, "doesn't your wife think you're fucking the gasoline attendant?"

The entire table fell silent in horror; Pai wasn't someone to trifle with. But Pai finally let his usual poker face curl into the hint of a grin—*"Heh . . . heh . . . heh"*—and everyone breathed a sigh of relief. But not for long: when the trader was transferred to Calgary, many assumed it was Pai's doing.

Around 1995, Lay, responding to complaints from a female employee, finally issued a memo announcing that Enron would no longer pick up the tab at topless bars. "When that memo came out," recalls a former ECT executive, "the trading floor went completely quiet. There was a pall for two days."

Pai kept expensing his excursions for months, until he finally received a rare personal scolding from Skilling. "Well, it's the old gas business," Pai protested.

"It's not part of the *new* gas business," Skilling replied.

Like all those in Skilling's small inner circle, Pai operated with his boss's unquestioning support. "Lou could do things that Jeff didn't like to do," says a longtime colleague. "Lou had no problem telling people they had stupid ideas." For years, the prickly Pai even treated Ken Lay's son, Mark, an early ECT employee (and an undistinguished performer) with undisguised disdain. Ken Lay complained to Skilling, agitating for Pai's head. But Skilling refused to serve it up. "If he's gone, I'm gone," Skilling told the Enron CEO. So Lay backed off.

But why? Why was Skilling so loyal to Pai, so willing to allow his greed and poisonous tactics to shape the culture of ECT? Skilling's response was simple: he left Pai alone because he always got the job done. But among Skilling's top executives, there were other theories. One was that Skilling liked having someone like Pai around, that he prized his blunt methods and the conflict they created. Another theory was that Skilling felt he had to give Pai a wide berth because he was a star performer and because he had the loyalty of the traders. "I think he became afraid of Lou, because of the power he had as the man who controlled the trading operation," says a former ECT executive. "He didn't want to do anything because they were making money."

Nor was Pai the only one who seemed to have his way with Skilling. Traders and deal makers alike came to realize that it was easy to hold up Skilling for a raise or a bigger bonus or more options: all they had to was threaten to quit, and Skilling would give in to their demands. Later, when Enron was flying high, the press portrayed Skilling as a Master of the Universe, in control of everything at the company. But the insiders always knew better. As smart as he was, he could be taken advantage of. And take advantage they did.

The day would come when the trading operation became enormous, when it posted the biggest profits in the company and when virtually all business activity at Enron revolved around the giant trading floor. But in those early years, it wasn't like that at all. In the beginning, the traders were their own small division, trying to build a business from scratch.

Their transformation from a support group to a powerful profit center was cemented by a key Skilling decision. Pai had originally been in charge of the financial traders, which then made up a small portion of the trading business. Skilling expanded his purview to include all the traders who actually handled the logistics of moving natural gas through pipelines for physical delivery. This meant they were now responsible for getting the gas to customers as well as using financial instruments to manage the price risk from the long-term sales contracts that Enron's marketers were negotiating. This gave Pai and his traders a wealth of intelligence about what was going on in the marketplace, information no other company's trading desk could match.

The traders became critical inside Enron. In effect, trading sat in the middle of the gas-sale transaction, between two groups of commercial deal makers. On one side were Skilling's gas bankers, busy offering financing deals to producers to lock up long-term supply. This group was headed by Gene Humphrey, Skilling's first hire, who had come from Citibank. On the other side were the marketers, who made big deals with utilities and industrial buyers of natural gas. Both kinds of deal makers were called originators, but in the early years, it was the marketing originators who got all the glory. Whenever ECT signed a long-term contract with a customer, it could immediately declare the profits for the entire deal on its income statement, thanks to mark-to-market accounting. In addition, Ken Lay's strategic goal was to create new markets for natural gas, and that's precisely what these originators did with their deals.

From the moment Enron Gas Marketing was put under his aegis, Skilling began pushing the originators to do something spectacular, to pull off a deal the likes of which no one had ever seen before in the natural-gas industry. The Holy Grail was a big deal with a power-plant developer, someone who would agree to build a plant that would buy gigantic amounts of gas.

And in January 1992, the Grail was found: Enron announced that it had agreed to provide the entire gas supply for a new 1,000-megawatt plant in upstate New York. Enron convinced the plant developer, Sithe Energies, to use natural gas instead of coal, but that wasn't what made it so important. As big as the Brooklyn Union deal had been three years earlier, the Sithe contract was of a different scale entirely. Enron would supply Sithe with 195 million cubic feet of gas per day for 20 years, an extraordinary amount for an unheard-of term. The estimated value of the gas: $3.5 billion to $4 billion. As Skilling saw it, this was his group's "bell-cow transaction," the one that made everybody stand up and pay attention. Both inside and outside the company, people were agog at what Skilling had pulled off.

The Sithe deal had ramifications that went well beyond its sheer size. For years, Sithe helped Enron meet its aggressive profit targets. Using mark-to-market accounting, Enron began booking profits even before the plant started

operating. It kept booking profits from Sithe well into the late 1990s by restructuring the deal on multiple occasions when the company was scrambling to meet
its quarterly projections. Later, the deal's complex machinations backfired, producing a huge liability that Enron never fully disclosed. But that was far in the
future.

The Sithe deal was the ultimate proof that Skilling's big idea was working. He
had said that his new creation would allow Enron to land giant deals, and now the
company had one in hand. He had said that Enron could supply huge amounts of
gas on a long-term contract, and now he'd committed to do just that. To make
Sithe work, Enron bought gas from dozens of locations and laid miles of fresh
pipeline into the plant from Canada. And the traders were suddenly engaged in
seeing to it that the Sithe supply never faltered and the price risk was managed;
indeed Sithe jump-started the trading operation like nothing that had come before
it. "In the beginning, we needed physical supply to trade," says Amanda Martin,
who began working for Skilling in 1992. "We had to originate transactions to give
the traders something to play with." It was a logistical triumph, proof that Enron
could deliver on a huge long-term gas supply commitment.

The lead originator on the Sithe deal was a man named Kenneth Duane Rice,
who soon became one of Skilling's closest deputies. Among Skilling's confidants, Rice stood out as conspicuously normal. A veterinarian's son from the
prairie town of Broken Bow, Nebraska, Rice was a wrestler at the University of
Nebraska, where he earned a degree in electrical engineering. Fifteen years later,
he retained the clean-cut good looks, wholesome manner, and boyish charm of a
college jock. Rice's father was a frugal and demanding man who made Rice earn
his spending money by yanking nails from old boards on the family farm and
helping out with midnight cesareans. Never an avid student, Rice later joked that
"it was easier to get a degree than tell my dad I wasn't going to go to college."
Rice married his college sweetheart, a future pediatrician, six months after going
to work as an engineer at InterNorth. He later earned an MBA at Creighton University in Omaha, then moved to Houston and started selling spot-market gas to
industrial customers. It became clear that he was a natural salesman.

Because of its size and importance, the Sithe deal also served as the bell cow
for Rice's career. It brought hefty bonuses, lots of options, and big promotions.
But even more than that, by vaulting Rice into Skilling's inner circle, Sithe put
Rice in a position to make tens of millions more. He went on to cut more big
deals, assume top jobs in ECT, and run Enron's high-stakes (and ill-fated) broadband venture.

Sithe made Skilling a big winner, too. In 1992, ECT's net income more than
doubled, to $122 million, making it the second-biggest contributor to En-
ron's bottom line. When the year was over, Enron bought out 30 percent of his
phantom-equity stake in ECT for $4.7 million in cash and stock. That meant that
the company was now valuing Skilling's two-year-old "start-up" at a staggering
$650 million.

• • •

Is it a surprise to learn that even as the originators were landing long-term supply contracts, they were increasingly coming into conflict with Pai's traders? Perhaps not. There is a natural tension in any such business over how to divide the spoils. But given the ethos Skilling was instilling at ECT and that Lou Pai was running the trading desk, bitter conflict was inevitable. There was simply too much money at stake.

The traders' power stemmed from a simple fact: they had a great deal of say in deciding just how profitable an originator's deal would be. That's because the deal's profits didn't depend just on the terms of the sale. Every bit as important was the spread between the agreed-on sale price for the gas and what it would cost Enron to supply that gas. Yes, the finance group was negotiating agreements with gas producers to buy some of what was needed, but the trading desk had to round up a lot more.

With each big new origination deal, more and more of the burden for meeting the demand—and hedging the price risk—fell to the traders. For short-term deals, the New York Mercantile Exchange prices provided a benchmark. But there was no NYMEX futures market beyond 18 months. Prices for 20-year deals like Sithe were set by deploying models and plotting curves, models and curves that were, at best, educated guesswork and, thanks to Pai's clout, set at the discretion of the trading desk.

There was some justification for the traders' power in setting prices. Long after the originators had gotten their big bonuses and moved on to other deals, the traders were still going to have bear the risk that the contract would become unprofitable. (It was impossible to fully hedge a deal like Sithe.) They needed to build in some cushion so that they could increase their chances of making money even if prices changed over time, as they surely would.

But the disputes that took place between the traders and the originators over how to price a deal went far beyond normal corporate infighting. They turned into pitched battles over how much each camp—traders, marketers, and finance—got to claim from a deal's profits. One executive likened the process to what happened when a village woodsman hauled in a big kill. "At Enron, you had hunters, skinners, and hangers-on. You'd get a big carcass that the organization would dive all over and strip of all the value—skin, bones, and meat."

If it meant more money for him and his group, Pai was more than willing to cheat his ECT brethren. One former trading executive recalls that when finance executives approached him on the trading floor to obtain prices for selling the gas they'd acquired from a producer, Pai, behind his back, would secretly signal thumbs-down, meaning that the trader should quote a below-market price. And when a marketing originator came to the trader to get a price for *buying* gas, Pai would give a thumbs-up, to quote an above-market price. The effect of this would be to steal some of the expected profit spread for the trading desk from the deal makers. "The line is you show them the same price you'd show anybody else that called on the phone or better," says the trading executive. "If you're showing them a worse price than you show Morgan Stanley, you're screwing them. Lou took me aside on more than one occasion for not taking enough money out of the transaction for the trading desk." Of all the corrosive things Lou Pai did at Enron, nothing did more to emphasize the mercenary nature of life at Enron and undermine any vestige of teamwork. But Skilling, ever the believer in creative tension, didn't see a problem.

The battles between the traders and the deal makers were also aggravated by cultural differences. The origination teams cultivated personal relationships with customers and hammered out deals with them over many months. The traders did business by phone and computer in a matter of seconds. The originators viewed the traders as bloodless mercenaries, who, as one prominent member of the group put it, "would sell their mom for a buck." The traders viewed the originators as dinosaurs, destined for extinction; they believed they were bringing harsh economic efficiency to what had long been a good-old-boy business.

This conflict climaxed every six months, the result of another innovation Skilling had imported from his consulting days: an elaborate peer-review system. At McKinsey, Skilling had served on the powerful committee that assessed the performance of all consultants worldwide. One of the first things he did upon joining Enron was set up a similar system, officially called the Performance Review Committee (PRC).

Early on, when ECT was still small, the PRC seemed a useful innovation. It swept out obvious deadwood and identified and rewarded up-and-comers. But over time, its goals were distorted, and the PRC had more to do with manipulating the system than with honestly evaluating talent. Employees called it "rank-and-yank."

Twice a year, every ECT employee (except Skilling), from managing director down to secretary, underwent individual review. It began with extensive written "feedback reports" from bosses and colleagues that assessed their performance on five sets of criteria. The real action took place at a string of marathon sessions held at local hotels, where panels would debate and rank each employee on a scale of 1 to 5—1 being the best and 5 the worst—while the individual's photo was projected on a screen in front of the group. Most of the ranking categories involved collaborative qualities, such as "teamwork/interpersonal" and "communication/setting direction." What really counted, though, was the bottom line. "If they were making money and being total jerks to people, we'd always forgive them for that," says one early ECT executive. "They might be a 5 in teamwork, but if they were a 1 in earnings, they were a 1. If you weren't doing deals, we had trouble valuing your contribution to the company."

Still, it wasn't all just about money. It was also about friendship. Executives simply refused to tell the truth about weak members of their team with whom they were friendly, knowing that all the other executives in the room were doing the exact same thing. Rather than reflecting a true meritocracy, the PRC became a perversion of it. "People manipulated the system," recalls a former top executive. "It became a question of who could argue better, who could debate better, and, in some cases, who could shout the loudest." Sometimes managers would purposely sabotage one candidate in order to ensure room at a higher level for one of their favorites.

For individual employees, the stakes were large. Those rated a 1 got huge bonuses. A ranking of 2 or 3 could cost a vice president a six-figure sum. And those at the bottom were supposed to be fired if they didn't improve their ranking at the next PRC. Because Skilling insisted that the ranking be distributed along a curve, at least 10 percent of the workforce had to be placed in the bottom group, marked for execution.

Predictably, the sessions got ugly. Because traders and deal makers with the same title were rated together, by representatives of both groups, the PRC became a place to duke out their mutual grievances and debate their relative worth. "A trader could go out and generate $5 million of earnings in a day," noted one early ECT hire. "The numbers can be huge. A lot of the controversy stemmed around the fact that for originators to generate the same type of earnings, the effort is ten times greater."

And so the argument went: should a hot trading hand be more richly rewarded than a gas-supply deal that had taken nine months to negotiate? Why should effort matter as much as profits? Every single ranking had to be unanimous, encouraging horse-trading and the occasional filibuster. The entire process consumed huge amounts of time for everyone involved. Sessions for executives, where the debate got the hottest, sometimes ran from 8 A.M. until after midnight. As Skilling and his defenders saw it, the PRC produced the best of Enron, rewarding brains, innovation, and dedication. But many thought it brought out the worst of Enron: ruthlessness, selfishness, and greed.

Of all the guys with spikes that Skilling gathered around him in those early days of ECT, none was as close to him as Cliff Baxter. Baxter's particular talent was in the arena of mergers and acquisitions; he was Skilling's in-house M&A specialist. Over time, Baxter's deals helped get Enron into the retail-energy-services business, electricity trading, and broadband. The two men lunched together several times a week. They regularly sneaked away from the company's smoke-free offices for a furtive cigarette in a parking garage across the street. And Baxter was one of the few who could barge into Skilling's office unannounced and say whatever was on his mind. After Baxter died, Skilling told friends: "I probably spent five times as much time with Cliff as anybody else."

A police sergeant's son from a Catholic family in Amityville, Long Island, Baxter had put himself through New York University then joined the air force, rising to captain. After leaving the military, he earned his MBA at Columbia University in 1987. He worked as an investment banker before joining Enron's

Washington office in 1991. Not long after that, Baxter approached Skilling to advise him that Enron was "wasting my talents." Skilling hired him.

Like Pai, whom he despised, Baxter was someone who could have thrived only at Enron. Blunt, blustery, and bombastic, Baxter had a towering ego and a volatile personality. He was a devoted friend and a generous mentor—he once loaned a new Enron arrival $40,000 to buy a luxury car—but he was also exceedingly sensitive to perceived slights involving his own status and compensation. He could be giddily happy when he was in the middle of a deal and go into a deep, unshakable funk when he wasn't. "He was," says one former executive, "a bundle of contradictions. He was very aggressive, but at the same time he was the most insecure man I've ever seen in my life. He'd present something in such a strident way, and then afterwards, he'd come up to you privately and say, 'Was that right?' "

He was also brutally honest. Almost alone among those close to Skilling, Baxter was quick to voice moral indignation, something he did frequently over the years. He didn't hesitate to tell others when they'd done something wrong. He clashed bitterly with other ECT executives, especially Pai.

Though he eventually made millions at Enron, he also complained frequently that he was underpaid and underappreciated. While Baxter had many fans, he was, in many ways, not an easy man to like.

But Skilling didn't care. Baxter, he later told people, "was the best deal guy I ever saw," and that's all that mattered. And Baxter *was* good. Meticulously organized, he planned out his deal strategies in tiny, neat handwriting and had a keen sense of how events might unfold. When he was in the middle of a transaction, he'd be transformed, as if the intensity of the deal was an intoxicant he couldn't resist. "Cliff Baxter is like an Indy race car," Ken Rice used to say about him. "If you wanna play, Cliff Baxter is the one you want. But you don't want to take him out of the garage to go to the 7-Eleven."

In 1995, in a dark mood after wrapping up a deal, he spent an entire lunch berating Skilling, telling him how he'd made a mess of his life. When Baxter finally stopped ranting, Skilling advised him to see a doctor. "Are you saying I'm *crazy*?" Baxter demanded. He was incensed that Skilling could suggest such a thing. "That's it—I quit!"

That summer, he took a job at Koch Industries, a big, privately owned commodities conglomerate in Wichita, Kansas. It was "a bungee trip," in the words of a former Enron executive. Koch Industries was a conservative midwestern company, and there was no way it could absorb Baxter's outsized ego. Shortly after arriving at Koch, he insisted that he could travel only on the corporate jet. "He just couldn't survive in a normal atmosphere," says a former colleague. Baxter had already bought a house and moved his wife and two children up to Wichita. But just weeks after he'd left for Koch, he was already putting out feelers about returning. He finally called Skilling himself. "What would you think about my coming back?" he asked. "A lot of people up here are real jerks."

Skilling wanted Cliff back; before Baxter left, he had given him an open offer to return. There was one hitch. Though Skilling was firmly in charge, he had
been promoting the notion that ECT operated like a professional firm, where top
executives acted almost as partners. So he submitted the issue to a monthly meeting of ECT's 13 managing directors and sought the group's blessing. But
Skilling, who knew there was sentiment within the group that Baxter was more
trouble than he was worth, wasn't going to take a chance that the answer would
be no. He made a point of greasing the deal with a rare personal appeal to Pai. "I
know you're going to raise a stink about this—*don't*," Skilling pleaded.

When Baxter got the official word, it was early evening. The next morning he
jumped in his car and started off on the 600-mile trip back to Houston, leaving
his family photos, Rolodex, and deal toys behind in his office. Koch executives
arrived the next morning to discover that Baxter, after just two months on the
job, had disappeared without a word.

There was one final piece of the puzzle. If ECT was going to grow as rapidly as
Skilling wanted, he needed more than long-term gas contracts and more than a
trading operation. He also needed a way to finance it all. Financing was his most
serious constraint, the one thing that could hold him back. Enron was reluctant to
pour money into ECT. Kinder had told Skilling that he wanted ECT to be able to
fund itself and that any capital Enron put into ECT would count against the
phantom equity the top executives held in the division.

The cash flow from the hard assets Skilling controlled didn't come close to
meeting his needs, given how many people he was hiring and how much he was
spending to make the new business grow. And he could hardly plow the profits
back into the operation: because of mark-to-market accounting, most of those
earnings were only paper profits. The actual cash wouldn't be seen for years.

That left the banks. But Skilling didn't want to depend heavily on bank loans
either. Part of the reason was that he couldn't: Enron already had lots of debt,
which put serious limits on how much any division could borrow. Besides, bor-
rowing itself was a constraint. Loans required collateral and had to be repaid;
loans had a way of tying your hands, not freeing them.

But there were other, newer techniques for raising capital, one in particular
that Skilling found especially compelling. Back when he was a consultant,
Skilling had been deeply influenced by a well-known McKinsey partner named
Lowell Bryan. Bryan was one of the pioneers of securitization: the practice of
pooling loans together and selling them to outside investors in the form of a security. For instance, a credit card company, instead of tying up its own capital by
keeping credit card loans on its balance sheet, could bundle them together and
sell them into the marketplace. Then it could use the capital it reaped from the
securitization sale to make more loans. In 1987, Bryan wrote that "securitization's potential . . . is great because it removes capital and balance sheets as con-

straints on growth." He believed that most financial-services companies would be greatly aided by securitizing their loan portfolios.

And that's exactly what Skilling was seeking to do: *remove capital and balance sheets as constraints on growth.* And since so much else about ECT was modeled on the financial-services industry, why not securitization as well? Why couldn't ECT bundle, say, the loans it was making to struggling gas producers? Why couldn't it use securitization techniques to generate capital that would allow it to grow faster than would otherwise be possible? Why couldn't Skilling transform this aspect of the national gas business as well? So that's what he did. Which is to say, that's how Enron first got into the business of setting up special-purpose entities.

Unlike some of the later special-purpose entities Enron created, these early deals were entirely aboveboard; the company even publicized them. The first such deal, completed in 1991, was called Cactus. Despite its many complex wrinkles, it was, at its core, a securitization deal. Enron bundled some $900 million of the money it had promised to front for gas producers and sold shares on those deals, as a package, to a group of high-powered investors, including General Electric. Under the terms of the deal, the group would then sell the gas back to Enron, which would resell it to wholesale customers like Sithe Energies. As a result of Cactus, the debt was eliminated from Enron's balance sheet and ECT was handed cash to accelerate its growth.

The next big deal was a landmark event for Enron. In 1993, the California Public Employees Retirement System (known as CalPERS) agreed to put $250 million in cash into a new off-balance-sheet investment partnership that Enron would run. For its 50 percent stake, Enron would contribute $250 million of its own stock. The money would be used to make energy-related investments (which is indeed what it did over the course of the next four years). With an investment portfolio of $130 billion, CalPERS is the largest public pension fund in the country and it is also among the most respected institutional investors in the world. A CalPERS imprimatur isn't quite on a par with Warren Buffett's deciding to put money into a company, but it's pretty close. Enron touted the partnership in press releases, and internally there was enormous pride in what the deal represented. It meant that Enron was finally joining the big leagues.

The partnership was called JEDI. Officially, the acronym stood for Joint Energy Development Investments. But it was also a sly nod to the *Star Wars* films; the man who devised the partnership was a *Star Wars* devotee, a finance executive named Andrew Fastow, whom Skilling had hired three years earlier. Though Skilling was enamored of him, Fastow hadn't yet made much of an impression on the rest of Enron.

With the financial piece in place, nothing could stop ECT, and nothing did. By 1996, in its sixth full year of existence, Skilling's division made $280 million before interest and taxes, more than 20 percent of Enron's earnings. Trading was rapidly becoming the company's biggest profit center. At the same time, Skilling was firmly established as the company's resident genius.

"Everyone believed what he said because he hadn't been wrong," recalls one ECT executive. "It was death if he raised his voice. He was brilliant at asking questions. He made people feel inadequate. People spent days getting ready for a meeting with him." When Skilling stepped out for a stroll in the trading room, the word went out as though Elvis were in the building: *"Jeff's on the floor!"*

■   ■   ■

Skilling himself later spoke of his days building ECT as his favorite time at Enron, the time when he had the most fun. But among those who worked for Skilling, fun was one of the last words they would associate with him.

Everyone in those years worked brutal hours, which took an inevitable toll, and no one worked harder than Skilling himself. Ever since he was a teenager, Skilling had been a workaholic, with little time for idle chitchat or variation in his routine. In his years at McKinsey, he arrived every day at 7 A.M. and ate breakfast—Twinkies and a Diet Coke—at his desk. Lunch was always the same: ham and cheese on white bread with mayo and a bag of Cheetos. He worked until about 8 P.M. on weekdays and came into the office every Sunday afternoon.

In 1990, Skilling had negotiated his move to Enron while his wife was in labor with their third child, reviewing drafts of his employment contract in the hospital labor-and-delivery room between Sue's contractions. After he arrived at Enron, he worked even harder. "I'd wake up at three o'clock in the morning in a cold sweat and say, 'What have I *done*?' I was working like a fool, an absolute fool," he later told friends. "It was fun, but it wasn't good for you." One Friday afternoon, Skilling bumped into gas-marketing executive Dan Ryser, who explained that he was hustling out to coach his kids' soccer team and get his mind off business. "What do you do to get your mind off the business?" the executive asked. "Nothing," Skilling responded.

Skilling built a vacation home in Utopia, in the Texas Hill Country. He relished his visits there partly because the four-hour drive from Houston gave him time to think about work. One weekend in 1995, while rock climbing there Skilling fell 20 feet and seriously hurt his ankle. A local doctor told him that he could do nothing: the ankle was so badly mangled that Skilling needed to go to a big-city hospital for surgery. Scheduled to leave the next day on a four-day trip to Germany, Skilling bought a set of crutches and hobbled onto the plane. The surgery took place a month later; reassembling his ankle required a bone graft, two pins, and three screws. Skilling later looked on his decision as "setting an example for the organization: things need to get done."

Inevitably, Skilling's family bore the brunt of his work habits. In the mid-1990s, with his marriage on the rocks, Skilling approached Lay and the Enron board for their approval of a last-ditch attempt to patch things up with his wife Sue. He would work half time, two weeks on the job, two weeks off, and spend the rest of his time trying to work things out at home. Ron Burns, an Enron pipeline executive, would serve as co-CEO to help run ECT. Skilling changed his title to managing director and accepted the 50 percent pay cut demanded by Kinder; he envisioned acting much like a management consultant, letting Burns handle the day-to-day operations. The Enron board thought the arrangement odd but approved it.

As a manager, Burns was everything Skilling wasn't. He motivated people not by throwing money at them but by taking an interest in their lives and making them feel appreciated. He had exquisite people skills. As one ECT employee put it, "He could fire you and you'd feel good about it." Though Burns lacked Skilling's crackling intelligence, he had the kind of practical management skills that most companies treasure—and that Skilling never had. He also had little tolerance for the kind of outrageous behavior and free spending that Skilling routinely indulged, or for guys with spikes. "He was the human part of the team," says an old ECT hand.

So naturally the arrangement was doomed. Part of it was that Skilling's marriage was too far gone to be saved. Part of it was that rather than valuing Burns for his management skills, Skilling viewed him as an intellectual lightweight and was openly dismissive of him. "Ron doesn't get it," he would tell his inner circle. Taking his cue from Skilling, Lou Pai began a campaign to undermine Burns.

In August 1995, Burns resigned to become president of the Union Pacific Railroad. Skilling, who had returned to work full time, assumed, once again, the title of chairman and CEO of ECT. Then he plucked one of his inner circle to be ECT's new number two: Lou Pai.

CHAPTER 6

The Empress of Energy

Until the mid-1990s, most people who had heard of Enron had no idea who Jeff Skilling was. To the outside world, the person who *was* Enron, who had a reputation for turning impossible concepts into glittering realities, was not Skilling. It was Rebecca Mark. When she stepped off Enron jets in remote spots in third world countries, she was welcomed like a celebrity and surrounded by throngs of reporters. Mark was a high-profile woman in a very male industry at a time when building power plants and pipelines across the globe was thought to be one of the most glamorous, profitable businesses ever, a little like the Internet in the late 1990s. And she reveled in it, embraced it with every fiber of her being. "In her ambition, her drive, and her tenacity," says a former Enron executive, "she was truly spectacular."

Mark, who was put in charge of something called Enron Development upon Wing's departure, not only kept her former lover's legacy of ferocious independence; she furthered it. Her team's offices were in downtown Houston—but across the street from Enron's headquarters, not in it. The decor was all glossy wooden furniture and expensive Oriental rugs, a dramatic contrast to Skilling's stark modernism. Mark's fiefdom had its own compensation system, one that would make her incredibly rich regardless of the ultimate success of her projects. It had its own books, its own accounting system, and its own risk-management system. And it had its own culture, where the ex-military guys she liked to hire sought to outdo each other at parties featuring elephants, motorcades, and belly dancers, and where Mark herself once came roaring in on the back of a Harley to the beat of "Eye of the Tiger."

It's actually one of the more stunning things about Enron that Mark's international business and Skilling's trading business could coexist within the same company. Skilling wanted to figure out ways to separate energy from the hard assets needed to produce it; Mark's business was nothing *but* hard assets. Trading was all about hedging away risk and quickly capturing profits. International development, where it could take a decade to recoup your money, meant taking on uncontrollable risks—everything from natural disasters to popular uprisings— and living through the inevitable trauma that comes with constructing a giant power plant in inhospitable territory. "Foreign direct investment," says a former executive in Mark's group, "is a matter of faith." That was anathema to Skilling. "We were absolutely on opposite ends of the spectrum," he once acknowledged. "Put us both in a room and we'd start screaming at each other."

Within Enron, it was obvious early on that Mark and Skilling were on a collision course. The contempt they had for each other's business was well known, and there was—and still is—a bitter divide between those who worked for Skilling and those who worked for Mark. Both have always insisted that their rivalry was a business issue, not a personal one. But for them, business *was* personal. Mark and her deputies thought that Skilling was a financial manipulator who wasn't capable of running a real, dirty-fingernails business. Skilling saw his rival as someone who was so busy jetting and glad-handing and playing the Enron glamour girl that she couldn't be bothered to understand the numbers. She snowed people, he believed. "Harvard Business School doesn't teach you accounting or finance," Skilling once said about Mark. "They teach you how to be convincing." Mark, in turn, came to believe that Skilling would go to any lengths to sabotage her. In time, she was proved right, not that she didn't give him plenty of ammunition.

Perhaps part of the problem was that, in many ways, they were very much alike—and not just because they were the same age and had Harvard MBAs. They both came from modest midwestern backgrounds. They had both been brought up to believe in the virtues of hard work, which, as adults, they took to extraordinary lengths. They were both driven to succeed. And they both believed they were creating new worlds, where anything was possible. Both also wrapped their business goals in the lofty language of idealism. Skilling loved to say that in trying to create a new kind of energy company, Enron was doing "the Lord's work." Mark struck a similar tone in talking about her business. "We are brought together with a certain amount of missionary zeal," she told Harvard for a case study. "We are bringing a market mentality and spreading the privatization gospel in countries that desperately need this kind of thinking."

Mark and Skilling also have this in common: both are blamed for Enron's downfall—by ex-employees, by outside observers, and by each other. Mark's critics contend that the shockingly poor performance of the assets she built stripped Enron of its financial strength and that, in being so richly rewarded for building those assets, she looted the company along the way. Nor is the harsh criticism limited to those from Skilling's side of the company. "Ego-driven empire-building," is how one former international employee describes Mark's tenure. Mark "worked very hard at self-promotion," says an early executive. "She had a lot of drive and personal ambition, but I'm not sure it was always directed toward the company." And this, from the former CEO of a major oil company: "The failure of Enron before all the accounting scandals can be seen in the results overseas."

The first comment people make about Skilling invariably involves his brains. With Mark, the first thing people mention is her looks. That's partly because she operated in the all-male energy industry and partly because the world can still be a sexist place. But it's mostly because of Mark herself. She happily played up her physical attributes, which included long blond hair, big brown eyes, and a dazzling smile. At Enron, she viewed her outfits—usually high heels and short skirts—as part of the show. *Forbes* writer Toni Mack once noted that Mark would sometimes change clothes as often as three times a day. "High finance with a touch of theater," Mack called it. Mark unapologetically viewed being a woman—a smart, charismatic woman—as a way to "get privileges that other people don't get, and . . . audiences that others could never hope to achieve," as she told one reporter. Her gender was not an obstacle to be overcome but an advantage. As she liked to put it, "I'll take all the advantages I can get."

The image of blatant opportunism that such a quote conveys doesn't really do Mark justice. Yes, she was opportunistic, but she was also genuinely charming—all down-home warmth, not big-city glamour—with a gift for remembering personal details and a girlishness that put people at ease. Mark had a way of talking that made listeners feel as though they were being taken into her confidence. "If you meet her and she turns on the charm, you'll be absolutely reduced to mush," says a former Enron executive who is not a fan. It's easy to see how those who worked for her could believe that anything was possible.

Mark's defining characteristic, though, was her optimism. She always had faith in herself, faith that the world was a place where she could make things happen, and faith that no matter how bad things seemed, all would work out just fine in the end. In her many interviews, she was so upbeat that she sounded positively sappy: "We were taught to believe that if you worked hard enough at anything, you could accomplish it," she told one reporter. "Many times the biases against women are those of our own creation," she told another. "If you approach people thinking that you're not going to be discriminated against, most often you're not." This wasn't just pap she fed the press; it was what she really believed. One of her favorite books was Paulo Coelho's *The Alchemist*, essentially a fable about the good things that happen if you follow your dreams.

Born Rebecca Pulliam, the second of four children of devoutly Baptist parents, Mark grew up on a farm in the small community of Kirksville, Missouri, about 150 miles east of Kansas City. Just as Ken Lay used to talk about his upbringing in moralistic terms, so did she. The farm, she later said, was where she learned the importance of hard work and where she got her first understanding of business. Even as a child, she preferred what is usually considered man's work—mucking out stalls, for instance—over, say, sewing. Mark was a good student, and like her siblings (not to mention Ken Lay and Jeff Skilling) she put herself through college. She spent her first two years at William Jewell College, a private Baptist school near Kansas City, before transferring to the Baptist-run Baylor University in Waco, Texas.

Mark did not leave the farm intent on going into business. On the contrary:

she dreamed of becoming a clinical psychologist and earned a BA in psychology in 1976. She took an internship working with juvenile delinquents, but it was not a happy experience; the job simply didn't mesh with her natural optimism. She later described it as "personally depressing—the antithesis of everything I learned growing up: that you can control your own destiny." What drew her to business was precisely her sense that it was an arena where she could control her destiny, where her willingness to work hard and dream big could pay off. By 1977 she had a master's in international management from Baylor.

By an odd coincidence, Mark ended up working in the same place that Skilling did after college: Houston's First City National Bank, where she began her business career as a commercial-lending officer. As she has pointed out, Skilling was upstairs operating in the rarefied world of portfolio theory while she was down on the floor making loans. That is to say, she was getting her fingernails dirty. (It was also during her stint at First City that she met and married an Arthur Andersen consultant named Thomas Mark.) In 1982, she joined the treasury department at Continental Resources, an energy company that was bought by Houston Natural Gas in 1985 shortly before the InterNorth merger. She ended up working in Enron Cogeneration, where she desperately wanted to prove that she could work just as hard as the guys and where she learned, as one of her colleagues put it, to never "melt into the shadows."

By 1991, Rebecca Mark felt that her time had come at Enron. The Teesside deal had been completed, it was a triumph for all concerned, and she believed she'd been a big part of it. She'd gotten her Harvard MBA. She was free of John Wing, who had been removed by Lay and the board from his Enron empire, lucrative consulting contract in hand. Her relationship with Wing, she believed, had toughened her up. She believed that she deserved to replace Wing as head of Enron Power, and she fervently hoped that Lay and Kinder would agree.

Much to her dismay, they didn't. Instead, they decided to carve up Enron Power into three divisions: Europe, the United States, and an emerging-markets business called Enron Development. Mark got Enron Development. The only problem was that Enron didn't *have* an emerging-markets business: Mark had been handed a division without a single asset and with only a handful of employees. And that wasn't the only indignity. Instead of reporting directly to Lay, she was told that she would be reporting both to Bob Kelly, who was put in charge of Enron Europe, and Tom White, the new CEO of Enron Power. Mark was furious at the decision; years later, it still rankled. When someone once mentioned the success Skilling had in building his trading operation, she scoffed. Unlike him, she replied tartly, she "didn't start off with the largest gas-pipeline system in the United States."

Emerging markets: in the early to mid-1990s, there was no more seductive siren call in all of American business. Developing nations, long overlooked by Western corporations, had enormous populations and tremendous needs. Their governments were becoming more open to free-market ideas and to the notion that Western investment could help generate jobs and improve standards of living. Many governments were even privatizing state-run enterprises. Banks were salivating over the prospect of loaning billions to third world development projects.

One thing developing nations needed was energy—cheap, plentiful, reliable energy. If they hoped to lure other forms of development, if they just hoped to provide for their growing populations, they needed energy before just about anything else, which meant more pipelines, more power plants, more everything. In the early 1990s, Enron predicted that worldwide power plant requirements would grow by a staggering 560,000 megawatts over the next decade. Government development agencies such as the Overseas Private Investment Corporation (OPIC) and the Export-Import Bank were willing to loan money to fund big energy projects, as were the big banks, which meant that companies like Enron had to invest only a tiny sliver of their own capital to get a project off the ground. Wall Street analysts talked about the potential for 30 percent returns on equity, about triple what U.S. pipelines were earning.

In the gold rush that followed, all kinds of companies raced in to stake their claims. And the projects were massive. In 1994, for instance, General Electric announced that it had teamed with financier George Soros to invest $450 million in power projects abroad; GE said the figure could eventually exceed $2.5 billion. In 1996, when Bolivia auctioned its state oil and gas company, some two dozen foreign companies bid. More often than not, the winning company took the initial up-front risk, with plans to extract some quick profits by selling off pieces to other buyers once the project was under way. In some ways, that was prudent business: it was a way to diminish the risk. Yet that kind of business plan was predicated on the belief that someone else would always be willing to pay a higher price. On Wall Street, this is known as the greater fool theory.

So while Mark may have been handed a division without any assets, she did have the wind at her back. And there was no doubt what she was expected to do: plant the flag for Enron in as many developing nations as she could. Mark's team quickly put together a string of flashy, first-of-their-kind deals. One of the earliest took place in late 1992, when Enron bought a 17.5 percent stake in Transportadora del Sur, a pipeline in southern Argentina that the government was privatizing. By early 1994, Mark also had power plants in the Philippines, Guatemala, and Guam and had struck deals to build plants in India and the Dominican Republic. Within the next few years, her team was busy laying a pipeline in Colombia (where Enron had to hire hundreds of soldiers to guard workers against guerrilla attacks), constructing a plant in China, and evaluating opportunities from Indonesia to Yemen. Enron also announced grand plans to develop enormous gas fields in Mozambique, lay a pipeline to South Africa that would feed a multibillion-dollar steel plant there, and construct a power plant in Vietnam.

Mark was particularly excited about South America, which she (along with everyone else) thought was bursting with opportunities. "I want to *conquer* Brazil," she told a Brazilian energy consultant in 1993. Pumping abundant Bolivian gas into perennially power-starved Brazil, where it could fuel new electric plants, was always thought to be impossible. By the mid-1990s, Enron had orchestrated the start of construction on a $2 billion pipeline that stretched 1,875 miles, from Santa Cruz, Bolivia, across swampy bayous and craggy mountains to Porto Alegre, Brazil. Just as Wing had done at Teesside, Mark positioned Enron not as the low-cost option but as the solver of the unsolvable problem.

Indeed, for years the specter of John Wing hovered over Mark's operation. He had given Enron its great Teesside triumph; now she was determined to come up with projects that were even bigger and better than his. Wing had established extraordinary autonomy. So did she, not showing up for staff meetings run by her nominal superiors, Kelly and White, and taking her business issues directly to Ken Lay, who was board chairman of Enron Development. Wing liked to hire can-do ex-military types. So did she. Oh, and one other thing: for the first few years Rebecca Mark raced around the globe looking for projects to build on behalf of Enron, John Wing did the same thing with his new Enron-backed business. Mark's former lover was now her competition.

It was almost comical the way the two of them spent the next several years bumping into each other all over the globe, as they tried to lay claim to this country or that on behalf of Enron. Government officials would meet with one, then the other, and have no idea who was actually supposed to be representing Enron. The result was chaos. "It was a free-for-all," recalls one former executive. In 1992, when the Wing Group announced that it was jointly developing Turkey's first private power plant with Enron Europe—run by Wing's former deputy Bob Kelly—Mark was irate. "The world isn't that big," she complained to Lay, telling him that he needed to make decisions on territory. Lay's response was classic Lay: everyone should just get along.

The conflict came to a head around 1994 in Shanghai. The Wing Group had just won a letter of intent from a nearby provincial government for a major power project. Wing's staff had heard rumblings that Mark's group was also sniffing around. Mark, who was in the city to give a speech, had no idea that Wing had just laid claim to China. Just before lunchtime, she appeared in the lobby of the Portman Shangri-La Hotel, where she and her team spotted some members of the Wing Group, who were staying there.

The encounter quickly escalated. "Ken told us *we've* got China!" "No," replied Mark, "He told me *I* have China!" "Nobody hit anybody," remembers one combatant, "but it was ugly." Wing's group and Mark's team continued to battle in the coffee shop, racing back and forth to the lobby pay phones to call Houston. By the end of the day, Mark and Wing had both reached Lay. His decision? They could both proceed. But from that point on, Rich Kinder was assigned to help divvy up the world on a monthly basis. A year or so later, Wing decided that the emerging markets had become so overheated that building projects there no longer made economic sense, and he exited the business.

By the mid-1990s, Enron Development was viewed internally as an enormous success, and Rebecca Mark was widely acknowledged as the woman who had made it all happen. Her charm, her drive, her knowledge, and, above all, her optimism made her a fabulous marketer, far better than Wing. "She was able to convince people of things that no one else could, because she believed them," says a former executive. Many of her employees worshiped her, in no small part because no matter how hard they worked, they knew she was working harder. At one point, she was traveling 300 days a year while still trying to be a mom, racing from the Far East to Houston to attend her children's school plays. Glowing profiles—a woman doing this?—ran constantly. The head count at Enron Development, which had about 25 people when Mark began, grew to 10,000.

And in 1996, Rebecca Mark got her reward: she became the new CEO of Enron International, leapfrogging both Kelly and White. EI, as it was called within Enron, encompassed all of the developing world as well as Kelly's former territory in Europe. Mark now ran more than a dozen pipeline and power-plant projects costing billions of dollars, with even more in the works. She was indeed controlling her own destiny.

Yet under the gleaming surface, there were problems at EI, problems that got only worse over time. Mark, who at first ran and reran numbers to make sure her deals made economic sense, became sloppy, says one person who worked with her closely. Because she was tearing all over the world trying to juggle a million balls, important details fell through the cracks. And while Enron International executives loved putting deals together, the business had a flaw that was endemic to Enron: no one felt responsible for managing the projects once they were up and running. Mark's developers saw their role as getting the deal done: "We are in the business of doing deals . . . this deal mentality is central to what we do," Mark told an interviewer for a Harvard Business School case study. Indeed, Enron treated Mark's division almost as if it were an outside development team whose job was simply to find deals. Mark and her deputies couldn't commit Enron's money without approval. But Enron itself had no great interest in managing projects because its emphasis was also on deal making. And because the developers were trying to do so many deals, in some quarters Enron got a reputation for dropping the ball. "Enron could talk a good game, but they didn't deliver," says a former Big Oil CEO. "Big Oil, we don't operate that way. If you say you're going to do something, you do it."

To make matters worse, Enron International was an incredibly expensive business to run. It often took years to land a project, years during which teams of developers had to fly back and forth across the globe and live abroad for weeks at a time. Among the developers, a belief took hold that the time it took to manage expenses just wasn't worth it. No one ever thought about where the cash would come from to pay for it all. "People treated Enron like a bottomless trough for a long time," says a former EI executive. Mark, for her part, would insist that she cared about keeping costs under control, yet she herself got a reputation for spending a fortune when she traveled. Local teams would shudder when her jet touched down, dreading the huge amounts their project would be charged for a short meeting.

One of the core ideas behind Mark's business was that most of the money for the projects it put together would come from non-Enron sources, from bank loans to governments, say, or investments from companies hankering to get in on the emerging-markets gold rush. That would keep debt off Enron's balance sheet and put a minimal amount of Enron's own capital at risk. But in the rush to do deals, that wasn't always the case, and Enron often ended up guaranteeing some or all of the debt, at least for a time. For the Subic Bay, Philippines, plant that Enron was developing, the company guaranteed all $105 million in debt; on a second Philippines plant, in Batangas, Enron guaranteed 25 percent of the principal and interest on a $50 million loan. In addition, Enron provided tens of millions of dollars in letters of credit to support cost overruns. One executive remembers that on one project, the banks had a list of conditions that, once they were met, would eliminate the need for an Enron guarantee. But no one at Enron bothered to meet the conditions and thereby get rid of the guarantee.

Then there was the question of what happened to the large sums spent on projects that didn't go forward. Here was an early example of Enron's willingness to stretch accounting rules. The money Enron poured into projects that never were built—and such a failed deal could soak up tens of millions—was supposed to be written off. In Vietnam, for instance, one accountant says that Enron spent some $18 million trying to build a power plant, only to see the project canceled. Yet Enron International often booked such costs as an *asset* on the balance sheet, in what came to be known around the company as "the snowball." Usually the rationale was that there was no official letter saying the project was dead, so therefore, officially, it wasn't. Rich Kinder had a rule: the snowball had to stay under $90 million. But it eventually ballooned to over $200 million.

A second problem: the assumptions Enron made to justify its deals assumed that nothing would ever go wrong. Of course, the banks financing the deals were making the same assumption; this was a mania, after all. But building energy projects in poor countries—often run by dictators and where capitalism was still a new concept—was absolutely fraught with peril, and it was absurd to believe that everything would play out according to plan. Things went wrong all the time. Who could say for sure that a plant in the wilds of Brazil that wasn't even supposed to be operational for years would ever generate the monster profits Enron was anticipating? What if there were cost overruns? What if Brazilians couldn't afford the cost of the new energy? What if the government decided to nationalize the project? With every emerging-markets project, there were a million what-ifs.

Take the Dominican Republic, where Enron had invested $95 million to own 50 percent of a barge-mounted plant off Puerto Plata on the northern coast. It turned out that the Dominican Republic wouldn't pay for the power. The plant was next to a hotel called the Hotelero del Atlántico; the prevailing winds blew soot from the plant onto the guests' meals, blackening their food—and not in a stylish way. The winds also blew garbage from nearby slums into the plant's water-intake system. For some time, the only solution was to hire men who paddled out to the intake valve in boats, where they would push the garbage away with their paddles. In 1995, the hotel sued, alleging damages and loss of customers. For Enron, the deal was a complete bust; through mid-2000, the company had collected a pathetic $3.5 million from its $95 million investment.

In part, the rush to do deals was a natural outgrowth of Mark's personality. Her inherent optimism led her to push forward where others might have at least hesitated. Over time, naysayers in her operation were relegated to lesser roles. People who worked for her say she trusted her gut far more than any spreadsheet, as she would tell anyone who tried to say no to her by citing a project's questionable numbers. As Mark saw it, she might make mistakes from time to time, but that wasn't necessarily a bad thing because all the motion and activity would lead to something better. One former Enron International executive calls some of EI's exploits "a triumph of chutzpah over common sense."

But the most poisonous explanation for the mad rush to do deals was money, not the money Enron would make but the money the developers would make. What one former international executive calls the "fatal flaw" in the business was the compensation structure. Developers got bonuses on a project-by-project basis. The developers would calculate the present value of all the expected future cash flow from a project. This was also the model the banks used to lend money. When the project reached financial close—that is, when the banks lent money but before a single pipe was laid or foundation was poured—they were paid.

No wonder the developers were so eager to move on to the next deal; they had no financial incentive to follow through on the one they'd just completed. And the money they stood to make was stunning, amounting to some 9 percent of the project's total value. In other words, if the developers estimated that the project would ultimately bring Enron $100 million, the developers took home $9 million. In a sense, they were paid on the basis of mark-to-market accounting—just like the traders in Skilling's group.

It was crazy. Kinder had come up with this scheme in an effort to avoid giving direct equity in projects to the developers, as John Wing had had with Teesside. Wing's deals usually required that his projects return a certain percentage, and his payouts took place over years. Thus Wing and his team wouldn't get their full payout unless the project actually worked.

But under this new pay arrangement, the only thing that mattered was making the deal happen. The more deals Enron International did, and the bigger they were, the richer the developers got. The system encouraged international executives to gamble without risk. The deeper problem, one that emerged in later years, was that no one was held responsible for the operation of a project, yet it was the *operation* that produced the real money. (Around 1994, Kinder changed the compensation structure; the developers were paid 50 percent at the financial close, the rest once the project was operational.)

Why were Lay and the board so eager to spend shareholders' money on risky projects around the globe? In part, it was because the international business played to their own desires. The board loved the idea that Enron was providing power to people who desperately needed it. So did Lay, who was always looking for ways to increase the use of natural gas. It also gave him the perfect opportunity to employ such luminaries as Henry Kissinger and James Baker as consultants, sending them to such far-flung locales as Kuwait and China to open doors for Enron. And Lay loved meeting heads of state. "Ken had no international stage to play on until we created one for him," says one former executive.

There was another reason for Lay's unwillingness to apply the brakes. Although Mark has always disputed this, Lay had a blind spot about Enron's glamour girl. Lay, who sometimes accompanied Mark on her global jaunts, saw her at her best: marketing. He took great pleasure in the glowing press clips she generated. Acutely conscious of appearances, he loved having a female star in a male business. Lay always wanted to cheer on his favorite employees, not say no to their projects. "Ken had pets," says one former Enron board member. "And Rebecca was one of them."

For all its problems, the international business would be remembered differently today if just one deal had turned out differently. Indeed, all of Mark's other failures and successes are dwarfed by a single project, a project that was supposed to be her Teesside but instead made Enron controversial years before its bankruptcy.

In Dabhol, India, about a hundred miles south of Bombay on a remote volcanic bluff overlooking the Arabian Sea, sits an enormous modern power plant. On one side of a fence is a decrepit third world village, awash in grime and poverty. On the other is this *thing,* this gleaming monstrosity that dwarfs everything around it. The plant was the largest-ever foreign investment in India and it was supposed to be Enron's first step in a grand, $20 billion scheme to reshape India's energy sector. Instead, it is a white elephant. And critics such as the novelist Arundhati Roy, who called the Dabhol project "the biggest fraud in India's history," have seized upon it as the ultimate symbol of the failure of globalization. An Indian Wall Streeter says, "I've never been to another country where every single person hates one company."

Investing in India was Enron at its most contrarian. India's energy sector has always been run by the government and is a bureacratic quagmire. All power is sold through state electricity boards, most of which totter on the edge of bankruptcy because so much power is either stolen or given away to farmers. The boards can't raise rates because India's politicians don't want to ask its citizens to pay more for power. When Enron first thought about building a plant in India, the country's foreign reserves were dwindling and Moody's, the credit-rating agency, had just downgraded India's debt. Enron's own strategic planners had put India on the top of a list it compiled of countries the company should avoid. But Ken Lay liked to say that the company made its money by going where the strategic planners said not to go. So, naturally, Enron went to India.

The Dahbol saga began in early 1992, not long after Mark became head of Enron Development. An Indian delegation, led by the country's power secretary, came to the United States touting the government's program of economic reforms, and seeking investors to help India address its chronic energy shortages. Many American energy companies, wary of the problems that came with doing business in India, held only cursory meetings with the delegation. Not Enron. Mark spent an entire day with the Indian delegates. Eventually she told them that Enron would be the country's first investor, but only if India were willing to meet three conditions. It would have to work with Enron on an expedited basis, it would have to commit to using natural gas, and it would have to back up any deal with ironclad government guarantees.

On June 30, Enron signed a letter of intent with the electricity board in Maharashtra, India's wealthiest and most heavily industrialized state, which was desperately in need of power. That summer, on one of her now-frequent trips to India, Mark spent three days with Maharashtra officials driving down the coast in search of the perfect site for the plant. The spot they chose was so remote that the project would have to develop its own roads, hospital, housing, and port. Enron was awarded the right to develop the site without competing bids.

Eighteen months later, in December 1993, Mark inked a 20-year power-purchase contract with the Maharashtra State Energy Board (MSEB). The terms called for Enron to build an enormous, 2,015 megawatt plant—bigger than Teesside. The construction would be done in two phases at an estimated cost of $2.8 billion. The two sides agreed that power prices in the region would rise once the plant was up and running, in part because, for environmental and reliability reasons, the fuel would be imported liquefied natural gas, an expensive fuel. The bill for the power would be calculated in dollars, so that the MSEB, not Enron, bore the currency risk. Finally, the MSEB promised to buy 90 percent of the power Dabhol produced for the entire 20-year period. Its ability to pay was guaranteed by both the state and the central government.

It is astounding, in retrospect, that no one on the Enron side could envision the kind of resentment and backlash such a one-sided agreement would engender. To many Indians, the deal came to represent nothing less than a huge giveaway to a rapacious multinational corporation. But even putting that aside, the deal was a huge gamble for Enron. If the MSEB was ever going to be able to pay for the power on its own, the Indian government would have to push through serious economic reforms, reforms that would put state electricity boards such as the MSEB on a firm financial footing. But such reforms were politically contentious because they would mean increasing the price of power for some consumers. On top of the normal economic risk was a frightening amount of political risk.

Still, at first, Mark seemed brilliantly ahead of the pack, just as Wing had been with Teesside. After Enron signed its letter of intent, other companies worried that they might be missing out. During 1992 and 1993, almost 200 memorandums of understanding were signed to build plants in India. (Very few were ever built.) And Mark began unloading some of Enron's exposure, insisting, for instance, that GE (which was selling turbines to Dabhol) and Bechtel (which was constructing the plant) each put up 10 percent of the equity. They agreed.

Then the problems started mounting. The first big hurdle was financing. For years, the World Bank had held a near monopoly on financing infrastructure investments in India. But the bank objected to the project, warning that Dabhol was "too large" and "not economically viable" and would "place a heavy financial burden on Maharashtra."

Mark and her team fumed that the World Bank, which was the biggest lender to Maharashtra, didn't want its position usurped by private developers. It took Mark almost two years, but in February 1995, after two government reviews, nine court cases, and reviews by over a hundred outside lawyers, advisers and bankers, Mark finally got her financing. Dabhol received a total of $643 million for Phase 1 of the project from sources as varied as OPIC, a syndicate of Indian banks, and Bank of America.

Just weeks after Bechtel bulldozers began flattening the red rock hillside in Dabhol, there was an ominous development. In Indian state elections that took place in March 1995, the ruling Congress Party in Maharashtra lost to a Hindu nationalist coalition that had campaigned on an anti–foreign investment platform and a promise to "push Enron into the Arabian Sea."

Suddenly, questions that had been bubbling in the background erupted. How could a project the size of Dabhol have been approved without bribes? Just where did the $20 million that Enron said it spent on "educating" the Indians about capitalism really go? Why had the Enron contract been negotiated in secrecy, without a competitive bidding process? How was MSEB ever going to be able to afford to buy all that power? "India's status will be enhanced, not lowered, if it tells the world that it is no pushover, no banana republic ready to accept an atrocious deal," opined the *Times of India*. The new ruling party immediately began a review of Dabhol.

The situation soon got uglier. In May, hundreds of protesting villagers swarmed over the site, and a riot broke out. Human Rights Watch and Amnesty International eventually charged security forces guarding Dabhol for Enron with human-rights abuses; Human Rights Watch blamed Enron for being "complicit." Meanwhile, various Clinton administration officials, including Treasury Secretary Robert Rubin, weighed in on behalf of Enron; in June, the Department of Energy issued a statement saying that canceling Dabhol could have an adverse effect on India's ability to attract foreign investment.

On August 3, the Maharashtra state government ordered the project halted because of "lack of transparency, alleged padded costs, and environmental hazards." Construction ground to a halt; by then, some $300 million had been spent on the project. "What we are experiencing here is every investor's worst nightmare," Mark told the newspapers. "I'm in grief."

Over the next year, an Enron senior management group, spearheaded by Kinder, convened every day at 8 A.M. to review the company's options. Meanwhile, Enron fended off two dozen lawsuits from various Indian entities trying to undo the Dabhol contracts. Enron's stock, which had been on a tear, stalled, as the deadlock at Dabhol cast broader doubt on Enron's international strategy.

What followed can be described as either a triumph of Mark's negotiating prowess or as a disastrous doubling of an already risky bet. While the lawyers in Houston dug through the contracts, Mark got on a plane to India and spent the next six weeks there. She later described it to one friend as refusing to "listen to negativity." She and her team talked to over a thousand people, offering to renegotiate the price of the power, the capital costs of the plant, even offering to switch to a cheaper fuel. After nearly two months, the Indian team agreed to reopen negotiations.

Mark had breathing room, but only if the entire project, not just the first phase, were renegotiated. Over the previous four years, costs for much of the major equipment had plunged, allowing Enron to slash its costs on the second phase, whose equipment had not yet been purchased and which India had not yet approved. That meant Enron could offer a major overall rate reduction while preserving the economics of the deal, but only if *both* parties doubled their bet.

On February 23, 1996, Maharashtra and Enron announced a new agreement. Enron cut the price of the power by over 20 percent, cut total capital costs from $2.8 billion to $2.5 billion, and increased Dabhol's size from 2,015 megawatts to 2,184 megawatts. And both parties formally committed to developing the second phase. On December 10, 1996, Enron announced that the financing for Phase 1 had again been secured, and that construction had resumed.

The MSEB also won the right to be able to purchase a stake in the venture; it eventually owned 15 percent of Dabhol. If the foreigners were going to make so much, India wanted a piece of the action. But the MSEB's obligations still remained mammoth. Under the revised terms, it was required to purchase more power than before, by some estimates as much as $30 billion worth over the life of the contract. It was a preposterous sum. Critics in India, meanwhile, continued to hammer away, complaining that Enron's estimated return, which by some calculations could be as much as 30 percent, was shockingly high. Accusations of bribery and corruption, though never proven in court, never went away. Mark's team hung in through it all. The first phase began producing power in May 1999, almost two years behind schedule, and construction started on phase 2. Costs would ultimately climb to $3 billion.

Then everything came to a stop. The MSEB refused to pay for all the power, and it became clear that getting the government to honor the guaranteees would not be an easy task. Although Maharashtra still suffers from blackouts, it says it does not need and cannot afford Dabhol's power. (The *New York Times* calculated that the cost would exceed Maharashtra's entire budget for primary and secondary school education.) And India's power sector still loses roughly $5 billion a year. Today, Dabhol, in which Enron invested some $900 million, sits silent, a gigantic, wasted marvel of modern technology.

But that became clear only much later. For Rebecca Mark, the near-term effects of Dahbol were entirely different. For one thing, it made her rich. One executive remembers a conference call between Mark and Ken Lay to discuss Mark's bonus for Dabhol. The cash-flow estimates she had prepared assumed, naturally, that everything would go smoothly, but Lay offered no objections to her spreadsheet. The project team split $20 million, of which she received a huge chunk. Soon she was zipping around Houston in a ruby-red Jaguar XK8 convertible. She had a Land Rover for the kids, a lake house, a ten-acre retreat in Taos, and an apartment on Manhattan's Upper East Side.

The near-miraculous resurrection of Dabhol made Rebecca Mark into even more of a rock star. The press was fawning: "From near disaster, Mark and Enron have wrested a victory," wrote *Forbes*. Pulitzer Prize–winning energy historian Dan Yergin told *Fortune:* "Rebecca is tops in her business." Jeffrey Garten, the dean of the Yale School of Management, said to *Institutional Investor:* "Enron has gained tremendous respect for their manner abroad. . . . What developing countries want, especially in sophisticated energy industries, is first-rate American companies with the best of American management and technology. That's what Rebecca gives them." Garten added that Mark and Lay were "clearly willing to take major risks before they know what the endgame is in a business with huge capital requirements, and they are willing to stick it out through the ups and downs." Both inside and outside the company, there was speculation that Mark would be Enron's next CEO. Enron International accounted for more than 15 percent of the company's earnings in 1996, and Enron was soon predicting that its earnings from International would grow at 20 percent a year for the forseeable future.

At least one person other than Skilling was not convinced: Rich Kinder. Ever the hard-core numbers guy, Kinder was skeptical of everything, but he was especially skeptical of Mark's business. There was no way he could evaluate its performance, because so much of the profits were on the come. But globalization had caught on, the board belonged to Ken Lay, and Mark was his star. To other Enron executives, it appeared as if Kinder was afraid to take her on, because he realized this was one battle that he would lose.

Events were brewing under the surface, however, that would change everything—and inside Enron, decisions were being made that would set the company on a very different course.

CHAPTER 7

The 15 Percent Solution

By the mid-1990s, it all seemed to be clicking, at least on the surface. Enron now had a story Wall Street loved, the story of a company transforming itself into something new and shiny and different, a company that relied as much on trading screens as on pipelines and that landed breathtaking deals in far-flung places. With every passing year, it seemed, Enron was posting record profits, from $387 million in 1993 to $453 million in 1994 to $520 million in 1995. The community of Wall Street analysts and institutional investors that followed the energy industry was enthralled with the company and rewarded Enron the only way it knew how: by buying the stock. From mid-1990 to late 1995, Enron's stock price tripled.

And who was responsible for this remarkable transformation? Why, it had to be Ken Lay, didn't it? Certainly, that's what most people outside the company assumed. He had long since begun the process of raising his profile, in Houston, on Wall Street, and especially in Washington, D.C.; in the process, he crafted an image as a thoughtful and visionary businessman, a caring community leader, and the philosopher-king of energy deregulation. It didn't hurt that the philosophy Lay had long espoused had largely become accepted wisdom, not just by Republicans but by Democrats as well. "Ken is a profound thinker, a great long-term strategist who has been on the forefront of the natural gas industry for many years," said a PaineWebber analyst named Ron Barone in 1996. "He knew where this industry was going ten years before it happened." Such accolades were typical by the mid-1990s.

But inside the company, especially among the top executives, it was a different story. Lay was a pushover when it came to negotiating pay and bonuses and could always be held up for more money. Even though Skilling's business was transforming the company, Lay's understanding of how ECT worked was fuzzy at best. He usually seemed at one remove from the nitty-gritty of the business itself. In his early years as CEO, Lay had been a workaholic who usually traveled with a bulging briefcase. Now, increasingly, he appeared more invested in his outside endeavors, from the Houston charities he was involved in to the campaigns he raised money for to the Washington think tanks whose boards he sat on, than in

Enron. "If you wanted to get Lay to attend a meeting," recalls a former executive, "you needed to invite someone important."

The person who usually ran those meetings was Lay's tough number two, Rich Kinder. It could have been the perfect arrangement, with Lay as Enron's Mr. Outside and Kinder as Mr. Inside. But such arrangements work only if each man respects and values what the other brings to the table. And they only work so long as the number two is content to remain behind the scenes while the CEO is taking all the bows. By the mid-1990s, that was no longer true of Ken Lay and Rich Kinder.

When did Ken Lay even have the *time* to run Enron? Turning himself into a public figure was pretty much a full-time job. Like many prominent CEOs, he sat on other corporate boards, joining Compaq's board of directors in 1987 and adding Eli Lilly's in 1993. He and his wife, Linda, were fixtures on the charity dinner circuit. They were among the premier hosts in Houston, throwing cocktail parties for important people passing through the city. The Lays and their personal charitable organization, the Linda and Ken Lay Family Foundation, gave millions to local causes. They also gave generously to out-of-town organizations, such as the Baptist Church in Columbia, Missouri, the Character Education Partnership in Washington, D.C., and Aspen's Biochemical Research Foundation. He served as chairman of the Greater Houston Partnership and raised money for the Houston United Way.

For local politicians, getting an audience with (and a donation from) Ken Lay was practically a rite of passage. Indeed, anyone involved in Houston's civic life simply had to get to know Ken Lay: he was the man who could make things happen. In 1996, when Lay read that the city's National League baseball team, the Houston Astros, might move unless it got a new stadium, he raced into action, working tirelessly to get a referendum passed authorizing construction of the stadium. In 1999, Enron agreed to pay $100 million over 30 years to have the stadium named Enron Field; Enron also got a 30-year contract, which it valued at some $200 million, to manage the stadium's energy needs. On the first day of the 2000 season, Lay was invited to throw out the first ball, while both generations of George Bushes and their wives cheered him on from their seats behind home plate.

Though he'd lived in Houston since the early 1980s, Lay had never lost his taste for Washington, D.C. Now, as a wealthy and prominent CEO, he could indulge it. He traveled to Washington frequently—often without informing Enron's Washington public-affairs office—arriving on a company plane and staying at a swanky hotel. He would be chauffered around town. His assistant, a commanding woman named Nancy McNeil—"the little general," some people at Enron called her—was considered a key go-between for politicians, all of whom knew her, and Lay. Lay, though, didn't often spend time with run-of-the-mill politicians. He preferred high-ranking executive branch officials.

He had become close friends with Charls Walker, the brother of his old mentor Pinkney Walker. Charls Walker was one of the most well-connected lobbyists in the capital. He joined Enron's board in 1985, and his firm was retained to lobby for the company. Realizing that Lay was an unusual asset—a CEO who had once been a government policy maker and understood the byways of the capital—Walker recruited him that same year to cochair something called the Coalition for Jobs, Growth, and Competitiveness, which lobbied against any increase in taxes for corporations. In the mid-1980s (and again in the year 2000), Lay served on the board of Resources for the Future, a respected environmental-policy development organization. And in 1995, Lay was elected to the board of the American Enterprise Institute, a right-leaning think tank that is a meeting place for Washington's conservative elite. Future vice president Dick Cheney was also a trustee; his wife, Lynne, is still a staff scholar there.

Of course, it wasn't just Lay's personality that won him friends in Washington; he also had Enron's money to spread around. Between 1989 and 2001 Enron and its executives contributed nearly $6 million to political parties and candidates, two-thirds to Republicans, according to opensecrets.org., a site that tracks political contributions. Over that same period, Ken and Linda Lay individually contributed over $880,000, of which 90 percent went to Republicans. Enron was a major supporter of Tom DeLay, the House Republican leader from Texas, and of Senator Phil Gramm, another Texan. And Enron was one of George W. Bush's biggest supporters.

Indeed, one of the reasons the Enron scandal burst from the business page onto the front page was its political dimension: Lay was said to be a good friend of the new president. In truth, although George W. Bush gave Lay the chummy nickname Kenny Boy, Lay was never especially close to him; his real friendship was with Bush's father, former president George H. W. Bush, who lived in Houston. Of course, Lay also knew Cheney: Cheney had served as CEO of Halliburton, a large Texas-based energy company. Later, when Cheney ran for vice president, Enron helped throw him a lavish luncheon. During the first Bush administration, Ken and Linda Lay were invited to sleep in the White House, and in 1991, Bush even offered Lay the position of commerce secretary when the incumbent, Texas businessman Robert Mosbacher, announced he was stepping down. Lay declined, telling Bush that he wasn't ready to leave Enron. In fact, although Linda was vocal about her desire to be a top Washington hostess, Lay thought he could do better than commerce secretary; he wanted to be treasury secretary. Walker had told him that was the only government position a man of his stature should even consider.

But Lay made a fatal miscalculation with George W. Bush that permanently strained the relationship. In 1993, when Bush was preparing to run for governor of Texas, he had made the ritual pilgrimage to Houston to get Lay's blessing. Bush asked Lay to serve as the Houston finance chairman for his campaign. Lay, however, rebuffed the candidate, explaining that it wouldn't be appropriate since he was then serving as chairman of the Business Council for Ann Richards, the Democratic governor. Richards was a popular governor and Bush a neophyte politician; nobody gave him much of a chance of winning. Somewhat condescendingly, Lay expressed the hope that even if Bush were defeated, the experience "wouldn't prevent him from running again." Still both he and his wife wrote checks to Bush for $12,500. Rebecca Mark and Jeff Skilling also contributed to the Bush campaign.

As election day drew near and the polls showed that Bush might well score an upset, Lay called Bush's finance chairman and said his wife was going to write another check for $12,500. Although Enron and the Lays ended up giving far more to Bush than to Richards, Lay's lukewarm embrace left its mark. George W. Bush's finance chairman that year was Rich Kinder. Years later, when George W. Bush was running for president against Al Gore, Lay was named one of the Pioneers: people who had raised at least $100,000 for Bush's presidential campaign. The leader of the Harris County Pioneers, however, was once again Kinder.

Was there a business purpose to all of Lay's Washington schmoozing and fund-raising? Of course there was. Enron's business needed favorable rulings and legislation to thrive, and that meant it needed the government to institute rules and laws to help spur deregulation along. But Washington was also a personal indulgence for Lay. He spent so much time there because he loved the world of policy and politics and he truly believed in the virtues of deregulation. He argued consistently that deregulation would save consumers money; he used to claim that between 1985 and 1996, consumers had saved some $30 billion a year as a result of the lower natural gas prices deregulation helped usher in. "He knew his stuff, and he spoke from the heart," recalls one person who worked with Lay on policy issues. Always, he cast himself as on the side of the angels. After all, wasn't natural gas helping to wean America from its dependence on foreign oil? Wasn't it helping control pollution? Yes, increased reliance on natural gas helped Enron, but it helped everybody.

There were times when Lay's lobbying seemed at odds with his oft-stated belief in free-market solutions. A classic example was Enron's dependence on such government agencies as the Overseas Private Investment Corporation and the Export-Import Bank, which provided loans and loan guarantees for development projects in the third world. In many cases, these agencies were an important source of financing, since banks were often leery of the risks. Rebecca Mark's business would have been much smaller without such backing; between 1989 and 2001, some 20 governmental or quasi-governmental agencies, including OPIC, the World Bank, and the Export-Import Bank, approved $7.2 billion in public financing for 38 separate Enron International projects in 29 countries, according to a study done by the Washington, D.C., Institute for Policy Studies. Skilling, who was always Mark's biggest critic, used to heap scorn on her reliance on government-backed financing, claiming that it was hypocritical for a company that supposedly worshiped at the altar of the free market.

But Lay had no such qualms. In congressional testimony in 1995 he said, "Public finance agencies are the only reliable sources of the financing that is essential for private infrastructure projects in developing countries." The following year, amid threats to cut funding for OPIC and the Ex-Im Bank, Lay warned that such moves "will change our strategy." And in early 1997, he asked Bush, then the governor, to lobby on behalf of OPIC and the Ex-Im Bank, saying that "these export credit agencies . . . are critical to U.S. developers like Enron."

As Enron grew, so did Lay's paycheck. In 1990, Lay owned some 300,000 shares of Enron stock and his total cash compensation amounted to about $1.5 million. By the mid-1990s, his salary alone was approaching $1 million and his annual bonus usually exceeded $1 million. And that was just the start. He owned 3 million shares of stock. He had options worth tens of millions. Every year, the board of directors showered him with more options, and every year, Lay realized millions more by exercising some of those options. He had a $4 million line of credit from Enron. He also got something called performance unit payments, which paid Enron executives in cash if the company's stock outperformed certain other investments. Those payments put even more millions in Lay's pocket. And just as quickly as he made money, Ken Lay spent it: he owned a high-rise multimillion-dollar condominium in River Oaks, the most exclusive section of Houston, which was decorated by Linda with the best of everything. He bought multimillion-dollar vacation homes in nearby Galveston and in Aspen. He generously subsidized the spending habits of children, stepchildren, and relatives. "Ken," says an old friend, "liked the complete lifestyle."

Just as he wanted outsiders to see him as a good and thoughtful man, he wanted Enron employees to see him the same way. He was the keeper of Enron's "vision and values," which Lay later defined as "respect, just treating other people the way we want to be treated ourselves; integrity, making sure that we do have absolute integrity, we're honest, we're sincere, we mean what we say, we say what we do. . . ." In one memo sent to staff, he wrote, "As a partner in the communities in which we operate, Enron believes it has a responsibility to conduct itself according to certain basic tenets of human behavior that transcend industries, cultures, economics, and local, regional and national boundaries." He added that "Ruthlessness, callousness and arrogance don't belong here. . . . We work with customers and prospects, openly, honestly and sincerely. . . ."

But at the very top of the company, the handful of insiders who dealt with him regularly had a hard time taking all this seriously—in no small part because Lay's own actions at times belied his stated creed. He rarely said something difficult to an underling, because he hated unpleasantness. The result was that his key executives found that he could be deceitful, willing to say things that just weren't true in order to keep people from getting mad at him. Most executives believed Lay's makeup included an unhealthy capacity for self-delusion: he tended to deceive himself about harsh truths he didn't want to face. "He invents his own reality," says one.

His top executives were also dismayed at the way he and his family openly fed at the Enron trough. "If you're the CEO of a public company, it isn't yours," says a former executive, but Lay seemed oblivious of such distinctions. Over the years, he seemed to have cultivated a powerful sense of personal entitlement. Not only did he use the company's fleet of airplanes for his private use; so did his children. Enron employees called the planes the Lay family taxi, so frequently did family members use them. Linda Lay used an Enron plane to visit her daughter Robyn in France. Another time an Enron jet was dispatched to Monaco to deliver Robyn's bed.

An even bigger issue was nepotism. Ken and Linda Lay had five children between them; four of the five worked at either Enron or Azurix, a water company Enron started in 1998. Enron employees were encouraged to make their travel plans through Lay/Wittenberg Travel Agency in the Park, which was 50 percent owned by Lay's sister Sharon. In fact, Lay himself initially owned a minority interest in the travel agency, which he sold after being warned about the impropriety. Early on, following the advice of an Enron lawyer, Lay agreed to put Enron's multimillion-dollar travel account out to bid. On one occasion, according to two people involved in the process, when an overzealous Enron administrator hired an outside consultant to oversee the bidding process, Lay's sister actually lost. So she was then given an opportunity to match the low bid. Travel Agency in the Park retained Enron's account as long as Ken Lay remained at Enron. In just two years, 1997 and 1998, Sharon Lay's agency earned $4.5 million in commissions thanks to Enron.

And then there was Lay's son, Mark, who was one of Skilling's first employees. After leaving Enron, he eventually joined a small company called Bruin Interests, which had contracts to store natural gas in facilities owned by Enron. In late 1994, lawsuits were filed alleging that Bruin's executive team, including Mark Lay, had embezzled more than $1 million from a bankrupt company that Bruin had bought earlier that year. According to the *New York Times*, the U.S. attorney decided not to pursue the criminal case, but Mark Lay paid nearly $315,000 to settle a related civil suit. (He later told the *Times* that he "trusted the wrong people and ended up in a transaction that everybody decided was wrong.") While some of this was still going on, Enron decided to do a deal with another small company that Mark Lay had gotten involved with. Enron agreed to reimburse over $1 million of this company's expenses; as part of the deal, Mark got a three-year contract with Enron guaranteeing him almost $1 million in salary and bonuses, plus 20,000 Enron options.

• • •

Ken Lay's increasing distance from Enron didn't matter very much to the executives under him. After all, Rich Kinder was running the show.

Kinder had mellowed a bit since his early days as chief operating officer. Though he still presided over a brutal weekly divisional meeting every Monday morning, he no longer reduced employees to tears, as he once had. Even so, he remained a demanding boss. Once, during a performance review, he told an employee that she'd done a great job, but then only gave her 2 on a scale of 1 to 5. Why, she asked, hadn't he given her a 1—which stood for excellent? "Nobody's excellent," Kinder responded.

Unlike Lay, Kinder was an utterly practical businessman who saw his job as solving problems and making sure Enron delivered on the earnings targets it promised to Wall Street. Every year, he created a list of Enron's top ten problems—its alligators—and spent the rest of the year working relentlessly to kill the alligators. He understood the innards of Enron's various businesses, even the new one Skilling was building. And he commanded respect from Enron's top executives in a way that Lay never did. "Lay was not a good manager," says one former executive flatly. "Kinder was a good manager."

Although they got along, there was always some underlying tension between the two men. Lay seemed to look down his nose at Kinder, according his talents limited value, and viewing him as having too many rough edges. "Ken was the visionary, and Rich was the deep-down operator, who would go beat up people," says a former high-ranking executive. "It was like the patrician who has to hire the Mafia." Kinder seemed to resent Lay's condescension. The Enron CEO failed to appreciate that it was the company president—and his willingness to roll up his sleeves—who made his grandiose lifestyle possible. "There are lots of visionaries," says one longtime friend of Kinder's. "There are very few people who can actually run a company."

Kinder had another issue: he badly wanted to be Enron's CEO. In the early 1990s, Lay had promised to hand over the top job to Kinder but had second thoughts, and concluded that he wasn't ready to give up his position. At the time, Kinder agreed to stay on as his number two, but in his next employment contract, he negotiated a provision stating that if he and Enron were "unable to agree upon an acceptable employment position," Kinder could leave the company, and his outstanding loan would be forgiven. Though it wasn't spelled out any further, both Lay and Kinder understood what the language meant: that at some point in the not-too-distant future, Lay would make Kinder the CEO of Enron. From Kinder's perspective, that was the only "acceptable employment position." And, according to Enron executives close to both men, Lay had assured Kinder that would happen when his own contract expired at the end of 1996.

In the aftermath of the Enron bankruptcy, there are many in and around the company who embraced the theory that it might have been avoided if Lay had kept his promise and made Kinder CEO. Many former Enron executives believe that he tempered the company's natural aggressiveness and brought a sense of discipline it badly needed. He was also the one person at the top of Enron who looked skeptically at things, consistently asking, "Are we smoking our own dope? Are we drinking our own whiskey?" After Kinder left, this theory goes, the inmates were running the asylum.

But to view Kinder simply as the white knight who got away is to ignore a more complicated reality. In truth, some of the seeds of Enron's downfall were sown on Kinder's watch. It wasn't just Ken Lay and the board who signed off on Skilling's use of mark-to-market accounting; so did Kinder. And if Kinder ever actually confronted Lay about his own blind spots, it doesn't appear to have produced tangible results.

Kinder was also every bit as focused as Lay and other Enron executives on making Wall Street happy, thus ensuring that the stock would go up. Analysts and investors, many of whom viewed Lay as useless ("Ask a candid question, get a canned answer," says one), vastly preferred dealing with Kinder. He was the one who told them what numbers to expect and the one who delivered on that promise. He knew how to sell the Enron story, which he did (along with Lay and other Enron executives) at extravagant ski retreats Enron threw for analysts and big institutional shareholders.

Kinder was also the one who told Enron's division heads the earnings they were *really* expected to deliver each quarter. Invariably, Kinder would accuse them of "sandbagging" him with lowball estimates and force them to stretch. "That's bullshit," he would say. "My grandmother could make $50 million. You can make $60 million." For this, the Enron COO made no apologies; he believed in setting the bar high and forcing people to jump over it.

But given the kind of company Enron was, the bar was hard to jump over consistently. And thus did Enron begin turning to aggressive accounting tactics, tactics that planted those dangerous seeds. The things Enron did in those early years were not illegal, nor did they push the boundaries anywhere near as far as it did later in the decade. But they did help mask certain unpleasant financial realities, and they pushed the company into accounting's gray zone. Kinder, though, had a sense of where the limits were—and he knew how to maintain control. Had he stayed, Enron's highs would never have been as high. But the lows would never have been as low.

Fifteen percent a year. That's what Enron was promising investors: that its earnings per share would grow at a clip of 15 percent a year.

That was an admittedly aggressive target, but if Enron could deliver, the company would be handsomely rewarded. Companies that grow at double-digit rates are classified by investors as growth companies, and they tend to have higher stock valuations than slower-growing companies. This was never truer than during the bull market of the 1990s, an era when growth companies were the only kind of companies investors wanted to buy. Internet stocks were growth companies, of course, and so were big technology companies like Microsoft and Cisco and Sun Microsystems. Every company, it seemed, was striving to become known as a growth company. The problem is that whenever a growth company disappoints Wall Street—when it announces earnings that don't meet the aggressive target it has set for itself—the punishment is usually severe. As rapidly as growth stocks can run up when the news is good, they can spiral downward just as quickly when the news is bad.

At Enron, as at many companies in the 1990s, a big incentive for achieving double-digit earnings growth was that it would make its executives rich. With so much of their compensation tied up in stock options, Enron executives cared deeply about seeing the stock rise as rapidly as possible: a rising stock had the potential to make them millionaires. For Kinder and Lay, it was even more explicit: it was written into their employment agreements. In early 1994, the Enron board awarded the two men enormous options packages: 1.2 million options for Lay and another million for Kinder. The vast majority of the options—80 percent—did not vest until the year 2000, meaning that the two men would not be able to cash in the options until then. But there was another provision: if Enron delivered at least 15 percent annual growth, a third of their options would vest each year. That one clause was worth millions to each man.

But how was Enron going to hit that growth target? It wasn't easy. Despite Skilling's traders and Mark's international deal makers, it was still an energy company, with an energy company's issues. The pipeline division had become solidly profitable, but it was never going to be a fast-growing part of the company. In 1993, the pipeline division made pretax profits of $382 million; the next year, pipeline's profits rose to $403 million—for a growth rate of just over 5 percent. Enron had a division called Enron Oil and Gas, its exploration and production arm. That part of the business was downright turbulent, with profits plunging one year, skyrocketing the next. Volatile earnings may reflect the way many businesses work, but they're not rewarded by Wall Street, which values consistency above all else. Skilling's ECT was generating the kind of fast-growing earnings Enron wanted, but that brought its own set of pressures: every time Skilling's group found a new profit center, competitors would quickly copy it, and the easy profits would vanish. And though Teesside was generating big profits, many of Mark's international deals were not yet money-makers. Theoretically, the vast bulk of international profits would come once her power plants and pipelines were up and running.

One way Enron managed its earnings, even then, was by reworking its long-term supply contracts—which would then allow it to post additional earnings, thanks to mark-to-market accounting. The company also sold assets and made other·"nonrecurring" moves to meet its earnings targets. But it didn't always label these as nonrecurring events; Enron simply declared them part of its ongoing operations. For instance, between 1994 and 1996, Enron reduced its stake in Teesside from 50 percent to 28 percent and folded the gains it reaped from selling the stake into its earnings. Back in 1989, Enron had raised needed cash by selling a minority stake in Enron Oil and Gas through a public offering; six years later, the company sold more Oil and Gas shares to the public, generating an additional $367 million in pretax profits.

Were these transactions hidden from the investing public? No. Enron's brass didn't go out of their way to point them out, but for anyone willing to wade through the company's financial documents, the numbers were clear. From time to time, an analyst would ask some tough questions or a reporter would write a story that raised what would seem now to be obvious objections to Enron's modus operandi. In 1993, Toni Mack published a story in *Forbes* entitled "Hidden Risks," in which she questioned the use of mark-to-market accounting in Skilling's business. "If you accelerate your income, then you have to keep doing more and more deals to show the same or rising income," an Enron competitor told Mack. A few years later, a journalist named Harry Hurt III wrote an article in *Fortune* about, as he put it, Enron's "allegedly byzantine methods of managing earnings." Hurt noted that when you stripped a few of the onetime gains out of Enron's seemingly healthy 1995 earnings, including the profit Enron recorded for selling shares of Enron Oil and Gas, 1995 hadn't been such a good year after all. Without those gains, Enron's profits actually *fell*. But stories like that were soon forgotten.

There's another tactic Enron used during the Kinder years that deserves special attention; in retrospect, it was a harbinger of things to come. In 1994, Enron created a spin-off company called Enron Global Power and Pipelines (EPP). Its stated purpose was to purchase Rebecca Mark's assets from Enron, thereby taking them off Enron's balance sheet and freeing capital for Enron to reinvest. (For instance, Enron planned to sell EPP 50 percent of Dabhol.) There is nothing remotely illegal about this; in fact, Coca-Cola spun off its bottling system for much the same reason. But there was also a second benefit: by selling assets to EPP, Enron could realize profits at once, which would help it hit its earnings targets instead of waiting for them to drift in over the years. In a sense, it was analogous to Skilling's use of mark-to-market accounting for ECT.

Here was the rub, though. Enron couldn't simply sell the international projects outright. Why? Because the various agreements it had with its lenders and partners often required it to maintain a majority ownership of the assets. Yet under accounting rules, if Enron were deemed to control EPP, it would not be allowed to realize profits when it sold stakes in the assets to EPP. It was a classic catch-22, difficult even for clever accountants and lawyers to get around. Nevertheless, Enron and its accountants at Arthur Andersen (and its lawyers at the blue-chip Houston firm of Vinson & Elkins) managed to find a way. Enron, they decided, would retain slightly more than 50 percent of the assets, but it would set up an oversight committee consisting of three directors who would independently approve every transaction. Astonishingly, Arthur Andersen agreed that this would mean Enron didn't control EPP and could therefore book profits when it sold assets to EPP. It was, all in all, a remarkably sleazy solution. For their work, Arthur Andersen was paid $750,000 and V&E $1.2 million. Oh, and the chairman of EPP? That was Rich Kinder.

In November 1994, EPP sold stock to the public at a price of $24 a share, raising a total of $225 million, money that bolstered Enron's 1994 earnings. Of course, in substance, Enron *absolutely* controlled EPP, which the EPP offering document flatly stated. That same document also said that the relationship with Enron "may result in conflicts of interest" when EPP and Enron's interests diverged. Indeed, it did. Not only was Kinder the chairman of EPP; its CEO was Rod Gray, a managing director of Enron. After the public offering, Gray's stake in Enron continued to be larger than his stake in EPP, and Enron continued to pay part of his salary. (The rationale was this was a good thing because Gray would have an inside scoop on the assets.) The CFO was Jim Alexander, who had been one of Enron's investment bankers at Drexel Burnham.

But EPP didn't work out as planned, partly because certain projects weren't completed and partly because Jim Alexander, who quickly became the fly in the ointment, complained that Enron was pressuring EPP to overpay for assets, particularly the troubled Dominican Republic power plant. Alexander even met with Lay to complain about the rampant conflicts. He also says he told Lay that there were problems with the accounting in Enron's international business, including the compensation system and Enron's practice of "snowballing" development expenses for projects that had ground to a halt. Lay said he'd have Kinder look into it and ushered Alexander out.

Alexander also complained to other Enron executives. They, however, told Lay that he was overreacting and that the conflicts were being well monitored. They also felt Enron's internal accounting issues were none of his business. Alexander worked for EPP, after all.

Weeks later, EPP entered into a cost-sharing agreement with Enron, which meant, among other things, that EPP's accountants now worked for Enron. Alexander left EPP as did several other EPP officials, all in the same week. Alexander says today: "They were people who couldn't take no for an answer. They couldn't even take no from reality." Once Alexander departed, Enron sold a 50 percent interest in the troubled plant in the Dominican Republic to EPP.

In August 1997, Enron announced that it would buy back EPP. Several former executives contend that the problem wasn't that the gatekeeper didn't work, but that it worked too well. EPP wasn't paying enough for the assets it bought, and the process was viewed as more trouble than it was worth. There had to be a better way—and soon there was.

Enron ultimately paid about $35 a share for EPP, which represented about a 14 percent annual return to EPP shareholders. It was a premium price, but Enron wanted Wall Street to think that its investments were stellar. But the buyback wasn't Kinder's doing; he was gone by then.

• • •

There was one part of the business that Ken Lay always kept to himself: the care and feeding of Enron's board of directors. Over time, most of the old board members he'd inherited from InterNorth had been replaced with people Lay handpicked. Charls Walker joined in 1985. So did Charles LeMaistre, the president of the famous Houston cancer hospital, M. D. Anderson. In 1993, Lay added Wendy Gramm, who had just finished a stint as chairman of the Commodities Futures Trading Commission (CFTC) and was married to Texas Senator Phil Gramm. (Several notables declined to join Enron's board, including former commerce secretary Robert Mosbacher, one of Lay's old Houston friends, who decided against it after asking some associates in the energy business about the wisdom of Enron's strategy. And despite two separate invitations from Lay, Robert Rubin, Bill Clinton's former treasury secretary and later the chairman of the Citigroup executive committee, also turned down a chance to sit on Enron's board.)

The board had its share of conflicts, all of which received withering scrutiny after Enron's bankruptcy. Enron employed Walker's lobbying firm. Just after Wendy Gramm stepped down from the CFTC, that agency approved an exemption that limited the regulatory scrutiny of Enron's energy-derivatives trading business, a process she had set in motion. (At the time, both Enron and Gramm denied any kind of mutual back-scratching.) Enron donated hundreds of thousands to the M. D. Anderson Cancer Center. It gave a $72,000-a-year consulting contract to Lord Wakeham. Several directors did business with Enron. And John Urquhart actually owned 0.1 percent of Enron Power's phantom equity through a consulting arrangement he had with the international business. Enron bought him out in 1993 for over $1 million but also gave him a fresh batch of options on Enron stock. In 1994, for instance, he earned $596,354 consulting for Enron and reaped another $931,000 through his options.

But Enron was hardly the only board in America rife with conflict, and in any case, the real problem with the board wasn't merely the conflicts. It was that just about every member of the board seemed to believe that Ken Lay walked on water. The Great Man persona he presented to the world at large was also what the Enron directors saw. Walker later described Lay as a "unique individual"— "charitable work, leadership in the community, leadership in the Republican Party, a preacher's son." To their way of thinking, Ken Lay was the one indispensable person at Enron.

The flavor of the board meetings only reinforced the notion that all was perfect at Enron. The day before the board met, the Enron jets would pick up the directors and fly them to Houston, where they would sometimes head to the Lays' condominium for a cocktail party. The meetings themselves were clubby affairs, with soothing conversation and long dinners, "more like a family gathering than a board meeting," recalls a former director. Enron executives would deliver what Walker recalls as "very, very well-rehearsed" presentations. (Indeed, throughout the years, few, including the accountants, ever hinted that anything fell short of perfection.) Lay would share his vision with the group. And the outcome was never in doubt. "Whatever Ken wanted them to okay, they did," says a former executive. Which goes a long way toward explaining what happened next.

Kinder had been operating under the belief that he would be elevated to CEO at the end of 1996. In the interim, though, Lay had begun to sour on his number two. He still believed that Kinder lacked the appropriate polish. He had hoped Kinder would "grow into the job," he later told several Enron executives, but in Lay's opinion that hadn't happened. And of course Bill Clinton was headed toward a second term as president, which meant that Lay's dream of becoming treasury secretary would have to wait at least four more years.

In 1995, as Ron Burns was preparing to leave the company, Lay asked whether Kinder was the cause of his departure. Burns thought it was a strange question, and it made him wonder if Lay was looking for reasons to hold back Kinder. Then, in the fall of 1996, as the time approached for Kinder to take over as CEO, Lay went to at least one other top executive and said that he planned to tell the board the executive wouldn't support Kinder—and he wanted to be sure this person would back Lay up if asked.

Finally, there was this: in the fall of 1996, Lay heard that Kinder, who had recently divorced his University of Missouri college sweetheart, was romantically involved with Nancy McNeil, Lay's trusted assistant (and by then an Enron vice president) who had also recently been divorced. Lay was dismayed, to say the least: he grilled another Enron executive about whether the relationship had been going on before their respective marriages had broken up. And he was furious that his number two had a pipeline into his office. "I've lost Nancy's loyalty," he declared.

Whatever lingering relationship Kinder and Lay still had pretty much dissolved with this discovery. Lay was voicing moral outrage; never mind that he'd had an affair with his own secretary or that both Kinder and McNeil denied persistent rumors that their relationship had begun before both were divorced.

The climactic board meeting—the one in which Kinder expected to be promoted—was held in New York in mid-November. Early on the morning of the meeting, one of the directors saw Kinder arrive at the hotel accompanied by McNeil. During the meeting, as the board discussed Kinder's qualifications to be CEO, the romance was brought up. According to Walker, two of the directors said that they couldn't support Kinder: he lacked Lay's character. (When asked why Kinder's affair was different from Lay's, one director says: "Some people would make the point that it was his own secretary, versus the boss's secretary.") After the meeting, Lay told Kinder that he had asked the board to promote Kinder to CEO but that the directors had refused to accept his recommendation.

Here's a telling comment on the way Lay was perceived in the upper ranks of Enron: very few of the company's senior executives believed him. People at the top of Enron believed that Lay was hiding behind the board because he didn't want Kinder to be CEO but lacked the guts to tell him so directly. As one executive put it, "Any time there was a tough issue, Ken would blame it on the board." Certainly that's what Kinder believed. After getting the news, Kinder angrily told one senior executive: "Ken fucked me! He fucked me. He's blaming it on the board. That's *bullshit!*"

On Tuesday, November 26, 1996, Enron announced that Lay had agreed to a new five-year term as chairman and CEO and that Kinder was leaving. Lay got a new contract guaranteeing him a base salary of $990,000 in 1996, rising to $1.2 million the next year. And even though Enron's earnings only grew 11.6 percent that year, the failure to hit the 15 percent earnings target didn't cost Lay. The board simply amended the compensation provision to include "at least double-digit earnings per share growth annually," instead of 15 percent. In addition, Lay got a new grant of 1,275,000 options. There was again a provision that would enable Lay to cash them in quickly. But this time, it wasn't tied to earnings: Enron's stock simply had to outperform the S&P 500. Those options alone would later be worth as much as $90 million.

In typical Enron fashion, Kinder was well taken care of, too. He got $2.5 million in cash, and forgiveness of an outstanding loan of almost $4 million. He also took $109,472 in unused vacation pay. Despite the earnings failure, most of his options vested, too. Kinder quickly sold over 1 million shares of Enron stock, worth $40 million.

On his way out the door, Kinder took one other thing, the most important of all. He cut a deal to buy Enron's interest in something called Enron Liquids Pipeline for about $40 million in cash. There was no fairness-opinion done, and Enron sought no competing bids (though it had had the stake on the block for some time). "He knew that system [the liquids pipeline] better than anybody else and he cut one hell of a deal when he left," says a former executive.

That he did. Within a matter of months Kinder had joined up with his old University of Missouri classmate Bill Morgan to form a company called Kinder Morgan. The assets he bought from Enron were the foundation of the company; they included interests in two natural-gas liquids pipelines, one carbon dioxide pipeline and a rail-to-barge coal-transfer terminal. They were the sorts of assets Enron didn't put much value in anymore, but Kinder, says one friend, "always loved those assets."

By early 1998, Kinder Morgan had a market value of over $1 billion. Since 2001 Kinder has been on *Forbes*'s list of the 400 richest in America. By mid-2003, Kinder Morgan's stock was worth over $7 billion. Nancy McNeil left Enron around the same time Kinder did; the two soon married. Their philanthrophic activities soon rivaled those of Ken and Linda Lay; for instance, the Kinders gave $3 million to the DePelchin Children's Center. To this day, Kinder refuses to allow Kinder Morgan to own a corporate jet; though he leases a hundred hours of airtime on a private jet each year, he pays for it out of his own pocket.

For his part, Lay told the senior staff that he was not planning to replace Kinder, and the company announced that starting on January 1, 1997, Lay would assume Kinder's old title of president while continuing as CEO and chairman of the board.

One former board member says that "it was one of the saddest days for Enron when Rich Kinder left." And that director wasn't the only one who felt that way. Though long gone from the company, John Wing still held millions in Enron stock. When he learned that Kinder was leaving, he sold most of his shares.

CHAPTER 8

A Recipe for Disaster

Early in December 1996, just days after Kinder's resignation was announced, Ken Lay had lunch with Ron Burns in a private room at the River Oaks Country Club, Houston's most exclusive enclave. After leaving Enron to become president of the Omaha-based Union Pacific Railroad, Burns endured a rocky stint that lasted only 15 months. He'd orchestrated a graceful exit when Union Pacific merged with another railroad. He had been out of work about a month when Lay invited him to Houston.

"I'd love to have you back," Lay told Burns, adding that if Burns were willing to return to Enron, Lay would restore the stock options and other benefits he'd forfeited; it would be as if he'd never left. Lay didn't specify what job he had in mind for Burns, but that wasn't unusual. Even after all these years, Lay still had a habit of hiring people he liked, then figuring out what to do with them later. Burns, for his part, told Lay that there was only one position he'd consider: Kinder's old job. He also told him that if he became Enron's president, his first order of business would be to rein in the company's two warring superstars, Skilling and Mark. "If you're willing to deal with them," Burns told Lay, "I'll talk." Lay was noncommittal, and the negotiations went no further. But that evening, Burns bumped into some old friends from ECT at a Houston restaurant and over dinner and a few drinks casually mentioned that he'd met with Lay earlier in the day.

When Skilling heard the news, he reached a predictable conclusion: the two men had to be talking about Burns returning as president and COO of Enron. That also sparked a second worry—that his rival, Rebecca Mark, might also be trying to maneuver herself into the position.

During the time his marriage was disintegrating (the divorce was final in 1997), Skilling would tell colleagues that he felt burned out, that he even sometimes thought about calling it quits. But nobody at Enron took this seriously; Skilling had always been too driven. Just nine months earlier, Skilling had signed a new five-year contract, bumping his annual base pay to $400,000 a year and providing that Enron would work with him to find "an enhanced position and job title." If a new job title couldn't be agreed upon by February 1997, Skilling would be entitled to a $1 million payment.

Now that Skilling sensed that Kinder's job was up for grabs, he knew exactly which enhanced position he wanted. Quickly, he and his forces swung into action. Skilling met with Lay and used the classic Enron tactic: he told the Enron CEO that if anyone else got the job, he'd quit. What's more, he declared, if Lay named Rebecca Mark as president, "there will be revolution in the ranks—70 percent of the merchant business will quit the next day." On a business trip a few days later, amid speculation that Lay might be considering Mark for the post, Skilling said to an ECT colleague, "I'll tell you one thing. If that bitch gets it, I'm outta here." Lou Pai also did his part to drive the message home. In a meeting with Lay, he told the Enron CEO that only Skilling could keep the traders happy.

How did Lay respond to these threats? He caved. Mark might be his fair-haired child, but he just couldn't afford to let Skilling walk out the door. Thus, on December 10, 1996, barely two weeks after announcing that Lay would assume Kinder's duties, Enron made a new announcement: Jeff Skilling would become the company's new president and chief operating officer instead.

In his physical appearance, Skilling was a dramatically different man. He'd always been disheveled in a nerdlike way, and over the years, his poor eating habits and lack of exercise had taken their toll; at the time his marriage was bottoming out, he'd ballooned to nearly 200 pounds. After a scare from chest pain, he resolved to get in fighting trim. Skilling began lifting weights and dropped 65 pounds in a couple of months. He later started using a hair-growth drug to recarpet his balding scalp. At the age of 43, he'd never looked better.

But as a business executive, Skilling really hadn't changed at all. Even though he'd been running ECT for six years, he still thought like a consultant, enamored, always, of the Big Idea, with surprisingly little appreciation for how one got things done in the real world. He had zero interest in the nuts and bolts of operations. He was as incapable of getting tough with his core group as Ken Lay was with Enron's top executives. He had a narrow, even selfish, view of what constituted success that revolved solely around ECT; he was largely indifferent to the rest of Enron.

Yet suddenly he was in charge, running a company that was generating $13 billion in annual revenues, employed 11,700 people, operated in 22 countries, and had an array of problems that needed to be fixed. "It was a recipe for disaster," says an early ECT executive. "You had Lay, who was disengaged, and you had Skilling, who was a big-picture guy and a terrible manager." And this isn't just hindsight speaking. There were many Enron executives, even at the time, who felt that Skilling was miscast in Kinder's old job. One of them, Forrest Hoglund, who ran Enron Oil and Gas, even told him so directly. "You're a very bright guy," Hoglund said to Skilling shortly after the appointment had been announced. "But when you become president, you're going to have nine different masters. I'm sorry, but based on your temperament, you're not going to be very good at that."

For his part, Ken Lay never appreciated what big shoes he was asking Skilling to fill. "Lay had a lack of understanding of just how much Kinder did," says a longtime corporate officer. "He felt anybody he selected could run that company the same way Rich did." When he maneuvered to prevent Kinder from becoming Enron's CEO, Lay made a big mistake. Now he had compounded his mistake by naming Jeff Skilling as the company's new president.

Between 1989 and 1994, Enron's stock consistently outperformed the Standard & Poor's 500. In each of those years, the company had met or exceeded its earnings targets, and Wall Street had responded by pushing up the stock; during that time span, the stock rose 233 percent, compared to the S&P 500's 65 percent. Enron's record of regularly beating the market's most important barometer was a point of enormous pride for the company; Lay and Kinder never tired of boasting about the accomplishment.

In 1995, the streak was broken. Though the stock rose a healthy 25 percent, the S&P 500 did better, rising some 34 percent. But it was 1996 when it became clear that Wall Street was having second thoughts about Enron. That was the year that Enron missed its earnings target, as profits rose only 12 percent instead of the expected 15 percent, and for the second year in a row, Enron lagged the market index. In fact, the earnings miss was only part of the problem. The huge Dabhol contract had fallen apart, and it was only at year-end that Rebecca Mark had miraculously managed to get the project back on track.

Wall Street was even raising questions about Enron's quality of earnings, meaning that stock analysts were beginning to look askance at some of the steps that Enron had employed to hit its earnings targets. "One of the biggest concerns consistently voiced about Enron is the complexity of its operations and how those interrelationships affect the quality of its earnings," wrote a Morgan Stanley analyst in the spring of 1997.

When investors are in love with a stock, they'll forgive a lot. The analysts will ignore potential problems, and they'll accept management's word that, say, a nonrecurring charge really is nonrecurring and not part of the ordinary course of business. They'll work hard to put a positive gloss on even the most ho-hum corporate announcements. But when Wall Street goes negative on a stock, the opposite phenomenon takes place: a remorseless skepticism takes hold, as investors search for clues that more bad news is on the way.

Such was the case with Enron as Skilling took over as president. Analysts who'd had strong buys on the stock during most of the Kinder era were downgrading Enron to a hold—which is Wall Street's code for sell. Carol Coale at Prudential Securities—one of the leading analysts of Enron—downgraded in October 1996, pointedly noting that in the third quarter, four cents a share of the company's profits had come from selling a stake in Teesside. An analyst at Dean Witter Reynolds, who had downgraded Enron a few months earlier, cited "Dabhol uncertainty."

One of Enron's looming problems, which the analysts had belatedly begun picking up on, was the old J-Block contract. Remember J-Block? That was the terrible deal Enron signed in March 1993 in the wake of its Teesside triumph. With the approval of Lay and Kinder, the company had agreed to a long-term contract committing it to purchase a huge amount of gas, as much as it had bought for Teesside. The gas would flow from a part of the North Sea called J-Block, which would be ready to come on line in 1996.

What made the deal so foolish was that it was a classic take-or-pay deal. Back then, during the early giddiness over Teesside, Enron officials had assumed that it would be easy to find customers for the additional gas. Bob Kelly, Wing's old deputy, who was then running Enron Europe and had negotiated the J-Block deal, even thought he might be able to use the gas to fuel a second Teesside-type plant he hoped to build.

But all of the assumptions the international team made turned out to be horribly wrong. The problem was that Enron had committed to a price near the top of the market. By 1995, the spot-market price had dropped far below what Enron had agreed to pay. That meant it was no longer possible to sell the gas at a profit, and it simply didn't make economic sense to use it for another plant.

Which is not to say that the company hadn't had its chances to unload the gas. In the months after the deal was signed, Enron had numerous chances to sell the J-Block gas at about the price it had committed to pay. But Kelly had been transferred back to Houston in 1993, and his successors in Enron's London office turned down the suitors, holding out the hope that the market would soon resume its climb, allowing them to book a profit. Executives who had not been involved in the original J-Block deal later stumbled across an inch-thick file of letters from companies inquiring about the gas with the standard Enron reply saying that the gas was not for sale.

By 1995, Enron's exposure was approaching $2 billion at a time when Enron's total market value wasn't much more than $5 billion. J-Block was posing a serious threat to Enron's survival. Kinder had grown increasingly frustrated, at one point pounding his fist on a conference table: "You mean with all this goddamn high-priced talent in this room nobody can tell me what is going on with this fucking J-Block contract?"

Kinder had dispatched a series of teams from Skilling's ECT to grapple with the problem. One executive was so shocked after reviewing the drafts of the contract—every negotiating point seemed to have been resolved against Enron—that he hired a private investigator to explore whether someone on the company's negotiating team had taken a payoff. (Ultimately they found no evidence of impropriety.)

Kinder even flew to England to try to negotiate a settlement himself. But after a stormy meeting with the producers, led by Phillips Petroleum, the talks collapsed and everyone headed for the courthouse. Enron sued to void the deal, using a number of technical excuses. But the most it could get from the courts was a temporary reprieve: Enron, the courts ruled, wouldn't have to take the gas until late 1997. By then, the atmosphere between the two sides had become so ugly that Enron executives regularly had their London offices swept for bugs. As the date to start delivery loomed, J-Block was still some $1.5 billion in the hole.

Though the company was eventually forced to discuss J-Block in its public SEC filings, Enron minimized the problem, insisting that it did not expect the contract to have a "materially adverse effect on its financial position." London-based insiders shook their heads at this assertion; one later called it "mind-boggling."

And in their newly skeptical mode, the securities analysts who followed Enron weren't buying it either. Several began to make inquiries in England and raised tough questions in their reports to clients. Although they never discovered the full magnitude of Enron's J-Block exposure, they certainly sensed that it was much bigger than Enron was letting on. As the Dean Witter analyst succinctly put it, "J Block contracts add additional measure of risk . . . with the price of gas under the contracts now well above the market price."

With Kinder gone, J-Block was now Jeff Skilling's problem, and he wasn't a bit happy about it. It wasn't so much the size of the problem that bothered him or even that Wall Street was breathing down his neck to take care of it. It was that he just hated having to fix a mess that someone else had made. Never mind that he was now the president of the entire company and that solving other people's problems was a big part of his job.

But Skilling knew it was critical to get rid of the problem, so he moved quickly. Though the spot price of natural gas had begun to rise in 1997, Skilling decided that it was too risky to hope that price alone would bail Enron out of J-Block. Instead, Skilling decided to negotiate his way out of trouble. Virtually the first thing Skilling did upon becoming president of Enron was fly to Bartlesville, Oklahoma, where Phillips was headquartered, and meet with his Phillips counterpart, James Mulva.

Skilling told Mulva he wanted to negotiate a settlement—and the Phillips president agreed to talks, grueling ones, which dragged on for months. Because Skilling was willing to pay a big price to make the problem go away, he was able to do what Kinder hadn't: come up with a new J-Block agreement. It was announced in June. Enron would make a $440 million up-front cash payment to Phillips and the other producers of the J-Block. In return, the pricing was restructured to float with the market (though Enron still had to take the J-Block gas and find buyers for it). Enron booked a $675 million pretax charge as the total cost of cleaning up J-Block.

At the end of the quarter, hoping to get all the bad news out at once, Enron also took a $100 million charge against another problem Skilling had inherited—a bad investment the company had made in a Houston ship channel plant producing something called MTBE, a chemical additive that made gasoline burn more cleanly. The two charges wrecked Enron's annual profits. For 1997, Skilling's first year as COO, Enron made only $105 million. That was a staggering 82 percent drop from the year before. Not since 1988 had Enron made so little money.

Skilling hated breaking the news to Wall Street. "I never want to have another analyst meeting like the one we had second quarter last year," he later told *Fortune*, "telling a crowd of people that we were writing off $550 million. Well, there were not a lot of happy campers, and I took it kind of personally."

In an effort to bolster the stock, Lay and Skilling announced a share buyback program. (When a company buys back its own shares, it means that there are fewer shares outstanding, which improves the closely watched earnings-per-share number.) They also vowed to simplify Enron's finances and end the company's quality-of-earnings problem. In the short term, at least, the moves didn't help. In a year when the S&P 500 index rose some 31 percent, Enron's stock declined by almost 4 percent. In explaining the plunge in profits, Lay and Skilling said that the poor results were primarily the result of "nonrecurring charges" needed "to clear the decks of key business uncertainties." They began their annual report by declaring the year's stock price performance for 1997 "unacceptable." And they promised better things ahead.

Inevitably, now that he was in charge, Skilling began the process of refashioning Enron in his image or, rather, in the image of ECT. He would jettison those divisions that didn't fit his vision of what an Enron business should be and start exciting new ones to take their place. He would emphasize intellectual capital and promote risk taking. And he would make sure to place his loyalists in key spots all over the company. Thus, it wasn't long before Lou Pai, Ken Rice, Cliff Baxter, and other important ECT managers were handed senior positions at Enron, along with big raises and more stock options. By the end of Skilling's first year, Skillingites filled 11 of the 26 slots on Enron's management committee, including such disparate positions as finance and governmental affairs.

Making Enron more like ECT meant creating new, modern businesses while putting less emphasis on the old legacy operations like pipelines and natural-gas production, which Kinder had always loved. Skilling's original idea to trade natural-gas contracts had been such a huge triumph, bringing not only earnings but acclaim, that one could hardly blame him for wanting to replicate it. But his vision also grew out of necessity. As early as 1993, profit margins in the gas-trading operation had begun to slip as competitors, such as the Natural Gas Clearinghouse (later renamed Dynegy), El Paso, and a host of others had flooded into the business, establishing their own gas-trading desks.

What's more, the basic business had changed. No longer did gas producers need Enron to front them money. The banks were making loans again and squeezing Enron out. And at the other end of the business, big industrial users of natural gas were far less interested in signing long-term origination deals with Enron, like the old Sithe agreement. After all, they could use their own traders.

So even though Enron had become the biggest player in the business of buying and selling natural gas contracts, controlling some 20 percent of the market, Skilling was fretting about the future. His solution? To do even *more* trading and extend it beyond natural gas. He wanted Enron to trade electric power. This was his next Big Idea.

Skilling later described his decision to push Enron into electricity trading as a "no-brainer." But that was just Skilling being Skilling. It was true that Enron was a pioneer in starting up power trading, just as it had been in setting up a trading market for natural gas. But unlike natural gas—where Skilling understood the business and had a clear sense of how trading would work and what value it would add—he had no special insight into electricity trading. Instead, his rationale went something like this: the wholesale electricity market (that is, the power that was sold back and forth among electric utilities) was huge—by Enron's estimates, about $91 billion a year, triple the size of the market for natural gas. Assuming the company could create an electricity-trading business and claim 20 percent of it, the payoff would be enormous. As the first big entrant in the power-trading business, Enron would be able to create liquidity and exploit the big early profit margins that result from a young, inefficient market. Plus, the federal government was about to pass a law opening the way for deregulation of electricity. Skilling quickly commissioned a consulting study (from McKinsey, naturally) which confirmed his initial assumptions. "It was déjà vu all over again," he declared.

Except that it wasn't. In the natural-gas business, Enron was a charter member of the club. In electricity, Enron was an outsider. A fraternity of local electric utilities dominated the electric power business. Under the new federal law partially deregulating the industry, the utilities were supposed to make their transmission lines available to anyone, much as the natural-gas pipeline companies had been required to provide open access. This provision was critical to making electricity trading profitable: during the summer, for example, Enron might want to buy cheap power from underused plants in balmy New England and move it to sweltering Florida for sale at higher prices.

But as Enron soon learned, the logistics of moving power were incredibly complex, and the utilities, unhappy about the new law, threw up countless roadblocks. They had other advantages, too. States had enormous regulatory power over the utility industry, and most of them were far less eager to deregulate than the federal government. And through their access to the nationwide electric grid, utilities could tell in an instant when a plant anywhere in the country had gone down, a move that might spike a region's prices in a matter of minutes. To put it another way, they had precisely the kind of information advantage Enron had in natural gas. And there was one more big difference between the two businesses: unlike natural gas, electric power can't be stored. This meant that electricity prices were highly volatile, far more than natural gas. That volatility increased the potential for big profits—and big losses.

Skilling threw his crack troops into the power game, but the early years were tough. With Lou Pai leading the charge, Enron had begun trading in June 1994, even before the federal open-access rules had passed. The originators, led by Ken Rice, began trying to make long-term power deals with the utilities, both to buy and sell electricity and to arrange for access to their transmission lines. But the industry simply wasn't interested in letting Enron into the club; many utilities wouldn't even talk to Rice's deal makers. Skilling then dreamed up the idea of forming a consortium with a dozen far-flung utility companies. As he envisioned it, the utilities would build and manage the power plants; Enron would market the electricity they generated, do the trading, and use its lobbying resources to widen deregulation. He even had a vaguely ominous name for it: NAPCON, for North American Power Consortium.

But Skilling's grand scheme went nowhere. Utility executives weren't about to hand over the keys to their kingdom to Enron. Skilling's notion was naive and presumptuous. "You'll never get 12 utility executives to agree on anything," one of his deputies tried to tell him. "Why not?" responded Skilling. "This makes perfect sense!" So Skilling sent some of his people to shop the idea around. "We talked to a dozen utility executives, and they all kicked us out of their offices," recalls one of his former aides. "Jeff didn't have the practical experience to realize there are some things you can't do." Skilling finally came to appreciate the state of affairs. "They hated us," he later admitted. "The electricity guys were scared to death of Enron. It was very hard to break into the electricity market."

So Skilling went in another direction: he decided to buy his way into the club by having Enron purchase a utility. He wanted one in the West, with access to the California market, in part because that market was so big and in part because it was one of the few states up to that point to pass any form of retail deregulation allowing direct access to consumers of electricity. He had other criteria as well: he wanted a utility with no nuclear power plants (a political nightmare), one that wasn't too big (so Enron could swallow the acquisition), and one that had a short position in power (Enron was expecting prices to fall).

Once again, he met with stiff resistance. Cliff Baxter, his chief deal maker, approached dozens of utilities, none of which wanted anything to do with Enron. Finally, though, he found one: a midsize utility in Oregon, called Portland General.

To get the utility to agree to a buyout, Enron offered a price—$2.1 billion plus the assumption of another $1.1 billion in debt, which represented a 46 percent premium to its market price. (Because of the high price, Enron stock dropped nearly 5 percent on the news.) That was yet another difference between Skilling and Kinder: once Skilling got his eye on the prize, price was no object. He believed that the business he would build with the asset would make so much money that it didn't matter if he overspent in the beginning.

In fact, the real price of Portland General was even higher. In the wake of the June 1996 announcement, Enron was so high-handed with the Oregon Public Utility Commission, whose approval was required, that one commissioner publicly upbraided the company's management, with Lay in attendance, for treating the state officials like rubes. "We don't ride around in turnip trucks here," the commissioner declared. Responding to the company's refusal to provide documents or make concessions, the panel's staff actually recommended rejecting the acquisition until Cliff Baxter presented an offer to give Oregonians a $141 million rate cut. The deal didn't close until July 1997.

The purchase gave Skilling what he wanted: entrée to California's power grid and a copy of the utility industry's secret playbook. It also gave him a big supply of electricity to trade. In both the United States and overseas, Enron's originators were now pitching electric power *and* natural gas—often to the same big customers. By 1998, it was the biggest power merchant in North America.

No longer satisfied with being "the world's first gas major," Enron had adopted a new, more aggressive corporate goal: to become "The World's Leading Energy Company." Skilling even had vanity license plates made for his car with the initials WLEC.

Then there were the divisions that Skilling felt no longer deserved a prominent place in Enron's portfolio. These were largely the parts of the company that Enron had been built on—the old-fashioned parts of the old HNG and InterNorth, such as the pipelines. Skilling, in fact, considered selling the pipeline division itself, though he eventually backed away from that idea.

In other cases, when he saw an opportunity to shed an old business, he took it—even when that business was profitable and brought cash in the door. Consider the case of Enron Oil and Gas, or EOG, as everyone at Enron called it. Though it was a separate company with its own publicly traded stock, EOG was, in effect, Enron's in-house oil and gas production unit. (Enron held a majority stake in it.) EOG made its money by drilling wells in search of hydrocarbons, as wildcatters had been doing in Texas since the turn of the century. You could not find a better-run part of Enron; under CEO Forrest Hoglund, who'd had the job since 1987, EOG's production had tripled and costs had been cut to the bone. It had long provided Enron with both cash flow and profits. But Hoglund was fiercely independent and no fan of Jeff Skilling.

Over the years, EOG had played two important roles for Enron. First, it had provided a backup source of natural gas for Enron's customers. Second, thanks to a series of well-timed public offerings, it had been instrumental more than once in allowing Enron to hit its earnings targets. Along the way, Enron Oil and Gas had also made its shareholders very happy. In 1994, with the stock soaring, Hoglund himself had cashed in $19 million worth of options, a development Lay touted as evidence of Enron's entrepreneurial environment. ("If Forrest creates enormous value for the shareholders and receives enormous compensation for it, then Godspeed to him. I'm not afraid to hire someone who's smarter, more creative, prettier, more handsome, or more highly paid.")

But with trading now the dominant motif at Enron, the company no longer felt it was necessary to have a homegrown supply of natural gas. As an EOG executive summed it up: "They didn't feel they needed the gas wells and the people. If they wanted to go long gas, they could just do it on the trading floor." As for the profits Enron had reaped from those stock sales, well, Skilling felt pretty sure he wouldn't be needing those anymore either, not after he finished remaking the company. What he especially disliked about EOG was that its profits were erratic and volatile, which made it that much more difficult to show Wall Street the kind of smoothly rising earnings that would move the stock.

In late 1998, Enron was approached by Occidental Petroleum, which wanted to buy Enron's majority stake in EOG. It was a shrewd move by Occidental; because of a deep slump in gas prices, EOG's shares had sunk to $14, the lowest they'd been in years. The oil company saw a chance to grab a great asset at a below-market price. Which it very nearly did. Skilling (and Baxter, who, as always, conducted the negotiations) very quickly cut a deal with Occidental. Under the terms, EOG would be dismembered: Occidental would get its North American assets, Enron would get its international properties. Occidental would pay with a combination of stock and cash. Enron, however, would get all the cash, and EOG shareholders would get the stock. When you added it up, the sale price amounted to a small premium over the market price but nowhere near the $25 a share the company had been worth early the previous year.

Hoglund was livid when he learned about the deal. The price was much too low, he said. And the EOG shareholders were being cheated by having to take Occidental stock when Enron itself was getting cash. Hoglund quickly hired Goldman Sachs as an outside adviser, demanded a review by EOG's independent directors—who voted down the deal—and threatened a public fight. It took him five months, but Hoglund killed the deal. (As a result of this conflict, Enron for years largely excluded Goldman from consideration for its lucrative investment-banking business.)

Now it was Skilling's turn to be furious. More determined than ever to unload EOG, Skilling sent Baxter to negotiate with Hoglund directly. After weeks of bitter talks, Hoglund won EOG's independence. Enron would sell the bulk of its stake in EOG, mostly back to the company. In return, Enron would get $600 million in cash and EOG's holdings in China and India. At the time of the deal, EOG stock was valued at about $22 a share. When the brutal negotiations were finally over, Baxter, who was largely outmaneuvered by Hoglund, sent his crusty adversary a huge bouquet of flowers, accompanied by a conciliatory note: "Forrest: We finally got the right deal done." Hoglund sent Baxter a droll response: "Dear Cliff: There's no question we finally got the right deal done. But what you need to understand is that I'm from the Midwest, and I think this means we're engaged."

After the EOG spinoff was complete, Hoglund retired, turning the company over to his second in command. Sure enough, by the end of 2000, EOG's stock had risen to $54 a share, more than twice the value at which Enron had sold it. In his eagerness to unload Enron's EOG stake, Skilling had left more than $1 billion on the table.

Don't think for a minute that Skilling had forgotten about Rebecca Mark—or that she had forgotten about him. Mark was furious about Skilling's promotion. It meant that Ken Lay had lied to her: he had said that he wasn't going to replace Kinder anytime soon.

With Skilling in charge, Mark's charmed career at Enron was not likely to be charmed much longer. Skilling had long been her chief in-house critic, disdainful and suspicious of her deals and her operation. But as long as they'd been equals, she'd been able to fend him off. Now that Skilling was her boss, she darkly suspected that her days at Enron were numbered. In this, she was completely right. Over the next two years, the two became locked in the business equivalent of guerilla warfare. It was a war Rebecca Mark never really had a chance to win.

In later years, the media explained the divide between Skilling and Mark as a fundamental difference of business philosophy: Skilling believed Enron's future lay in what came to be known as his asset-light strategy, driven by brainpower not physical infrastructure. As Mark herself liked to put it: "Oh, Jeff just hates assets." And of course Mark's division was nothing but hard assets.

But that was never quite right. Physical assets were always the foundation for Skilling's own business success. Enron's pipeline system revealed the secrets for making a fortune trading natural gas; the Portland General acquisition provided entrée into the new world of electricity trading. Later Skilling bought paper mills so Enron could start trading pulp and paper, and a billion-dollar fiber network launched broadband trading. Skilling thought he had it down to a formula: Enron would buy the infrastructure needed to crack the code, build a new trading business—and then unload the assets when everybody else started to pile in. During his tenure at the top of Enron, the company spent billions on physical assets.

His problem with Mark's overseas plants and pipelines was that he simply didn't believe her deals made sense. There was no particular strategy driving her empire-building; she would strike deals in any country that would have her and for just about any kind of power or energy project. "When they found a deal, they did a deal," recalls a former Enron executive. "It was buckshot all over the globe." Mark used to speak nobly about helping the world's underdeveloped nations. But, as this same executive pointed out, "bringing technology and light to people in darkened states is not a business." Skilling believed that Mark's projects could be justified only if their returns were extraordinarily high, because the risks she was taking in volatile emerging markets were enormous. And in his opinion, the returns just weren't there.

Not that he had any way of knowing for sure. That was another of his beefs: her international deals routinely sidestepped internal corporate review. Skilling complained it was impossible to get good numbers from Mark. Even as her peer, back when he'd been running ECT, Skilling had argued that his own risk-control group should be charged with reviewing her deals. Intent on maintaining her autonomy, and suspicious of Skilling's motives, Mark had beaten back the effort. But Skilling had managed to make other incursions. In 1993, he took over responsibility for all North American power plants, which had been part of Wing's old empire. Soon he was given responsibility for England as well.

Then there was the matter of compensation. Nothing bugged the executives at ECT more than knowing that Mark and her developers were paid huge bonuses without regard for how their deals turned out. Mark, for example, received bonuses of $1 million to $2 million, even for some small Enron International projects. As the ECT side saw it, this provided a mindless incentive for the developers to keep building—and gin up a rosy projection to justify it.

Valid as the criticism was, it contained a large element of hypocrisy. After all, ECT's traders and originators were also richly rewarded up front based largely on their own long-term profit projections, which could be every bit as rosy. And unlike the traders, the international developers often put in years of work on a project before getting a bonus at all. One former Enron executive says: "It was basically prima donnas accusing other prima donnas of being a bigger prima donna."

Still, bringing Mark to heel was not going to be easy; her projects had enormous momentum. Nonetheless, Skilling began the process of slowly clipping her wings. His first big move after becoming president was to pitch Lay on the idea of giving him responsibility for all of Enron's operations in western Europe. His reasoning was that Enron's plants could be used as a platform for building a regional trading and marketing business, in essence, a foundation for a global ECT. Besides, the plant developers needed ECT's trading and risk-management expertise. Hadn't the J-Block disaster proven as much?

Mark objected bitterly and lobbied Lay to let her keep that part of her empire. The fight came to a head at an Enron off-site meeting in San Antonio, where Lay convened a meeting with the principals. Mark made the case that her people knew Europe and Enron's projects there best; she viewed Skilling's proposal as a brazen power grab. "As soon as we build something," she said, "you want to take it away!" When it became clear that Lay was siding with Skilling, Mark and her deputy, a former military man named Joe Sutton, got up and stormed out of the meeting.

Mark later described the resulting encounter with Lay to friends. "I've never had anyone walk out on me in my whole business career," he told her.

"Ken," Mark responded, "all you want is what Jeff wants."

To the outside world, Rebecca Mark was still riding high. *Fortune* put her on its list of the 50 most powerful women in American business. Media profiles gushed that she had a shot at eventually replacing Lay as CEO.

But Mark knew the battle was lost. She was desperate for a way out of the company and away from Skilling. She was contemplating quitting when another idea landed in her lap: selling Enron International to Shell. Skilling agreed to consider it, as long as Cliff Baxter served as lead negotiator. Discussions went on for months. Lay, in the summer of 1997, sat down for lunch with a top Shell executive. A price tag was even batted around: as much as $3 billion for a 50 percent stake. But there was never a formal offer on the table. A Shell negotiator says the company was worried about the cultural fit, among other things. Mark blamed Baxter and Skilling for mismanaging the negotiations.

During that same period, something truly curious happened. During the summer of 1997, Mark invited Skilling to spend a week with her touring development prospects in South America, and he accepted. She had employed this tactic before, with board members. She'd taken them overseas, wined them and dined them with high-ranking officials, given them tours of the projects, and explained the good they might do someday. It worked like magic.

Amazingly, her tour had the same effect on Skilling. He came back eager to pour money into the continent's southern cone. Of course, he used the classic Skilling rationale: if Enron could build a critical mass of infrastructure in South America, it could leverage those assets into a big new trading business. "South America—awesome story," he gushed at an Enron employee meeting in May 1999. ". . . South America may be our strongest network in the world. . . ." Skilling was so jazzed about his visit he even bought a beach house in Brazil with an executive from Enron's South American operations. The transformation was so dramatic that rumors started flying that the ever-beguiling Mark had—literally and figuratively—seduced him. (Both have denied any personal involvement.)

Nevertheless, Skilling continued to make Mark's life miserable, gradually stripping Enron International of its independence. By May 1998, she'd finally had enough. Mark handed her post as CEO of Enron International to Joe Sutton while remaining EI's chairman. She also became an Enron vice chairman, a title known internally as "the ejector seat" because it was viewed as the first step out the door.

And yet when you look back on the two years the two battled for control of Enron International, one striking fact stands out above all else: in all that time, Rebecca Mark kept striking deals and building power plants. And Skilling, for all his talk about how poor her assets were and how unreliable her numbers, never shut off the flow of Enron's cash—and never shut down her deals.

Skilling later explained that it was politically impossible for him to stop Enron International dead in its tracks. In addition to Lay's favor, Mark had strong support from the board. "I should have thrown myself under the truck on some of them," Skilling later told friends. "But what would it have accomplished? I didn't feel like I was in a position to stop it." But the irony remains: Skilling, who today blames Mark for spending Enron into bankruptcy, signed off on many of her projects.

• • •

Enron being Enron, Mark got a rich new contract when she left her job running International, with a $710,000 salary and 450,000 additional stock options. (In 1998 and 1999, Enron also forgave over $1.6 million in loans.) And Mark being Mark, though she'd been relegated to the sidelines, she didn't stay there for long. Just a month after her appointment as vice chairman, she proposed to the board that it allow her to lead Enron into a business it was already contemplating: the business of water.

Mark wanted to buy a British water utility, called Wessex, as the opening move in building a new Enron subsidiary that she would run. The cost would be $2.4 billion. Water was a treacherous game, dominated by the French giants Vivendi and Suez Lyonnaise des Eaux. The politics of water were complicated, the profit margins razor thin. The companies that succeeded in the business understood how to keep costs to a minimum, not exactly Enron's strength.

But Mark made a compelling case. "The world's running out of water," she declared. The water business was going to be deregulated—right up Enron's alley. It was an unparalleled opportunity, she insisted. Mulling over the issue, the directors wondered what their fellow board member, Jeff Skilling, thought about the idea.

"If it works," he said coolly, "it could be a good business." What Skilling thought to himself but didn't say aloud was that approving this deal would get Rebecca Mark out of his way, once and for all. The price of the acquisition was steep (as Skilling figured it, she was overpaying by about $200 million), but that never bothered him. Besides, under the terms of her deal, she'd have to raise all additional capital on her own. If she failed, well, that would be her problem. For all these reasons, it seemed to Skilling that it was worth doing, regardless of whether it made sense for the company.

Even with Skilling's blessing, not all the directors were convinced. When it came time to vote, two directors voted against the acquisition, the only time in recent memory that an Enron board vote was not unanimous. Still, it went through, and Rebecca Mark was back in business.

She originally wanted to call her new company WaterMark. Instead, she chose Azurix, a name that was devised by a brand consultant. It would only take a few years before Mark's new company, with its fancy new name, would provide the first visible crack in Enron's facade.

CHAPTER 9

The Klieg-Light Syndrome

It is utterly beyond question that in reshaping Enron after he was named its president, Skilling turned it into a place where financial deception became almost inevitable.

In no small part, that's because there were so many other kinds of deception taking place. Skilling created a freewheeling culture that he touted as innovative—but didn't rein in the excesses that came with it. He preached the gospel of intellectual capital, claiming that it was critically important to give smart people the resources and freedom to let creativity flourish, but looked the other way when this became a license for wastefulness and self-indulgence. He bragged about Enron's sophisticated controls but undermined them at every turn. He was openly scornful of steady, asset-based businesses that grew slowly but generated cash—then swept them away to make room for a series of ever-bigger, ever-riskier bets that brought in almost no cash at all.

Worst of all, Skilling created impossible expectations and unbearable internal pressures by holding Enron out to Wall Street as something that it simply wasn't. He created a wild, out-of-control experiment yet presented it as a well-oiled machine that generated steadily growing profits. He offered the world a powerful, even charismatic, vision of the new Enron. But the Enron Skilling was describing—and which by 1998 Wall Street and the press were once again lapping up—wasn't even close to reality.

Consider the issue of risk. It would be hard to think of a more important concept for Enron than managing risk. Traders risked losing money every time they made a trade. Signing long-term contracts to provide gas and electricity required understanding all kinds of risks—pricing, delivery, credit, and so on—and knowing how to hedge those risks. Figuring out whether a deal was worth doing was nothing if not an exercise in calculating risk: did the size of the potential return justify the risk of all the things that could go wrong? That's a question that every executive at every company has to be willing to tackle. A company that lacked the ability to manage risk properly simply had no business doing the kinds of deals Enron did on a daily basis.

When reporters and analysts inquired about the company's risk-management abilities, Skilling had a ready answer: he pointed to Enron's Risk Assessment and Control department, known inside the company as RAC. Though Skilling had had small risk-management teams at ECT, he set up RAC as a stand-alone unit in 1996. Skilling knew Wall Street wanted to see a strong system of internal controls and after he was named president, he made RAC a centerpiece of management presentations to Wall Street analysts, investors, and credit-rating agencies. RAC was the part of the company that had the analytical skills—and presumably the authority—to prevent Enron from doing anything stupid. Skilling imposed a requirement that RAC had to review virtually all Enron deals—even international ones—and he bragged constantly about the sophisticated oversight that RAC provided, which he portrayed as sacred. "Only two things at Enron are not subject to negotiation: the firm's personnel evaluation policy and its company-wide risk-management program," Skilling told a corporate-finance journal.

On paper, RAC sounded terrific. Its mission was to assess the economic, financial, credit, and political risk in every Enron deal of more than $500,000. Its analysts pored over numbers, challenged assumptions, tested models, checked price curves, and monitored portfolios. It employed former bankers, accountants, statistical wizards, and MBAs—a crack team of experts in every aspect of a commercial transaction. RAC had resources, too: by the late 1990s, a $30 million budget, access to a $600 million computer system, and 150 professionals. Most of all, as Enron described it, RAC had independence and clout. The formal mechanism for expressing its findings was a document called a deal-approval sheet—or DASH. The DASH, which contained space for signatures of everyone who needed to approve the project, summarized the deal, the range of projected returns, and the risks that it presented. Later iterations of the form included a box for RAC's recommendation: it could approve the transaction or it could tell management "do not proceed."

The top man at RAC was Rick Buy, who had joined Skilling at ECT in 1994 after years as a vice president in the energy department at Bankers Trust. Buy was named the company's chief risk officer in 1998 and promoted to senior vice president of Enron in early 1999, at the age of 46. Skilling described Buy as Enron's "top cop" and frequently pointed out that he reported regularly to the audit committee of the Enron board. No one flat-out declared that RAC had veto power over a deal. But this was, after all, Enron's *control* group. The implication was clear: if Buy thought a deal was too risky, Enron wouldn't do it.

Thanks to RAC, Enron was able to portray itself as a company that could safely take on *more* risk than other companies, precisely because it had the right controls in place. As Buy himself once put it: "You won't make money these days without taking on risk. We want to take on risk—a lot of risk—subject to prescribed limitations and insight into the associated outcomes. If the outcomes are palatable, we've got an appetite." Indeed, Enron claimed that its risk systems were so good that there was no need to slow the frantic pace of deal making. "We move fast around here; things *cook*," Buy explained in a promotional videotape for Arthur Andersen, Enron's auditing firm. "I mean, it's a high-stress, high-pressure, fast-moving place. You don't want anyone . . . that's going to slow you down or bog you down or not be value-added. . . ."

Wall Street was dazzled. "We rely heavily on Enron's risk-management ability," Todd Shipman, an analyst with the Standard & Poor's credit-rating agency, told *Fortune*. "You can't overemphasize how important that is. It's the underpinning to everything. . . . It gives you a nice, warm, fuzzy feeling. . . . Even though they're taking more risk, their market presence and risk-management skills allow them to get away with it. . . . Enron has such extraordinary risk-management capabilities that we look at them differently." Rick Walker, managing director in the Houston office of Chase Manhattan Bank, added: "Rick has figured out how to profit from risk. Consequently, Enron has become a company defined by the way in which it handles risk."

But how much of the RAC story reflected the reality of life inside Enron? It was certainly true that RAC had substantial resources and talented analysts. But the part about RAC being a serious force within the company, able to stop bad deals dead in their tracks: that part wasn't even close to the truth. And everyone in the company knew it. "RAC was a hurdle, a speed bump, but not an obstacle," says a former Enron managing director. "If a deal had overwhelming commercial support, it got done. I treated them like dogs, and they couldn't do anything about me. The process was there, sure, but the support wasn't. If RAC had complained about me and I got paid $100,000 less bonus, I would have changed. Never happened. I told my guys to fuck 'em." A former RAC vice president agrees: "We didn't approve shit," he says.

RAC's ineffectiveness was largely a reflection of the executive Skilling picked to run it. Rick Buy was a pleasant, paunchy man with glasses—a soft-spoken sort, uncomfortable with confrontation. When his analysts raised issues with a deal, Buy would dutifully take them up the chain of command. But in a head-to-head with the company's senior traders and originators, it was no contest, as those on both sides of the table recognized. "RAC existed to keep analysts happy, to keep the story alive," says one veteran originator. "Buy was a decent guy but not smart enough or strong enough to be in that position." A former senior Enron executive says: "Rick's the right guy to evaluate the risk. He's not the right guy to stand down the guys who want their deals done. They'd ram it down his throat."

It is business wisdom that many of a company's best deals are the ones it doesn't do. That was never the belief at Enron, a place that was defined by deal making. "The corporate culture was such that you never said no to a deal," says a Buy friend who worked in corporate finance. "It was 'how do you make a deal work?' " Buy, she adds, "didn't want to be seen as someone saying no to a deal." In fact, Buy later insisted that saying no wasn't even part of his job description. He eventually told his staff that RAC's charge was simply to describe a transaction, analyze its risks and possible returns, and tell senior management: "you guys make your mind up."

There were times when frustrated RAC executives refused to sign off on a bad deal, but Buy would overrule them. In 1998, John Hopley, who served for four years as one of Buy's top deputies, opposed a deal promoted by ECT executives in Europe, who wanted to invest about $20 million in a British company named Techboard, which made fiberboard for kitchen cabinets. Hopley opposed the deal because the company was in the British equivalent of bankruptcy and even the originators' projected returns—which assumed the company would be able to navigate its way out of the mess—were small. He refused to sign the DASH. So Buy signed it instead. Three months after signing the agreement, the company went into liquidation, and Enron wrote off its entire $20 million investment. "Rick and the group were under a tremendous amount of pressure," says a former RAC executive. But Buy, he adds, "was not as forceful as he could have been in laying down the law."

According to RAC employees, the deal makers were often allowed to set absurdly optimistic assumptions for the complex models that spat out the likelihood of various outcomes for a transaction. "Every attempt was made to really strong-arm RAC with regard to the assumptions," says one RAC vice president. After completing its analysis, RAC had to circulate its draft comments for the DASH on a given transaction—and the deal makers actually had the right to *edit* them. When RAC employees complained, they were told to negotiate what they would say in the DASH with the deal makers. "In many instances," says the vice president, "the actual drafting of the language was done with an originator at the same table, very much suggesting the language that should go in there."

Often, entire deals went to RAC just a few days before the close of the quarter, leaving little time to scrutinize transactions involving hundreds of millions of dollars, and putting enormous pressure on RAC to sign off, because the company needed the deals to hit its numbers. "The mentality was to do whatever they can to go over, under, and right through us; that was the objective," says one RAC veteran.

The performance-review process was another way the deal makers beat RAC into submission. Incredibly, traders and originators sat on panels that ranked the same RAC executives who reviewed their transactions. Everyone was supposed to act honorably, but there were clear opportunities for retaliation ("he doesn't cooperate; he's hard to deal with"), and Buy wasn't able to protect them. "If you really pissed off an originator, that came up in the PRC," says a RAC vice president. "Those guys could really tag you and tag you hard. You could get knocked down from the first or second group to the third or fourth group," for some RAC executives, enough to make a six-figure difference in their annual bonus. And some originators didn't hesitate to use this very threat as a club during negotiations with RAC, warning the deal analyst: "This deal's going to get done whether you like it or not. If your name's not attached to it, it's going to look bad for you."

Buy agonized constantly over his situation. One Enron originator remembers him complaining over lunch in early 1999 that "he had a real problem with the job: he felt like he didn't matter. I said, 'Quit!' " the dealmaker recalled. "He said, 'I have to stay because I'm making a ton of money.' " Buy's cash compensation hit $400,000 in 1999, but his big money loomed from stock options, and he'd need to stick around for a couple of more years for most of them to vest. (In 2001, Buy unloaded Enron shares worth $4.3 million.)

Did Skilling realize how ineffectual Buy was? In fact, he did. He used to tell associates that Buy wasn't strong enough to stand up to the deal makers; when Skilling left Enron, he even told Ken Lay to replace Buy with someone tougher and more aggressive. But if he understood that, why didn't Skilling replace Buy himself? In private meetings with those who raised this issue, Skilling argued he could personally make up for Buy's weakness because he was so aggressive in challenging deals himself.

This was one of Skilling's delusions, though. In fact, in his own way, Skilling was as big a problem as Buy. He personally approved some deals even when he was openly skeptical, especially if they were backed by one of his trusted deputies. "I don't like this deal. I *hate* this deal!" Skilling would announce in a meeting. Then he'd look over at the senior deal maker backing the transaction and tell him he was getting a pass: "If you really want to do it, this is your silver bullet, but I'm going to hold you responsible." After recounting how the scene too often played out, one RAC executive slowly shook his head: "There were a lot of silver bullets."

After Enron fell, Skilling continued to defend his system, blaming RAC's weakness on Buy for failing to use the power he'd been given. But Amanda Martin, the former Enron executive who once presided over the ECT deal makers, believes that Skilling's selection of a "meek" chief risk officer was no accident: "If Buy had said, 'I will not sign off—I will go to the board,' Jeff would have caved and killed the deal." As Martin sees it, Buy's refusal to press the issue allowed Skilling to maintain that he always respected the integrity of RAC. If Buy had gone to the board, she says, "He would not have had the plausible deniability he wanted. Jeff played chicken, and he never got run off the road."

So much of the culture Skilling instilled at Enron was just like RAC: it sounded great in theory, but the reality was something else entirely. Skilling used to say that a culture that supported innovation, as Enron's did, needed to be willing to accept failure: "I'll take a smart, thoughtful guy who fails over a person who is successful," he declared in one interview. But what company can afford to hang on to executives who fail too often? At Enron, though, there was virtually no consequence for cutting a bad deal. Skilling might say he was going to hold deal makers responsible, but he rarely did, and the deal makers all knew it. On the contrary, by the time it was clear that the deal had gone south, the originator would have gotten his bonus and moved on.

Another Skilling precept: a company that worried too much about costs would discourage original thinking. "I don't think we should be doing stupid things," he later explained, "but I don't think a penny-pinching environment is one that fosters creative ideas. We are not the Wal-Mart of the natural-gas business. We are the Mercedes-Benz of the natural-gas business." An Enron managing director summed up the philosophy this way: "If you are focusing on costs, you're fucking up."

How did this play out in the daily lives of Enron employees? Not surprisingly, people began spending as if every day were Christmas. Expenses soared, for items large and small. Want a new PalmPilot? No problem; it was on your desk in hours. Fancy a new flat-panel monitor for your computer? It would be waiting for you the next day. On many floors in the Enron building, catered lunches arrived daily.

The sense of entitlement, bankrolled with corporate cash, was shared by many at Enron, from Ken Lay to the secretarial staff, most of whom carried Enron-purchased cell phones. There was no requirement to use a particular vendor; if you didn't want to wait for something, you could just pick up the phone and order it yourself. Anyone with a half-baked idea to launch a business in Europe could hop a plane and fly to London. Hundreds of deal makers made a habit of flying first class and staying in deluxe hotels; no one seemed to care. Even junior executives didn't hesitate to hire expensive consultants; sometimes different business units hired different consultants to study the same idea. The corporate administrative types gave up trying to keep a lid on things. "These people literally did not understand what they were doing and what they were spending," says Mary Wyatt, who worked as vice president for administration until 1998. "People just did what they wanted."

Nor did Skilling's Enron seem to care how much it cost to land a deal. A former Enron vice president, Bob Schorr, a company veteran who worked as a gas-marketing executive in ECT, says: "If you met your earnings target, you'd get your bonus, even if you spent twice your budget for expenses." An executive who worked in London adds: "If you're told to make $25 million and you do it, you're in great shape. It doesn't matter how much it costs you to make that $25 million."

One Enron executive estimated the company's worldwide overhead at a staggering $1.8 billion. It wasn't until 2000 that the company finally started to get a grip on expenses. A veteran Enron executive, George Wasaff, was named procurement czar. Wasaff was appalled to discover that Enron was spending upward of $750 million annually just on consultants and professional services with virtually no controls. He centralized purchasing, required approval for consultants, and imposed reasonable limits on travel and other expenses. Travel costs alone dropped by 25 percent.

Here was another Skilling theory: if you hired smart people, it didn't matter whether they had any experience. In fact, it didn't even matter if they stayed in one job long enough to learn it. Job assignments at Skilling's Enron could change from month to month. The company started and folded new businesses—and reorganized old ones—constantly. Some didn't last a year. ("Intellectual businesses: the life cycle is short," explained Skilling.) Speed was of the essence: everything moved so fast there was no point in long-range planning. "Other companies set goals for a person for a year, but the market moves so fast that we don't know what someone should do in July," said Skilling.

In the early ECT days, support staff would complete all the necessary employee moves around the building—known at Enron as churns—once a week, on Friday nights. By 1998, special "move teams" were carrying out churns *every night*. Enron spent more than $6 million a year just on relocating offices and cubicles, according to Wyatt: "I had a million square feet I was moving around every day." It was not unusual for someone in the merchant business to move three or four times a year. The shifting and blending and renaming of business units took place so often that human resources managers joked about the "reorg du jour" and date-stamped incoming organizational charts.

This was terribly disruptive, of course. New recruits barely had time to learn the fundamentals of one new job before rushing off to another department. There were always plenty of fresh troops. Taking yet another cue from Wall Street, Skilling had begun an analyst-associate program in the early 1990s, bringing in a handful of top students from the best undergraduate and MBA programs. These were supposed to be the company's prize recruits, but by 1999, the company was awash in them, hiring upward of 400 a year. In the early years, a former executive says, the associates and analysts were like the Delta force. By the end, they were like the reserves.

As Skilling saw it, experience in any one part of the business really wasn't important: smart people who "got it" could work anywhere. "I don't want anyone sitting in the same position for five years and getting bored," he said. "Fluid movement is absolutely necessary in our company."

Most of this movement was self-directed, with workers, in effect, transferring themselves. This flowed from yet another Skilling theory: that employees helped Enron figure out which businesses it should be in by voting with their feet. Those new businesses that attracted lots of staff were obviously the most promising; those that went begging for people were ones that Enron needed to shut down. Of course, this ignored the simple reality that employees went wherever they thought the action was—which was defined by Skilling's public pronouncements. This made Skilling's indicator self-fulfilling. "I called it the 'klieg-light syndrome,' " says Bob Schorr. "Wherever Jeff was, talent would flock. The activity was following the light." Says a former company vice president: "The best way to describe Enron was as a constant job search."

This freedom of movement intensified the political wrangling during the rank-and-yank process. Bosses needed to win top ranking for their best talent to keep them from going somewhere else in the company. "Managers have to deliver good bonuses to their best guys to keep them," says Hamd Alkhayat, an Enron associate who worked closely with Skilling. "Everyone's horse-trading—'I need this guy; I'll vote for your guy if you vote for mine.' "

In retrospect, one wonders why Wall Street and the press were so willing—so eager, even—to swallow the idea that Enron was reinventing corporate culture. Part of it was that Skilling—and Lay, too—could make it all sound so *perfect*. Skilling liked to use the phrase "loose-tight" to describe Enron's culture, a phrase borrowed from *In Search of Excellence*. The company, he said, could be managed loosely because of its tight internal-control mechanism.

It was also, in part, that the world had entered the era of Internet mania, an era in which there was a complete suspension of healthy skepticism and disbelief. Brand new dot-coms—companies that barely had revenues, much less profits—were going to pose serious threats to big, established companies. The dot-coms, too, had newfangled cultures, which featured spending without controls and strategies that changed on the fly. Everybody talked about moving at Internet speed. Much of what Skilling was selling had the effect of positioning Enron as a company that had more in common with the dot-coms than with an old energy giant like Exxon. Of course it also helped that no one suspended disbelief more than Skilling himself: he seems to have truly thought the culture he was establishing would give Enron a huge competitive advantage in the new age.

But to many of those on the inside, the new Enron culture made it, quite simply, an unpleasant place to work. Many who had joined ECT in the early 1990s looked back on those days with great fondness. *That* Enron had been an exciting, even magical, place to work, where the powerful sense that they were changing the world was intoxicating. The Enron of the early 1990s really had felt new and different. But that place was gone. At the Enron Skilling wrought in the late 1990s, money seemed to be the only thing that mattered. Gradually, people who prized teamwork were weeded out by the PRC process, and those who stayed and thrived were the ones who were the most ruthless in cutting deals and looking out for themselves.

By the late 1990s, says one executive, "corporate killers" had come to dominate Enron. "You always had to look out for someone stabbing you in the back because the prize was so big," says another. Enron operatives sometimes dropped big sums competing against one another to launch the same business idea and took special delight in outmaneuvering other Enron subsidiaries. "If you made money at the expense of other business units, it was good," says Amanda Martin. "To put one over on one of your own was a sign of creativity and greatness."

There was no incentive for making reasonable assumptions about how a deal would play out. A former Enron managing director says: "The mentality on most of this stuff was they did deals and moved on. They closed one deal and moved on to another one to try to find some more income for themselves." And if you couldn't get it done quickly, you abandoned the idea, even if it looked promising. "If you hold onto a deal too long, it looks like you've got nothing better to do," says John Allario, an MBA who went through the analyst-associate program. "That's the one thing you didn't want to be associated with at Enron: something that lingers." People became "deal machines," says Amanda Martin. "All you had to do was bring them in the door."

Little attention was paid to customer relationships, since nobody was going to get a big bonus for keeping the customer happy. "We managed to screw and piss off every major utility customer we had," says Martin. The word was out, she says: " 'Don't do business with Enron: they'll steal your wallet when you aren't looking.' "

The old ECT veterans could only shake their heads at the brutality of the new culture. By comparison, the first generation of executives—Pai, Baxter, Hannon, Rice—were "gentlemen-rogues," says one former managing director. The next generation "were screamers. They would cut you off at the knees and make you bleed."

It had become a culture of excess, where nothing was too over-the-top.

During his years running ECT, Skilling had led small groups of Enron executives and customers (all male, of course) on daredevil expeditions to the Australian outback; to Baja, Mexico; and to the glaciers of Patagonia. His goal, Ken Rice said later, was to find an adventure "where someone could actually get killed."

The Baja trip—a 1,200-mile road race in jeeps and on dirt bikes—was particularly hairy. Only three members of the group (including Rice and Skilling) finished the entire course. Rice put a tooth through his lip when he slid off his bike. Another man barely escaped death when his 4x4 jeep flipped end over end. A third broke several ribs after wiping out on his motorcycle; the first one on the scene was Andy Fastow, who promptly tumbled off an embankment and landed on a cactus. Others arrived to find the injured rider plucking cactus spines from Fastow's behind. The journey ended at a huge rented mansion in Cabo San Lucas called the Villa Golden Dome, where a chef had prepared a gourmet meal and a team of masseuses awaited the weary executives. Everyone was flown back to Houston on a chartered jet, and photo albums showcasing the expedition's highlights were later handed out. These trips entered Enron lore, serving as symbols of the company's macho, risk-taking culture.

For those at the top of Enron, excess was a part of daily life. Enron had a fleet of corporate jets, limousines on constant call, and even its own concierge, who would pick up busy employees' dry cleaning, water houseplants, and shop for anniversary presents. At bonus time, there was a rush on Houston's luxury car dealerships; flashy wheels (Porsches were a particular favorite) were de rigueur for top earners. Many built new homes and bought vacation properties or ranches. After living modestly for several years following his divorce, Skilling began construction on an 8,000-square-foot Mediterranean villa in River Oaks, full of modernist touches and with black-and-white decor. In Enron's work-hard, play-hard culture, the scent of sex was unmistakable; affairs flourished inside the company.

"Money went to those guys' heads," says a longtime Enron executive. "I used to walk off the company plane after being picked up and being dropped off by limousine, and I'd have to remind myself I was a real human being. You start living that life long enough, if you don't have very strong morals, you lose it fast. Enron was the kind of company that could spoil you pretty well."

That phenomenon clearly affected Ken Rice, the Nebraska farm boy who had once yanked nails for spending money. In the years after the Sithe deal, Rice found himself a multimillionaire while still in his mid-30s. He became caught up in the Enron whirl. Rice was one of the ringleaders of the daredevil trips Skilling organized; he developed a fondness for fast cars and motorcycles. Rice also had a reputation as a womanizer, and in 1996, while still married to his college sweetheart, he fell into Enron's most celebrated affair. The relationship became widely known because of the high-profile participants and because it lasted for three years.

Rice's mistress was Amanda Martin, who had worked at Enron since late 1991. A slim, stylish woman who had been raised on her family's sugar plantation in Zimbabwe, Martin had trained as a lawyer and come to ECT from Vinson & Elkins, the giant Houston law firm with close ties to the company. After starting out as an in-house lawyer, she ran a new group managing Enron's power plants worldwide for more than a year, then returned to ECT as a deal maker. In early 1995, she became ECT's first female managing director. In 1996, Martin was named president of North American origination and finance.

Martin's rapid rise was striking in ECT, with its lingering fondness for strip bars and its well-deserved reputation as a boys' club. One day in 1996, Martin received an interoffice envelope with an anonymous message: "Just thought you'd be interested to see this." Inside were computer printouts of the salary and bonus history of the male executives who had been promoted to managing director along with her. Everyone in the group had been promoted at the same time; all of them, including Martin, had consistently received a 1 performance ranking. Yet the printouts showed all the men were being paid $300,000 a year—Martin's base was $225,000—and had gotten bonuses that were at least $100,000 higher than hers for two consecutive years.

Martin immediately brought the documents to Skilling, who had often given her what he intended as a considerable compliment: "Amanda, you're one of the smartest women we have here." Now, insisting he knew nothing about the pay discrepancy, Skilling promised to look into it. Two weeks later, she received a check for $300,000. "Enron," says Martin, "was a hard place for a woman to work. It was like a boys' locker room."

At about the same time, though, Martin also made matters considerably more awkward for herself by beginning her relationship with Rice. The situation was messy. Both were married, with children (though Martin was separated from her husband). Rice was also Martin's boss. Not surprisingly, as the relationship became known, coworkers muttered that sleeping with the boss had accelerated her advance. One disgruntled ECT originator named Brian Barrington did more than mutter: he filed suit against the company and Rice, blaming the relationship for Rice's refusal to overturn Martin's decision to demote him. (The litigation aired some embarrassing discovery about Rice's sophomoric behavior before it was finally settled out of court.)

Skilling had first picked up complaints about the relationship a few months after it began. He confronted Rice, who denied that he was involved with Martin. But Skilling eventually realized that Rice had lied to him. Rice and Martin came clean and began appearing together in public, generating even more bitter complaints of favoritism. To deal with the complaints Skilling dispatched Martin to Rebecca Mark's new water company, Azurix. And Ken Rice? Nothing happened to him.

For his part, Skilling also began seeing someone from Enron, a woman named Rebecca Carter, a former Andersen accountant who worked on the trading floor as a risk manager. Skilling actually asked the board for permission to date her (after, according to several sources, their relationship had already begun). Skilling also gave her a big promotion, naming her to the powerful post of corporate secretary, which put her in charge of organizing board meetings and taking the official minutes, among other duties. By the time she left Enron, her salary and bonus approached $600,000.

Which was yet another problem with Skilling's Enron. He still had his favorites, and they could still do no wrong. Skilling's handful of direct reports, noted Alkhayat, the COO's Egyptian-born aide, operated with his "blessed hand"; it was as if they'd been anointed by the leader as infallible and holy.

But they didn't consider Skilling infallible. It was a given, of course, that he was brilliant and that he could get to the essence of an issue faster than anybody. But once he felt he understood the strategy, he lost interest. Execution bored him. "Just do it!" he'd tell his subordinates with a dismissive wave of his hand. "Just get it done!" The details were irrelevant.

Many times, it wasn't even clear what Skilling wanted. He sometimes praised deals that had been carried out against his orders. He became enraptured with businesses he had initially dismissed. And he sometimes insisted he'd always opposed deals that he had actually embraced. When he gave specific directions, those unaccustomed to dealing with him sometimes made the mistake of following them too precisely. One longtime Skilling deputy says the boss's instructions at times required translation. "We'd understand where Jeff wanted to go and what he wanted to do. A lot of people who came over later would take him literally. They'd say: 'Jeff wants me to do this.' I'd say, 'Well, Jeff doesn't want you to do something *stupid*! He wants the end results. He doesn't know how to get there.' "

And always, hovering over everything and everyone at Enron, was Wall Street. During the Kinder era, of course, Enron executives had cared a great deal about pleasing the Street and watching the stock move upward. In the Skilling era, the stock became something else entirely: it became Enron's obsession. A stock ticker in the headquarters lobby offered a constant update on the price of Enron shares. TV monitors broadcast CNBC in the building elevators. Employees were repeatedly encouraged to buy Enron shares; on average, they kept more than half their 401(k) retirement holdings in Enron shares. In 1998, when the stock price hit $50, Skilling and Lay treated it as a major corporate milestone, handing out $50 bills to every Enron employee. Later Lay announced a new personnel initiative: if the company hit performance targets over several years, every employee would get twice his annual salary in Enron shares.

For Skilling himself, says a former aide, "the stock price was his report card." When it rose, he was exultant; when it dropped, he was glum. Whenever he was on the road, Skilling would call several times a day just to check on how the stock was performing. Lots of corporate executives were fixated on their companies' stock price during the bull market of the 1990s, but Skilling's obsession went beyond most of them. As a businessman, his thought process revolved almost entirely around the stock, to the point where he began to believe that Enron's market capitalization—that is, the total value of the company's stock—was the only measure the company should be concerned with. Eventually, he would justify business decisions entirely on the basis of what it would mean to Enron's valuation.

Enron was back in Wall Street's good graces by 1998. That year, the S&P 500 had yet another big bull market run-up, gaining 27 percent. Enron easily outpaced the market index, rising 37 percent. The analysts had all restored their buy recommendations on the stock and were once again singing the company's praises. Enron was once again posting steady annual earnings increases of 15 percent and above. The company was beating its quarterly numbers with such regularity that it seemed almost effortless.

In fact, it was anything but effortless; there was nothing at Enron that required more effort, more cleverness, more deceit—more *everything*—than hitting its quarterly earnings targets. As out of control as Enron was on a day-to-day basis, the place went practically bonkers when the end of the quarter grew closer. For this, Skilling deserves the lion's share of the blame.

By the late 1990s, Enron had made a fundamental shift: trading and deal making were its core. By the estimation of one former executive, of the 18,000 people Enron employed in 1999, a stunning 6,000 were doing deals of one sort or another. And the vast majority of them—perhaps 5,000—were traders and originators working in Skilling's merchant business, the descendant of ECT. "That was our business," Skilling would later say. "We bought and sold stuff."

But that was something Skilling could never admit to the outside world. Partly that was because if Wall Street understood anything, it understood the inherent dangers of a trading operation. Back in December 1995, Skilling had gotten a taste of just how jittery Wall Street could be about trading. That month a rumor swept the Street: Enron had suffered a huge loss from shorting the gas market in the face of a cold snap that had sent prices soaring. What's more, the rumor had it, Skilling had been led off the trading floor in handcuffs. The story was false, but it was a tale the market was more than willing to believe; Enron's stock plummeted 2⅞ points in a single day, wiping out $750 million in market value. The next morning, Lay, Kinder, and Skilling, who had all been skiing in Colorado, were forced to convene a conference call, where they refuted the rumors and insisted that Enron's tight system of risk controls made such a catastrophic loss impossible. More than 170 anxious institutional investors and analysts listened in on the call.

But it wasn't just Wall Street's nervousness that caused Skilling to skirt the truth about its core business. This was Enron's dirty little secret: a company built around trading and deal making cannot possibly count on steadily increasing earnings. Skilling may have sold EOG in part because of the unpredictable nature of its earnings, but what he refused to acknowledge is that there is nothing more unpredictable than a trading desk. A trading desk can make or lose tens of millions of dollars in the blink of an eye. As one former Enron managing director says, "A business that had stable and predictable earnings that's primarily engaged in the trading of commodities is a contradiction in terms."

Precisely because of their volatile earnings, companies whose business is primarily trading invariably have low stock valuations. Goldman Sachs, widely viewed as the best trading firm in the world, has a price/earnings multiple—the key valuation gauge—that rarely goes above 20 times earnings. (That means that the price of a share of the firm's stock is 20 times the amount of its annual earnings per share.) Goldman Sachs never even attempts to predict its earnings ahead of time. It can't.

Enron's valuation was twice that size by the late 1990s, and Skilling wanted to make it go higher still. So instead of admitting that Enron was engaged in speculation, he claimed it was a logistics company, which merely found the most cost-effective way to deliver power from any plant anywhere to any customer anywhere. There was some truth to that, it just wasn't the whole truth. The Enron trading desk, Skilling added, always had a matched book—meaning that every short position precisely offset every long position—and made its trading money merely on the commissions, not on speculative risk. Right up until the end, Skilling and his lieutenants stuck to that line, long after it had become demonstrably false.

That's one reason why hitting the company's earnings targets was so hard:

it wasn't in a business that naturally generated steadily growing earnings. Here's the second reason: Skilling's method of arriving at Enron's quarterly and annual targets was downright perverse. Instead of going through a rigorous budget process and arriving at a number by analyzing all the business units and their prospects for the coming year as Kinder used to do, he would impose a number based solely on what Wall Street wanted. He would openly ask the stock analysts: "What earnings do you need to keep our stock price up?" And the number he arrived at was the number Wall Street was looking for, regardless of whether internally it made any sense.

Under Skilling, the budget process at Enron was "a giant game of chicken," recalls a former executive. "The numbers trickled down. You wanted to say, 'Wait, I can't do that.' But you weren't doing yourself a service if you did that." Another executive adds, "It was just the allocation of big numbers. The budget process was last year's number, plus x percent growth."

Invariably, as the quarter drew to a close, Enron's top executives would realize that they were going to fall short of the number they'd promised Wall Street. At most companies, when this happens, the CEO and chief financial officer make an announcement ahead of time, warning analysts and investors that they're going to miss their number. In other words, the reality of the business drives the process of dealing with Wall Street. Not at Enron. Enron's reality began and ended with hitting the target. And so, when the realization took place that the company was falling short, its executives undertook a desperate scramble to fill the holes in the company's earnings. At Enron, that's what they called earnings shortfalls—"holes."

Calls went out from Skilling and chief accounting officer Rick Causey to the heads of the various company businesses. "We need an extra $15 million!" What rabbits could they pull out of their hats? Deal closings were accelerated so that earnings could be posted by the end of the quarter. This usually required capitulating on key negotiating points, which, over the long term, would likely cost the company millions. But that wasn't the point: at least they'd make the quarter.

Enron also relied heavily on mark-to-market accounting to help it reach its earnings goals. Originally, mark-to-market had been used only in the accounting of natural gas futures contracts—that, after all, is what the Securities and Exchange Commission had agreed to back in 1991. Over the years, Enron had quietly extended the practice. It marked-to-market its electric power contracts and trades after it got into that business. Then, in 1996, it began booking profits on its 50 percent portion of JEDI—the partnership it had established in 1993 with CalPERS—using mark-to-market accounting. By 1997, Enron had extended mark-to-market accounting to every portion of its merchant business. It even began using the approach to book profits on private equity and venture-capital investments, where values were extraordinarily subjective. By the end of the decade, some 35 percent of Enron's assets were being given mark-to-market treatment.

Enron employed other tricks. Deal makers regularly revisited large existing contracts—some more than five years old—to see if they could somehow squeeze out a few million more in earnings. Sometimes the contracts were restructured or renegotiated; other times, they were simply reinterpreted in ways that made them appear more profitable. "When the last-minute call for earnings went out," says one high-level deal maker, "I'd go: 'Which contracts did I do five years ago that had potential value?' A lot of them you could remark." Skilling himself labeled the contract portfolio "a gold mine."

Earnings projections on mark-to-market deals, based on complex models, were reexamined. Was it possible to be a little more optimistic? A small move in a long-term pricing curve could generate millions in extra accounting profits. The curves often went so far into the future that drawing them was already little more than an educated guess. The danger was that skewing curves to generate more profits was not only improper but also raised the likelihood that the curves would turn out to be way off base, producing a big mismatch between Enron's projections and a reality it would eventually have to face. But that, of course, was a future concern, far removed from the crisis of the immediate quarter.

Another trick was to delay recording losses. At the end of each quarter, for example, Enron was supposed to write off its dead deals. To review what needed to be booked, Causey met individually with the heads of the origination groups. At one meeting, an executive recalled, Causey kept coming back to a dead deal and asking: Was it possible the deal was still alive?

It wasn't, responded the executive.

"So there's no chance of it coming back?"

No.

"Is there even a *little* bit of a chance of it coming back?" asked Causey. "Do you want to look at it again?"

Finally the executive took the hint—and the deal was declared undead. Enron deferred the hit for another quarter. "You did it once, it smelled bad," says the executive. "You did it again, it didn't smell as bad."

Enron also generated earnings through tax-avoidance schemes. Beginning in 1995, the company executed 11 mind-numbingly complex tax transactions that allowed Enron to bank some $651 million in profits. The deals were cooked up in Enron's tax department, whose head count grew to 250. The department was run by a grizzled tax lawyer named Bob Hermann, who had begun with Houston Natural Gas back in 1981. The first of the deals, dubbed Project Tanya, involved setting up a special entity to manage deferred compensation and benefit programs, which then issued preferred stock that was transferred back to Enron. It generated $66 million in earnings.

The point man on the special tax deals was a conspiratorial CPA and lawyer named R. Davis Maxey, who quietly traveled the country meeting with tax specialists at banks and law firms to come up with new ideas. One by one, he teed up deals, which often took as much as a year to develop and were supposed to generate savings that stretched over a period of as long as 20 years. Enron's high-priced tax advisers—a law firm might earn a fee of $1 million for a single transaction and a bank could earn as much as $15 million—had urged the company to keep a low profile on the schemes, lest they attract the ire of the Internal Revenue Service. But after Skilling became Enron's COO, the company increasingly turned to its tax department to act like just another profit center—and help the company hit earnings targets by taking more and more of the tax savings early. "In effect, we have created a business segment for Enron that generates earnings," Maxey wrote in an e-mail.

Whatever the propriety of these maneuvers, they all had one clear effect: they rolled Enron's problems further into the future, where the issues slowly accumulated.

Like many companies during the bull market, Enron began to invest in other businesses—a few dozen private and public companies. Skilling called this part of the business Enron's merchant investment portfolio. Not surprisingly, as the company's holes grew larger, the equity portfolio became yet another earnings-management vehicle.

Take, for instance, Enron's investment in Mariner Energy, a privately owned Houston oil and gas company that did deepwater exploration. Enron took control of Mariner in 1996 in a $185 million buyout. Private-equity investments are often tricky to value since they're not publicly traded; and deepwater drilling is highly speculative. In the years that followed, this made the precise value of the company uncertain. Enron exploited this uncertainty by periodically marking up the value of Mariner as needed to fill earnings holes. Such valuation increases could immediately be booked as mark-to-market income through an aggressive approach called fair-value accounting that Enron began using about that time.

When Enron got in an earnings bind, says one Enron vice president familiar with the situation, "People were asked to look and see if there's anything more we can squeeze out of Mariner." And squeeze they did. Indeed, Mariner served as a sort of piggy bank for Enron earnings. By the second quarter of 2001, Enron had Mariner on its books for $367.4 million, by any reasonable measure, an absurdly high amount.

Mariner was a prime example of how Enron executives made a mockery of the RAC process. A postbankruptcy review by Enron's new chief accounting officer concluded that the company's Mariner investment was really worth less than a third of what Enron had claimed. (This resulted in a write-off of $256.9 million.) In fact, even while the Mariner investment was being marked up to book profits, RAC analysts consistently challenged the valuation. According to the accounting review, Enron, during much of 2001, justified its inflated figure using "a model that was not supported by RAC" and was rigged with outlandish assumptions. Enron carried Mariner on its books throughout this period for about $365 million; its own internal-control group placed its value in a broad range between $47 million and $196 million.

The review noted: "The accounting for Mariner in the second and third quarters of 2001 used valuations not endorsed by RAC in accordance with the Company's internal control system." It added that there was "no documentation justifying this control override" and that "this exception to the established internal accounting control procedures [was] not brought to the attention of the Audit and Compliance Committee for consideration or review." In fact, according to RAC executives, their own boss, Rick Buy, refused to press the matter of Mariner's inflated valuation with Enron's top executives. Buy, a former energy banker, certainly knew the investment well: Enron had appointed him to the Mariner board.

There was also a part of the merchant portfolio known as the Industrial Group. The twenty or so deal makers who made up this group were led by an Enron executive named J. Kevin McConville. Their job was to make equity investments outside the energy industry but with an eye toward energy-intensive businesses, where Enron might be able to cut related deals to provide their plants with electricity, coal, or gas.

Beginning in 1997, McConville's group cooked up a series of such complex deals. They bought equity in a paper manufacturer called Kafus, a steel maker named Qualitech, and a Thai steel mill company called NSM, among others. Ultimately, the only thing the Industrial Group's deals had in common was this: they all lost money.

Every Monday morning, a team of RAC analysts met to examine how Enron's investments were performing. The list of portfolio assets was color-coded: green meant okay, yellow meant the deals needed work, and red meant big trouble. Increasingly, McConville's investments were turning up red. In several cases, Enron hadn't just bought equity in each of these companies; it had invested in other ways as well. Take NSM, a $650 million project to redevelop a troubled steel mill in Chonburi, Thailand. Enron not only bought 52 million shares of NSM stock and taken a seat on the NSM board; it also swallowed at least $20 million of a private $452 million junk-bond offering. Long before the plant could be redeveloped, though, the company went bankrupt, generating extensive litigation. Kafus and Qualitech were disasters too. Yet even as his deals deteriorated, McConville was promoted to managing director.

McConville, a veteran Enron executive, attributes much of the criticism about his deals to jealousy over his rapid promotion. He says that if the energy-supply portion of the projects is considered—on which Enron routinely booked profits—about 30 percent of them made Enron money. He acknowledges that several, such as NSM ("a horrible failure"), turned into disasters.

What really made his deals look worse than they were, says McConville, was that Enron recorded gains on the private-equity investments to book profits, just as it did with Mariner. "Every one of them was written up [in value]," he says. This meant the paper loss Enron faced was bigger than the cash investment the company had made. And Enron, of course, was loath to acknowledge any losses.

That had always been the case with Skilling, who loved the gains his private-equity investments could generate but hated having to record the hit when they went south, as was supposed to be done under mark-to-market accounting. As early as 1996, when ECT had moved from merely financing energy companies to making equity investments in them, Skilling fretted over this very issue to his portfolio management advisory committee. One of Fastow's deputies, then known as Sherron Smith (she later rose to postbankruptcy fame, after getting married, as Sherron Watkins) recalls Skilling saying: "I don't want to be the one to go tell Enron's board we've had a big loss when we're supposed to be such great risk managers."

Skilling was always looking for a hedge—even an imprecise "dirty hedge"— for Enron investments that, by normal standards, couldn't be hedged. In one such case, he tried to protect a gain in some securities that couldn't be sold by ordering Enron's traders to buy S&P 500 puts. At one point, Watkins recalls, Skilling tried to hire an expert to develop new hedging techniques for locking in gains on Enron's private-equity investments. After meeting with everyone involved, the candidate refused to take the job, explaining that the venture was doomed to failure because Skilling wanted to accomplish the impossible. "It's called equity *risk* for a reason," he told Watkins.

For McConville, the day of reckoning arrived in 1999 after RAC toted up the industrial portfolio's losses: they came to more than $400 million. McConville soon left the company. Belatedly, Skilling decided to pull the plug on new industrial investments. "We understand oil and gas a whole lot better than the steel business in Thailand," he told his subordinates. "We learned our lesson pretty expensively."

Still: *$400 million!* Even for Enron, that was a big hole, not easily papered over. How was it ever going to be able to cover that amount without wrecking earnings? Deep inside the company, there was another team working on that very problem.

CHAPTER 10

The Hotel Kenneth-Lay-a

Reported earnings follow the rules and principles of accounting. The results do not always create measures consistent with underlying economics. However, corporate management's performance is generally measured by accounting income, not underlying economics. Therefore, risk management strategies are directed at accounting, rather than economic, performance.

—Enron in-house risk-management manual

When, exactly, did Enron cross the line? Even now, after all the congressional hearings, all the investigative journalism, all the reports, lawsuits, and indictments, that's an impossible question to answer. There have been accounting frauds over the years where companies created receivables out of whole cloth or shipped bricks at the end of a quarter instead of products. In such cases, someone at a company has to consciously consider the fact that he or she is about to commit a crime—and then commit it.

But for the most part, the Enron scandal wasn't like that. The Enron scandal grew out of a steady accumulation of habits and values and actions that began years before and finally spiraled out of control. When Enron expanded the use of mark-to-market accounting to all sorts of transactions—was that when it first crossed the line? How about when it set up its first off-balance-sheet partnerships, Cactus and JEDI, with such reputable investors as General Electric and CalPERS? Or when it categorized certain unusual gains as recurring? Or when it created EPP, that "independent" company to which Enron sold stakes in its international assets and posted the resulting gains to its bottom line?

In each case, you could argue that the effect of the move was to disguise, to one degree or another, Enron's underlying economics. But you could also argue that they were perfectly legal, even above board. Didn't all the big trading companies on Wall Street use mark-to-market accounting? Weren't lots of companies moving debt off the balance sheet? Didn't many companies lump onetime gains into recurring earnings? The answer, of course, was yes. Throughout the bull market of the 1990s, moves like these were so commonplace they were taken for granted, becoming part of the air Wall Street breathed.

Besides, the big Wall Street investment banks, not to mention the nation's giant accounting firms, had a huge vested interest in the kinds of moves Enron was making to create accounting income. Even before the dawning of the 1990s bull market, a new ethos was gradually taking hold in corporate America, according to which anything that wasn't blatantly illegal was therefore okay—no matter how deceptive the practice might be. Creative accountants found clever ways around accounting rules and were rewarded for doing so. Investment bankers invented complex financial structures that they then sold to eager companies, all searching for ways to make their numbers look better. By the end of the decade, things that had once seemed shockingly deceptive, such as securities that looked like equity on the balance sheet but for tax purposes could be treated as debt, now seemed perfectly fine. Securitizations exploded, with everything from lotto winnings to proceeds from tobacco lawsuits being turned into securities that could be sold to the investing public.

In the wake of Enron's collapse, the mood changed virtually overnight, and creative became a very bad word, synonymous with deceptive. But it's important to remember that it wasn't always that way. That statement in Enron's risk-management manual perfectly captured the sentiment of the times. In fact, the material in the manual, developed with the help of a consulting firm, was used throughout the energy-trading industry.

Of course it wasn't *only* the times that caused Enron to get ever more creative. It was also necessity. A company like General Electric might employ a little financial ingenuity to hit its earnings target on the nose quarter after quarter (as, indeed, it did), but even without such strategies, GE had a hugely profitable business. That wasn't true of Enron. Especially in the latter part of the 1990s, Enron didn't have anywhere near enough cash coming in the door. Eventually, the whole thing took on a life of its own, with an insane logic that no one at the company dared contemplate: to a staggering degree, Enron's "profits" and "cash flow" were the result of the company's own complex dealings with itself. At which point, of course, there could hardly be any doubt: Enron had most certainly crossed the line.

But if it's impossible to mark the moment Enron crossed the line, it's not hard at all to know who led the way. That was Andrew Fastow, the company's chief financial officer. He was 28 years old when he first joined Enron in late 1990, hired as one of Skilling's early finance guys at ECT. Skilling wanted him precisely because he knew how to set up complicated financial structures, specifically securitizations. Fastow became Enron's Wizard of Oz, creating a giant illusion of steady and increasing prosperity. Fastow and his team were the financial masterminds, helping Enron bridge the gap between the reality of its business and the picture Skilling and Lay wanted to present to the world. He and his group created off-balance-sheet vehicles, complex financing structures, and deals so bewildering that few people can understand them even now. Fastow's fiefdom, called Global Finance, was, as Churchill said about the Soviet Union, a riddle wrapped in a mystery inside an enigma that was Enron's string of successively higher earnings. "Andy was a master at walking in, always at the end of the quarter or the end of the year," says Amanda Martin. "The fat was in the fire and about to ignite. He'd say, 'give me the ball,' and he'd come through every time. That's why Jeff and Ken loved him." Like everyone at Enron, Fastow was handsomely rewarded for this work. But for him it wasn't enough. So over time Fastow found other ways to pay himself. Some of these ways his superiors knew about. Others they didn't know about—but should have.

Andrew Fastow grew up in New Providence, New Jersey, a suburb about 25 miles from New York City. His father, Carl, was a buyer for drug-store and supermarket chains; his mother Joan worked as a real-estate broker once the children were grown. The second of three sons, Fastow was a huge *Star Wars* fan and played tennis and trombone; he was well liked enough to be elected student council president his senior year of high school.

Even as a high school student, Fastow burned with ambition. It was an odd kind of ambition, though: not necessarily to be the best but to be *seen* as the best. A high school English teacher later described him as a "wheeler dealer" because he would try to negotiate better grades. He was also part of a group that lobbied the New Jersey Board of Education to have a student named to the board. Fastow was that student. (After graduation, he came to one board meeting smoking a pipe.)

Fastow seems to have never had a moment's doubt that he was destined for business, specifically for finance. At Tufts, where he went to college, Fastow majored in economics and Chinese—the latter because he thought it would aid his business career—and graduated summa cum laude in December 1984. Tufts is where Fastow met his wife, Lea Weingarten. She was a sophomore and had come a week early to serve as a host adviser for the incoming freshman, one of whom was Fastow. Upon sighting him, she confided to a friend, "God, I think he's cute, but he's only a freshman. Should I date him?" The two soon started dating.

Weingarten is a name many Texans know instantly. For decades, the Weingartens have been one of Houston's wealthiest and most prominent families. Lea's great-grandfather founded a supermarket chain that dominated southeast Texas; though the family sold the business to Grand Union in 1980, an offshoot, the publicly traded Weingarten Realty Investors, owns shopping centers throughout the Southwest. (Jack Weingarten, Lea's father, worked for the chain but never ran it.)

Despite her wealth—or, perhaps, because of it—Lea Weingarten had a far more difficult childhood than her future husband. Her mother, Miriam Hadar, whom Jack married in 1961, was a beauty queen who had been named Miss Israel and was a semifinalist in the 1958 Miss Universe contest. In 1968, when Lea was six years old, her parents' marriage disintegrated, and they became enmeshed in an ugly divorce that consumed the better part of three years. Miriam accused Jack of being physically and verbally abusive, dependent on drugs and alcohol, and "unstable emotionally"; Jack countered that Miriam missed the "glitter and high living" of her previous life and was guilty of "misconduct with other men during her entire marriage." The divorce was granted in late 1970, with Jack Weingarten getting custody of Lea and her brother, Michael. The judge said that the children should grow up in Houston, a city "in which their name is associated with the finest of Jewish example and tradition." Miriam moved back to Israel.

In high school, Lea Weingarten was a sensitive and insecure girl who struggled with her weight. In college, she was still heavy but dressed well and appeared to be upbeat and happy. As she got older, she slimmed down and became a woman whom friends describe as "unpretentious" and "gracious."

Just three months after graduating from college, Andy Fastow married Lea Weingarten in a low-key Houston ceremony. (Years later, the two renewed their vows at the Elvis Wedding Chapel in Las Vegas.) The newlyweds then headed to Chicago, where both were enrolled in the training program at Continental Bank, a midlevel commercial bank that was just emerging from one of the biggest business scandals of the 1980s, the so-called Penn Square scandal. (It revolved around bad loans made to the oil patch during the oil boom of the early 1980s.) Rather than work a few years then take a few years to go to business school—the normal route to an MBA—the two accelerated the process. They both earned MBAs at Northwestern's Kellogg Graduate School of Business, which they attended at night, after work.

Fastow was instantly unpopular with his peers at Continental. He came off as arrogant, ambitious, and more than a bit of a dandy, wearing Hermès ties and Gucci shoes. Had he worked at a New York investment bank, none of these traits would have been remarkable, but at a quiet, Midwestern commercial bank like Continental, Fastow stood out. "He invoked a lot of jealousy because he was clearly on the make, almost nakedly so," says a former boss, who also thinks there was another element to the dislike: "Both Andy and Lea were smart and gorgeous."

In early 1987, Fastow took a short, unsuccessful detour. He left Continental for a small, publicly traded company called CCC Information Services, which maintained a computerized database to help insurance companies set a value on cars that had been stolen or involved in accidents. Founded in 1980, CCC had almost 300 employees by the time Fastow joined and was growing like mad. "CCC couldn't hire people fast enough in those days," recalls one former employee. Around the time Fastow joined the company, the stock hit a high of almost $15 per share.

That August, CCC cut a deal to sell itself for almost $100 million. But the deal fell through, and by late 1987, the stock had dropped to $6 a share. The following January, the company was sold to another bidder, a privately held company, for roughly $80 million, and Fastow beat a hasty retreat back to Continental. Although he'd been at CCC for less than a year, he claimed on his résumé that he had "launched and managed an automotive industry database management company. First year operating profit of $1 million on revenues of $7 million," which would have represented a significant amount of CCC's profits and revenues during that time period. Yet CCC's financial documents don't even mention Fastow's operation, and former senior officials say there was nothing remarkable about his brief tenure there.

It was during his second go-round at Continental that Fastow found his calling. Rehired as a loan officer, he sat across the credenza from a small team of executives who were doing pioneering work in securitization. He immediately gravitated to that team and maneuvered to become its newest member. He was like a "pig in shit," recalls one of his former bosses.

This same man claims that Fastow was "incredibly talented" at securitization, but that is hardly a unanimous view. "He was a good average performer, but you weren't held in awe of his intellect," says another former Continental executive. "You didn't marvel every day at what smart things he came up with."

What is certainly true was that Fastow loved being on the cutting edge of finance and reveled in the work. In the late 1980s, securitization was just getting started and Continental was doing deals the likes of which no one had ever seen before. A deal led by a Continental banker named Michael Woodhead was named one of *Institutional Investor* magazine's "Deals of the Year" for 1989. Woodhead had figured out a way to bundle the outstanding debt from leveraged buyouts and sell a fresh security backed by the interest on those bonds. This, in turn, freed up capital for the banks involved in the LBO game to make new loans. The deal was known as FRENDS.

What people noticed about Fastow, even then, was how willing he was to push the limits. Because securitization is so complex and so ripe for abuse in the wrong hands, hundreds upon hundreds of pages of rules were being written to mandate what was allowed and what was not. Fastow, says one of his former bosses, "was rules-driven from day one." By that, he meant that the future Enron CFO took it upon himself to figure out if he could accomplish his goals while following the precise letter of the rules, even if it meant violating their intent. "Andy was really into just pushing the parameters of the possible," this person says. "I don't know that he ever had a moral compass." While at Continental, Fastow never crossed the line, but that was largely because his superiors were far more risk-averse than he and turned down his ideas if they thought he went too far. To this former boss, it was easy enough to see how things could have gotten out of hand at Enron: "You put Andy in an environment where he is on the same side as his manager, with the same objectives, it's a Molotov cocktail."

On his resume, Fastow bragged about FRENDS and took full credit for himself. ("Created and sold first security backed solely by senior LBO bank debt. . . . Sourced assets from ten banks and placed securities with investors in 23 countries. . . . Directly responsible for pretax profit contribution of $12.8 million.") But this, too, was an exaggeration. "Andy was the number two guy in a two-man group, but it was not his idea and he was the follower not the leader," says a former Continental hand.

Meanwhile, over at Enron, Jeff Skilling, newly hired to get the Gas Bank up and running, decided he needed a finance executive who knew something about securitization. Skilling, after all, wanted to free up capital so he could do more natural-gas deals, and he thought that securitization was one way to do that. An executive search firm found Fastow, who was more than ready to leave the bank for Enron. At Continental, promotions and pay raises were slow in coming, bonuses were small, and a young executive on the make had to be willing to spend long years in the trenches. Not yet 30 years old, Fastow was already getting impatient. Besides, Houston was his wife's hometown.

Skilling was dazzled by Fastow's résumé, never for a moment questioning whether any of it was exaggerated. Fastow's experience "launching and managing" a business at CCC meant that the young finance whiz had an "entrepreneurial bent," Skilling concluded. His work "creating and selling" FRENDS meant that he could come up with new ideas to free up capital. And he had other attributes, too. For instance, Fastow claimed on his résumé that at Continental he was responsible for "continuing education of commercial bank lending and portfolio officers regarding accounting and risk adjustment implication of asset securitization." "I just went agog," Skilling later said. "He was perfect. Absolutely perfect."

Gene Humphrey, who was then Skilling's finance head, was less certain. He was actually more impressed with Lea Fastow, whom Enron brought into the company's treasury department. (Indeed, many people at Enron thought she was the smarter of the two.) Still, this was 1990 and Enron was still a pipeline company; star corporate finance prospects weren't exactly rushing to apply for the position. In November, Skilling offered Fastow the job, and he took it. His title was manager, his starting salary was $75,000, up from the $68,000 he'd made at Continental, and his signing bonus was $20,000. He was also guaranteed a bonus of at least $25,000 in the following year. He began work on December 3, 1990.

Early on, one of the gas-bank executives took Fastow to meet a crusty Oklahoma oil producer. It was instantly clear that Enron's new finance guy was out of his element. The oilman had a wad of chewing tobacco the size of a baseball in his cheek and periodically interrupted the conversation to spit a stream of brown juice into a tin can, leaving Fastow in a state of shock.

For the most part Fastow didn't stand out in his first few years at Enron— certainly, not many people would have guessed that he would one day ascend to become the CFO of a Fortune 500 company. "I thought he was a strange little guy . . . he didn't talk much, but he came up with creative structures," says one executive. "He might not have been the brightest guy in the world, but he was very, very hardworking," says another. Not long after he arrived, one executive assistant says, he skipped a vacation cruise the Weingarten family had planned to the Galápagos Islands because he was too busy with work. Fastow was also a big practical joker who would throw slimeball goo against glass walls as a joke and kept Frisbees and other toys all over his office.

ECT was small in those days, and Fastow rose rapidly. He worked on the first Cactus deal, was the leader in developing the JEDI partnership, and helped devise the EPP strategy. In 1992, Gene Humphrey wrote in a performance review that "Andy is and is continuing to develop into one of the strongest financial innovators that I have worked with. He has a strong and solid future at Enron." (Humphrey noted, however, that Fastow needed improvement in the "personal relationship skills useful in the heat of negotiation. Sometimes a kind word is more useful than a blunt assertion.") By mid-1993, Fastow was a vice president, and his performance reviews were increasingly positive. In 1994, Fastow received raves for his "creativity, vision, persistence, initiative, presentation skills" and his "innovative thinking on new deal structures." He was told, though, that he needed to develop "strong lasting relationships" with capital providers such as banks and insurance companies and to "negotiate with a win/win attitude." By late 1995, Fastow had become a managing director, with a salary that topped $225,000.

And yet he was unhappy. Why? Because even though he was making more money than he'd ever made in his life (and was married to an heiress), he could see plainly that his pay wasn't even close to what the big earners at Enron were raking in. Even worse, it probably never would be. The people who made the big money at Enron were the executives who either ran divisions or landed big deals. John Wing, Lou Pai, Ken Rice, Rebecca Mark, and others were already millionaires, thanks to their Enron compensation deals. They got huge bonuses, tons of stock options, pieces of their deals or businesses—you name it. But executives like Fastow, in finance, were never going to make that kind of money. And that's because the finance department, important though it was to ECT's success, wasn't a profit center in its own right. It didn't contribute directly to Enron's earnings; as they say in business, it didn't have its own P&L. (The letters P&L stand for profit and loss. The phrase means that a division isn't just a cost center; it makes money for the company.) "The whole story about Andy is that if you didn't have a P&L at Enron and you didn't add a lot of money to the P&L, you weren't a man," says a former colleague.

Desperate to prove that he belonged among Enron's heavy hitters, Fastow began lobbying Skilling to give him a division to run. And because he had become one of Skilling's favorites, Fastow got his wish. By 1996, Skilling had put Fastow in charge of a new division he'd recently set up. It was supposed to be Enron's first foray into the retail-energy business, an effort to sell electricity and gas directly to the consumer. But nobody had figured out how, precisely, Enron was going to do that; Fastow was told to come up with the business plan for the new unit.

Try as he might, he simply couldn't do it. Fastow's business plans were so poor that Skilling kept sending him back to the drawing board. "He had lots of big ideas and went in lots of different directions," recalls a former colleague. "He would talk a big game." But he never came up with anything that had a real shot at being a business. Within nine months, after many shouting matches with Skilling, Fastow was back in finance. Fastow saw his failure as a major humiliation, potentially fatal for his career at Enron. There was no glossing over the fact that he failed miserably. Some of the traders started calling him Andy Fast-Out.

But within a matter of months, Skilling sent a clear signal to the rest of the organization that Fastow was not going to be punished for his failure. On January 13, 1997, just weeks after replacing Kinder as Enron's president, Skilling named Fastow a senior vice president, in charge of treasury, risk management, pricing capital, and funding for all of Enron's business. Fastow was also named to Enron's management committee. He was now part of the inner circle. (Shortly after Fastow was promoted, his wife Lea, who had risen to assistant treasurer, left Enron after giving birth to their first son.)

To many who knew him well, Fastow seemed an incredibly insecure man. There were many people at Enron who kissed up to Skilling, but few did it as overtly as Fastow. "Gratuitous annual self promotion" reads an entry on Skilling's calendar next to a meeting with Fastow. Fastow named his first son Jeffrey; after the birth, as Fastow was passing out cigars in the office, he had to fend off jibes accusing him of being a "suck-ass" for naming his son after his boss. According to one former managing director, Fastow replied, "Hey, who's done more for me other than my mom and dad?"

Fastow frequently complained about money: how he wasn't making as much as he should. After getting his promotion to senior vice president, Fastow hired a personal image consultant to help him dress like a corporate executive; later, he started wearing double-breasted designer suits, buttoned up, making him a dandyish figure in the halls of Enron, where people tended toward 1990s-style casual cool (khakis and open-collar shirts). Before he bought a new Porsche, he polled women in the office to see whether he should buy a blue car or a black one.

Fastow also seemed to have a split personality; he was Enron's version of Dr. Jckyll and Mr. Hyde. "He was so mean in business but so personally delightful," says one banker who knew him well. In a company full of strident Republicans, he was not. Years before it became a public issue, Fastow turned down a coveted invitation to attend the Masters golf tournament because women weren't allowed in the club. He was a devoted and doting father. He was also a health nut who was known for taking long runs. And he took care of employees—certain employees, that is—whom he needed on his side. "You always knew Andy was out for himself, but as long as you made him look good, he always looked after you," says a former colleague.

But Fastow was also greedy and out for himself—a "take-no-prisoners political animal," according to a former colleague—who had no qualms about taking credit for things others had done. And he had a vicious temper. "You could tell when he was about to twist off," says one banker. "That mouth would go in a certain way, and then he'd stretch his neck. You knew he was going to explode, and it would be terrifying." To the bankers and Wall Streeters he dealt with regularly, Fastow's volatile fist-pounding manner came to exemplify Enron's culture. And over the years, it only got worse. "As time went on, Andy changed," says an early senior executive. "People started to become afraid of him and afraid to speak out. It almost created a fear factor between Andy and people who did not agree with him."

In late 1997, Skilling decided to search outside the company for a CFO. He met with a handful of candidates and took a particular shine to Denise McGlone, the former CFO of Sallie Mae, who in 1997 was named one of *Euromoney*'s top 50 women in finance for her work in risk management and derivatives. He went to New York to talk to McGlone and was impressed enough that he had her fly to Houston to make the rounds at Enron. Fastow, recalls a former colleague, "freaked out." She continues: "I was sitting in my office. He'd been acting really weird. Skilling walked by with this woman, introducing all of us. Andy really almost had a meltdown over it. He was in his office, staring at his desk, not reading anything, not doing anything."

Rick Causey, Enron's chief accounting officer, was almost as upset as Fastow. For both men, their worry was the same: a new CFO would inevitably get between them and Skilling. They each went to Skilling and told him that either one of them would work for the other but neither would work for McGlone. They got their way. Lay told Enron's board that he felt the best candidate was an internal one: rising star Andy Fastow. In March 1998, Fastow, just 36 years old, was named CFO of Enron. Once again, Enron had installed the wrong man in the wrong job for the wrong reason.

"Andy didn't have the knowledge base required to be the CFO of a major company," says one of his former bosses at Continental. He had a narrow set of skills—creating financial structures—and lacked the experience and judicious temperament the job required, the willingness to say no to deals and the attention to basics necessary to insure that the company's balance sheet remained strong. "Andy didn't have a risk-control bone in his body," says Sherron Watkins.

He lacked something else: the knowledge that being a CFO demanded. Fastow knew so little about accounting that one person who knows him wasn't even sure he could dissect a balance sheet. "It amazes me that you'd take a corporate finance asset-backed guy and make him CFO," says his former boss. "That's not what a CFO's job really is." Of course, the man had never worked at Enron.

• • •

Though he now held the exalted title of chief financial officer, Andy Fastow's job didn't really change at all. He still saw his primary role as creating the financial structures that would allow Enron to hit its profit targets. And even though he was now CFO, Fastow was never supposed to be able to do whatever he wanted without any oversight. There were others, both in and outside the company, whose job was to act as a check on Fastow, to perform the same kind of role as his old bosses at Continental. To put it another way, there were people whose job it was to say no to Andy Fastow when he wanted to cross the line.

Ostensibly, the person inside Enron who was supposed to help keep Fastow in check was Rick Causey, the company's chief accounting officer. At most companies, the chief accounting officer reports to the CFO. But that wasn't true at Enron. Aware of Fastow's shortcomings, Skilling made Causey his equal and gave him many of the day-to-day responsibilities that a CFO normally handles. Causey reported directly to Skilling.

One of Causey's responsibilities was to determine how Fastow's transactions were reported on Enron's financial statement. He was also the go-between between Enron and its outside accountants at Arthur Andersen. Had he been willing to declare that Fastow's transactions didn't pass the smell test, it would have been impossible for Fastow to do what he did. On paper, at least, he had the authority to stop Fastow from going too far. But Rick Causey didn't see his job in those terms. Instead, he saw his role as *facilitating* Fastow's transactions. Ultimately, he was every bit as weak in his role as Rick Buy was as chief risk officer.

A University of Texas graduate, Causey joined Arthur Andersen straight out of school and spent almost nine years there, the last half of which he worked primarily on the Enron account. In 1991, Causey joined Enron as assistant controller at a salary of $100,000 and helped do the accounting work for JEDI and Cactus. Though he never made partner at Arthur Andersen, he was promoted to chief accounting and information officer at Enron at the age of 37. To a large extent, Enron was all he knew.

Within the company, people used to call the roly-poly Causey "the Pillsbury doughboy." Soft-spoken, considerate, salt of the earth, he loved playing golf and attending University of Texas football games. He wasn't a bully, either—not the way Fastow was—but he knew what he had to do, and he did it willingly. Not that he had much choice. "If he didn't figure out a way to make things happen, he'd be fired," says a former finance person.

One of Causey's big responsibilities was to keep track of where Enron stood in relation to the earnings targets Skilling had promised Wall Street. He had an army of CPAs that eventually numbered around 600, most of them spread out in Enron's various business units. The accountants would alert Causey of impending earnings or cash flow holes so that Causey could figure out what deals needed to close where. And he would coordinate with Fastow's finance team to figure out a way to fill the holes. "Any company worth its salt uses accounting rules to smooth small peaks and valleys," says one former Enron accountant.

"But with Enron, it got to a point where it was so prolific." Says another former Enron accountant, "Budget shortfalls weren't just business issues, they were accounting issues. There was an absolute conviction at Enron that clever accounting could alter the business reality."

Causey also had a smaller team of some 30 accountants in Houston and London called transaction support. Instead of being back-office types, these people, some of whom came from the Financial Accounting Standards Board (FASB), which writes new accounting rules, worked side by side with the finance team to structure deals. These accountants saw themselves as advisers—even gatekeepers—who guided the deal makers by telling them what the accounting ramifications would be. They also knew all the latest rules and the loopholes—and how best to exploit them—and there was often pressure from the deal makers to do just that. To this day, few of the in-house accountants believe they did anything wrong. They knew that they stretched and twisted the rules to Enron's advantage, but they saw their actions as creative rather than misleading. And that seems to be Causey's view as well. People who worked for him agree that he was a capable accountant who acknowledged he was pushing the limits but didn't believe he was stepping over the line. "I always thought he had at least one foot on solid ground, not that he couldn't stretch!" says one.

What they were doing—what some might even privately admit they were doing—was gaming the system. By the 1990s, it took literally tens of thousands of pages to list all of the nation's accumulated accounting rules, known as General Accepted Accounting Principles, or GAAP. (When a company presents its financials to the public, the numbers must be in compliance with GAAP.) Every time the Financial Accounting Standards Board wrote a new set of rules, it did so to help ensure that a company's books reflected its underlying reality.

But interpreting those rules has always been more art than science, reliant in no small part on the good faith of those applying them in everyday situations. For very smart people who saw the rules as something to be gotten around, well, it wasn't all that hard to do—in fact, some former Enron employees argue that the rules themselves provided a road map. And Enron, which prided itself on employing only the very smartest people, took that view further than any company that's ever existed. "We tried to aggressively use the literature to our advantage," admits a former Enron accountant. "All the rules create all these opportunities. We got to where we did because we exploited that weakness."

Here's how another former employee describes the process: "Say you have a dog, but you need to create a duck on the financial statements. Fortunately, there are specific accounting rules for what constitutes a duck: yellow feet, white covering, orange beak. So you take the dog and paint its feet yellow and its fur white and you paste an orange plastic beak on its nose, and then you say to your accountants, 'This is a duck! Don't you agree that it's a duck?' And the accountants say, 'Yes, according to the rules, this is a duck.' Everybody knows that it's a dog, not a duck, but that doesn't matter, because you've met the rules for calling it a duck."

And there was the ultimate problem. With Enron's financial team working feverishly to exploit the rules, there was no one willing to say that the duck was still a dog. Because they could come up with plausible rationales for why a given structure was technically valid, they believed they were on the right side of the law. They were, in fact, proud of what they were doing. In their view, they were doing what every other company was doing, except that they were doing it better and smarter, because they were Enron, where everything was done better and smarter. But while people at Enron were smart about bending the rules, they were not smart at all about understanding where all that bending was taking them.

Besides, hadn't the outside auditors at Arthur Andersen signed off on the transactions and structures Fastow and his crew were devising? Hadn't Enron's longtime accountants bestowed their blessing on all that financial cleverness? For that matter, hadn't Arthur Andersen been intimately involved in helping Enron set up these structures—as well as helping to devise the accounting treatment? After all, the outside auditors are the ones who sign off on publicly filed financial statements, giving their word that they "present fairly, in all material respects" the financial condition of a company. They are supposed to be stick-in-the-muds who say no far more often than they say yes.

The accountants should have been a potent check on Fastow. But Andersen, despite having more qualms than Causey or any other high-ranking executive inside the company, had great difficulty saying no to Enron. The accountants in Arthur Andersen's Houston office worked so closely with Enron that they came to see the world in the same way as Enron executives. Nor did they want to risk losing one of their biggest clients. This was also part of the modern bull market: a gradual disintegration of the high standards that accountants had once proudly upheld.

There is a sad irony in the fact that Arthur Andersen was brought down by the Enron scandal. For much of its history, Andersen was the most upright of the nation's accounting firms and took enormous pride in that reputation. An accounting firm's primary allegiance is supposed to be to the investing public, not the company whose books it is auditing. No firm took that mission as seriously as Arthur Andersen. It was founded in 1913 by a Northwestern University professor (whose name, naturally enough, was Arthur Andersen). One of the firm's early mottos was "think straight, talk straight," a saying from his Norwegian mother. Andersen was a principled, even self-righteous, man, and the firm's lore is full of stories about his standing up to the corporations that employed his accountants. Once, in the firm's young and lean years, Andersen auditors told a railway company client that it had to change a certain accounting practice, to the detriment of reported profits. When the company's president demanded that the firm reverse itself or lose the account, Andersen famously retorted that "There is not enough money in the city of Chicago" to make him change the firm's decision. (Throughout its life, Chicago was Andersen's home base.) Andersen lost the account. Months later the railroad company was bankrupt.

Arthur Andersen started the first training school for accountants, recruiting young men straight out of college so he could indoctrinate them in the Andersen way. They all had to dress the same, use the same methods, offer the same level of service, and uphold the same high standards. Competitors seethed at what they saw as Andersen's arrogance and labeled its staffers Androids. The founder could not have cared less.

Andersen's successor, Leonard Spacek, who ran the firm from 1947 to 1963, was every bit as principled and every bit as self-righteous, often publicly scolding his profession for—as he put it in a 1957 speech—"failing to square its so-called principles with its professional responsibility to the public." He regularly berated the Securities and Exchange Commission for not doing a good enough job rooting out accounting fraud, claiming that the SEC was "at best a brake on the rate of retrogression in the quality of accounting," and continued his crusade for high standards even after he'd retired from the firm. The Financial Accounting Standards Board, which was formed in 1973, came about largely because of Spacek's incessant lobbying.

Spacek was also interested in computers and technology, and when employees came to him with an idea—that Andersen should help corporations figure out how to use these complicated new machines—he helped push it forward, setting up the industry's first consulting arm. What he failed to realize was that consulting would play a major role in corrupting both the accounting profession and Andersen itself.

Over time, consulting became the tail that wagged the dog. Consulting divisions—which included not only computer assistance but business strategy and risk management, among other things—grew much faster than the auditing divisions, which at many firms became practically loss leaders to help get the consultants in the door. The consultants themselves generated far more money than their accounting counterparts and had far more status. Along with the rise of consulting came a new focus on the bottom line. Accountants hired to audit a company's books were also expected to help persuade their clients to use the firm's consultants as well. By the 1990s, there were few firms willing to quit an account on principle, as Arthur Andersen had done so long ago; there was simply too much money at stake. Not surprisingly, accounting standards eroded, and accounting fraud mushroomed.

At Andersen, the growth and success of its consulting division, Andersen Consulting, led to a long, simmering feud between the accountants and the consultants. In a partnership where profits were shared, the situation became so bitter that in 1989 the consultants were spun off into a separate business unit, but they were still required to share their profits with their poorer audit cousins. (In 1997, the consulting side produced 56 percent of the firm's revenues—and consulting was growing at nearly twice the rate of auditing.) As a firm, Andersen had two cultures, the sleek, self-satisfied consultants—and the downtrodden auditors who only had to look across the hallway to see that they weren't keeping up. In December 1997, after several years of open warfare, the consultants voted to split off entirely. The auditors demanded over $14 billion; in 2000, a judge ruled that they would get just $1 billion. The Andersen accountants, left with a slow-growing audit business—it was the smallest of the Big Five accounting firms—began aggressively building a new consulting arm of their own. The pressure to generate fees was intense, and so was the pressure to hold on to clients. Even before Enron, Andersen had been embroiled in several high-profile accounting scandals, including Sunbeam and Waste Management.

In the Waste Management case, Andersen paid $75 million to settle civil lawsuits, agreed to pay a $7 million fine to the SEC, and promised not to repeat its conduct. In the wake of its settlement with the SEC, the firm circulated a memo to all its partners: "One of the most important lessons from litigation involving our profession is that client selection and retention are among the most important factors in determining our risk exposure. . . . have the courage to say no to relationships that bring unacceptable levels of risk to our firm."

Andersen had long since abandoned its founder's old motto, "think straight, talk straight"; instead, its new slogan was "simply the best." But by the late 1990s, "simply the best" had a different meaning than it might once have had at Arthur Andersen. Those partners who were viewed internally as simply the best were the ones who kept their clients happy, especially the handful of clients Andersen labeled its crown jewels. Enron was one of them.

Practically from the day Enron was formed, the company was a big client for Andersen's Houston office. Between 1988 and 1991, Andersen earned $54 million in fees from Enron. By the late 1990s, that number had skyrocketed; in 2000 alone, Enron paid Arthur Andersen $52 million, over half for consulting services. Enron was one of Andersen's top four clients, and it dominated the attention of the Houston office, which, thanks to its aggressive energy practice, was the largest and most profitable office in the firm. Within Andersen, the Houston office had a reputation: it was the place to go if you wanted to make partner quickly, and the Enron account was a large part of the reason why. In addition to its external auditing, Andersen at various times also had consulting contracts to handle Enron's internal auditing and was in charge of auditing Enron's internal-control system.

Even that doesn't begin to describe how close Andersen and Enron were. Over the years, Enron hired at least 86 Andersen accountants, who were lured by the promise of higher pay and Enron stock options. Over time, many important finance jobs at the company were held by people who had worked on the Enron account at Arthur Andersen. Andersen often complained that Enron was raiding its staff, but the firm was also rather proud of it. Although Arther Andersen's Houston office was just a few blocks from the Enron building, most of the 100 or so Andersen employees who worked on the Enron account spent almost no time there; *their* offices were at Enron, where they worked alongside the company's own accountants. They adopted the same business-casual style that was prevalent at Enron, making it hard to tell who was the auditor and who was the client. "It was like these very bright geeks at Andersen suddenly got invited to this really cool, macho frat party," Leigh Anne Dear, a former Andersen accountant, told the *Chicago Tribune*.

In April 2000, when Arthur Levitt, then the SEC chairman, tried to force accounting firms to separate their consulting and accounting practices, Enron leapt to its accountant's defense. "For the past several years, Enron has successfully utilized its independent audit firm's expertise and professional skepticism to help improve the overall control environment within the company," wrote Ken Lay to the agency. "I believe independent audits of the internal control environment are valuable to the investing public. . . ." After a bitter fight, Levitt largely backed down.

Enron and Andersen even bragged about their closeness in a promotional video. "We basically do the same types of things . . . we're trying to kinda cross lines and trying to, you know, become more of just a business person here at Enron," said one Arthur Andersen accountant in the video. Added another, "Being here full time year round day to day gives us a chance to chase the deals with them and participate in the deal making process. . . ."

The person who best symbolized the unseemly closeness between the company and its accounting firm was David Duncan, who was just 38 years old when he was put in charge of the Enron account in 1997. Born in Lake Charles, Louisiana, and raised in Beaumont, Texas, Duncan joined Andersen's Houston office in 1981, straight out of Texas A&M. Rick Causey started at the firm around the same time, and the two men became fast friends. That didn't change after Causey moved to Enron. They often lunched together at Nino's, an Italian restaurant frequented by Enron and Andersen employees. They co-chaired the Open Heart Open, a Houston golf tournament that benefited the American Heart Association. On at least one occasion, Causey took Duncan and a handful of Andersen accountants to the Masters. Duncan also served on the American Council for Capital Formation—one of Charls Walker's groups—with Ken Lay.

Did this bother anyone at Andersen? Actually, it did, but not the people who mattered. There were accountants among the rank and file who thought that Duncan was far too close to his client. But most of Duncan's bosses viewed him as a rising star who did exactly what he was supposed to do—generate 20 percent to 25 percent in additional fees from Enron each year. Duncan had become a partner in 1995 and took over the Enron account two years later; by 2000, his annual salary hovered around $1 million. He was on Arthur Andersen's firmwide strategic advisory council and in the fall of 2001 was invited to join chairman Joe Berardino's advisory council, which consisted of just 21 partners. At the time of Enron's collapse, he had a shiny life with his wife and three daughters and an expensive house in Houston's affluent Memorial area. All thanks to the Enron account.

The problem, of course, wasn't merely that Duncan was going to the Masters with Causey; it was that he saw things the way the client wanted him to see them and gave his assent to Enron accounting treatments that bore little relationship to economic reality. Did he know how far out on the edge Enron's accounting was? Of course he did. But he was being rewarded at Andersen for keeping the client happy—and that meant becoming every bit as creative as Enron was.

Within the firm, Enron was labeled "high risk." That in itself was not unique; Andersen had other clients in the same category. But over the years, the firm's internal notes on Enron showed just how high risk this client was. "Client is a first mover, and expects to push the edges of established convention, and where they can, create new convention . . . often in very gray areas," wrote one partner in early 2001. "The transactions are complex, and there is no clear written literature with respect to these transactions," noted another. Enron, said Andersen, had a "dependence on transaction execution to meet financial objectives." An internal Andersen appraisal of the client noted that Enron's "accounting and financial risk" were "very significant." Andersen said the same thing about Enron's use of "form over substance" transactions.

"There are a number of areas," the firm pointed out to Enron's board in a 2000 audit update, "where accounting rules have not kept up with the company's practices. . . . Categorization of activities between certain segments, operating vs. non-operating or recurring vs. non-recurring can be highly judgmental." Duncan's own appraisal of Enron's accounting? "Obviously we are on board with all of these [transactions]," he jotted in a handwritten note after Andersen had completed its 1998 audit, "but many push limits and have a high 'others could have a different point of view' risk profile."

But just like the Enron executives, Duncan couldn't see where the cumulative effect of his decisions was leading. Yes, all the incentives inside Andersen pushed him to see things the way the clients wanted him to see them: his big salary, his rapid rise, his status inside the firm were utterly dependant on keeping Enron happy. But he had started smoking the dope, too, abandoning the auditor's role of skeptic and becoming a believer himself. Enron was a great company, wasn't it? Enron's finance executives were whizzes. They were all on the cutting edge. Sure, they were stretching the rules, but the Andersen team always had a rationale as to why they weren't *breaking* the rules. Given the firm's experience with the Waste Management scandal, the firm could hardly afford another big accounting scandal. Yet in signing off on one risky accounting treatment after another, that was the very large risk Duncan was taking. And he never seemed to realize it until it was much too late.

What about those times Andersen did object to an Enron transaction? At such times, Enron put the firm under intense pressure. There were times when Causey and others would ask that certain accountants who weren't "responsive" enough be moved, and Duncan complied. Knowing just how important the $1 million-a-week account was to Andersen, Enron also kept competing firms lurking in the wings. From time to time, Causey would throw a small bit of business to Ernst & Young or PricewaterhouseCoopers, just enough to remind Andersen who was running the show. Inside Global Finance, Arthur Andersen was viewed as "a manageable issue," says a former Enron employee. "They were pretty easy to push around and bully into doing whatever we wanted them to do." A midlevel Andersen accountant named Patricia Grutzmacher later testified in court, "When you look at a deal and you give the answer no, and then they appeal the no, and the answer ends up being yes, you just wonder, you know, why are you even there?"

Andersen had a small elite group that formed something called the Professional Standards Group, which was supposed to make independent rules on particularly tricky accounting issues. Starting around 1999, more and more of the PSG's time was consumed by Enron; at one point, Andersen's Houston office was calling the PSG practically on a daily basis. The PSG was supposed to have the final word on any technical accounting question. If the client team wanted to reject the advice, the issue was supposed to be settled by higher-ups at the firm. In addition, the team was supposed to speak to the client with one voice. But Causey understood how the PSG worked and insisted that he be consulted when Enron accounting issues were brought to the PSG's attention. As Duncan told his partners, Enron demanded "more face time with Chicago to ensure their views are heard directly." Causey expected Duncan to be Enron's advocate in dealings with the PSG. Duncan obliged.

These weren't just issues that cropped up at the end. The cross-fertilization between client and firm, the willingness of Andersen to push the envelope on accounting decisions, the aggressiveness with which Enron pressed the accountants to see things its way—those were there, in one form or another, for years. As early as 1995, back when Kinder was still president of the company, a Houston-based Andersen auditor named James Hecker decided to have a little fun at Enron's expense. Hecker never worked on the Enron account, but at lunches and other social occasions, he would hear auditors on the Enron account talk about strategies to "minimize losses" and take liabilities "off the balance sheet." He heard chatter that Enron was, as he later put it, "very opportunistic in trying to achieve objectives." Hecker later used the word "shambolic" to describe Enron's accounting, not that it was completely a sham but that it was substantively illogical, like a duck that's really a dog. One day, Hecker wrote a parody, which he showed to a few colleagues. Sung to the tune of "Hotel California," he called it the "Hotel Kenneth-Lay-a":

Welcome to the Hotel Mark-to-Market
Such a lovely face
Such a fragile place
They livin' it up at the
Hotel Cram-It-Down-Ya
When the suits arrive, bring your alibis

Mirrors on the 10-K, makes it look real nice
And she said, we only make disclosures here
Of our own device
And in the partners' chambers
Cooking up a new deal
3% in an SPE
But they just can't make it real

Last thing I remember I was running for the doors
I had to find the entries back
To the GAAP we had before
"Relax," said the client
"We are programmed to succeed
You can audit any time you like
But we will never bleed"

Just as the cozy relationship between Enron and Andersen wasn't a secret, it was also no secret on Wall Street that Enron was an aggressive user of structured finance devices such as special purpose entities (that's the SPE in Hecker's song), securitizations, and off-balance-sheet partnerships. "If there was a whiz-bang structure somebody had, the place to sell it was down there on Smith Street, because they were buying," says one banker. Andy Fastow's team, says another banker, were "black belts in structured finance."

"It started out as pure, clear, legitimate deals," says a former senior Enron executive. "And each deal gets a little bit messier and messier. We started out just taking one hit of cocaine, and the next thing you know, we're importing the stuff from Colombia."

CHAPTER 11

Andy Fastow's Secrets

In the spring of 1998, shortly after Andy Fastow became Enron's chief financial officer, he approached Jeff Skilling about using the equity markets to raise money. Selling new shares of stock is one of the most common ways a corporation can raise capital, and in the middle of a roaring bull market, it's one of the easiest ways as well. Unlike debt, the money never has to be paid back; investors are betting that the company will use the capital wisely and that the stock will go up as a result. If it doesn't, the investors, not the company, take the hit.

Although Enron clearly needed capital—it had by then billions in debt and was preparing to spend billions on new business ventures—Skilling and Lay were cool to the idea. Skilling, in particular, was opposed to anything that might hurt the stock price, even temporarily. That's always the danger when new shares flood the market: the new supply can outstrip the demand for the stock and push the price down. Additional shares also make it harder to hit an earnings-per-share number because there are more shares outstanding. As they say on Wall Street, existing shareholders are diluted.

But Fastow countered that the stock market would easily absorb the shares; Enron hadn't sold a significant amount of stock in five years, and its executives could surely tell a compelling story. Eventually, Skilling and Lay relented, and Enron raised some $800 million in the offering. Less than a year later, Enron sold more stock. But after that, although Andy Fastow and his group at Global Finance generated billions of dollars of new capital for Enron, never again did they do a financing as simple and straightforward as an equity offering. By then, the era of Enron's financial subterfuge had begun in earnest.

In Finance 101, there are only three ways for companies to fund their growth. They can take on debt, issue stock, or draw from their existing cash flow. Enron had committed to Wall Street that it was going to grow rapidly; that was an essential element of the Enron "story." But all three of these tactics were ruled out at Enron. The company couldn't put too much debt on its balance sheet because that would hurt its credit rating (and banks would stop lending if Enron's debt ratios got out of whack). Nor could it use existing cash flow, since Enron didn't have much real cash flow. And although the equity market was, indeed, available, Skilling had made it clear that he didn't want to tap it often.

Yet Enron continued to fund its growth—to the tune of billions of dollars each year—through the miracle of structured finance. Structured finance enabled Enron to raise capital off its balance sheet to an extent no one imagined possible. According to an Enron board presentation, Fastow's Global Finance group was raising around $20 billion worth of capital a *year,* mostly through structured finance deals. As Fastow himself once told the board, his job was to "feed the beast."

In business terms, it was as if the company had discovered a way to defy the laws of gravity. Using off-balance-sheet vehicles and other complex transactions, Enron seemed to be able to make money magically appear without either adding debt or issuing stock. And that's precisely how many Enron executives felt, especially those who worked directly for Fastow: they thought they *were* magicians, reinventing corporate finance, rewriting the rules of the game, thumbing their nose at the way business had always been done.

One wonders now whether Fastow recognized that he was creating an illusion, especially as the pressure increased, and the sums became larger, and the chicanery required to pull it all off grew more brazen. For the most part, Fastow seemed to exhibit great pride in the work he was doing—he even bragged about some of Enron's more clever structures. But every once in a while, he would show that he could glimpse a more terrifying reality. Once, a banker asked him what would happen to Enron if the deal flow ever stopped.

"It implodes," Fastow responded.

Fastow's role made him the kind of figure he'd always wanted to be at Enron: truly indispensable. He had never stopped seething over the fact that people in finance weren't considered as important at Enron as the deal makers or the traders, and part of his motivation was to change that perception. Thus, within months of taking on the CFO role, he tripled the finance staff to over 100 and, as he later boasted, "transformed finance" into an internal capital-raising machine. He set up the group to resemble nothing so much as an investment bank, up to and including selling its services to other parts of the company. (In fact, Enron even set up a small group that tried to capture underwriting fees on the company's own deals.) One in-house presentation laid out all the things that Global Finance could do for Enron's divisions. The aim, the presentation declared, was "to craft solutions to help business units achieve their goals. . . . Common business unit goals include earnings, fund flows . . . balance sheet management, return on invested capital." Later, after explaining the various vehicles Global Finance had at its disposal to "craft solutions," the presentation added, "There is no obligation to use these vehicles. They are one option for achieving business unit goals." But of course almost every part of Enron used them, even the divisions run by executives who detested Fastow.

Like its leader, the top executives in Global Finance all had chips on their shoulders. Their attitude, says a former finance executive, was that "we're working really hard to fix the mistakes the rest of the company is making." They worked terrible hours. To anyone who crossed them, they could be verbally abusive: one person described theirs as a "bully culture." The finance executives resented having to clean up behind the deal makers who dug the holes and resented even more, as one employee put it, "that the people who dug the holes walked off with the loot." Because they were the ones who saved the company every quarter, they saw themselves as heroes. As an in-house lawyer named Kristina Mordaunt, who worked for a period in Global Finance, later told investigators: "Everyone was applauding the finance team for its efforts. Enron was hiring smart investment bankers, creating new structures, and getting the market used to them. . . ."

One of the few high-ranking Enron executives who ever expressed concern about Fastow was Cliff Baxter, though he, too, found times when he had to rely on Global Finance. He'd often complained to Skilling that Fastow was a little too clever. Baxter used to say that it was always worth paying a little more to ensure that a deal was clean. With Fastow, he'd add, you could never tell whether deals were clean because they were so complicated.

Even with his new higher profile, Fastow remained a shadowy figure to the rank and file. He didn't seem to care whether people outside his own small circle liked him. He spent most of his time with members of his own group and with the bankers and investment bankers who aided and abetted the Global Finance team. Under his leadership, Global Finance was tight-knit, secretive, and seemingly untouchable. Soon after taking over corporate finance, Fastow began freezing out Bill Gathmann, the corporate treasurer, by holding meetings without him. (Gathmann was soon replaced by an executive named Jeff McMahon.) And while the Global Finance staff could sit in on meetings taking place in other parts of Enron, outsiders were not allowed to attend Global Finance meetings. Just as Skilling had gathered loyalists around him, so did Fastow.

The most important Fastow disciples were a pair of executives named Michael Kopper and Ben Glisan. Kopper, who was three years younger than Fastow, arrived at Enron in 1994. A Long Island native, he went to Duke and the London School of Economics and was working in structured finance for Toronto Dominion bank when Enron came calling. He was 29 when he joined the company.

Kopper wasn't the person from Toronto Dominion whom Enron wanted to hire. Enron had been recruiting Kopper's boss, a more senior banker named Kathy Lynn; she brought him with her into the company. (Although Kopper joined at a fairly junior level, he still got a signing bonus of $20,000 and a salary of about $85,000 a year.) But Kopper quickly leapfrogged Lynn, becoming fast friends with both Fastow and his wife, Lea. In an early performance review, Rick Causey noted that Kopper was a "valuable asset to Enron" and good at "keeping the banks focused on Enron's goals"; he ranked him in the top 10 percent. Later reviews add that Kopper "conveys a win-win attitude." (Perhaps as testimony to how worthless the reviews could be, Kopper's reviews also claim that his "deals are structured so that they are always clear . . . no unnecessary complexity," that "risks are clearly identified," and that Kopper "sacrifices personal good for others and the team.") The only critical comment: "customers sometimes think you negotiate too hard." Of course at Enron, that wasn't necessarily a bad thing. In 1996, Kopper signed a new employment agreement, giving him a salary of $135,000, a signing bonus of $100,000, and guaranteed bonuses of $100,000 for each of the next two years. By 1997, Kopper headed Fastow's special projects group.

Kopper was gay, and over the years, he became more open within the company about his sexuality. Fastow could not have cared less; his reaction upon learning that Kopper was gay was "So what?" Kopper and his partner Bill Dodson, who worked in finance at Continental Airlines, lived in a starkly contemporary house that featured a glass staircase. The two traveled widely, and within Enron, Kopper was known as a jet-setter and a fashion hound who favored Prada suits. Although Kopper made over $1 million in cash salary and bonus in 2000—and had millions in Enron stock—those who know him could see how it wouldn't be enough. "Given the opportunity to make money, he wouldn't spend much time thinking about it," says a former executive.

Within Enron, Kopper was even less well known than Fastow. After Enron's bankruptcy, Ken Lay said he didn't even know who Kopper was. Some of those who did know him, though, disliked him intensely. He was temperamental and difficult to work with—and in doing his boss's bidding, he amplified Fastow's flaws. "He would wind Andy up, tell tales, and make it worse," says one former executive. "People wouldn't cross him because they knew there would be an explosion from Andy." People who knew them both also considered Kopper smarter than Fastow; some view Kopper, not Fastow, as the brains behind the most complicated of Enron's off-balance-sheet vehicles. Says one former executive: "Kopper would make the bullets, and Fastow would fire them."

The other Fastow disciple, Glisan, joined Enron as a 30-year-old accountant in late 1996. Like Kopper, Glisan also shot through the ranks. But to insiders, Glisan didn't seem anything like Kopper or Fastow—at least at first. When he joined Enron, he wasn't arrogant or hot-tempered, and he got along with just about everybody. A native Texan who grew up in a blue-collar neighborhood outside of Houston, Glisan seemed thrilled to have made it as far as he had—at one point, Kopper described him as a "workhorse carrying one of the heaviest loads in the group." He struck many people as a Boy Scout who wasn't capable of imagining a dishonest deed, much less carrying one out.

Glisan came to Enron the same way so many others did, through Arthur Andersen's Houston office. He attended the University of Texas, where he majored in finance, graduating in 1988. After working as a lending officer at Bank One in Austin, he went back to UT for his MBA, where he earned a 4.0 grade point average. He then joined Coopers & Lybrand in Dallas as one of two MBAs hired into a pilot management development program to provide "audit and consulting services on high-risk engagements" (a small irony). In January 1995, Glisan accepted a position in Arthur Andersen's Houston office, where he worked mainly on ECT. He stayed for only a year and half, at a salary of $66,000, before being recruited to Enron, where his salary increased to just over $100,000. (He also got a signing bonus of $15,000 and, of course, the promise of lots of options.)

Glisan was a highly skilled accountant who understood all of the nuances of his craft. "He was very clued up about accounting," says another Enron accountant. "He knew exactly what to say to bankers and accountants to appease any concerns they might have." In a 1999 review, Kopper wrote that Glisan knew "exactly when and how to make trades and negotiate a deal." (He also wrote that Glisan was "always working to create solutions with Enron's best interests in mind.") One person who worked closely with Glisan saw something else. If he saw something unethical, says this executive, "Ben was not mature enough to make a noise and stop it." Another former executive puts it this way: "He wasn't willing to be his own guy." Over time, Glisan's affability slowly morphed into the swaggering arrogance that characterized so many Enron executives. "It was painful when he didn't get his way," says an ex-colleague. "He would browbeat people."

Like many Enron executives, Fastow used the semiannual Performance Review Committee to push his people ahead and buy their loyalty. Though the original purpose of the PRC had become largely perverted, most executives at least went through the motions. Fastow didn't bother. "People were expected to cite anecdotal evidence and provide rational backup," says one former senior executive. "Andy didn't do that. He just dug his heels in." Skilling was the only one who could get Fastow to back off, but if he didn't rein Fastow in, the group would often just cave and give Fastow's people the top ranking so they could move on and go home.

The public high point for Fastow came in 1999, when *CFO Magazine* gave him a CFO Excellence Award, an honor he'd actively campaigned for. "Our story is one of a kind," Fastow told the magazine. He explained that Enron couldn't dilute its shareholders by issuing equity, and couldn't jeopardize its credit rating by issuing debt. He went on to describe how Enron issued off-balance-sheet debt, backing it up with Enron stock. This was the tactic that later triggered Enron's final crisis. But in 1999, with Enron's stock on the rise, its credit-rating intact, and its earnings headed ever upward, there wasn't so much as a whisper of doubt or complaint. On the contrary. "He has invented a groundbreaking strategy," said a Lehman Brothers banker quoted approvingly in the story. An analyst at one of the credit-rating agencies touted Fastow's ability to "think outside the box." And Skilling took the opportunity to publicly celebrate his protégé. "We needed someone to rethink the entire financing structure at Enron. . . . [Fastow] deserves every accolade tossed his way."

• • •

There are several different ways to think about Andy Fastow's deals. One is in terms of what was disclosed. Contrary to popular belief, many of the entities Enron created to play its financial games were not only revealed in the company's publicly filed financial documents but were things Fastow was only too happy to boast about. Wall Street analysts often mentioned the company's "innovative" financing tools in their reports. Credit-rating agencies knew about much of Enron's off-balance-sheet debt. But there were other deals in which the circle of outsiders in the know was small—and the disclosure in Enron's financial documents was purposely vague—because Enron knew that real disclosure would raise too many questions. And finally, there were deep, dark secrets that no one knew about except Fastow and his closest associates, including Kopper and Glisan.

A second way to think about the deals is in terms of their purpose. All the structured-finance deals Fastow and his team cooked up were meant to accomplish a fairly simple set of goals: keep fresh debt off the books, camouflage existing debt, book earnings, or create operating cash flow. At their absolute essence, the deals were intended to allow Enron to borrow money—billions upon billions of dollars that it needed to keep itself going—while disguising the true extent of its indebtedness. What made Enron's transactions so bewildering was not their purpose so much as their sheer multiplicity. Enron would mutate every vehicle it created to strip more and more accounting benefits from it and would often use one vehicle as a building block for another, so that unraveling one transaction would mean unraveling a half-dozen others. "It looks like some deranged artist went to work one night," is how Enron's postbankruptcy CEO, Steven Cooper, summed up the resulting tangle.

To see how Enron used these building blocks—and how they mutated in complexity—consider a structure called Whitewing. Whitewing began life in December 1997 as something called a minority-interest transaction, which took advantage of various accounting rules governing the way business ventures with third parties are reported in a company's financial statements. Enron borrowed $579 million from Citigroup and then raised another $500 million, mostly debt from an entity affiliated with Citi, plus a sliver of equity from other investors. Whitewing, in turn, used this money to buy $1 billion in Enron preferred stock. (The remaining $79 million was used to help pay the investors their return.)

The Whitewing structure was not a secret—it was disclosed in Enron's financial statements—but the $500 million showed up on the financial statements not as debt but as a minority interest in a joint venture. "The primary purpose of the transaction had been to convert debt to equity" is how corporate treasurer Jeff McMahon later described the transaction to Enron's board. That was true only in a technical sense. The $500 million hadn't been converted; it had only been disguised. Enron was still responsible for paying the money back. This was one of the first times that Enron used its stock—the value of the preferred shares in Whitewing—to support an off-balance-sheet financing. It was not the last.

This time, the bet on Enron stock was highly successful. Within a few years, the value of the preferred stock Whitewing owned had risen substantially. So Fastow's team decided to pay back Citigroup, issue yet more debt, and remove Whitewing from Enron's balance sheet altogether. It did so in a fall 1999 deal that Ben Glisan put high on his list of accomplishments for that year. In order to move Whitewing off its balance sheet, Enron needed more independent equity. So it created an entity called Osprey, which, through yet another entity, raised $100 million in "equity" (actually, certificates that paid a fixed return) from various banks and insurance companies. At least $1 million of that supposedly independent money came from a handful of investment bankers at Donaldson, Lufkin & Jenrette, the firm that was paid to sell the deal. Then, Osprey sold another $1.4 billion in debt to institutional investors. That $1.5 billion was used to buy a "limited partnership interest" in Whitewing. Under accounting rules, Whitewing now qualified for off-balance-sheet treatment: it was partly owned by that ostensible third party, Osprey. About one-third of the new money went to pay back Citigroup's original Whitewing loan. The remainder was set aside to purchase assets from Enron. Whitewing was precisely the kind of vehicle that Fastow's Global Finance team marketed internally to help business units meet their financial goals.

And what was supporting that $1.4 billion in debt? (Which was also not a secret: in fact, the credit rating agencies *rated* that debt.) Mainly, it was the value and dividends from the Enron preferred stock plus the value of the assets Whitewing bought. But that wasn't all. Enron also promised that if the assets in Whitewing weren't sufficient to pay back the money—which would come due in early 2003—it would make up the difference by issuing stock. And if it couldn't issue enough stock, it would pay cash. There were also triggers built in to reassure investors: If Enron's credit rating fell below investment grade and, in addition, its stock fell below $28, the investors could demand to be paid back immediately. In other words, although the Osprey debt was technically off-balance-sheet, investors and rating agencies knew that the obligation ultimately belonged to Enron. As if there was any doubt about whose debt it really was, all they had to do was flip open the Osprey offering document, which is all about . . . *Enron*. Later, in 2000, Osprey sold approximately $1 billion in additional debt. As part of the inducement to new investors, Enron raised the trigger price on its stock to $59.78.

Thus was Enron stock supporting a pool of debt that was being used to buy Enron's assets and create cash flow. If that sounds like impossibly circular logic, in commonsense terms it was. According to the court-appointed examiner in the Enron bankruptcy case, the company used the Whitewing structure to buy at least $1.6 billion in assets from various divisions in the company. The examiner also says that Whitewing was, in effect, used to refinance hundreds of millions in Enron debt.

Another kind of minority-interest transaction took place toward the end of 1999, when Enron was desperate to show cash flow. In a deal called Project Nahanni, Enron, in essence, borrowed $485 million from Citigroup and raised a sliver of equity ($15 million) through a minority-interest financing, used that money to buy Treasury bonds, sold the Treasury bonds, and booked the proceeds as cash flow from operations under the pretext that buying and selling bonds was part of Enron's day-to-day business. That $500 million represented a staggering 41 percent of the total $1.2 billion in operating cash flow that Enron reported that year. Then, right after the first of the year, when the camouflage was no longer necessary, Enron repaid Citi. Over the years, there were many more minority-interest financings, with names like Rawhide, Choctaw, and Zephyrus, all done with Wall Street's help, that allowed Enron to pretty up its financial statements.

A second tool Enron relied on was Skilling's old friend, securitization (which is also known by the accounting statute, FAS 140, that governs it). By the late 1990s, securitization was no longer considered an exotic form of financing. All kinds of companies were using securitizations for all kinds of purposes. Banks, of course, securitized credit card loans, and retail companies securitized receivables. Composers were also securitizing song royalties; states were securitizing the proceeds from tobacco litigation. Anything, it sometimes seemed, could be securitized. The point of the exercise had not changed: instead of waiting for money to trickle in over time, the owner of the asset estimated the value of the future cash flow, sold it off to investors at a discount, and pocketed the money it took in from the sale. To use a word Skilling loved—and that became a term of the art at Enron—it was a way to "monetize" assets.

As securitizations gained popularity, new wrinkles developed. One of the most important ones was the use of so-called special purpose entities, which were set up by companies specifically to purchase the assets being securitized. The original idea behind SPEs was to isolate risk by setting up an independent legal entity that owned just one asset—say, credit card receivables. The investors who controlled the independent entity would reap the gain, but they would also have to accept the risk of something going wrong. In any event, the asset was isolated from the rest of the company's business risks.

But if the companies themselves set up the SPEs, what exactly constituted independence? Amazingly, the rules developed by the accounting gurus stated that as long as 3 percent of the capital in the SPE came from an independent source and was truly at risk—meaning that it could all be lost if the deal went awry—the SPE qualified as independent. In other words, even if 97 percent of the capital consisted of debt raised by the company selling the assets, the company didn't have to include that debt on its balance sheet. (Don't search for the logic behind the 3 percent threshold. There isn't any. For years, there were some, including a few high-ranking accountants at Arthur Andersen, who argued that

3 percent was absurdly low.) Ken Lay later told investigators that while he could read a balance sheet, he did not understand the accounting requirements for SPEs until October 2001.

But though most of Enron's SPEs technically included the 3 percent of independent money, in fact, its entities were rarely truly independent. Enron gave implicit—sometimes explicit—guarantees that it would take care of the lenders. In addition, Enron often tossed a derivative called a total return swap into the mix. This security, in essence, meant that Enron guaranteed the investor a debtlike return; in exchange, Enron kept almost all of the real return. (Adding a classic Enron twist, the company would then mark-to-market the estimated value that it expected to receive from the asset.) To put it another way, Enron had "sold" something and booked earnings and cash flow from the "sale." But the asset wasn't truly gone; now there was a big slug of additional debt that had to be paid back within a few years. The court-appointed bankruptcy examiner later concluded that much of Enron's liquidity was the "result, in effect, of loans to Enron for which Enron retained the ultimate liability." He also contends that Enron did not properly disclose that liability to investors. People in RAC called these deals "boomerangs."

Over time, Enron securitized just about everything that wasn't nailed down— fuel-supply contracts, shares of common stock, partnership interests—and even some things that *were* nailed down. For instance, Enron securitized the profits it expected to generate from many of Rebecca Mark's international assets, including plants in Puerto Rico, Turkey, and Italy. In total, from 1997 to 2000, according to one analysis, Enron booked $366 million in net income from such power-plant securitizations.

Securitization, at least the way Enron did it, provided a great short-term boost. But as with so many other Enron deals, it created ticking time bombs of debt, debt that was rarely supported by the true value of the asset, because it was often based on unreasonably optimistic assumptions about what would happen over a period of years. "It was a purported sale, but it looked and smelled like a financing," as a former Enron International executive puts it. It also created holes for the future. After all, if you've generated earnings and cash from selling something, you can't claim those earnings or cash flow the next year or any year afterward. "Enron borrowed from the future until there was nothing left to borrow," says one Enron executive. "If shareholders understood the extent to which the future was being mortgaged . . ." ponders another. At the time of its bankruptcy, Enron had over $2 billion in off-balance-sheet debt related solely to securitizations.

While securitizations generated both cash and earnings, cash was too critical to the company to be a mere by-product. So Global Finance had a separate area that specialized in creating cash flow. As early as 1997, for instance, Enron came up with a convoluted way to raise cash by "selling" some of the gas stored in its huge Bammel facility to an SPE backed by Enron guarantees. The result: $152 million in cash, 72 percent of the total cash that Enron's operations generated in 1997.

The most important of Enron's cash-generating devices, though, was something called a prepay. The Enron bankruptcy examiner later called prepays the company's "quarter to quarter cash flow lifeblood." While there were many variations on the theme, here's how a typical one worked: Enron would agree to deliver natural gas or oil over a period of time to an ostensibly independent offshore entity that was, in fact, set up by one of its lenders. The offshore entity would pay Enron up front for these future deliveries with money it had obtained from the lender. The lender, in turn, agreed to deliver the same commodity to Enron; Enron would pay a fixed price for those deliveries over a period of time.

On the surface, these looked like separate transactions. But in reality, the commodity part of the deal canceled out, leaving Enron with a promise to pay a lender a fixed return on money it had received. In other words, it looked suspiciously like a loan with interest. Nevertheless, Enron listed prepays not as debt but as trading liabilities that were supposedly offset by trading assets. And although there are Enron finance executives who to this day claim that prepays *were* trading liabilities, one would be hard pressed to find an independent observer who would agree that they shouldn't have been classified as debt on Enron's books. The Enron bankruptcy examiner certainly didn't view them as legitimate. "These delivery requirements went from party to party around a circle with the result that the apparent assumption of price risk was illusory," he wrote in a report released in March 2003. "Thus, the transactions were in substance debt, funded by either large financial institutions or institutional investors."

Enron, which began using a version of prepays as early as 1992, quickly got hooked. According to an analysis done by the Senate Permanent Subcommittee on Investigations, Enron engaged in $8.6 billion (and possibly much more) of these transactions, mainly with a Chase Manhattan–sponsored entity located in the Channel Islands known as Mahonia and a Citigroup-backed entity called Delta. Not incidentally, these were lucrative deals for the banks: the *Wall Street Journal* estimated that Chase earned as much as $100 million in fees and interest from these deals.

In congressional hearings, both J. P. Morgan Chase and Citigroup denied that prepays were, technically speaking, loans, adding that Arthur Andersen had signed off on Enron's accounting—and that in any case they weren't responsible for Enron's accounting. (Chase Manhattan merged with J. P. Morgan on December 31, 2000. J. P. Morgan's dealings with Enron over the years were dwarfed by Chase's relationship with the company.) Another institution that transacted prepays with Enron, Credit Suisse First Boston (which acquired Donaldson, Lufkin & Jenrette in 2000), was concerned at one point about what its bankers called the "reputational risk" of one deal. Enron promised that its treasurer or CFO would sign off on it. So CSFB went ahead. Later, one banker described the prepay in an e-mail as "Ben's pet project."

But their internal e-mails and discussions leave no doubt that the banks understood what Enron was doing with prepays—and why:

"Enron loves these deals," wrote a Chase banker in a 1998 e-mail, "as they are able to hide funded debt from their equity analysts. . . ." And a Chase banker in a 1999 e-mail: "They are understood to be disguised loans and approved as such. . . ." In a deposition taken in a lawsuit that resulted from these transactions, a J. P. Morgan Chase employee recalls a senior Chase executive named Bob Mertensotto referring to the prepays as "smoke and mirrors." Citigroup understood the deals the same way Chase did. "E gets money that gives them c flow but does not show up on the books as big D Debt," a Citigroup banker wrote in a 2000 e-mail.

And both banks worked to reduce their own risk to Enron. Chase entered into some $1 billion worth of insurance contracts that were supposed to pay in the event Enron didn't. (After Enron's bankruptcy, J. P. Morgan Chase sued the insurance companies when they refused to pay. The insurers said that they hadn't known that the transactions were really loans.) For its part, Citigroup sold its risk to public investors through a series of notes. In its internal calculations of Enron's total debt, Citigroup included the prepays. But when it came to selling the risk to investors, it used Enron's financial statements—which were supposed to comply with GAAP accounting—and lumped prepays in with trading liabilities. Thus, while Citigroup didn't want to assess its own risk without seeing the full picture, it was perfectly willing to sell investors a more pleasing image. GAAP accounting, noted Citigroup internally, was the "least conservative analysis." ("Legal but sleazy" is what one senior Wall Streeter says.) Citigroup ultimately issued over $2 billion worth of such securities. From Enron's perspective, this was highly desirable, because now Citigroup could lend it even more money.

In contrast to structures like Whitewing, the prepays were very hush-hush, and Enron went to great lengths to keep it that way. An internal Enron presentation of one of the Citigroup deals touts its "unique 'black box' feature" and talks about "limiting disclosure." At one point, an institutional investor who bought the Citi securities learned something about the offshore entity Delta and began to make phone calls posing troublesome questions. An Enron e-mail to Citi read: "We need to shut this down."

How was Enron, which was perennially short of cash, going to pay off these loans, which had to be repaid on an ongoing basis? In theory, the company would use future cash flows from outstanding trades to pay them back. But that does not appear to have happened. Instead, Enron used fresh prepays to replace earlier ones. One executive says that before Kinder's departure in 1996, prepays never got above $200 million. After he left, they exploded. At the end of 1998, Enron had $1.3 billion in outstanding prepays; at the time of Enron's bankruptcy, it had almost $5 billion in outstanding prepays. In 1999, Enron's cash flow from operations would have been negative without prepays and Project Nahanni. "The banks liked it because Enron got addicted," says one former risk executive. "Enron had to repay the loan, but the cash flow didn't materialize. So it snowballed." Another Global Finance executive argues that as discrete transactions, the prepays make sense: "The problem is, Enron did them on steroids."

Actually, the problem was that nobody inside Global Finance thought any of this was a problem. Though the company was piling up truly astounding levels of debt—by the end, Enron owed some $38 billion, of which only $13 billion was on its balance sheet—the executives who made up Fastow's team seem to have barely thought about it. They certainly never added it all up, though that's precisely what responsible finance executives are supposed to do. Instead, the Enron finance executives thought about how much smarter they were than everybody else in American business. They also convinced themselves and their accountants that they were complying with GAAP accounting, though the mental gymnastics required to get there were often tortured, to say the least.

Indeed, they thought their work was giving the company a competitive advantage. In an in-house memo written toward the end of 1999, Kopper listed Glisan's goals for the year 2000. The only thing he mentioned was the need "to continue to provide innovative mechanisms for raising capital for Enron."

In another telling in-house memo, an executive named Joe Deffner, who was in charge of the prepays and became known as Enron's cash czar, wrote a self-evaluation in 2000 to his boss. Cash flow, he noted, "is probably the single most critical and difficult metric for Enron to achieve to maintain its BBB+ rating." (BBB+ is several notches higher than the minimum for a company to be considered investment grade.) He then noted that of the aggregate $9.7 billion of operating cash flow reported by Enron for 1995 to 2000, the SPE transactions he had worked on had accounted for 56 percent.

"To maintain our credit rating, if Enron were to finance itself primarily or solely through simpler on-balance-sheet reported structures, 40 percent of each transaction would be funded by the issuance of new debt and 60 percent through retained earnings or new equity," Deffner wrote; ". . . for 2000 I was responsible for the Global Finance team that generated approximately $5.5 billion of overall off-balance-sheet financing, which at a 60 percent equity allocation would have required $3.3 billion of new equity capital in 2000 to support a BBB+ rating. The value of avoiding . . . equity dilution is difficult for me to quantify although, as a shareholder, I know it's reflected in the valuation. . . ."

Far from worrying that he was helping Enron misrepresent the business, Deffner clearly believed that he deserved a big bonus.

Is it clear by now that Fastow and his Global Finance group could not have done what they did without plenty of help? They needed accountants to agree that prepays were a trading liability. ("Enron is continuing to pursue various structures to get cash in the door without accounting for it as debt," an Arthur Andersen employee wrote in 1998.) They needed lawyers to sign off on deal structures. They needed the credit-rating agencies to remain sanguine in the face of frightening levels of off-balance-sheet debt. Most of all, though, they needed the banks and the investment banks to help them carry out their machinations. Every bit as much as the accountants at Arthur Andersen, the banks and investment banks were Enron's enablers.

At the top of the list were two of the biggest banks in the country, Chase Manhattan and Citigroup. Enron's relationships with the two giant banking institutions went back practically to the company's beginnings. Chase had helped finance the merger between HNG and InterNorth that created Enron. Marc Shapiro, Chase's vice chairman in charge of finance and risk management, was well acquainted with Ken Lay; in the 1980s, he headed Houston-based Texas Commerce Bank, which Chase acquired in 1987. (Lay sat on the board of Texas Commerce for a period.) For its part, Citi helped Ken Lay fend off the corporate raider Irwin Jacobs back in 1987 by loaning Enron part of the $350 million it needed to buy out Jacobs's stake in the company.

It wasn't just Enron that had changed dramatically since those days; so had the two banks. They were both eager participants in the ongoing process of bank consolidation that swept the country throughout the 1990s, a process that created a small handful of giant national financial institutions. Chase, for instance, had been formed through a series of acquisitions that included three of the largest banks in New York: Chase Manhattan, Chemical Bank, and Manufacturer's Hanover. Citigroup, the parent company of Citibank, had transformed itself into the largest financial institution in the world; it included Travelers Insurance Group and the Salomon Smith Barney brokerage house.

More to the point, perhaps, both banks could offer their corporate clients not only loans but a full range of investment banking services, including stock underwriting and research. For decades, the Glass-Steagall Act had prevented banks and investment banks from encroaching on each other's turf, but during the 1980s and 1990s, Glass-Steagall had gradually been chipped away until Congress, in the face of furious lobbying, finally repealed it in 1999. Once that happened, the nation's big banks began using their lending prowess to land investment banking deals.

Few banks were as aggressive as Chase and Citigroup. From the banks' point of view, this made perfect sense: lending, though the most fundamental of banking activities, had devolved into a low-profit, low-margin enterprise, while investment banking, with its outsized fees, was one of the most profitable endeavors known to man. And few clients were as profitable as Enron. Fastow and his team were always in a hurry to complete a deal, and their deals were always far more complicated than a plain-vanilla underwriting. And there were so many of them. "There was something to play in, if you wanted, every month," says one banker who did business with Enron. "Behind every closed door, there was a deal going on at Enron," says another. The result was that Enron was willing to pay fees that few other companies would contemplate. By the late 1990s, Enron had become one of the largest payers of investment banking fees in the world. According to the company's own calculations, it paid out $237.7 million in fees in 1999 alone. By the end, Citi was reaping some $50 million a year from Enron.

This increased competition for investment banking fees made the banks not just eager to land business but practically desperate. Objectively, the party that should have felt desperate was Enron; it simply had to have a steady infusion of capital just to keep operating. But there were so many banks clamoring for those Enron fees that Fastow could keep them on a string just by playing them off against each other. This he did brilliantly. He tapped into their own greed, pitting banks against one another, forcing them to curry favor with him, and in so doing, he crafted one more Enron illusion. He made it appear that he was the one who held all the cards.

Part of the banks' desperation stemmed from Enron's place in the Wall Street nexus. Investment bankers, as a rule, tend to think they're a lot smarter than the company executives they're advising, but they didn't feel that way about those they were dealing with at Enron. Global Finance executives acted just like investment bankers. They spoke the same language. And the Enron people were just as smart as the bankers, or so the bankers believed. Since on Wall Street you are known by the people who choose you to do their business, it thus became a badge of honor to have a piece of the Enron account. "You weren't an energy banker if you weren't banking Enron," says one.

It was also true that the ethos of many investment banks was not all that different from the essential Enron mind-set. The ethics of their deals with Enron were never much of a concern among the bankers. "In investment banking, the ethic is, 'Can this deal get done?' " says a banker. "If it can and you're not likely to get sued, then it's a good deal." In their internal correspondence, it's almost impossible to find an instance of investment bankers' worrying about the propriety of what they were doing. When they worried at all, they were concerned about the perception. An e-mail from the head of risk management for Citigroup's investment banking division warned about one deal: "The GAAP accounting is aggressive and a franchise risk to us if there is publicity." The deal was done anyway.

Fastow worked exhaustively to squeeze everything possible from Enron's— and his own—relationship with the banks. This prerogative he guarded jealously, screaming at any Enron executive outside his fiefdom who dared to initiate contact with a bank without his permission. Baxter, in particular, chafed at this restriction; it was one of the key reasons for his animosity toward Fastow. Eventually both he and Dave Maxey, the hunter of lucrative tax deals, were allowed to call bankers without clearing it with Fastow.

In managing the banks, Fastow never missed an angle. He and his group knew how to hint that another had already agreed to do a deal, which of course made the bankers even more eager to land the business. He sometimes cast deal proposals as a "favor" that would be rewarded with more lucrative business later. He did not take no graciously. As CSFB banker Osmar Abib wrote after turning

down an Enron deal: "I am about to . . . get my head taken off by Michael Kopper and Kathy Lynn at the charitable dinner tonight sponsored by Enron . . . we
should all expect a blistering call from Fastow once he gets the feedback. . . ."
And there was no mistaking that Fastow was the man they had to please. Skilling
would sometimes drop in on meetings Fastow was holding with bankers, but he
was mostly window dressing. His appearances, says one banker, were mainly
meant to convey "I know the answer, and I'm right. I'm Jeff Skilling. And I'm
Enron—are we all clear here?" (Skilling later told people, "I'm not particularly
interested in the balance sheet. It seemed to be doing well. We always had
money.")

Fastow's most aggressive tactic was his internal ranking of the 70 or so banks
that did business with Enron. Fastow had his minions keep meticulous track of
the number of deals each had done with Enron and how much they'd received
in fees. The Global Finance team would look at the capital the banks had extended versus the investment-banking fees that they had earned. Enron saw the
investment-banking fees not as the price for advice—Enron, after all, didn't need
advice—but as a return on the capital. Then he divided all the banks into three
categories—Tier 1, Tier 2, and Tier 3—based on their willingness to do his
bidding.

As a 58-page document prepared for a January 2000 internal "relationship review" meeting of Enron's top finance executives describes it, the Tier 1 banks
had to be willing to lend large sums to Enron "when needed," be willing to "un-
derwrite $1 billion in short period of time," give Fastow ready access to their top
executives, and have a relationship officer "capable of delivering institution"—in
other words, someone who could make sure the bank didn't say no to an Enron
request. In return, says the document, "Enron will manage to a minimum 20%
ROE." Though Enron did not hold many people accountable internally, Fastow
was like Rich Kinder when it came to the banks. At that same relationship
review—which was an annual event—members of the Global Finance team discussed each bank's performance, and whether the bankers had gotten the "previous message" about what they needed to do to enhance their relationship with
the company. The session ended with cocktails.

Tier 1 status didn't necessarily go to the biggest or most prestigious banks.
The issue was explicitly how much you did for Enron—and how often you came
through in the clutch. One banker recalls Fastow's explaining just what it meant
to come through for him: "Giving us credit when we need it, typically at quarter-
end or year-end, when we need to sell assets. We'll buy them back and give you
a return on your capital." So Morgan Stanley and Goldman Sachs—two of the
most prestigious names on Wall Street, investment banks with conservative lending rules—sometimes found themselves consigned to Tier 3, with the likes of the
State Bank of India. Meanwhile, little-known firms like West LB and ABN Amro
were among the nine firms in Tier 1, right up there with Credit Suisse First
Boston, Citigroup, and Chase Manhattan. Fastow conferred Tier 1 status as

though it were something to be coveted, and he wasn't shy about telling banks that weren't in the top bracket what they needed to do to get there. "You guys have got to put up a little more capital if you want to make it to the big leagues," a Tier 2 banker recalls Fastow telling him.

Every year, Tier 1 bankers (no spouses, thank you) got invited to join Fastow and his top lieutenants on an expensive jaunt to some fancy locale. This was their reward. On one outing to Miami Beach, a Brazilian-themed dinner for 60 featured performances by a quartet of Capoeira acrobats, a pair of carnival dancers, and hand-rolled cigars. The entertainment alone cost $13,000. At another Tier 1 outing, this one to Las Vegas, Enron rented a fleet of 15 helicopters to fly the bankers over a mountain for dinner at a Nevada vineyard, to see the casino strip lit up at night, and to the Grand Canyon for a picnic. The total tab for one of these annual outings ran as high as $130,000.

Fastow even expected the banks that got Enron's business to contribute to his pet charities. A February 1998 Chase memo from Rick Walker, who was the relationship manager for Enron, reads: "In addition to our business relationships, Chase has endeavored to be supportive of the charitable causes sponsored by Enron and its executives. . . ."

Some bankers resented Fastow's manipulations—and his constant browbeating—even as they scrapped for the company's business. "Every once in a while, we had to step back and count to ten and say the client is the client, but . . ." remembers one banker. "They'd beat the crap out of the lawyers, they'd beat the crap out of the investment bankers, they'd beat the shit out of the accountants. There's zero loyalty to anything but that trade. It was hell doing business with them, but you had to because they were so big."

There were also lots of whispers in the banking world that Enron consumed incredible amounts of capital, that the company was way overleveraged, that, as one internal Citigroup e-mail explicitly put it, "Enron significantly dresses up its balance sheet for year-end." But despite the whispers—indeed, despite knowing far more than most people about what was really going on inside Enron—few bankers were willing to stop doing business with the company. They were hooked, too.

One of the things investment bankers get to do is invest their own money in deals they're working on; it's one of the sweeter perks of the job. That's one reason the investment bankers from Donaldson, Lufkin & Jenrette were able to put up some of the equity when Enron was putting together the Osprey deal. And it's why, over the years, investment bankers from Merrill Lynch and other Wall Street firms sometimes invested in Enron's deals. Since Andy Fastow saw himself as running his investment bank within Enron, he wanted to be able to invest in Enron's deals, too. Even though he was making, by the late 1990s, upward of $1 million in salary and bonus annually and had millions more in stock options, he wanted more. More than that, he felt that he *deserved* more.

This was not some belated itch Fastow suddenly needed to scratch. As early as 1995 he had approached investment bankers about setting up a partnership, with himself as its head, to buy Enron assets. The idea went nowhere. A few years later, Enron's law firm of Vinson & Elkins called a meeting to discuss the possibility of allowing Enron employees to make investments in company deals after Fastow brought it up again. A lawyer named Ron Astin said that he didn't think it was a good idea at all: such a partnership could appear to be a vehicle for favored employees and was likely to exacerbate rivalries between business units.

Fastow pressed the issue. After all, he said, investment bankers did it. Astin countered that Enron *wasn't* an investment bank; it was an energy company. He also told Fastow that if he insisted on pursuing the idea, he needed to get the explicit approval of both senior management and the board. Even so, he didn't think such a partnership was appropriate given Fastow's position as Enron's top finance executive.

What Astin didn't know—indeed, what almost no one outside a tiny circle of Global Finance executives knew—was that Fastow and several others were already investing in deals. One of the difficulties in setting up the off-balance-sheet vehicles Enron had come to rely on was finding that independent investor who would put up the 3 percent equity slice. And the more vehicles Enron set up, the harder it became. "Think about trying to raise equity and explain these deals on a true third-party basis," says one former Global Finance executive. "There's no way you could have done it."

So starting in the early 1990s, the Global Finance team pulled together a small group of investors known internally as the Friends of Enron. When Enron needed to find that 3 percent equity investor, it turned to the friends. One friend was a real-estate broker named Kathy Wetmore, who had helped many Enron executives find their homes, including Fastow and Kopper. Another was a woman named Patty Melcher, who was a friend of Fastow's wife, Lea. Fastow approached Melcher about investing in eight deals; she told the *New York Times* that she made investments ranging from $100,000 to $2 million in five deals. Of course, given the nature of their relationships with Enron executives, the "friends" were independent only in a technical sense. Though they made money on their investment, they hardly controlled the entities or the assets within them. Which, of course, was precisely the point.

In 1997, Fastow decided to take it one step further. That January, Enron bought a company called Zond, which owned some wind farms. Because wind farms provide alternative energy, they enjoy a legal status as qualifying facilities (QFs). QFs get certain government-mandated benefits, such as higher rates from electric utilities, which are required to buy power from them. However, those benefits disappear if the QF is more than 50 percent owned by a utility. In early 1997, Enron wasn't a utility, but it was about to become one, because of its pending acquisition of Portland General.

From Enron's point of view, the solution was simple: set up a special-purpose entity that would purchase Zond. That way, Enron would retain full control of the asset while the wind farms would be able to keep their government-granted benefits. (So much for the free market.) In May, Fastow and Kopper created two special-purpose entities known as the RADRs. The RADRs bought 50 percent of Enron's wind farms for approximately $17 million, 97 percent of it a loan from Enron. This time, instead of turning to the friends, Fastow and his wife, Lea, supplied most of the required $510,000 in independent equity themselves—but they hid that fact. In May 1997, according to the government, Lea Fastow wired $419,000 to Kopper, who then funneled the money to two other investors, one of them also an Enron employee.

No one probed deeply enough to uncover this deception. In fact, no one probed at all. Fastow told Enron's board that most of the money was a loan from Enron and that the transaction was "not a sale for book purposes": Enron retained all the risks and rewards associated with the projects and retained an option to repurchase the shares. In other words, the board was informed that Enron was using the RADRs as a place to park the wind-farm assets in order to retain government benefits to which it wasn't entitled. But according to the minutes of that meeting, not a single board member asked where the equity was coming from or challenged the transaction. The Federal Energy Regulatory Commission was given much of the same information but still approved the continuing QF status for Zond. (Later, Southern California Edison, which had to buy power from the Enron wind farms, complained that it was overcharged by as much as $176 million from July 1997 to April 2002.)

When investment bankers invest in a deal they're working on, the cards may be stacked in their favor, but the deal isn't rigged. The RADRs, though, were rigged; Fastow had seen to it that Enron guaranteed the RADRs a minimum return. In July 1997, the RADRs began to make distributions. According to the government, the investors of record paid Kopper, who in turn secretly paid Fastow, transferring, in late August, $481,850 from his Bank One account to a bank account in the name of Lea and Andrew Fastow. That represented an effective annual return on the Fastows' investment of over 50 percent. To the government, these payments were kickbacks, pure and simple. But to Fastow, who operated within the warped world of Enron, they were just commissions. After all, he'd given others the opportunity to invest, so they owed him.

Over the next three years, according to the government, the RADRs generated about $4.5 million in proceeds, from which Kopper and his lover Dodson paid more than $100,000 back to Fastow and his family in increments that were always no more than $10,000 so that they could be classified as gifts. Fastow told Kopper that if anyone ever asked about the $10,000 transfers, he could explain them by saying they were close friends. The government also alleges that the Fastows did not report any of this money on their income tax returns.

That same year, Fastow and Kopper did a second, bigger deal that was remarkably similar in character. You'll recall that years before, Enron had convinced CalPERS to invest in one of its first off-balance-sheet joint ventures, JEDI. By 1997, all the money in JEDI had been invested, and Enron urgently wanted CalPERS to set up a second fund. CalPERS was willing to do so only if Enron could find a buyer for its stake in JEDI. The two parties agreed that $383 million, which represented a 22 percent annual return for CalPERS, was a fair price. (This return later helped Enron convince others to invest in its deals.) But although Fastow and his team did look, Enron wasn't able to find an outside buyer.

Once again, Fastow's Global Finance came to the rescue by setting up a special-purpose entity to buy out CalPERS. It was called Chewco, named after the *Star Wars* character Chewbacca. Fastow first tried to persuade Jeff Skilling that Lea's family should be allowed to put up the necessary 3 percent equity and that Fastow should be allowed to manage the partnership. But Skilling said it was "too messy." So Fastow again turned to Kopper, whose involvement did not have to be disclosed publicly because of his lower rank, to manage the partnership and invest in it. The Enron accountant who worked on Project Chewco was Ben Glisan.

Skilling, who signed off on Kopper's involvement, later said that he thought he had discussed it with the board. Although that's not reflected in any board minutes, there is one sentence about Chewco in Enron's 1999 annual report that implies that it wasn't a secret: "In addition, an officer of Enron has invested in the limited partner of JEDI and from time to time acts as agent on behalf of the limited partner's management." Another Enron employee sent diagrams of the deal showing Kopper's stake to Vinson & Elkins. And while there were no official announcements about Kopper's involvement, there were plenty of whispers within the company about Fastow's favoritism toward his top deputy.

The closing of the Chewco deal was sheer panic. CalPERS insisted that the deal close quickly, or it would demand more money. Kopper was scrambling to come up with the $125,000 he was supposed to invest—people later surmised that he was waiting for a distribution from the RADRs. Barclays, the large British bank that was supposed to provide the outside equity, was proving to be a difficult partner. Barclays didn't want to put real equity into this deal. So Enron proposed what looked like a loan, although it wasn't called a loan, but rather equity certificates. This alone probably should have disqualified Chewco for off-balance-sheet treatment. But then Barclays insisted that the loan be *collateralized*, meaning that nobody could claim that the equity certificates constituted money that was truly at risk, as accounting rules require. "It is implausible," an investigator later concluded "that he [Glisan] (or any other knowledgeable accountant) would have concluded that Chewco met the 3 percent rule." Yet Glisan signed off on the deal, as did Arthur Andersen.

What's amazing, given the problems Chewco later caused, is what small sums of money were involved. Chewco's final structure consisted of a $240 million loan from Barclays—a loan that was guaranteed by Enron—and a $132 million advance from JEDI. All that Fastow's team needed to do was find $11.49 million in independent "equity" to meet the 3 percent threshold. Instead, of the required $11.49 million, most of the money came from Barclays, and it was backed up by Enron collateral worth $6.6 million. Kopper supplied the remaining $125,000, $100,100 of which represented reinvested proceeds from the RADRs, according to the government. On December 18, 1997, Kopper transferred part of his interest to Dodson, presumably in order to avoid the appearance that he controlled Chewco. They must have believed no one would ever look more deeply.

Even today, it's murky who knew what when. Glisan later insisted that he did not know about the collateral or that Kopper was the only other outside investor. Others, however, say he was present in meetings in which it was discussed, and handwritten notes that investigators say were his cite Chewco's "unique characteristics" as "extreme leverage . . . minimization of third party capital." The form transferring the collateral into the reserve accounts was signed by an Enron executive named Jeremy Blachman, who had helped Glisan land his job at Enron. Blachman later said that he didn't know the details. The Arthur Andersen partner who worked on Chewco, Tom Bauer, had been Glisan's boss before Glisan moved to Enron. Bauer later said that he didn't know about the collateral or about Kopper's involvement, either. Although Ken Lay and several other board members later said they didn't remember Chewco, the executive committee of the board approved it on November 5, 1997.

It's very clear who benefited. One executive says that it was the Chewco deal that helped secure Fastow the CFO job—who else could have pulled it off? And Enron did well, too. Keeping JEDI off its balance sheet boosted its earnings by hundreds of millions of dollars over the next few years. Enron used JEDI to book income from various derivatives trades related to the appreciation of the Enron stock that JEDI held—$126 million in the first quarter of 2000, for instance. Enron also found other ways to book earnings from Chewco: by charging it a $10 million structuring fee on the loan it extended and by marking-to-market the ongoing management fees it charged Chewco. (That alone added over $20 million to earnings in 1998.) Later, Enron used the increased value of its shares in JEDI to raise hundreds of millions more in off-balance-sheet debt. And Chewco also provided a chunk of the independent equity in Whitewing—meaning, of course, that Whitewing probably wasn't really independent, either.

All those benefits help explain why everyone was willing to look the other way. And while they averted their eyes, Fastow and Kopper profited. On January 6, 1998, just seven days after the deal closed, Chewco borrowed more from JEDI and paid a management fee of $141,438 to Kopper and Dodson. In other words, they recovered their investment and then some in the space of a week. Kopper was paid $500,000 a year to manage Chewco, $1.5 million in total. In December 1998, Fastow had Enron pay Chewco a $400,000 nuisance fee to amend an agreement. According to the government, Kopper kicked

$67,224 back to Fastow, his sons, and the Fastow Family Foundation, a purported charity he set up. They did not report this money to the IRS, either, the government claims. The government also says that some $54,000 was paid to Lea Fastow as "administrative fees." Much later, at Fastow's direction, Enron repurchased Chewco. Kopper got some $13 million, despite arguments from others at Enron that the Chewco stake was worth no more than $1 million. No one understood why Fastow was willing to push so hard on Kopper's behalf.

This was the deep, dark secret buried within Global Finance.

CHAPTER 12

The Big Enchilada

Enron's accounting games were never meant to last forever. All the frantic gim-micks and desperate machinations—rushing deals, restructuring contracts, set-ting up off-balance-sheet partnerships, monetizing power plants, generating cash through prepays—all that was meant merely as a bridge, a sort of giant corporate Band-Aid. The goal was to maintain the impression that Enron was humming until Skilling's next big idea kicked in and started raking in *real* profits.

Skilling had a special name for the sort of transcendent business idea he was counting on. He called such a business "the big enchilada." Gas and power trad-ing, of course, each received this designation. But in the years after he was named president of Enron, there were two big new hopes that Skilling bet on above all.

The first was Enron Energy Services (known as EES), aimed at capturing the retail side of the market: providing electricity, gas, and energy management di-rectly to businesses and homes. Skilling put one of his most trusted deputies, Lou Pai, in charge of EES. The second had nothing to do with energy at all: it was Enron's venture into the high-tech world of broadband. It was run by an-other key Skilling lieutenant, Ken Rice.

The company's ambitions for these two new divisions were nothing short of astounding: Skilling used to publicly predict that EES would one day be bigger than all the rest of Enron, while Ken Lay proclaimed that Enron's broadband venture would "dwarf" gas and power trading. In classic Enron fashion, the company spared no expense getting these businesses off the ground, spending billions. But Skilling also put Enron in a terrible bind: having spent all that money and having raised expectations so high, the big enchiladas simply had to work. There was no room for failure.

In Skilling's mind, though, there was no way he was going to fail. He had al-ways succeeded before, and his successes had transformed the company. Why would it be any different with EES and broadband? "I *am* Enron!" he once ex-claimed over drinks, in a moment of euphoria. As Rich Kinder might have put it, he was indeed now "smoking his own dope."

• • •

In retrospect, it's a little surprising that Skilling would put so much emphasis on EES, for Enron's retail effort was not some late-1990s brainstorm. It had a long and tortured history at Enron. This was the piece of the company Andy Fastow had tried to run back in 1996, when he'd spent nine months unable to devise a business plan before finally returning to finance, his tail between his legs. (His replacement was Rick Causey, who had an even shorter stint before being promoted to chief accounting officer.)

For years, Enron's retail business wasn't much more than a vague concept, revolving around the idea that just as the wholesale electricity market had been deregulated, so, too, would the retail market one day. And when that happened, Enron needed to be in a position to sell power (and even gas) directly to consumers nationwide, cutting America's utilities out of the picture. It was a given that Enron would make money doing so, because, well, Enron always made money in the wake of energy deregulation.

It's also surprising because unlike natural gas or wholesale power, there was no big move afoot to deregulate the retail energy market. This was never a case of Lay and Skilling's seeing what was coming, then trying to get out in front of it. Retail electricity (which was the primary focus of Enron's effort) was regulated at the state level, and states were exceedingly wary of introducing uncertainty into something so important to voters. Nor were federal legislators much interested in getting involved. Instead, this was a case of Enron's hubris getting the best of it. Because Skilling and Lay believed retail power *should* be deregulated, they convinced themselves they could make it happen. They would use Enron's lobbying might and their own powers of persuasion to bring around a reluctant Congress. Anybody could see that power deregulation was a no-brainer.

Both Skilling and Lay naturally came to the issue with a strong free-market bias in favor of deregulation. Skilling viewed it primarily in business and economic terms: it would be a good thing for the capitalist markets—and a good thing for Enron—if retail electricity were freed from government oversight. But Lay turned it into much more than that. He cast the issue as a *cause*.

Utilities were "cozy monopolists," who used their protected position to gouge consumers, he declared. In Lay's dreamy vision, once electricity was deregulated, opening the door to competition by companies like Enron, prices would tumble, saving consumers (according to an Enron-funded study) from $60 billion to $80 billion a year. Lay liked to call the potential savings "one of the largest tax cuts in U.S. history." As he saw it, Enron would earn the nation's gratitude for having served as "the people's cops"—breaking the grip of the utility industry, creating a new world where consumers would be able to choose their own energy provider. "It will be just like with the different competing telephone companies who offer a full line of telecommunications services today," Lay said. "You'll be able to call up and order all your energy from Enron."

In the press coverage surrounding the Enron bankruptcy, a myth has sprung up, according to which Ken Lay always got his way in Washington. Though he did win plenty of favors over the years, on this critical issue—the issue that probably meant more to his company's future than any other—Lay got nowhere. By the mid-1990s, Enron was putting its Washington muscle behind an audacious idea: a piece of legislation that would preempt the states, forcing them to deregulate whether they wanted to or not. Enron built up its already formidable lobbying office, took out newspaper ads, and spent millions.

It is conceivable—not likely, but possible—that had this bill passed, the Enron story would have turned out differently. But it didn't pass; at every turn, Lay and Enron were roundly rebuffed. This was partly because the utilities had far closer ties to legislators than Lay did, and they fought back fiercely. Congressmen who had regularly taken Lay's campaign contributions refused to back Enron's deregulation bill. Far from being a no-brainer, in Washington, the bill was a nonstarter, something Enron was utterly unwilling to accept.

Another problem, though, was Skilling. Unlike Lay, Skilling had no patience for the capital. On the contrary, his contempt for Washington was palpable. "How can you stand your job?" he asked an Enron Washington lobbyist after a meeting on Capital Hill. "These guys are absolute idiots." One senior member of the Enron government staff says: "Jeff thought you could throw money and buy people and they did what you told them to do."

By 1999, Enron's annual government affairs budget had climbed to more than $37 million. Yet it couldn't even get a retail-energy bill out of committee. Skilling took his case to Texas Republican Joe Barton, chairman of the House Energy and Power Subcommittee, who was preparing legislation offering incentives for states to embrace electricity deregulation. Barton was a natural Enron ally, and his bill was a small measure of progress.

Not good enough, Skilling told Barton in a meeting in the congressman's office; he expected the congressman to support an Enron-backed bill that would set a firm deadline for requiring deregulation. Such a bill didn't have the votes to pass, Barton responded, and he didn't favor preempting the states anyway.

"You need to change your opinion," Skilling scolded. As horrified aides for both men watched, Skilling started lecturing the congressman. Wasn't it *obvious* what needed to be done?

"I may not have as many millions as you do, but I'm not an idiot," Barton bristled. "You can run your company the way you want, and I'm going to run my committee the way I want." The meeting was soon over.

By then, though, Enron was already deploying Plan B, hiring scores of lobbyists in a massive effort to promote deregulation before each of the 50 state legislatures. As far back as July 1996, in fact, Lay had written a "Dear George" letter to Texas Governor Bush, urging his support for a state law to deregulate the retail market quickly. "We can't afford to wait," Lay warned. "Delay is dangerous. . . . It's time to let the forces of the market work their magic. . . . The nation's new energy system is being installed now." Incredibly, Lay, who was at that very moment working to *preempt* state regulation, argued that Bush needed to act because Texas ought to have the opportunity to craft the new rules for itself. "Our place in the new system will be decided by us, or for us," Lay wrote. "I want that decision to be made in Austin, not in some other state's capital, or in Washington."

Again, the local utilities fought back fiercely, keeping deregulation at bay. Still, a handful of states did begin to open up. Limited pilot programs were approved for electricity in New Hampshire and Pennsylvania and for gas in Ohio. And one state did enact a law to deregulate energy at the retail level. That state was California; the new law was set to go into effect in 1998.

Eager to establish itself as a national alternative to the utilities, Enron plunged into the early pilot programs. In 1996, Skilling dispatched 20 sales representatives to Peterborough, New Hampshire, where the Board of Selectmen had chosen the Houston company as its "preferred" electricity provider after meeting with executives and scrutinizing Enron's environmental record (and after the company donated $25,000 for community improvements and $1,000 for a Miss New Hampshire scholarship, among other gifts).

Although the town had only 5,300 residents, Enron decided to use Peterborough as the centerpiece for its first national advertising campaign, spending $30 million on a series of ads aimed, according to a company press release, at making Enron "one of the most recognized names in the world." Lay's ambition was to turn Enron into a consumer brand for energy. Ogilvy & Mather designed the ads; the famed graphic designer, Paul Rand, came up with a cool new Enron logo, the tilted, multicolored design that later became infamous as the crooked E. The company celebrated it all with a typically over-the-top Enron party, complete with fireworks, spotlights, and Elizabeth Taylor and Whoopi Goldberg look-alikes.

Philadelphia was another city where Enron tried to make inroads, offering to cut electric rates by 20 percent through 2000 if it were allowed to become the city's default provider of energy. Enron hired political consultant Ralph Reed, former executive director of the Christian Coalition, to help its effort. But after a fierce lobbying campaign and a garish media war in which Enron executives were portrayed in ads as Texas hucksters by the lying Joe Isuzu character, the state regulators turned down the company's plan, calling it unworkable.

Finally, there was California, the one state that was deregulating at the local level, thus theoretically allowing Enron to sell power directly to consumers. Even before deregulation took effect in January 1998, Enron began offering an eye-catching deal: it would cut customer rates by 10 percent for two years and throw in two weeks of free electricity. In the green-friendly state, Enron pitched itself as the environmentally sensitive provider, stressing its use of solar energy and wind farms, including the wind projects it continued to control through the shady RADR transactions. It spent more than $20 million, blanketing the state with direct mail and ads, in an effort to drum up customers.

Part of the California strategy involved the use of two-way wireless electric meters, which could be read remotely and eventually used to turn air-conditioning and lighting systems on and off by telephone. Enron bought thousands of them as well as millions of dollars' worth of wireless airtime in anticipation of deploying them in California homes and businesses. But few of the meters ever made it out of the warehouse. Instead, Enron employees ended up getting Skytel pagers because the company had already paid for a massive block of airtime that it didn't need.

Despite several months of intensive marketing, Enron signed up just 50,000 households in California, about 1 percent of the market. Contrary to Ken Lay's expectations, consumers weren't willing to go to the trouble of switching from their reliable old utility, even with Enron's offer of a rate discount. All that grassroots outrage about monopoly power that Lay talked about, the pent-up rage at the utilities—it simply didn't exist.

In March 1997, two months after becoming president, Skilling upped the ante. He broke out retail as a separate business, named it Enron Energy Services, and designated Lou Pai as its chairman and CEO. Skilling and Pai had a lot personally riding on EES; both men received sizable stakes in an EES phantom-equity plan, and Enron harbored hopes of one day taking EES public as a separate company. (Skilling and Pai later exchanged their phantom stakes for big blocks of Enron shares.) A few months later, Tom White, the retired general who had managed the construction of Teesside, was named Pai's number two.

Pai got a new three-year contract, giving him an annual salary of $400,000 and an annual bonus of up to $300,000. If EES hit performance targets, Pai was eligible for a long-term incentive bonus of $700,000 over a two-year period. Later he also received $70,000 worth of free personal use of Enron's corporate jet fleet each year. If no plane was available, Enron would charter a jet for him.

But how was this new team going to turn things around? Enron had lost $35 million on the retail business in 1996. The following year, with a hiring binge under way and the growing advertising costs, EES appeared headed for a $100 million loss. Wall Street had become agitated over the money Enron was pouring into the retail business; it was yet another reason why the stock languished in 1997.

"At the heart of the valuation of Enron as an investment today is the assessment of the move into retail energy marketing," wrote Jefferies & Company energy analyst Larry Crowley that September. ". . . This effort has generated significant investor debate surrounding the strategy itself, the attendant risks and rewards, and its potential for ultimate success or failure." Crowley's own view was that EES could become "a major home run." But he acknowledged that investor concern over "the size of the bet" resulted in Wall Street giving Enron "zero value" for EES.

Enron was already taking steps to change that, using one of its tried-and-true tactics. In mid-1997, Andy Fastow's finance group began working on a plan to sell a piece of EES to some institutional investors. The buyers Fastow ultimately found were the Ontario Teachers' Pension Plan and JEDI II, Enron's 50/50 partnership with CalPERS. Together, the two investors agreed to take a 7 percent stake in EES for $130 million.

This sale did three big things for Enron. First, it helped offset the retail business's start-up costs. Second, Enron used the investment to establish a franchise value for all of EES, the reasoning being that if 7 percent of the business was worth $130 million, the entire effort was worth $1.9 billion—about $5.50 per Enron share. Although EES wasn't close to making a profit—it wasn't really even much of a business yet—Lay and Skilling hoped Wall Street would start giving Enron credit for this value and push up the company's stock. At an analysts' meeting that took place a few weeks after the deal was announced, Skilling tried to make that happen, arguing that Enron's share price should be at least $5 higher.

Here's the third thing the deal did: it allowed Enron to book a $61 million profit in 1997. That amounted to 58 percent of the company's net earnings for the year, keeping the 1997 results (which included the big J-Block write-off) from being even more dismal than they already were. Enron booked the entire gain from the deal, even though EES received its money in three annual installments (and an Arthur Andersen in-house expert had advised the Enron audit team that only one third of the gain should have been recorded in 1997). But Enron needed the earnings in 1997, so that's what happened. A group of finance officials scrambled to close it by December 31. Some circulated a list of Top 10 Reasons Why We Thought That It Was a Good Idea for You to Spend Your Christmas Holidays and Year End with Us. (Number 9: "One of your 1997 New Years' resolutions was to make sure that Enron made its earnings targets.")

Only a few months after Enron booked this gain from selling part of EES, the company finally threw in the towel on its residential energy campaign. Lay and Skilling acted partly on the recommendation of a newly hired consumer-marketing expert named Jim Badum, a veteran of Pepsi and Taco Bell. Just three months after coming to Enron, Badum, with Pai in agreement, told them that the company "needed to slow things down." States simply weren't deregulating fast enough, and Enron was spending so much on landing customers that none of the early ventures had a prayer of turning a profit. "They wanted to go into the markets and hope the markets would get better," says Badum. "We said, 'Maybe it's time to take a wait-and-see approach in these states.'" Lay, who had relished his role as populist crusader, seemed crushed. "This is the last thing I expected from this meeting," he said, pushing his chair back from the table. Says Badum, "When it came to the simple realities of the consumer business, Enron simply didn't get it."

Reluctantly, Enron stopped signing up new residential accounts in California and returned its hard-won customers back to the hands of the "monopolist" utilities in most of the states with pilot deregulation programs. And it returned its customers—all 300 of them—in Peterborough, New Hampshire, too.

Not that Enron was about to back away from EES—how could it, after Skilling and Lay had touted it to Wall Street and the company had sold a piece of the division to some highly reputable investors? No, Enron would just have to shift strategies, that's all. Instead of targeting homes, it would target businesses, from hospitals to fast-food chains to big corporations with scores of office sites around the country. And instead of just selling them power, it would subcontract to take care of all of their energy needs.

Can you see how this would be an alluring notion for a big company that spends tens of million of dollars each year to light, heat, and cool its offices? Just as consultants had cropped up to handle the complicated computer needs of large corporations, saving them money in the process, Enron was promising to do the same with energy. Its ability to lock in prices on the trading floor would eliminate the worry that volatile energy costs would blow a hole in a company's budget.

In addition, Enron was promising to use its energy know-how to make efficiency improvements that would save even more money. "That was the pitch," recalls an early EES executive: " 'You go focus on building your widget, and we'll worry about the energy side of the business. We're the energy experts.' " Depending on the size and term of the contract—some ran as long as 15 years— EES was promising savings of anywhere from 5 percent to 15 percent.

The more perplexing question is why this would be an alluring idea for Enron. The commodity part of this new business—providing electricity and gas at a discount to customers—was often a money-loser at the retail level because most states were still refusing to deregulate retail energy. That meant the only way Enron could cut the cost of energy for a customer was to buy electricity from a local utility and resell it at a loss.

Amazingly, Enron was willing to do this because it remained convinced— despite much evidence to the contrary—that the states would soon open up their markets and the company would begin making money at the tail end of long-term contracts. When it started its retail push, back in 1996, Enron had forecast that half the U.S. retail markets would be open by 2001. Then by early 2000, it pushed back its projection of hitting that mark to 2004. In fact, by 2001 only a quarter of the U.S. power market had opened up and the deregulation effort had ground to a standstill.

What's more, this new thrust by EES was taking Enron somewhere it didn't belong. A business like the one EES was launching requires attention to detail, devotion to customer service, and a willingness to understand—and care about— the nitty-gritty of a company's energy issues. Enron was promising, for instance, to make energy-efficiency improvements, many of which would require big

up-front expenditures. But what did Enron executives know about energy efficiency? Nothing. Enron was promising to run the cooling and heating systems,
hire the energy-maintenance staff, change the lightbulbs, and pay the bills. Enron had never shown that it could manage that sort of operation.

Pricing energy costs for customers was especially tricky. In a typical long-
term EES deal with a large corporation, Enron had to establish models with
multiyear tariff curves—predictions about how dozens of factors would affect
electric rates—for every utility in every locale the customer had a business site.
In just one of its contracts, Enron was required to manage 252 properties in 36
states. "It's like duplicating the rate department for every single utility in the
country and having to do it on the fly and keep it updated," says an electrical engineer who worked on the EES tariff-risk desk.

One thing Enron *was* good at quickly came into play, though: cutting deals.
EES started out signing pure commodity contracts—selling gas or electricity to
companies. When it became clear these weren't going to generate big profits,
EES started bundling the sale of power and gas with energy-management services, in what it called total energy outsource contracts. Offering big customers millions in guaranteed savings, EES began rapidly signing up high-profile
clients.

The University of California and California State University systems signed
up for four years to let Enron provide electricity and efficiency projects for their
31 campuses. (Enron had promised to provide them electricity at 5 percent below the utilities' rate, saving a projected $16 million.) Lockheed Martin struck a
four-year deal for electricity and energy infrastructure. The San Francisco Giants
signed a ten-year commodity contract "totaling $60 million" for their new ball-
park; Ocean Spray, a $116 million ten-year agreement; Owens Corning, a ten-
year contract said to be worth $1 billion; the Simon Property Group signed up
for a ten-year $1.5 billion "alliance" to manage energy needs for its malls. Chase
Manhattan Bank and IBM each signed ten-year contracts. Tom White won EES
the first contract for privatization of utility management at a U.S. military base.
Enron even claimed the blessing of the Roman Catholic Church: a seven-year
energy deal with the Archdiocese of Chicago. In 1998, Enron announced, EES
had signed contracts with a total "value" of $3.8 billion. By the end of 1999, the
company had signed up so many new customers that the "total contract value,"
according to Enron, was a stunning $8.5 billion.

It's important to note, however, that this "total contract value"—the phrase Enron was using to keep score—bore no relation to either revenues or profits. The
term merely represented Enron's calculation of the cost of all the energy and infrastructure needs a customer had outsourced to EES over the life of the contract.
If Enron agreed to supply $500 million worth of electricity to a large corporation
over a ten-year period, that $500 million was included as part of the total value
of the contract, even if Enron was likely to lose money on the sale. But the num-

ber was still useful to the company: it was a way to show growth and to dazzle Wall Street.

In fact, this new metric had been cooked up for that very purpose. In September 1997, a high-level EES executive named Dan Leff sent out a memo proposing that Enron adopt a new term he called TCEE—total customer energy expenditure. "The overall objective of creating and deploying TCEE is to communicate, in a simple manner, the size, growth and success of EES to investment analysts, the investment community, shareholders, employees, and customers. We will endeavor to create a new index . . . where Enron is number one out of the box, as the metric is announced." Leff proposed refining the metric for formal presentation to Skilling two weeks later. By the time it was unveiled, TCEE had been changed to TCV: Total Contract Value. Just as the new dot-coms had such uneconomic measures as "eyeballs" and "hits," Enron now had TCV. Enron used the term so freely—in press releases, earnings announcements, and annual reports—that it made some of the company's accountants nervous. "It was a PR message embedded in a financial disclosure," says one former divisional EES accountant. "That even made Rick Causey cringe." It served the same purpose as the dot-com metrics: it gave Wall Street something to focus on besides profits.

For most of 1998 and 1999, EES was still reporting losses: $119 million in pretax losses in 1998, another $68 million in 1999. Skilling, as ever, raised the bar. He'd promised the Street that the division would go "earnings-positive" by the end of 1999. Sure enough, in the fourth quarter, Enron announced a $7 million profit, and management promptly declared victory. "In 1999, we proved that Enron's retail business works," Lay and Skilling declared to shareholders in Enron's annual report, written in early 2000. "Enron Energy Services achieved positive earnings in the fourth quarter, and its profitability is expanding rapidly."

Swallowing Enron's story, Wall Street analysts declared victory, too. Goldman Sachs's David Fleischer gushed: "Enron has redefined the worldwide energy marketplace with its vision for both the wholesale and retail markets." In April, Credit Suisse First Boston's Curt Launer calculated that EES alone was worth a staggering $19 billion, about $24 per Enron share. Four months later, he raised his valuation target on EES *alone* to $30 per share.

Back in January 1998, at a time when Skilling was intent on convincing Wall Street that EES was taking off, Enron invited the analysts who covered the company to Houston for an annual meeting with the company's top executives. As part of the event, Enron officials gave the analysts a tour of the company's operations, including EES. The group was escorted to the sixth floor of Enron headquarters, where they were shown what was described as the EES war room.

There, they beheld the very picture of a sophisticated, booming business: a big open room, bustling with people, all busily working the telephones and hunched over computer terminals, seemingly cutting deals and trading energy.

Giant plasma screens displayed electronic maps, which could show the sites of EES's many contracts and prospects. Commodity prices danced across an electronic ticker. "It was impressive," recalls analyst John Olson, who, at the time, covered the company for Merrill Lynch. "It was a veritable beehive of activity."

It was also a veritable sham. The war room had been rapidly fitted out explicitly to impress the analysts. Though EES was then just gearing up, Skilling and Pai had staged it all to convince their visitors that things were already hopping. On the day the analysts arrived, the room was filled with Enron employees. Many of them, though, didn't even work on the sixth floor. They were secretaries, EES staff from other locations, and non-EES employees who had been drafted for the occasion and coached on the importance of appearing busy. One, an administrative assistant named Kim Garcia, recalls being told to bring her personal photos to make it look as if she actually worked at the desk where she was sitting; she spent most of the time talking to her girlfriends on the phone. After getting the all-clear signal, Garcia packed up her belongings and returned to her *real* desk on the ninth floor. The analysts had no clue they'd been hoodwinked.

Just as Enron's financial executives convinced themselves that their financial shenanigans stayed within the rules, it seemed, so EES executives reasoned that this deception wasn't a problem. Eventually, EES really would use all that space. Eventually, there would be hundreds of busy employees working the phones and trading energy and the division would be every bit as fabulous as they were telling investors. It just wasn't quite there yet. In many ways, Skilling's little Potemkin Village stood as the perfect metaphor for EES: so much of what outsiders were led to believe about the operation was at odds with what was really going on. Listening to Skilling and Pai describe it, EES sounded like a business that made sense; that's one reason all the analysts were so willing to buy in. But it never made sense for Enron.

For instance: if you tell all your highly aggressive deal makers that the only thing that matters is total contract value and add to that horrible controls *and* an extreme urgency to get deals done quickly *and* a compensation system based on the projected profitability of long-term deals, you're inevitably going to get an awful lot of bad contracts. That's precisely what Enron did.

Despite Skilling's oft-stated horror at the way Rebecca Mark's international deal makers were paid, he instituted virtually the same system at EES. The EES originators—they eventually totaled 170—got huge bonuses not on the basis of how a deal worked out over time but on how profitable it *appeared* on the day the contract was signed. Margaret Ceconi, a 40-year-old former GE Capital manager who joined the EES origination staff in November 2000, says headhunters were recruiting former bankers for EES sales jobs with the prospect of making $1 million or more a year.

With that kind of incentive, EES executives used all the standard Enron tricks to make their deals look better than they were. Even though state-by-state deregulation was largely stalled, they priced contracts as if it were inevitable, thus making losing deals appear to be winners. They signed 15-year contracts that even they acknowledged would lose money for the first ten years—but included a wildly optimistic price curve that showed steep profits at the end, making up for all the losses. (Tilting the curves, this practice was called.) They underestimated the cost of and overestimated the savings from efficiency improvements. They stomped all over Rick Buy's risk assessors.

To make life easier for the sales force and give himself more opportunity to wheel and deal, Pai also insisted that his division have its own trading and risk-management staff. Shockingly, Pai's team was allowed to establish pricing curves that were different from the ones used by the wholesale traders. In other words, different parts of Enron were making different long-term pricing assumptions, then booking millions in mark-to-market profits based on those different guesses.

Knowing how critical it was to land big-name companies that would lend credibility to EES, Enron cut some deals that looked like losers on the day the contracts were signed. Pai was perfectly fine with this state of affairs; he even encouraged it. Signing big deals fast was what counted. If any contracts turned out to be stinkers, he told his staff blithely, they could simply restructure and sell a longer-term deal later on. "We'll just blend and extend," is how he used to put it. One EES executive says the business's early mantra was: "After all the marquee names, we'll get the profitable ones."

EES even *paid* companies to sign contracts—in one case, $50 million. "We bought the business," says an EES vice president. "It was easy to get people to do deals, if you pay them up front." In many cases, this was structured as a pre-payment on part of the savings expected over the life of the contract. Owens Corning got a $2 million promotional payment from Enron, in exchange for permission to use its brand and even its trademark Pink Panther in EES marketing materials. Enron paid Simon Property Group millions to lease its existing energy equipment. To sweeten the deal with Simon even more, Enron also agreed to provide a $4 million "equity infusion."

Even after it started reporting quarterly accounting profits, EES was hemorrhaging cash. After all, its operating expenses were huge, many of its deals wouldn't make a dime for years, and it was writing multimillion-dollar checks to win contracts. Then there was the matter of making energy improvements, a huge capital expense, which included such big-ticket items as replacing chilling systems and boilers. Enron was supposed to make the money back over the life of its contracts by sharing in the savings from cutting customers' consumption of energy.

But it soon became apparent that many of the improvements wouldn't pay for themselves or couldn't be done on the rapid timetable the company had promised. Starwood, the large hotel chain, had been promised $42 million in efficiency improvements, says Ceconi. When it became clear that the spending wouldn't pay off, Enron balked at moving forward.

EES even pitched its deals as offering opportunities for earnings management. Tyco's contract, for example, guaranteed 15 percent annual energy savings and provided the company "with ability to monetize," according to an EES document; this meant Tyco had the option of asking for the savings in an up-front payment. The Owens Corning deal even involved an off-balance-sheet partnership. To cook up such deals for retail, Andy Fastow formed an EES Structured Finance Group.

Ken Lay himself helped EES rope in prominent corporations. His calendar is dotted with meetings and phone calls with top executives of other companies, opening doors for the division: Larry Bossidy of Allied Signal in December 1998; Tyco's Dennis Koslowski in May 1999; Owens Corning in July 2000. With Lay's help, EES struck a big deal with Compaq, where he served on the board. Whenever the EES deal makers had trouble getting in to make their pitch to a prospect, they would call on Lay. "Ken can get us in," Pai would say.

As ever at Enron, there was always another powerful incentive for getting deals done quickly and making them appear profitable. EES needed to feed the Wall Street beast. Internally, company executives were explicit about this. A document detailing EES's 1999 business plan, prepared that February, included this reference to Skilling's public vow that the division would turn a profit in the fourth quarter: "Q4 EBIT Positive is Nonnegotiable." The document added, "We have a gap—and it must be filled. . . . We must change the way we operate—NOW."

Sure enough, the division's deal makers began racing to get contracts signed so that they could make the quarter. The haste caused bad deals to become that much worse, as Enron's originators gave up negotiating points to sign contracts and as they played with the price curves and other assumptions to disguise reality. They also used those price curves and assumptions to book mark-to-market profits based on the life of the contract.

After getting the word that EES needed to close another deal by the end of the quarter to make its numbers, one senior executive recalls persuading a customer to sign a simple commodity agreement while putting the more lucrative outsourcing agreement on hold. "I knew I had to get creative," he says. "To get deals done, we just said, 'Shit, we're going to have to talk these guys into doing part of the deal, so we'll do the second piece later.' The quarter was riding on it." This same executive recalls an instance where he closed a deal that had a total contract value of $500 million, only to see Enron issue a press release claiming the contract was worth $1.3 *billion.* "You don't know what to do in that case," he said. "Do you beat on Lou Pai's door and say, 'What are you smoking?' "

EES would presumably have to pay the real cost for fulfilling its contracts someday. But the sales team, which was paid up front, wasn't worried about what would happen five years down the road. One senior sales executive used to joke about how he'd close deals, then "throw them over the fence" to let the back-office staff worry about actually making them work. "People would say to me: 'Hey, it's not your problem,' " recalls Ceconi. " 'You're not going to be around. Why do you care?' "

Here, though, may have been the biggest problem of all: once Enron had the contracts, it had to start fulfilling the terms. Partly, that meant selling power to big companies at cut-rate prices. But it also meant that Enron had to start implementing all those energy efficiencies, hiring all those maintenance workers, changing all those lightbulbs, and paying all those bills. This was a massive undertaking. At its peak EES was managing 28,000 different sites all across the United States and Europe.

Lacking that kind of management expertise, Enron decided to go out and buy it. EES made a string of acquisitions of energy-management and facilities companies, assembling a massive energy-maintenance operation, and becoming the biggest HVAC (heating, ventilation, air conditioning) contractor in the country. Even though this expertise was desperately needed, the company's culture remained as contemptuous as ever of people who had to manage and execute; Enron's fast trackers dismissed these acquisitions as "butt-crack businesses." One Enron analyst scouting for new purchases even had a cap made up, reading Butt-Crack Acquisition Team.

One Enron employee assigned to the operations side spent time researching whether the company could buy financial instruments to hedge the possibility of rising labor costs. That was the Enron way of dealing with labor costs. Meanwhile, promised energy-saving projects were never started, unpaid utility bills piled up, and EES tried to wiggle out of provisions it had agreed to that were either too difficult to perform or too expensive.

Take the California public universities' contracts, which required EES to bill the university system for energy use on each of their 31 campuses. According to David DeMauro, a Cal State administrator who helped manage the schools' deal with EES, Enron routinely made major billing errors and submitted its bills late. In fact, says DeMauro, from the very first month that the contract went into effect, EES *never* got it right. "There were no situations," he says, "where the bills were either on time or correct. People either didn't get the bills or they got incorrect bills. We went all four years without receiving timely or accurate bills. We figured a company like this could do something as easy as turning out timely, accurate bills. They were never able to do so."

"The problem was so widespread over our campuses," says DeMauro, "we decided that our strategy would be that we would not pay Enron until they could deliver us an accurate bill. We probably went five or six months without paying Enron at all. I would guess our accounts payable was approaching $40 million or so."

Enron never delivered the energy-efficiency projects it had promised, either, says DeMauro. The one constant in dealing with Enron, he says: "People we worked with were always making promises that weren't kept."

Enron also had a contract with the giant HMO Kaiser Permanente to handle utility bills for hundreds of facilities in several states. But EES habitually paid the wrong amounts and ran up late fees as well. At one point, while Enron tried to straighten the mess out, boxes of unpaid Kaiser bills stacked up in EES's offices.

EES's cash management was so poor that it took months to invoice customers for reimbursement of utility bills it had already paid. "We were basically paying their utility bills and giving them loans," says an Enron managing director who studied the situation. According to EES executives, the float was costing the business more than $50 million a year.

"How are we actually going to do all this shit that we're selling?" an EES back-office manager named Glenn Dickson recalls asking. "The approach was, 'Let's sell it—and we'll figure out everything else later.' They touted themselves as a risk-management company, but they never asked what could go wrong. It was a free-for-all—a chaotic, fucking free-for-all."

Yet Skilling remained oblivious. At an employee meeting held in February 2000, the Enron president told the assembled staffers that "EES has turned the corner." Then, later in the meeting, he added almost off-handedly, "The next challenge in this business is going to be execution. This stuff sells. Now we have to actually get out there and do something for the customers. That's the easy part." For Skilling, like everyone else at Enron, customer service was little more than an afterthought.

Arthur Andersen had been warning Enron executives about EES's management problems. In an April 26, 1999, memo to the EES board, which included Skilling, Pai, and Fastow, the auditing firm noted "significant deficiency in the internal control structure of the company," problems that included "few defined accounting policies and procedures . . . to ensure account balances and transactions were properly reported in a timely manner." At year-end, according to an Enron accounting executive, EES's Andersen auditors were so concerned they were threatening to take the extraordinary step of giving the division a "qualified" accounting opinion.

A few months later, in response to Andersen's complaint, a special team was assigned to look into EES's problems. Nobody at the top of Enron expected them to find anything serious.

And then there was the other big enchilada: broadband.

This, too, was a business that might seem, at first glance, to be a surprising choice for Jeff Skilling's Enron, and not just because it had nothing to do with energy. For a man who liked to think of himself as on the cutting edge of American business, Skilling was pretty much a Luddite. During his years at Enron, he never learned to surf the Internet. He stubbornly refused to use e-mail; his secretary printed out the messages he received. Though he had two computer terminals on his desk, he used them only to track stock and commodity prices. "He didn't even know how to turn them on," his secretary told people.

But of course anyone who remembers the Internet mania of the late 1990s will understand perfectly why Skilling touted broadband as the Next Big Thing for Enron. Internet stocks had taken off; companies would go public in the morning and have a $100 share price by 4 P.M., when the market closed. Valuations were so high they bore no relation to profits or revenues—which, for many Internet companies, were non-existent. If Skilling was going to get Enron an Internet-style valuation—and there was nothing he wanted more—he'd have to convince Wall Street that Enron was becoming, at least in part, an Internet company. He may not have known how to surf the Web, but the relationship between the Internet and the stock market was something he understood all too well.

The part of the company that became Enron Broadband began life as an afterthought: it was a tiny start-up inside Portland General, called FirstPoint Communications. When Skilling learned in 1996 that the Oregon utility had just launched a telecommunications business that was laying fiber-optic cable around Portland, he was distinctly unenthusiastic. He gave the business zero value, and his intention was to sell the operation or shut it down once Enron completed the Portland General acquisition.

Portland General was one of several utilities that had jumped into the telecom business with the idea of using their existing right-of-way to lay a fiber network—a system of glass strands that acts as an underground highway for moving Internet data at high speeds. Joe Hirko, Portland General's CFO, had taken over the small telecom business in 1997. Following the merger, Skilling remained skeptical. But after a group of trusted Enron deputies came back excited from a scouting trip to Portland, he authorized Hirko to spend up to $20 million to expand his network.

Then, of course, he began to see what happened to the stocks of Internet companies. He also had a second reason for changing his mind: Enron's traders had gotten enthused about the idea of trading bandwidth—capacity on the fiber-optic networks that Enron and others were building. It made at least theoretical sense: Internet data moved along fiber networks that crisscrossed the country, just like natural gas and electricity. Why couldn't Enron trade bandwidth capacity in the same way it traded natural gas?

Suddenly, Hirko's little telecom business was starting to look like a knock-off of the power-trading business—only better. According to Skilling's back-of-the-envelope calculation—"horseshoes and hand grenades," he liked to call it—Enron's market value would increase by $20 for every dollar the company invested in a broadband venture. Thus, a $1 billion investment would add $20 billion in market capitalization. Whether the business would bring in cash or profits (and how long that might take)—those were different issues. If broadband could quickly get him another $20 billion in market cap, he was all for it. "I've always believed there's no such thing as a free lunch," he later told associates, "but this looks like a free lunch. I've never seen economics like these numbers."

In the summer of 1999, Skilling flew west and met with the employees of the new division in the lobby of their start-up offices above the beer vats at a popular restaurant in a historic building in downtown Portland. (Internet companies all had to have funky quarters; it was part of the ethos.) Skilling told Hirko's staff that he had great news: they were about to become a core business for Enron. This meant two things. First, Enron was prepared to spend up to $1 billion to build the business. Second, it meant that its center of gravity would inevitably shift to Houston. "We're all going to make a lot of money together," Skilling happily declared.

But the Enron president didn't get the exultant reaction he'd expected. Hirko's troops were looking for an even quicker payoff. They had stakes in the broadband subsidiary and had been hoping Skilling was going to announce that Enron planned to spin them off through one of those hot tech IPOs. Skilling's announcement meant they'd end up with shares of *Enron* stock instead. There was another issue, too: none of them wanted to move to Houston.

Back in Texas, however, the word quickly spread: broadband was Skilling's new "it" business. The klieg-light syndrome immediately kicked in. Tracy Smith, the Portland division's marketing director, recalls arriving in Houston, where she began spending much of her time, and finding dozens of new employees, none of whom had any experience in technology or telecommunications. "Whole groups from other business units, with 20 people, would transfer in," says Smith. "You'd ask them what they were going to do, and they'd say, 'I don't know.' It was their job to figure out what they should do. They'd come up with minibusiness plans."

The Portland staff soon grew to 300. Enron moved them from their cool offices above the brewery to more expensive digs in a downtown office tower. But because so much of the business was being conducted in Houston, many of the employees didn't spend much time in their new offices. An Enron jet began a regular shuttle service to Texas, leaving Oregon Monday morning and returning Friday afternoon.

There was another big sign of how much Skilling was making broadband his own. In mid-1999, he asked Ken Rice to leave his top job at ECT—which had been renamed Enron North America—and run this new business instead. Worried that the engineers and the rest of the Portland staff would bolt, Skilling also wanted to keep Hirko on in Portland, with an informal arrangement that he and Rice serve as co-CEOs.

Rice wasn't enthusiastic about the idea. A skilled deal maker for many years, Rice by then was 41 years old. He was rich, and he was tired, and he was in the throes of a midlife crisis. His relationship with Amanda Martin, which was finally over, had taken a toll. Martin and her husband had divorced in 1997, and that year Rice had filed to end his own marriage, too. But he delayed the suit after discovering that his wife was pregnant with their fourth child, and the Rices later reconciled. In the midst of it all, he'd entered counseling and begun taking antidepressants. Unwilling to keep working long hours, he'd also found other distractions: he was planning a vacation home in Telluride, Colorado; he'd started cutting out early to spend time with his kids; and he'd developed a fascination with racing Ferraris and expensive motorcycles. These were his passions now, not Enron.

Rice didn't like the awkward co-CEO arrangement either. But Skilling pleaded with him. So much was at stake: he was desperate to plant a trusted ECT hand in this new broadband business. Skilling promised to make Rice an offer he couldn't refuse. "You know I'm going to take care of you," he told Rice. "Just make it work."

Rice finally relented—and Skilling did take care of him. The following February, his amended contract was approved by the Enron board. Rice received a base salary of $420,000. He would get a cash bonus of $1.75 million. And he received a stunning package of almost 1.8 million stock options, which he'd be free to cash in unusually early. Some 346,154 of the options would vest immediately, another 771,154 in just a year, and 425,000 more in just two years.

Running Enron's broadband business would add tens of millions to his fortune. Still, Rice came to regret having given in to Skilling's pleas. Accepting the job, he later privately confided, "was probably the biggest mistake I could have made."

It didn't take the new broadband employees long to learn what it meant to work for Enron. Dozens of them who lived out of town were put up in corporate apartments, at $3,500 a month each. A midlevel salesman on a business trip to Los Angeles rented the penthouse suite at one of the most expensive hotels in town. Small tech companies were acquired, consultants were retained, reports were commissioned, parties were thrown. "No expense was spared," recalls Tracy Smith. "It was just the Enron culture."

Because she was new to Enron, Smith was struck by things that most Enron employees had long since taken for granted. The abrasive, cutthroat culture. The condescension toward anyone who didn't work at Enron. And always, the obsession with the stock price at every level of the company. "Everywhere you looked, the stock ticker was going," said Smith. "In the lobby of the building. In the lobby on your floor. It was on the screen of your computer. Everybody was focused on the stock price. You couldn't get away from it. When the stock wasn't doing well, the mood changed."

By late 1999, Skilling thought Enron had the makings of a hot new business. Its foundation would be the sophisticated cross-country fiber-optic system it was building; they dubbed it the Enron Intelligent Network. Enron claimed that its system would transform the Internet by providing bandwidth and switching capacity to distribute TV-quality video and other content rapidly and at a reasonable price. And it had other plans, too. It would create a market in bandwidth trading, which it believed it could launch, then take to critical mass in the span of just two years. Finally, Enron had a team working to develop content, to figure out how to send high-quality entertainment and other video over the Internet with no delay.

In late 1999, Skilling began making plans to unveil this vision to Wall Street. He had laid the groundwork with a flurry of press releases, announcing an assortment of minor acquisitions, alliances, and developments. In December, Enron announced that it had executed the first bandwidth forward trade, with Global Crossing. "This is Day One of a potentially enormous market," Skilling told a Houston reporter.

The big splash was to come at Enron's analysts' meeting, scheduled for January 2000. The business was set to debut with a brand new name. Up until then, the business had been known as Enron Communications. The new name was Enron Broadband. It conveyed exactly the right message. "Wall Street was into broadband," says marketing director Smith, recalling the thought process behind the new name, "and if we put broadband into our name, that would mean everything."

And for a little while, it did.

CHAPTER 13

"An Unnatural Act"

Enron's top executives may well have believed their own rhetoric about the company's two big new businesses—that they would one day be huge and successful and generate billions in real profits. And that, in turn, might allow the company to wean itself from the machinations it so depended on to book earnings and impress Wall Street. But in the here and now, EES and broadband had exactly the opposite effect: because they chewed up so much capital while generating so little cash, their existence made the company even more dependent on Andy Fastow.

In his two years as corporate-finance czar, Fastow had employed creative forms of financial chicanery to dress up Enron's financial statements. He'd also figured out how to use his power—and his closest associates—to secretly line his own pockets. Now he established new ways to accomplish both of those ends, on a far larger scale, at once.

His mechanism was a private equity fund—a series of funds, actually—that Fastow named LJM and that he ran even while serving as Enron's CFO. The name signaled how important they were to him. His earlier entities, JEDI and Chewco, were named after *Star Wars* characters; the letters *LJM* were the first initials of Andy's wife and two sons: Lea, Jeffrey, and Matthew.

Fastow, you'll recall, had long harbored the desire to set up a fund that could invest in Enron deals. But over the years, whenever he had broached the idea, he'd been shot down—and with good reason. A special fund open only to certain favored employees would surely be enormously divisive, and having the CFO himself running it would create an obvious conflict of interest. When Enron wanted to sell an asset to the fund, Fastow would be in the position of negotiating with himself.

But by the late 1990s, Enron was making such frequent use of SPEs that finding the necessary outside equity investors was becoming nearly impossible. There were only so many trusted Friends of Enron, after all. So Fastow began promoting the idea of setting up a big standing private equity fund—a sort of permanent Friend of Enron—that would raise enough cash from institutional investors to provide the all-important 3 percent independent equity for dozens of Enron deals. This was an elegant solution, Fastow argued. It would avoid the messiness of having to find new investors every time. It would allow Enron to close deals faster than ever. It would even save money on banking fees. And, Fastow argued to Skilling, it wouldn't distract from his regular duties at Enron.

By August 1998—just five months after becoming CFO—Fastow was actively exploring the idea with investment bankers at Merrill Lynch. Enron's key Merrill contact was a Houston investment banker named Schuyler Tilney, whose wife Beth was an Enron executive and a Ken Lay confidante; the Fastows and Tilneys were good friends. As Fastow initially presented the fund idea to the Merrill bankers, Enron would contribute half the equity, just as it had with JEDI, in the form of company stock. But unlike JEDI, where CalPERS was the only outside partner, this fund would solicit dozens of private investors, all of whom would be expected to contribute cash. Despite the Fastow-Tilney friendship, though, Merrill didn't bite. In an e-mail report back to New York after the meeting, one Merrill banker wrote: ". . . we just listened to Andy and . . . we all—at least I did—got headaches trying to analyze an Enron stock contribution from an investor's viewpoint and what kind of commitment it really was given that Enron can 'manufacture' stock—even Schuyler observed that we were probably asking investors to consider 'an unnatural act.' "

Fastow pushed ahead anyway. By May 1999, he was floating the idea with Enron's accountants at Arthur Andersen. Even they thought it was a bad idea—though they kept this view to themselves. In a May 28 e-mail to colleagues, Benjamin Neuhausen, a member of the elite Professional Standards Group at Andersen, wrote: "Setting aside the accounting, idea of a venture entity managed by CFO is terrible from a business point of view. Conflicts of interest galore. Why would any director in his or her right mind ever approve such a scheme?"

David Duncan, Andersen's Enron relationship partner, expressed similar skepticism, writing back: ". . . on your point 1 (i.e. the whole thing is a bad idea), I really couldn't agree more." Duncan said that he would insist that the plan be approved by Enron's CEO, general counsel, and board—and he expressed hope that would put an end to it. ("None of this communication has yet to occur and this thing could get killed when it does.") It was clear, however, that Fastow wasn't going to give up easily. Noted Duncan: "This thing is still very much in the brainstorming stage, but Andy wants to move through it very quickly to get all this done, if possible, this quarter. Andy is convinced that this is such a win-win that everyone will buy in. We'll see."

Through Duncan, the accountants were setting in motion a game of dodging responsibility. They privately agreed the idea was terrible but were expecting Lay and Skilling—or, surely, the board—to kill it. For their part, the board and management would later point to Andersen's silence in justifying their conclusion that Fastow's scheme was perfectly okay.

Fastow finally brought his idea to life by seizing an opportunity to prove just how handy such a fund could be. The occasion involved a $10 million investment Enron's fledging broadband unit had made back in March 1998 in a tech start-up called Rhythms NetConnections, one of the first high-speed Internet providers. Enron had bought 5.4 million pre-IPO shares at $1.85 per share. On April 7, 1999, a year later, at the height of the Internet frenzy, Rhythms went public at $21 and promptly skyrocketed to $69 by the end of the day. By May, Enron's $10 million investment was worth about $300 million.

Skilling convened a meeting of ten Enron executives to discuss the dilemma this presented. As ever, Enron needed an earnings boost, so it wanted to book the entire gain right away. But if it did so, Skilling complained, Enron would get no credit in its stock price from Wall Street because it would be booking the wind-fall as a onetime gain. "We need to figure out how to make it a recurring item on our income statement," he told the group.

Then Skilling turned to the broader issue: even after Enron booked the Rhythms gain, it couldn't just unload the stock. To get the pre-IPO shares, it had signed a lockup provision preventing it from selling until November. Who could say where the price would be in November? Skilling was eager to find a way to lock in the gain, to hedge against the very real possibility that Rhythms shares would drop sharply before the lockup expired, which, under mark-to-market accounting, would then require the company to book a *loss*.

The meeting ended with everyone scratching his head; by conventional methods, what Skilling wanted to do was impossible. Buying some kind of traditional hedge, such as a put option—an obligation to buy the volatile Rhythms shares at a set price—from a legitimate third party would be prohibitively expensive. Besides, Rhythms was so thinly traded and Enron's position so large—it controlled about half the shares available in the market—that it would be exceedingly difficult for any buyer to unload. No outside buyer would assume such enormous economic risk.

Into the breach stepped Fastow, who let it be known that he was willing to create a new SPE to hedge the Rhythms position for Enron, but *he* needed to control it. Here's how it would work: Fastow would start his first fund, LJM1 (also known as LJM Cayman), with $1 million of his own money. An additional $15 million would be contributed by two big outside investors. LJM1 would then set up a subsidiary, called LJM Swap Sub. Swap Sub would sell a put option on the entire Rhythms stake to Enron, giving Enron the right to force Swap Sub to buy the Rhythms stock from Enron in June 2004 at $56 a share. To compensate Fastow and his partners for taking this extraordinary risk, Enron would arrange the transfer of 3.4 million shares of its own stock, worth about $276 million, to LJM, which then moved almost half the holding (as well as several million dollars in cash) into Swap Sub. LJM also gave Enron notes for $64 million, which helped Enron by adding to its reported cash flow.

In essence, Enron was using the value of its own stock to buy the hedge. This meant that it wasn't truly hedging its risk at all. If Rhythms fell, the only way it could pay off the hedge was by using Enron stock. But if the shares dropped, Swap Sub would have no way of making good on its obligation to Enron. Like so many of Enron's questionable transactions, the Rhythms deals was rooted in the fundamental belief that Enron stock would never fall. The entire arrangement was an accounting artifice, protecting Enron from having to book an accounting loss but doing nothing to protect it from an actual economic loss.

Fastow and Kopper, in fact, were quite proud of the structure they'd created for the Rhythms hedge, so much so that they later tried to sell the concept to at least one other Houston energy company, El Paso. They thought El Paso might want to do a deal with LJM. After listening to the two men explain the complex structure, the El Paso executive, a former investment banker himself, scratched his head. The accountants would never approve it, he said.

Sure they will, Fastow and Kopper told him. "We can get you an opinion letter."

"How do you determine valuation?" he asked.

Fastow and Kopper grinned. "It's whatever you want it to be," one of them replied.

In early June, as Fastow was hatching this scheme, Rick Buy phoned Vince Kaminski, head of Enron's Research Group, for help in pricing the Rhythms options. Kaminski's 50-member group was part of RAC, a team of high-powered quant jocks who built Enron's complex derivatives-pricing models. The Polish-born Kaminski was a former Salomon Brothers vice president with an MBA and a doctorate in mathematical economics who read daily newspapers in five different languages. He was universally respected for his raw brainpower—at Enron, no small compliment—and equally renowned for his bluntness.

Buy was calling Kaminski with Jeff Skilling in his office. The chief risk officer was vague about what was really up, but Skilling told Kaminski the project was urgent. A short while later, Skilling appeared in Kaminski's office—an exceedingly rare event—to try to explain the transaction. When Kaminski later presented the problem to members of his group, everyone in the room laughed; that kind of put option, they all knew, would be impossible to buy on Wall Street. Still, they did what they were told and came up with a price.

The next day, Kaminski told Buy that his group had produced a number but that he viewed the idea of transferring Enron shares to an outside partnership as foolish. In fact, Kaminski declared, "This is so stupid that only Andrew Fastow could have come up with it." That's when Buy told him that Fastow *had* come up with the idea—and that the CFO was planning to run the partnership himself. Now Kaminski was even more certain the idea was stupid. What about the conflict of interest? After hearing more about the structure, Kaminski returned the following week with more arguments. The hedge simply wouldn't work. And the payout cheated Enron shareholders in favor of Fastow, Kaminski said; it's "heads the partnership wins, tails Enron loses." After all, Enron was funding the hedge almost entirely with its own shares, giving LJM virtually no exposure. Buy listened with his usual sense of grim anxiety, then told Kaminski he would try to stop the deal. "The next time Fastow is going to run a racket," the Enron risk officer nervously joked, "I want to be part of it."

At 10 A.M. on the morning of Friday, June 18, Skilling and Fastow walked over to Ken Lay's office for a discussion of the deal that would give birth to LJM. Fastow's role in the new private partnership would require an exemption from Enron's code of ethics, which barred employees from profiting from any company that did business with Enron but allowed the CEO to waive the provision if the arrangement "does not adversely affect the best interests of the Company." Lay agreed to grant the waiver but wanted the board of directors to ratify his decision.

Ten days later, LJM was brought before a special meeting of the Enron directors; most participated by phone. As Fastow explained it, his personal involvement in the new partnership was an act of altruism, an unfortunate but necessary ingredient to attract outside investors to LJM and essential to Enron's goal of hedging the Rhythms investment. Fastow insisted that LJM would provide the hedge "at no cost to Enron." And in materials that had been sent to the directors, he insisted that, even though he would serve as LJM's general partner, he would personally receive "no current or future (appreciated) value" from the Enron stock it held; if Enron's shares continued to rise, those gains would all go to his limited partners.

Fastow did note, however, that he would receive a $500,000 annual management fee plus more than half the returns on any other assets in LJM. Fastow also told the board that PricewaterhouseCoopers would be issuing a fairness opinion affirming that the deal was fair to Enron. (Fastow neglected to mention that the firm was also being paid by LJM to work on the deal.) With nary a dissenting vote—or even any discussion of how to monitor the conflict—the directors passed a resolution exempting Enron's CFO from the company's code of ethics. Even with several other items on the agenda, the meeting was over in just an hour.

Neither David Duncan, Enron's auditor, nor Rick Buy made any attempt to get in the way, despite their muttered complaints to outraged colleagues. Buy later told Vince Kaminski the project had too much momentum for him to stop it. And in fact, Fastow had clearly viewed the board approval as a mere formality. He had teed up the entire transaction before the board even met—and closed it two days after the vote.

As for Kaminski, in the aftermath of his objections to LJM's first deal, his entire group was removed from RAC and placed in Enron North America, where it was no longer in a position to stand in the way of anything Andy Fastow wanted to do.

As it turns out, the finances of LJM1 and Swap Sub soon moved in Fastow's favor. The increase in Enron's shares meant that Fastow's new partnership was sitting in a sizable gain.

Fastow's happy limited partners were two of his Tier 1 banks: Credit Suisse First Boston, which had invested through an entity established in the Cayman Islands named ERNB (the initials stood for Enron's Rhythms Net Bet), and Greenwich NatWest, a British bank that had named its Cayman Islands subsidiary Campsie Limited. Each had sunk $7.5 million into the venture—and as the size of the gain became clear, Fastow agreed to a series of complex transactions that guaranteed each a profit of more than $20 million.

NatWest was represented by a colorful trio of United States-based Brits from the structured-finance department: Gary Mulgrew, Giles Darby, and David Bermingham. The three men's exploits had been chronicled in a British novel by a former colleague named Robert Kelsey, *The Pursuit of Happiness: Overpaid, Oversexed and Over There,* that told how they courted an especially aggressive Houston energy giant named Hardon. In the book, the bankers schmoozed the company's officials "and made sure they got what they wanted. And what they wanted was usually a round of golf, a nice dinner, and a visit to a local strip club."

In late 1999, as the NatWest bankers were working up proposals to extract the bank's profits from LJM, they began turning their attention to Swap Sub as well, allegedly with an eye toward lining their own pockets. Detailed federal court filings, including lengthy e-mail excerpts, offer a vivid account of what government prosecutors later charged was an elaborate fraud.

For months, the limited partners had officially written off their stake in the Swap Sub as worthless; that's because they assumed that after it had paid off the put option, there would be nothing left in the entity. But Enron's stock had risen so fast that it covered the put option with millions left over, and no one at the bank seemed to have noticed. In late January, Bermingham e-mailed his NatWest colleague Darby that he had been studying the bank's stake in Swap Sub and realized that "there is quite some value there now. The trick will be in capturing it. I have a couple of ideas but it may be good if I don't share them with anyone until we know our fate!!!" The three men had reason to be worried about their future: two bigger banks were in a bidding war to gobble up NatWest's parent.

By February 19, the government charges, the three were at work on a Power-Point presentation for a meeting with Fastow where they would present ideas on how they could restructure Swap Sub—and split the spoils. "For your info," Bermingham e-mailed Darby and Mulgrew, "our minimum profit per these slides would be $8m, rising to $17m for the middle bit, and then finally up to around $30m. Everybody wins." The following day, Bermingham wrote Mulgrew that they would do well to assure Fastow a hefty payout. "If I knew there was a realistic way to 'lock in' the $40m and give him $25m, we would also jump all over it I guess, since it would give us $15m. . . . I will be the first to be delighted if he has found a way to lock it in and steal a large portion himself." Bermingham added: "We should be able to appeal to his greed."

The three men were soon covering their tracks with their colleagues. Responding to a query from another NatWest banker, Bermingham claimed that he and his two colleagues were traveling to Houston to do a deal and their boss was "in the loop" but that he should "not speak to anyone" about the matter and "just act dumb please." Then he wrote his coconspirators: "This is an attempt to head the obvious off at the pass and keep the lid on the thing. Large numbers of people are asking what we are up to. I hate lies."

On February 22, the three British bankers arrived in Houston. Fastow had scheduled plenty of time for them: a leisurely dinner that evening and four more hours the next day. According to the government, the bankers sat down with the Enron CFO and offered a slide presentation laying out several illicit scenarios. One involved selling Swap Sub's Enron shares for cash, then buying them back a few days later (presumably to get around the prohibition on Fastow's profiting from the Enron stock). But that wouldn't work, the bankers' slide presentation noted: "Problem is that it is too obvious (to both Enron and LPs) what is happening (ie, robbery of LPs), so probably not attractive."

By the time the bankers left Houston on February 24, they had allegedly come up with a plan. Working hand in glove, Fastow, Kopper, and the trio from NatWest would orchestrate the bank's sale of its valuable interest in Swap Sub for a relative pittance, then secretly transfer most of the stake to themselves and split millions. When he got back to New York, Mulgrew told his boss, according to the government, that Fastow had informed him that Enron was willing to pay NatWest $1 million for its Swap Sub stake. Mulgrew added that this sum was all the stake was worth and urged his boss to accept the modest return. Mulgrew got the go-ahead.

Over the next two months, the government charges, Fastow, Kopper, and their bank collaborators operated on two levels: openly generating the paperwork and winning the approvals needed to complete the official transactions with their respective employers and simultaneously carrying out the covert maneuvers needed to divert the deal's riches to themselves.

A key part of the machinations was ensuring that Enron would unwind Swap Sub on generous terms. Fastow took care of that. By spring, Enron was ready to liquidate its position. The lockup had expired; the Rhythms shares had started to fall (the company was heading toward bankruptcy). It took Enron several months to unload its Rhythms position.

But the Enron shares held by Swap Sub had soared to $70, up from $56. Fastow proposed to Causey that Enron pay Swap Sub $30 million for the return of the remaining shares. Mike DeVille, an Enron finance executive who worked for Causey, thought Fastow's partnership was "making a killing." Investigators also later concluded that Enron substantially overpaid in the deal. Neither Rick Buy's RAC nor any outside accountants reviewed the terms. Fastow told Causey the $30 million was going to the limited partners: $10 million to CSFB and $20 million to NatWest. In fact, while CSFB was indeed getting $10 million, NatWest's share was only $1 million.

Meanwhile, Fastow, Kopper, and the NatWest bankers were busy laying their plans. On Wednesday, March 1, after calling ahead to discuss arrangements for a fly-fishing excursion, Fastow left Houston for a five-day trip to the Cayman Islands. There he met with Darby and Bermingham, who participated in a Campsie board meeting authorizing Darby to negotiate the official deal to sell NatWest's stake. Over dinner, according to the government, Fastow privately told Bermingham that they had to "move quickly" on their private transactions. Kopper, who was handling many of the details, wrote in his work notebook: "Gary Mulgrew—spoke to AF, everything moving as planned."

The purchaser for both the NatWest and CSFB stakes in Swap Sub was a newly formed partnership, called Southampton Place, controlled by Kopper. This partnership was named for the upscale Houston neighborhood where both Fastow and Kopper lived. It paid the banks for their Swap Sub shares in late March. After it did so, it still had about $19 million in secret profits to divvy up. According to the government, this is how it was done. Fastow and Kopper transferred about half the equity in the now valuable Southampton into yet another partnership, Southampton K. On April 27, the NatWest bankers bought Southampton K by wiring Kopper a token $250,000 from Bermingham's account in Moorgate, England.

The next day, prosecutors say, Fastow called Mulgrew, who was in Toronto, to give him the happy news: they had just made $7 million. The money—$7,352,626, to be precise—arrived on May 1 by wire transfer to a Cayman Islands account. The three men split the money, about $2.4 million apiece. By late July, all three had resigned from their jobs at NatWest and entered a genteel retirement. (The three men were later indicted. "Really sorry, but no comment," said Bermingham when contacted in England. Mulgrew and Darby could not be reached for comment.)

The rest of the windfall went to a select handful of people Fastow had chosen to reward. Though no one else at Enron knew it, Fastow had invited six limited partners into the partnership; most were deeply involved in the ongoing dealings between LJM and Enron. Everyone hit the jackpot: the Fastow Family Foundation, set up by the CFO and his wife, invested $25,000 and received almost $4.5 million. Kopper, who also plunked down $25,000, also got $4.5 million. Ben Glisan, the deal's accountant, and Kristina Mordaunt, then general counsel for Enron Global Finance, each chipped in $5,800 and walked away with $1 million. Three other Enron and LJM employees—Kathy Lynn (Michael Kopper's old boss), Anne Yaeger, and Michael Hinds—put up less than $3,000 each and banked between $416,000 and $520,000.

Altogether, the Southampton investors received $12.3 million on a collective two-month investment of a mere $70,000. When asked later how they justified receiving such outrageous returns, the employees essentially explained that Fastow and Kopper had assured them it was all right so they didn't ask any questions.

The big Southampton score was only a fraction of the Fastow family's take from its $1 million investment in LJM. In July 2000, Fastow received an $18 million distribution from LJM1. His management fees from the fund, which did just two more deals with Enron, totaled another $2.6 million. The Fastows' total secret take, just from this one partnership, ultimately reached a staggering $25.1 million.

Michael Kopper was doing well in LJM1 also. His take from the fund totaled $12 million.

About a month after the payments arrived, Fastow flew the entire group to the Mexican resort of Los Cabos for a four-day midweek celebration. Michael Kopper and Bill Dodson were there; so were Ben Glisan and his wife; Kathy Lynn; Kristina Mordaunt and her husband; Anne Yaeger and her Enron fiancee, Trushar Patel; even Kopper's Enron secretary and his LJM assistant, along with their husbands. Everyone had a glorious time in the sun.

And why not? LJM picked up the $52,000 tab. And most of them had just made a fortune.

For Fastow, LJM1 was merely the warm-up. Just months after the entity was up and running, he returned to the Enron board, seeking approval for what he'd really wanted all along: a big, all-purpose private equity fund. Named LJM2, this fund would have far more outside money to play with—Fastow hoped to raise a minimum of $200 million—and do lots of Enron deals. As he described it in materials submitted to the directors, the fund was designed to help Enron by providing a "source of private equity for Enron to manage its investment portfolio risk, funds flow, and financial flexibility."

This time, there were a few questions about controls on the CFO's plans to greatly expand his personal business dealings with Enron. But Fastow had anticipated all of them. Rick Causey and Rick Buy were to approve all transactions between Enron and LJM, he said. The audit committee of the board would review all LJM transactions yearly. And Fastow would receive nothing more than "typical" private-equity-fund fees and the modest "promote" normally granted its managing partner on his personal investment. *What did Andersen think?* They're fine with it, responded Causey, running interference for Fastow. *But the conflict* . . . Not a problem, insisted Causey. The partnership agreement gave the investors the right to oust Andy, thus keeping him from having too much power.

As he'd done with LJM1, Lay exempted Fastow from the Enron code of ethics; on October 12, 1999, so did the Enron board. It is clear that Fastow regarded this second board vote as yet another formality. He had already retained Merrill Lynch, which had no objections to Fastow's latest approach, to market the fund to wealthy investors. And he had begun with friendly banks to start lining up commitments. Merrill formally released the placement memo on October 13, the day after the Enron board's vote.

Over the course of the next 18 months, as LJM2 completed more than 20 transactions with Enron involving hundreds of millions of dollars, Enron's full board and its finance committee received several updates on the fund's rapid-fire activity. Throughout that time, the directors remained utterly sanguine about the CFO's role. Indeed, each presentation seemed only to reinforce their sense that Fastow was engaged in selfless behavior, risking his own capital and committing his own time, all for the good of Enron. "Gosh, Andy, it sounds like you're the meat in the sandwich," remarked director Jerry Meyer during one meeting. Meyer was so impressed with the CFO's presentation that he worried Enron was *exploiting* Fastow. "Why do you want to put a busy guy in this position?" he asked Lay.

Throughout, Fastow insisted to the board that both his personal time commitment and his investment profits were limited. Seven months after winning approval for LJM2, he informed the board's finance committee he was spending only three hours a week on the partnership. And he repeatedly claimed that his compensation from the fund was modest, far less than the money he made from Enron. Fastow emphasized the care he was taking to avoid improperly exploiting his powerful role at Enron for the benefit of LJM2. Always, he insisted that his real goal was to *help* Enron.

Fastow was telling a very different story to Wall Street, however. While reassuring the board that he was safeguarding Enron from any damage resulting from his conflict, he was bragging to investors about how they could *profit* from it. In fact, this was LJM2's main selling point. The partnership's intimate ties to Enron, boasted the LJM2 placement memo, would provide "an unusually attractive investment opportunity." After all, it noted, LJM2 would be managed "on a day-to-day basis by a team of three investment professionals who all currently have senior level finance positions with Enron." The team was the Holy Trinity of Enron Global Finance: Fastow, Kopper, and Glisan. (Neither Kopper nor Glisan, who later insisted his inclusion in the prospectus was a "mistake," had requested waivers for their own conflicts.)

Just how would their involvement translate into fat returns for investors? They would provide privileged access to Enron's deal flow ("opportunitities that would not be available otherwise to outside investors"), they'd exploit Enron's desperation to close deals quickly (LJM2 "will be positioned to capitalize on Enron's need to rapidly access outside capital"), and they'd bring to the fund their "familiarity with Enron's assets and their understanding of Enron's objectives."

The memo explicitly boasted that Fastow's insider status "will contribute to superior returns." The partnership's goal, it added, was to generate an annual internal rate of return for investors "in excess of 30%" after payment of all fees. On the issue of compensation too, the offering memo was instructive: Fastow and company would receive an annual fee of 2 percent of investors' capital—at the fund's projected $200 million minimum, that amounted to $4 million a year just for starters—plus 20 percent or more of the partnership's total return.

Although this offering document had been completed well before the board meeting at which LJM2 was approved, it was never shown to the board, not then or at any other time. The directors and top Enron executives who presumably were supposed to be overseeing Fastow's conflict—Lay, Skilling, Buy, and Causey—all say they never asked to see any LJM2 partnership documents. One Enron director, Robert Belfer, later said he received the LJM2 placement memo in the mail, offering him the opportunity to invest, but that he threw it away without reading it. Finance committee chairman Herbert (Pug) Winokur later explained that he didn't need to see the memo because it had been reviewed by Enron's lawyers at Vinson & Elkins.

A month before the board vote, Fastow had been even more explicit about how he planned to run LJM2. With Kopper in tow, Fastow addressed salesmen from Merrill's private-equity team in a remarkable September 16 meeting at the firm's offices near the World Trade Center in lower Manhattan. He spoke to them for almost an hour. His remarks were preserved on videotape. There was no talk during this meeting about limiting his efforts to three hours a week. On the contrary, Fastow openly described LJM as his ticket out of Enron. "This is what I'd like to do," he declared. "Being CFO of Enron is as good a CFO position as anyone could have in America, I think. This is what I want to be my next step. I want to run an investment business. This is a unique opportunity to set it up, with unique access to deals."

The Merrill group seemed taken aback at the sheer audacity of it all. Just how would all this work? Would Fastow get to see competing bids for Enron deals? Standing in front of the room, Fastow shuffled his feet and offered a cat-that-ate-the-canary grin. "It's very hard for me *not* to see competing bids." As CFO of Enron, didn't he have an obligation to represent the company in negotiations? "I will always be on the *LJM* side of the transaction," he replied. Fastow continued: "Do I know everything that's going on? Do I have to sign off on every deal that goes in there? *Yes*." He would be in the "unique position" of being able to "know everything" about all of Enron's assets.

The sheer volume of Enron deal flow would allow him to cherry-pick great opportunities, Fastow added. ("You've got $7 billion in assets coming in every year; that roughly means I've got $7 billion in assets coming out the other side.") And so would Enron's eagerness to unload assets ("If we want to sell an investment, we want it done by the end of the quarter.") The deal selection would be "truly staggering," Fastow promised. "The prime hunting ground is going to be highly complex structured deals that have to be moved in a short time frame"—something that was never in short supply at Enron. As for how Fastow planned to recruit fund investors, a Merrill executive stated the obvious: "Andy, as chief financial officer of Enron, is heavily banked." This was an amazing opportunity, Fastow declared. "We have a real opportunity here to bust it wide open."

In the midst of this explanation of how he would play his hand in a game where he got to see all the cards, Fastow allowed himself a special moment of giddy, smug delight. "The only thing that's amazing to me," he said with a sly grin, "is that our really smart investment bankers didn't figure this out first."

After Fastow's appearance, even his friends at Merrill wanted a word of additional assurance that Fastow wasn't straying too far from the Enron reservation. On October 7, Tilney and Rob Furst, a second Texas-based Merrill banker, presented Fastow with a short list of questions for Skilling.

Had he considered how much time "Andy and his team" would be spending on LJM2? If they raised even more than the anticipated $200 million, was Skilling still comfortable with the situation? And finally, was he comfortable with "the internal mechanics put in place to resolve the conflict of interest issue?"

Four days later, the Merrill bankers got the reply they wanted to hear. "It was apparent that Jeff Skilling has spent a great deal of time with LJM matters," Tilney and Furst reported, in a brief memo to the "LJM due diligence File." They added:

> Jeff is comfortable with the conflict of interest issue for the following reasons:
> 1. Andy has no control of asset sale decision.
> 2. Rick Causey, EVP and Chief Accounting Officer, will review all transactions.
> 3. Audit Committee of the Board will receive LJM2 financial statements.

The memo offered one final observation: "Jeff stressed how important transparency and disclosure will be to the success of the arrangement."

In fact, LJM2 hadn't yet even gone to the Enron board for approval; over the duration of the fund's life, the audit committee received none of the fund's financial statements.

As CFO of Enron, Andy Fastow was indeed "heavily banked"—and he didn't hesitate to use this leverage as he set about raising money for LJM2. For the banks, the calculation was simple: Fastow maintained a stranglehold on doling out Enron's extraordinarily lucrative banking and financing work—and he kept score. Ponying up for LJM2 was a price the banks needed to pay to retain his favor. Fastow made the connection overt: his annual appraisal of individual bank performance explicitly noted their level of participation in LJM.

Fastow had begun hitting on banks to commit to LJM2 months before the fund had even won board approval. One of his prime targets was Chase Manhattan Bank, which was hungering for more Enron business. The maneuvering that preceded the bank's inevitable decision to pony up illustrates just how openly Chase viewed LJM2 as a ticket to more Enron business.

Chase Manhattan's Houston relationship manager, Rick Walker, was almost as close to Fastow as Merrill's Schuyler Tilney. Fastow wanted the bank to commit to a $20 million investment in LJM2. In August 1999, Walker sent a long memo to his two bosses, Jimmy Lee, head of global investment banking, and Todd Maclin, head of the global oil and gas business, supporting Fastow's request that Chase serve as an "anchor investor" for his fund.

The request should be viewed as "a relationship-driven exercise," Walker wrote. While Fastow was anticipating 30 percent returns, Walker was eyeing other benefits, such as "substantial financing and M&A opportunities" from LJM2 and "continued deal flow from Enron Corp." Noted Walker: "Andy has always performed on his promises to help Chase with its investment banking strategies. . . ." Though Walker knew Fastow was likely to hand the job of marketing LJM2 to Merrill, the CFO had hinted that Merrill's role might be "limited" and Chase might get future LJM business. "This is a carrot from Andy to Chase," reported Walker, "and one I think we should consider taking."

Walker advised his bosses that money invested in LJM2 was practically a sure bet. "Andy's position with Enron affords him superior insight into Enron's merchant portfolio," he noted, and the fund's ability to move quickly "will command a premium from Enron." Unlike the Enron board, Walker also harbored no illusions about Fastow's motivation. The CFO's involvement, he noted, would have "significant impact on [Fastow's] wealth."

Walker didn't just send the memo to his bosses. He also quietly faxed it to Fastow, with a personal message on the cover sheet: "Andy—Following is my draft memo—most of which I wrote last week. I'm looking forward to your comments and also discussing your schedule—do you still want to meet with Jimmy Lee next Wednesday morning? I'm currently holding my schedule open so that I could be there with you . . . Rick."

Maclin, who had recently joined Walker on a weekend fishing trip with Fastow, strongly backed the investment. Their time with Fastow, he wrote Lee in a follow-up memo, had made it clear that a $20 million commitment to LJM would produce "deal flow out of the fund" for Chase and "a closer relationship with Enron leading to more M&A and corporate finance opportunities with the company." When Lee scheduled a meeting with Fastow, Maclin noted: ". . . he is very important to the business flow out of Enron. . . . The $20 million investment in his LJM2 fund is important to him, and I believe it will buy us a lot from Enron in return, especially since it's Andy's baby."

But after meeting with Fastow, Lee had some doubts. He forwarded the LJM materials to another bank executive with the hand-scrawled message across the cover sheet: "Will you please look into this with Rick Walker. It is a 'captive' fund to Enron. I am skeptical because this guy running it is inexperienced & sounds very naïve. However, this relationship is very big and important. We 'may' have to do a little. J."

Ultimately, Lee agreed to put $10 million in the fund. After getting the news, Maclin jotted a note to Walker reminding him that the bank was expecting a quick payoff: "Rick—Now that you got your $10 mil, we need an M&A mandate—something big & high profile. When do we go ask Fastow for this order??" It didn't take long for the returns to start flowing. Within months, Chase had received $650,000 in LJM underwriting fees.

In the midst of these internal deliberations, an Enron executive named Gene Humphrey—coincidentally, the man who hired Andy Fastow—approached Chase with a request for an equity investment in another fund. This one was sponsored directly by Enron and was aimed at providing venture capital to inner-city businesses owned by women or minorities. The Enron Economic Development Corporation, as it was called, was close to Ken Lay's heart. But Fastow quickly advised Walker that the bank could feel free to ignore it; LJM was the real priority. Andy made it "crystal clear" that "there is absolutely no pressure on Chase to invest in this fund concept," Walker e-mailed his bosses. "Andy was also very emphatic that he did not want anything to detract from our efforts to work with him on his LJM2 investment fund."

Fastow was putting the hard sell on all the financial institutions that did business with Enron. "All of our significant relationships are coming," he advised one Houston banker while soliciting a big investment. The message was clear: if the bank didn't kick in, it might not remain "significant." So the commitments poured in: First Union, $25 million; CIBC and J. P. Morgan, $15 million; Chase and Credit Suisse First Boston, $10 million apiece; Donaldson, Lufkin & Jenrette, $5 million. Merrill signed on for $5 million, and the hallway buzz about the fund was so strong that 97 individual Merrill employees agreed to invest another $17.6 million. (Merrill received a $3 million placement fee.) Citigroup, whose annual fees from Enron exceeded $40 million, committed $10 million. An internal e-mail later noted: "The initial investment in the fund was based solely on Enron's relationship with Citigroup, not potential investment returns." Lehman Brothers was so shocked that the Enron board would approve such an arrangement that it insisted on receiving a certified copy of the board resolution approving Fastow's conflict. Then it signed on for $10 million.

For the most part, financial institutions and insurance companies provided the early money, but there were plenty of other blue-chip institutional investors: Weyerhaeuser, the MacArthur Foundation, the Arkansas Teacher Retirement System, and the Institute for Advanced Study in Princeton. By the time he was done, Fastow had roped in 51 investor groups and raised capital commitments of $392 million—almost twice his original goal.

With the board's blessing and its coffers brimming, LJM2 leaped into action, instantly becoming the single most powerful tool for managing Enron's earnings. Fastow proudly informed the board that in less than six months his two LJMs had contributed $229.5 million to Enron's earnings, generated more than $2 billion in cash flow, and, he insisted, saved Enron $2.3 million in fees. In 1999, LJM had also participated in Enron's usual end-of-year frenzied deal making, which Fastow reported this way: "Q4 1999: 8 days/6 deals/$125 million."

What's remarkable about all this is that Fastow wasn't using his inside information to cherry-pick Enron's best deals, as he'd promised his investors. The projects he was steering LJM into were among Enron's *worst,* the dogs the company couldn't unload on anyone else. Yet even when these investments further deteriorated in LJM's portfolio, Fastow's fund almost always somehow managed to make a profit.

The reason was simple: the game was rigged. LJM was really just doing Enron's dirty work: warehousing troubled assets, allowing Enron to get them off its balance sheet and book the profits and cash flow it desperately needed to please Wall Street. LJM's real business was making Enron look good. And in return, LJM was getting paid handsomely for its troubles through secret special arrangements with Enron.

Consider, for example, Cuiabá, a deeply troubled power project Enron was building in Brazil. The plant, which was being built in phases, was supposed to hook up to a natural-gas pipeline that Enron was laying from Bolivia to Brazil, through an endangered tropical forest. By the fall of 1999, Cuiabá was experiencing major problems, and Enron wanted to sell down its stake in the project. Not surprisingly, there were no interested buyers.

Enter LJM1. In September, Fastow's first partnership bought a 13 percent stake for $11.3 million in the joint venture that owned Cuiabá. By cutting Enron's stake, LJM allowed Enron to keep $200 million in debt from the project off its books and record $65 million in mark-to-market profits on a gas-supply contract with the plant. After the sale to LJM1 was completed, the plant's situation—and, presumably, its market value—continued to worsen. Rick Buy, Enron's chief risk officer, later recalled being delighted that Enron had reduced its stake in the plant. Cuiabá was in a group of troubled assets that Fastow's finance team referred to as "Enron's nuclear waste."

Yet about two years after the sale, with Cuiabá in far worse shape, Enron bought back LJM's stake, handing the CFO's partnership a $3 million profit. Skilling later insisted that Enron's Brazilian staff had made misrepresentations to LJM that obligated Enron to buy back the fund's interest.

But at the time (according to a later investigation), Fastow told a subordinate that Enron had made a secret handshake agreement with LJM1 that guaranteed repurchase of the Cuiabá interest, even if its value declined. Indeed, it wasn't even all that much of a secret: a June 1999 e-mail from an Enron accountant named Kent Castleman described LJM as a "short-term equity warehouse" for the Cuiabá stake. Kopper later disclosed that the buyback provision had even been included in drafts of the original Cuiabá sale documents. One thing was certain: the deal provided yet another windfall for LJM's investors. When the transaction was completed, the fund's general partner (by then Michael Kopper) received $7.3 million. LJM1's limited partners, CSFB and Royal Bank of Scotland (which had acquired NatWest), got $2.7 million apiece.

Another example: On December 21, LJM2 bought a 75 percent interest in an Enron power plant being built in Poland, the country's first independent power project. Fastow's fund invested $30 million in equity and debt in the plant, which allowed Enron to book $16 million in fourth-quarter profits. The company had agreed that it would try to find a buyer for LJM2's interest after the quarter closed, but when the plant malfunctioned during a test, Enron couldn't find one. So, just three months after selling to LJM2, Enron, through two different subsidiaries, bought it back for $32 million.

For a price, LJM2 made all sorts of accommodations to Enron, even backdating documents. The legal documents on one LJM2 transaction showed that the fund bought a set of financial instruments from Enron on December 29 and sold them to another Enron-related entity the very next day—in time to remove them from Enron's balance sheet in the company's 1999 financial statements. But investigators later found that the deal didn't actually occur until two months later. Fastow had originally demanded that LJM2 be paid $1 million for its troubles. But he dropped his price to $100,000 after complaints from Enron treasurer Jeff McMahon.

In another late-December deal, LJM2 paid $26.3 million ($1 million in cash, the rest in a note) for an offshore natural-gas gathering system. According to an LJM internal memo, the deal allowed Enron to book $2.5 million in earnings and another $25 million in cash flow on a related gas contract when "no other 3rd party would take . . . the exposure in the timeframe that LJM did." Enron bought back the interest three months later, giving LJM a $500,000 profit.

As the pace of LJM's deal making accelerated, Fastow made little effort to dampen the conflicts of interest he and other LJM officials faced. On the contrary: he positively embraced the conflicts and flaunted them inside Enron. For instance, under an agreement Fastow struck with Causey, Enron employees were allowed to work full time for LJM while keeping their Enron benefits and even remaining in their Enron offices. The arrangement institutionalized their divided loyalties: LJM was to pay Kopper's bonus while Enron would cover his base salary, Kathy Lynn would get her salary and bonus from LJM and her benefits from Enron, and the salary and bonus for Anne Yaeger would be divided between LJM and Enron. The LJM executives sat next to colleagues who were sometimes negotiating with them on behalf of Enron. At times, it was unclear who was negotiating for Enron and who was negotiating for LJM.

Fastow himself had no compunction about pressuring Enron finance executives—officials who reported to him in his capacity as Enron's CFO—to cut more generous deals for LJM. In at least 13 transactions with LJM, Enron employees who reported either directly or indirectly to Fastow found themselves on the other side of the table from their boss. Time and again, he told Enron negotiators they were bargaining too hard against LJM, that they needed to wrap up a deal, even if it meant giving the partnership more generous terms. Notorious for beating up bankers, Fastow proved just as nasty to Enron employees negotiating against LJM. Crossing Fastow, they knew, could cost them a large part of their year-end bonuses.

Fastow's partnership made out handsomely. Almost all of LJM2's deals—21 of 23—were related to Enron. Excluding five assets LJM2 held at the time of Enron's collapse, the fund made money on all but one of them, generating $85.3 million in profits. Of the 16 Enron-related assets that LJM2 sold profitably, 14 went straight back to Enron (or a related entity), most in a matter of months, even when their value had dropped.

This pattern spurred rumors that Skilling and Fastow had made a secret deal to guarantee that LJM2 wouldn't lose money. Government officials later charged in court papers that Fastow had forged just such an arrangement with Causey, called the Global Galactic agreement. Under the accord, the government alleges, if LJM lost any money in its deals with Enron, the company promised to make it up later. Many Enron hands believe that Causey wouldn't do anything this significant without Skilling's blessing. Though all the principals involved (including Skilling) have denied the existence of such a pact, Causey's calendar shows a 30-minute meeting with Fastow at 9 A.M. on September 6, 2000. It bears the notation "Global Galactic deal."

It's safe to conclude that LJM's investors were led to believe that Fastow had received certain, shall we say, commitments. An executive at the Royal Bank of Scotland, an LJM lender, returned from a meeting with Enron executives with written notes of their informal assurances: "Enron's senior management are consistent in strongly representing verbally that Enron will do everything in their power to protect the investors and lenders involved." In an e-mail to his colleagues, a Citigroup executive later described a similar assurance offered from the LJM side: "LJM2 principals argue that Enron would make the Fund whole should it suffer losses because the vehicles that the Fund invests in are critically important to Enron's ability to manage its earnings."

Enron's court-appointed bankruptcy examiner later noted that there was "no evidence of any effort to determine and use fair market values" for the sale of assets to LJM2 or their subsequent repurchase by Enron. "LJM2's function in the Enron related transactions was as a lender," he added. "Its 'investments' were more like loans than arm's length sales to third parties. . . ." Many of the transactions, he concluded, "had no valid business purpose from Enron's perspective, other than to achieve desired financial statement reporting." A lengthy investigation by outside lawyers hired by Enron's board concluded that LJM's investments simply were never at risk: "As a matter of economic substance, it is not clear that anything was really being bought or sold."

As for the controls, they were a joke. None of those who were supposed to be providing oversight of Fastow's conflict took the responsibility seriously. Causey and Buy were supposed to be reviewing all transactions with the partnership, but some of the deals were never even submitted to them. And when he did review LJM transactions, Causey—whose fiftieth-floor office was next door to Fastow's—later explained, he viewed his job as merely making sure that the appropriate people had "signed off"; never mind that *he* was the appropriate person. Buy, who was also supposed to provide oversight, said he limited his involvement to assessing Enron's risk; he later complained to Vince Kaminski that he was getting so many approval sheets to sign on LJM deals at his New Hampshire summer home that he'd had to buy a new fax machine. Some LJM2 deals went through without any approval sheets being generated; in other cases, required signatures from Enron executives were never obtained or the approval documents were prepared after the deal had closed.

In February 2000, the board audit committee conducted its first annual review of LJM transactions. It received a single sheet of paper titled "LJM Investment Activity 1999" listing eight partnership transactions; two others (including Cuiabá) weren't even included. Causey described the deals and assured the directors that all the transactions had been negotiated on "an arms-length basis." The discussion lasted 15 minutes. A few months later, the board's finance committee took its turn, listening to Fastow discuss how much his fund was doing for Enron. When one director asked why Enron's CFO was spending so much time on an outside partnership—*didn't he have enough to do?*—Fastow replied that he had hired employees to run the fund and it was now occupying only about three hours of his time a week. Anticipating the subject of his compensation, Fastow told the finance committee that LJM2 was projecting that its investors would receive an annual return of a relatively modest 17.95 percent. What Fastow didn't mention was that *on that very day,* the Enron investors in his Southampton partnership were receiving wire transfers divvying up more than $12 million—with the Fastow Family Foundation alone receiving a return on its investment of *17,765 percent.*

Even with the existence of LJM2, Enron was still having trouble making its numbers as 1999 came to a close. Though investors and outside observers didn't realize it, the company was having a tough year. It was spending a fortune on EES and broadband and seeding an assortment of Skilling's other new ventures. And trading was having a mixed year.

There was so much at stake. Enron's shares were climbing again—they rose 55 percent in 1999—and salaries and bonuses were soaring. Every high-level Enron executive held options worth millions. There was even a long-term incentive plan to provide yet another payoff built on Enron's share price: if the company's stock performance between 1997 and 2001 ranked among the top six companies in the Standard & Poor's index, everyone in upper management would get a special cash bonus.

So as Enron headed into December and as the company's finance executives realized the company was still short of its earnings targets, it undertook two deals that were egregious even by Enron's standards. Both involved Merrill

Lynch; it wasn't lost on anyone that Merrill was helping Fastow raise money for LJM2.

In the first transaction, Merrill agreed to participate in an energy trade with Enron that would generate $50 million in fourth-quarter profits. The government later called the transaction fraudulent. The deal was initiated by Cliff Baxter, who had become CEO of Enron North America earlier that year.

As originally conceived, the deal involved two commodity trades between Enron and Merrill in something called heat-rate swaps. The paired trades were perfect mirror images of one another, but they had different accounting treatments. As a result, Enron would book the profits it needed immediately on the first trade while deferring a loss on the mirror-image trade until later. Merrill was to make $8.5 million from the transaction. But Arthur Andersen refused to approve the accounting because neither party had any true risk in the deal.

The problem was solved by setting up a second set of trades, where the paired deals were different enough to justify the separate accounting treatments—or were, at least, as long as Enron and Merrill didn't cancel both trades at the same time. To get Merrill to go along with this arrangement for booking profits, Baxter had agreed to double the bank's fee to $17 million.

The key Merrill advocates were the usual suspects: Schuyler Tilney and Rob Furst, the firm's top Enron contacts. They explained to a firm committee reviewing the deal that it presented no risk to Merrill and that they had extracted the oversize $17 million profit because Enron was desperate to hit its Wall Street targets. One Merrill executive, according to a later SEC complaint in the matter, expressed reservations: *wasn't this earnings manipulation?* Merrill, responded a senior executive, has "17 million reasons" for doing the deal.

After Merrill executives insisted on speaking to Causey, Enron's accounting chief explained that the company needed the trade's earnings to hit its numbers; millions in executive bonuses were riding on it, Causey added. At Merrill's request (according to the SEC), Causey agreed to sign a warranty letter prepared by Merrill stating that Arthur Andersen had approved the deal and that Merrill Lynch had played no part in its accounting. Causey faxed the signed letter back to Merrill on December 31, literally only hours before the clock ran out on the fourth quarter. For its part, Arthur Andersen said that Enron would have to restate the numbers if the trades were later unwound.

Sure enough, less than two months later, Enron told Merrill it wanted to unwind the trade early. The SEC later charged that this early unwinding had been part of an "understanding" between Enron and Merrill all along. Still, there was squabbling over the arrangements. Enron wanted Merrill to forgo its fee, which wasn't due until the fall; Merrill wanted the entire $17 million. Tilney wrote his Merrill colleagues for guidance: ". . . they knew what we were making at the time and we were clearly helping them make earnings for the quarter and year (which had great value in their stock price, not to mention personal compensation). What would you think was a fair number . . . ?" Ultimately, they agreed to split the difference: in June, Enron paid Merrill $8.5 million for its help in manu-facturing earnings. Arthur Andersen never followed through on its threat to force Enron to restate the $50 million if the trades were later unwound.

The second deal was cooked up to solve a familiar Enron problem: assets it couldn't sell. In this case, Enron was trying to unload a trio of 3,600-ton floating power plants, turbines placed on barges destined for a lagoon off the Nigerian coast. These barges, still under construction, were supposed to provide elec-tricity for Nigeria's national grid.

In mid-December, Enron treasurer Jeff McMahon contacted Furst about buy-ing an interest in the barge project. According to the SEC, Enron wanted to sell so it could book another $12 million in earnings and $28 million in cash flow. The proposed deal would work like this: if Merrill would take the stake in the barges off its hands by year-end, Enron would arrange a profitable buyback later. Merrill would get a $250,000 up-front fee, a 15 percent annual rate of return on a $7 million equity investment (Enron would finance $21 million in interest-free debt), and an oral guarantee that Enron would "facilitate" Merrill's "exit from the transaction" by June 30, 2000. Merrill's internal deal memo captured the es-sential dynamic: "Enron has strongly requested ML to enter into this transaction. Enron has paid ML approximately $40 million in fees in 1999 and is expected to do so again in 2000."

Nonetheless, inside Merrill, there was considerable anxiety about the ar-rangement. If the buyback guarantee were real, the sale was a sham. On the other hand, if Enron wasn't really guaranteeing the buyback, Merrill was risking $7 million on an asset—Nigerian barges?—that no one there wanted to own. Mer-rill hadn't even done any due diligence on the investment.

Enron's promise, of course, had to remain informal. The guarantee couldn't be made in writing because doing so would disqualify it from the accounting treatment Enron sought. And indeed, Merrill later denied that the guarantee was part of the deal even though the obligation was cited in draft deal documents as well as in e-mails circulated by both Merrill and Enron executives, according to the SEC. Inside Merrill, in fact, executives referred to the deal as a $7 million "handshake" loan to Enron.

For a few days, Merrill hesitated. Some of its bankers harbored qualms about the appearance of the transaction, if nothing else. One executive who'd reviewed the deal scribbled a handwritten note: "Reputational risk i.e. aid/abet Enron in-come stmt manipulation. . . ." But to most at the firm, the real issues were risking $7 million and displeasing Enron.

To resolve these delicate matters, Dan Bayly, global head of investment bank-ing, led a group of Merrill bankers in a conference call with Fastow. The Enron CFO had been putting the heat on Merrill to do the deal—"bear-hugging," Fastow liked to call it. Now Bayly wanted to make sure they understood one another. Bayly wanted Fastow to know that Merrill was considering the deal as a special

favor to Enron; he hoped the CFO would appreciate this act of friendship and presumably reward it with future business. According to the government, he wanted
Fastow's personal assurance that Merrill's money really wasn't at risk, that the
firm would be taken out in six months' time. After Fastow told Bayly what he
wanted to hear, the Merrill executive ordered his bankers to close the deal.

The following May, as the deadline for the barge buyout neared without an
outside purchaser in sight, an Enron executive noted the consequences of Enron
having to repurchase the stake itself: ". . . The investment in the barges will be
placed on the balance sheet. This will not only have income implications but require a level of damage control with AA [Arthur Andersen]. As you know, ML's
decision to purchase the equity was based solely on personal assurances by Enron senior management to ML's Vice Chairman [Bayly] that the transaction
would not go beyond June 30, 2000."

A few weeks later, with the investment bankers wringing their hands, Enron
informed Merrill that it had found a buyer for the barges. It was none other than
LJM2. Fastow's fund purchased Merrill's equity stake for $7,525,000, exactly
the promised return, and assumed the $21 million debt as well. Merrill walked
away from the deal with a $775,000 profit. And LJM2 bought into the Nigerian
barges with its own take-out promise from Enron. As a deal-approval sheet explained: "LJM2 expects to be bought out by Enron within 7 months. . . ." Instead, Enron managed to find a *real* outside buyer three months later. Andy
Fastow's fund cleared $650,000.

On January 18, 2000, Enron issued a press release announcing its fourth-
quarter results: ENRON CONTINUES STRONG EARNINGS GROWTH. The company
reported earnings of $1.17 per share—matching Wall Street's expectations. The
LJM and Merrill deals had contributed more than half of the quarter's profits.
Without the transactions, Enron would have missed its number. A near catastrophe had been averted.

Jeff McMahon, Enron's treasurer, had good reason to wish LJM2 well. McMahon owed his job to Fastow, who had installed him as corporate treasurer in
1998, bringing him back from London, where he'd spent three years as CFO of
Enron Europe. Fastow had also told him that if LJM2 succeeded, he would put
together an even bigger fund—LJM3—and might leave Enron to run it. Then,
Fastow explained, he would recommend that McMahon replace him as CFO. It
was just the sort of carrot Fastow loved to dangle, yet another way to wield
power. Only later did McMahon learn that Fastow had made the same promise to
Rick Causey.

McMahon was no innocent. Like virtually all Enron finance executives, he'd
helped put together his share of funny deals over the years to help the company
hit its earnings targets. He also didn't have any particular qualms about the idea
of a captive private fund that the company could tap to supply equity for Enron-
created SPEs. But when Fastow decided that he would run the fund himself, that,

to McMahon, was taking things too far. Bankers were soon complaining to him that his boss was, in effect, blackmailing them into investing in LJM; one even said his firm had been promised Enron's next bond deal in exchange for an investment. McMahon was also shocked by Fastow's claims to the board that he was spending less than three hours a week on LJM matters. McMahon knew that the CFO had spent weeks on the road selling his fund to investors.

McMahon had also expressed skepticism about Enron's decision to buy back some of the LJM deals. On one approval sheet, he'd written: "There were no economics run to demonstrate this investment makes sense" before crossing out the remark and initialing his approval. It bothered him that Fastow and Kopper were so blatantly exploiting their knowledge of which deals Enron needed to close to meet its budget numbers. He saw how executives were afraid to negotiate too strenuously against LJM, fearing that Fastow and Kopper would retaliate at bonus time. McMahon had complained to Fastow about LJM issues, and he firmly believed that it had cost him. McMahon's 1999 bonus had been lower than he'd expected; Kopper's, by contrast, had been off the charts.

On March 15, McMahon met with Fastow again, complaining about the conflicts and the distraction the partnership presented and telling him that the LJM staffers need to be moved "out of the Enron building." Fastow had spent part of the morning in a meeting about LJM1's Rhythms hedge; he would spend most of the rest of his afternoon on LJM meetings and document signings. "I hear you," he told McMahon. "I'll fix it." Unconvinced, McMahon—acting on the advice of Cliff Baxter, who told him that only Skilling could resolve the "Andy problem"—immediately made an appointment with the Enron president for the following day.

To prepare for the meeting, McMahon sat down and jotted down two pages of notes about his problems with his boss. When McMahon arrived for the 30-minute meeting with Skilling, he later recalled, he followed his script closely.

"Untenable situation," the notes begin. "LJM situation where AF wears two hats and upside comp is so great creates a conflict I am right in the middle of. I find myself negotiating with Andy on Enron matters and am pressured to do a deal that I do not believe is in the best interests of the shareholders," McMahon's notes continued, "My integrity forces me to continue to negotiate the way I believe is correct." If he had to continue doing this, McMahon told Skilling, according to his notes, "I MUST know I have support from you and there won't be any ramifications." If Skilling couldn't make that promise, McMahon wanted a transfer. "Will not compromise my integrity," McMahon wrote. He also didn't want to be punished for it financially, either. "Bonuses do get affected," he noted, citing his own treatment compared with Kopper's.

McMahon spoke almost nonstop for 30 minutes. When he was finished, Skilling assured him he would take care of it.

Skilling later presented a dramatically different account of the encounter. He insisted McMahon's primary concern wasn't the ethics of the situation but the awkwardness of negotiating with his own boss and how that "might impact his compensation package." He said that he'd advised McMahon to "take a baseball bat to Andy" when negotiating on behalf of Enron and that he wouldn't pay a price for it at bonus time.

In any case, the matter was soon resolved. On March 30, Fastow angrily demanded a meeting with McMahon. They met in the CFO's office at 7:30 the next morning. "I'm not sure we can keep working together," Fastow told him. Why had McMahon gone behind his back? Didn't he know everything he told Skilling would get to Fastow?

The following week, McMahon was approached about transferring into a new business the company was starting, called Enron Net Works. Despite the problems with Fastow, McMahon wasn't interested, because the new job was a demotion: he liked being the corporate treasurer of a major corporation too much to let go of it easily. But a few days later, Skilling himself came to McMahon's office to persuade him to take the new job. The future of Enron was in businesses like NetWorks, Skilling insisted. He should take the opportunity.

As McMahon saw it, the message was clear: what Skilling was really doing was accepting the "or else" portion of his ultimatum. Clearly, the Enron president wasn't willing to do anything about Fastow and his conflicts, so he was arranging McMahon's transfer. (Skilling later insisted McMahon's move represented a promotion and was entirely unrelated to his complaints about LJM.)

After accepting the transfer, McMahon gave Fastow a list of three candidates he recommended to replace him. None of them got the position. In May 2000, Fastow named his favorite accountant, 35-year-old Ben Glisan, as Enron's corporate treasurer.

CHAPTER 14

The Beating Heart of Enron

Inside his warped world, Andy Fastow believed he deserved all the money he was taking out of Enron through the LJM partnerships. After all, he and his Global Finance team were the ones whose deals were creating the illusion of a company that could do no wrong. Fastow, Kopper, Glisan, and the other key members of the Global Finance group saw themselves as the core of Enron.

But there was another group at Enron who believed precisely the same thing, who thought *they* were the smartest and the best; who thought, in fact, that they represented the beating heart of the coolest company on earth. These were the wholesale traders.

Almost from the moment Skilling set up the old Gas Bank, the traders had viewed themselves as a breed apart. From the start, Skilling had grafted MBAs and former Wall Streeters onto an organization that was largely made up of old-time oil and gas hands, executives more comfortable with drilling rigs than pricing curves. With Skilling's encouragement, the traders soon came to see themselves as Enron's true elite.

Over the years, though, the culture of the trading floor had undergone some subtle and none too pleasant changes. In the early years, the traders' feelings of superiority came from the sense that they were creating a new industry from scratch. In later years, although the sense of mission—even, in some cases, the idealism—about the greatness of markets remained, it was overshadowed by the money it was so easy to make. Toward the end of the 1990s came unprecedented volatility, and for traders, volatility is one of the necessary ingredients for making outsize profits. And as trading profits soared, the traders became convinced of their own invincibility. "It was zealotry to greed to arrogance to demise," says one former executive.

Arrogance was present in spades—and not just in Enron's dismissive attitude toward the rest of its industry. It was their work, the traders believed, that was papering over the failures elsewhere inside Enron. *Global Finance?* Kopper used to complain about the lack of respect he got from the traders. The traders ridiculed Fastow, both for his slight speech impediment—"Willie Whistle," one used to call him—and for his fondness for a buttoned-up suit. Fastow rarely set foot on the trading floor. "If Enron was arrogant to the industry," says one former trader, "then we were arrogant to the rest of Enron." The other Enron businesses, even the sexy new ones like EES and Broadband, were nothing more than "a collection bin of castoffs," full of employees who couldn't make it on the trading floor, adds another trader. In time, the traders became nearly impossible to control.

That was true even for Skilling, who used to lament that dealing with the traders was like "herding ducks. Traders are not just right but absolutely right," he would add. "Everything is a negotiation. If you asked them to turn left, even if they wanted to turn left, they'd say, 'Well, how much are you going to pay me to turn left?' " Though Skilling was their boss, he seemed intimidated by them. They were like a powerful high school clique that terrorizes even the principal. "They didn't appear menacing," says a former executive, "but they were a mob."

The traders *were* smart, by and large, and they were good at what they did. But their insular culture had a dangerous edge; not only was it self-righteous, but it could never see beyond its own value system. The culture that evolved allowed the traders to justify making money in ways companies should never countenance. Most companies with trading desks don't allow the traders' ethos to trump all other values, and they don't allow the traders themselves to run amok. That both happened at Enron was not so much a failure of the traders but of Enron's top management, which was supposed to keep them in check but wouldn't—or couldn't.

The head of Enron North America—as the part of the company that included trading was now called—had always been a member of Skilling's old guard. For years, of course, Lou Pai had been in charge of the traders. In 1997, when Pai left to take charge of the fledgling EES, Skilling installed Ken Rice as his replacement. Even by then, the trading culture was changing, and the new breed of traders had begun to view Skilling's old guard as a handful of has-beens who happened to have their umbrellas open when it rained money. They particularly loathed Ken Rice. His proudest accomplishment, the old Sithe deal, had become a millstone around the necks of the traders. His affair with Amanda Martin was also a cause of ire. It wasn't the affair itself the traders objected to; Martin's rapid rise through the ranks was an affront to their belief that they were operating in a meritocracy. The traders were convinced that she was getting ahead solely because of her relationship with Rice. She certainly didn't think like a trader, and they were not about to acknowledge that she might have had some skills as a businesswoman. What the traders also didn't see is that the world they were creating wasn't perhaps such a pure meritocracy, either. After all, most of the people who got ahead were the ones who looked and acted like them.

The third member of the old guard to be put in charge of the traders was Cliff Baxter. He took over in the middle of 1999, when Rice departed for the new broadband division. This was Baxter's first try at running an Enron business, something he'd openly hankered for. Like Fastow earlier in the decade, he wanted to prove his mettle as a manager who could generate big profits for the company. But by the time he arrived on the scene, the trading culture had hardened. Although the traders liked him well enough, Baxter wasn't one of them; the traders knew they could safely ignore him. And so they did. Besides, they already had a leader. His name was Greg Whalley. He didn't have Baxter's title, but he was their real boss, the one they listened to and the one who truly commanded their respect.

A former army tank captain, Whalley personified the trader's view of the world. He saw everything in terms of split-second economics; if he couldn't buy or sell something *right this second*, it seemed to have no value to him. His favorite book was Ayn Rand's *The Fountainhead*, which extols individual achievement and drive over the will of the group. He believed in a culture that maximized the ability of individuals to make their own decisions and reap their own rewards. "People were able to take risks the way they wanted and be accountable for it, which is the most sacred thing in a trading shop," says a former trader. Whalley had the trader's ability to strip his decision-making of all emotional content, which he viewed as noneconomic. That's why another executive says that Whalley "would have been content to interact with a computer 360 days a year." Even more than Skilling, Whalley believed that he could create a pure meritocracy. He instilled a culture on the trading floor that was ruthlessly mercenary.

Yet he was also a man who commanded enormous personal loyalty and admiration. Part of it was that he was witheringly smart; Skilling often described Whalley as "probably the smartest person I know." Part of it was that others admired his abilities as a trader. But it was also that he had the kind of personal presence that made people want to follow him, a rarity at Enron. Equally rare was that Whalley, at least in the view of his admirers, did not put his own paycheck above everything else. Not that he was looking out for everyone. The needs of his own clan were Whalley's top priority: it was "us first," not "me first." To his supporters, his black-and-white view of the world did not come across as self-serving but rather as reflecting a genuine intellectual belief. Many of the traders worshiped him. "Whalley is a screaming stud," they'd say. "He's everything you would want in a boss or a friend." "People would run through walls for him."

The driven, workaholic son of a pilot for Federal Express, Whalley graduated from West Point in 1984 with a degree in economics and spent the next six years in the army, serving in Germany and Kentucky. In 1990, he resigned to go to Stanford Business School, then joined Enron in one of the first classes of associates. One person who interviewed him was struck by his passion for the trading business, not just the trading itself but the esoteric intellectual arguments that went along with it. He was 30 by then, older than most of his fellow associates, and he immediately stood out for his intelligence and his tremendous confidence, two of the greatest assets an Enron employee could have. Whether through ambition or curiosity, he was always looking outside his own sphere for another problem he could fix. That was another rare trait at Enron, and it helped Whalley rise rapidly. He was a natural trader, and even after he became a top executive, he never completely stopped trading, running his own oil trading book right up to the end. (One set of Enron daily position reports shows that he was down about $30 million for the year when Enron collapsed.) In 1996, Whalley was chosen to help start Enron's trading operations in Europe. Two years later, he returned to Houston, and though he held a number of different titles over the next several years, everybody at Enron understood what his real job was. Whalley controlled the traders. The old guard—Baxter, Rice, and Pai—used to refer to him as "the union boss."

Whalley was another "guy with spikes." He was unusually blunt for a corporate executive; indeed, that was part of the reason the traders adored him. "Whalley was very rough around the edges," says someone who used to work in the Enron executive suite. "If his mind thinks it, his mouth says it." Those who disliked him—and there were many outside the trading floor—criticized him for being arrogant and immature. ("He is just a *jerk*," says someone who dealt with him at corporate functions.) He could usually be found wearing rumpled khakis and a casual shirt, and he liked to hang out with fellow traders at a Houston bar named Kenneally's, drinking beers and debating.

At work, he forced the traders to defend their ideas, even when he already agreed with them. He took that same approach even when he wasn't working. It didn't seem to matter to him which side of an issue you took; Whalley leaped to the other side, even on such contentious political subjects as abortion, gun control, or gays in the military. He would say, "I love the NRA" or "people who own guns are idiots," then abruptly switch sides if someone agreed with him too quickly. It was as if he had no particular moral beliefs himself; it was just a big game. He had zero patience for those he felt lacked the kind of pure intellect he admired and could instantly reduce just about anyone to red-faced, quivering shame. "Whalley had a vicious intelligence to him," says a former colleague. "If you didn't know what you were talking about, he would pick you to pieces."

Whalley was also a gambler. In the mid-1990s, before he left for London, he ran an NCAA betting pool from the trading-room floor. Many of the Enron old guard put money in the pool, including Pai and Rice. So did outsiders, including some of the McKinsey consultants assigned to the Enron account. The pot grew to more than $100,000. Whalley and others claimed that the pool was an intellectual exercise designed to teach young traders about risk and reward. But when Lay found out, he was furious. At the next PRC, there was a fierce debate over whether Whalley should be denied a promotion for running a betting pool. He wasn't.

As Whalley rocketed through Enron, he brought along a handful of acolytes. One was a Canadian named John Lavorato, or Lavo, as everyone called him, who eventually ran trading in North America. He was known for his aggressive attitude and his odd physical tics, which including grabbing onto the shoulders of his shirt, twitching, and scratching. Lavo "played pretty loose" with the rules, as Skilling once put it. Not that this tendency ever concerned his bosses at Enron; Lavo rose through the ranks even as he was being investigated for manipulating power prices in Canada. (He was later cleared of the charges.) Lavorato was another who saw the world as a place where everything was tradable; it came as a major shock to him to learn that Enron's venture-capital investments in small private companies couldn't be sold at a moment's notice. Another Whalley aide was John Sherriff, a former gas trader who ran Enron Europe. The Sherriff legend was that he had made an enormous amount—tens of millions—in a single bet on short-term gas prices back in the mid-1990s, when the business was still in its early stages and such a windfall was not believed possible. All the members of Whalley's core group shared a short-term mind-set, and all of them reveled in taking huge risks.

One thing the traders all loved about Enron was the sense they had of operating in the purest environment that had ever been created in corporate America. By pure, they meant that the trading floor operated strictly by the dictates of the free market. The company's credo had always been that free markets worked best, of course. But the traders grabbed onto that belief with a cultlike fierceness. They could be positively self-righteous about it. They *loved* the idea that they were inserting competition—and not just any competition but brutal, Enron-style competition—into such formerly sleepy industries as the utility business. They believed that free markets made the world a fairer place, one where price dictated deals, rather than relationships or other "noneconomic" factors. To them, the lines were clearly drawn: it was visionaries versus Neanderthals. "Enron," says a former trader, "was all about changing the world, showing up every day to be a pain in the ass to every incumbent."

More than that, though, they believed that the market was the ultimate judge of their work and their worth. The market created a true meritocracy: you either made money because you made good trading decisions or you lost money because you made bad ones. Enron traders didn't concern themselves with ethics or morality apart from the unyielding judgment of the markets. Maximizing profit was not inconsistent with doing good, they believed, but an inherent part of it, and the judge of good and bad was the immediate consequence of a split-second trade. The highest compliment a trader could pay a colleague was to call him intellectually pure. The worst insult was to accuse someone of making a deal that wasn't economic.

There was another component, too. Because the traders thought they were creating a new world, they looked upon existing rules not as guidelines to be respected but as mere conventions to be gotten around in whatever creative fashion they could devise.

Whalley was so intent on trying to remove the human element from trading that he once had a robot programmed to trade futures contracts. He wanted to see whether a market with enough liquidity could run on autopilot. He even gave the robotrader a name: George. Skilling was entranced with Whalley's experiment and would wander down to the trading floor every few hours to see if George was making any money. "How's George doing?" Skilling would ask. "Down another $50,000," Whalley would reply. George lost about a million bucks before Whalley finally pulled the plug.

The traders' belief system did not make the Enron trading floor a warm and cuddly place. "We were an enormous collection of Type A personalities," says an ex-trader. "We were very competitive, and we just didn't feel that we could fail a lot." An executive named Bill Butler used to stalk the floor with an eight-foot-long black bullwhip in hand, jokingly threatening traders who didn't seem to be spending enough time on the phone. Their esprit was such that the traders took great pleasure in outsmarting other parts of Enron, and they didn't show much mercy for one another, either. "If you showed any weakness, the antibodies would attack," says a former trader. "Life at Enron," says another, "was the purest form of balls-out guerrilla warfare."

This sense of the world as an endless competition, a chance to one-up some-one else, permeated the trading floor. Betting was a way of life and not just during March Madness. Traders would make bets on whether someone could down a sack of Big Macs or make consecutive free throws or eat two slices of bread (without water) in under a minute. Sometimes the stakes got very high. Every year, on the annual retreat to the Hyatt Hill Country Resort in San Antonio for vice presidents and above, a group of traders would play a poker game called Omaha (where the lowest hand and the highest split the pot) at the same table in the lobby of the hotel. The pot was usually around $1,000, but in the final year it was played—2000—three players thought they had good odds of winning. The pot grew to $33,000, as the crowd gathered and the tension built into the early morning hours. One player had both the high hand and the low hand. He bought a new BMW. The other two—one of them London chief John Sherriff—were out $11,000 each.

The one member of the old guard the traders admired was Skilling himself. Though they cringed when he said things like "we're on the side of the angels"— what an emotion-laden thought!—they agreed wholeheartedly with the underlying sentiment. "What Skilling did so well was to motivate other people to his vision," says a former Enron trader. "I still believe in a lot of the things he said." Several of the traders did think that some of Skilling's personal habits, such as hanging out in Houston dive bars until the wee hours, were strange. But they liked that in a way, too. "Enron people, who cares about normal?" asks another former trader. "We don't like normal. People at Enron didn't want a typical CEO." And in a way, Skilling was just like them. He too had a penchant for taking business gambles. As Whalley himself once put it, "The biggest gambler of them all sits on the fiftieth floor."

Still, it gnawed that Skilling refused to publicly acknowledge the traders' importance to the company's profits. They were proud of their success as speculators. But Skilling continued to tell Wall Street what he always had: that Enron was a logistics company and that its trading profits were merely a predictable function of the volume of energy it sold to customers. There was a kernel of truth to this, but it became increasingly less true over time. By the late 1990s, origination, which had been the impetus behind the creation of the trading desk, had started to wither away. Part of the reason was that some of the big, old origination deals had turned into massive headaches. "Half of what kept origination in business was cleaning up their own messes," says one former executive in a typical comment.

The Sithe deal was a classic example. Under the original terms of the 20-year deal, Sithe and Enron had set up something called a tracking account, which reflected amounts owed either side as energy prices fluctuated. It was assumed that over the long haul, the tracking account would never get too far out of balance. Over time, though, the tracking account became extraordinarily unbalanced, to the point where Sithe was projected to owe Enron about $1.5 billion over the life of the contract. Yet the only collateral was a share of the cash flow from the plant and the plant itself, which RAC estimated were worth just over $400 million. In other words, Enron was not going to be able to collect some $1 billion it was owed. Under mark-to-market accounting, that should have been reflected on both the company's balance sheet and in a charge to reported profits. Yet according to a postbankruptcy review conducted by Enron's new chief accounting officer, that charge was never taken.

In the meantime, Enron was also losing money on various pieces of the contract. Restructuring Sithe became a regular endeavor; every few years or so, the giant Sithe contract would land on some hapless young associate's desk, and he was told to figure something out.

Besides, origination required so much *work* and for so little payoff. Competition in the industry was brutal and margins had plummeted. Old-fashioned origination had become, in the opinion of the traders, noneconomic. "Origination," sighs a former executive. "You'd bust your balls for six months and make $2 million or $3 million. A junior trader was swinging that in just a few days. The trading shop was making so much money that everything else was a waste of time."

So while Whalley was running the trading shop, another Young Turk named Dave Delainey took over origination and made it more closely resemble trading. He and his team turned power plants themselves into a kind of trade, building then quickly flipping them for a profit. They also bought hundreds of millions of dollars worth of turbines, which are the biggest expense in a power plant, then quickly resold them to power developers. ("We were going to corner the turbine market," says one former RAC employee.) Both these efforts were supremely successful, and Delainey became a star. In 1999, Enron did do one old-fashioned deal, signing a five-year contract to supply People's Gas & Electric of Chicago with all its gas. Executives would cite that as an example of the sort of deals Enron did. In fact, by that point, People's was one of the few new deals of its kind. Instead of customers, the new Enron had counterparties.

Yet the fiction persisted. One trader remembers watching Skilling and Ken Lay on CNBC on December 13, 2000. When CNBC anchor Maria Bartiromo brought up Enron's trading prowess, Skilling quickly responded that "trading is just a small portion" of the company's business. The week before, there had been an Arctic air mass over Canada moving toward Texas; the traders called it the "polar pig." Many were long gas, expecting the ensuing cold weather to drive prices upward. Instead, the pig petered out and prices unexpectedly plummeted. On December 12, the day before Skilling and Lay appeared on CNBC, the traders lost $550 million, according to one report, and $630 million, according to another report that was sent to both men. If a Wall Street firm lost that kind of money, the news would make headlines. There wasn't so much as a peep outside Enron. Inside was a different matter. "There wasn't anybody in the company who thought we weren't speculators," says one former trader. An internal document explaining the loss chalked up part of the reason to "weather conditions ease—blizzard expected to hit the North East does not arrive." Logistics, indeed.

Not even Lay seemed to really believe that the Enron traders were indifferent to commodity prices. Once, Lay was asked at an employee meeting if he regretted the sale of Enron Oil and Gas, whose stock had bounced back since Enron had gotten rid of the company. "No," Lay said. "We've made manyfold more money out of the rise in gas prices through our wholesale business in the last six to nine months than we ever could have owning EOG."

In late 2000, a 26-year-old superstar trader named John Arnold—who was revered for being able to do complex mathematical equations instantly in his head—hit a bad losing streak and went from being up $200 million to being down $200 million in the space of less than a month. On Wall Street, such a performance might well have gotten Arnold fired. But when Skilling heard what had happened, Whalley told him that everything was cool. And so Skilling came down to the thirty-second floor, where the traders worked, and put his arm around Arnold in a public show of support.

On the trading floor, where the two pieces of required reading were *When Genius Failed,* about the collapse of the giant hedge fund Long-term Capital Management, and *Reminiscences of a Stock Operator,* about the adventures of a turn-of-the-century speculator, Skilling's "we're just a logistics company" spin was a source of both amusement and annoyance. "Logistics company? Complete freakin' lie. Biggest crock ever," says a former trader. "Logistics company?" says another. "That's complete and utter bunk." But they understood why he was doing it. In the early years, whenever the traders complained to him about how little credit they were getting, Skilling would explain that he was positioning the business in the way that was best for Enron's stock. In the latter years, nobody needed to ask; they understood. "Jeff couldn't let go of 'we're just a logistics company,' because if you did, the stock was going to get nailed," says a former senior originator. "People found it incredible, but we thought, more power to Jeff if he can sell it to the Street," adds another former executive. Then he pauses. "But it was fundamentally misrepresenting the business to the people who own it: the stockholders."

The Enron board was also aware of the increasing amount of speculative risk the traders were taking. Remember the old Enron Oil days, when the Enron directors were so fearful of trading losses that they instituted a $4 million trading-loss limit? That era was long gone. But the board still had to approve every increase in trading limits. As the head trader, Whalley pushed hard to get the limits increased—and the board repeatedly went along. Even at the end of 1998, a presentation to the board shows, Enron was willing to risk, as a percentage of its net income, more than five times the amount that Morgan Stanley would. By the end of 2000, the board roughly tripled the amount of capital the traders were allowed to risk, according to one key measure; the following year, it was raised again. By the end, Enron was willing to risk losing some $3 billion over the course of a year, according to one knowledgeable risk manager.

And even those increases couldn't keep up with the risks the traders were actually taking. According to a document prepared by RAC, in the first six months of 2000, the traders committed 64 "limit violations . . . where no tangible action was taken to adjust commercial personnel views regarding the importance of a risk management framework and risk control environment." In other words, Enron's traders were violating the trading limits frequently—with absolutely no meaningful consequences.

Trading, as we've noted earlier, begets trading. That's true not just of stocks and natural-gas futures but also of baseball cards and rare books and just about anything that someone believes has value. If enough people want to trade a commodity, a market will develop. "If you have a puff, then another puff, then you have a gale, then you have a tornado," says the chief credit officer of a top Wall Street firm. "It feeds on itself."

In leading the charge into trading gas and electricity, Enron didn't just create a different kind of energy company; it created an entire industry. Other energy companies jumped in to take advantage of this new profit-making activity. They had names like Dynegy, El Paso, and Mirant. They all traded energy derivatives with one another and with the handful of Wall Street firms that also got into the business. They marked-to-market their trading gains, just like Enron. Most of the companies in this new industry were based in Houston, just like Enron, where they operated in the long shadow of the industry leader. They took to calling Enron the "evil empire."

Enron executives chalked up such talk to jealousy, and in large part they were right. Despite the new competition, Enron remained, by far, the most powerful force in the business. It constantly came up with new wrinkles that its competitors were forced to copy. Several institutional investors say that Dynegy CEO Chuck Watson used to tell them that his company's strategy was to keep tabs on Enron. If a new Enron idea appeared to be working, he'd have the same business up and running six months later.

One of Enron's key advantages over its competitors was information: it simply had more of it than its competitors. Its physical assets provided information, of course. And Enron didn't stop there. It employed former CIA agents who could find out anything about anyone. Instead of tracking the weather on the Weather Channel, the company had a meteorologist on staff. He'd arrive at the office at 4:30 A.M., download data from a satellite, and meet with the traders at 7:00 A.M. to share his insights. (The traders would also call him for weather reports before they left for vacation.) Early on, Enron employees paid farmers located near power plants to let them put cameras on fences to monitor activity. Later, the stunts grew more elaborate. Once, the company sent an analyst to pose as a porta-potty salesman. His task was to figure out how long a plant was supposed to be under construction so the traders could learn when it might start producing power. Enron sent analysts to meetings of the Washington State's electric commission, where policy makers talked about the level of water in various dams. When the level was high, that meant there was plenty of hydroelectric power, so the traders might short electricity. "Lo and behold, the dam would release water, prices would drop, and we'd make a ton," says one former executive. "We just sat there dumbfounded, thinking, this can't be that easy."

By the late 1990s, these research efforts were herded together into something called the fundamentals group—fundies in trader parlance. The fundies group produced intelligence reports and held morning briefings on everything from new power plants to the state of the economy to production levels at different E&P companies. They analyzed gas storage levels, the demand coming from important industries like fertilizers and chemicals, and outages at power plants. Individual traders could digest that information and establish whatever positions they saw fit. The traders considered the fundies group a huge advantage.

But the biggest information advantage was something called Enron Online. Enron Online, which went live on November 29, 1999, was the next iteration in energy trading. Amazingly, until then, a trader who wanted to buy an energy contract negotiated the price by calling another trader who wanted to sell a contract or by talking to a broker. The kind of widespread information-sharing that had long been commonplace in the world's big stock markets—where computer screens listed all the bids and asks for any stock—didn't yet exist in the energy trading business.

Enron Online changed that. At last, market participants could see prices on a screen, just like stock traders—and they could actually trade by hitting a key. Very quickly, every energy trader in the country had EOL up on their screens; "It was free, it was easy, and it was addictive," says a former Enron executive. "It

was a revolution," adds another trader. But there was one difference between Enron Online and, say, the New York Stock Exchange: the stock exchange wasn't
controlled by one important market participant, like Merrill Lynch or Goldman
Sachs. With Enron Online, Enron controlled the energy exchange completely.

The story of the creation of Enron Online became an instant corporate legend
and a key part of the Enron myth, testimony to how Enron's culture fostered an
entrepreneurial spirit that was at the root of the company's success. The press
trotted it out as an example of Enron's cutting-edge management style, and some
professors at Harvard Business School based one of the school's famous case
studies around it. It helped that the hero was a young woman and that in setting
up EOL, she operated in stealth mode. It also helped that EOL was unveiled at
the height of Internet mania, when any business conducted online had to be a
good thing, almost by definition.

The woman in question was named Louise Kitchen. An Enron employee
since 1994, she had become a top gas trader in the United Kingdom, where she
worked for John Sherriff. Loud, aggressive, and profane, she fit right in with the
predominately male trading culture and was completely unafraid to tell her
bosses, including Whalley, exactly what she thought. According to the legend,
EOL was her creation, but that's not quite true. In fact, Lou Pai had brought up
the idea of online trading in the mid-1990s, and Sherriff had been quietly working on it for a few years. By early 1999, with the Internet explosion, Whalley decided that Enron needed to move its trading operation onto the Internet. He and
Sherriff approached Kitchen, and while she resisted at first—she was worried
about what would happen to her career if she failed—she eventually agreed to
take on the project. The part of the myth that is true is this: even though they
were about to spend millions getting EOL off the ground, chew up people's time,
and plot to radically change Enron's business model, the coconspirators felt no
need to seek approval from Skilling or Lay.

With Whalley urging her on, Kitchen enlisted a team of some 350 Enron employees to help develop EOL, which they did in addition to their regular jobs. "I
never went to people's bosses to ask their permission," Kitchen told the Harvard
professors. "I just went directly to the people I needed. Some of the senior
managers didn't even know their people were working on this." (Harvard named
the case study Louise Kitchen: Intrapreneur.) Harvard also noted that Kitchen
"spared hardly a moment's thought for what the new system would cost to develop." As Sherriff later said, "The overriding philosophy at Enron is that if
you're going to do something, don't dabble. Do it in a big way, and do it fast."

Skilling had a vague notion that a team led by Whalley was working on an
online trading system, but he was skeptical. He envisioned something like eBay,
an open marketplace that brought together buyers and sellers and took a small
commission whenever something was sold. It wasn't until September 1999—
barely a month before the launch—that Sherriff met with Skilling to explain the
concept. Enron Online, he told Skilling, was *not* like eBay. Instead, anyone who

used the EOL system could trade only with Enron. It would serve as the counter-party for every single trade. And that meant that Enron would know what each of its competitors was doing at all times. Now Skilling "got it." Sherriff was re-lieved to have the boss's backing, because he and Whalley had already rolled out versions of the system in several European countries. Later, Sherriff told Har-vard that keeping Skilling informed "never occurred to Greg or me, either. As long as you are growing your business rapidly, you get a lot of latitude here. I couldn't conceive of Jeff not going along with this."

Unlike other Enron ideas, EOL was a brilliant innovation, but it had a hidden cost. Because Enron was involved in every trade, it dramatically increased the capital requirements of the trading business. Just how dangerous this was would become all too apparent—much later.

But at the time, because Enron could trumpet EOL as part of its embrace of the Internet, it helped the stock. Most of all, EOL gave the company's traders a viselike grip over the energy markets. It's usually estimated that Enron did some 25 percent of the trades in gas futures and electricity, but some competitors claim that, thanks to EOL, Enron was actually involved in over half the gas trades in the United States. ("All I'm asking for is one side of every trade," Whalley once told an associate. "Is that too much to ask?") John Arnold would sit with a phone in one hand, a mouse in the other, a headset blaring prices into his right ear and trade well over $1 billion worth of energy futures every day, an average of 5,000 contracts on the NYMEX alone per day. EOL made Enron as close to omniscient as any traders have ever been or ever will be again. It allowed the traders to speculate more safely, and speculate they did. The FERC later estimated that En-ron traders made more than $500 million as speculators in 2000 and 2001—just in business done through EOL.

EOL also made a mockery of other people's attempts to compete with Enron. At Kitchen's insistence, the EOL office area featured a huge poster of Dynegy's competing system, Dynegy Direct, which—surprise, surprise—was launched just months after EOL. Kitchen loved the poster because in the background you could clearly see that all the Dynegy traders had the EOL Web site on their screens. At one meeting to discuss EOL, Whalley said: "I want all the money outside the building *inside* the building."

The power Enron wielded did not go unnoticed. Its competitors worried that Enron could effectively determine prices for certain energy contracts, especially those that were thinly traded. "It was a very easily controllable market if you had the *cojones* and the money to do it," says a trader who worked for a competitor. "There were places where Enron controlled the market, and there was nothing you could do." "Their domination in parts of the market led them to think that they could do anything," says the chief credit officer at a competing company.

Much later, FERC would conclude that the oft-noted idea that EOL gave En-ron the equivalent of the house advantage in a casino game was, if anything, an understatement. "A card game in a casino has set rules and all players can clearly see who they are competing against," said a FERC report. The report added that this was never the case with EOL, where the only thing outsiders could see was the price Enron was posting. Only the Enron traders could see everything. The FERC also claimed that because "the use of EOL enabled Enron to post any price it wanted," Enron "was able to present or influence the market in any way it wished." And the FERC also asked whether Enron was able to use its information edge to "create monopoly profits for itself, at the expense of its trading partners."

Did Enron manipulate the market? "Yes, we moved markets," says a former trader. "We wanted that sucker up, it went up." In performance reviews, Arnold praised a trader who was able to "further exploit our dominance." He noted approvingly that another trader was "learning how to use the Enron bat to push around the market" and was a "position taker and market manipulator" who was still learning how to "use position to force markets when it's vulnerable." (Arnold later told investigators that he didn't actually think Enron was manipulating the market and that he now sees his comments "in a different environment than what I meant it at this time.")

Early in EOL's life, someone asked Whalley if he was worried about a Microsoft-like market power issue. "That's a high-class problem," Whalley replied. It continued to be a topic of discussion on the trading floor. But Arnold's bravado notwithstanding, most of the Enron traders didn't believe they were doing anything wrong; this was the way all markets worked. From their point of view, taking a big position—using the Enron bat—might move the market temporarily, but that was all. "Supply and demand drive the market," says one former trader. "What traders do does not determine the long-term price." If outside traders were too scared of getting run over to not go along with EOL's pricing, was that Enron's fault?

In addition, on EOL, the Enron traders had to take either side of the trade—either buy or sell—at the prices they posted, which entailed huge risks. And despite the FERC's complaints, if a counterparty came in and accepted a price, didn't that have to mean, by definition, that it was the market price? Besides, nobody *had* to use EOL; in the view of Enron's traders, it certainly wasn't their fault that others just couldn't come up with anything better. (Enron's argument was not unlike that of Drexel Burnham Lambert, which also had a near monopoly in market-making for and trading junk bonds in the late 1980s.) And it wasn't just the industry that was lazy: in the glory years, regulators like the FERC and the CFTC did nothing to rein in Enron, either.

EOL cemented Enron's dominance in gas and power trading, but dominating gas and power was no longer enough. It hadn't been enough for a while. Even before the advent of EOL, some of the traders had begun to believe that they could trade anything. Creating new markets where none had existed before—that was what they *really* did. In other words, it wasn't their understanding of the energy business that gave Enron's traders an edge; they believed they had an edge because they were smarter than other people. "Look at pulp and paper," Skilling once told *BusinessWeek*. "Look at all those salesmen who play golf all day. For a commodity, for crying out loud. You don't need to play golf to sell a commodity." And they certainly didn't need to understand the business they were entering; that was unimportant. "We almost believed that you could create a market by sheer force of will," says one former trader. "If I want it to happen, it will happen."

Some of the commodities Enron started trading were part of the energy world. In 1997, Enron began trading coal. There was a fair amount of internal opposition to the idea: it cut against Enron's image as an environmentally friendly natural-gas company. A meeting was held in Skilling's office to discuss coal. Some 15 people were gathered, ready to debate, when Skilling weighed in. "Coal? I like coal," he said. And so it was done.

Other commodities Enron tried to trade had less to do with energy. By the end of the decade, Enron was trying to create markets for steel, pulp and paper, lumber, freight, metals, weather derivatives, you name it. Often, the decision to dive into such a market was driven by that classic Enron calculus: if the market is x, Enron will invariably grab y percent of it and make lots of money.

Of course, establishing a market meant spending money, but that was never a problem at Enron. To build its pulp-and-paper business, which one Enron executive took to calling "pulp fiction," Enron bought a newsprint mill in Quebec City and one in New Jersey. In fact, Enron bought at least $500 million worth of pulp and paper assets alone.

To get into the metals market, Enron paid $415 million plus the assumption of $1.6 billion in debt for a metals company in the United Kingdom. That was a Greg Whalley deal; since Whalley was now one of Skilling's trusted lieutenants, Skilling gave him one of his famous silver bullets and let him go through with it. (Metals, after all, was a $120 billion market.) The acquisition, done with just four days of due diligence, most of it done with heavy drinking in London bars, according to several Enron Europe employees, was an utter disaster. "I wish I could hire the person who sold it to them. He must be the best salesman ever," says the head of commodity trading at a Wall Street firm. "Why else would you pay $415 million for a business that's worth maybe 10 percent of that?" Whalley was still promising to fix it when Enron went bankrupt.

Not that any of this seemed to matter in Enron's glory days. "Paper, steel, metal, oil—they sucked," says one former trader. "So that guy lost $25 million. But who cares? His bonus will suck, but it won't affect the company." Another trading executive adds, "We needed a growth vehicle to be perceived as more than an energy company. There was a mania and a sense of bravado, and it truly reached a level of lunacy."

Apart from the amount of money Enron flung at things, some of the markets the company tried to create bordered on the absurd. Over at Enron Broadband, executives tried to steal some of the traders' thunder by developing their own new markets, such as offering PC makers a way to hedge the price risk of semi-conductor chips and the media industry a way to protect against an increase or decrease in advertising rates. "Enron didn't have a clue about how the industry worked," says one publisher who met with a group of young Enron executives. (Their cards read Enron Media Services.) He adds, "They were very gung-ho but clueless. Young MBAs reading textbooks on advertising. Wall Street would say things like 'Enron is going to take over your business.' I'd say, 'Have you *met* these guys?' "

Enron got into the business of trading credit derivatives: financial contracts that are triggered when a company's credit rating is downgraded. In a stinging irony, it even tried to launch a new kind of contract that would be triggered by bankruptcy rather than a mere downgrade. But credit derivatives were hardly an example of Enron trying to create a market where none existed before; rather, it was a case of Enron trying to elbow its way into a long-established market that was dominated by the big Wall Street firms. The Wall Street traders—who, admittedly, weren't going to welcome Enron with open arms—could never figure out Enron's motives for jumping into the business. Wall Street had the same edge in credit derivatives that Enron had in energy futures: it had information, in the form of huge research networks supporting the traders. "It was like amateur night," says one competitor. "Enron was not in touch with the community. We wouldn't compete in energy trading with them."

Indeed, by the end of the decade, Enron seemed to have forgotten the core rule of trading: information is even more important than brains. In a twisted way, it was EOL, which had done so much to cement Enron's position in gas and power, that provided a powerful incentive for that way of thinking. EOL could be a platform for all kinds of markets. "We could be the market maker for the world!" Skilling exulted.

Other experts echoed him. "Like Microsoft created DOS, Enron is creating MOS: the market operating system. And they can apply it everywhere," raved management guru and best-selling author Gary Hamel. In the spring of 2000, Whalley and Lavorato persuaded Skilling to let them begin using EOL to trade sugar futures, coffee futures, hog futures, grains, and a variety of meat futures. Trading volumes for these products remained near zero, but at Enron they believed there was nothing they couldn't do. "It was euphoria," Skilling later told friends. "It was absolute euphoria. I felt it too."

Blinded by their belief that they could do no wrong, the traders failed to see that their business had some of the same flaws that characterized other Enron divisions. The overhead was obscene; one executive estimated that the North American trading operation alone spent between $650 million and $700 million a year just in overhead. Expense accounts were over the top, but nobody dared try to rein them in. "If you told them to stop spending," says a former trader, "they would stop earning."

And their earnings? By 2000, the trading floor didn't have to undergo that frantic search for earnings that was so common elsewhere at Enron, but there were still so many ways to manipulate earnings that it was hard to say what, precisely, constituted earnings. There were reserves, such as credit reserves in case a counterparty couldn't pay, that were at least somewhat discretionary. "Expectations created the need for hiding money and pulling it out at different times," says a former origination executive. "We just viewed the rules differently than other people."

Then there was the issue of the "market" in mark-to-market pricing. To value some trades, companies could look at price indexes printed by the trade press (such as *Gas Daily* and *Inside FERC*), much the same way an investor might look at a quote for shares of IBM. But the indexes for energy prices were a lot less solid than the price for a share of IBM. Individual traders could tell the trade press anything they wanted—and they did. Sometimes, they made up spreadsheets showing pricing for trades that never happened. They did it to make their own books look better, and they did it because everyone in the industry thought everyone else was doing it. Valuing long-term trades was even murkier. Companies used their own proprietary models to estimate the value of trades. But they didn't use the same models. If company A declared $100 million in profits resulting from a trade with company B, company B didn't necessarily declare a $100 million loss.

Enron, partly thanks to EOL, which provided market prices for many trades, played these games less often than smaller players did. But it is impossible to know how real the values on EOL were, either. Although the Enron traders mocked the rest of the industry for its lack of intellectual purity, they were part of the same industry, with some of the same issues. For instance, at one point, Enron's biggest contract was a long-term deal it had with TXU Europe, which by mid-2001 was valued at almost $2 billion. Prices had moved dramatically in Enron's favor, but one former RAC employee familiar with the contract says that Enron still overvalued its gains by hundreds of millions. More important, much of the gain turned out to be illusory: TXU Europe declared bankruptcy shortly after Enron did. In truth, the entire new industry that Enron helped create was built on a quicksand of assumptions, which helps explain why all energy traders struggled just to survive after Enron's bankruptcy.

What's more, just because the traders were reporting earnings under mark-to-market accounting, it did not necessarily follow that cash was coming in the door. As North American gas and power trading became increasingly short term in nature, there was more immediate cash, but the same was not true of the other things Enron traded. The net result was that the trading floor was also dependent on Andy Fastow's machinations. "I called it cashless prosperity," says a former risk manager.

Not that this was anything any of the traders ever thought about. At Enron, it was bookable accounting profits, not dollars coming in the door, that mattered.

"People did not know the difference between mark-to-market earnings and cash," says a former trader. "No one ever talked to me about cash," says another. "It wasn't on our annual review or included in our targets. It had nothing to do with how we were measured for our bonus. It was nothing we were paid for, so who cares?" He adds: "I knew we had no cash and that our earnings were susceptible to manipulation. *This is a game*. I know that, everyone knows that. But it was a game we were winning."

There was one final issue. Even though trading was an enormously volatile business, Skilling nonetheless expected the traders to generate steadily increasing earnings every year. Vince Kaminski, Enron's probability guru, used to warn Skilling that he shouldn't have earnings expectations when it came to the trading business; in any given year, profits were as likely to go down as to go up. Skilling would respond that people always told him that, but the traders had always come through. And he assumed they'd keep coming through. So every year, trading was handed a budget that was substantially higher than the year before.

In 2000, the traders were told they needed to make $1.4 billion. When Cliff Baxter saw that number, he hit the ceiling. "There's no way," he told Skilling. "And if I do make the number, I want to be paid!" Though he'd had responsibility for the trading operation for less than a year, he was deeply unhappy with the job. Baxer had little power. Among other things, he lacked the authority to promote employees in his division or even to set their compensation. For someone who cared so deeply about status, the whole situation was humiliating.

One day, early in the summer of 2000, during a meeting of about 25 top Enron executives, Baxter complained to Skilling about Pai's compensation, always a sore point with him. Skilling turned to Dave Delainey and said, "Is he right about that?" Baxter, always sensitive to perceived slights, was offended; as he later told an investigator, he felt that Skilling had publicly undermined his authority.

After obsessing over the matter, Baxter decided to leave both his post and Enron. But Skilling talked him out of quitting the company, offering him the title of chief strategy officer, and later Enron's vice chairman.

By the end of 2000, Greg Whalley had become the chief operating officer for the entire wholesale business. That meant that aside from EES, broadband, and the pipelines, Greg Whalley, the ultimate trader, now had day-to-day oversight for all of Enron's businesses.

CHAPTER 15

Everybody Loves Enron

At practically every employee meeting in the late 1990s, Ken Lay would trot out what he once described as "one of my most favorite slides." The slide compared Enron's stock performance against that of the S&P 500 during the 1990s. It was, unquestionably, a glorious sight to see, and one that only got more glorious with almost every passing quarter. By May 1999, Enron had returned over 600 percent to its investors, one and a half times the return of the market's most important index. By early 2000, Enron's return had hit 1,000 percent. And by October 2000, Lay's favorite slide showed that Enron had returned a stunning 1,400 percent since 1990, more than three times the gain of the S&P 500.

Enron's stock slump of 1997 was ancient history. In the heady days of the late bull market, it was hard to recall a time when Enron's stock hadn't gone straight up. In August 1999, with the stock closing in on $88 a share, the company announced a two-for-one split, its first since 1993. For the year, Enron stock returned a startling 58 percent.

Enron's ever-rising share price, of course, was serving as the underpinning for the many special-purpose entities Andy Fastow and his Global Finance underlings were devising to help the company raise capital and hit its quarterly earnings targets. It had a number of other consequences as well. At the tail end of a bull market that had run for nearly a decade, any company with a flashy stock chart and an eye-popping price-to-earnings ratio took on an aura of invincibility, none more than Enron. "Enron is literally unbeatable at what they do," raved David Fleischer, a securities analyst at Goldman Sachs. "The industry standard for excellence," chimed in Deutsche Bank's Edward Tirello. "Enron is the one to emulate," wrote the *Financial Times*.

Any remaining vestiges of skepticism were washed away in the torrent of praise that showered over the company and its top executives. Enron's nearly incomprehensible financial statements? Nobody worried about them. The related-party transactions buried in the footnotes? Who bothered with footnotes? That Skilling himself sometimes seemed unable to give a coherent explanation of Enron's business—at times, he got by with saying "We're a cool company"—bothered no one. All that mattered was that the stock was going up. Because the stock was rising, Enron's executives were seen as brilliant. Because they were viewed as brilliant, all their new ideas had to be winners. "They had the aura of whiz kids, of golden boys who could do no wrong," says Thomas Kuhn, the president of the Edison Electric Institute, the powerful trade association for the nation's electric utilities. Skilling and Lay found themselves mentioned in the same breath as GE's Jack Welch, Microsoft's Bill Gates, Apple's Steve Jobs, and the very small handful of other celebrity businessmen.

The people inside Enron were as caught up in the frenzy as any outside investor. It was fun to read the stories about how smart they all were. Because the market rewarded every new move they made, Enron's employees started to think they couldn't make mistakes. One top executive says, "We got to the point where we thought we were bulletproof."

Enron was hardly the only company to see its stock ascend on a cloud of hype as the 1990s came to a close. But it was different from most such companies in one critical respect. The circle of people who knew—or should have known—that Enron's glittering surface masked a different reality was surprisingly large. Much of what Enron did—such as generating billions in off-balance-sheet debt—was out in the open. Many of the analysts knew full well that the company's earnings far outstripped the cash coming in the door. The bankers and investment bankers, who worked for the same firms as the analysts, certainly understood what Enron was doing; indeed, they made Fastow's deals possible. The credit-rating agencies knew a lot. The business press, which could have looked more closely at Enron's financial statements, couldn't be bothered; the media was utterly captivated by the company's transformation from stodgy pipeline to new economy powerhouse. And of course there were any number of Enron's own employees who could see for themselves how the company was making its numbers. And yet, they all chose not to make the logical leap, to see where it was inevitably headed. Instead, they all chose to believe.

Everyone loved Enron.

Start with the analysts. The securities analysts who covered Enron knew a great deal about how the company really operated. Here, for instance, is a J. P. Morgan analyst named Kyle Rudden, writing in mid-1999: "ENE is not a cash flow story. . . . Enron has significant flexibility in structuring contracts and hence booking earnings . . . contracts can be structured to recognize the economic value of projects long before they are operational and cash is coming in the door. . . . This has two effects: front-end loaded earnings that bias the denominator in the PE ratio, and a timing disconnect between projects' cash and earnings effects. . . ." (ENE was Enron's stock symbol.)

Rudden noted, for instance, that a plant Enron built had not become operational until 1999, but Enron had booked the income it expected to generate from it two years earlier. In other words, the analyst saw clearly that Enron's stated profits had more to do with its accounting than with the reality of its business. The analysts also knew that Enron had an enormous amount of off-balance-sheet debt, which they occasionally mentioned—but never stressed—in their reports. From time to time analysts would quiz Enron's investor relations department about the LJM partnerships, which were, after all, disclosed in Enron's financial documents. But they refrained from pointing them out in the reports they issued to investors.

Analysts who worked for Wall Street banks later claimed that they had been deceived by Enron. But if they were indeed victims, they were willing ones. "For any analyst to say there were no warning signs in the public filings, they could not have read the same public filings that I did," Howard Schilit, an independent analyst who is the president of the Center for Financial Research and Analysis, later told Congress.

For a securities analyst working in late 1990s, there was no percentage in making much of such potential problems. Wall Street research had changed a great deal during the previous two decades. Once a sleepy backwater, research departments had evolved into one of Wall Street's glamour professions. Top-ranked analysts made millions of dollars. Their calls—that is, their upgrades or downgrades of individual stocks—moved the market. Some of the most prominent analysts, such as Henry Blodget, who covered Internet stocks for Merrill Lynch, and Jack Grubman, Salomon Smith Barney's telecom analyst, became even better known to the public than the CEOs whose companies they covered.

But analysts got to be rich and famous only if they were bullish. That's what got them appearances on CNBC, not to mention loving profiles in *The New Yorker,* an honor accorded Morgan Stanley's famed Internet analyst Mary Meeker. As the market rocketed upward, bearish analysts who dared to buck the crowd were putting their jobs in jeopardy. Many were replaced by more bullish souls. In Internet chat rooms, individual investors flamed analysts who downgraded their favorite stocks. Even sophisticated institutional investors—the analysts' primary clients—often became angry at research analysts who turned bearish on stocks they held. It didn't matter if the analyst's insight was correct or perceptive; all that mattered was that he or she had hurt the stock.

In truth, many Wall Street researchers had largely stopped doing anything that resembled serious securities analysis. That was a second way the role of a Wall Street analyst had changed during the bull market. Once upon a time, an analyst saw his job as trying to assess a company's long-term prospects. The modern analyst, however, was more a marketer than a researcher and was almost entirely consumed by short-term considerations. Above all else, analysts focused on earnings per share. They regularly consulted with the company's investor relations executives, who quietly gave them what came to be known as earnings guidance. Using that guidance, the analysts came up with their earnings estimates for the next quarter (or the next year), which they would then market to their big institutional clients. The estimates of the various analysts were also fed to an organization called First Call, which blended them together to form the consensus earnings estimate. That consensus earnings figure was the number companies needed to meet or beat to keep Wall Street happy—and ensure that their stock would keep going up.

The crucial point is this: so long as a company met or beat its earnings-per-share estimate, nothing else mattered. Cash didn't matter. Off-balance-sheet debt didn't matter. Even *on*-balance-sheet debt didn't matter. And meeting or beating its quarterly estimates was exactly the game Enron had mastered. In the giddiness of the bull market, no analyst was going to spoil the party by asking tough questions about how it had pulled this off.

Analyst Curt Launer, who was then at Donaldson, Lufkin & Jenrette, told CNN in May 1999 that "the growth rate of Enron is 15 percent to 18 percent per year, very reliable, visible earnings growth." Of course, Enron's earnings growth was hardly visible, nor, beneath the surface, was it even reliable. But no matter.

Launer was a longtime, well-respected natural-gas analyst. But by the late 1990s, his career had become a perfect example of the rewards an analyst could reap by playing the game according to the new rules. In his reports, he didn't seem to have any particularly deep insights into Enron's business. His understanding of the business was such that he told at least one investor that Enron was "a 'trust-me' story." Some at the company didn't think much of him. "He loved going to lunch with Skilling and Lay," recalls one former top executive. "He was never into the numbers. And he didn't understand the trading business even after we spent years explaining it to him." But he pounded the table for a soaring stock. In both 1998 and 1999, Launer was named *Institutional Investor* magazine's number one–rated natural-gas analyst, largely on the strength of his "longstanding buy signal on Enron." Number one–rated analysts tended to make $1 million a year or more.

Why were analysts so maniacally focused on quarterly earnings estimates? In large part, because that's what many of their most important clients cared about. The bull market brought with it the rise of a new breed of institutional investor: momentum investors, who bought stocks primarily because they were rising and whose stock-picking discipline was built solely around whether a company beat its earnings-per-share number. With its rapid earnings growth, Enron had become a classic momentum play by the late 1990s. The company's single largest investor was Denver-based Janus, which operated a high-flying family of mutual funds, most of which invested in the fastest-growing companies their fund managers could find. At the peak, Janus owned some 8 percent of Enron's shares.

The problem with momentum investors is that they don't necessarily understand the business and at the first sign of trouble, they don't stick around to hear explanations. Just as they can help drive a stock higher with their buying, they can also accelerate a downward push with their panic selling. Convinced that Enron's stock would never go down, neither Skilling nor Lay was worried about the influx of momentum players. As Lay put it during one employee meeting, "Increasingly it [Enron's stock] is being bought by the growth portfolio managers, and of course even the momentum portfolio managers. But this is probably the world we are in now. And I would rather be in this world with a 50 PE than in that more stable world with a 20 PE."

What if an analyst tried to get beyond Enron's pat explanation of its business? Executives would imply that they were slow and stupid, and most of the other analysts would agree with that assessment. "If you weren't with Enron, you were against them," is how one former investor sums it up. Plus, Enron's business was all so new, which provided another perfect excuse for the lack of clarity. As analyst Jeff Dietart at Simmons phrased it at the time, "It's more the nature of the business than Enron not giving analysts the information they need."

Skilling, in particular, was infamous for dividing the world into those who "got it" and those who didn't. Internally, it was part of the company's code; Enron itself was divided between those who got it (the traders; the deal makers) and those who didn't (the old-line pipeline executives). Outsiders who came into regular contact with Skilling hungered to be included on the list of those who got it. This was especially true of Wall Streeters, who pride themselves on their smarts. On the rare occasions when Skilling was pressed, he would react with scorn. "He did not want to be crossed in any manner, shape, or form," says one major investor. "He had a good McKinsey trick," says another. "If you asked a question that he didn't want to answer, he would dump a ton of data on you. But he didn't answer. If you were brave and said you still didn't get it, he would turn on you. 'Well, it's so obvious,' he'd say. 'How can you not get it?' " So the analysts and investors would pretend to get it even when they didn't.

Besides, the Enron story, when Skilling told it, sounded so good; otherwise intelligent people were reduced to nodding their heads in agreement. Skilling listened to what the market wanted and sold Enron that way. As he had proved in his McKinsey days, he was a master presenter. He knew how to convey the sense of limitless opportunities and supercharged growth that investors wanted to hear. "Think of us as getting into power trading now and being the J. P. Morgan of the 1870s," he told one investor around 1998. And when Skilling said things like "I think strategic planning is the antithesis of building a corporation," everyone thought he sounded like a visionary, not an atrocious manager.

For the analysts, there was a final reason they needed to keep their buy ratings on Enron: the ugliest and most powerful reason of all. There was simply too much investment-banking business at stake *not* to have a screaming buy on the stock. In an earlier age, Wall Street research and investment banking had been separated by a so-called Chinese Wall. Researchers were supposed to be able to make independent stock calls without worrying about the potential effect on the investment-banking side of the firm. But the Chinese Wall had long since broken down, and during the bull market, analysts became increasingly instrumental in helping their firms land banking business.

When a company was trying to decide which investment-banking firm to choose for an IPO, for instance, analysts would accompany the bankers, and help pitch the business. More important, analysts would promise to produce favorable research on the company once it went public. Without question, an analyst who made this promise was betraying investors to help his firm land banking fees. And in the aftermath of the bull market, analysts were raked over the coals for having done so. (Both Blodget and Grubman were fined millions of dollars and barred from the securities industry for life.) But in the late 1990s, any analyst who spent much time worrying about the obvious conflict wouldn't be a Wall Street analyst for very long.

Over time, many companies came to *expect* buy recommendations from analysts; it was often a prerequisite for getting banking business. And the more banking business a company did, the more leverage it had over the analysts who covered it. Enron, which paid some of the highest investment-banking fees in corporate America, had an immense amount of leverage, which it used shamelessly. "Enron has a simple attitude: 'We do over $100 million of investment-banking business a year. You get some if you have a strong buy,' " says one analyst. Among investors and analysts, one story in particular became part of the Enron legend. It was a cautionary tale about what happened when an analyst refused to play along.

The analyst in question was John Olson; in the late 1980s, he covered Enron for Credit Suisse First Boston. Although CSFB did a good deal of banking business with Enron, Olson had stubbornly stuck a hold rating on the stock—which, as everyone on Wall Street knows, is a polite way of saying sell. Olson also had a habit of asking persnickety questions that made his feelings about the company clear, which Enron also didn't like.

Ken Lay had complained to the CSFB investment bankers—led by a man named Rick Gordon—about Olson, but the issue didn't explode until the fall of 1990, when *Forbes* published Olson's five top stock picks. Enron was not one of them. "They weren't earning enough to pay their dividend," Olson recalls. Lay was furious that Olson hadn't recommended Enron to *Forbes,* and Gordon, who did not think that Olson was an "effective advocate of the [Enron] story," made it clear that he wanted things to change. Gordon today denies pressuring Olson, but others saw it differently. "At First Boston, the analysts knew they'd get whacked if they got out of line," says a former member of Gordon's team. Although Olson felt he had the support of senior executives, he also knew that the growling from the investment bankers would make his life miserable. So when Goldman Sachs came calling, he leaped at the opportunity.

Olson stayed at Goldman for less than two years before receiving a lucrative offer from Merrill Lynch. It was an ill-fated move. In March 1993, some six months after Olson was hired, Merrill hired Rick Gordon and his team of Houston-based energy investment bankers, including his top deputy, Schuyler Tilney. "He ran from us and we caught him!" says the former member of Gordon's team gleefully. Gordon quickly became one of a handful of the most influential Merrill executives; he knew Ken Lay socially. But Olson was still lukewarm on Enron, and as a result, Merrill got less than its proportionate share of Enron business. Even so, at the time, Merrill still had a reputation for protecting its analysts from its bankers. Olson kept his job.

He kept it, that is, until 1998, when Merrill was about to be left out of one of Enron's last equity offerings. On the evening of April 17, Fastow called Gordon and Tilney to give them the news. He said that the decision to leave Merrill out was "based solely on the research issue and was intended to send a strong message as to how 'viscerally' Enron's senior management" felt about John Olson, according to a Merrill Lynch memo. The Merrill bankers felt that it would be deeply embarrassing to be excluded from a deal that size.

The next day, Gordon and Tilney wrote a memo to Merrill's president, Herbert Allison, complaining about Olson. "He has a poor relationship with Jeff [Skilling] and, particularly, Ken [Lay]," they wrote. "John has not been a real supporter of the company, even though it is the largest, most successful company in the industry." Enron, they added, complained that Olson's research was "flawed" and said that Olson often made "snide and potentially embarrassing remarks" about the company. Gordon and Tilney also pointed out that every firm that was going to get a fee from the equity offering had a buy rating on the stock. Allison quickly called Lay, and Merrill got a slice of the business. "We never leaned on Olson," insists Gordon. "Frankly, having worked with him at First Boston, it wouldn't have worked anyway." But that summer, Olson was fired. (Tilney soon took over the energy group from Gordon, who was retiring.)

As for Olson, he wound up at a small Houston firm called Sanders Morris Harris, where he remained mostly skeptical about Enron's prospects. On the wall of his office is a framed letter sent by Ken Lay in early 2001 to Olson's boss, Donald Sanders. "Don—John Olson has been wrong about Enron for over 10 years and is still wrong. But he is consistant [*sic*]. Ken." (Olson says, "I may be old and worthless, but at least I can spell the word consistent.") At Merrill, Olson was replaced by an analyst named Donato Eassey—who, while more cautious about Enron than many of his peers, started his coverage with an accumulate on the stock. Though Eassey did downgrade the stock when he felt it was warranted, he also wrote paeans to Enron's "culture that stresses innovation, competition, and unrelenting drive . . . an impressively deep resource of some of the best and brightest minds around."

"Enron had Wall Street beaten into submission," says one portfolio manager. "You know that term, 'regulatory capture'?" asks Andre Meade, who covered Enron for Commerzbank. " 'Analyst capture' is probably a legitimate term."

On a human level, it's understandable, though still troubling, that analysts and investors lost their heads as Enron's stock price spiraled ever upward. It takes discipline not to develop a rooting interest in a stock you own or follow. But there was one group of watchdogs that should have had that discipline, that should have been able to remain aloof from Enron's rising stock price and even unimpressed by it. Those were the analysts who work for the nation's two major credit-rating agencies, Moody's and Standard & Poor's. Credit-rating analysts are not supposed to care about stock prices or about earnings per share or about astronomical revenue growth. They're supposed to care about one thing only: the ability of a company to generate enough cash to pay back its debt. How could they have failed to point out the risks in Enron's jerry-built financial structure?

To understand how important the rating agencies were to Enron, you first have to understand a little about the odd role that they have come to play during their nearly one hundred years of existence. A rating from Moody's and Standard & Poor's is an absolute necessity to sell most forms of debt; in fact, in certain cases, it's a legal requirement. And that's not all. Credit ratings have become woven into the very framework of the capital markets. The office of the comptroller of the currency uses them to determine the capital adequacy of banks. Certain money-market funds and pension funds use ratings to determine which bonds are safe to own.

If a bond falls below a level known as investment grade, some investors *have* to sell it. A downgrade by the agencies can cause a company to default on its loan agreements with its banks; it may also act as a trigger in structured finance deals that requires the immediate repayment of debt. (This was the case, for instance, in Enron's Whitewing transaction.) Precisely because a downgrade can have such dire consequences, the credit rating agencies are often slow to act, critics say; many times, the market passes judgment long before the rating agencies do. The agencies respond that their job is to take a long-term view rather than react to every vicissitude. Even so, their analysts are supposed to be ever-vigilant for signs that a company is running into trouble. Unlike stock analysts, they have no built-in conflict of interest. That's what they're paid to do.

For Enron, maintaining an investment-grade credit rating was even more important than getting buy recommendations from Wall Street analysts. Enron's credit rating was the lifeblood of its trading business. Whalley later said that Enron's "business model [did not] exist below investment grade." By doing business with Enron, all its counterparties were, in effect, accepting its credit. After all, if you enter into a ten-year gas swap with a company, you want to know that company is going to be around for ten years. It is virtually impossible to operate a trading business without an investment-grade credit rating; to do so would require providing enormous amounts of collateral. Most Wall Street firms have, at a minimum, an A rating. (The best rating, held by about a dozen companies, is AAA.) As early as October 1993, Enron's board discussed the "importance of achieving an A debt rating" to support its trading operations.

But to get an A rating would have meant, at the very least, cutting debt, controlling costs, and funding fewer big enchiladas, and that Enron was not willing to do. The highest rating Enron achieved was BBB+, just a few notches above junk-bond status. And though Enron told the agencies that it would do whatever necessary to boost its credit rating, the truth is that the company deliberately walked a dangerous line. As Skilling told employees in October 2000, in a rare moment of candor about the company's debt rating: "We want to be as leveraged as we can be and still keep that credit rating . . . last year, we were on the ragged edge, as we are every year."

Of course, that wasn't the story Enron told Moody's and Standard & Poor's. Fastow and other members of Global Finance made repeated visits to New York over the years to urge the agencies to upgrade Enron. In a January 29, 2000, presentation given by Jeff McMahon, Enron offered a David Letterman–like top-ten list of why it deserved an upgrade. The number one reason: "Enron's credit rating is critical to the maintenance and growth of its existing dominant market share business." (Translation: It's important to us; therefore we should have it.) Enron also cited its "no secrets policy" with analysts, investors, and credit officers and added that it "proactively manages its balance sheet to achieve target rating."

It's not unusual for companies to meet with the credit-rating agencies. What was unusual is the extent to which Enron saw the agencies as just another part of the system it could game. Agency analysts have certain criteria they use to measure a company's health, ratios such as cash flow to interest expense and total debt compared with total assets. If a ratio was in balance, it was easy for the analysts to simply check it off and move on to the next one. In fact, a big part of the reason Enron used structured finance was to show the credit analysts the ratios they wanted to see. And if the analysts didn't ask precisely the right question to get under the smooth surface, well, then, Enron wasn't about to give a meaningful answer.

A presentation that Ben Glisan and another Global Finance executive gave as an educational seminar to accountants at PricewaterhouseCoopers offered a perfect illustration. It was entitled "Enron: Managing Off-Balance-Sheet Financing." The "key takeaways": "Equity and debt analysts generally 'appreciate' structures. Debt analysts understand credit effects—can give 'equitylike' credit for 'debtlike' transactions. Equity analysts understand income statement effects— can give favorable recommendations based on strong ratios/profits. However, the best off-balance-sheet transactions are 'seamless' (e.g., the public is not even aware of the full benefits/ramifications)."

Later, the rating agencies said that Enron duped them. S&P analysts claimed that they didn't know that Enron's prepays—which were a huge tool in showing the agencies the cash flow they wanted to see—were really just disguised loans. Moody's analysts claimed that they didn't know about the existence of the prepays at all; if they had, Enron would have had a junk rating. The rating agencies also point to an Enron document called the "kitchen sink" analysis, which they say was supposed to contain a list of all of Enron's off-balance-sheet debt. The prepays are not included. The S&P analysts also claimed that they didn't know about LJM or Fastow's involvement in the fund. When investigators pointed out that both of those items had been disclosed in Enron's publicly filed

1999 proxy statement, the S&P analysts responded, incredibly, that they had not read the document. At least the Moody's executives didn't make that claim; to Enron executives, one Moody's analyst used to privately joke about LJM, calling it "Andy's secret fund."

Enron executives heatedly dispute the notion that they misled the rating agencies. "Lying sons of bitches," says one former senior Enron executive. He claims that the credit analysts knew full well what the prepays were and how they were booked; he also says that the kitchen sink analysis, despite the name, was not represented as showing all of Enron's debt.

In any case, the agencies had no illusions about Enron's substantial off-balance-sheet debt or its "aggressive use" of structured finance, a term used by S&P analyst Ron Barone (no relation to the equity analyst Ron Barone who covered Enron). Nor did they have any illusions about the complicated nature of Enron's business. In fact, Enron used to joke about it with the agencies. One slide in that January 2000 presentation features a cartoon character saying: "Can they make a more confusing annual report? Hmmm . . . off-balance-sheet debt, structured finance, nonrecourse debt, guarantees." And if the agencies didn't know about all of Enron's off-balance-sheet debt, they knew about a great deal of it. They rated it, after all.

The agencies argue that Enron's BBB+ rating appropriately reflected all of these risks, that it was Enron's lies that caused the problem. But even that doesn't excuse their optimism. They are supposed to scrutinize a company's publicly filed financial statements, footnotes included. And if they didn't understand something, they certainly had the leverage to get more information. "We are hard-pressed to recall a situation where the rating agencies held so much sway over a company and had such commanding leverage to extract information and yet were so ineffective at doing so," Glenn Reynolds, the CEO of an independent credit-research firm called Credit Sights, later told Congress. Yet even as Enron's debt ballooned, as the related-party disclosures in its financial statements grew longer and more incomprehensible, as the numbers got ever bigger, as more and more profits came from the inherently volatile trading operation, the agencies didn't sound the alarm.

Why not? It wasn't the money. The agencies earned a couple of million dollars a year from Enron. Companies have to pay the rating agencies for their work on a debt issue; it was hardly enough to risk their reputations.

Part of the explanation was that the credit agencies got caught up in the Enron hype just like everyone else. "This is a very, very, very well run company, a strong, strong management team," said Fitch analyst Ralph Pellechia in Enron's heyday. (Fitch is the third rating agency, smaller and less powerful than Moody's and S&P.) Part of it was that the credit analysts include a company's access to capital in their analysis—and Enron seemed to have an open spigot from the banks. But the real problem was that while the credit analysts saw many of the pieces that made up Enron's convoluted financing structure, they never added them all up—and so they never realized how truly precarious it was.

And so, instead of acting as the ultimate watchdog, the credit analysts unwittingly served the opposite purpose: they gave all the other market participants a false sense of security. Stock analysts and investors alike took solace in the fact that the credit analysts gave Enron an investment-grade rating. After all, the credit analysts had access to lots more information than the equity analysts, so if *they* thought Enron was secure, then surely there was nothing to worry about. Thus did the responsibility to truly analyze Enron land nowhere. And thus the stock continued its climb.

It's not as if Enron employees were laughing at the gullibility of the outside world. Certainly there were executives who worried about the company's financial maneuvers, but the vast majority of people who worked for Enron simply assumed that the Global Finance team and Enron's accountants at Arthur Andersen—not to mention the stock analysts and credit analysts—knew what they were doing and that there was nothing for them to worry about. Some skeptics in individual units, like EES, saw that their own part of the company was struggling. But even they assumed that elsewhere at Enron things were humming along nicely.

It was so easy to believe, for signs of success were everywhere. Enron was building a flashy 40-story skyscraper, designed by the architectural superstar Cesar Pelli, at a cost of about $200 million—complete with a $1 million, hand-etched relief map of the world that hung from the atrium ceiling on 18-foot glass panels. Lay told employees that the building "may become kind of the landmark for downtown Houston." (It was still under construction when Enron collapsed; the building was sold for $102 million in 2002.) In London, Enron's expensive new offices overlooked Buckingham Palace. "You walked through the offices every day and thought, 'Someone is paying for this,' " says a former Enron Europe employee. "We all had faith based on empirical observations."

Harvard Business School professors were practically swarming over the premises, working up case studies about the company's triumphs. (There were at least five touting the Enron model.) Management gurus like Gary Hamel made the pilgrimage as well; a half-dozen management books published beginning in the late 1990s contained admiring discussions about Enron. *Fortune* named Enron Most Innovative Company six years in a row. *CEO* magazine picked Enron's board as one of the top five in corporate America. (Enron's board "works hard to keep up with things," the magazine said. "We are heartened by the overall corporate governance structure.")

Enron also had the blessing of the world's preeminent consulting firm: McKinsey, which called Enron employees "petropreneurs." "Enron has built a reputation as one of the world's most innovative companies by attacking and atomizing traditional industry structure," wrote McKinsey consultants David Campbell and Ron Hulme, in one of many laudatory pieces McKinsey published on Enron. (Hulme was the lead partner on the Enron account.) Many of Skilling's theories, from "loose-tight" management to "asset light," came from McKinsey. Enron continued to be a top McKinsey client, paying some $10 million a year for advice, but more importantly for the firm, Enron's stunning success became a kind of validation of McKinsey's brilliance. McKinsey got it, too.

The adulation suited Ken Lay perfectly. He devoted little time to the actual running of the business. Instead, Lay embraced his role as a business visionary, traveling the world—China, India, Russia—and offering his wisdom on everything from energy deregulation to corporate ethics to the future of business. Eminent people, ranging from the *Weekly Standard*'s editor, William Kristol, to economics star Paul Krugman (now a columnist at the *New York Times*), came to Houston twice a year to share their thoughts with Lay in a boardroom adjacent to his office on the fiftieth floor. (They were each paid $50,000 a year to do so.) In conjunction with Rice University, Lay even established the Enron Prize for Distinguished Public Service. Recipients included Nelson Mandela, Colin Powell, Mikhail Gorbachev, and, in 2001, Alan Greenspan. That such famous and important people would come to Houston to accept the award was yet another validation of Enron's success.

A story in the *Economist* in June of 2000 recounted a speech Lay gave to a gathering of top oil and gas executives in London. As he extolled the virtues of deregulation, people in the room could only nod in agreement; after all, Enron's market value had increased ninefold over the past decade. "We'll do it again this coming decade," Lay said. After the speech, Lay told an aide, "Some of these guys finally seem to get it." She replied, "Yes, they're even using some of our language."

The perks the company handed out, which were excessive even by the standards of an excessive era, also reinforced the feeling of heady success. There was the elaborate health club in the basement of the headquarters, the free computers provided at home for every Enron employee, the subsidized concierge service.

And there was the pay. How could this be a company in trouble with the salaries it was doling out? Senior people were paid eye-popping sums. Of course, nobody did better than Lay and Skilling. By early 2000, Lay owned 5.4 million shares of Enron stock, worth some $380 million, and Skilling owned 2.3 million shares, worth about $160 million. For his work in 1999, Lay got a $1.3 million salary and a cash bonus of $3.9 million, plus another $1.2 million under the performance unit plan, which handed out money based on the performance of Enron's stock relative to other investments. The board also handed Lay almost a million additional options and shares of restricted stock. Skilling, whose salary was $850,000, got a cash bonus of $3 million.

And it wasn't just the top-tier executives. According to an analysis by the

Joint Committee on Taxation, in 1998, Enron's 200 most highly compensated employees took home a total of $193 million in salaries, bonuses, and various forms of stock. In 1999, that leaped to $402 million; in 2000, they took home $1.4 billion. For their work in 2000—the last full year before Enron went bankrupt—each of the top 200 employees made over $1 million; 26 executives made over $10 million. In 2001, the year Enron went bankrupt, at least 15 employees made over $10 million.

Most of all, there was an attitude that permeated Enron, an atttitude that Enron people were simply better than everybody else. At conferences, Skilling would openly sneer at competitors. The big oil companies, he would say, were dinosaurs, destined for extinction. At Arthur Andersen's annual energy symposium in late 2000, he told the audience that companies like the newly formed ExxonMobil "will topple over from their own weight." In a December 1999 employee meeting an employee asked Skilling if Enron would ever consider merging with a company like Mobil. The Enron president responded: "Well, unfortunately, Mobil has just merged with Exxon, so it won't be Mobil, which really disappointed me, because if we could have merged with Mobil then we could have been MORON."

He was no kinder to smaller competitors, companies like Dynegy and El Paso. At an energy conference in Wyoming, Skilling unabashedly boasted that Enron was going to "bury" the competition. "We're up here—and everybody else is down there," he declared. Spotting Dynegy CEO Chuck Watson in the audience, he cited the smaller competitor as one of Enron's certain victims. Watching it all, Watson wondered if Skilling had bothered to contemplate a world without real competitors. Later, he told Skilling, "Jeff, you can't make money trading with yourself."

An Enron trader named Jeff Shankman once e-mailed Skilling with a thought that exemplified the Enron attitude. "I wanted also to tell you about this recurring dream I've had (three times now)," he wrote. "Your buddy Lee Raymond's company [ExxonMobil] bought Enron, and you both become co-CEO (money on you), and our mgmt team gets to apply our way of business to ExxonMobil, and unbelievable wealth and shareholder value is created. Odds?"

One outside public-relations consultant tried to ask Enron employees where they thought they were vulnerable. All he got in return were blank stares. People at Enron simply didn't believe they were vulnerable.

And of course there was the stock. If there was one reason above all others why Enron employees believed, it was that the market was telling them their belief was justified. Many of them were getting rich working for Enron, at least on paper. Early ECT employees owned huge amounts of stock; some owned so much that they were almost (but not quite) indifferent to their salary and bonus.

In employee meetings, Lay and Skilling touted the stock relentlessly. In mid-1999, for instance, when Enron shares were trading at $84 before the split, an employee asked when the stock price would reach $100, an almost 20 percent increase. "I think it's very possible before year-end. . . . I think there is a fairly good chance we could see the stock price double again over the next year to 18 months," responded Lay. "Now that's what's exciting. You do that math on your Enron stock."

Five months later, at that December 1, 1999, employee meeting, the very first question was about the stock price, which was selling for about $38 a share after the August stock split. "Why," an employee asked, "has our stock price decreased over the past several weeks, and what is management doing to get it back up?"

Lay's message was unchanged: "I don't want us to ever be satisfied with a stock price; it should always be higher. . . . Indeed, we still think that over the next several months that there's a good chance that the stock price could be up as much as 50 percent, and I think there's no reason to think that over the next two years we can't double it again . . . particularly depending on how this whole message on our communications business plays out over the next several months."

Later in that same meeting, Cindy Olson, who ran human resources, took the podium to answer questions. One written on a card was handed up to her. "Should we invest all of our 401(k) in Enron stock?" she read. She looked up at the auditorium full of employees and replied, "Absolutely! Don't you guys agree?" She smiled at Lay and Skilling.

The whole room laughed appreciatively. "You're doing good," Skilling said with a grin.

■   ■   ■

On January 19 and 20, 2000, Enron held its annual analysts meeting. For the company, this event had become one of its key rituals of seduction. It was during the 1998 meeting that Skilling and the EES executives had pulled their little Potemkin Village stunt, creating a fake tableau of bustling employees who appeared to be putting together deals for the new retail operation. Over the years, as Enron had reported ever-better earnings and the stock had risen ever upward, the annual get-together with analysts had become, in the words of one participant, "practically like a revival meeting."

As always, the conference began with cocktails at the Four Seasons Hotel in the evening, followed by a full day of presentations. The previous afternoon, Enron had announced its 1999 results. Enron's revenues hit $40 billion—up almost nine times from the beginning of the decade. Earnings were up 18 percent. (That is, before nonrecurring charges.) Europe, where Enron had launched a trading business, was "absolutely exploding," Skilling had reported in the conference call. EES, he'd added, was "just rockin' and rollin.' " There was no hint of the frantic deal doing with Merrill Lynch or the business with LJM that had made those numbers possible. At the cocktail party, there were no hard questions. The mood was one of adulation.

The next day, Skilling and the other executives reviewed the performance of each of the business units, as they did every year. The highlight of the meeting was the unveiling of Enron's new broadband strategy; the company had set aside two full hours, from 12:30 to 2:30, to give the analysts the complete dog and pony show. The name change, from Enron Communications to Enron Broadband, was just the beginning. Enron announced that the Enron Intelligent Network, which would be the "industry standard," would help Enron become both "the world's largest buyer and seller of bandwidth" and "the world's largest provider of premium broadband delivery services."

"Today's message," read a slide in the presentation, is that "the broadband explosion is real, it is here *now*. . . . The Enron business model, which emphasizes open, robust networks and markets, will enable Enron to develop the most efficient broadband delivery network in the world." In fact, "Enron Broadband has *already* established *the* superior broadband delivery network."

When the executives talked about the Enron Intelligent Network, they made it sound as if it were working already. "This software layer, is this a pipedream, is this something that we're going to get done in the next five years?" asked Joe Hirko, co-CEO of the business. "No, this is something that exists today." He also said that Enron could "deliver an Internet experience that has quality of service that's appropriate for the content being transmitted. It basically allows us to achieve the vision of the Internet that was never possible because of the way it was originally architected."

For his part, Rice talked about the way the EIN could identify applications that required a higher quality of service and how Enron, thanks to its proprietary software, could switch customers between its broadband network and other networks.

To bolster the company's claims, Enron trotted out a surprise guest, Scott McNealy, the CEO of Sun Microsystems, who announced that Enron would buy 18,000 Sun routers to help build its network. "Instant credibility," Goldman's David Fleischer later noted. Ken Lay took to the podium to predict that bandwidth trading would dwarf Enron's gas- and power-trading businesses. And Skilling told the crowd of analysts just how they should value the nascent business. The U.S. market for bandwidth "intermediation," he said, would hit $68 billion in 2004. Enron would quickly control 20 percent of this market plus some of the international market. This business, Skilling predicted, would generate operating income of over $1 billion by 2004. The content-services side would generate global revenues of $11.7 billion by 2008, producing another $3.5 billion in operating income. By his calculation, the two parts of the business were together worth $29 billion, or $37 a share that was not accounted for in Enron's stock price. Skilling, of course, did not mean that the business would be worth $29 billion in six or seven years. He meant that it was worth that much *today*.

The room practically exploded at the announcement. Some 200 securities analysts and institutional investors rushed out to the hallway to call their trading desks. By the close of the market, Enron's stock had risen 26 percent—*in a single day*—to a new high of $67.25.

The late afternoon tour of broadband services on the forty-fourth floor of the Enron building, which had been outfitted with flat-screen TVs and servers in glass boxes, capped the hysteria perfectly. That night, an Enron executive standing in line at the airport found himself behind two analysts; as he eavesdropped, they raved about how Enron was the last undiscovered technology play. "It got everyone excited about how we could play the Street," says a former Enron executive. "When they wheeled out McNealy, we all sat and watched the stock fly."

Over the next few days, as the analysts issued their reports on Enron's meeting, the drumbeat only intensified. Analyst Carol Coale at Prudential Securities cited the "impressive story" that Enron had told and raised her target price on Enron shares from $52 to $85. Ray Niles of Schroder & Company—who later moved to Citigroup's Salomon Smith Barney—raised his price target to $100. "We see validation in the sheer technical excellence that was obvious from our walk-through of Enron's facilities," he wrote. Credit Suisse First Boston analyst Steven Parla: "For Enron to say we can do bandwidth trading is like Babe Ruth's saying, I can hit that pitcher. . . . The risk is staggeringly low, and the potential reward is staggeringly high." Brownlee Thomas, an analyst at Giga Information Group: "Absolutely it will succeed." Deutsche Bank: "All we can say is WOW." Merrill's Donato Eassey: "Although this is still an energy company, in our view, Enron fits the description of a 'New Economy' stock. . . ." Having Enron viewed as a new economy stock, of course, was precisely Skilling's goal; new economy stocks got valuations that energy companies could only dream of.

One analyst, Hugh Holman of Robertson Stephens, even apologized for failing to "do justice" to the business in his note, writing that "we suspect that most attendees at today's conference, like ourselves, are being asked to venture fairly far afield from their home turf (natural gas, power, energy) . . . it's not that we don't get it, or are unexcited by the prospects laid out for us; rather it's that we have no highly tuned critical filter to apply. . . ."

With each passing month, the hype seemed only to intensify. On an April 2000 conference call, Skilling told analysts about EOL. "It is astounding. . . ." Skilling said. "I feel a little bit like we have been swamped with new opportunities, and we are just trying to sort them out and figure out what we do with all of them." In July, he commented, "I've said this, but I'm afraid it just continues to be true . . . I've never seen the company in better shape. Our core markets are just absolutely moving from strength to strength." And in the fall of 2000, Skilling said about the wholesale business, "If we can maintain or build a 25 percent market share worldwide, this business by itself could have revenues of over a quarter trillion dollars a year!"

On August 23, 2000, Enron's stock closed at $90—its all-time high—giving Enron a market valuation approaching $70 billion. As the stock ran up, analysts raced to raise their price targets; Launer put his at $115 a share. As McKinsey's Hulme and

Ken Lay in late December 2000, when Enron was on top of the world and Lay was widely viewed as a business visionary. *(Pam Francis, Sipa Press)*

Jeff Skilling at the height of
his power and fame, outside
Enron's gleaming headquarters
in downtown Houston.
(Wyatt McSpadden)

Rebecca Mark was Enron's
most glamorous executive—
and Skilling's fiercest rival.
*(Barron Claiborne, CORBIS—
Outline)*

Andy Fastow, the mastermind behind the financial schemes that helped bring the company down, made more than $60 million from the two private funds he ran. *(Gamma)*

The "crooked E"—Enron's famous logo outside its headquarters. *(Gamma)*

Enron's massive trading floor. In 2001, trading profits covered up huge losses in EES.
(Paul S. Howell, Liaison)

Skilling deputy Ken Rice ran the
ill-fated broadband division—and
was later charged with fraud and
insider trading.
(Brett Coomer, GettyImages)

Lou Pai, another trusted Skilling lieutenant, was best known for two things: cashing out of Enron at the top of the market and his infatuation with strippers.
(Wyatt McSpadden)

Cliff Baxter was Enron's moody, hypersensitive deal maker and Skilling's closest friend at the company.
(Gamma)

Above: A storage tank in Dahbol, India, under construction in 2001. It was part of Enron's most audacious, and most troubled, power project ever. *(Sherwin Crasto, AP)*

Right: Rebecca Mark, who struck the $3 billion Dahbol deal, lights a ceremonial candle at the plant in early 1997. *(Pablo Bartholomew, Liaison)*

Fastow lieutenant Ben Glisan created many of Enron's most fiendishly complex financial structures.
(David J. Phillip, AP)

Michael Kopper, Fastow's other top deputy, was involved in many of Fastow's sleaziest deals.
(Mark Wilson, GettyImages)

Skilling led small groups of Enron executives and customers on daredevil expeditions, including this one, in 1996: a twelve-hundred-mile road race in Jeeps and on dirt bikes called the Enron Baja Off-Road Rally. *Above:* The bikes line up for the day's race. *Below:* Skilling (*left*) and Fastow share an exultant moment.

Above: Fastow at the dinner table.

Below: A midrace lunch break (Skilling is standing in background; Fastow is standing in foreground).

Skilling (*left*) catches some sun after a day on the race course.

Ken Rice gets nine stitches. He wiped out on his bike, putting his tooth through his lip.

Rick Causey, Enron's chief accounting officer, pushed Arthur Andersen hard to see things Enron's way.
(Gamma)

Rick Buy, the head of Enron's risk assessment and control department, agonized over his inability to stop bad deals.
(Gamma)

Longtime Enron executive Amanda Martin says that the company managed to anger virtually all of its big customers. The word was out, she says: "Don't do business with Enron. They'll steal your wallet when you aren't looking."

Greg Whalley was the only one who could control the unruly traders. He became Enron's president when Skilling left the company.
(Landov, Bloomberg News)

Skilling and Fastow were among those who built enormous houses with their Enron wealth. *Above:* Skilling moved into his 8,120-square-foot house just before he quit Enron. *(Michael Stravato, Gamma)*

Below: Fastow's house was still under construction when he was indicted. *(Pat Sullivan, AP)*

Ken Lay in better times: (*left*) at a company celebration in 1998 and (*bottom*) with his wife Linda at an Alexis de Tocqueville Society reception in early 2001.
(Left: GettyImages; bottom: Dave Rossman, Gamma)

Federal Reserve Chairman Alan Greenspan received the Enron Prize for
Distinguished Public Service from Lay in November 2001, less than
three weeks before the company filed for bankruptcy. *(David J. Phillip, AP)*

Even before she wrote her
memo to Lay in August 2001,
Sherron Watkins told an Enron
friend, "Andy and Causey are
going to jail."
(Steve Liss, Gamma)

Fastow and his wife Lea leave the courtroom in May 2003 after she was indicted and he was charged with new offenses. *(David J. Phillip, AP)*

Laid-off Enron employees wait outside company headquarters on December 3, 2001, the day after the bankruptcy filing. *(David J. Phillip, AP)*

Skilling on a break during his combative appearance before the Senate Commerce
Committee in February 2002.
(Robert Trippett, Sipa Press)

Campbell wrote a few months later, "Enron has convinced Wall Street of the favorable long term prospects of its new businesses; about half its current market cap is attributable to businesses that have yet to generate annual earnings. As a result of this persuasiveness, Enron trades at a PE multiple of 60"—four times the industry average. When people asked Jeff Skilling about the chances of the stock tumbling, he had a ready answer: "I can't worry about comets hitting the building."

There was, however, at least one person who didn't believe it was going to last. Not long after leaving the company, Forrest Hoglund, the former head of Enron Oil and Gas, began warning friends who owned Enron shares. "Nobody knows how they get their numbers, but as long as they make them, the market's going to accept it," Hoglund said. "But if they ever stumble, the stock'll fall twice as far as your worst bad dream."

CHAPTER 16

When Pigs Could Fly

As Enron's stock was rising to new heights and the acclaim for Skilling and Lay was reaching new crescendos, where was the company's former superstar, Rebecca Mark? Although Skilling had managed to push her out as the head of Enron International, she had convinced Enron's board of directors to set her up in the water business, in a new Enron subsidiary named Azurix, which she'd run herself as chair and CEO. The operation was launched in July 1998, with Enron's $2.4 billion all-cash purchase of a British water utility called Wessex.

Mark spent the next two years doing what she'd always done: racing around the globe like a madwoman, working harder than seemed humanly possible to put deals together. She wanted to run something on her own, apart from Enron, and prove to the world that she could succeed. But it was not to be. Azurix was handicapped from the start, and everything Mark did over the next two years only made matters worse. On August 25, 2000, just two days after Enron's stock hit its high, Mark was forced to resign as CEO of Azurix and leave Enron as well.

Unlike other Enron problems, though, this one wasn't buried. Mark's humiliation played out in full public view, as a kind of reverse story line to the Enron tale, served up by the business press as a stark contrast to Skilling's string of seeming successes. "Their respective fates stand as testimony to the effectiveness of their competing business strategies," declared Rebecca Smith and Aaron Lucchetti in the *Wall Street Journal*. Skilling himself seemed practically gleeful when Azurix failed, even though he served on Azurix's board. In a videotaped interview he gave for a case study at the University of Virginia, he said, "Azurix was in some ways—and this is going to sound terrible—probably good, because it resolved the discussion. It was absolutely clear it was not the direction to go."

Many people at both Azurix and Enron came to the dark view that Mark had been set up by Skilling. "He wanted to give her some rope to hang herself," says a former senior RAC official. "His objective was to see her fail," adds another high-ranking executive. Mark herself later complained that she'd been abandoned by Enron and hung out to dry. But Mark also avoided seeing what was clear to everyone else: that she had mismanaged Azurix terribly, turning a difficult situation into an impossible one. Skilling's failings as a businessman and a manager remained hidden for another year. With Azurix, Mark's failings were on vivid display, for anyone to see.

Rebecca Mark later told friends that she almost backed out of Azurix several times before it got off the ground. It bothered her that there had been two dissenting votes on the Enron board for the Wessex acquisition; it made her wonder how committed the board really was to her new business. It bothered her even more when she heard Lay announce that Enron would not give Azurix any additional capital after it completed the Wessex deal.

In fact, Mark's longtime deputy, Joe Sutton, who took over at Enron International after she'd left, advised her against launching Azurix. At Enron, he told her, there was "no goodwill" toward her new venture. But she pushed aside the doubts and forged ahead with the kind of single-minded determination that had always characterized her. The global water business, she told herself, played to her strengths. With the capital it was committing to the Wessex acquisition, Enron had too much skin in the game, she believed, to abandon Azurix. Besides, it wasn't in her nature to walk away from a challenge.

What was it that made Rebecca Mark—and, for that matter, the executives who signed up with her—believe that they could build a water company from scratch? And not just any water company but, as she put it early on, "the global leader in the water industry." A lot of it was hubris, the same kind of hubris that preceded every new Enron venture. Neither Mark nor Enron had any experience in the water business nor any real sense of how it worked. They also thought they saw a huge opportunity. Water was a big business, with some $300 billion in global revenues. But it was veering toward crisis, and they believed that Azurix could both profit from the crisis and help alleviate it. The World Bank estimated that a billion people around the globe had poor access to clean drinking water and three billion lacked sanitary sewage facilities; there were predictions that shortages would become increasingly common. Both water and wastewater treatment facilities were often old and outmoded and badly needed to be upgraded or replaced. Mark and her team cited studies that suggested that $600 billion would need to be invested in global water and wastewater infrastructure in just the next decade, hundreds of billions in the United States alone.

All around the globe, water utilities operated as small local businesses, usually run by municipal governments. A small chorus of experts were saying that the world's water woes would not be solved until the industry was privatized because municipalities lacked the money and the expertise to provide solutions on their own. Mark quickly joined the chorus. "The only way to bring capital to solve the problem is to place it in private hands and increase accountability," she told the trade publication *Global Water Reporter* in March 1999.

The two biggest players in the industry, Vivendi and Suez Lyonnaise des Eaux, both French companies (France had privatized its water sector decades ago), made substantial amounts of money by operating municipal water systems for local governments. Surely, as privatization efforts around the world gained momentum, Mark and her team at Azurix would be able to grab a large chunk of the business.

Her plan of action was not much more than a carbon copy of what she'd done at Enron International. She'd jet off to one continent or another, meet government officials, persuade them that privatization was the answer to their water troubles, and cut deals to buy water utilities, wastewater treatment facilities, the rights to operate a municipal system—whatever she could pry loose. Where would she get the capital to do all these deals, especially now that Enron wasn't going to provide it? Her audacious plan was to acquire companies quickly and use their cash to build the business. She also assumed that Azurix would go public and that she could tap its stock, which she was sure would be high-flying, as currency to do even more deals. The key was to move fast—"in a time frame that would wow everybody," as a former Azurix official later put it. Unfortunately, this person adds, "She picked an industry that is the antithesis of moving fast."

In fact, although privatization of the water business was on the horizon, it was already proving to be a slow, drawn-out affair. Privatizing municipal water systems cuts against the grain; for most people, water is a sacred entitlement, and there is an inherent resistance to the idea of having a private company profiting from selling people water. Water is also regulated at the local level, which makes the politics much different and much closer to the bone. "Unless you give it five years, it's not going to work," one former Azurix executive warned early on. But that kind of time horizon just wasn't Enron's style.

Mark's other miscalculation was underestimating the French. Vivendi and Suez had been in the business since the days of Napoleon III, who put the French water industry into private hands. What made Azurix think it could outsmart them? Why did Azurix executives believe that the industry giants would simply play dead and yield their territory to an arrogant newcomer? And what made Azurix think a municipality would choose it over a company with far more experience?

None of these potential stumbling blocks deterred Azurix's grand plans. Early in 1998, well before the Wessex purchase, Enron had thought about getting into the water business by putting together a venture with a fast-growing California company called USFilter, a provider of water equipment and services and the largest American company in the business. But when CEO Richard Heckmann met informally with Mark and other Enron executives, he was baffled by what he heard. Mark told him that Azurix, once it attained scale, would eventually be able to move water from one area to another; in essence, Azurix would make a market in water, just as Enron did in natural gas and electricity.

"If they can do what they're saying, then it really is a new economy and I don't get it," he said afterward. Mark, he thought, was either brilliant or crazy. He recalls thinking that "if Azurix is this far off base, then Enron has to be off base, too." (In March 1999, Vivendi announced that it would buy USFilter for over $6 billion. Heckman says that at the party to celebrate the close of the deal, J. P. Morgan and Salomon Smith Barney—USFilter's bankers—displayed a huge chart showing the company's history. In the upper left-hand corner was a sinking ship. On the ship's bow, it read "Enron.")

Does it need to be said that Mark and Enron also miscalculated the value of the Wessex purchase? Overpaying for acquisitions was practically an Enron trademark. Wessex was a heavily regulated, publicly traded utility. Though its stock had run up 20 percent over the previous year or so, Enron's $2.4 billion offer, cobbled together by Mark and Cliff Baxter, still represented a 28 percent premium for Wessex's investors.

But the rich price wasn't the real problem. While Wessex gave Mark her entrée into the water business, it just wasn't a good vehicle around which to build a fast-moving, fast-growing company with global water know-how. Though it was one of the most profitable utilities in the United Kingdom—Wessex made $232 million in operating profits on just $436 million in revenues the year before Enron bought it—government regulators were considering the imposition of rate cuts, which could dramatically reduce profits. Wessex was also supposed to provide Mark with the water expertise she lacked. But what did utility executives in the south of England really know about managing water systems in the third world? As it turned out, not much.

There's one more reason why Azurix was in trouble from the start, and it had to do with the way cash-strapped Enron had financed the $2.4 billion Wessex purchase. Enron did not use much of its own cash, nor did it use stock to buy Wessex. A chunk of the money—$800 million—came from new debt (which went on Azurix's balance sheet, not Enron's). Mostly, Enron relied on sleight of hand, cooking up a deal intended to create the appearance that Azurix would have no immediate—or even long-term—impact on Enron. Fastow and his Global Finance team created an off-balance-sheet vehicle called Marlin, similar to the Osprey/Whitewing off-balance-sheet partnership. In late 1998, Marlin sold over $1 billion of debt plus $125 million of equity certificates—basically, stock that paid a fixed return—to institutional investors. Marlin, in turn, used that money to buy a 50 percent stake in a new entity called Atlantic Water Trust. Enron, which contributed Azurix to the trust, owned the other 50 percent of Atlantic Water Trust, meaning that it owned 50 percent of Azurix. Then, some $900 million of the money Fastow had raised was paid back right back to Enron. The remainder went into a trust to help pay interest to the Marlin investors.

Why would investors be willing to buy the Marlin debt? Because once again, Enron promised that if Azurix couldn't pay it would make up the difference by issuing stock or buying back the debt itself. As was the case with Osprey, investors got extra protection: if Enron's debt rating fell below investment grade and its stock fell below $37.84, the company would be obliged to pay off all the Marlin debt at once. Once again, even though Marlin was sold to investors as Enron's responsibility, the rating agencies treated Marlin as off-balance-sheet debt, not as Enron's obligation. Nor was there anything secretive about this transaction: it was disclosed in Azurix's public documents. To *CFO Magazine,* Fastow even boasted about the innovative contingent equity structure he used to finance Azurix.

Marlin had both near-term consequences and long-term repercussions. It created a Chinese box of debt—debt that resided neither on Azurix's balance sheet nor on Enron's but that one or the other nevertheless had to pay. Although Azurix (which soon had plenty of its own debt) was ostensibly independent, the Marlin investors were in the game to collect interest on what they saw as an Enron obligation. The fact that the money was going to Azurix was largely immaterial to them. Indeed, they cared so little about Azurix that even though they had the right to appoint half of Azurix's board, they never bothered; all of the outside directors on Azurix's board were Enron appointees, including Ken Lay, Jeff Skilling, and Pug Winokur.

Yet to a surprising degree, Enron wasn't all that invested in Azurix's success, either. The company had taken so much money out already—in addition to the $900 million in Marlin money, two executives say that Enron also kept $330 million it reaped from the sale of one of Wessex's assets—that it fooled itself into thinking that even if Azurix failed, it would have no appreciable effect on Enron. This turned out to be a terrible miscalculation.

Given these facts, though, is it any wonder that some people came to believe that the entire expensive episode had all been a grand conspiracy to do Mark in? Her new company was barely off the ground, and Enron had already sucked out over $1 billion in cash while loading it up with debt. Instead of being freed from Enron, Rebecca Mark remained tethered to it. And instead of getting away from Jeff Skilling, she now had to deal with him on the Azurix board.

On the other hand, Mark took a bad situation and made it worse at every turn. For instance: you would think that a company that didn't have a great deal of cash would hoard what it had. But most of Mark's business career had been at Enron, where the mantra had always been "spend today." Like Enron, Azurix was a high-cost operation. (One executive recalls meeting with Lay while deciding whether to accept an offer to work at Azurix. "I've decided that budgets and management oversight is the wrong way to go," Lay told this person. "You spend so much time looking over shoulders.") Although Azurix was a start-up, Mark paid herself the same base salary she'd made at Enron—$710,000—and hired Enron executives, which meant she inherited their rich Enron contracts. They included Amanda Martin, who was named president of the North American business and paid $400,000 a year. (Martin also got an additional $350,000 just for transferring her contract to Azurix.) CFO Rod Gray, who also came from Enron, was paid $430,000 a year. They, along with other executives, all got long-term, guaranteed contracts. As befitted an Enron company, Azurix had all the trappings of success. In the year before Enron bought Wessex, its general overhead was $29 million. By the end of 1999, Azurix was spending $118 million on overhead. Mark, for example, continued to use Enron's corporate jets that year. "Many of us said 'You can't do that,' to her, but when it finally sank in, it was too late," says a former Azurix executive.

Mark quickly hired an army of developers—a corporate staff of over 70—to seek out water deals. "How are you going to do anything without people?" she said at the time. But others had a different view of the buildup. It was "a monster hooked on to the side of Wessex," recalls Chris Wasden, a former Azurix executive. Early on, new people were showing up almost every day. Naturally, they weren't the standard gray-haired engineers who dominated the water industry. Mark, like Skilling, believed that talent outweighed experience, and in Enron's world, talent meant thirty-somethings with MBAs from all the best business schools. What did it matter that they didn't know a thing about water? They were smart; they would figure it out. "What am I going to do, hire a $50,000 water engineer from Detroit?" she'd ask.

Azurix people worked hard, and no one worked harder than Mark herself. She was always in her stilettos, always urging her employees to get deals done, and always, always, courting people. "She could talk up to ambassadors and down to rednecks," says one former Azurix executive admiringly. But to what end? The rap on Mark when she ran Enron's international business was that she was so intent on landing the deal—*any* deal—that she didn't fully consider whether the deal made sense.

At Azurix, the search for deals had a more desperate quality; after all, the company *needed* to do deals. That was the story it had sold investors. But the competition was brutal and prices were sky-high; and Azurix was behind from day one. Yet Mark never lost that sense of boundless optimism, her unshakable belief that she could make the company work. "We spent millions chasing things with little likelihood of success," says one executive, who remembers jumping on a plane and flying to Guam for a dinner meeting. Others would tear out of the office at a moment's notice and spend three weeks investigating deals in far-flung places.

Almost immediately Azurix needed more money. Mark, with the help of Skilling, Lay, and Fastow, tried first to raise several billion dollars from private-equity firms, even approaching Chase Manhattan about helping the company find partners. But that effort went nowhere; this was the era when people put $20 million into an Internet start-up and took $200 million out six months later. Nobody wanted to tie up billions in a heavy-asset company like Azurix. So instead, Mark told the investment bankers at Merrill Lynch that she wanted to take the company public. Indeed, she *had* to take Azurix public; otherwise the company would soon be out of cash.

It was a very risky move, especially in a stock market that had zero patience. After a public offering, the brand-new company would be naked, forced to reveal itself four times a year, like every other publicly traded corporation. It would have no Enron shield to hide behind and no room for even small stumbles. Azurix had yet to complete a single deal aside from the original Wessex purchase. To some people inside Azurix, it was obvious that the company wasn't ready to go public. "Enron took the pie out of the oven way too soon. It wasn't cooked in the middle," says a former Azurix employee. Amanda Martin says she even went to Jeff Skilling to tell him that Azurix wasn't ready to go public. "I don't care," she says Skilling replied; Enron was determined to see Azurix fund itself.

One thing Mark never lost was her ability to sell snow to Eskimos—as she proved again during the IPO process. As she met with potential investors in advance of the IPO, Mark made extravagant projections, projections that were unprecedented in the water industry. Azurix was going to earn a 20 percent return on equity, double the industry average. With all the acquisitions she planned, operating profits, she claimed, would skyrocket, from $300 million to $800 million in 12 to 18 months. Azurix's profit margins would far outstrip those of its older, stodgier competitors. Azurix, she said, would revolutionize the water business, just as Enron had done in natural gas and electricity.

But *how?* How was Azurix ever going to be able to grow that fast? By doing deals, that's how! Indeed, Azurix's prospectus listed dozens of possibilities, from Tunisia to Ecuador to Illinois. Here, though, was a problem even Mark's vaunted salesmanship couldn't overcome: Azurix still hadn't done any deals, and investors were hardly going to flock to the stock until she could prove that her deal-oriented strategy would work. Its one ongoing business, Wessex, was hardly enough to inspire a big commitment from the investment community. By the time Mark and her team launched the Azurix road show—the grueling multicity tour in which the top executives and the investment bankers make presentations to rooms full of institutional investors—the situation was getting desperate. Azurix needed to compete a deal—fast.

And there was a big one out there for the getting. The political leaders of Buenos Aires province in Argentina decided to allow private water companies, including Azurix, to bid for the right to manage the water and wastewater needs in part of the province. The contract would run for 30 years. Even as Mark was busy preparing for the IPO, a team from Azurix was in Argentina, trying to gauge how much it should bid. (Mark herself didn't have the time to visit.) In mid-May, an Azurix board meeting was called to discuss the company's final bid. The mood was tense, with Azurix's officials worried that they might lose out to one of the French water giants, which were also bidding for the business. The numbers were already big, but one person present remembers Ken Lay asking if Azurix could support upping the bid another $30 million. The Azurix team said yes, and no one present said no. Azurix bid $439 million.

Days later, on May 18, 1999, Azurix was notified that it had won the rights to the Buenos Aires concession. Though Azurix bid for the right to manage two regions—2.1 million people—while most competitors bid for smaller pieces, the company's offer was more than three times higher than the next contender. "There was so much money on the table, the rest of the industry was laughing at us," says a former Azurix executive. But the deal was done—Azurix had shown it could do what it promised—and the prospective investors were none the wiser.

Three weeks later, on June 9, Azurix went public. Mark and CFO Rod Gray each bought $1 million worth of stock to show their faith. Azurix's shares opened at $19 per share; the sale raised just under $700 million. Once again, however, the big winner was not Azurix but Enron. Over half the shares—20.5 million—were sold by Atlantic Water Trust. Enron took $185 million of those proceeds; most of the rest of it went to pay down some of the Marlin debt. And Azurix? It wound up with $300 million. Most of that cash was quickly consumed by repaying an advance from Enron and funding the Buenos Aires deal.

Still, it seemed a triumphant moment. Over the next month, the stock rose to $23.88. Merrill Lynch earned some $25 million in fees on the deal; its analyst dutifully predicted that Azurix would achieve average annual growth of 30 percent over the next decade. As for Mark herself, the IPO made her controversial in England, where business writers pounded her for taking two million Azurix stock options.

But to most other observers, Mark seemed at the pinnacle, both personally and professionally. In July, she joined Enron's board, rekindling the old speculation that she might be in line to run the company one day. (She told friends that she joined the board mainly to protect Azurix's interests.) During an early September interview with Fox's Neil Cavuto, he pointedly asked her to address the rumors that she would be Enron's next chairman. She refused to comment but did say about Azurix, "This is a company that I think will grow exponentially over the next three to five years." Later that fall, Mark was ranked 29th in *Fortune*'s annual list of the 50 Most Powerful Women in Business. (The year before, she was ranked fourteenth. "Fierce and fearless," wrote the magazine that year, "Mark is like a character in an Ayn Rand novel.") *Fortune* also noted that she was "beginning a new five-year project: to consolidate the $300 billion global water market." And she became engaged to a Bolivian-born businessman named Michael Jusbasche, whom she married in October. On the surface, life appeared sweet for Rebecca Mark.

Just weeks after the IPO, Amanda Martin walked into Mark's office and said, "We've got a mess on our hands." The mess was Buenos Aires.

It was almost immediately apparent that the Buenos Aires deal would have been horrendous at any price. The Azurix team sent to Argentina to scout out the deal missed some important details, starting with the fact that the water system's headquarters wasn't included in the bid. Azurix employees had to scramble to find office space and hang a shingle on a storefront so people could pay their bills. So many records were missing that Azurix could bill only 60 percent of its customers. Many water users didn't pay at all, because they were friendly with the government, which protected them. The Azurix team hadn't even realized that basic maintenance work had been ignored for years; Azurix engineers later estimated that the company needed to spend $350 million on infrastructure over the next five years. Wasden remembers coming to a stomach-wrenching realization: "We're not *ever* going to make any money on this thing." He was right: over the next six months, Buenos Aires produced just $39.5 million in revenues and a pathetic $400,000 in operating profits; in 2000, the Buenos Aires operation had an operating loss of $11.6 million.

On August 5, Azurix had to report its quarterly earnings for the first time. Mark announced that the company had hit its profit target, with $20 million in earnings for the quarter. But that figure was entirely due to Wessex, and during the ensuing conference call with analysts, she conceded that the deals were coming a little slower than she had expected.

In June, Azurix had bid on a big contract to manage Berlin's water supply but lost out to Vivendi. Still, Azurix was attempting to put together projects in Bucharest, Tangier, and Peru, among other places, and she expressed confidence that all would be well. One by one, though, each of those deals was pushed back, and the stock began to slide. What deals the company did complete were small and scattered. They included a concession in Cancún, a Canadian water-service company, and a German construction company. None was a show-stopper and several were dogs. Within four months of the IPO, Azurix stock stood at $17 a share, two dollars below the original offering price.

It didn't help that Azurix seemed to sink into one political pothole after another. On September 21, 1999, Mark and several members of her team met with Florida's governor, Jeb Bush, to discuss the possibility of Azurix selling water from the Everglades in exchange for helping to fund a $7.8 billion restoration project. The project was supposed to capture storm runoff; some of it would stay in the Everglades and some of it would be sold. When Azurix's plan was leaked to the press, it caused an uproar, with the chairman of the Florida legislature's Everglades committee calling the idea "the most sinister business proposition the state has ever had." The proposal went nowhere.

A few weeks later, Azurix spent $31.5 million to buy 13,600 acres in Madera County, California, from a developer who, according to Public Citizen, had paid just $8 million for the land eight years earlier. Mark wanted to use the land to build an underground water-storage bank so that Azurix could collect water in wet years and sell it in dry years. Once again, Azurix executives underestimated the politics of water. Upon learning why Azurix had bought the land, the Madera County government immediately began drafting a set of rules that would require the company to obtain elaborate approvals before it could make a move. Organizations including the Sierra Club and a local farmers group berated Azurix, with the farmers calling the plan a "crime in progress" and a "theft of our water." That plan also stalled.

Even Wessex, Azurix's one solid asset, was sinking. An upsurge in the value of the dollar against the British pound hurt Wessex's reported earnings, which were calculated in dollars. In late 1999, the company was told by British regulators that it had to cut its rates by 12 percent starting in April 2000. The real killer was that like so many other older water utilities, Wessex needed to upgrade its own facilities—at a cost estimated to be upward of a billion dollars. "Within a year," says a former Azurix official, "you could make a good case that Wessex was worth about $1 billion less than we paid." By late October 1999, Azurix's stock had fallen to $13 a share.

The first real day of reckoning was November 4. Just five months after the company had gone public, Mark was forced to announce that Azurix's earnings would be dramatically lower than investors were expecting. She had wanted to make a more upbeat announcement—she was *sure* things were going to turn around—but the company's lawyers wouldn't let her. The tone on the resulting conference call was extremely negative. The stock promptly plunged 40 percent, to $7.75 a share.

In an effort to cut Azurix's costs, Mark began to let go of some of her high-priced talent. But because of the guaranteed contracts she signed in the company's heady early days, even the layoffs cost money. Though he'd worked at the company for only a short time, CFO Rod Gray's severance called for him to receive $3.5 million over four years. Azurix's strategist, Ed Robinson, also walked off with a $2.1 million payout when he left. Meanwhile, there were rumors that Azurix couldn't make its payroll. During the fourth quarter, Azurix announced a restructuring and took a $34 million charge.

Inside Enron, Azurix became a whipping boy. Some of the traders called it the "chick company." Although it had been in existence for only a year and a half, Enron executives were already writing it off. After an employee made a joke about Azurix's performance in a December 1999 all-employee meeting, Lay said: "What happened there is, in fact, too bad. It maybe in part couldn't have been prevented; maybe part of it could have been prevented. . . . Enron doesn't like to be associated with any company that's not successful. We're sorry that Azurix has not been totally successful. . . ."

With Azurix clearly in trouble, its directors were meeting more frequently. By November, there were monthly meetings, and they were in crisis mode. These were not polite, Enron-like affairs. Skilling used the meetings to lash out at Mark, arguing that Azurix had to stop spending money and instead follow an asset-light model, the strategy that was working so well for him with EES and Broadband. But neither did Skilling want Azurix to simply hunker down; he demanded growth. "You could just feel the tension between him and Rebecca," says one former Azurix employee. "Jeff would just attack, attack, attack. And

Rebecca was just dancing." Skilling would ask Mark, "What's your competitive advantage?" Mark had no good answer. "We're here to make things happen," was the best she could do.

In early February, Mark announced that the company had a new strategy: Azurix would now become an Internet company. Taking a cue from Skilling's broadband strategy, she announced plans to sell water equipment and trade water contracts and water-related products online.

Although the first part made sense—indeed, USFilter is doing it today—the idea of trading water was doomed. Water couldn't be easily moved from one place to another like natural gas or electricity. Even in the American West, where water is of critical importance, the system for getting water from one place to another is discrete; one can't suddenly decide to reroute water the way one can reroute gas or electricity. And unlike BTUs or megawatts, water droplets are not created equal; they differ in salinity and taste, for starters. These were fundamental facts, well known to anyone who had spent any time in the water business. Yet Mark didn't hesitate to predict that her way would work. She told the *Economist* that Azurix had "created something completely different, unlike the French who have piddled around with this industry for the past 150 years."

Given how poorly the company had performed in its short time as a public entity, here's the unbelievable thing: Azurix actually managed to get more money out of Wall Street. True, the money came in the form of junk bonds and bore an interest rate of over 10 percent. But still, it was $600 million, which was, amazingly, $100 million more than Mark had set out to raise. Once again, though, the deal didn't buy Azurix much time. It had to use all but $18 million of the proceeds to pay down existing debt, including a credit line it maintained with Enron.

That March, with the stock trading at between $7 and $8 a share, the Azurix management team pushed Mark to bring in some consultants from McKinsey. The consultants' mandate was to evaluate the company's worth and help it figure out a strategic direction. The McKinsey analysis was stark: Azurix, the consultants reported, was worth as little as $4 to $5 a share. And its only hope was to begin dramatically slashing costs.

In the wake of the report, Mark held a two-day meeting at a swank hotel called the Houstonian to discuss how to rebuild Azurix's value. During the second day, employees were divided into teams and given problems to tackle. One was: how do we get the stock to triple? This group, led by Chris Wasden, was the last one to present, and as the team members waited their turn, one bored employee began to doodle on a transparency. He drew a picture of a pig in the sky, complete with clouds and wings. When Wasden took his turn, the employee who drew the doodle came up to the podium with him and put the transparency up for all to see. "Chris is scared to tell you this," he said, "but the stock will only triple when pigs can fly."

When Wasden had finished, Mark took to the podium. "I grew up in Missouri on a pig farm, and I know a lot about pigs," she said defiantly. "And I'm here to tell you, sometimes pigs *do* fly."

That was the thing about Rebecca Mark. She would not—*could not*—admit defeat. Many of Azurix's problems she had brought on herself. Yet even knowing that, some Azurix employees found something both sad and admirable about her refusal to give up.

"She came into the office every day," says a former Azurix executive, "never acting like anything other than the fearless leader who would lead you out of the darkness." Mark once told this person: "You never ever wake up in the morning without saying, 'I will win today.' " That quality of unyielding optimism was her greatest strength. And it was also her greatest weakness.

The last straw came on April 2000, and there is rough justice in the fact that it emerged from that same Buenos Aires contract that had hobbled Azurix from the start. One day, the residents of the Argentine city of Bahía Blanca, which was part of Azurix's Buenos Aires territory, complained that their water was brown and stinky. "It smells and tastes like a pesticide," said a city spokesman. An investigation revealed that the water contained higher amounts of algae than was normal. Azurix blamed the problems on the government's failure to treat a reservoir it operated; the government blamed Azurix. The city's public health chief told reporters, "I've worked here for 25 years, and this is the worst water crisis I've ever seen." Azurix had to supply bottled water in trucks and agree not to bill customers for 50 days. The army was called out to deliver water to the elderly and schoolchildren. By the end of the year, prominent government officials were saying that Azurix should be removed as the operator of the concession.

On a Sunday in July, Mark planned a dinner for Azurix's top executives and its board at an exclusive Houston restaurant. Two prospective new board members were in attendance, and Mark had the Azurix team set to deliver its latest business strategy.

Almost before anyone could get a word out, Skilling went on the attack, firing off detailed questions about the numbers and the financing plans. It turned into a bloodbath, with Azurix executives unable to defend their business plan. One remembers Lay, ever the smiling glad-hander, telling the two prospective board members that they might want to reconsider. The Azurix team was mortified.

On Tuesday, August 8, 2000, Azurix warned yet again that it would not meet its earnings expectations. On the news, Azurix's stock fell another 20 percent, to $6.69 per share. Two weeks later, Azurix sent out a terse press release announcing that Rebecca Mark had resigned.

By the end of 2000, Azurix, which had begun its life some two years earlier with $232 million in operating profit, thanks to Wessex, was down to less than $100 million in operating profit, which didn't include a $402 million write-off for Buenos Aires. Its debt load had more than quadrupled, to almost $2 billion.

Azurix's stock slid to as low as $3.50 before Enron announced, in late 2000, that it would repurchase the publicly held shares. Enron wound up paying $8.375 a share, a total of $330 million, less than half the price the public had paid less than two years earlier.

At most companies, the failure of a highly touted offshoot would be a cause for dismay and sadness. Not at Enron. The *Wall Steet Journal* writers cast Mark's demise as validation that Skilling's way of doing business was superior. Skilling's trading activities, wrote the paper, "generate a much bigger rate of return while tying up less capital than do the kind of traditional infrastructure projects pursued by Ms. Mark." Ken Lay told the *Journal:* "A lot of capital has been chewed up. I think it's best for Rebecca to start afresh."

What no one seemed to appreciate was that Azurix's failure was not some distant event that Enron could dismiss with impunity. It had looming consequences. There was, for instance, the Marlin debt of $1 billion. Enron was now clearly on the hook for that debt, which was due in early 2002. What's more, the Marlin debt was a matter of public record—it was spelled out in financial-offering documents that any big investor could obtain.

And some did just that. As often happens when a stock makes a meteoric rise, Enron had caught the attention of several short sellers. Short sellers are investors who make money by betting that a stock will go down, not up. They do this by selling stock that they don't actually own—betting that they will later be able to buy it at a lower price and pocket the difference.

Short sellers tend to be a suspicious lot, and as they looked closer they began to wonder about Marlin and about how Enron was going to pay back that debt. They also started to wonder what the existence of that strange Marlin structure and the flameout of Azurix suggested about the rest of Enron.

■   ■   ▓

The Azurix saga represented the public part of Mark's downfall. There was a back story as well, one that played out in typical Enron fashion, with only the insiders aware that it was unfolding. The story came from the final chapters of the Enron International saga, and it had just as much to do with Mark's departure as the Azurix debacle.

Enron's international development efforts hadn't ended when Mark went to Azurix. Enron developers struck deals to build plants in war-torn regions that included Croatia and the Gaza Strip and went on buying sprees, snapping up, among other things, part of a gas-distribution business in South Korea for almost $300 million. Nowhere did Enron buy more than in Brazil, which began privatizing its energy sector in the 1990s. The privatization news had sparked a competitive frenzy, with energy companies racing into the country to land deals. In mid-1998, about the time Enron was buying Wessex to get Azurix up and running, the company announced that it had bagged a big prize: a controlling interest in Elektro Eletricidade, Brazil's sixth-largest electricity distributor. The cost was $1.3 billion.

As ever, the analysts gushed. "A lot of times what might seem surprising or illogical turns out to be right when Enron does it," wrote Schroder & Company's Ray Niles. But the acquisition was an almost immediate disaster. Just about six months after the deal was announced, Brazil devalued its currency. The move instantly sliced Elektro's value. But in March 1999, Enron increased its ownership of Elektro from 47 percent to 100 percent at an undisclosed cost, perhaps because if a third party had bought the stake, Enron might have had to write down its existing stake. Elektro's value continued to plummet as Brazil's economic problems worsened. (The Elektro purchase was funded partly by an SPE. Enron later repaid the banks that funded the SPE by selling 25 percent of Elektro to Whitewing for $461.5 million. A year later, Enron estimated the value of that stake at $245 million.) Enron's other South American assets—the same assets Skilling had been touting ever since he'd toured the region with Mark several years before—also sank in value.

Mark, of course, was running Azurix by then. No matter: Skilling needed someone to blame, and he blamed her. Never mind that both he and Lay had signed off on the Elektro deal, and Mark's signature was nowhere to be found. Never mind that Lay had been enthusiastic about the purchase. The executives running the South American division were Mark's acolytes; they wouldn't so much as lift a finger without her approval.

For most of the 1990s, Mark's business had been a story about the future. Although Enron earned development and construction fees, which it was able to book as earnings, the serious profit was supposed to come after its projects were up and running. And by the end of the decade, that future was supposed to have arrived. Wall Street analysts had been predicting for years—based on the guidance they'd received from Enron—that International would be producing upward of $350 million in earnings by 2000. In early 1999, Goldman's Fleischer predicted that EI would grow its earnings at a 25 percent clip for the forseeable future.

But with 2000 fast approaching, it was becoming obvious inside Enron that these figures were astronomically off base. Like most Wall Street frenzies, the international development craze was wildly overhyped. In the wake of the Asian crisis of 1998 and the resulting economic meltdown in emerging markets, the values of virtually all energy assets collapsed—it didn't matter who owned them. Even so, some of Enron International's assets were almost comically awful, and others were fields of dreams. A power plant it built in China was never commercially operated. The Dominican Republic plant was padlocked for a time. The plant in Cuiabá, Brazil, was hundreds of millions of dollars over budget. In Poland, there were difficulties getting the government to pay Enron for a plant it had built. A planned pipeline in Mozambique never happened, nor did a $500 million plant in Indonesia or a $200 million plant in Croatia. And that doesn't even include the greatest debacle of them all—Dabhol, the $3 billion project that remains shuttered to this day.

Skilling would rage at International's problems and at the woman he held responsible for them. As was always the case with Skilling, he deeply resented having to deal with "her mess." "It was not my vision," he told friends. "I built a business. Now, I'm spending all my time cleaning up messes. It's the last thing I want to be doing."

It was at a budget-planning session for the year 2000 that Skilling discovered just how bad things really were. He was expecting the international executives to present plans to bring in $500 million in operating profit; instead, they projected less than $100 million. He thought at first they were lowballing him, giving him a number they knew they could beat. He soon discovered that just the opposite was true: the $100 million was a stretch. "We invested $5 billion in equity to earn $90 million?" he asked in disbelief.

Amanda Martin remembers seeing Skilling around this time. He seemed more distraught than she had ever seen him. Although he had asked her to come by to discuss Azurix, he didn't want to talk about the water business. It was International's problems that were on his mind. "Just fix it," Skilling said about Azurix. "You're my friend. We can't take any more hits."

Not long afterward, a near miracle took place: an investor group from the United Arab Emirates expressed interest in purchasing 80 percent of Enron's international assets. It represented a potentially astounding escape: the initial offer valued all of EI at more than $7 billion. Enron called the deal Project Summer.

Cliff Baxter's handwritten notes show that the potential buyers were valuing Enron's Dabhol stake at $950 million at a time when it was on Enron's books for $714 million. And they put a value of $4.3 billion on the South American assets, compared with Enron's book value of $3.4 billion. Once Skilling concluded that the buyers were real, he got so excited that he assigned a team to help Enron figure out what it should do with the massive inflow of cash it would soon be getting from the Middle Eastern investors.

By that point, Enron was also planning to sell Portland General for $2 billion—Skilling had decided he no longer needed the hard asset to trade electricity—and so everyone thought they would soon be awash in cash. The Global Finance team believed the smartest thing to do with the money was to pay down debt to make the ratings agencies happy. Ben Glisan also observed in handwritten notes that the sale would get rid of the project finance debt associated with EI, which, he wrote, Moody's considered "a large overhang." Glisan also hoped the cash would allow Enron to sweep away some of the structured finance deals. "Scary places gone," he noted.

Still, Skilling had one final item on his agenda before the international assets went away. He was determined to show the board, once and for all, what a dismal failure Mark had been as the head of International. The Arabs might value EI at over $7 billion, but he wanted Enron's directors to understand that the assets weren't worth anything close to that amount. That summer, Skilling assigned an in-house accountant the task of evaluating the International division, and he personally supervised the work. The analysis the accountant came up with showed that Mark's business was earning a mere 2 percent return on equity—a pathetic amount, given the capital Enron had expended and the risks it had taken. And that didn't even include the huge potential liabilities associated with some projects, such as Enron's guarantees of debt.

When Mark learned what Skilling was up to, she promptly got her own numbers cruncher, who sat down the hall from Skilling's accountant, to work up a competing set of numbers. Mark's analysis showed, not surprisingly, that the international business had been a success, producing over $1 billion of cash and earnings and making a 12 percent compound annual return over its history.

It is astonishing, of course, that two high-ranking executives, working for the same company, sitting on the same board, and evaluating the same business, could come to such wildly varying conclusions. It spoke volumes about the murkiness of Enron's numbers, about the way this company viewed earnings and margins and all the other financial benchmarks by which we gauge American corporations. It also said a great deal about the inability of top executives at Enron to work together or even communicate. Everything was perception; nothing was real.

"Figures lie, liars figure," says one of the accountants who worked on the analysis. He adds that "if it had been Skilling that was being measured, he would have found a way to show a 20 percent return." Yet the accountant went on to note an even more astonishing fact: viewed through their respective prisms, they were probably both right. Skilling evaluated the international assets based on what they'd cost, how much they were earning at that moment in time, and what the market value was. He didn't include any of Andy Fastow's funny business: the accounting structures that were designed to book earnings from the international assets. On that basis, the returns were unacceptably low.

But as Mark never tired of pointing out, there *was* funny business, lots of it. Enron played the same accounting games with its international assets as it did with every other part of the business. Over and over again, Enron had monetized its power plants and other overseas projects, either through securitizations or by selling stakes in them to one of its many off-balance-sheet partnerships, including LJM, then booking the sale to its bottom line. Her analysis included some of these profits.

Although the company didn't break out International when it reported its earnings, both Lay and Mark used to boast about the division's importance to the company's bottom line. In 1997, according to one internal analysis, Enron booked $152 million in international earnings; the following year, earnings rose to $246 million. But those numbers didn't reflect ongoing profits; rather they were a case of stealing from the future. Because of these financing techniques, Mark's assets did bring cash into Enron, cash that her loyalists say was plowed into the enchiladas like EES and broadband. Her assets, she bitterly told one friend, "were just cannon fodder to feed the machine."

But the Enron board wasn't about to get into a debate on the subject. Skilling was still viewed as a man building great, profitable businesses, while Mark was viewed, suddenly, as a loser, a failure at a company that simply didn't believe that it could fail.

The climactic board meeting took place on Tuesday, August 8, 2000. As late as 6:30 Sunday evening, Mark had tried to argue her case privately to Lay. Lay, furious about Azurix, didn't want to hear it. At the board meeting, Skilling disemboweled Mark, laying out his case in clear, damning detail—the poor return on her assets, the projects that hadn't worked, the years of stumbles and mistakes.

When Mark asked for the chance to respond, nobody on the board would even look at her. They all looked down at the floor. Mark told the board that if there were better places to put the money—like broadband and EES—that was fine, but she didn't agree with Skilling's analysis. And then she left the boardroom, citing another meeting she had to attend. Later, it wasn't Skilling who made the harshest comments about Rebecca Mark: it was Ken Lay.

Lay spent the next weekend in Aspen and, after a brief business trip in the early part of the following week, went over to the Azurix offices to meet with Mark. That's when he told her that it was time for her to leave both Azurix and Enron. Mark agreed. But she insisted that she be paid the remainder of her $710,000 Azurix contract. Lay paid her.

And the Middle Eastern buyer? All summer long, the negotiations dragged on. Mark's old deputy, Joe Sutton, had found the prospective buyer and was planning to leave Enron and help the Arab investors manage the assets. If Sutton negotiated the deal for Enron, he would have an obvious conflict of interest, not unlike the conflict Fastow had with LJM. But in this case, Skilling wasn't about to look the other way; he brought in Cliff Baxter to finish the negotiations. There was a huge internal uproar when Sutton managed to get a guarantee from Lay that the international team's options would vest upon completion of the sale. Typically, Lay didn't bother to ask what the number was; when Skilling discovered that it came to $300 million, he threw a fit.

But he was ready to do the deal anyway. Skilling and Lay had the final papers drawn up, and Skilling even met with two Enron public-relations executives to prepare a press release. The last round of negotiations—which would culminate with the signing of the papers—was set to take place in London.

Then a final piece of bad luck: during that final round, the scion of the family making the purchase became deathly ill. Without his permission, no one had the authority to guarantee the purchase. The deal fell apart.

In October 2000, Joe Sutton was asked to leave. Over the course of the next few months, other international executives were fired, too. The irony was that their options all vested once they were let go and they were able to cash out, winding up with the same $300 million they would have received if Project Summer had gone through.

The following February, the company's international developers were summoned to Houston and told that Enron International was being shut down. If they wanted to stay at Enron, they needed to find new jobs at either EES or broadband. A few weeks later, EES held a job fair at the Hyatt—a typically lavish affair with a baseball theme, including fake grandstands and peanut salesmen. Many international employees ended up working for one of the two big enchiladas.

In the end, Rebecca Mark was one of the lucky ones: even though it hadn't been her choice, she got out at the top. Soon after she started Azurix, she had begun selling her Enron shares; by spring 2000, she had sold her entire stake, over $80 million worth. Had she stayed, that stake would have been worth nothing.

But she could never quite bring herself to see it that way. Instead, she continued to boil over about what Skilling and Lay had done to her. Without her projects, Enron would have been exposed years earlier, she would say; her deals gave the company real assets. Those were the assets the company put into its off-balance-sheet vehicles, thereby raising cash. Yes, the rate of return on some of her projects may have been low, but her side of the company was real, unlike Skilling's. Even Azurix, for all its problems, always made a profit, a *real* profit.

"My stuff was discounted because it *could* be analyzed," Mark told one friend. Skilling's team, she added bitterly, "lived off us for so many years, sucking our blood."

Mark also never stopped believing that success was just around the corner, and this was especially true of her tenure at Azurix. If only Enron hadn't been so eager to pull money out of the company . . . if only Skilling hadn't been such an impediment . . . if only Enron had been willing to commit more capital and given it more time.

"It just needed time," she told a friend years later. "With time, it would have all been fine, just fine."

CHAPTER 17

Gaming California

Aside from his age, Tim Belden didn't fit the profile of a typical Enron trader.

Thin and slightly balding, he favored the rumpled look of the academic researcher he'd once been. He had a master's in public policy from Berkeley and spent five years working as a researcher at the Lawrence Berkeley National Laboratory, where he coauthored papers on energy markets and lost money investing in environmentally friendly wind projects. His Enron colleagues called him a tree hugger because he rode his bike to work. He was 30 when he joined the company in 1997.

But looks can be deceiving. Not only was Belden an Enron trader, he was one of the leaders of a group of hyperaggressive West Coast electricity traders who operated out of Portland General, the Oregon utility Enron purchased in 1997. He was, as they liked to say at Enron, intellectually pure—a trader who believed in the beauty of free markets and had no scruples when it came to exploiting inefficiencies to make money. He struck others in the industry as very knowledgeable, and while he was affable enough to outsiders, he had traces of Enron mean. (He once asked an interviewee named Lynn Brewer what the square root of 363,000 was.) It wasn't long before Belden caught the notice of Whalley and the other top trading executives in Houston; within a year and half, he was named an Enron vice president.

Belden had always had a bit of the mad scientist in him, and in the late spring of 1999, he began working on an intriguing idea. Deregulation of California's energy market had gone into effect the year before, creating an enormous opportunity for energy traders, who were suddenly in the position of buying and selling a huge portion of the state's electricity. The sheer complexity of the rules governing deregulation seemed to make them exploitable in another way as well. Clever traders could find loopholes in the thousand or so pages of rules and game the system in much the same way Andy Fastow's team gamed the accounting rules. For instance: what would happen if a trader sold energy to the state for the next day but scheduled it in such a way that the electricity couldn't possibly be delivered? What would a move like that do to the price of electricity? That's what Belden wondered and what he set out to learn with his little hands-on experiment.

• • •

California. Outside of Washington, D.C., was there any place Enron spent more time maneuvering than California? California was so big, so important, so influential—and this big, important, influential state was also moving more quickly than most others to deregulate its retail energy markets.

Enron hired lobbyists by the bushelful. It doled out tens of thousands of dollars in campaign contributions to California politicians. Lay and Skilling made stump speeches touting deregulation's benefits. In one appearance before the California Public Utilities Commission (CPUC), Skilling claimed that the state would save $8.9 billion a year: "Let me tell you what you can buy every year," he said. "You can triple the number of police in Los Angeles, San Francisco, Oakland, and San Diego, and you could double the number of teachers."

Then, after energy deregulation took place in California, Enron's EES division spent millions more in an attempt to make itself into a high-profile energy retailer, selling electricity directly to consumers. Though that effort was a bust, deregulation still gave the company a tremendous vested interest in the state. And, finally, once the California experiment became an out-and-out debacle, bankrupting the state's largest utility and wreaking havoc on its economy, Enron had yet one more reason to focus on California: to defend itself from the near-universal belief among Californians that Enron was the company that turned out the lights. Although the accusations were only partially true—many of the other parties involved in this mess behaved no better—Enron's size and its undisguised disdain for the state's suffering made it the prime target.

In truth, for all Enron's lobbying, the new rules accompanying California's deregulation were a far cry from what the company had hoped to see enacted. As always, Enron had pushed hard for a completely deregulated marketplace, in which companies could cut whatever deals suited their needs. But there were so many powerful competing interests jockeying for advantage that the CPUC, which was in charge of designing the new rules, was never going to allow a completely free market.

For example, the state's three investor-owned utilities—Pacific Gas & Electric, San Diego Gas & Electric, and Southern California Edison—all had long-term contracts to buy power at high rates. If the state was no longer going to set electricity rates based on their costs, they wanted compensation for the losses that would inevitably ensue. Politicians, meanwhile, wanted guarantees that consumers would get their rates reduced. Otherwise, what was the point?

The result was a convoluted mishmash of compromises featuring more rules and regulations than ever. The utilities were forced to sell off their generating facilities and buy their power on the open market. They were also forbidden from entering into any significant long-term contracts; instead they had to purchase power in the spot market *every day.* This was supposed to lead to panic selling, thereby driving prices down. At the same time, though, the rates consumers were charged weren't deregulated, at least not in the short term. Instead, they were cut

10 percent, then frozen for five years. Because the CPUC was convinced that spot-market power prices would drop substantially more than 10 percent after deregulation, it wanted the utilities to be able to use the difference to recoup the losses on their long-term contracts. (Indeed, if the utilities recovered their losses before five years were up, consumer rates would be unfrozen. This actually happened in San Diego.)

But the true nightmare—and the opportunity for traders like Belden—lay in the market itself, which was really a handful of markets layered together in incredibly complex ways. To some extent, the very nature of electricity made that necessary. Getting electrons to go where you want them to go isn't a matter of loading them on a truck, driving them someplace, and letting the extra ones sit around until a buyer arrives. It's an engineering feat, one involving something that's essential to modern life. Supply has to be lined up ahead of time; and the path the electrons will take to get from Point A to Point B also has be planned ahead of time, because transmission lines have a limited amount of capacity. It's also impossible to store electricity; electrons can travel only in real time. So there also has to be a way to make sure that supply and demand match at all times.

This is complicated stuff to begin with, and California made it even more complicated. The state's new rules created two quasi-governmental agencies. One was called the California Power Exchange (Cal PX). Its job was to set hourly prices for electricity through auctions conducted the previous day and on the day of delivery. Sellers received (and buyers paid) the highest price needed to satisfy all the demand in any given hour. The second agency, the Independent System Operator (ISO), was in charge of managing the state's network of transmission lines to ensure reliability. It also conducted its own real-time auctions, which were just supposed to correct last-minute supply-and-demand imbalances and ensure adequate reserves.

The logic behind many of the new rules could be difficult to fathom. One example: when the ISO purchased last-minute power that was generated in California, the price was capped in early 2000 at $750 per megawatt hour. But if the power came from out of market, there was no price cap. Of course, the price caps could also easily turn into price targets: people knew just what the ISO was willing to pay.

Another example: if too much electricity was scheduled to flow on a transmission line—and the line became "congested"—the ISO would pay fees to whichever power company agreed to relieve the apparent congestion. There was no way to check if there was even enough real demand to cause the congestion in the first place. The potential for abuse was obvious. As early as 1996, a man named Eric Woychik, an adviser to the CPUC in the 1980s and later an ISO board member, wrote that gaming the market would be like "shooting fish in a barrel—not great sport, but lucrative." Even Belden himself, in an internal presentation he gave in May 2000, noted that "the ISO and the PX have a complex set of rules that are prone to gaming."

The new rules went into effect on April 1, 1998. At first, deregulation seemed to be a roaring success. It did exactly what everyone hoped it would do: it caused prices to drop substantially. There was so much competition among suppliers that electricity was actually free between 1 A.M. and 2 A.M. For most of the next two years, wholesale costs averaged around $33 per megawatt hour—well below the old regulated rates. They also stayed safely below consumer rates, allowing the state's big utilities to recover billions of dollars.

But to those in the guts of the market, it was clear almost immediately that some suppliers were not going to play nice. On July 9, 1998, just three months after the new rules went into effect, ISO employees were stunned to see the price for reserve power, which had been a dollar, suddenly spike for no apparent reason to $2,500 per megawatt hour, then to $5,000. Four days later, it happened again: the price soared to $9,999 per megawatt hour.

What had happened? Dynegy had simply offered to supply standby power at that price—and under the rules, since there were few other offers and the ISO was expecting high demand, the ISO was forced to take Dynegy's price. Jeffrey Tranen, then the CEO of the ISO, later told the *Sacramento Bee,* "All of us saw those numbers and realized . . . there was nothing to stop someone from bidding to infinity."

By any objective measure, Enron had a powerful self-interest in seeing the California experiment succeed. It had preached for years that deregulation would cause prices to go down and make life better for everyone. The Enron belief was that once California deregulated and showcased the virtues of a free market in retail electricity to the rest of the nation, other states would have no choice but to follow suit.

But if deregulation was a failure, Enron would be badly hurt. As an internal Enron memo put it, "If Enron doesn't do well in California, Enron will have a difficult time convincing anyone outside of California that they are capable of and committed to providing power services." Just as importantly, if the California experiment failed—no matter what the reason—other states were hardly likely to follow it into the abyss. A California failure could put an end to the push for broad, national power deregulation.

Yet from Ken Lay on down, Enron executives simply refused to see that their best interest lay in helping the state succeed. That kind of larger consideration was utterly foreign to the company's what's-in-it-for-me culture. This was especially true of the traders, who viewed such thoughts as lacking intellectual purity. Besides, everyone at Enron was annoyed at the way California had put deregulation into effect; the state hadn't followed the company's long-held position that a completely free marketplace was the only thing that made sense. Having failed to listen to Enron, the state therefore deserved whatever it got.

"If they're going to put in place such a stupid system, it makes sense to try to game it," says one former senior Enron executive, in a comment that perfectly summed up the prevailing attitude inside the company. That their actions might cause turmoil and hardship, that they might affect businesses up and down the state, well, from the point of view of the Enron traders, that was California's problem, not theirs. "It was the traders' job to make money, not to benefit the people of California," says another former Enron executive.

Thus, right alongside their rivals at Dynegy and elsewhere, Enron's West Coast traders began searching for loopholes. There were ultimately a hundred West Coast traders; they operated out of the Portland World Trade Center, where the company had built a copy of its Houston trading floor, down to the plasma TV screens and Nerf footballs. Belden, who was leading the effort to find exploitable loopholes, put in 14-hour days learning the arcane rules of California deregulation. By the spring of 1999, he thought he saw a flaw he could exploit. But first, he had to conduct his experiment.

Here's what Belden did: on May 24, 1999, at 6:10 A.M., he submitted four bids to sell a total of 2,900 megawatts—enough to run a city the size of Fresno for a day—to the Cal PX to meet demand in the peak hours the following day. At 7:01 A.M., the PX notified Belden that his bid was successful. At 7:29 A.M., Belden identified a transmission route called Silverpeak as the means for getting the electricity to the state.

The transmission route Belden had chosen begins at the Beowave geothermal energy facility in Nevada, where steam is pulled from subterranean cauldrons into a huge turbine, generating electricity. The electricity is carried across Nevada to a terminal in Silverpeak, a ghost town in the desert, where lines then transmit it over the Last Chance mountain range into Southern California. Here's the key point, though: the Silverpeak transmission lines can only carry 15 megawatts at a time.

In other words, Belden had scheduled 2,900 megawatts on a line that could only absorb a tiny fraction of that amount. Because the transaction was physically impossible, alarm bells went off in the offices of the ISO, which was responsible for both the transmission lines and for correcting supply-and-demand imbalances. At 11:17 A.M., an ISO scheduler called Enron to find out if there had been a mistake. Belden was expecting the call, which was immediately transferred to him.

> BELDEN: Um, there's a—there—we, just, um—we did it because we wanted to do it. And I don't—I don't mean to be coy.
> THE BEWILDERED ISO SCHEDULER: Cause, I mean, it's—it's—it's a— I mean . . . it's a pretty interesting schedule . . .
> BELDEN: It—it's how we—it makes the eyes pop, doesn't it?

It did indeed. Because there was no way for Belden's power to be delivered, the PX didn't have the supply it thought it had. And so the ISO, which handled such emergencies, had to hustle to find replacement supplies. Because the agency was forced to buy a substantial amount of power at the last minute, prices in California shot up by more than 70 percent, resulting in a cost of as much as $7 million to users. There was nothing subtle about Belden's gambit. "Someone played a game yesterday," reported a newsletter called the *Energy Market Report*. Almost immediately, complaints from other market participants triggered an investigation.

The investigation dragged on for almost a year. Belden's essential defense was that he wasn't trying to break the rules; he was simply performing an experiment. In fact, he claimed, he was doing the state a favor by pointing out such a huge flaw in its regulations. Enron's hypocrisy was stunning: Ken Lay wrote to the Cal PX in November 1999 that Enron "believes in conducting business affairs in accordance with the highest ethical standards . . . your recognition of our ethical standards allows Enron employees to work with you via arm's length transactions and avoids potentially embarrassing and unethical situations."

Enron's arrogance was equally stunning. Greg Whalley, Belden's boss, flew to California to argue Enron's position. In a meeting with a Cal PX economist, he went up to a white board and filled it with supply-and-demand charts, explaining all the while why the California market was flawed. "It was like Whalley was a college professor, lecturing him," recalls an Enron lawyer who was there. Whalley's position was that it wasn't Enron that was at fault; the problem was the foolishness of the rules, which were so easy to take advantage of. His argument was a little like an eight year old telling his parents that it was their fault he'd done something wrong because they weren't watching him closely enough.

In April 2000, the Silverpeak case was settled. Enron neither admitted nor denied the allegations that it had violated the market rules, but it agreed to pay a fine of $25,000 and promised to not "engage in substantially the same conduct." The agreement was signed in large, upright handwriting by Greg Whalley. "This 'experiment' clearly demonstrates a disregard for the Cal PX's primary goal of maintaining efficient and fair markets," concluded the Cal PX investigators. If Enron had really been worried about a flaw in the system, they added, "the appropriate response would have been to bring the matter to the attention of appropriate policy makers at the Cal PX rather than disrupt the market for its own education." But no changes were made to market rules. And internally, Belden wasn't even reprimanded for Silverpeak, though he had hardly been upholding "the highest ethical standards." Then again, why would Enron reprimand him? He was making money for the company.

In fact, even as Whalley was signing the settlement agreement, Belden and his team were busy devising similar schemes. These were subtler than the Silverpeak experiment—now that it was for real, it seems that the traders didn't want to get caught—but the purpose remained the same: to manipulate the rules and make money in the process. In one scheme, Enron submitted a schedule reflecting demand that wasn't there. The West Coast traders called that one Fat Boy. Another was a variation of the Silverpeak experiment: Enron filed imaginary transmission schedules in order to get paid to alleviate congestion that didn't really exist. That was called Death Star. Get Shorty was a strategy that involved selling power and other services that Enron did not have for use as reserves, with the expectation that Enron would never be called upon to supply the power or would be able to buy it later at a lower price. The point of Ricochet was to circumvent California's price caps. For instance, Enron exported power from California and brought it back in when the ISO was desperate and had to pay far higher prices. (This strategy, which was used by all the power traders, was more widely known as "megawatt laundering.")

When a trader found a formula that worked, he would send an e-mail around the office. On May 5, 2000, for instance, an Enron trader named Michael Driscoll sent an e-mail to his fellow traders. "The FINAL PROCEDURES FOR DEATH STAR . . ." read the subject heading. The e-mail, which contained detailed instructions on how to replicate the strategy, noted that "project deathstar has been successfully implemented to capture congestion relief across paths 26, 15 & COI." The e-mail concludes with "THANKS AND GOOD LUCK." (Driscoll's year-end list of accomplishments in 2000 noted that he had also "implemented the Round the West trade strategy—taking California power out in the Southwest, up the Rockies . . . and back into California" and that he was an "innovative trader.")

One advantage the traders had in playing their games was the use of Enron's own utility, Portland General. It wasn't long before the utility's transmission lines became a part of the company's machinations. For example, as Portland General later told the Federal Energy Regulatory Commission (FERC), some of the transactions it did during this time "may have resulted in the company purchasing power from the Cal PX and reselling power from its portfolio of supplies at prices higher than those paid to the Cal PX."

The U.S. Senate Committee on Governmental Affairs also says that transcripts of Portland General employees reveal transactions where the apparent purpose was "to assist Enron in exporting power from California with the intention of reimporting it back to the state at higher prices." It's not clear how complicit Portland General was, but several transcripts make it sound as if the old-line Portland General employees, unlike the West Coast traders, hated what they were being told to do. On an April 6, 2000, transcript of Portland scheduling calls, one Portland employee responsible for scheduling power transmission tells another: "I'll sure be glad when we're sold and they can't pull this [expletive] anymore." At other times Portland General transmission workers describe Enron deals as "messed up," "stupid," "the weirdest junk," "convoluted," and "bogus." Another says, "This is a scam and you know it." Even an Enron trader acknowledges that certain deals are "kind of squirrelly" and "nasty."

Indeed, Enron couldn't have pulled off many of its strategies without the help of third parties, which had access to generation and transmission lines that Enron itself didn't control. But that turned out to be not much of a problem; many competitors, as well as out-of-state utilities and power suppliers, were only too happy to oblige. There was money in it for them as well. According to a later FERC report, an undated Enron document notes that the traders were pursuing a strategy of "gaining control of a variety of small resources or capabilities around the west." By 2000, Enron had agreements with Montana Power, Powerex, El Paso Electric, and others. ("These prices provide extraordinary opportunities," Enron wrote to El Paso in July 2000.) An Enron Services Handbook contained a list of various market conditions that might arise, which of the "partners" to call, what steps to follow in order to take advantage of a particular situation, and an explanation of the profit-sharing arrangements.

"El Paso wants to play again," wrote an Enron trader in one e-mail. "They are willing to . . . profit share (fat boy) into the ISO. . . ." Over time, Enron noted, it would "store operational data" from its partners. It wanted, the handbook said, "to lock customers in—if they leave . . . their data stays here." This strategy of enlisting other players gave Enron more information, more market share, and more access to power generation and transmission. Under the rules, it was supposed to report resources it controlled to the FERC. The FERC says it didn't. It seems that the Enron traders simply didn't believe any outsider would ever be smart enough to connect the dots.

In addition to his short-term schemes, Belden had a long-term outlook on electricity. Despite Enron's predictions that prices would fall after deregulation, he had a different view. He had become convinced that the economics of power in California were such that prices were going to rise. His calculation didn't have much to do with gaming the rules of deregulation; it was rooted instead in his reading of several larger trends.

One trend was that the California economy had gone through a tremendous boom in the 1990s, a boom that had included an enormous expansion of computing power, thanks in part to the rapid growth of Silicon Valley. As computer companies and dot-coms grew, they used more power. At the same time, though, the state's strict environmental laws prevented major new power plants from being built. In other words, Belden believed, demand was growing and supply was not keeping up. Perhaps more important, Belden also believed that California had begun to rely far too much on an abundant supply of hydroelectric power. According to his analysis, hydro accounted for some 40 percent of the resources used to produce power throughout the West. What would happen if there were a dry year? Because of the way the California market was structured, with the utilities forced to buy most of their power on the spot market, any shortage could send prices spiraling upward. The result wouldn't be the panic selling the deregulation gurus had envisioned; it would be panic buying.

Acting on Belden's theory, the West Coast trading desk took a huge long position in electricity in late 1999. By the spring of 2000, Belden's prediction began coming true. Unseasonably warm weather boosted power needs. At the same time, because of lower snow pack, or snow density, there was less hydroelectric power available from Oregon.

Almost overnight, the surplus became a shortage, and California needed every megawatt it could get its hands on. Soon, the ISO, which was just supposed to balance supply and demand around the edges, was providing 20 percent to 25 percent of California's total energy needs and paying increasingly higher prices for power. On May 12, 2000, Belden e-mailed a colleague in Houston: "We long. Pricing keep going up. So far so good."

On May 22, 2000, the ISO was forced to declare a Stage 1 emergency, because its power reserves had dropped below 7 percent. Before May, prices had averaged $24 to $40 per megawatt hour; now they quickly hit the price cap of $750 per megawatt hour. Industry experts were in a state of shock: it wasn't even summer yet, and supply and demand were not wildly of whack. Why was the price of electricity going up so much?

It became frighteningly clear that May 22 was no isolated event. All through June, power prices remained at sky-high levels. Emergencies became increasingly common; the ISO wound up declaring 55 emergencies in 2000 and another 70 in 2001, compared with just 17 in 1998 and 1999 combined. Suddenly, utilities were bleeding money because they were forced to pay far more for their power than they could collect from customers, who were still paying regulated rates.

In mid-June, as temperatures in the Bay Area topped 100 degrees, Pacific Gas & Electric was forced to declare rolling blackouts—the first since World War II in California—in part because a plant that it sold to Duke Energy (as the new rules required) was taken offline for maintenance. Entire neighborhoods saw their power shut off for an hour to two hours at a time—at which point their power was turned back on and another neighborhood went dark. In just that one month, the total wholesale cost of electricity topped $3.6 billion, roughly half of what power had cost for all of 1999. The ISO, in search of a solution, lowered the cap on the price it would pay for power generated in California from $750 per megawatt to $500 and finally to $250.

And so it went, all summer long. In San Diego, the one city where consumer rates had been deregulated (that's because the local utility had earned back all its losses from those onerous long-term contracts), power prices doubled between May and August. Small businesses had to shut their doors because they couldn't pay their bills. State officials pleaded with companies and consumers alike to turn down their air conditioners and dim their lights. Schools that had obtained lower rates by signing contracts under which their power supply could be interrupted—never thinking that such a thing could happen—had to send students home because their electricity was shut off. Companies with similar contracts had to turn off their air conditioning entirely, even though it was approaching 100 degrees outside. The big California utilities were suddenly in deep financial trouble. People were enraged. Protests sprang up all across the state. By the end of the summer, California was in full-crisis mode.

And Enron was taking full advantage: Belden and his West Coast trading desk were booking profits the likes of which they'd never seen before, some $200 million just between May and August of 2000, according to a presentation Enron later gave to Moody's. That was roughly four times the profit the desk had made in all of 1999, according to the government.

But *why?* Why was this happening? To hear Enron and the other power sellers describe it, the whole debacle was California's fault. The state needed to build more power plants; that was the only way supply and demand would get back into balance. And it needed to stop trying to keep an artificial lid on prices, which only made things worse. Indeed, to Enron, the two issues were intertwined. As Belden put it in an e-mail to the ISO, "prices need to reflect market conditions in order to incent new generation."

Later, Belden addressed an industry conference, which was covered by the *Los Angeles Times*. "Is there scarcity?" he asked. "Is there a smoking gun? We still don't know. How did we get here? Well, first, these complex markets were designed by economists and engineers. If you want to trade power in California for Enron, the minimum requirements are, you need to have a law degree and a Ph.D. in engineering. You need to have done significant research in market theory and game theory." At which point, the audience laughed.

California regulators and politicians found such comments utterly infuriating. To them, the problem was simple: the big power companies, including Enron, were manipulating the market for their own benefit. And state officials wanted the federal government to do something about it. San Diego Gas & Electric filed a complaint with the FERC, requesting lower price caps. On August 10, the ISO issued a report, blaming the crisis on the exercise of market power; on August 17, representatives from the California utilities presented a detailed list of alleged trading abuses to the FERC, including the intentional creation of congestion and "megawatt laundering." The FERC denied San Diego's request, citing a lack of evidence. But on August 23, the FERC, under political pressure, did order an investigation.

At the time, the FERC was deeply unsympathetic to California's complaints. Most of the FERC commissioners were fundamentally proderegulation—that was the ethos of the times. They tended to agree with the power-trading companies that California had botched deregulation. On August 24, representatives from a group of power marketers met with the FERC to defend their actions. Enron sent Mary Hain, a regulatory affairs lawyer. The message she laid out—"The high prices in California were the result of scarce supply" and the FERC should be "discouraged . . . from taking any action that would hurt the vibrant wholesale market in the [*sic*] California and the rest of the West . . . ," as she later wrote in an e-mail—fell on receptive ears. That was what the FERC already believed.

Despite the FERC's willingness to side with the energy traders, the company had no illusions about what was coming. "We knew we were going to get sued," says Richard Sanders, who was head of litigation for Enron North America. "There was no way we weren't going to get sued." To steel itself for the coming legal battle, Enron assembled a team of outside firms, including Stoel Rives, a Northwest firm that specialized in energy regulations, and Brobeck Phleger, which had trial expertise in complex business litigation.

On October 3, 2000, the entire team—more than a dozen lawyers and regulatory experts—convened in Portland to get a handle on the problem. "We are not your lawyers," Sanders and the Brobeck lawyers warned Belden when the meeting started. "We are the company's lawyers." The message, of course, was that if Belden said anything incriminating, they would be looking to protect the company's interests, not his. Belden was unflustered. He quickly went to the white board at the front of the room and began sketching out in minute detail the strategies he and the West Coast trading desk had been employing.

For the next two hours, he went through them all. He explained how his traders employed Ricochet to move power out of California, then back in again at much higher prices. He detailed Fat Boy and Death Star and Get Shorty, too. "No one can prove, given complexity of our portfolio," he said at one point, according to handwritten notes taken by Mary Hain. (In a deposition she later gave, she said that she did not think this reflected chicanery, just the traders' belief that regulators wouldn't be able to figure out what was going on.) Far from being ashamed of what his group had done, Belden was proud of it. "I don't think they ever thought they did anything wrong," Sanders said later. "To them it was a big video game. . . . He [Belden] thought it was all just part of working the system to make us as much money as possible."

Sanders, however, was horrified. He didn't understand everything he was hearing it—it was very complicated stuff—but those nicknames sent chills up his spine. *Fat Boy? Death Star? Ricochet?* To Sanders, it scarcely mattered whether the strategies were legal or not. He was a litigator; California was in crisis; people were furious. He knew exactly how these nicknames would sound in court. "Is it too late to change the names?" he asked plaintively. "Can't you just call them Puppy Dog and Momma's Cooking?"

There was another issue, too. Enron had gotten requests from both the CPUC and the California attorney general's office, which wanted to know, among other things, exactly how much money Enron had earned in the state's power market. The profits that Belden ascribed to the short-term strategies—$5 million here, $3 million there—were small. (The FERC later estimated that Enron earned a mere $60 million from "congestion revenues" and that it was "highly unlikely" that the impact of Belden's strategies on spot prices "accounted for a substantial portion of Enron's total revenues." But as the ISO has also noted, it is impossible to gauge the "indirect and cumulative impact of these strategies on overall market prices and outcomes.")

But the company *was* making a fortune on Belden's long position. Enron executives, knowing how poorly that would play, were desperate to avoid disclosing the figures. Hain said she heard from higher-ups that Enron would "die on the Hill rather than provide that information." She also said: "They didn't want anybody to know how much money they were making."

Yet despite all of this—the certain outrage that would result from the discovery of the company's mammoth California profits; the legal headaches that would arise from exposure of the trading strategies' names; indeed, the possibility that the strategies were *illegal*—nobody told the traders to stop. With one exception: at Belden's request, Sanders did talk to a trader who had figured out that if he scheduled megawatt sales in fractions—say, 22.49 megawatts—the ISO would round down to 22 megawatts for the delivery and round up to 23 megawatts for payment, enabling Enron to skim the difference. Sanders told him to send the money—some $15,000—back.

Belden argued that all Enron's competitors were employing similar strategies, which was true. (In fact, other companies made much more than Enron did. But they were smart enough to avoid the headline-grabbing names like Deathstar.) He also blamed California's *real* problems on the companies that owned the power plants, a group that did not include Enron. Belden insisted that some strategies were even beneficial to the market. For instance, because the state's big utilities routinely underestimated their demand for the next day to force prices down, Fat Boy, which was a way of overestimating demand, made the system more reliable.

Mostly, though, he claimed that while his traders' strategies took advantage of badly designed rules, they didn't break them. In the energy trading world, "talking your book"—lying about your position in order to get the market to move your way—was common practice. That these practices made a mockery of Ken Lay's exhortations about Enron's high ethical standards was irrelevant. So was the long-term damage the traders were doing to Enron's larger goal of nationwide deregulation.

In trying to be so smart, Enron's West Coast traders were doing something incredibly stupid. But inside the Enron cocoon, they simply couldn't see that. "The attitude was, 'play by your own rules,'" says a former trader. "We all did it. We talked about it openly. It was the school yard we lived in. The energy markets were new, immature, unsupervised. We took pride in getting around the rules. *It was a game.*"

When Richard Sanders returned to Houston, he promptly went to see his boss, Mark Haedicke, the general counsel for Enron North America. "We have a problem," he said.

They certainly did. Gary Fergus and Peter Meringolo, two of the Brobeck lawyers who attended the session with Belden in Portland, noted that there were already at least six investigations into California energy practices and spelled out the potential consequences of the West Coast traders' actions in a memo to the Enron legal department.

"If Enron is found to have engaged in deceptive or fraudulent practices, there is also the risk of other criminal legal theories such as wire fraud, RICO, fraud involving markets, and fictitious commodity transactions. . . . In addition depending upon the conduct, there may be the potential for criminal charges prosecuted against both individuals and the company," they noted. "We believe it is imperative that Enron understands in detail what evidence exists with respect to its conduct in the California electricity market as soon as possible."

At the end of October, the two in-house lawyers, Sanders and Haedicke, along with two of the top executives in the Wholesale division in Houston, Dave Delainey and John Lavorato, held a conference call with Belden so that the Houston executives could hear firsthand about Belden's strategies. When he heard the nicknames for the schemes, Delainey could only shake his head. No one suggested shoving the problem under the rug—but, once again, no one said to stop, either.

On November 1, just days after the conference call, Enron got some good news: the FERC issued the results of its investigation. The investigators had only had three months and lacked subpoena power, so they had no way of knowing about Death Star and Ricochet. The FERC did note that rates were "unjust and unreasonable" and proposed a number of remedies. But the report largely exonerated the power trading companies, including Enron. While the FERC said that "certain market rules do interfere with the functioning of the market and, taken together, may permit sellers to exercise market power," that was as much a slap at California as it was the companies. And in any case, the investigators concluded that there was insufficient data to "support findings of specific exercises of market power." The FERC also declined to order immediate refunds to California as San Diego Gas & Electric was demanding. The report was met with fury in California. One consumer group said that the "FERC is fiddling while consumers are burning."

If not for what happened next, Belden's little tricks might have stayed a secret forever. On December 6, two lawyers—Christian Yoder from Enron and Stephen Hall from Stoel Rives—sent a memo to Richard Sanders and Mark Haedicke. Both had attended the meeting in Portland where Belden had laid out the traders' schemes and were deeply troubled by what they'd heard. Neither of the recipients had requested a memo, but according to one person involved, Yoder wanted to make sure that Haedicke, who had a reputation for being slippery and political, couldn't disavow knowledge of the Portland problem.

Using phrases like "the oldest trick in the book" and "dummied up" demand, Yoder and Hall walked through Fat Boy, Death Star, and the other techniques. When they got to Ricochet, Enron's strategy of exporting lower-cost California power out of the state then bringing it back in when the ISO was desperate, the lawyers wrote: "This strategy appears not to present any problems, other than a public-relations risk arising from the fact that such exports may have contributed to California's declaration of a Stage 2 Emergency yesterday."

By this time, Haedicke had California first on his list of the top ten legal risks that Enron faced, says Sanders. (LJM was also on his list: "Increased SEC scrutiny might lead to restatement of earnings," he noted.) The Brobeck lawyers soon drafted *another* memo, trying to soften the harsh language Yoder and Hall had employed. They noted that Yoder and Hall had made a number of errors and that the lawyers still didn't really understand what the traders were doing. But the damage was done. The Yoder and Hall memo, given to the FERC by Enron's board months after Enron's collapse, gave California the proof it had long sought that Enron had manipulated the market. Indeed, it caused many people to blame Enron for *creating* the California crisis.

But that came later. All winter long, as Enron's lawyers were grappling internally with their discovery of the West Coast trading schemes, California's power problems continued to escalate. The state, by then, was desperate for power. It didn't matter whether the weather was severe or not; the shortages were chronic, the declaration of emergencies more frequent. The ISO asked people not to turn on Christmas lights to save electricity. ("I know everybody says we're the Grinch that stole Christmas," said a spokesman, "but we're trying to keep power on in their homes.") Companies cut back on capital investment because they needed to make sure they had enough cash to pay their energy bills. Some factories were calling workers in at 2 A.M., so they could operate the plant when electricity was less scarce—and conserve it during peak hours.

At the same time, PG&E and Southern California Edison were drowning in debt. Lacking long-term contracts—and unable to pass on their soaring costs to customers, who, as a result, had no motivation to conserve energy—they were reduced to sending out pathetic press releases begging consumers to "turn off PCs, monitors, printers, copiers, and lights when not in use."

Stunningly, the companies that had bought the generation plants from the utilities—companies like Mirant, Duke, Dynegy, and Reliant, which also traded energy—were taking them off line for maintenance. By-mid November, nearly a quarter of the state's generating capacity was idle for maintenance or emergency repairs, nearly three times the outage rate of a year earlier. In fact, from May 2000 through June 2001, plants owned by the major generators ran at just over 50 percent of capacity, according to industry consultant Robert McCullough.

The companies insisted that the outtages were the necessary and inevitable result of running old plants hard. Governor Gray Davis and consumer advocates insisted that the outtages were a deliberate attempt to drive prices up. In fact, as it turned out, the hourly operations of many West Coast plants had for a time been posted on an energy-industry Web site; when the California attorney general learned about this, he demanded a list of everyone who had access to the site—a list that included Enron.

To make matters worse, the price of natural gas—a major component of the cost of electricity—was also soaring to strangely high levels at the California border. That, of course, helped power producers justify the high prices they were charging. The FERC later alleged that energy traders were manipulating the natural-gas market as well.

Every day, ISO officials would make frantic phone calls in a desperate attempt to find power. "We simply couldn't make enough phone calls. It was a Turkish bazaar. It was madness," COO Kellan Fluckiger told *Fortune* that winter. Even if the ISO found power, it couldn't always pay the price the seller was asking because of the price caps. Because of the financial instability of both the utilities and the ISO, which needed money from the utilities to pay suppliers, power producers began refusing to ship to California. (Perhaps it's no wonder that Fluckiger wanted to switch sides: that December, he approached Belden about getting a job with Enron.)

Statewide blackouts were narrowly averted at the last minute when U.S. Energy Secretary Bill Richardson imposed a state of emergency, requiring marketers to sell to California.

Incredibly, around the same time, Ken Lay telephoned Richardson and asked him to use his emergency powers to deregulate the nation's electricity transmission grid. "We don't think we can do that," Richardson replied. "We don't think it is appropriate." A former Richardson aide said, "I was floored by the request. I couldn't believe they were asking this." Even one of Enron's lobbyists later called it "a dumb idea."

During the first week in December, power had become incredibly scarce. Nearly a quarter of the state's entire system was off line, and the ISO was unable to buy in-state power that fell under the price cap because prices as high as $5,000 a megawatt in neighboring states were sucking supply out. The situation was so desperate that the CEO of the ISO finally asked the FERC to, in essence, abolish the price caps. The FERC complied on December 15. By the following week, prices had risen to as high as $1,500 per megawatt.

Inside Enron, meanwhile, the lawyers had held another two days of meetings in Portland on December 11 and 12. It was at these meetings—several months after first learning of the West Coast traders' strategies—that they finally told the traders to stop. The lawyers still hadn't decided if Belden's actions were illegal or not, but by that point, several lawsuits seeking class-action status had been filed in San Diego against Enron and other power companies. "We were stopping because the heat was too hot," says Sanders.

By then, though, Belden had other things on his mind: he and his wife were waiting for their first baby (a boy) to arrive. On December 21, a friend e-mailed him: "Hey you must be going crazy with the California energy crisis! Is SoCal and PCG going out of business or what???????" Belden wrote back: "any day now . . . the official due date is christmas. i'm ready. sue is ready. bring it on.

work is crazy! pcg and eix are running out of cash. it's not a pretty situation. those safe utility bonds aren't quite so safe anymore . . ."

Did the effective elimination of price caps end the California crisis? Not a chance. Though Enron had long argued that the caps were an impediment to the free flow of electricity in California, when they were finally lifted, the crisis seemed only to worsen. By mid-January, the credit rating of the utilities was sliding toward junk from fears that they would default on their debt. On January 17, rolling, hour-long blackouts swept through Northern California. For an hour at a time, modern life ground to a halt: elevators packed with passengers stopped between floors. Traffic accidents occurred because traffic lights suddenly shut down. Computers and ATMs went blank.

Governor Davis, who refused to allow the utilities to raise the rates they charged consumers, signed an emergency order permitting the state to buy power on behalf of its citizens. To keep the power California so desperately needed from flowing to other states offering higher prices, Davis and others began to call for regional price caps, a move that Enron vehemently opposed.

Meanwhile, the legacy of the entire mess was starting to be felt. In a *San Francisco Chronicle* survey, 92 percent of Californians described the deregulated energy market as a problem. In January 2001, according to a later Moody's presentation, Belden's West Coast power desk had its most profitable month ever: $254 million in gross profits.

It was around this same time that Belden's actions were publicly acknowledged by his superiors at Enron. No, he wasn't reprimanded—he was *promoted,* to managing director. Later, he was put on the powerful vice president's PRC committee, meaning that he evaluated the performance of the company's vice presidents, helped set bonuses, and recommended promotions. (Ben Glisan and Michael Kopper were also on the committee.) "i looked at that list and thought— wow, i'm hanging with the muckety mucks now . . . the down side is that i have to go to houston and hang out in meetings," Belden e-mailed a colleague. In 2001 alone, Belden was paid over $5 million in cash bonuses, ranking him among Enron's top earners.

The crisis didn't end until the summer of 2001. In April, Pacific Gas & Electric filed for bankruptcy. Two months later, the FERC finally decided to reverse course and instituted price caps across the Western market. Enron had lobbied furiously to prevent the caps from being approved, arguing, as ever, that they'd only make matters worse. (Of course, regionwide price caps would also eliminate such strategies as megawatt laundering.) But by then, the FERC was under too much political pressure from the other direction; it finally sided with California.

This time, the tactic appeared to work. By the end of June, prices were down to $43 per megawatt hour at one key hub, well below the cap of $92, according to McCullough. The last emergency took place on July 3, after which everyone began toting up the damage. During the crisis, California paid some $40 billion for electricity, more than quadruple the cost during a similar period a year earlier.

And yet, it's impossible to say with certainty that the caps themselves were what did the trick, just as it's impossible to say for sure what caused the crisis in the first place. Even now, opinion is widely divided on the question, and hard answers are nearly impossible to come by. Was the culprit California's flawed deregulation plan? Or was it the power companies, which learned to manipulate the market and took greedy advantage of the loopholes they found?

Throughout the crisis, this debate had raged on, with most Californians convinced that their state's power infrastructure had been abused by the companies that sold the state its electricity. "Why are prices on a Sunday in 1999 seven times lower than prices on a Sunday in 2000?" asked an executive at Southern California Edison, summing up the prevailing view for the *Los Angeles Times*. "Same load [demand], no plants are out or anything like that. What would do that? . . . As demand started going up, the marketers figured out a way that they could exercise market power."

Later, others argued that the energy companies were indeed exercising market power. After Enron collapsed, the FERC, while still blaming a "significant supply shortfall and a fatally flawed market design," also agreed with many of California's allegations, arguing that there was "clear evidence of market manipulation" on the part of many of the big energy traders, including Enron. The FERC also said that Belden's strategies were "forms of gaming based on price manipulation and the falsification of information." The FERC would also—long after it mattered—strip Enron of its ability to compete in gas and electricity markets. But even that didn't end the debate. It seems that no one agrees what the rules should be when it comes to a commodity that is essential to modern life.

But the academic debate was lost on Californians, who were enraged at the way the nation's energy executives and their political supporters had dismissed their pain so cavalierly. It was as if their complaints were the baseless grumblings of rubes who were incapable of fully appreciating the glory of the free market.

"The deregulation that wasn't," sniffed McKinsey, Enron's favorite consulting firm. "As they suffer the consequences of their own feckless policies, political leaders in California blame power companies, deregulation, and everyone but themselves," Texas Senator Phil Gramm (whose wife, of course, sat on Enron's board) told the *Los Angeles Times*. "Price caps are not a help," said Vice President Dick Cheney. "They take us in exactly the wrong direction." "California has done nothing to curb demand and nothing to help supply," said Dynegy CEO Chuck Watson. "Even an old econ major from Oklahoma State like me realizes that's a collision course."

No one was smugger or more dismissive than Enron executives themselves, and no one was more insistent that they had done absolutely nothing wrong. Skilling "clearly thinks Californians should be thanking Enron, not castigating it, for its role in trying to push open the state's power markets," wrote *Business-Week* in February 2001. "We're on the side of angels," Skilling said.

In an interview he gave to the online financial site the Motley Fool, Skilling said of California's degulation effort: "It is something I think that a central planner from the old Soviet Union would understand exactly." "You probably couldn't have designed a worse system," he told Reuters. And as late as June of 2001, he was still taking potshots at the state. At a conference in Las Vegas, Skilling offered up an astoundingly insensitive joke: "You know what the difference is between the state of California and the *Titanic*?" he asked, with a grin. "At least the lights were on when the *Titanic* went down." Later, in that same appearance, he added, "Please do not use the terms California and deregulation in the same sentence."

Ken Lay was every bit as dismissive. At one employee meeting, he said that California had "set up a system that was doomed to failure at the beginning . . . they're going to have a really, really tough summer, much tougher than they're talking about. . . . I mean it could be almost catastrophic from the standpoint of electricity shortages and blackouts . . . now we'll try to work with them and help them where we can, but indeed, we think they ought to be trying to make the system work effectively with competition and with markets."

In a March 27, 2001, interview with the PBS show *Frontline*, Lay cited the lack of new power plants as the primary cause of California's crisis and brushed off any suggestion that Enron might have done something wrong. "If we think there's market power, if we think there's manipulation by anybody in the industry, either inside the state or outside the state, then that ought to be attacked, and attacked aggressively," he said. The interviewer asked, "So you didn't see any market power being exercised this past winter in California?" Said Lay: "We did not . . . every time there's a shortage or a little bit of a price spike, it's always collusion or conspiracy. It always makes people feel better that way."

In speech after speech, Lay told Californians that they had only themselves to blame for having done such a dismal job of deregulating. And in private he could be even more withering. David Freeman, who during the crisis ran the Los Angeles Department of Water and Power, told the *Los Angeles Times* about a conversation with Lay in the latter part of 2000. Lay was trying to persuade Freeman that price caps weren't necessary; Freeman argued with him that they were. "Well, Dave, in the final analysis it doesn't matter what you crazy people in California do," said Lay. " I've got smart guys out there who can always figure out how to make money."

Long before there was an Enron scandal, there was at least one public figure who wanted to prosecute Ken Lay and the company. That was California Attorney General Bill Lockyer. In a May 2001 interview with the *Wall Street Journal*, he summed up all the fury Californians felt: "I would love to personally escort

Lay to an 8 by 10 cell that he could share with a tattoed dude who says, 'Hi, my name is Spike, honey.' "

Even though the crisis was over, the investigations were just beginning. The immediate threat lay in California, where a state senate committee was pushing hard on its own investigation. It had subpoenaed documents from Enron, but the company stonewalled; in fact, Enron sued, arguing that the committee had no authority to investigate Enron. Enron relented in late July only when it faced the possibility of contempt charges and financial sanctions. Of course, the real reason Enron was stonewalling was that its lawyers knew full well what the documents would reveal, and they wanted to delay the discovery of Deathstar and Get Shorty as long as they could—forever, if possible.

There was another issue the company didn't want to disclose. When the traders closed the books on 2000, Belden's West Coast power division had booked $460 million in profits. Most of that resulted from the large long position that Belden's team had taken. There was nothing illegal about that, but how profitable would the position have been if the market hadn't been manipulated, both by Enron and others? And how would it look if that profit was revealed? The West Coast gas traders—who also benefited from the crisis in California—made even more than Belden's group: $870 million. Overall, Enron's North American trading desk had made a staggering $2.2 billion for the year, according to the Moody's presentation.

Of course Enron wasn't just trying to hide this fact from the prying eyes of some investigators. It didn't want *anyone* to know how much it had made from trading—even its own investors. After all, it was simply not possible to make that kind of money acting as a logistics company. It could be made only by speculating. To reveal that number would be to reveal the truth.

And it found a method to avoid doing so. Enron also knew it had potential legal issues in California. As early as that fall, Belden noted that he had begun working with Houston trading executive John Lavorato to ensure that his books were "reasonably reserved for political exposure." So Enron took a huge amount of trading profit—upward of $1 billion, says one former executive—and booked it as a reserve against the potential liability it faced in California. This was not disclosed anywhere in Enron's books, although the company did repeatedly tell investors that it was "fully reserved" for any problems in California. Such is the murkiness of Enron that it's not clear if even the profits the company showed Moody's reflected reserves that had been put aside.

By spring 2001, even before the California crisis had ended, Enron's fundamentals group was forecasting lower energy prices and less volatility, partly because of the weakening economy and successful conservation. This view was extremely contrarian: other power trading companies were racing to build new power plants in California, but now the Enron team was arguing all that new power wouldn't be needed. Whalley didn't buy it at first, but after a trip to Portland, he came back convinced.

In the weeks that followed Whalley's trip, Belden's group began taking a large short position on western electricity. Star trader John Arnold also established a short position in natural gas. Other Enron traders began shorting competing power-trading companies—including Mirant, Dynegy, and Calpine—in their personal accounts. Some even started wondering about Enron itself.

The enormous profits Enron's traders made in 2000 and the first half of 2001 had raised a final, sobering question: how long could they keep it up? "Two businesses were profitable, trading and pipelines. And trading was not sustainable," says one former trader. He adds: "We all knew that the markets in 1999, 2000, and 2001 were impressive by any measure. But that type of volatility is not perpetual. We were afraid of that. We were throwing everything we could at trading, and it was maxxed out."

CHAPTER 18

Bandwidth Hog

That memorable analysts meeting in January 2000—the one where Skilling unveiled Enron Broadband, projected that its trading business would be generating more than a billion dollars in operating profits by 2004, and insisted that it *already* deserved an extra $37 in the price of every Enron share—presented a troubling problem for the executives who worked in the new division. Though Enron's stock started to jump within minutes, that was only because the analysts didn't know what the broadband insiders understood all too well: they didn't really *have* any business.

At that point, Enron Broadband was little more than a grandiose, untested plan. One part of the plan was to build a trading desk that would do for broadband what Enron had done for natural gas and electricity—turn bandwidth capacity into a tradable commodity. The second part was content delivery—streaming movies and other video into homes, taking advantage of a billion-dollar fiber-optic network Enron was building.

This plan required hundreds of millions of dollars in new investment. It required management expertise that Enron didn't have. It also required something else Enron lacked: patience. It was impossible to say for sure whether bandwidth could ever be made tradable in the same fashion as natural-gas futures; there were plenty of real-world impediments Enron would have to overcome. As for the business of delivering movies and other content over the Internet, it was still in its infancy in the year 2000; and though there were many people who believed it would eventually become a commercial reality, there was no way of knowing that for sure, either. And there was *certainly* no way of knowing just how big the business would be and how much of the new market Enron would be able to land.

But the analysts didn't appreciate any of this—in part because they were so terribly credulous, in part because they were simply misled. Enron had built its claims about the broadband business on the promise of its own high-speed network, with sophisticated technology driven by powerful new software that no one could match. In a press release back in April 1999, Enron started publicly claiming that its new system provided "virtually unlimited bandwidth" and "built-in intelligence" that would give businesses access to "a powerful new breed of Internet services." At the time, Enron had portrayed this network as "lit, tested, and ready." In fact, it wasn't close to operating on a commercial scale, and much of the promised technology never made it out of the lab.

For all of these reasons, Skilling's claims about the broadband business's value went well beyond mere hubris or even Internet-era hype, so common at the time. It was an act of staggering recklessness. "Jeff declared it a success when his own management team said it's not there yet," recalls a senior Enron executive. "You were creating another pressure cooker."

"Enron Broadband was a reasonably decent concept with reasonably decent technology," adds a former Enron managing director who worked in the business. "Given six years to develop the technology and the business plan, without making representations about a $29 billion market value, it had a decent shot of doing something unique. Demanding first-quarter results in a start-up communications business is really what led to some of the things that were done. They put out the projection, and then you've got to do some questionable things to make it happen."

In many ways, broadband stands as the logical evolution of the accumulating problems that ultimately brought down Enron. What Enron was trying to accomplish was bold, even inspirational. It looked dazzling in a hotel ballroom, presented to analysts by Skilling on PowerPoint slides. But in the real world, it ran headlong into the reality of a thousand technical, economic, competitive, and logistical roadblocks that keep any business plan—especially one so exceedingly ambitious—from unfolding perfectly. That was the problem with thinking about an elegant idea as profits in the bank (or at least on the income statement) from the moment it was conceived. The real world just doesn't work that way.

Although it ended in a welter of criminal charges, Enron Broadband didn't start out as deliberate fraud. Though few who worked there thought broadband was really worth what Skilling claimed, there were plenty among his minions who were convinced it would all work out in the end. If broadband's promises and valuation were miles ahead of reality, well, they would ultimately catch up. As Enron people saw it, this was how they always did things. "Our company was running downhill, with our arms pinwheeling, as fast as we can," says one former executive. "You get to a point where your legs can't keep up with your body. But we all believed we'd get to the bottom of the hill before we collapsed."

Skilling seemed oblivious of the practical challenges of turning his latest grand vision into reality and utterly unconcerned with the enormous pressures he'd created. What he saw was that the failure of Azurix and the contraction of the international business posed a threat to Enron's market capitalization, and he simply could not—*would not*—allow that to happen, no matter what. Broadband seemed as if it could work, and the payoff was off the charts. With the announcement of the broadband initiative, he later exulted, "We could get the market cap *fixed*. We *had* it fixed."

All this meant that Enron couldn't ever back away from Skilling's profit predictions, at least not without causing the stock to crater. Which left the broad-band executives facing a nightmarish scenario. They would have to somehow manage to build an entirely new industry from scratch in an incredibly short time against astonishing odds. And in the meantime, they would have to resort to cre-ating a portrait of a reality that simply didn't exist.

How big were the obstacles facing the new broadband division? They were enormous. Take trading first. Without question, the idea of trading bandwidth ca-pacity had appeal. At the time, purchasing bandwidth was an inflexible, expen-sive proposition, requiring business customers to lease a special dedicated line—usually for a year or more—with far more capacity than they needed. One former Enron broadband trading executive says: "It's like going to Sam's Club and asking for a single pack of gum."

Enron believed that broadband trading would make it possible for customers to buy only the bandwidth capacity they needed when they needed it. Businesses that required lots of bandwidth during a daytime peak period, for example, could sell their nighttime and weekend capacity for residential use. This kind of trad-ing would be more efficient than laying new lines and, in theory, bring prices down as well.

But as a practical matter, the kind of real-time switching Enron envisioned was impossible. Transferring high-capacity bandwidth meant sending workers out to change connections by hand, a process that took days—if it was possible to switch them at all. Two companies that leased lines had no way of hooking up to use each other's bandwidth. For all practical purposes, when it came to high-capacity bandwidth, the information superhighway was like a series of parallel roads that never intersected.

Enron claimed to be rolling out the capability to change that, through its En-ron Intelligent Network. This network, with its powerful new operating software, was the foundation for all of Enron's broadband promises, including instanta-neous electronic switching. Enron had claimed back in 1999 that its network of-fered a "highly reliable pay-for-what-you-need, bandwidth-on-demand way to deliver data." Enron's idea was to connect customers through a few dozen pool-ing points in key cities around the country, which would act much like transfer hubs in the gas-pipeline business. As a practical matter, this capability to deliver real-time bandwidth-on-demand was what made trading useful and attractive—and critical to Enron's prediction, in its 1999 annual report, that the "robust mer-chant operation" it was building would allow the bandwidth-trading market to "reach critical mass" by 2001.

In fact, the Enron network *couldn't* provide bandwidth-on-demand and never would. The switching capability was still under development, as were other ad-vanced features of Enron's system. Yet Enron continued to portray most of its key components as present-day reality. During 2000, according to the govern-ment, top broadband executives regularly discussed among themselves the Enron network's inability to do much of what the company claimed. Still, Enron kept issuing fresh press releases boasting about network capabilities that didn't exist.

There was another problem with developing bandwidth trading: the owners of the existing big broadband networks, mostly telephone companies, were largely uninterested in hooking into Enron's nascent system. They were already in the driver's seat; as they saw it, turning bandwidth into a tradable commodity could only cut into their profits.

The second part of Enron's master plan, assembling and delivering content for home viewing, was every bit as audacious and problematic. Enron was promising to establish a profitable new entertainment business by streaming programming for consumers, such as on-demand movies and sports events, over its global broadband network. The company would make money by charging consumers on a pay-per-view basis.

Never mind that Enron had no experience with this sort of thing; "video on demand" was full of gnarly problems that stymied even veteran entertainment companies. Most homes didn't even have the high-speed broadband telephone lines that Enron was planning to use for on-demand video. Those that did were connected to computers; the Enron plan called for video to be streamed into television sets. Providing such digital-TV video required a new kind of set-top box that would cost $500 apiece (while the boxes were under development, one of them burst into flames). And, not least, Enron was competing with the cable-television industry, a modern cabal if ever there was one, which had a giant built-in advantage: it already had wires and boxes in millions of American homes.

Attempting even one of these plans would have been an enormous undertaking for any company, requiring a tremendous commitment of resources, time, and talent. To try to do them all at once, without any previous experience, virtually overnight? It was *crazy*.

Nonetheless, Enron Broadband Services—EBS, it was called internally— exuded the company's version of brash cool. Its offices were vintage dot-com, with whiteboards that hung floor to ceiling and funky indirect lighting. Ken Rice's imprint was evident, too: he had placed a huge gleaming-red Hellcat motorcycle, custom-built in Louisiana for $30,000, outside the elevators of EBS's executive floor. It was inscribed with the words BANDWIDTH HOG.

In February 2000, star performers from other Enron businesses had been officially urged to sign on at broadband at a special internal job fair held at a hotel near Enron's headquarters. EBS's head count gradually climbed to 600, then 900, then over a thousand, eventually spilling onto three floors in the Houston tower and in more space in Portland. Eager newcomers kept piling in, then charging off to spend money exploring new ideas. In no time at all, EBS was churning through money at a burn rate of $500 million a year.

By the summer of 2000, the co-CEO experiment had failed. Joe Hirko, the former utility company CFO who had remained in Portland, left Enron in late

July; since the January 20 analysts meeting that sent shares soaring, he'd cashed in $35 million worth of Enron stock. Hirko's departure left Ken Rice fully in charge. Rice's top deputy at broadband was his number-two man at wholesale, chief operating officer Kevin Hannon.

While EBS was never what Enron claimed, certainly much of the work being done was real. Teams of engineers were struggling with the technology, trying to crack the code on the networking problems, testing video-streaming, spending hundreds of millions on hardware, and cobbling together the promised 15,000-mile fiber network, which Enron had pledged to extend to Europe (where it was putting yet another hundred employees). The traders were developing standard contracts, trying to drum up trading partners, and courting the phone companies. EBS's mergers-and-acquisitions team gobbled up software companies that might help the business along. Broadband even had its own venture-capital division, investing in start-ups and public tech stocks.

Considerable effort was also devoted to giving Wall Street the impression of rapid and dramatic progress. Enron sent out dozens of press releases, trumpeting every new partnership, equipment purchase, and video event. ("Enron to broadcast international cricket tournament live via the Internet.") The company made a point of creating the impression that its bandwidth-trading business was moving quickly toward critical mass—from 3 trades in the first quarter of 2000 to 236 in the fourth.

In fact, the trading really wasn't much more than a demonstration project. EBS's main trading partners were other companies that had followed Enron into the game and were just as eager to launch a market. But their activity served no commercial purpose for actual bandwidth users and generated no real profits. In practical terms, the continued lack of instantaneous switching rendered most bandwidth trading pointless.

There was another problem, too. Enron was hardly the only company trying to build a huge network of high-speed fiber-optic cable. During the Internet bubble, dozens of start-ups had sprung to life with this exact goal, and dozens of well-established companies had committed their own billions to building fiber-optic networks. As a result, there was a tremendous glut of fiber capacity, far outstripping the meager demand. Once the Internet bubble popped in the spring of 2000, prices plummeted. Soon enough, the entire telecom industry was in meltdown.

Though he'd committed $1 billion to laying thousands of miles of fiber, Skilling quietly slowed the build in 2000. He figured he'd lease or trade for whatever additional city-to-city links he needed, then cobble them together through Enron's pooling points, with EBS's own fiber, to assemble a virtual network.

While this decision saved money, it upset many of the Portland engineers, who saw the fiber network as the centerpiece of their efforts. Enron had spent millions on the expensive equipment needed to activate the network—to light it, as they say in the business—but it no longer made sense to do so. So Enron left much of its fiber dark and stuck the networking gear in a company warehouse. The equipment was helpful in one way, though: broadband job prospects were often given a tour of the warehouse stuffed with hardware to impress them with the size of Enron's commitment to broadband. (Enron was less forthcoming with local tax officials, who later indicted the company for dodging $1 million in county property taxes by submitting declarations that the warehouse contained about $500 worth of furniture and fixtures instead of computer and telecommunications gear worth more than $20 million.)

The biggest pressure of all, though, was the lack of time. In hyping the business, Enron told Wall Street that EBS would lose no more than $60 million for all of 2000. This meant that the division had to begin showing quarterly results right away.

It was an utterly impossible goal; Enron Broadband wasn't close to being ready to generate real income. But everyone at broadband knew that didn't matter: they had to deliver the number Skilling had promised. And if EBS executives couldn't come up with real earnings and revenues, they'd have to figure out a way to gin them up. Instead of focusing on building the business, they had to start playing accounting games. Here's what they did:

First quarter 2000: EBS announces $59 million in revenues. It gets almost the entire amount by exchanging surplus strands of fiber on its own network for strands built by competitors that expand its reach. This helps to build out EBS's virtual network, and it also taps into an accounting oddity that Enron is happy to exploit: the fiber Enron is selling can be accounted for as an immediate gain, while the fiber it is purchasing can be depreciated over 20 years. Though no cash changes hands, this produces an instant boost to the bottom line for both parties. These deals, popular among many telcom companies desperate to show revenue growth, become known in the industry as fiber swaps.

Second quarter: Ken Rice orders his deal makers to try to sell some of Enron's dark fiber so it can book the ensuing gain to the quarter's earnings. But the deal makers can't find any takers, so they turn to Enron's buyer of convenience—Andy Fastow's LJM2. Broadband just wants LJM2 to warehouse the fiber until the quarter is past and it can find a buyer. Fastow, of course, plays hardball with his own company: he wants the cap on his rate of return raised from 18 percent to 25 percent if EBS can't resell the fiber in two years. As the deadline starts closing in, two EBS finance executives, Mike Krautz and Larry Lawyer, find themselves in the deeply uncomfortable position of haggling on behalf of Enron—with Enron's CFO on the other side of the table. "Krautz, you cocksucker!" Fastow barks at one point over the speakerphone, seeking to bludgeon the Enron negotiators. Rice is finally brought in but winds up in a shouting match with Fastow. In the end, Fastow agrees to do the deal (called Project Backbone!) just before the quarter closes. He pays $100 million for the fiber—$30 million in cash and a $70 million note. Ken Lay personally signs the LJM2 approval sheets. And EBS books a $53 million pretax gain on the sale on its way to a loss of just $8 million for the quarter. (Enron finds a buyer for the dark fiber just a few months later.)

Third quarter: To make its numbers this quarter, EBS captures a huge gain on an investment in a tech start-up called Avici Systems, which makes high-speed routers. Several months before, in return for committing to purchase $25 million in hardware, EBS was allowed to buy almost a million coveted pre-IPO shares of the company. After Avici goes public in July, its stock skyrockets to $162.50, giving Enron a gain of more than $150 million on its $15 million investment. Enron uses one of its special-purpose entities to lock in its gain. (It can't sell the shares outright because of a 180-day lock-up provision.) Then EBS transfers its stake into a special-purpose entity, allowing it to book $35 million in third-quarter profits.

Then came the fourth quarter. . . .

There was no getting around it: by the end of 2000, things at the broadband division were starting to feel desperate. EBS's costs and head count had continued to soar; there were 24 people in the public-relations department alone. It was further bloated with refugees from Enron's hobbled water and international businesses. Everyone scrambled to come up with minibusiness plans. One came up with the idea of developing a risk-management system for movie studios to allow them to recover their losses if expensive new productions flopped. (Hollywood wasn't interested.) Another explored the idea of starting a futures trading market for film revenues.

The switching technology for the Enron Intelligent Network remained under development, and with bandwidth prices in free fall, the traders were fighting an uphill battle to build a market. The division still had virtually no cash coming in the door.

To make its numbers for the fourth quarter, Enron resorted to a positively breathtaking scheme, a truly brazen feat of accounting duplicity. Enron Broadband ended its year by booking $53 million in earnings on a deal that was well on its way toward collapse and hadn't produced a single penny of profit.

It involved the content business—developing video entertainment programming for streaming into homes. The content team was led by a flamboyant Enron deal maker named David Cox, one of the more unusual characters at Enron. Far from being the typical high-achieving MBA, Cox was a high school dropout and former commercial fisherman who had started out at Enron in the basement graphics department. While working on projects for Skilling, he'd managed to convince the Enron executive to have the company bankroll his own printing business—and give him Enron's printing work.

Cox later returned to Enron and was running its paper-trading venture when Rice tapped him to head the broadband content sales team. "You could take

David and drop him in the middle of the desert naked, and within a day, he'd figure out a way to make money," Rice liked to say of Cox. The EBS deal chief,
who had a reputation as a loose cannon, had clearly absorbed the Enron ethos.
"No one in the world can package this like we do because of all the financial engineering," he explained, in an interview with a *Fortune* writer. The company
philosophy, he noted, was: "No shots, no ducks. Nobody gets rewarded for
saving money. They get rewarded for *making* money."

Back in April, Cox had landed an exclusive 20-year agreement with Blockbuster, the nation's biggest video-rental chain, to collaborate on a new video-on-
demand service. Under the agreement's terms, Blockbuster would use its
Hollywood clout to obtain licenses for films and other content while Enron
would be responsible for figuring out how to stream it into homes.

In Blockbuster's first meeting with the Houston energy company, Cox—
acutely conscious of his company's extravagant promises for broadband—told
the Blockbuster negotiators: "I want to do a *really* big deal." The movie chain
had wanted to explore the video-on-demand business—though it had already
concluded that VOD was far too expensive and technically difficult to turn a
profit for years. Enron, however, offered a deal too good to refuse: Blockbuster's
job was to line up the movie studios to provide content and allow use of its
name and stores to market the venture; Enron would do pretty much everything
else and pick up the costs as well. Enron would receive about $1 for every
movie sold; all the rest of the proceeds (after certain expenses) would go to
Blockbuster.

As Blockbuster executives saw it, they couldn't lose. "Basically, the deal
was: we brand it, and they pay for it," recalls one. They did wonder about Enron's motives for bankrolling a venture that would take years to establish and
seemed certain to lose money even longer; but they figured the respected energy
giant would write off the red ink as a loss leader toward building the broadband
business for the long haul.

Blockbuster also warned that it would be tough to line up the movie studios,
which were wary of any new distribution channels they didn't control. In fact,
just nine days before the deal was to be publicly unveiled, Blockbuster CEO
John Antioco flew to Houston to have dinner with Lay, Rice, and Cox, where he
told them the video chain had concluded it would be easier to line up the studios
before going public with the deal. Blockbuster wanted to delay the announcement. But Enron was desperate for broadband to make a splash; Lay told Antioco they should go ahead. "I can help you crack the studios," Lay said. "I've got
a lot of influence."

When the deal was announced in July, the hype that accompanied it was impressive even by Enron standards. "For the first time, customers will be able to
choose from a large library of movies through their TV screens and enjoy VHS-
quality or better with VCR-like control (pause, rewind, stop)," boasted the Enron

press release. Ken Lay declared: "With Blockbuster's extensive customer base and content, and Enron's network delivery application . . . we have put together the 'killer app' for the entertainment industry." Blockbuster CEO Antioco pronounced the arrangement "the ultimate 'bricks, clicks, and flicks' strategy."

The two companies said they planned to introduce the service in "multiple U.S. cities" by year-end and roll it out to other markets, both in the United States and abroad, during 2001. On cue, the analysts swooned. "Signing a company like Blockbuster is a reassuring signal of the validity of their strategy," declared PaineWebber's Ronald Barone. He promptly raised his Enron rating, citing the "ongoing valuation upside" Enron Broadband offered.

Does it need to be said that there was almost nothing to back up the hype? As the court-appointed bankruptcy examiner later dryly put it, "This agreement reflected nothing more than an aspiration." Almost immediately, problems arose that made it obvious the dream the two companies shared was unlikely ever to become reality.

The first big stumbling block was that Enron quickly became impatient with the slow pace of lining up the studios; after several months, Blockbuster had signed up only one. Cox began camping out in Beverly Hills, trying to negotiate studio deals on his own. Blockbuster executives got wind of this, and when Blockbuster's general counsel Ed Stead ran into Cox in Los Angeles, he bluntly advised him: "If you're going around us, we're going to feed you to the fishes."

Enron, meanwhile, was having trouble delivering on its own promises. A big piece of the challenge for video-on-demand was solving what's known as the last-mile problem—getting the content from Enron's network into people's homes. That required negotiating agreements with the phone companies that provided local DSL service across the country. Enron executives, according to a Blockbuster official, had assured the video chain they had the phone companies "in our pocket"—and under the terms of the deal, Blockbuster had the right to walk away if Enron hadn't gotten them all on board by December.

When it became apparent that wasn't going to happen—and Blockbuster threatened to terminate the venture—Enron negotiated an extension on the requirement until March. Even then, according to government filings, it was so clear the venture was doomed that one lawyer who worked on the extension wrote a memo predicting that the partnership would enter a "termination scenario" in two months anyway.

Still, Enron somehow managed to introduce the service in four cities by year-end—which it promptly announced in yet another press release. Ken Rice, who had vowed to shave his head if the trial began on time, paid off his bet by showing up at a meeting of the Blockbuster project team with a female barber, who shaved his head clean to wild cheers. Ken Lay dropped in to offer his congratulations—and to enjoy the show.

What nobody mentioned was that the trial wasn't exactly what Enron and

Blockbuster had promised. Originally, the companies had planned trials in four cities—Seattle; Portland, Oregon; New York; and a Salt Lake City suburb called American Fork. But without all the phone companies on board, Enron was reduced to conducting testing in three of the cities using tiny providers. Only about 300 households were involved; in Seattle, the test was limited to just three apartment buildings. Much of the testing didn't even use standard DSL equipment.

Though Enron had boasted of allowing customers to choose from "a large library of movies," the trial offered a feeble collection of offerings. The standard fee was $5 a film—Enron's share was just $1.20—but many of the customers in the test markets weren't even charged. Even then, few used the service; each household watched an average of just 1.8 videos a month—half of what Enron expected. Broadband executives sat in meetings poring over reports on the pilot's comically pathetic results: *The Care Bears Movie:* seven purchases—$8.40. When Cox excitedly reported his movie proceeds at one gathering, another executive handed him a $5 bill and said, "I just doubled your revenue."

Just because the Blockbuster deal was doomed didn't mean Enron couldn't figure out some way to monetize it. Enron finance executives had been working to monetize the Blockbuster deal practically from the moment it was announced. The scheme they devised was called Project Braveheart—named for an Academy Award–winning Mel Gibson movie depicting a rebellion by thirteenth-century Scots.

Here's how it worked: even before the pilot program was begun, EBS calculated a value for the entire 20-year Blockbuster deal, based on projections—wildly speculative, of course—about future DSL use, customer video purchases, the speed of the rollout, market share, expenses, and other factors. Then, through a series of transactions, it sold most of its interest in the Blockbuster contract to an outside buyer. EBS then began booking profits up front.

What outsiders would buy into this arrangement? Friendly ones. In the first step of the transaction, the broadband division formed a joint venture, called EBS Content Systems, with two partners. One was a vendor involved in the Blockbuster trial called nCube—a tiny video-on-demand equipment company privately owned by Oracle CEO Larry Ellison. The other was an investment vehicle called Thunderbird, owned by Whitewing, the Enron-controlled special-purpose entity. As ever, to justify off-balance-sheet accounting treatment, nCube and Thunderbird had to contribute a total of at least 3 percent of the venture's equity, that investment had to be at risk, and the outside investors had to control the joint venture. To meet the 3 percent requirement, nCube chipped in $2 million and Thunderbird $7.1 million. EBS contributed its Blockbuster contract.

EBS Content Systems then sold almost all profit rights in the Blockbuster deal for $115 million to a *second* investment vehicle, called Hawaii 125–0 (a play on the old *Hawaii 5–0* television show and one of the accounting rules governing such transactions, known as FAS 125). Hawaii 125–0, in turn, was funded with $115.2 million from the Canadian Imperial Bank of Commerce in Toronto.

CIBC was supposed to get 93 percent of the Blockbuster deal's cash flow for the next ten years.

But neither nCube nor CIBC really wanted to invest in Braveheart—and neither apparently believed that it had any money at risk. According to government filings, nCube and CIBC were in the deal as a favor to Enron—a favor that Enron had promised to repay with the quick return of their capital plus a tidy profit for their troubles. Officials at nCube say that EBS executives promised they'd repay their investment in early 2001, with a profit of $100,000. Eventually, this promised profit grew to $200,000, because Enron asked nCube to stay in the deal for another quarter.

Officials at CIBC say they had a similar handshake agreement, the government charges. At the time, CIBC was falling over itself to please Enron. After investing $15 million in LJM2 and lending Enron hundreds of millions of dollars, it had finally made the leap onto Andy Fastow's coveted list of Tier 1 banks. Just a few months earlier, CIBC Houston banker Billy Bauch had written the Enron CFO a note of thanks "for the opportunity to work with Enron & LJM over the last year," adding, "To be named one of your Tier One banks is a noteworthy achievement for us, and we are sincerely humbled by your confidence." Bauch ended with a friendly word on the Fastow family's plans to build a huge new residence in River Oaks: "I trust that the house is coming together and will not cause you too much fiscal pain."

One CIBC banker later reassured nervous colleagues by telling them that Fastow had "given his strongest possible assurance that the risk won't be realized." A second banker elaborated in an e-mail quoted in government court filings: "Unfortunately, there can be no documented means of guaranteeing the equity. . . . We have a general understanding with Enron that any equity loss is a very bad thing. They have been told that if we sustain any equity losses, we will no longer do these types of transaction[s] with them. Not many other institutions are willing to take such risks so it is important to Enron to keep us happy. . . . We have done many 'trust me' equity transactions over the last 3 years and have sustained no losses to date." According to a government filing, this same banker, whose name was not disclosed, once remarked that someday Fastow would be "led away in handcuffs."

Such guarantees, of course, would mean that the equity investments weren't truly at risk and that Enron therefore couldn't legally report the revenues. But it did. According to the government, an Enron finance executive told CIBC officials point-blank that he couldn't put EBS's commitment on paper because it would "blow the accounting treatment" for the deal.

Kevin Howard and Mike Krautz, the EBS finance executives who headed Project Braveheart, deny they had any unwritten agreement, even though federal authorities say it was described in draft deal documents and e-mails. A memo Howard later prepared for Rice, for example, contains a passage titled CIBC Exit Strategy and notes "that by the end of 2001, Enron would need to replace CIBC with " 'true' outside equity, ie without ENE support." (The situation is complicated by the fact that neither CIBC nor nCube got back their money before Enron's collapse.)

The government also charges that the handshake arrangements with nCube and CIBC were hidden from the Arthur Andersen auditors who reviewed Project Braveheart. But if the firm were really doing its job, that shouldn't have mattered; even without that information, the auditors had more than enough to know that signing off on Project Braveheart required an incredible stretch of accounting rules. It was obvious that the deal was largely worthless. And even if it hadn't been, Enron was using assumptions to value the contract that were truly fanciful; it was the broadband equivalent of monkeying with a pricing curve on a long-term electricity contract. To book the profits it needed, Enron had to assume that by the year 2010 the company's content business would be operating in 82 cities, that 32 percent of the households in those markets would be using DSL lines, that 70 percent of DSL customers using video-on-demand would subscribe to the Enron-Blockbuster service—and that Enron would control 50 percent of the video-on-demand market. (This last figure came from "research" conducted by EBS and McKinsey.)

A top Andersen accountant named Carl Bass was upset with Enron's plans to book profits from Project Braveheart. Bass was an old-fashioned Andersen hand, an acerbic, skeptical veteran who was highly regarded inside the firm for his technical expertise. In late 1999, Bass was appointed to Andersen's Professional Standards Group (PSG), which was supposed to offer independent rulings on particularly tricky accounting issues. At Duncan's request, Bass was spending much of his time on Enron issues, since the company was by far the riskiest accounting client Andersen had. But Duncan came to regret seeking Bass's involvement, for Bass quickly became the leading in-house critic of Enron's financial maneuvers. A typical Bass comment was one he made in an August 2001 e-mail about an Enron deal: "Help me out here," he wrote. "How do you sell an asset and generate operating cash flow?"

To Bass, the accounting treatment for Project Braveheart defied common sense. ". . . I was told that they were going to have some $50 million gain on the sale of this venture interest immediately after the contract was signed and the venture was entered into. Furthermore, the other venture partner was not contributing anything," he wrote in an e-mail. "In effect, this was a very risky transaction. . . ." But as Bass also noted, Duncan and his team "did not follow our advice on this." The only concession Andersen was able to wring out of Enron was a promise that the company would obtain an independent appraisal of the value of the Blockbuster contract. But Enron never bothered to get the appraisal—and Andersen approved the deal anyway.

For Enron, all the machinations produced the desired result: EBS booked the revenue it needed to meet Wall Street's expectations. Kevin Howard, EBS's vice president for finance, had originally intended to book just $20 million on the

Braveheart deal. But as the end of the year approached, EBS's earnings hole kept growing—in late November, COO Hannon calculated that the business was $100 million behind budget—and so did the amount the company needed to milk from Braveheart. In the end, EBS claimed a $53 million gain on Braveheart for the fourth quarter, representing 84 percent of the broadband division's revenues. Broadband closed 2000 reporting a loss of just $60 million for the year, meeting Enron's promise to analysts.

Everyone in broadband, of course, was acutely attuned to the stakes involved in pleasing the market. ("EBS has released key metrics to the analysts on Wall Street and must now deliver on those metrics," explained a 91-page internal document detailing broadband's "strategic vision," completed in November 2000. "Each group within EBS must learn to focus on these and make certain EBS meets or exceeds them to keep Wall Street interested in the proper valuations of Enron. This is now a very important part of the daily routine of EBS going forward.") And though they knew full well that they had met their numbers only by using smoke and mirrors, more than a few regarded the illusion they were creating as a genuine accomplishment. That, after all, was what Enron valued. That's what got them bonuses and promotions.

Indeed, at the Enron Broadband Christmas party, members of the finance group put together a PowerPoint presentation that celebrated, in mockumentary style, their earnings "achievement." "Since this is the largest earnings deal for EBS in the 4th quarter with over $50 million in earnings, the Blockbuster Team are now heroes. Congratulations," it began.

A series of slides then recast popular films to portray the exploits of several of the EBS executives who'd worked on the Blockbuster deal. One of them was called "Mike Krautz and The Search for the Holy Monetization." "Mike scours the globe in search of the holy mark-to-market—I mean monetization," the narrative read. "This monetization is supposed to bring everlasting life, but Mike soon discovers that his immortality lasts for only one quarter."

Another slide offered up a variation on *Thelma & Louise*, starring two EBS employees: "After Kevin tells them that they are responsible for unwinding the Blockbuster deal next quarter, the two decide to make a run for the border. In the end, they both drive over a cliff, choosing the more attractive exit strategy."

Blockbuster's inability to obtain first-run videos inspired the casting of Kevin Howard as Forrest Gump ("A monetization effort is like a box of chocolates, you never know what you're going to get"), with a buddy who "has all kinds of content—'kids' movies, action movies, animal movies, home movies, shrimp movies, just no hit movies.' "

And finally, the presentation portrayed the Arthur Andersen accountants who had objected to the deal as "The Grinch Who Stole VOD," starring "Arthur Andersen as the Grinch and Enron's Accounting Team as the Who's in Whoville," in "the story of how the mean, heartless auditors tried to ruin the deal for Little ConnieLeeWho:

> One Deal, Two Deal, Red Deal, No Deal
> You cannot do it without GAAP.
> You cannot do it because it's crap.
> You cannot do it for 25. What the hell, let's go for 65.

After the party was over, EBS's alarmed general counsel, Kristina Mordaunt—the same Kristina Mordaunt who had hit the $1 million jackpot in the Southampton investment with Andy Fastow—reportedly instructed Howard to destroy all copies of the presentation.

Two months after booking $53 million in profits from Project Braveheart, Enron announced it was ending its 20-year deal with Blockbuster. Enron publicly blamed Blockbuster, saying the video giant had failed to provide the "quantity and quality" of movies the project needed. Here's the most amazing part, though: Enron's spin machine, which had shamelessly hyped the Blockbuster deal to the analysts, now labored to dismiss the significance of its implosion—*and the analysts bought it!* ENRON EXPANDING ENTERTAINMENT ON-DEMAND SERVICE; TERMINATES EXCLUSIVE RELATIONSHIP WITH BLOCKBUSTER INC., blared the Enron press release. The company cast the venture's failure as a kind of liberation, reasoning that it was now free "to initiate discussions with various content providers" for movies, games, television programming, and music.

Blockbuster was less sanguine. Enron, which had signed a noncompete agreement, was openly seeking new partners, a process it had secretly begun even before the contract was formally terminated. As Blockbuster saw it, it had always made clear that lining up content from the studios would take time; it had actually signed a second major studio deal (with Universal) in early 2001. Yet Enron was blaming the venture's breakup on the video chain. The two sides took their dispute into secret arbitration. Enron settled a few months later by paying Blockbuster $5 million.

One person who took particular note of the dissolution of the Blockbuster deal was Carl Bass at Arthur Andersen. "One would think," he e-mailed a colleague, "there should be a loss reported." But that was hardly Enron's style. Instead of writing down the value of the deal, the company's finance executives reasoned that its broadband content business was worth *more* without Blockbuster, since it wouldn't have to share the proceeds. (As the bankruptcy examiner wryly noted: "Apparently, Enron's intention 'to initiate discussions' was even more valuable than its 'exclusive relationship with Blockbuster.' ") EBS booked an additional $58 million from Braveheart—more than two-thirds of its reported revenues for the first quarter of 2001. Thus was one last quarter saved. Blockbuster executives say they were astounded to find out months later that Enron had booked $111 million in profits on their unprofitable venture.

David Cox and his deal-making colleagues kept hustling. They vowed to develop more "killer apps." They promised to sign three more Blockbuster-like deals before year-end. (The World Wrestling Federation and the NFL were their top targets.) The company's lobbyists began laying plans to force the cable business to accept content distribution deals by demanding so-called open access to cable systems. But it was all for naught. "We were trying very hard to pump blood into this patient, and we ran out of blood," says an EBS vice president.

Inevitably, as broadband's inflated promise stood revealed, many in and out of Enron pointed the finger at Skilling's old lieutenant, Ken Rice. Much was riding on broadband's success but Rice had never risen to the challenge. He just didn't have it in him any longer to work the kind of hours an exceedingly ambitious start-up required. Like many Enron deal makers, Rice also hated managing— and it showed. An internal EBS document noted that the organization was characterized by "chaos" and "a perception of 'inability to get things done.' " Rice occasionally appeared in a T-shirt, biker jacket, and jeans; he seemed uninterested and distracted. "The last couple of years, a lot of us got lazy," he later acknowledged to friends. Rice felt trapped by broadband's enormous expectations. He was managing a business that had spent more than a billion dollars but hadn't produced a penny in real profits.

The government later charged, however, that there was one area where Rice had played the broadband game like a master—pumping and dumping Enron's stock. Government filings say that Rice was repeatedly warned that EBS was spending far too much and making far too little and that just days before the company's January 25, 2001, meeting with analysts, an outside consultant Rice hired had advised him that prospects for the year remained poor.

But that didn't stop Rice from presenting a remarkably upbeat forecast to Wall Street. In his presentation, the government noted, "Rice stated, among other things, that EBS's strategy was right on target; EBS's content delivery business had an outstanding year; Blockbuster was EBS's 'anchor tenant' with a 20-year deal" and that broadband was even further along than Enron had expected. Rice announced that he was anticipating an annual loss for 2001 of just $65 million, even though, according to the government, he'd received an internal estimate just three days earlier projecting broadband's losses as totaling $149 million for the first quarter alone.

Then there was the critical question of just how much the broadband business was really worth. Before the 2001 analysts meeting, an EBS team prepared a valuation of the content business, placing its worth at about $8 billion. According to government filings, Rice sent the group back to come up with a higher number, saying he wouldn't give the analysts a figure that was less than the $18 billion he'd fed them a year ago. Rice got just what he wanted: a valuation of $21 billion, which he then offered up to Wall Street. All of broadband, he told the analysts in 2001, was now worth $36 billion—an increase of more than 20 percent from its value just one year earlier. Rice, noted the government, also failed to disclose that the Blockbuster deal was in danger of cancelation—and that Enron, through the Braveheart deal, had already sold most of any future profits it might generate.

Inside Enron, there were, as always, plenty of rationalizations for this behavior. For instance, there were many valid methods for estimating a value for EBS—one of which really did generate a figure of $36 billion—and that Rice regularly received conflicting reports about the business's state of affairs. Those who defend Skilling and Rice excuse the giddy claims made for the business, in press releases and analysts meetings, as a combination of excessive optimism and puffery—typical for the Internet era. And after all, the Wall Street analysts didn't have to accept any of it. "If they're going to send everyone to jail that was optimistic in 1999 about broadband," Skilling later railed to friends, "they would have to incarcerate half of San Jose."

As the government saw it, Rice's behavior belied his insistence that his only crime was excessive optimism. It was during his time running the broadband business—between February 2000 and February 2001—that Rice cashed in a big chunk of his giant Enron stake, unloading shares and options valued at some $53 million.

■   ■   ■

In February 2001, Rick Causey convened a routine budget meeting with the top number crunchers from the company's operating divisions. The group of about 15 managers gathered in Enron's cavernous fiftieth-floor boardroom, which is darkly paneled with rare woods and dominated by a huge table.

Causey was in an upbeat mood. Everything was looking great, he announced to the team. The traders had made so much money in California that all Enron would have to do was reverse some of the giant reserves it had squirreled away from that late-2000 windfall and it could pretty much count on making its numbers for the entire year. "From an accounting standpoint," he declared, "this will be our easiest year ever. We've got 2001 in the *bag*."

When the session ended, a woman named Wanda Curry asked to have a private word with Causey. A long-time Enron accountant—she'd served as chief accounting officer of Enron Wholesale, among other assignments—Curry had been working for months on a special project. Now she and Causey sat back down in the leather boardroom chairs, waiting until everyone drifted out. "Rick," Curry finally began, "we've got some serious problems at EES."

With a small team, Curry had been digging for months into things at the retail division—and the situation was plenty ugly. There were huge, unacknowledged, speculative trading losses. Records were in chaos. The division's exposure to credit risk was far greater than anyone imagined. And finally, there was the matter of EES's contracts. Deals for which the company had booked $20 million in profits were actually $70 million underwater. Curry showed him a one-page document she'd prepared to try to calculate the size of the entire disaster: though she'd completed only a fraction of her audit, her calculations already showed that EES was in the hole by at least $500 million.

Wanda Curry had previously run afoul of Cliff Baxter when she'd worked at

Enron Wholesale. She had joined Andersen in objecting to his plans to book the questionable back-to-back energy trade with Merrill Lynch in the closing days of 1999. As a result, the trade had been reconfigured, and Curry had been transferred out of the division. She had been burrowing into EES's affairs since April 2000, when Causey asked her to look into complaints from Arthur Andersen about the division's poor controls.

After assembling a team of eight accountants, Curry soon discovered she'd stepped into a quagmire. The first issue was trading. At Lou Pai's insistence, EES maintained its own trading desk and made up its own sets of pricing curves, some of which were different from the ones used by Enron's own wholesale traders. Unlike the wholesale traders, the EES traders really were supposed to use trading purely as a hedging device.

The contracts it signed with its large business customers committed EES to supplying natural gas and electricity at preset prices. It was a prime responsibility of the EES trading desk to hedge this price risk, to, in effect, ensure that the contracts would not cost the company money even if the price of power rose. Trading, though, was in Pai's blood, and instead of hedging, he made a huge speculative bet. At the same time that Tim Belden and the wholesale traders were betting that power prices would rise, Pai was betting they would *drop* and that when they did, EES would reap a windfall. As it turned out, Belden made the right bet and Pai the wrong one. When California electricity prices soared in late 2000, EES incurred staggering losses.

Enron's corrosive culture quickly kicked in. The wholesale traders not only took pleasure in watching Pai flounder; they even participated in EES trades—on the other side. They brazenly pushed the EES desk off the wholesale floor and gleefully outtraded them on a regular basis. This only fueled the contempt that Whalley's new generation of wholesale traders harbored for old-timers like Pai as well as for the company's other divisions. One executive who worked in both Wholesale and EES says: "Retail is Wholesale times ten in complexity, and they had Wholesale divided by ten in talent."

The second issue Curry and her team uncovered was the EES contracts themselves. Her group had planned to dig into 90 EES deals that made up 80 percent of the business—"deep dives," she called them. By the time Curry met with Causey, her group had scrutinized just 13 but had already uncovered a gap of at least $200 million between the numbers EES had reported as earnings and the far starker reality. Of the 13 contracts, all of which EES had claimed were profitable at the time of signing, every one was now millions of dollars underwater.

Part of the problem was that EES hadn't done much more than guess at the energy loads its customers would require. Part of it was those faulty price curves, with their excessively optimistic assumptions. Part of it was the failure to hedge. And part of it was that EES hadn't recognized the enormous credit risk it faced in California. When the California energy crisis threw Pacific Gas & Electric into bankruptcy, the utility owed Enron hundreds of million of dollars. Much of that money was owed to EES.

As Curry began uncovering problems—and word filtered up from other sources—Rick Buy also became deeply concerned. "Is there light at the end of the tunnel?" he fretted. "Can we come out of this?" Buy established a special EES RAC task force, charged with a list of projects he labeled Points of Light. Eventually he assigned two dozen staffers to the effort, noting in an e-mail: "This is a huge commitment of staff from RAC and will strain us no end, but it is necessary." He noted that it would require "commitment of Skilling to fund the overage to the RAC budget, which I am under huge pressure to reduce, not increase."

All who were involved in these inquiries had their work cut out for them. That fall, an EES employee stumbled across trays containing hundreds of envelopes crammed under the trading desk. They turned out to contain uncashed checks from utility companies, about $10 million worth.

The management disarray was so bad that Skilling later received an e-mail from an Enron employee whose sister managed new buildings in Texas for J. P. Morgan Chase, an EES client. The bank was building a call center in San Antonio, and the city's electric utility, she noted, "wants to charge us a $50,000 deposit for new power because 11 out of the last 12 payments made by Enron have been late, and late fees have been paid. . . ."

Curry, meanwhile, kept discovering more land mines—and kept bringing them to Buy's attention. In January 2001, Buy e-mailed her, Whalley, and other executives to voice his dismay. Subject: "Another $40 million":

> I go away for a day and come back to yet another $40 million of PGE exposure. I guess the lesson is to not go away. Where does this end? Please inform all "deal doers" at EES that they better have RAC review their deals . . . in detail before they sign. This is more out of control than anything else we have at Enron.

Skilling, who had promised huge things for EES, recognized belatedly that its problems started with the business's top management. Though Skilling was loath to admit it, Ken Rice wasn't the only executive who had let him down. So had Lou Pai.

In fact, Pai had virtually disappeared from EES. Vice Chairman Tom White remained the business's front man, pressing the flesh with high-level customers and acting as a cheerleader with staff. Pai didn't even show up for most of EES's quarterly staff meetings. By mid-2000, he was rarely even in the office.

For years Pai had maintained a secret relationship with a woman named Melanie Fewell, a former exotic dancer. Fewell and Pai had had a child together, and Pai had divorced his wife and married the ex-stripper. He bought a ranch outside of Houston, where they kept and bred top-dollar dressage horses, including a legendary Appaloosa named Pay-N-Go, who put in an appearance at the New York memorial service for Paul McCartney's wife Linda. With partners, Pai also bought himself a huge ranch—77,500 acres—in southern Colorado, where he could comfortably retreat into seclusion. The property included a 14,047-foot-high peak, which the locals dubbed Mount Pai. Pai flew there regularly on an Enron jet, which he reportedly summoned from its hangar at Houston Intercontinental to an airport near his home in suburban Sugar Land, so he wouldn't have to make the 20-mile drive.

Now, Pai's sexual and mercenary appetites fed one another. While EES ran out of control, Pai was cashing out. The canny trader had shrewdly hung on to every Enron stock option he'd received during his years at Enron. He tried to cash out his phantom-equity stake in EES, but the dollar buyout was so huge that Skilling persuaded him to take company stock instead. Those shares soon soared, and Pai began selling large blocks, just as Enron's shares were heading toward their peak. Pai later explained that he sold his stock to settle his divorce.

That same year, while still head of EES, Pai had begun spending time on a new opportunity for a personal windfall: the New Power Company, Enron's second crack at the residential side of the retail energy market. Enron had spun off the business with an IPO in October 2000. Pai, who served as chairman, was given two million shares of New Power and bought another 463,000 at a pre-IPO price of about $11. When the stock climbed right after going public at $21 a share, his stake was briefly worth more than $66 million. (It soon plunged below the offering price.)

All this, of course, left even less time for EES. The Young Turks in retail had been grumbling about Pai's absentee management for years—especially given his enormous pay packages. They weren't the only ones: Cliff Baxter, who'd never liked Pai, was upset as well. Pai was robbing the company, Baxter declared. By early 2001, Skilling had reluctantly resolved to make a move. Fittingly, when Skilling called down to EES to break the news to Pai, he wasn't there. He called back from his ranch in Colorado, and Skilling told him it was time for him to go.

Even then, Pai got one last big payoff. In moving Pai out of EES, Skilling gave him a new job as chairman and CEO of the newly formed Enron Xcelerator—"to drive the formation and development of new businesses at Enron." Though it wasn't much more than a part-time job, Pai nonetheless got phantom equity along with a $1 million bonus. Pai's deputy, Tom White, also left EES, to join the George W. Bush administration as secretary of the army. He sold his Enron stock for $14 million and began building a multimillion-dollar beachfront home in Naples, Florida, after paying $6.5 million for the property.

The man who replaced Pai that February was Dave Delainey. An ambitious, talented, young Canadian who'd run the wholesale origination business, Delainey was a Skilling favorite and Greg Whalley's foremost rival. He saw the tough EES assignment as his best opportunity to leapfrog Whalley for one of Enron's top jobs.

But that was before he realized just how bad things were. "This is a *disaster,*" Delainey told an Enron consultant after he'd been there a few months. "They didn't know what their receivables were. They didn't know what they billed." He suddenly wasn't thinking about leapfrogging Whalley; he was worried mainly about surviving the experience.

The big question was what to do about the losses—both from the speculative trading and from the grossly overvalued contracts that Curry's group uncovered. Under mark-to-market accounting, all this was supposed to be booked immediately. But Enron wasn't about to book a loss that would likely total more than $500 million—especially in EES.

The retail division had just started reporting profits in the fourth quarter of 1999, and Skilling boasted regularly to analysts about the business's rapid progress. To show a loss now would be catastrophic, especially if it got out that Enron's vaunted trading and risk-management teams had lost their grip on the operations of an entire division. "If at any point they said EES was losing money, that would have been the nail in the coffin," says a veteran Enron executive. "It would show they didn't know what was going on. It went to the heart of what the company claimed as its core business acumen—trading and risk management."

Skilling and Delainey cooked up what seemed like a clever solution. The trading losses would be recorded but hidden—buried in the wholesale traders' overwhelming profits, through their assumption of all of EES's trading functions. The move was publicly cast as an overdue consolidation; it simply didn't make sense for EES to run its own trading desk. With the trading disaster moved off its books, EES reported a $40 million profit for the first quarter of 2001.

EES sales executive Margaret Ceconi, who had gotten her undergraduate degree in accounting and worked in finance most of her career, was among those who were bewildered at how the division could have reported a profit. Why hadn't Enron had to disclose the trading losses in EES, which informal office gossip placed at a minimum of $500 million? In late July, Ceconi e-mailed a query to the SEC, filling out a form on the agency's Web site. Leaving her phone number but not disclosing where she worked, she posed the following hypothetical question:

A public company owns an ice cream business and a popcorn business. The popcorn business is losing money, but the ice cream business is very profitable. If you move the popcorn business into the ice cream division, under accounting rules, can you avoid reporting the popcorn business's losses?

Two days later she was awakened at 7 A.M. by a phone call from an SEC staffer. The size of the popcorn business's losses and the impact of moving them needs to be fully disclosed and clearly explained, the SEC officer said—otherwise it would distort the financial results of both businesses. Ceconi didn't disclose why she was calling, and, amazingly, the SEC staffer didn't press the matter. But

Ceconi later checked Enron's public filings; there was no disclosure of how much money EES's trading operation had lost.

This manipulation was no secret inside Enron, though. The wholesale traders were furious. John Lavorato vented to John Arnold. As Arnold later described it in a deposition: "He would express frustration with the other divisions at Enron that were losing money and that the trading group was being looked upon to make its own budget and cover the losses of the other divisions." Asked why EES's trading desk was merged into wholesale, Arnold went on to say: "I had the sense that it was done because there was a large liability at EES that they were going to hide with Enron profits" from the wholesale trading business. Arnold said he had heard "rumors" that characterized the EES issue as "a billion-dollar liability," which made him concerned about the accuracy of Enron's financial statements.

The second problem—the overvalued contracts—was largely blustered away. In the weeks after EES's trading group was absorbed into wholesale, Wanda Curry was shunted aside. The deep dives project she led into EES's contracts was turned over to others and never completed. Through the time of her removal in April 2001, the losses her group had uncovered on the first 13 EES contracts had not been booked.

Delainey tried to stop the bleeding at EES, but all he could do was staunch the flow. He barred new deals in all but the handful of states that were already deregulated. He ended up-front payments to customers who signed contracts. Curves were adjusted downward, infuriating the originators, who suddenly lost their ability to make losing deals appear to be winners. He reluctantly closed a deal with J. C. Penney that arrived on his desk just days after he took over: the new curves showed it would be yet another loser. He sent his deal makers out to try to renegotiate the most egregious existing contracts.

Some things at EES didn't change, though. Shortly after Delainey's arrival in early 2001, EES signed a $1.3 billion, 15-year contract with Eli Lilly that had been in the works for more than a year. The agreement established a joint venture, owned by Enron and Lilly, to which Lilly would make payments for energy-saving improvements. Enron then transferred its interest in the joint venture into—what else?—a special-purpose entity. The result? A gain of $38 million—95 percent of EES's reported first-quarter profits.

The utter disarray of the business was impossible to overcome. After the purge of the Pai regime, a veteran trader from wholesale named Don Black was brought in to take over the trading desk. After he'd been there for a while, Black summed up his EES experience this way to a colleague: "It's like going to work every day with your hair on fire and nothing to put it out with but a hammer."

■   ■   ■

Inside Global Finance, Ben Glisan's promotion to corporate treasurer in May of 2000 had been cause for celebration. Young, smart, ambitious—and intensely loyal to his boss, Andy Fastow—Glisan replaced Jeff McMahon, who had quarreled with Fastow over the propriety of LJM. Not long after the promotion was official, everyone gathered at Ruggles, a popular Houston nightspot, for a few celebratory rounds of Kamikazes. Kopper picked up the $7,123 bar tab—and promptly put it on his Enron expense account.

Along with Kopper, Glisan had become Andy Fastow's go-to guy. He was the chief designer of the fiendishly complex structures Global Finance created, and he was the technical mastermind behind Fastow's most audacious scheme yet to manage Enron's earnings, which he'd devised just before he became treasurer. Emerging from months of brainstorming with other Enron executives, accountants from Arthur Andersen, and lawyers at Vinson & Elkins, Glisan had worked an accounting miracle. He called it Project Raptor.

Project Raptor was inspired by the Rhythms deal, in which LJM1 helped Enron use the value of its own shares to avoid booking losses on the decline of a high-flying investment. Glisan was deeply involved in Rhythms, and his participation, Rick Buy later recalled, made him "a hero."

Skilling was eager to do the same sort of thing on a monster scale—to lock in the gains from the winners in Enron's billion-dollar merchant portfolio (mostly energy and tech investments) while keeping the losers, like Kevin McConville's investments in underperforming steel mills, off the company's books. Vince Kaminski, Enron's resident derivatives genius, insisted this couldn't be done. But Fastow told Skilling what he wanted to hear: with Project Raptor, it *could* be done.

Glisan's creation would allow Enron to hedge assets worth billions of dollars—that is, allow the company to lock in paper profits the company had already booked. Though Skilling, Lay, and the Enron directors who approved the plan insist they never knew it, Raptor also guaranteed Fastow's LJM2 a mind-boggling return. It all seemed too good to be true. Project Raptor—for a time—was viewed as Global Finance's most brilliant achievement yet.

And so in 2000, Enron rolled out four new special-purpose entities—Raptors I, II, III, and IV—with the sole purpose of avoiding the need to record mark-to-market losses on its books. Like Enron's stake in Rhythms, many of these assets were impossible—or prohibitively expensive—to hedge in normal circumstances. A hedge, it's important to remember, is a little like taking out insurance. For a small amount of money, you're buying a derivative contract that commits the seller of the contract to pay you a preset price for the asset. If the price of the asset falls, the counterparty has to pay off your contract—and he takes the financial hit that you've avoided. If it doesn't fall, the counterparty keeps the money you've paid for the contract, and that's his profit. Conventional hedges work only for highly liquid assets, like large-cap stocks or corporate bonds, where derivatives traders can make money by writing lots of such "insurance."

In practical terms, you can't hedge the value of debt in a troubled steel mill or a private stake in a deep-sea drilling company, in large part because you'd never find a counterparty to take the other side of the hedge. The chance of losing a lot of money is too high. But Enron wasn't really hedging against a true economic loss; rather, it was using the Raptors to hedge against an *accounting* loss. It did this through a dizzyingly complex series of derivative transactions that essentially amounted to tapping, once again, the value of its own shares. As the underperforming assets placed in the Raptors continued to decline in value, the Raptors would have to pay Enron—therefore giving Enron a *gain* that would offset the loss. *Voilà!* The company had avoided having to report a decline on its income statement.

In truth, Enron was really just covering losses in one pocket by taking money from another pocket. As a board report put it after Enron's bankruptcy, "In effect, Enron was hedging risk with itself." The report added: "Were this permissible, a company with access to its outstanding stock could place itself on an ascending spiral: an increasing stock price would enable it to keep losses in its investments from public view; which, in turn, would spur further increases in stock price; which, in turn, would increase its capacity to keep losses in its investments from public view."

But what if Enron shares fell? If that happened, the entire structure would collapse under its own weight, and Enron would finally have to book its losses. Few at Enron worried about that, though. In early 2000, when a member of Vince Kaminski's group completed a statistical analysis concluding that there was a 25 percent probability that Enron's stock would fall below $40, the finance group reacted with outrage.

Raptor I, also named Talon, was born on April 18, 2000. Talon's chief asset came from Enron, through a subsidiary—Enron shares and stock contracts valued at about $537 million. But Talon was actually run by LJM2, which invested $30 million, providing the 3 percent outside equity required for off-balance-sheet treatment. Enron executives calculated that Talon had the capacity to offset almost $217 million worth of losses through the derivatives that hedged Enron assets.

In fact, it was Fastow's partnership that was going to be cashing in. Under terms negotiated between Glisan and Kopper (Glisan representing Enron; Kopper negotiating for LJM2), Enron was required to pay LJM2 $41 million—repaying its entire $30 million investment plus a 37 percent return. And this would have to happen before the Raptor did anything. Though LJM would have all its money back up front plus an $11 million profit—and thus face *no risk at all*—a series of extraordinary accounting maneuvers, all approved by Arthur Andersen, maintained the fiction that LJM hadn't withdrawn its 3 percent at-risk equity investment.

What was the rationale for the $41 million payment? Enron described it as a premium for a put option on the Raptors' Enron stake. But as a board investigation later put it: "The transaction makes little apparent commercial sense, other than to enable Enron to transfer money to LJM2 in exchange for its participation in vehicles that would allow Enron to engage in hedging transactions." Though the original put agreement required Enron to wait six months before it started hedging, Fastow convinced Causey to amend the terms in early August, allowing LJM2 to get its $41 million sooner. And that wasn't all: Enron picked up the tab for LJM2's legal and accounting costs and paid Fastow's partnership a $250,000 annual management fee.

Much later, Enron's top executives and directors insisted that certain key information about the Raptors—information that would have set off alarms—was deliberately withheld from them. This appears to be true. Indeed, while promoting the Raptors to the board, Causey privately confided to an Enron lawyer that he thought the structure had just a 50/50 chance of passing muster with the SEC. Still, the information they did have should have been more than enough to get those alarms ringing.

An Enron deal summary sheet on Talon, dated April 18, explicitly noted the windfall for Fastow's partnership: "It is expected that Talon will have earnings and cash sufficient to distribute $41 million to LJM2 within six months. . . ." Skilling later insisted he had no idea his CFO's partnership was making such returns; the line for Skilling's signature on an attached LJM2 approval sheet was left blank. (It did, however, contain the signatures of Glisan, Buy, and Causey.)

Glisan presented the Raptors to the finance committee of Enron's board in May. The presentation took place immediately after Fastow had finished reassuring the board that he was spending only three hours a week on LJM2. Then, with Lay and Skilling looking on, Glisan described the Raptors as a "risk-management program to enable the company to hedge the profit and loss volatility of the company's investments." His presentation noted that Talon would be capitalized with "excess [Enron] stock" and provide "approximately $200 million of P&L protection" to Enron.

On the subject of LJM2's compensation, the written board presentation was brazenly deceptive. It reported that LJM2 would "be entitled to 30% annualized return plus fees." It didn't say that the actual compensation language provided LJM2 with a 30 percent return or an up-front $41 million—*whichever was greater.* It was clear, though, that the risk-management program was an accounting artifice. Taking notes on the presentation, Enron's corporate secretary, Rebecca Carter, wrote: "Does not transfer economic risk but transfers P&L volatility." Among the risks Glisan presented: "accounting scrutiny"—and a substantial decline in Enron stock price. Glisan also noted that "the transaction had been reviewed by Causey and Andersen." Raptor I was quickly approved by both the finance committee and the full board.

After LJM2 got its $41 million, Talon began hedging, through $743 million in derivatives, called total return swaps, on Enron merchant investments. Investigators later concluded that many of the documents involved had been backdated.

Much of it was likely a simple (if improper) matter of convenience. But in one case—the hedging of Enron's Avici shares, the Internet company that the broadband unit had taken a stake in—the backdating was less benign. The transaction date was set as of August 3—which happened to be the very day Avici hit its high of $162.50 per share. By dating the swap with Talon on Avici then, Enron locked in the maximum possible gain on its books. By September 15, about the time the agreement actually appears to have been signed, Avici had already fallen below $100. This is precisely the sort of maneuver a normal counterparty would never allow, for it dramatically increased Talon's liability. Indeed, according to government filings, executives working on the deal for LJM and Enron referred to the backdating as "the Enron time machine." But LJM2, which was running the Raptor, had little reason to care. Its $41 million was already in the bank.

On June 22, the executive committee of the Enron board approved Raptor II. Named Timberwolf, this one was structured just like Talon. According to the board minutes, Fastow told the board that Timberwolf would "provide approximately $200 million of P&L protection." The CFO said the second Raptor was needed because of simple demand—"there had been tremendous utilization by the business units of Raptor I." In fact, as of that date, Enron hadn't even begun hedging with Talon. After sailing through the board, the new Raptor went through the same arcane machinations as the first, orchestrating LJM2's second $41 million payment.

On August 7, Glisan advised the board finance committee that Raptor I "was almost completely utilized," Raptor II wasn't yet ready for action, and that a new Raptor—called Bobcat—was needed to increase "available capacity." In swift order, LJM2 collected its third $41 million.

As Enron saw it, the beauty of the Raptors was that they wouldn't just lock in gains on winners—they could also bury the losses on losers. Indeed, one of the reasons the Raptors were so useful is that the traders were refusing to bury losses like those on Kevin McConville's disastrous investment portfolio, according to a former Global Finance executive. So the bad assets were stashed in the Raptors instead. Though some of them had already been written down, the Raptors insulated Enron from having to book even bigger charges. Dave Delainey used to call them "the critter deals."

On September 1, an Enron lawyer named Stuart Zisman, who had been reviewing the Raptor project, wrote a memo sharply questioning this strategy: "Our original understanding of this transaction was that all types of assets/securities would be introduced into this structure (including both those that are viewed favorably and those that are viewed as being poor investments). As it turns out, we have discovered that a majority of the investments being introduced into the Raptor Structure are bad ones. This is disconcerting [because] . . . it might lead one to believe that the financial books at Enron are being 'cooked' in order to eliminate a drag on earnings that would otherwise occur under fair value accounting. . . ." Of course, that's precisely what was happening. After receiving the memo, Mark Haedicke, a senior Enron attorney, called Zisman to his office and scolded him for using "inflammatory" language.

Zisman was right, though. The Raptors were absorbing much of Enron's "nuclear waste"—and, by the fall of 2000, with the collapse of the tech-stock craze, even the high fliers in the portfolio were starting to deteriorate. Enron's stock price was slipping, too. This meant that one of the Raptors—Talon—was running out of credit capacity. The situation was getting worrisome. Causey ordered his accountants to monitor the numbers closely.

And still, there was another: the last Raptor, called Porcupine, was created in November, and this one was even more bizarrely conceived than the rest. Porcupine was created to lock in a single large Enron investment—a $370 million Enron gain that was tied to the price of shares in the New Power Company, Lou Pai's residential energy spinoff, in which Enron had a 75 percent stake.

But instead of being funded with Enron stock, this Raptor held warrants in New Power—the very investment that it was supposed to hedge. This meant that if the price of New Power fell, Porcupine's obligation to Enron would grow at the same time that its ability to pay on the hedge was dropping. Thus, "this extraordinarily fragile structure" (as the special board report later described it) was "the derivatives equivalent of doubling down on a bet." Porcupine could survive only if New Power shares, which were about to go public, climbed in the aftermarket.

But they didn't. On October 5, one week after Porcupine got the New Power stock, the company went public at $21 per share. It was up $6 a share in the first day of trading, but within a week, New Power had fallen back below its offering price—and at year-end was below $10. This produced what one investigator called "a double-whammy effect" on Porcupine. Its obligation to Enron soared while its only real asset to pay the obligation plummeted. Of course, by then, LJM2 had recouped its stake in Porcupine, investing $30 million, then pocketing $39.5 million one week later.

By October 2000, Andy Fastow was entering the homestretch on what was turning out to be a lovely year. Back in February, he promised the Enron board that his Global Finance division would be a profit center—just like trading and the pipelines. Among his "key responsibilities," Fastow declared, was to contribute to Enron's earnings targets. He'd even given the board a projection of the profits his group could generate—$140 million.

Now, in early fall, he'd already blown that number away. In 2000 alone, the Raptors alone shielded Enron from more than $500 million in losses. In their brief lifespan, they allowed Enron to avoid booking an astonishing $1 billion worth of losses—effectively *tripling* the profits Enron reported to investors during that period. Not even Tim Belden could make such a claim.

If the Raptors were good to Enron, they were even better to Fastow. After barely a year in operation, LJM2 was already reaping impressive returns for its investors—including Fastow himself. Millions were flowing into his pocket in partnership distributions and management fees.

In fact, Fastow's partnership was doing so well that he was ready to ask the board to launch LJM3. He'd already started hitting up the banks, advising Chase's Rick Walker that he was preparing to launch the new fund "at Skilling's request"—and wanted to know about the bank's participation. LJM3, of course, was the fund he'd once described as his ticket out of Enron. Lay and Skilling didn't know that was his goal; they'd already given their approval for his third exemption from Enron's code of ethics. But he'd talked about raising a billion dollars for LJM3—and if he could pull that off, who could blame him for walking away?

The Enron board was holding its October meeting in Palm Beach, Florida, at an opulent Italian Renaissance-style hotel called the Breakers. Fastow's discussion of LJM3 was the featured item in his report to the October 6 meeting of the finance committee. Fastow displayed a chart showing the growth in Enron's off-balance-sheet assets. Since 1997, when he'd moved to corporate, Enron's balance-sheet assets had grown by 50 percent, while its off-balance-sheet assets had doubled. All this had resulted in a business of mind-boggling complexity. By then, Enron had generated 3,000 separate corporate entities, more than 800 of them in offshore jurisdictions like the Cayman Islands. Enron's corporate tax return for 2000 ran to 13 volumes.

But such details weren't of concern to the Enron board. In Palm Beach, Fastow didn't hand out any LJM documents or approval sheets to the directors, as he routinely did on Enron deals—and none of the board members demanded any. He didn't mention the proposed size of LJM3 or discuss the returns or his personal compensation from his first two private partnerships. But he did explain how Enron had "largely mitigated" his conflict—and would do so in the future. Enron's management or board could ask him to resign from LJM whenever it wanted, Enron had "no obligation to transact with LJM," and the audit committee reviewed LJM annually.

Among Fastow's list of reasons as to why his conflict was "largely mitigated," two involved Skilling. The CFO told the board that Skilling was among the executives who had to "approve all Enron-LJM transactions." The second: "Review of A. Fastow economic interest in Enron and LJM presented to J. Skilling." The minutes of the committee meeting, taken by Rebecca Carter—who was dating Skilling—reflect that he was present during the discussion (as was Ken Lay). Carter's handwritten notes from the meeting even show that Skilling spoke up in support of Fastow's proposal, explaining that Enron needed LJM3 "to get accounting treatment" and that "third-party transactions would take much longer to do."

But Skilling, who later publicly discussed these matters in congressional hearings, claimed that he might have been absent during the part of Fastow's presentation that cited his role in reviewing LJM transactions because of a power failure at the hotel that resulted in people running in and out of the meeting room. He added that he never heard Fastow's presentation that cited his oversight responsibilities for LJM, nor did he ever see the board minutes. In fact, Skilling later insisted: "I was not required to approve those transactions."

And, indeed, Skilling didn't sign many LJM approval sheets, even though they contained a line specifically for his signature. Even when he did sign, he said later, he merely signed if Causey and Buy had already done so, without giving the deal any independent assessment. In other words—contrary to what the board was told—he wasn't accepting any oversight responsibility at all.

And as for his review of Fastow's economic interest in LJM? Skilling was fuzzy about those details, too. But he did say that at some point, he sat down to discuss this subject with his CFO. Skilling had always been oddly squeamish when it came to personnel matters, and this time, by his own description, he let Fastow set the terms for the discussion. As Skilling described it, Fastow presented him with a one-page handwritten sheet, offering a back-of-the-envelope calculation comparing, over a five-year period, his probable compensation from the partnership with his likely take from his job as CFO of Enron. The figures, Fastow said, reflected assumptions that his Enron stock would appreciate at 15 percent and that LJM would earn a 25 percent return.

"You know, you're not going to make 25 percent," Skilling told Fastow. It would surely be much lower than that.

"I know," Fastow said, smiling. "I'm being conservative."

By Fastow's calculation, Skilling said later, the CFO expected his LJM proceeds to total "something on the order of $5 million." In fact, Fastow had already pocketed several times that amount. But Skilling never asked Fastow directly what he had already made—and he never asked him for any kind of documentation. Skilling left the meeting, he later said, convinced that his CFO's outside compensation would be modest and that Andy Fastow's personal interests would remain aligned with those of Enron.

Nineteen days later, Andy Fastow returned to Palm Beach, this time for the first annual meeting of LJM investors. This gathering was held at an even jazzier venue—the Ritz-Carlton—with Fastow the master of his domain, presiding over the event with a deep sense of satisfaction.

Among those listed as being in attendance was an eight-member contingent from LJM, including four of the beneficiaries of the secret Southampton deal: Michael Kopper, Kathy Lynn, Michael Hinds, and Anne Yaeger. LJM's lawyers were there, from Kirkland & Ellis, and its accountants, from Pricewaterhouse-Coopers. And there were the limited partners, including bankers from Chase and, of course, Merrill Lynch.

Fastow had good news for his guests. LJM was capitalizing on Enron's need to "deconsolidate assets" and "create structures which accelerate projected earnings and cash flow," he explained in materials handed out to the investors. "This leads to opportunities for LJM."

And how LJM had seized those opportunities! To Skilling, Fastow projected 25 percent returns. In front of his investors, he told a different story: he was projecting an annualized net return of 69 percent. And the individual investment details were even more extraordinary. LJM had racked up a 194 percent return on something called Yosemite. On the first three Raptors, he was showing returns of 156 percent, 248 percent, and *2,500 percent*! On the fourth Raptor, Fastow had forecast another 125 percent. All were deals with Enron.

Happy as they were to be making money, the LJM2 investors in attendance— several of them Enron bankers—couldn't help but wonder: *was LJM ripping off Enron? How could Fastow get away with this? Did Skilling know what was going on?* As usual, Fastow had anticipated the need to head off skepticism. His guest speaker for the end of the day was none other than . . . Jeff Skilling!

Enron's president had spent the day in New York, talking to the rating agencies. He had wanted to fly directly to Dallas for an SMU homecoming party with college friends the following afternoon. But Fastow insisted that he make an appearance at the LJM meeting.

When Skilling arrived, the LJM investors had already received copies of Fastow's 44-page presentation, detailing the partnership's extravagant returns. Skilling insisted to the SEC, many months later, that he'd never seen the document—*a 2,500 percent return, negotiating a deal against Enron?*—and that if he had, he'd have gone ballistic. Instead, Skilling popped in for his 30-minute appearance and reassured his CFO's investors that Enron stood squarely behind Andy Fastow and everything he was doing at LJM.

"LJM," Jeff Skilling told them, "is very important to Enron."

CHAPTER 19

"Ask Why, Asshole"

On December 13, 2000, Enron announced the inevitable: Jeff Skilling would succeed Ken Lay as Enron's CEO. The official transfer of power was set to take place in February. "I'm glad to see that Ken Lay has had the presence of mind to allow Jeff, who's really been running this show for a couple of years anyway, to go ahead and take over," Merrill Lynch analyst Donato Eassey told the *New York Times*, summing up the consensus view. In the analyst community, there were rumors that Skilling had forced Lay's hand by hinting that he had another job offer. Indeed, earlier in the year, Skilling renegotiated his contract with a trigger: If he was not named CEO by the end of 2000, he could leave the company and collect a payout of over $20 million. Lay himself was also rumored to be moving up—to Washington, where he would join the cabinet of the incoming Bush administration. But that rumor turned out not to be true.

By all appearances, Skilling was on top of the world. *BusinessWeek* celebrated his new position with a worshipful cover story, featuring Skilling precisely as he wanted the world to see him, dressed in ultracool black, electricity sizzling through his body. *Worth* magazine described him as "hypersmart" and "hyper-confident"—and named him America's second-best CEO (just behind Microsoft's Steve Ballmer) before he'd even been on the job three months. Merrill Lynch's Rick Gordon e-mailed Skilling to tell him that David Komansky, the firm's CEO, was searching for "potential new board members"—and wanted to "get together" with him.

Besides, these were the Enron glory days. Remember 1999, when the stock had returned 58 percent? In 2000 it did even better, returning a startling 89 percent, a gain that generated huge payouts to all the top executives, thanks to the company's performance-unit plan. In addition to his salary and his stock-based compensation, Skilling got a $7.5 million payout. Lay got a total of $10.6 million in cash. Other executives, including Cliff Baxter, Andy Fastow, Rick Causey, and Rick Buy, also got seven-figure payouts. The numbers the company was hitting were just as eye-popping. Revenues topped $100 billion, twice what they were in 1999. Earnings hit $1.3 billion—up 25 percent from the previous year on a per-share basis. (That is, before a $287 million onetime write-off—the result of Azurix's Buenos Aires disaster.)

On the conference call to announce the results, Skilling couldn't stop using words like "outstanding," "fantastic," and "tremendous." The 2001 analysts meeting, held, as always, in late January, was every bit the love fest it was the previous year, when the company unveiled its broadband strategy. The crowning moment came when Skilling presented his analysis of the value of Enron stock. The pipelines, by his analysis, were worth a mere $6 a share. EES, he said, was worth $23 a share. The wholesale business was worth $57 a share. And broadband was worth $40 a share. In the world according to Skilling, Enron stock was really worth $126 per share—more than 50 percent above its current level. The day of the meeting, the stock closed at $82, up 3 percent. Enron "management did not let the optimists down," noted Goldman Sachs analyst David Fleischer, who reiterated his $110 price target on the stock.

A month later, Skilling and Lay held one of their regular employee meetings. They took the opportunity to announce Enron's new vision. Clearly, the World's Leading Energy Company was no longer grand enough. The management committee had held a half-dozen meetings to brainstorm. The American executives loved the World's Coolest Company, but many of Enron's foreign employees didn't know what it meant. Instead, they chose the World's Leading Company.

Later in the meeting, Skilling explained how one measured the World's Leading Company—not that there was ever any doubt. "When we talk about becoming the 'World's Leading Company,' the target I think we all ought to have in mind is how do we become the company with the highest market value of any company in the world," he said. At that time, those honors belonged to General Electric, which had a market value of $400 billion—almost six times larger than Enron's.

Skilling had another thought as well. "Got to change my license plate from WLEC to WLC," he said. Everyone laughed.

Skilling later insisted that, appearances to the contrary, he never wanted to be the CEO. The trigger, he claimed, was not the naked power play that it appeared to be. Rather, he said it was Lay's idea—Lay realized that Skilling was restless. Even so, Skilling half expected that Lay would do to him what he'd done to Kinder four years earlier. But as it became clear that Lay had every intention of turning over the job to him, Skilling felt he had no choice but to accept the position. "Drive and ego, control and power," says a former Enron executive who was close to Skilling. "You want the next job. Then, on the other hand, you want a life." In this friend's view, Skilling was genuinely conflicted, but he wasn't able to walk away from the prestige of being Enron's chief executive.

Skilling had a variety of reasons for why he didn't want the job. He felt the board was always going to be in Lay's back pocket. After taking a trip to Africa with his brother Mark and his son Jeffrey, he realized he wanted to spend more time with his children. That trip was the first vacation he ever had where he was not eager to return to work at Enron. And, he confided to his inner circle, he wasn't having fun anymore. "I hate what I'm doing," he told people.

For all of Skilling's public bravado about how great everything was at Enron, he spent most of his time dealing with a host of serious problems, the part of the job he had always despised. Part of him was caught up in maintaining the illusion that Enron was, indeed, the World's Leading Company. But it seems likely that another part of him was being forced to confront the darker reality. Holding those two conflicting notions in his head at the same time—at a minimum, it had to be exhausting.

Take the underperforming international assets. Although Skilling had disbanded the international team, he had yet to unload the assets. Enron had placed its hopes on Project Summer—the $7 billion deal with the Mideast investor that fell through at the last minute. After the buyer went away, Skilling put Baxter in charge of selling the assets piecemeal. He told investors that Enron would sell $2 billion to $4 billion of international projects by the end of 2001. But there were no takers.

Dabhol had also resurfaced as a nightmare. By this point, Enron had almost $900 million invested in it, but Maharashtra stopped footing Dabhol's bills. Indian officials were complaining loudly about the high cost of Dabhol's power and the resulting "exorbitant profitability" to Enron. By the spring of 2001, Dabhol was dark and silent, construction had been halted on Phase II, and Enron had launched arbitration proceedings.

Ken Lay personally chaired the Dabhol task force, and Ben Glisan served as the Global Finance liaison. Rebecca Mark—who believed the problem was that Enron, having fired all the international executives, didn't have anyone left who understood the business—offered herself up as a savior, calling Lay to volunteer to salvage the situation. After Skilling told Lay that he would quit if Mark came back, Lay wouldn't even return her calls.

The problem was both incredibly simple and impossible to fix: the MSEB said it did not need and could not afford the expensive power that Dabhol produced, there was no one else to buy it, and the project would run out of cash by the summer. ("Plant of questionable value," Glisan noted.) Skilling joked to one fund manager that his preferred solution would be to confiscate Air India planes when they landed at JFK International Airport. Lay later told India's prime minister that he would settle for $2.3 billion, an amount that he called "exceptionally reasonable." Publicly, however, Enron insisted that Dabhol would not have a material effect on its finances.

Skilling could blame Rebecca Mark for the problems with the international assets. But he had no one to blame but himself for broadband. The market for tech and telecom stocks was melting down—there wasn't going to be anyone left to trade with. The content business remained a joke. And the broadband team, with its huge overhead, had run out of ways to create earnings. *This* was a business worth $36 billion?

Enron had negotiated the sale of Portland General to Sierra Pacific for $2.1 billion. It was supposed to be a sure thing. But as a result of the new California laws triggered by the state's energy crisis, Sierra Pacific was barred from selling generating plants it needed to unload in order to fund the acquisition. It took until April for Enron to announce what everyone already suspected: the deal was off.

California was troublesome in other ways. Questions were swirling about how much money Enron's traders were making, and on Wall Street, there were just many questions about how much money EES was losing in the state. Skilling insisted that Enron was fully "reserved" for any California problems, but he refused to disclose any details, insisting it was competitive information. On the year-end conference call, he said, "Now, for Enron, the situation in California had little impact on fourth-quarter results. Let me repeat that. For Enron, the situation in California had little impact on fourth-quarter results."

Six months later, the folly of Enron's California stance was underscored when its longtime investor, CalPERS, halted ongoing negotiations to amend JEDI II, meaning that JEDI II would have less money to extend to Enron. "This action is a direct result of the continuing power crisis in California and the threat of a backlash, which could lead to the reregulation of the energy industry," explained a Global Finance executive in an e-mail. "More pressure," replied Rick Buy succinctly.

And Andy Fastow's team had its own cancer in the making. Their clever concoction, the Raptors, had immediately gone sour. In late 2000, as the assets in the SPEs declined, the Raptors owed Enron money. But the New Power warrants that Porcupine was supposed to use to repay Enron had virtually collapsed. And the assets in the first Raptor had declined so dramatically that Enron needed its stock to continue to climb dramatically to cover the losses. But the stock had stalled. Since two Raptors couldn't pay what they owed, Enron would have to declare losses—which defeated the very purpose of the vehicles.

Naturally, Rick Causey and his in-house accountants tried to come up with a solution that avoided that dire possibility. They first argued that under a "probabalistic" analysis—the chief probability being that Enron's stock would climb—there was no need to declare losses. Andersen refused to go along with that, arguing that Enron's stock price was what the market said it was. (Enron was not a fan of the market when it meant taking losses.) Next, Enron argued all the Raptors could, in essence, be viewed in the aggregate—meaning that the healthy vehicles could use their excess credit capacity to support the sick ones. Under that scenario there would be no need to declare losses.

This solution should never have passed muster under any circumstances. The Raptors had already contorted the rules of accounting. This made a complete mockery of them. Indeed, Andersen refused to go along—or rather, Carl Bass refused to go along. He insisted that there was no rational basis for LJM to agree to use some SPEs to prop up others."Heads I win, tails you lose," as Bass described it. (Of course Fastow had already gotten his money out, so it made no difference to him.)

As year-end approached, both Enron and Arthur Andersen were desperate. And so, David Duncan, with the support of his immediate superiors in the Houston office—Mike Odom, the practice director, and Mike Lowther, the head of the firm's energy practice on the audit side—agreed to "bridge" the Raptors through the end of the year. Without telling Bass, they cross-collateralized the four Raptors for 45 days, enabling Enron to avoid reporting $500 million in losses. (LJM2 was paid $50,000 for its trouble.) Of course, the fix didn't really fix anything. It only pushed the problem further off and added another tangle to the fragile web of accounting deception.

On February 5, 14 senior Arthur Andersen partners, including eight based in Houston—David Duncan among them—held a meeting to discuss whether to retain Enron as a client. Andersen has insisted this was a routine meeting, but the topics seemed to be anything but routine. At the meeting, there was "significant discussion" about LJM, about Fastow's conflicts, and about whether Enron ever got any competing bids for assets that were sold to LJM, as a memo documenting the meeting noted. The Andersen accountants called Enron's use of mark-to-market accounting "intelligent gambling." The high-level group fretted over "Enron's dependence on transaction execution to meet financial objectives."

But they also noted that it "would not be unforeseeable that fees could reach a $100 million per year amount." They concluded that despite the rising fees, they could maintain their independence—so they would keep the account. They decided to tell Enron's board to establish a special committee to monitor the fairness of the LJM transactions. In fact, Duncan never made that request. One week later, Enron's board met, but Duncan and a second Andersen partner in attendance never breathed a word about their concerns. Instead, Duncan reassured the board that Andersen's "opinion on the Company's internal controls . . . would be unqualified."

Arthur Andersen reached another decision, too. In late February, Andersen CEO Joseph Berardino paid a visit to Houston, where he met with Causey and Duncan. The visit was a courtesy call, but perhaps inevitably, the subject of Carl Bass came up. Causey was angry that Bass had refused to sign off on Project Braveheart and the Raptors. Duncan scribbled notes: "Carl. Too technical. Client satisfaction involved in Blockbuster." Other notes conveyed Causey's feelings about Bass: "negative view of Carl" and "Some push by client to get Carl out of engagement team."

About a week later, the firm removed Bass from any further direct dealings with Enron. When Bass found out what had happened, he wrote a three-page e-mail to his boss, John Stewart. "You should at least have a version of what I know about this Enron 'thing' from me," Bass began. He denied harboring "some caustic and inappropriate slant" in dealing with Causey or Enron. In questioning transactions like Project Braveheart, he was doing his job—upholding accounting standards and protecting both the firm and the client. Bass also complained that Duncan's group had allowed Enron to know "all that goes on within our walls" instead of keeping his internal advice private. He recalled a meeting where a low-level Enron employee "introduced herself to me by saying she had heard my name a lot—'So you are the one that will not let us do something.' "

John Stewart was furious. "I thought it was unprofessional for Enron to make such a request," he later said. Stewart, who had been at the Professional Standards Group since 1980, also said he viewed Bass's removal as a defining moment. It was a request no client had ever made before, and one the firm should never have granted. "We should have been more independent," Stewart later said.

The bull market was over. It ended in the spring of 2000. The dot-coms were in free fall; many were soon out of business. The telecoms were in similar straits. Where investors had once cheered the market's every move, now they grew angry as their savings dwindled and they realized they had gotten caught up in a classic bubble.

As stocks sank, the game changed. Momentum investors were selling instead of buying. Skeptical voices that had been ignored during the great bull run were suddenly getting a hearing. And companies that hit or beat their earnings target could no longer be assured of a rising stock price. Investors were newly curious about how companies had arrived at those earnings. They were digging deeper and asking questions. In the bull market, investors always saw the glass as half full; now, for the first time in years, they were seeing it as half empty.

For all his brilliance, Skilling never seemed to understand this new dynamic. After peaking in August 2000 at $90 a share, Enron stock had sunk as low as $65 that fall, largely because of worries about California. It gained much of that back—helped, as ever, by the analyst meeting in January—but it never really jolted upward again the way Skilling thought it should. It was certainly not climbing inexorably towards $126 a share. Skilling was, if anything, more obsessed with the stock than ever; in the words of one of his executives, he had "morphed into more of a stock promoter than a businessman." He kept thinking that as long as Enron made its numbers, the stock would start climbing again. But he was wrong.

It was short sellers who first asked tough questions about Enron. Their interest was sparked by the tremendous run-up in the stock, which can suggest that a company is overvalued. It was fueled by the hype about broadband and the collapse of Azurix.

And it was also triggered by Enron's use of mark-to-market accounting, which had been largely ignored since Toni Mack and Harry Hurt III pointed out its dangers in the mid-1990s. On September 20, 2000, Jonathan Weil, a reporter in the Dallas bureau of the *Texas Journal*, a regional supplement to the *Wall Street Journal*, published a story that focused on the degree to which all the energy trading companies relied on mark-to-market accounting. Weil noted that outsiders had no way of knowing the assumptions that companies like Enron, Dynegy, and El Paso used to book their earnings. He also pointed out that a hefty portion of those earnings was not cash. Weil's story ran only in Texas; inexplicably, his editors chose not to run it in the national edition. But at his desk in New York, a man named Jim Chanos came across the story.

Chanos and his hedge fund, Kynikos Associates, are not well known the way that giant mutual fund complexes like Fidelity and Vanguard are. Hedge funds cater to institutions and wealthy individuals—Chanos's fund requires a minimum investment of $1 million—and they don't advertise. But to the Wall Street cognoscenti, Chanos is very well known indeed. Kynikos has been around for almost 20 years—an aeon in hedge-fund terms—and is one of the few funds focusing exclusively on short selling to have survived the long bull market. Chanos is always on the lookout for overvalued stocks, but more than that, he's a kind of financial sleuth, who scours balance sheets and financial documents searching for clues that something might be awry inside a company. Although he doesn't get them all right—in 1995, Chanos was run over shorting AOL—his batting average in recent years is high. Today, he manages over $1 billion.

Like Skilling, Chanos is from a midwestern family—his father ran a chain of dry cleaners in Milwaukee—and like Skilling, he was always interested in the market. When he was young, his father would take out books from the library on the market for him to read. Unlike Skilling, Chanos was conservative with his money and didn't invest on his own until college, when he bought shares of oil stocks and airlines—companies that were in the Dow Jones industrial average or the S&P 500. He attended Yale, where he began as a premed major but soon became fascinated by economics, accounting, and a book called *The Contrarian Investor*, which stresses fundamental analysis and the importance of ignoring the crowd. After graduation in 1980, Chanos began working as a numbers cruncher for a small investment-banking firm. His epiphany came when he did an analysis showing that a client about to issue equity should actually be buying back stock instead. "You cannot mention that," yelled his boss. "We are in the business to promote the sale of equity."

And so Chanos moved out of investment banking and into a small research firm. His life changed forever when he began looking into a company called Baldwin United. Baldwin, which had been formed from the merger of a piano maker and an insurance company that sold annuities, was one of the hottest stocks of that era. After months of dogged research, Chanos realized that the high-flying Baldwin was, in essence, a giant Ponzi scheme that raised money secretly through subsidiaries, turned the money over to the parent to support its enormous capital consumption, and used aggressive mark-to-market assumptions on its portfolio of annuities to create fabulous earnings growth. When it comes to stock-market frauds, history does repeat itself.

In August 1982, the 24-year-old Chanos put out a sell report on Baldwin United. The report was extremely controversial, for Baldwin, just like Enron, had wide and vocal support among the analysts. Merrill Lynch and many of the other firms made hefty commissions pushing Baldwin's annuities on its retail customers. Chanos's work was denounced up and down Wall Street. But by the fall of 1983, Baldwin had filed for bankruptcy, and the scandal had burst into the open. In 1985, Wall Street firms settled with the annuity holders for $140 million. That same year, Chanos founded Kynikos, named after a sect of ancient Greek philosophers that believed the key to life was self-discipline and independence of thought.

After Chanos saw Jonathan Weil's story in the fall of 2000, he flipped open Enron's 1999 10-K. He read: "The market prices used to value these transactions reflect management's best estimates." He thought: "A license to print money." He began talking to Enron's competitors, Wall Street analysts, and virtually anyone else he thought might have information on the company—though not to the company itself, which he viewed as a waste of time. ("You can call the analysts and get the company party line," he says.)

The more Chanos poked around, the more he felt that the Enron story didn't make sense. Chanos had made a fortune researching—then shorting—telecom stocks. He knew how much trouble they were in. How could Enron's broadband unit be doing so well when the rest of the industry was on life support? "We know telecom cold," he says. "And here's Enron bleating about this great opportunity."

Enron's return on invested capital was abysmally low, around 7 percent—and that figure didn't even include the billions upon billions of off-balance-sheet debt. "They were chewing up capital," says Chanos. He was struck by a three-paragraph disclosure in Enron's third-quarter 2000 filing about its dealings with a related party. No matter how many times he read it, he still couldn't understand what it said. He showed it to derivatives specialists, corporate lawyers, and other experts; they couldn't figure it out either. Chanos thought: "They must be trying to hide something." And then there were the insider sales. Lay was consistently selling about 2,500 shares a day. Skilling was also selling in big chunks.

Chanos and the others who shorted Enron's stock didn't have any special information that wasn't available to the bulls. "As soon as anyone looked, they could see the stuff we saw," says Chanos today. At first, he adds, "We didn't think it was some great hidden fraud. We just thought it was a bad business." By November 2000, he had begun taking a big short position in Enron stock.

Because of Chanos's record, reporters call his office regularly, looking for story ideas. A few weeks after Enron's 2001 analysts conference, Chanos and

Doug Millett, Kynikos's chief operating officer, told *Fortune* writer Bethany McLean (co-author of this book) that they were skeptical of Enron. Millett, a gregarious former Yale football player, laughingly described Enron as "a hedge fund sitting on top of a pipeline." After pointing out how low Enron's return on invested capital was, he added, "Would you put your money in a hedge fund earning a 7 percent return?" Chanos said, "Read the 10-K and see if you can figure out how they're making money." The two men also noted that Enron was a speculative trading shop, which meant that, at an absolute minimum, its outsize price-to-earnings multiple made no sense. "You don't give these things a 50 multiple even if it's the Goldman Sachs of the energy business," said Chanos.

Chanos was right: when you took the time to pore through Enron's financial documents, it wasn't hard to find scratches on its shiny surface. While Enron's reported earnings were growing smoothly, the business didn't seem to be generating much cash—and you can't run a business without cash. In fact, Enron had *negative* cash from its operations in the first nine months of 2000. (It was impossible to analyze the full year because Enron released an income statement only when it announced earnings—not a balance sheet or a cash-flow statement. Only when the report was filed with the SEC a month or so later could anyone really dig through the numbers. This soon became a huge issue.)

There were other warning signs. Enron's debt was climbing rapidly—$3.9 billion of debt was added on the balance sheet in the first nine months of 2000 alone—which didn't make sense if the business was as profitable as Enron was claiming. It was also clear that Enron was selling assets and booking the proceeds as recurring earnings. In fact, publicly filed documents showed that nearly 40 percent of Enron's earnings in 1998 and 1999 came from gains on sales of assets rather than from ongoing operations.

McLean soon realized that there was growing skepticism toward Enron in the investment community, though few were willing to express it on the record. "It's hard to believe they're not taking losses in California [on EES], but they'll cover it up somehow. Enron is especially good at that," said one portfolio manager under the cover of anonymity. "The last two years, about half the quarters they've had some kind of issue, but no one on Wall Street will challenge them." Another portfolio manager said: "Volatility and pricing are going to go down in California. How can you pull the same numbers out of trading?"

Commerzbank analyst Andre Meade, one of the few who had a hold rating on the stock, worried that Enron was "liquidating its asset base and booking it as recurring revenue." Another analyst, Robert Winters, then at Bear Stearns, wrote in a report dated January 26, 2001, that "the ability to develop a somewhat predictable model of this business for the future is mostly an exercise in futility." Yet another analyst when asked about Enron's accounting said: "You don't have a clue, I don't have a clue, and I'm not sure they have a clue. Enron," he added, "is a big black box."

On February 14 at 10 A.M., McLean and Skilling spoke for about 20 minutes.

Skilling, who had been CEO for all of two weeks, was not in a good mood. "Enron is *not* a black box," he said emphatically. "It is very simple to model." Enron was a "logistics company," not a trading company, he insisted. Off-balance-sheet debt? Virtually all of it, he said, related to international assets, and Enron was not on the hook to pay it back in any case. With every question McLean asked, Skilling became increasingly agitated. "I can see where you're going," he said finally and then went on almost a stream-of-consciousness rant. "I would really appreciate it if you would sit down with our finance and accounting teams. It is unfair to us and unethical [if you don't take the time to understand our business] . . . we are doing it purely right . . . people who raise questions are people who have not gone through our business in detail . . . people who don't understand want to throw rocks at us . . . we have explicit answers, but people want to throw rocks at us . . . anyone who is successful, people would like to take them down based on ignorance." With that, he hung up the phone.

Mark Palmer, Enron's head of PR, promptly called back, offering to come to New York the next day with Enron's CFO, Andy Fastow. "We want to make sure we've answered all of your questions completely and accurately," he said. With Mark Koenig, Enron's head of investor relations, in tow, they flew to New York the next morning, arriving at *Fortune* around ten. The three Enron executives were shepherded into a small, windowless conference room, where they sat down with McLean and two *Fortune* editors.

Fastow's explanation of Enron's business did not exactly provide the promised clarity. On the contrary. Here's how Fastow explained Enron's business model: "We create optionality. Enron is so much more valuable—hence our stock price—because we have so much more optionality embedded in our network than anyone else." Fastow then compared Enron to Toyota; Enron, too, was an "assembler" rather than a "manufacturer." "Our disclosure is more complete than anyone's," Fastow insisted. A moment later, he seemed to say precisely the opposite: "We don't want to tell anyone where we're making money." Like Skilling, Fastow insisted that Enron did not make its money speculating. "It's not trading, it's optimization," he said. The proof? Enron's earnings record in the wholesale business. "We have for 20 straight quarters exceeded the previous one. There's not a trading company in the world that has that kind of consistency."

When McLean asked Fastow about the related-party transactions, he replied, "One of our senior executives runs that fund. It's confidential who it is." (In fact, a line in Enron's 1999 proxy statement disclosed that the senior executive was Fastow.) Why did Enron need to do business with the related party? "We're always looking to hedge risks, to sell risks," Fastow replied. "We want to sell, but we don't want the information to get into the market . . . it adds to our optionality." And "we strip out the price risk, we strip out the interest-rate risk, we strip out all the risks. What's left may not be something that we want. We want the contract, but we don't want the power plant. We're not investing for the whole thing—we wanted the optionality. Once we've gotten that piece, we want to sell off the other pieces."

After two hours, the meeting came to a close. Koenig and Palmer left the room; Fastow lingered for a moment. After he gathered up his things, he paused. "I don't care what you say about the company," he said finally. "Just don't make me look bad."

In retrospect, the story that ran in *Fortune*, which was published on February 19, barely scratched the surface. Headlined "IS ENRON OVERPRICED?" it asked far more questions than it answered: "How exactly does Enron make its money? . . . 'If you figure it out, let me know,' laughs credit analyst Todd Shipman at S&P. 'Do you have a year?' asks Ralph Pellecchia, Fitch's credit analyst, in response to the same question." The story noted Enron's lack of cash flow and climbing debt. And it quoted some analysts defending the company. "Enron is no black box," says Goldman's Fleischer. "That's like calling Michael Jordan a black box just because you don't know what he's going to score every quarter." The *Fortune* story didn't even mention Enron's odd dealings with the related parties.

At Enron's February 21 all-employee meeting, there was one question about the story. To Enron's employees, Skilling not only admitted that the company was a black box—something he'd flatly denied to McLean—but he seemed proud of it. "Yes, it is a black box," he said, "but it is a black box that's growing the wholesale business by about 50 percent in volume and profitability. That's a good black box. And we've been absolutely up front with the analysts."

He later added: "People will take shots at us because the p/e ratio is high. I personally believe that the p/e ratio is justified because we're growing very quickly in earnings and revenues and we have the strongest position in every market that we're in. But it is going to take a little while to get that across and I think we can expect these kinds of articles to come out over the next couple of months because we really are the only ones left with this high p/e ratio. I personally think it's justified. . . . I think we're going to have a great year this year, and I think that's going to push the stock price up."

Enron's stock, which had been at $82 after its analyst conference, sank to $68.50 by February 28.

With Enron's stock sputtering, the Raptors again began springing leaks, and the desperation kicked in all over again. This time, Causey and Fastow, with the help of other Enron accountants, including a young ex-FASB intern and Arthur Andersen alum named Ryan Siurek, came up with what they thought was a permanent solution. The Raptors were restructured so that they could prop each other up forever. In other words, as long as one Raptor could pay for the losses sustained by the others, Enron could avoid disclosing the losses. To do this, Enron had to contribute yet more stock and more derivatives on its shares. In exchange, the Raptors gave Enron $828 million in notes receivable.

How did Enron overcome the objections of Andersen's Professional Standards Group? Simple: this time, Duncan didn't even consult with Andersen's experts. "We decided to accept the client's position," he later said. In total, Andersen was paid about $1.3 million for its Raptor-related work.

The Raptor restructuring closed on March 26—just in time. Four days later, the first quarter came to a close, and the Raptors had shielded another $200 million in losses. And though the word Raptors was never used—and there was never any precise description of what these entities accomplished—the restructuring itself *was* disclosed in Enron's first-quarter filing. Mind you, it wasn't disclosed in a fashion that any outsider could interpret. But if you took a skeptical eye to the sentence in Enron's first-quarter SEC filing that read "Enron received notes receivable from the Entities totaling approximately $827.6 million," you might suspect that something enormous had happened.

Skilling later claimed that he knew very little about the Raptor restructuring. Most people don't believe him. On the afternoon of March 26, just after the deal closed, Skilling called Siurek to thank him for his work. He has claimed that he did this at Causey's urging and that he was only vaguely aware of the situation. "It's conceivable that Andy could pull the wool over Jeff's eyes," retorts a friend. "But if Causey knew there was an earnings impact, then Jeff knew." Causey himself told investigators that he was "certain that he told Skilling about the shortfall in the Raptor vehicles." The investigators added: "When they found what Causey felt was a solution, Causey sought and obtained Skilling's approval. Causey updated Skilling before executing the Raptor restructuring, during development of the restructuring plan and after determining the solution to the problem."

There's a second reason why Skilling's explanation does not ring true. He was a man obsessed with Enron's quarterly numbers. Although the traders were making a fortune during this period—enough to cover earnings shortfalls—the losses inside the Raptors would still likely have had to be disclosed to investors. Skilling later insisted that Enron could have simply taken the hit—everyone was writing down high-tech investments. But not everyone was using structured finance to prop those earnings up, and the market would certainly not have taken a write-down lightly. Could Skilling really have been only dimly aware of something with such potential to crush the stock?

Enron's board members also insist that they were kept in the dark about the restructuring—it was never included on a list of Enron's top credit exposures, for instance. Still, since the restructuring was disclosed in Enron's financial statements, there are only three possibilities. They are lying. They did not bother to read Enron's financial statements. Or they read the financial statements—but like so many others, they didn't understand what they were reading.

On March 21, Enron's stock fell a stunning $5.06, to $55.89. The next day, it hit an intraday low of $51.51. Enron executives, feeling blindsided by the stock's downturn, struggled to figure out how to get it back up. Though the end of the quarter was barely a week away, the company took the unusual step of issuing a press release announcing that it would meet earnings estimates. The next day, Skilling held a conference call. "I just came in from South America this morning—got in at 5:30—so I'm in a really lousy mood, so I hope we get the message across quickly," he began testily. "Enron's business is in great shape." Rumors had been floating in recent days that Enron would need to do an equity offering to raise money; Skilling went out of his way to flatten the rumor. "From a credit standpoint, there is absolutely no need to issue additional equity, either this year or for the foreseeable future," he said. "So overall, I have no under-standing of why [our] stock price is in the $53, $54—that's just crazy."

After the call, Enron's stock rebounded to $59.40. "$102 target likely a late 2002 event," wrote analyst Ron Barone in what passed for conservatism—he had been predicting that the stock would reach that level in the ensuing 12 months. A few days later, Goldman's David Fleischer added, "Investors have focused on is-sues we view as almost insignificant to future valuation."

About a month later, with its stock stuck around $60 a share, Enron an-nounced another stunning first quarter, beating its earnings estimates by two cents a share. The next morning, Causey, Koenig, Rice, and Skilling gathered at the conference table in Koenig's office for the conference call following the earnings release. Skilling had just returned from a college tour with his daughter, Kristin; he was in an upbeat mood. "Just an outstanding quarter, another out-standing quarter," said Skilling. We are "very optimistic about each of our busi-nesses and confident that our record of growth is sustainable for many years to come."

In the middle of the question-and-answer period, a man named Richard Grubman was given the floor. Grubman, who runs a hedge fund called High-fields Capital, is another well-known short seller. Like Chanos, Grubman had taken a large short position in Enron. Koenig promptly slipped Skilling a note, informing him that the questioner was a short seller. Grubman didn't care about Enron's earnings. He wanted to see a balance sheet, which would have far more detailed information than the income statement Enron put out the day before.

Skilling: "We do not have the balance sheet completed. We will have that done shortly when we file the Q. But until we put all of that together, we just cannot give you that."

Grubman: "I'm trying to understand why that would appear to be an un-reasonable request, in light of your comments about daily control of all your credits?"

Skilling: "I'm not saying we can't tell you what the balances are. We clearly have all of those positions on a daily basis, but at this point, we will wait to dis-close those until all . . . the right accounting is put together."

Grubman: "You're the only financial institution that cannot produce a balance sheet or cash-flow statement with their earnings."

Skilling: "Well, you're—you—well, uh, thank you very much. We appreciate it."

Grubman: "Appreciate it?"

Skilling: *"Asshole."*

Rice, who was half asleep, bolted awake. Jaws dropped around the table. A horrified Mark Palmer, listening in on the conference call with the rest of Enron's public-relations team, immediately ran upstairs with a note to Skilling, urging him to apologize right away. Skilling looked at the note and then slipped it under a pile of papers in front of him.

The call had been piped onto the trading floor. When Skilling called Grubman an asshole, the whole floor burst into applause. Afterward, the traders gave Skilling a sign that played off Enron's motto, "Ask Why." It read: "Ask Why, Asshole." Skilling proudly displayed it behind his desk.

Ken Lay, who was already upset by the declining stock, was aghast. So was Enron's board. Big institutional shareholders called Lay to complain. "It didn't go over well," Skilling later admitted to friends while steadfastly maintaining that the comment was justified: "I don't like shorts promoting their position." But he also claimed that at that point, he didn't care: "I was tired. I was beat."

Over at Kynikos, Jim Chanos was in hysterics. He had never heard the CEO of a Fortune 500 company lose it like that. After listening to the conference call, Chanos was more convinced than ever that Enron was hiding serious problems. Even owners of Enron stock thought Grubman's questions were perfectly valid—and if they hadn't been, Skilling should have dealt with them more adeptly. "Any CEO should be able to handle the hardest of questions from the most aggressive of shorts," says analyst Meade.

Skilling's act was finally starting to wear thin. "After eight or ten conference calls, I started to lose faith," says one analyst. "It was always exactly the same thing. There was never anything wrong. Four quarterly conference calls and the annual meeting, all exactly the same. It's all great. The company is ahead of everyone. It will only get better."

Another money manager found himself increasingly disturbed by Skilling's stock-price fixation. In meetings with this person, he would spend 15 to 20 minutes of a one-hour presentation talking about the stock and grousing that investors weren't recognizing Enron's greatness. "I asked internally, have you ever come across a CEO so obsessed?" says the manager.

Skilling's explanations for the few problems that were visible were losing credibility. For instance, Skilling used to blame Enron's low return on capital on Mark's international assets. Skilling claimed that the return on Enron's other businesses—*his* businesses—was far higher. But he wouldn't offer any proof. That was fine during the bull market—but this wasn't a bull market anymore. Investors complained to Enron's investor-relations department that they didn't want to hear excuses if they couldn't see evidence.

Another major fund manager had loaded up on Enron stock mainly because he believed in the company's deregulation story. Even in the midst of the California debacle, Skilling and Lay continued to insist that the trend towards deregulation was unstoppable. Skilling went so far as to say that the fiasco would "push forward more open competitive markets." Few agreed with him. The mutual fund company began dumping its Enron shares.

As people began to question Skilling's credibility, other things began to matter—such as the whole logistics company rationale. Many had never believed it. On Wall Street, people knew people who traded with Enron; to them it was obvious the company was speculating. But during the bull market, they let Skilling have his conceit. Now, it became one more reason to doubt him. "He's either compulsively lying, or he's refusing to recognize the truth," one portfolio manager remembers thinking.

Skilling knew that his credibility was slipping. "Am I the liability here?" he asked several analysts. In early May, he and Rebecca Carter flew to Turkey for the wedding of his brother, Mark, who had moved there to become a writer. Upon his return, Enron's stock was still stuck at around $60. Skilling was beside himself.

Someone inside Enron finally became uncomfortable enough about LJM to try to do something about it. In October 2000, Fastow had booted out his general counsel at Global Finance and brought in a lawyer named Jordan Mintz, who had spent the previous four years in Enron's tax department.

Like many Enron employees, Mintz had known of the existence of LJM. Now, in his new post, he began to learn the gory details—and the more he learned, the more panicked he got. LJM, he thought, was "potential dynamite." His first impression was simply that everything was a mess. Files were an absolute shambles. Documentation was scattered; required signatures on approval forms were missing. In addition, LJM people and Enron people were working side by side, and one could scarcely tell who was wearing which hat—and when. "This is certainly a shit load of dysfunctionality," Mintz thought.

Mintz also worried that the disclosure about LJM in Enron's public filings was inadequate. Though he understood, as he later put it in an e-mail, that Enron's goal was "to be as innocuous as possible in terms of description, detail, etc.," he maintained that they would all be better off if Enron provided "evidence of Senior Management and the board's carrying out their fiduciary duties, absence of a 'sweetheart deal', and the 'legitimacy' of the financial treatment resulting from the transaction."

Finally, he was concerned that Enron was not disclosing how much money Fastow was making from LJM, as the law seemed to require. As a rule, if top executives are making substantial sums from an entity that does business with the company, they have to tell shareholders. Although there's some murkiness surrounding the rules—and Mintz knew that Enron relished murky areas—he felt that the company's failure to disclose Fastow's LJM income was hard to justify.

At the end of 2000, he talked to Fastow. "You want to know how much I've made?" Fastow asked playfully. He told Mintz that he probably shouldn't tell him until he'd talked to his lawyer at Kirkland & Ellis. "Let's figure out a way not to disclose it," he said. Then, Fastow said, "Hell, if Skilling knew how much I made, he'd have no choice but to shut LJM down."

On March 8, Mintz sent a memo to Causey and Buy—which he copied to Fastow—listing all the problems he saw with LJM. "Enron does not consistently seek to negotiate with third parties before it transacts with LJM," he noted; thus, there was little evidence of either "accounting substantiation" or of the board carrying out its fiduciary duties. He also talked to them about Fastow's compensation. Causey was unperturbed. "I don't care how much Andy's making," he told Mintz. "This is a win-win situation for the company."

Rick Buy had his own problems. Late in 2000, Skilling had formed a new übergroup called the Policy Committee. It consisted of a dozen male Skillingites—but not Buy, who was deeply upset by his exclusion. He was all too aware of his impotence. In frustration, he told Mintz he was considering leaving Enron to work for LJM. Yet at other times, he complained that LJM made him uncomfortable. Then, that winter, doctors discovered a tumor on his tongue. Buy had surgery and took a vacation to recuperate.

Mintz did get a reaction—a huge one—from Fastow. Michael Kopper came storming into Mintz's office with the memo, flung it across his desk, and said, "What do you want to do, shut us down?"

When Enron's 2000 proxy was filed in late March, it contained no information about Fastow's pay. Mintz, relying on lawyers from Enron and Vinson & Elkins, had used a loophole to avoid disclosing what Fastow was earning. Because not all transactions between LJM2 and Enron had officially settled, the lawyers maintained that they couldn't calculate Fastow's income yet. Never mind that Fastow had received millions in partnership management fees and distributions.

The last thing Mintz wanted, though, was for Fastow to relax. And so he sent another memo, this time directly to Fastow, the next day, telling him that the lack of disclosure likely couldn't continue and that "the decision not to disclose in this instance was a close call; arguably, the more conservative approach would have been to disclose the amount of your interest."

In early May, Skilling gave Fastow an additional responsibility: he became head of corporate development—incredibly, this was the group in charge of finding buyers for projects Enron wanted to unload. This new conflict didn't bother Fastow any more than any of the old ones. In a staff meeting, Fastow said bluntly, "We're going to start selling a shit load of assets to LJM." For Mintz, that was the last straw. Looking for more ammunition, Mintz sent a letter to a lawyer he knew in the Washington office of Fried Frank Harris Shriver & Jacobson, a tony New York law firm. Mintz was referred to an SEC expert at the firm, to whom he sent a huge pile of Enron and LJM documents, seeking his opinion on the adequacy of the company's public disclosures. (Fried Frank later opined that Enron should "consider supplementing the prior disclosures . . . especially on such points as the purpose of the specific transactions entered into and the 'bottom-line' financial impact on the Company and the LJM Partners.")

Mintz also took another, far more drastic step. He resolved to take his concerns directly to Skilling. Buy warned him against doing so. "Jeff is very fond of Andy," Enron's chief risk officer said. "I wouldn't stick my neck out." But Mintz did exactly that. Because Skilling had not signed many of the LJM2 documents, Mintz, on May 22, sent him a memo in a "personal and confidential" envelope. The memo informed Skilling that Mintz had a batch of LJM approval forms awaiting Skilling's signature and that he would "arrange to get on your schedule" so the CEO could sign them. Mintz hoped that the forms would alert Skilling to the "dysfunctionality" involving LJM2 and hoped the ensuing conversation with the CEO would make him reconsider whether Fastow's partnership was really such a great idea.

To this day, the fate of Mintz's memo remains a mystery. Mintz insists that after he got no response, his secretary called Skilling's office three times over a two-week period trying to set up a meeting. The lack of response was later viewed as deliberate, an attempt by Skilling to maintain his distance from the messy details of LJM. But Skilling and his assistant, Sherri Sera, have both denied to investigators ever receiving the memo or Mintz's calls. "I would have met with Jordan in an instant," Skilling has said. "Why didn't Jordan come up and talk to me?"

Though Mintz didn't know it, things were already changing. Skilling told confidants that he was beginning to worry that Fastow was spending far more than three hours a week on LJM2. "We used to talk about Enron most of the time, and now we're spending most of the time talking about LJM and the balance sheet," he complained. And the criticism from the investment community was intensifying. It was becoming quite clear that the existence of LJM2 was not helping Enron's stock. If nothing else got Skilling's attention, that certainly did.

And so, on a Friday afternoon that spring, Skilling called Fastow into his office. LJM was taking up too much of the CFO's time, Skilling said. Now, Fastow had to make a choice. "Do you want to be CFO of Enron," Skilling asked, "or do you want to run LJM?" Fastow asked for the weekend to think about it. On Monday, he gave Skilling the answer: "I want to be the CFO of Enron."

Mintz later described the moment Fastow told him that he had decided to sell his interest as "melodramatic." "I created LJM," Fastow said. He seemed almost heartbroken at the thought of giving it up and giving up as well his dreams of

LJM3. "I'm really sad I've got to divorce myself." Fastow said that the partnership agreement gave him free rein to sell his interest to anyone of his choosing. He put Credit Suisse First Boston in charge of setting an appropriate purchase price.

In late July, Fastow sold his interest in the two LJM funds. The buyer was none other than Michael Kopper, whom Fastow had persuaded to leave Enron to take over the partnership. Causey, the government later alleged, assured Kopper that the deal would be lucrative, because Enron would continue to do plenty of business with LJM to meet its financial reporting goals.

Kopper paid Fastow a total of $16.35 million. Of that amount, $15.5 million was cash; the rest came in the form of Kopper's house, valued at $850,000, which he turned over to Fastow. (Fastow planned to give the house to his parents.)

Where did Kopper get the cash? He got a loan from Citigroup, which, according to the government, noted in a memo that the loan should be approved because "many [Enron] transactions will continue to flow through LJM." According to the terms of the loan, though, Kopper had to repay at least $8 million by the end of 2001. That too was easy. When LJM1 sold its Cuiabá stake back to Enron, Kopper, as the new general partner, was entitled to a distribution of $7.3 million. He apparently used the proceeds to repay Citi. (Kopper's total take from Chewco and the LJM partnership amounted to $33.5 million.)

Naturally, Kopper also was paid to leave Enron. Under the terms of his separation agreement he received $905,000. In addition, his departure was termed an involuntary termination, which meant that all of Kopper's options and restricted stock vested. On his way out the door, Kopper asked to be able to stay in his Enron office, and he wanted all of the legal and accounting expenses he incurred in connection with the LJM purchase to be paid for by Enron. Though his request to keep his office was denied, Enron agreed to pick up the tab for Kopper's expenses. (He kept his Enron cell phone, too.) In late August, Global Finance held a going-away party for Kopper at the Ruggles Grill. The charge was $4,815.76. Enron paid, of course.

Few at Enron knew that it was Michael Kopper to whom Fastow had sold his interest in LJM. Enron's shareholders weren't told. The directors say they weren't told, either, but they didn't ask. Nor did the board ever ask how much Fastow had made from selling his interest. As far as the board and management were concerned, Fastow's exit from the partnership had brought an easy end to any problems anyone might have with the company's involvement in LJM.

On May 6, Enron's "mindnumbingly complex" financial disclosures became one of the subjects of a skeptical report written by Mark Roberts, a well-respected short seller and researcher who runs a firm called Off Wall Street Consulting.

Roberts dug deeply into Enron's financial report for 2000, which had been released in late March. He noted Enron's increased reliance on trading and the seeming cluelessness of the Street analysts who were recommending the stock. He scrutinized the related-party transactions and noted that none of the "numerous industry experts and analysts" he asked were able to explain the footnotes to him. He also noted other oddities revealed in that filing, such as the information that Enron had received $2.4 billion in proceeds from securitizations, and that Enron, by using swaps, appeared to be retaining an unknowable amount of risk. "These are, in effect, sales with recourse to Enron," Roberts wrote.

One of Roberts's most devastating revelations had to do with Enron's cash flow. In 2000, Enron reported an unprecedented $4.8 billion in operating cash flow. Roberts noted that almost $2 billion of it was from customer deposits—because energy prices were so high, Enron's counterparties had to provide more collateral. But this money didn't really belong to Enron. If prices fell, it would have to be returned to the counterparties. Roberts also noted that another $1 billion in cash flow had come from a onetime sale of inventory. (Although Roberts didn't know it, another $1.5 billion in cash flow was the result of prepay transactions.) In other words, much of the $4.8 billion in cash flow wasn't cash flow at all. It was merely the illusion of cash flow.

Though most of the mainstream business press was unaware of Roberts' report, it was widely circulated among hedge-fund managers and other large institutional investors. A reporter named Peter Eavis, who wrote for the popular online financial site, TheStreet.com, followed up on Roberts's research and began writing a string of negative stories about Enron. Slowly, the heat was being turned up.

There was yet another disaster brewing: broadband. All through the winter and into the spring, even as telecom and Internet companies were collapsing, Skilling continued to insist that Enron Broadband Services was right on track. On March 23, when he conducted that conference call to assure Wall Street that Enron would hit its earnings targets, he claimed that the broadband trading business was "absolutely developing, it is ahead of plan." He also said he was "very optimistic" about the content business. Falling prices, Skilling insisted, were helping Enron gain access to network capability at lower prices, decreasing the required capital expenditures.

A few weeks later, Skilling gave a presentation at a Salomon Smith Barney investment conference in Manhattan and insisted, yet again, that collapsing prices would be good for Enron's broadband traders. Chanos attended the conference; it was the one time he saw Skilling in person. As he listened to him explain why collapsing prices were good, Chanos thought, "Are you crazy? There won't be anybody left for you to trade with!"

Inside Enron, the mismatch between rhetoric and reality was becoming increasingly stark. In fact, EBS quietly spent much of the first quarter redeploying people out of the division. In late March, Peter Eavis wrote a story for TheStreet .com citing the redeployments as evidence that EBS might be underperforming.

That day, the stock fell over 8 percent. Two days later, CBS MarketWatch, another online financial site, quoted Skilling as saying that the rumors of broadband job cuts were "absolutely not true"; Enron's PR department said the redeployments were "standard daily practice" and went so far as to say there were sixty job *openings* in broadband.

In late March, one EBS employee sent an anonymous letter to *Fortune*. "When Jeff Skilling says that it is 'absolutely not true' that there are job cuts in Broadband Services, he is not telling the truth. There have been job cuts of about 30%. These are 'redeployments,' which means that the person has 45 days to find a job elsewhere at Enron or they are terminated. Unfortunately, the other parts of Enron are also 'redeploying' people so that you are being laid off. I asked my boss who is a senior person in Enron Broadband Services about Mr. Skilling's quote. He said that he could not believe that Jeff had said this to the media. He said that he was in the meeting with Jeff where these decisions were made and that the job cuts might have been twice as large except for the need to maintain the perception that the Broadband Services business unit was being successful. I am sorry that I can't provide my name, but I don't want to be redeployed also. Employees at Enron know what the truth is. All you need to do is ask them."

During the next few months, EBS had its last gasp. A handful of executives argued that Enron needed to either acquire another company—in other words, buy a real business—or shut down EBS. Several people pushed the idea of acquiring PSI Net, an Internet service provider. (It later declared bankruptcy.) Skilling and Rice opposed the deal. Then, the Enron team briefly toyed with the idea of buying WorldCom, but they quickly realized that the combined debt made the deal impossible. With that, executives who had options elsewhere at Enron began to flee.

During this period, Skilling's moods seemed to swing wildly. In Portland, where dozens of people were redeployed, Skilling gave a mid-March speech telling them that the industry was in a meltdown. Yet that spring, Skilling also gave a pep talk to the broadband troops in Houston. Some 50 to 100 broadband employees stood around him as he spoke. "We are perfectly positioned in broadband," Skilling insisted. "This is just like gas." One executive recalls, "I could look around and see people saying, 'This is bullshit.' People thought he was nuts. Everyone was tired of hearing him say everything was just perfect."

Throughout 2001, as Enron was besieged by business issues, Skilling was also besieged by internal political issues. It was now obvious that his longtime lieutenants, like Rice and Pai, were costing the company more than they were contributing. The long-simmering resentment that Enron's young guns felt toward them was getting uglier. Yet Skilling—who took such pride in Enron's kill-or-be-killed culture—was reluctant to take any action.

When Skilling became CEO, it was assumed that one of his first tasks would be to replace himself as the company's chief operating officer. There was no way that Skilling could choose one of his old compadres to succeed him as COO. They didn't really want the job—but even if they had, Whalley and the other top traders had made it clear that there was only one acceptable candidate. That was Whalley himself. But Rice, who had been threatening to leave for some time, told Skilling that he was definitely gone if Whalley became COO.

For his part, Skilling didn't believe that Whalley was ready for the COO job. His stone-cold brilliance notwithstanding, Whalley was rough around the edges, and he knew little of the company beyond the trading organization. Some argued that he was "reckless" and pointed to such disasters as the metals deal. Executives in Enron's other divisions were panicked at the possibility that Whalley would be chosen. There was a perception that he was not encouraging to women, Louise Kitchen notwithstanding, and Skilling was worried about reinforcing the widespread view that Enron's culture was a macho one.

Yet Skilling knew that he no longer had the blind loyalty of Enron's traders, the major source of the company's profits. Whalley did. So Skilling dithered. To one insider, it appeared that he was hoping something would give and the decision would magically take care of itself. By letting the situation simmer, says one former executive, "Jeff was tightening the noose around his own neck."

By early 2001, Pai and Rice were largely no-shows, yet they continued to hold important titles and take down millions in compensation. Rice and Pai were both in charge of deeply troubled businesses. The wholesale traders' profits were hiding EES losses. The traders thought this was a grave injustice, and their resentment soon hardened into outright viciousness. One former executive from the trading side, asked to describe Ken Rice, replied: "Scumbag motherfucker." Another trader says, "We sat around asking, why Pai? Why Rice? As motivating as everything at Enron was, to see people like that getting paid . . ." He paused for a moment, then added, "We had no respect for their intellectual capital." In an effort to defuse the rage, Whalley used to tell his crew that the huge compensation the two were reaping should be rightfully thought of as founder's pay, their reward for having worked so hard in the early years to make Enron what it had become. The traders didn't want to hear it.

Finally, in 2001, the old guard started to leave. The first to go was Cliff Baxter. Baxter had always been a bundle of resentments, and it had only gotten worse over time. He viewed himself in rivalry with Fastow, and he saw the CFO's close relationship with Skilling as usurping his own position with the boss. He was also upset with Fastow's LJM deals. He would rage about Fastow, "He's a goddamn master criminal!" Baxter had also been humiliated by his treatment as head of Enron North America, where he complained about his lack of authority.

Baxter's last assignment at Enron was to sell the international assets after Project Summer fell through. It was an impossible task. The market for overseas assets was deteriorating; buyers simply couldn't be found. Baxter always had an odd arrangement with Skilling—he could work the hours that he chose, which often meant twenty-hour days followed by vacation time. But by the end of 2000, the widespread perception was that Baxter wasn't working anymore. Certainly, his heart wasn't in it.

And so, in late April, the two men agreed that Baxter would leave. The press release announcing Baxter's departure went out on May 2, noting that he was leaving to spend more time with his family. At the end of May, all the top Enron executives and their spouses—including Andy and Lea Fastow—attended a farewell dinner held in Baxter's honor.

There was no press release announcing Lou Pai's departure. He was largely a no-show in his last Enron job, running the Xcelerator. Pai had an office the size of Ken Lay's on the fiftieth floor. Xcelerator was on the fifth floor. If he came in at all, he showed up at ten and was gone by two. He spent far more time at his ranch in Colorado. The new breed of traders had once respected Pai, but now they grew angrier and angrier at his sinecure. Skilling could no longer look the other way. In June, he called Pai to tell him it was time to go.

Pai had continued unloading his shares. Just between May 18 and May 25, 2001, he sold almost a million shares. When he had finally parted with his last share, Pai had sold over $250 million worth of Enron stock—more than anybody else at the company.

And then there was Ken Rice, who had always been considered Skilling's golden boy. This was the most delicate of the three, because Rice was still running what was supposed to be a successful business, Enron Broadband Services.

Back in 2000, one of Whalley's deputies infiltrated the broadband ranks. His name was Jim Fallon, and he was a hard-nosed nuclear engineer who had become a CPA, worked at PricewaterhouseCoopers, gotten an MBA from Columbia, and joined Enron as an associate in 1993. On the trading floor Fallon had a variety of nicknames. One called him the Janitor, because he had a reputation for being able to clean up messes. Another called him J. Edgar Fallon. The rumor on the trading floor was that before he made the move to broadband, he sent a young associate down to the broadband offices late at night to snoop around people's desks and see what information he could pick up. "You always know where Fallon is standing," says another trader. "Behind you with a knife."

Fallon soon began to agitate about the staggeringly high costs in the broadband business. Along with Greg Whalley, he came up with a plan, which the two men presented to Skilling. They would take over Broadband, chop the costs dramatically, and bury it in the wholesale business. Though Rice was planning on leaving, the idea of reporting to Whalley infuriated him. Rice told Skilling that he wouldn't work for Whalley. Here was the climactic confrontation between the old guard and the new, but it was so preordained it was largely anticlimatic. At a meeting on June 15 with Rice and Fallon, Skilling made his decision: broadband would merge into wholesale. The young guns had won.

The next day, Fallon headed down to the EBS floor and began firing people; eventually he fired 50 percent of the staff. He walked into David Cox's office and said, "Get out." He also fired Kristina Mordaunt (who soon rejoined Fastow at Global Finance). EBS executives were calling Rice frantically; Rice, in turn, called Fallon to tell him that was not the way to do things. Fallon stormed into Skilling's office and asked, "Who's really in charge here?" The firings continued.

A few days later, Rice phoned Skilling to say that his decision was final: he was leaving. Skilling said, "Well, I was afraid I was going to have to fire you anyway." Rice felt betrayed. "One or two years ago, Skilling would have told Fallon to get the fuck out," he later told a friend.

Yet even so, Skilling was unwilling to cut the cord. Over a breakfast, he asked Rice to stick around, telling him that they'd come up with something else for him to do. "Don't go," Skilling said. "I know how you feel. Why don't you stick around? We'll have some fun, and we'll leave together."

Skilling started to wipe tears from his eyes. "The traders have taken over," he told Rice darkly. "These guys have gotten so powerful that I can't control them anymore." Rice agreed to stay through the end of the third quarter—he had options vesting. But in truth, Rice was gone. When you added up all the stock he had cashed in over the years, it came to over $70 million.

The official announcement that Broadband would be merged into Wholesale went out on July 12. The debacle had cost Enron some well over $1 billion.

A few people were starting to rethink their life at Enron. One veteran executive had seen the way Enron changed people. "You could see the green MBAs coming in, so happy-go-lucky and innocent," he said. "Within six months, they'd become assholes." When broadband's failure was announced, this same executive was shocked to see people from other divisions trading high-fives. *Weren't they all part of the same company?* The PRC sickened him, too. "This place has bad karma," he told his boss.

In late June, Skilling flew to California, where he was the keynote speaker at San Francisco's Commonwealth Club. It was about a week after he'd made his widely publicized crack comparing California to the *Titanic*. Just two days earlier, the FERC had imposed price controls all across the West in an effort to stem the power crisis. Politicians were vowing to punish wrongdoers. For Skilling, this was decidedly hostile territory; many Californians saw him as the person most responsible for their suffering. He insisted on going anyway—he believed his words could convince people to see it Enron's way.

Before the speech, Skilling asked Richard Sanders and Mark Haedicke for an update on PG&E's bankruptcy plans. At the end of a brief meeting, Sanders told Skilling about Death Star, Ricochet, and Fat Boy. Skilling lowered his head. Sanders does not think he had known about the schemes before then.

When Skilling arrived at the Commonwealth Club, it was surrounded by protestors. Many of them wore pig masks and waved signs saying "Skilling is a pig!" A security guard told him, "We don't know if we can protect you." A few minutes into his speech, a woman in the third row got up from her seat, ran up to him, and smashed a raspberry pie in his face. Skilling had pie everywhere, dripping down his face and all over his suit. He wiped off his face and managed to finish his speech. Although he stayed calm at the time, the incident rattled him. "I was exhausted. I was just fucking beat," he later told friends. "This is nuts."

That day the stock closed at $44.05. Never again did Enron stock close above $50 a share.

CHAPTER 20

"I Want to Resign"

"I hereby resign my position as Chief Executive Officer of Enron Corp." So begins the handwritten note addressed to Enron's board of directors. That first line is scratched out. In his small, barely legible handwriting, the writer starts over: "After much consideration [crossed out] *evaluation and consideration,* I have decided [crossed out] *concluded* that I cannot be effective in carrying out my duties as President and Chief Executive Officer of Enron Corp. Please accept my resignation effective immediately. . . ."

Jeff Skilling wrote his first resignation note on April 30, 2001, just three months into his tenure as CEO. He never sent it. But from the day he took the job he secretly had one thing uppermost in his mind: quitting.

In all the time he had been at Enron, Skilling had always seemed supremely confident; there was never so much as a crack in the facade he presented to the world. But now that he was CEO, the facade was crumbling; there was something raw about Skilling's angst. He never seemed so alone as he did once he took the job—and once things started to go awry. His old allies were leaving, and he missed them terribly—missed the good times that they represented, when they were all so excited to come to work every day and invent a new industry.

Earlier that spring, another old buddy, Amanda Martin, came to see him. She knew Skilling well, and she could see that he was falling apart. "You've got a problem," she said. "The people you're closest to and loyal to, you've made too much money for them. The next layer down, the Whalleys, the Fallons, they will slit your throat if it means they'll get to the trough faster." Once, Skilling would likely have thrown her out of his office for making a remark like that. Not now. Skilling stared out the window in silence for a few moments and then said in a sad voice, "Mandy, you're most likely right."

Another colleague remembers telling him, "Ken Rice and Lou Pai are not your friends," and he replied, "They're all I've got." Now he didn't even have them anymore.

The stock price had fallen by nearly half since August. Skilling kept doing what he'd always done—talking it up to analysts and institutional investors, making it sound as if Enron was still the greatest, coolest company ever. But they weren't buying it anymore. People in the investment community were asking tough questions and were no longer so willing to accept Skilling's tried-and-true answers. The Enron CEO had always embraced the idea that the stock market was his ultimate report card. Now that it had gone against him, he felt enormous pressure to turn it around. But he couldn't.

Then there were the pressures of actually trying to run the business. Ken Lay was nearly useless. Lay was in exit-strategy mode, planning his retirement from Enron and, as ever, preoccupied with the trappings of his office. Just before Skilling took over as CEO, Lay appeared in his office. The stock had already started to fall, the broadband business was in meltdown, and the entire state of California was blaming Enron for turning out the lights. In the midst of all this, there was Enron's chairman, holding fabric swatches for decorating the new $45 million G-5 corporate jet he'd ordered for Enron. "What interior configuration do you like, Jeff?" Lay asked.

Among the executives who reported to Skilling, the battle raged over who would become the new chief operating officer—a post he seemed incapable of filling for fear of driving away someone he thought he needed. The traders were far more loyal to Whalley than to him. And suddenly, Skilling was no longer infallible. Always before, when Skilling said the stock would go up, it went up. But not this time; now, his insistence that the stock was worth $126 a share had the scent of desperation. Skilling now hated riding in the elevator with employees.

Always before, Skilling was able to come with a new big enchilada to drive the business—and the stock price. That was the part of being a businessman that he loved. But he was out of big ideas. Righting Enron required lowering everyone's expectations—something he could not bring himself to do—and fixing problems, which he hated. "It was getting hard," says a former executive, "and Jeff doesn't do hard."

To those around Skilling, the signs of his emotional distress were clear. "He was spiraling," says one. In the best of times, Skilling was a volatile, moody character. A few years earlier, when he was still COO, he gave the finger to an employee who had almost run into his car during the morning parking rush. It was hardly the sort of gesture one expected from a big-time corporate executive. But Skilling blew off complaints about the incident, word of which spread like wildfire. "I'm an entrepreneur, not a politician," he said.

Now, in the wake of broadband's failure, some speculated that he suffered from depression. He sometimes came to work unshaven and looking haggard, as if he hadn't slept. Instead of providing ballast for Enron, he seemed to be sinking with the ship.

Skilling had always liked passing his time at little bars where he could be anonymous. Now, he was spending more and more time smoking cigarettes and drinking white wine at a handful of bars around Houston, especially one called Muldoon's. The owner didn't know who he was, at least, not until much later. But Skilling was such a regular that he gave him a nickname. "Quiet Jeff," he called Skilling.

Mark Palmer, Enron's top public-relations executive, who was himself under growing pressure trying to fend off the avalanche of bad press, had a meeting with Skilling one day. "There are mornings when I want to curl up in a ball," Palmer said.

"Man, I know *exactly* what you mean," Skilling replied and then launched into his own complaint. "I'm not having any fun," he said. "I don't like what I'm doing. I don't like this place. I'm having a hard time coming to work."

"I'm not having any fun." For much of the time he was CEO, that was Skilling's refrain.

A few days after Skilling had the pie pushed in his face in California, he and his son Jeffrey left for a trip to Spain and Morocco. They were gone from June 27 to July 8. In Enron's early years, Skilling seldom took vacations; he didn't like being away from work. During the trip he took to Africa with his son the previous year, for the first time he'd felt reluctant to return. This time, his reaction was even more severe. "I didn't want to come back," he told a friend. "I just flat out didn't want to come back."

Skilling returned in time for the release of Enron's second-quarter earnings. Some on Wall Street were speculating that Enron's traders were caught in an enormous, wrong-sided bet, that the trading desk had stayed long even as energy prices plunged. At a minimum, investors were anxious to know what the decline meant for Enron's business.

On the morning of July 12, Skilling announced that Enron had beaten Wall Street's earnings expectations for the second quarter by three cents a share. Net income was up 40 percent from a year ago. The numbers were made in the usual fashion. In May, Enron sold three power plants for just over $1 billion and included the onetime gain on that sale in its recurring earnings. In addition, traders on Tim Belden's West Power desk and John Arnold in Houston had sensed that the market was about to turn and taken big short positions ahead of the decline.

But, in fact, the rumors were partially correct, according to an internal presentation, dated May 22, concerning the performance of the wholesale business. It showed that the *gas* traders, as opposed to the power traders, had been in a huge hole. The report says that as of May 18, the gas traders were down $162 million for the quarter. Although the North American power traders were up almost $300 million—thanks to Tim Belden—hundreds of millions in additional EES losses were chewing up their gains. In all, the wholesale business was nearly $1 billion under its budget of $431 million. Yet in the last two weeks of the quarter the power and gas traders rang up an astonishing string of gains. Was it a reversal of some of the reserves stashed away from the huge gains of 2000? Or was it a sign that Enron traders, by buying or selling in huge quantities, could at least temporarily drive energy prices in the direction of their choosing? Or was it just serendipitous trading? No one may ever know.

But while the traders were able to save earnings, there was nothing they could do about the company's cash flow, which was melting away. In fact, they were the source of the problem. Remember the nearly $2 billion in customer deposits Enron had booked as cash flow in 2000? As energy prices collapsed, Enron had to send it all back to its counterparties and then some. As Glisan jotted in his notebook, "Margin & inventory has eaten convert proceeds." This referred to $1.3 billion in convertible debt Enron raised earlier in the year. He continued, "Giving back margin we previously took in. Should be offset from the cash of the transaction liquidating through the book, but we have not seen that yet."

Yet during the conference call and the round of media interviews that followed, Skilling was his old self. "If investors played the old Bob Newhart drinking game and had to refill their mugs every time Skilling said 'outstanding' in relation to second-quarter performance, they would have been drunk before the question-and-answer period," one commentator joked. The CEO pointed out that Enron had met or exceeded analysts' earnings expectations every quarter for the past four years.

Although Skilling finally had to publicly admit defeat on broadband— "there's a meltdown out there"—he reassured investors that Enron would quickly reduce costs to "match the revenue opportunities available." To Bloomberg News, which asked about Dabhol, Skilling insisted that Enron had "zero intention of taking any economic loss on the project. Zero." He was also quick to downplay the importance of broadband to the company's prospects. "The real story for Enron," he told CNNfn, "is this strong, strong growth and strong profitability of our energy business."

But neither sixteen straight quarters of increased earnings nor the reiteration of buy ratings from the analysts did anything for Enron's stock, which stubbornly refused to climb above $50 a share.

Instead, in private deliberations in sequestered boardrooms, major institutions were beginning to reevaluate their position on Enron. Unlike the public buy recommendations from the equity analysts, though, these private decisions never came to the attention of the small investor. Between March and the end of June, four large holders—Janus, Fidelity, American Express, and American Century— sold a total of 21.3 million shares, according to an internal Enron document.

One major Wall Street firm that traded with Enron began to watch its exposure more carefully and ever so slowly cut back the amount of money it would allow Enron to owe at any point. "We thought Enron was a very funky animal that kept getting funkier and funkier," says a credit officer there.

Remember the credit derivatives market that Enron had hoped to break into? Many banks use that market to hedge their exposure to loans. Buying credit protection is a very private way to protect themselves against the possibility that a company's credit might slide. Derivatives on Enron's credit had always been expensive—which meant there had long been higher-than-normal nervousness about its credit worthiness. Now, according to Creditex, a credit-derivatives firm, the premiums to buy an Enron credit-derivative began to skyrocket, which meant that the market's perception of the risk was increasing dramatically.

Enron's bankers at J. P. Morgan Chase were especially nervous. On the day of Enron's earnings announcement, Anatol Feygin, the J. P. Morgan analyst, re-iterated his buy rating on Enron shares in an upbeat report. On that same day, James Ballentine, a J. P. Morgan banker, sent an e-mail to a number of other executives at the bank, including Ken Lay's old acquaintance Marc Shapiro, who was vice chairman in charge of risk management. The executives wanted to know "what has been done on Enron," and Ballentine was updating them. He sent them a list of the bank's current exposure, which included loan commitments of $605 million and counterparty exposure of $275 million.

Ballentine also told his colleagues a stunning fact. "Net short positions add up to $295 million, which is one of the five-largest short positions in the North American corporate book," he wrote. In other words, one of Enron's biggest lenders was also betting against it. "We will look to add to our short positions on an opportunistic basis. . . ." Ballentine added.

Something else happened on July 12—something important because it shows the extent to which Enron's enablers became complicit in the deception. Remember Marlin, Enron's oh-so-clever way to get the Azurix debt off its balance sheet? The debt, which amounted to almost $1 billion, was due at the end of 2001, and just as the short sellers had long suspected, Azurix wasn't worth nearly enough to pay it back. Which meant, of course, that Enron itself was on the hook for the money.

Back when Marlin was set up, in 1998, Enron promised to issue stock if the assets backing Marlin proved insufficient to repay the debt. But now that the moment was arriving, Enron was adamant about *not* wanting to issue new stock. Given the questions that were swirling around the company, that was the last thing Enron wanted to do.

Once again, Enron's enablers came to the rescue, allowing Enron to refinance the Marlin debt. In a CSFB-led deal, Enron raised a fresh $1 billion to pay off old investors and extend the terms of the debt for another two years. This new deal contained the same provisions as the old one: all the debt came due at once if Enron lost its investment-grade rating status—and if its stock fell below $34.13.

The most shocking fact was this: there was clear evidence that Enron would have to pay the Marlin debt in some fashion, because in the offering documents, bankers estimated the value of the Azurix stake supporting it at a maximum of $700 million and as little as $50 million. Yet the rating agencies didn't sound any alarms, and the accountants still allowed Enron to classify the Marlin debt as "off-balance-sheet."

• • •

On Friday, July 13, the afternoon after the earnings announcement, Skilling went to Ken Lay's office. Lay had just gotten back from a trip to India in yet another effort to resolve the ever-worsening problems at Dabhol. He already knew Skilling was unhappy; his CEO had been complaining to Lay for several months. "How are you doing?" Lay asked. "I'm not doing great," Skilling replied. "I want to resign."

Lay was stunned. "Why?" he asked. Skilling's first response was that he wanted to spend more time with his family; his children were approaching college age, and if he didn't spend the time with them now, he would never have the opportunity. Lay later said that when he pushed further, Skilling told him that he was under a great deal of pressure—he was taking the stock price decline personally, and he couldn't sleep at night.

What happened next is still a mystery—one that only two people know the answer to. The common perception is that Lay was horrified at the prospect of losing Skilling. It wasn't that he was happy with his CEO's performance; he blamed Skilling for the falling stock price just as much as Skilling blamed himself. But what sort of message would it send to the already shaky market if the new CEO left after only six months? And since Skilling had not yet picked a chief operating officer, the only obvious successor was Lay himself. Lay hadn't had much to do with running Enron for years; he really didn't know much about the inner workings of the company. On top of that, he was contemplating leaving the company himself; rumor had it that he would make a graceful exit by running for mayor of Houston. Lay has said that he asked Skilling to reconsider over the weekend.

When the two met again on Monday morning, Skilling was still adamant about resigning. Lay called another board participant and told him Skilling was resigning. This person replied: "Don't let this happen. You don't want this to happen." Lay told some board members that Skilling was going through a bad patch and that he was working very hard to keep him. He later claimed that some of the members of the board spoke to Skilling and urged him to stay.

Skilling has told a very different story. He has claimed that Lay made no effort to convince him to stay and that he would have been willing to stay for up to six months to ease the transition. He has also told friends that not one board member ever called him.

If Skilling had indeed been willing to stay for a transition period, the board never knew that. One former outside board member recalls, when he first learned that Skilling wanted to resign, expressing his concerns to Lay. "I thought Skilling's resignation would hurt the company's credibility and told Lay to try to talk him out of it. If he couldn't, I asked Lay to try to get Skilling to stay on for an additional six months to a year to facilitate a smooth transition. This would have given us time to rebuild our senior management team. Lay apparently raised this with Skilling, because he told me well before the August 2001 board meeting that Skilling said he wanted to resign after the second-quarter earnings release and was unwilling to stay on for even a day after the August board meeting."

Not having fun anymore? Whoever said being a CEO was supposed to be "fun"? Board member John Duncan later told investigators that he was "disappointed" with Skilling's decision. "Skilling had been with the company for ten years and knew what being CEO entailed," Duncan also said.

What is clear is that Skilling's decision was kept very, very quiet.

After meeting with Lay, Skilling had lunch with Cliff Baxter. Baxter looked fabulous. He was spending time on his boat and clearly enjoying his new life. A few days later, Skilling took his daughter, Kristin, on vacation. They didn't return until July 22.

Ken Lay had a great deal more on his mind than Jeff Skilling's unhappiness. Although it seems almost unfathomable, Lay was fighting off his creditors. To the outside world, Lay was the very picture of corporate success, as Enron itself had been for so long. But in truth, here was a more telling way in which Lay personified the company he led: like his company, Lay's financial strength was an illusion.

Even in retrospect, Lay's financial catastrophe is hard to fathom. Over the previous few years, he had realized over $200 million from salary, bonus, and the exercise of Enron stock options; as of early 2001, he owned some five million Enron shares that were then worth $350 million. In 2001, as part of a plan to diversify his holdings, he was cashing in options—almost $30 million worth in the first six months of the year. And as chairman, he was still being paid an annual salary of $975,000.

Lay's finances, however, were built around the belief that Enron's stock would never go down. During most of the 1990s, Lay had most of his net worth in Enron stock. In 1999, his advisers began pestering him to diversify. But he did so in a manner that wound up, in effect, doubling his bet on the stock. Here's what he did: Lay pledged almost all of his portfolio of liquid assets—primarily Enron stock—as collateral for bank and brokerage loans. According to the *New York Times*, Lay had loans from PaineWebber, First Union, and the small Compass Bank, in addition to multiple lines of credit from Bank of America: a $40 million line for him and Linda, a $10 million line for his family partnership, and another $11.7 million line that allowed him to buy a piece of Houston's new professional football team. By early January 2001, Lay owed $95 million to his various creditors.

Lay then used the money he had borrowed to make other investments. He turned some of it over to various money managers. He also made a series of high-risk illiquid investments. (At the same time, Kopper and Fastow were putting their ill-gotten gains into municipal bonds.) With his son, Mark, Lay invested in privately held technology companies, including one called EterniTV, a start-up that planned to deliver video services over the Web, and EC Outlook, a supply-chain-management software company. (EterniTV was supposed to deliver its services by Enron Broadband.) He invested nearly $20 million in Questia, a Houston company that sold access to online books. He was so excited about Questia that he joined the board and pushed Skilling to invest, too. (Skilling declined.)

The parallel was eerie: to a stunning degree Lay's personal finances resembled Enron's dealings with the Raptors. But in a sense, Lay was making an even bigger bet on Enron stock than Andy Fastow had. Because so many of his investments—including his three multimillion-dollar homes in Aspen—were illiquid, Enron stock was the primary means by which he supported his loans. So long as Enron stock kept rising, Lay was fine. But if Enron's stock went south, Lay was in big trouble, and the further it fell, the deeper his trouble.

And Lay had left himself very little room to maneuver: as was the case with many of Enron's own deals, Lay's arrangements with his banks contained triggers, according to the *New York Times*. If Enron stock fell below $80, he faced margin calls. If the stock fell below $60, he would almost certainly be in violation of his loan terms. In 2001, as Enron stock hit the $80 trigger and then the $60 trigger, Lay, just like his company, became desperate.

Frantic for a way out, Lay decided to secretly take advantage of a little-known quirk surrounding executive loans: they can at times be paid off by selling stock back to the company. What's more, unlike regular executive stock sales, which have to be disclosed almost at once, these sales don't have to be disclosed until after the end of the year. Back in May 1999, Lay had modified his loan agreement to include this loophole; starting in November 2000, Lay began repeatedly drawing down a $4 million line of credit he had with Enron, using it to pay off his creditors and then repaying the loan by selling stock. As Enron's stock fell and the margin calls came faster—he got 15 written margin calls in total—Lay used it with increasing frequency. In June alone, he took out a total of $24 million in loans from Enron, repaying them by selling stock. By late July, he had sold $52 million in stock this way. One board member later called the practice Lay's "ATM approach."

Lay later argued that his stock sales were not a sign that he no longer believed in the company; rather, he sold because he had no choice. By using the secret loans to pay the margin calls instead of selling shares outright, he was bettting that Enron's stock would rebound and he would thus have to sell fewer shares to repay the company. In order to avoid selling Enron stock, Lay got at least one creditor to accept illiquid collateral instead. He began trying to sell his interest in the football team. That summer, Lay converted some 200,000 options into stock—and didn't sell. At the end of July, he also stopped his daily sales of 2,500 shares because he thought that Enron shares, then around $45, were underpriced.

But it's hard to believe that Lay didn't have another motive in choosing this method for repaying his creditors: he could keep it secret, at least for a while. He did not tell Jim Derrick, Enron's general counsel. He did not tell Enron's directors; they publicly professed horror when they found out. As director Charles LeMaistre later told a congressional committee, "One of the lines in the Enron code says that you will do nothing to hurt the interest of Enron, and taking this much money out and repaying it with stock when the stock is declining certainly is very devious. It is very difficult for me to understand why that did not hurt Enron." Nor did Lay tell investigators who explicitly asked him about his stock sales shortly after Enron collapsed. Instead, he said that *Enron* decided whether loans were to be repaid in stock or cash and that he had "made some payments for the loan toward the end of 2001."

What's impossible to know is how Lay's financial crisis factored into his feelings about Skilling's performance as CEO. Today, Lay insists that it didn't. But given how critical Enron's stock price was to his own fortunes, how could it not?

After returning from his trip with his daughter, Skilling continued to act like the CEO. He handled the PRC meetings at the St. Regis Hotel on the twenty-third and twenty-fourth of July and then flew to New York along with investor-relations head Mark Koenig and Andy Fastow—who was fulfilling his promise to act more like a CFO—to meet with analysts and investors. In the meetings with investors, Skilling was as arrogant and prickly as ever. He bragged that Enron's market share in natural gas and power was over three times higher than its next competitor, Duke. "We will hit those numbers, and we will beat those numbers," he told attendees, in response to worries about Enron's earnings.

During the meeting, the Enron team also showed a slide entitled Recent Investor Concerns. The list included California, India, Broadband, Cash Flow & Financing Vehicles, and "Trading" in Enron's Business Model. The executives told investors that LJM was no longer a cause for concern, because Enron was "eliminating the related-party relationship with LJM." As for all the other problems, Skilling dismissed them. "All of these are bunk," he said. "These are not issues for this stock."

That weekend, Skilling went to Aspen with Rebecca Carter; he had asked her to marry him back in June, when he was already thinking seriously about leaving Enron. Upon his return, Skilling had lunch on consecutive days with Ken Rice then Lou Pai. He did not talk about work at all—which was extremely rare for Jeff Skilling.

On August 3, Skilling appeared at EES for one of his periodic state-of-the-business floor meetings. As one hundred employees gathered around, Skilling climbed on a desk and offered his usual gung-ho speech. Everything was going great, he said. EES was going to be one of Enron's shining stars, maybe even its top division. Why in three years, Skilling predicted, EES was going to be making a half-billion dollars!

But even inside Enron, the old Skilling magic wasn't working anymore. The questions were skeptical. *How'd we make our numbers this quarter? Why are you selling so much of your own stock?* And finally, from Margaret Ceconi:

"You say we're going to make half a billion a year, Jeff. How in the world are we going to do that? What's your strategy?"

"Well, that's what you guys are for," Skilling responded. "You guys are the creative ones—you've got to figure it out." That afternoon, EES laid off three hundred people, including Ceconi.

If Skilling did have any second thoughts about his decision to leave Enron—and he has insisted that he did not—something happened that cemented his decision. On August 8, there was a massive explosion during routine maintenance work at Teesside. Three workers were killed; another man, gravely burned, was sent to the hospital. Roughly two hundred employees had to be evacuated, as black smoke billowed everywhere.

Skilling heard the news when he arrived at work that morning. He was visibly shaken and disturbed. He immediately took a company plane to England, where he met with all the Teesside employees, visited the surviving man in the hospital, and went to see the families of those who had been killed. He later told people it was the "worst day of my life." He seemed traumatized by the deaths. "It was just awful," he said. "These guys were good guys. The day before they were good guys, and the next day they were dead."

It was at the end of this week that the news began to circulate inside Enron. Lay finally told another senior Enron executive that Skilling was leaving. That person was shocked. "Don't be," Lay said. "This has been an issue for a while."

Over the weekend, Mark Palmer, Enron's head PR man, met with Skilling at the home of Steve Kean, Enron's chief of staff, to help draft the resignation press release. "You have to be prepared for people to be angry with you," Palmer told Skilling. Skilling later called Palmer. He sounded deeply depressed. "You just have to trust me," he said. "I had to do this."

On August 13, Enron held its regularly scheduled board meeting. Skilling attended the day-long session in his role as CEO and board member. One of the subjects the board talked about were four new disaster scenarios Rick Buy and his risk-assessment group had put together at Skilling's request. One scenario Buy presented envisioned a truly chilling chain of events. It begins with the announcement that Enron would miss its quarterly-earnings target, triggering a massive stock sell-off. This, in turn, leads to the collapse of the company's balance sheet, because it forces the unwinding of all the off-balance-sheet vehicles that were capitalized with Enron stock, which prompts downgrades in Enron's credit ratings, which trigger the material adverse change clauses in the company's trading contracts, which cause its trading partners to start demanding that Enron post cash collateral, which of course it doesn't have. All of this, in turn, wipes out Enron's remaining liquidity and destroys investor confidence.

But Skilling and Ben Glisan dismissed the odds of this ever happening. Enron, the executives noted, had plenty of committed sources of emergency cash.

• • •

That evening, there was a working dinner in the Austin Room at Houston's Four Seasons Hotel that included board members and Enron's top executives. The dinner began at 7:30. Forty minutes later, Lay called for an executive session, meaning that only the board members could stay in the room. Causey, Fastow, Koenig, and Rebecca Carter left the meeting; Lay stayed. That's when Skilling announced his resignation.

It was a short and extremely emotional meeting. Skilling was in tears. He wept openly as he told the board how much he loved Enron but also how guilty he felt that he hadn't "been there" for his children. He insisted, however, that the press release announcing his resignation not say anything about his family, because he did not want his children to feel responsible. He refused to allow the board to say that he was resigning for health reasons, even though everyone present was worried about Skilling's mental health. Ken Lay later said that Enron's directors tried to convince Skilling to stay, but he was adamant. He had already agreed to forfeit his severance pay and to repay a $2 million loan. At 8:40, Skilling left the room. It had taken all of a half-hour.

The next day, the board concluded its business in the morning. Skilling left the meeting at 11:35. "I've resigned," he told his assistant, Sherri Sera. The news flew through the halls of Enron.

After the stock market closed that day, the press release announcing Skilling's resignation hit the wires. The explanation given for Skilling's decision to quit was both curt and bewildering. "I am resigning for personal reasons," Skilling said in the statement. "I want to thank Ken Lay for his understanding of this purely personal decision. . . ." Mark Palmer argued to Lay that the company needed to say something more to calm the markets: "Ken, 'personal reasons' ain't going to fly. Is Jeff sick?"

"It depends on how you define sick," Lay replied.

That evening, Enron held a conference call with analysts and investors to discuss Skilling's resignation and to announce that Lay would be stepping back into his old job. Again, company officials refused to offer any explanation beyond the vague one already given. "The numbers, the earnings show that the company is just in excellent shape right now," Skilling told investors. "There is nothing to disclose, the company is in great shape, and I just want to reinforce it . . . the company is in great shape . . . everybody that has looked at the numbers knows, this is an entirely personal decision . . ."

Lay sounded equally sanguine. "If anything, there seems to be even a little acceleration in the company's both financial performance and operational performance," he said. Investors pressed for more. "Could you confirm that there are no accounting issues?" asked one person on the conference call. Lay replied: "There are no accounting issues, no trading issues, no reserve issues, no previously unknown problem issues. I think I can honestly say that the company is probably in the strongest and best shape that it has probably ever been in."

In after-hours trading, Enron's stock plunged to about $40 a share.

To the outside world, the whole thing was bizarre. A hyperaggressive CEO walks out the door with little warning barely six months into the job? (Although Lay had known for a month that Skilling was leaving, he told reporters that he and Skilling had discussed the matter for only a few days. "I certainly didn't expect it," he said.) No one in the press could shed any light on what the personal reasons were. The math made it even more puzzling. Skilling was walking away from some $22 million: an outstanding loan of $2 million, which would have been forgiven had he merely stayed until the end of 2001, and a severance package worth $20 million. His strange resignation fueled another round of intense speculation that something was terribly wrong inside Enron. Otherwise, why would he be so desperate to get out?

One analyst, Prudential's Carol Coale, wrote a tough note to her clients the next morning, openly questioning whether Skilling was really leaving for personal reasons. She pointed out that he was gettting married soon and had moved into the house he'd just finished building. She pointedly suggested that his departure might well mean that there were deeper problems at Enron than the company was acknowledging.

Coale, who is based in Houston, was one of the most influential Enron analysts. She formally warned the company that she was considering downgrading the stock; Lay was supposed to have lunch with her to allay her concerns. But when she arrived at Enron's headquarters and got to the executive suite, she bumped into Skilling, who had begged Lay to let him talk to her. He told her that he was so sure Wall Street wanted him gone that he was surprised the stock hadn't gone up on the news. Coale told him that she didn't buy his story. In vague terms, Skilling began to talk about the personal reasons he had for leaving. "He was close to tears," Coale recalls. "It was very emotional. And it made me very emotionally upset. I walked out of the meeting, and I was very shaken." She was convinced enough by his explanation that she wound up not changing her rating on the stock.

Most of the analysts reiterated their buy ratings as well. "Intensive meetings with ENE management continue to show no truth to any of the speculations," said CSFB's Curt Launer, who also kept his price target at $84 a share. But by now, even some of the bulls on Enron stock had become nervous. UBS Warburg's Ron Barone kept his buy rating but offered a warning instead of his usual reassurance. "The reality is Enron has lost substantial employee talent over the past 12 months," he wrote in a note to his clients. "In addition . . . the company has been plagued with a series of negative issues while its overall quality of earnings has deteriorated, its level of behind the scenes engineering has increased, and its overall standing with the Street has plunged." Merrill Lynch's Donato Eassey actually downgraded the stock.

Over at Kynikos, Jim Chanos, who once thought the bottom for Enron's stock was some $30 a share, shorted what he calls an "aggressive" amount of stock.

Chanos had uncovered something new. Skilling's departure coincided exactly with the release of the second-quarter 10-Q, which showed that despite Enron's stellar earnings, its cash flow from operations was a *negative* $1.3 billion for the first six months of the year. That day, Enron's stock fell 6 percent, to $40.25. Premiums in the credit derivatives market shot up almost 20 percent.

If the outside world was mystified by the personal reasons, most people inside Enron were equally bewildered—and worried. For years, everyone at Enron had banked on Skilling's brilliance. Mark Palmer's catchphrase was, "I'm not necessarily long Enron, but I'm long Jeff Skilling." Others felt the same way. In many quarters, the confusion quickly turned into caustic anger. "You don't do that," says a former executive, meaning "quit." "You don't do that if you're running the 7-Eleven on the corner."

On the trading floor, some decided that his abrupt departure wasn't that surprising after all. "With that type of personality, there's the wild-card factor," says one former trader. "There's a little secretiveness and a lot of unknowns." Some decided they didn't care; watching Skilling hype broadband all the way down had dented their faith. "The bloom was off the rose," says one. Yet other traders quickly came up with their version of a *Titanic* joke: "Women and children first—right after Jeff."

But true to trader form, they didn't waste a lot of time worrying about why Skilling had left. Almost immediately, it was yesterday's news, and now, Skilling was definitively no longer one of them. "You're either in the fight or you're not," is how one former trader puts it. Besides that, they had something far more important to worry about. Who was going to take Skilling's place in Enron's office of the chairman and get in line to be the CEO when Lay stepped aside?

The already difficult task of explaining Skilling's departure became even more difficult the next morning, when the *Wall Street Journal* printed a story by reporter John Emshwiller, who had interviewed Skilling. Instead of sticking to the script, Skilling told Emshwiller that Enron's stock had been "kind of an ultimate scorecard"; the *Journal* cast the plunging stock price as the main reason for his resignation. Skilling said that if the stock had stayed up, "I don't think I would have felt the pressure to leave." The story infuriated Ken Lay, who saw Skilling's comments as a betrayal of the company. Who was going to believe "personal reasons" after that?

So *did* Skilling have personal reasons beyond the falling stock price? In conversations with friends, he has blamed a number of things. He has claimed that he was burned out, just like Rice and Pai and Baxter. ("I had to do this. I had to do this. I could not continue to work. This was brutal. This was a brutal ten years. I don't think anyone realizes how hard it is to build a company.") He has talked about the problems in his personal life. ("I broke up my marriage. I didn't pay attention to my kids.") He has talked about the way he felt handcuffed by the board. ("I didn't like the fact that the board was Ken's. No matter what I did, I was never going to be in a position to run the company.") And he has blamed Baxter's departure. ("That hurt.")

If indeed there was one specific personal reason, no one, not even his closest friends, knew what it was. But the explanation at the other end of the spectrum— that Skilling saw what was coming and tried to escape—is also probably simplistic. It is difficult to find any evidence that Skilling—who once told *BusinessWeek* that he had "never not been successful at work or business, ever"—has ever admitted that he failed at Enron. Not even to himself.

What seems clear is that Skilling's comment to the *Wall Street Journal* came the closest to the truth: no matter what the real condition of Enron's business, if the stock had continued to climb, Skilling would not have quit. Skilling wasn't lying when he said he was leaving for personal reasons—the stock's steep fall *was* personal. For Jeff Skilling, Enron's stock price was one of the most deeply personal things in his life.

The day after Skilling resigned, his brother Mark flew in from Turkey. When he left on August 23, Skilling also left town for a rafting trip with his son. Meanwhile, Rebecca Carter began working out the details of her separation agreement from Enron. She negotiated a severance of $875,000.

Skilling told friends he had lots of plans. He wanted to go to Africa for a few months and drive from Cape Town to Nairobi. He wanted to learn to speak a foreign language fluently. He was talking to universities about teaching. Of course, true to Enron form, he was also continuing to collect money from the company— Ken Lay couldn't even cut Jeff Skilling off. In return for consulting services, Skilling was slated to get office space, an assistant paid for by Enron, and $60,000 a month. (He never got any of this money.)

Skilling also took care of his own finances. Since May 2000, he had sold over 450,000 shares of Enron worth some $33 million. In mid-September, he sold another 500,000 shares, bringing his total proceeds to over $70 million.

As for Skilling's mood, it seemed to oscillate between depression, righteous indignation, and manic excitement about the next big enchilada. When he came by Enron's office on August 22 to show his brother what a cool company he had run, an Enron veteran named Jim Schwieger, who had worked at the old Inter-North, saw him. Schwieger says that Skilling's eyes were bloodshot and he was unshaven. Schwieger ran after him down the hall just to say, "Jeff, we're all adults. People had the option to sell at $89. You can't take responsibility for that." Skilling shook his hand. He later told a friend he was surprised by the weird quiet in the halls. He had expected people to be high-fiving him, congratulating him on his new life.

A few days later, the *Houston Chronicle* published an interview with Skilling in which he ranted about how people couldn't get that he had quit for personal reasons. "I deserve a break. I honestly believe that." He added, "If people come back and write the history of Enron Corporation, they'll look at my tenure as

CEO. It was not great for the stock price. I wish it wasn't that way. It is what it is. I think what I would ask, and I would hope people would look at, is what earnings did."

Skilling also told the paper that his business career wasn't finished. "I think that there will be some new big idea," he said. "I don't know what that big idea will be." To find it, he planned to rent office space—with Ken Rice and Lou Pai.

CHAPTER 21

The $45 Million Question

Two days after becoming CEO of Enron once again, Ken Lay arrived for an all-hands meeting at the Imperial Ballroom of the Hyatt Hotel, just down the street from Enron headquarters. There, he found himself greeted like a Roman hero, returning from genteel retirement to resume command of the republic at a fateful moment. Hundreds of Enron employees packed into the ballroom jumped up to applaud—and kept applauding—until Lay, wearing shirtsleeves and an aw-shucks grin, finally quieted down the room. "Well, I'm delighted to be back," he announced.

Of course, he'd never been gone. Ken Lay had been the one constant at Enron since its birth in 1985 and had been richly rewarded for his role. But that was lost on most of this crowd—especially the older hands—who held Skilling responsible for all that had gone awry. With Enron's stock below $38 a share, they were desperate for a savior.

As in ancient times, there were plotters in the room. The traders, led by Greg Whalley, were particularly wary of Lay's "return." Furious as they were at Skilling for abandoning them, they'd always viewed Lay as little more than a political fixer, not really a part of Enron's actual business. All that really mattered to them was who Lay named as chief operating officer. Rumors were already flying, and there weren't many names the traders deemed worthy of their respect.

Earlier, Lay had signaled his view of Enron's condition—and his mission—in the e-mail he wrote announcing Skilling's departure. "I want to assure you I have never felt better about the prospects for the company. . . . One of my top priorities will be to restore a significant amount of the stock value we have lost as soon as possible. . . . Our performance has never been stronger. Our business model has never been more robust; our growth has never been more certain."

Now, standing before the faithful, Lay insisted that there was nothing wrong with Enron that a good dose of PR couldn't cure. "I'm excited," Lay declared. "I think we've got a lot of great stuff going on. We're not getting much credit for it in the marketplace for damn sure, but we will."

Lay sounded remarkably glib, even dismissive, about any business issues; it was as though he were reading from one of Skilling's leftover scripts. California was to blame for its problems. ("Now, I will tell you what I think about California. No, I really *won't*—probably not in mixed company.") Dabhol was a mere annoyance. ("Well, India's India, and that's about the best we can do. . . . It seems to pop up about every five years."). EES, which had just announced lay-offs, "just keeps banging away and just keeps growing at a tremendous rate." Lay even waxed optimistic about broadband and repeated Skilling's mantra to Wall Street: "We are not a trading company; we are a logistics and service company." Enron, he declared, has an "unassailable competitive advantage unless we shoot ourselves in the foot."

In fact, as Lay described it, there was really just one area where things needed to change—values. "I think we slipped a little bit on this recently, and we've got to restore it," Lay declared. "Values are incredibly important to the fiber of this company."

Finally Lay turned to the topic uppermost on everyone's minds—the collapse of the stock. When he agreed to return as CEO, the board awarded him a big new slug of Enron stock and options. (Under continuing pressure from creditors, Lay also persuaded the board to give him $10 million cash in exchange for two annuities he owned, even though a board consultant concluded that the cash value of the contracts was just $4.7 million.)

Now, to loud applause, Lay announced a special onetime options grant, vesting immediately, to every Enron employee, amounting to 5 percent of base salary. The stock was surely near "the bottom of this cycle," Lay said, and "we want you to enjoy the ride back up."

About an hour after the employee meeting, Lay boarded an Enron jet and flew to New York. He was headed to a hastily called dinner meeting at the Four Seasons to calm the analyst community. Andy Fastow met him there; the Enron CFO had flown up that morning to meet with rating-agency analysts and to have lunch with two LJM investors who had recently learned of Fastow's decision to sell his interest in the partnership and turn it over to Michael Kopper. Fastow, who harbored aspirations of becoming COO himself, was conspicuously making the point that he'd cast his lot with Enron. That very day, he later let it be known, he'd bought 10,000 shares of Enron stock on the open market.

Enron shares had slipped six dollars just since Skilling had quit. Eager to convince the two dozen invited analysts that Skilling's departure did not signal some big problem at Enron, Lay detailed (off the record, of course) how Skilling had unraveled under the pressure of the job; one analyst later told a reporter that Lay said Skilling had been going "kind of nuts." Lay promised more open communication with Wall Street and clearer financial reports and repeated his pitch about the health of the business. The analysts came away convinced, standing behind their buy ratings. "The Enron machine is in top shape and continues to roll along," Lehman's Richard Gross advised investors. CSFB's Curt Launer pointedly stuck by his $84-a-share target price.

Responding to all the intrigue about his departure, including rumors that Lay had forced him out, Skilling offered himself up for a phone interview with a

Dow Jones energy columnist, insisting that he had left the fast track behind to get in touch with the important things in life, like family, building houses for poor people, and serving as a spokesman for the city of Houston. "I've spent the last 34 years working really hard," said Skilling, then 47, dating that period back to his days as a 13-year-old TV-station production assistant in Aurora, Illinois. "It's not true that I was cracking up," he said. "Do I *sound* like someone who is cracking up?" As for Enron, Skilling insisted: "The company I built is doing great."

Sherron Watkins wasn't so sure. A midlevel Enron veteran, Watkins, 41, had traveled a familiar path to Enron—through the revolving doors of Arthur Andersen. Hired in 1993 by Fastow, she was like many Enron employees: bright, mercenary, and ambitious. Like many, she'd made the rounds at the company, moving from Enron Gas Services to International to Broadband. Also like many of her colleagues, Watkins had earned her biggest payday—a $175,000 bonus—from a big deal (in 1999, in Korea) that ultimately lost money. But long before that became apparent, she'd sunk the bonus money and her Enron stock options into a heady new lifestyle: a $500,000 home in Southampton, just a few blocks from Kopper and Fastow; vacations in Italy and Mexico; and a green Lexus SUV. Her base salary was about $150,000.

Caught up as she was in the Enron whirl, Watkins nevertheless possessed a deep contrarian streak. She was stubborn and blunt, with a mouth that could embarrass a trader ("dickweed" and "circle jerk" were among her favorites). Trained as a CPA, Watkins was quick to grasp the larger meaning of numbers. Inside Enron, she was called the Buzzsaw.

By June 2001, Watkins was an Enron vice president, married with a two-year-old daughter, and the chief breadwinner in her family. Amid broadband's collapse, she had nervously accepted redeployment back to the domain of Andy Fastow, whom she'd never really trusted. Fastow had recruited her to work as his "eyes and ears" in corporate development. Her first task was surveying scores of Enron assets to see what could be sold.

It didn't take Watkins long to start fixating on all the losers Enron had hedged with the Raptors. She saw the cryptic footnotes in Enron's SEC filings suggesting Enron had used the SPEs to avoid $500 million in losses in 2000 alone. In the few months since the Raptors were restructured, the value of the hedged assets had continued to fall (Avici, for example, had fallen some 90 percent). Of course, that mushrooming obligation in the Raptors—hundreds of millions altogether—was supposed to be covered with millions of Enron shares, but their value had plummeted too. Watkins was also concerned about the Whitewing SPE, also known at Enron as Condor. Its debt was coming due in 2002—and its assets no longer had enough value to pay it off. This meant that Enron would be on the hook to cover the obligation, which it would be able to do only by issuing several million more shares. Her concern was turning into panic. How could all this have passed muster with Arthur Andersen? *Did anyone else know?*

Watkins was not the sort to keep issues to herself. She spoke freely about it within her circle of friends, who included Kristina Mordaunt and Kathy Lynn—both secret Southampton investors—and Jeff McMahon, then running Enron Industrial Markets, whom she'd known since their days together at Arthur Andersen. About this time, she also called a friend in Global Finance. "Enron's going down," she announced: "Andy and Causey are going to jail."

Watkins was no babe in the woods. She'd helped manage the JEDI partnership for Fastow, she'd witnessed the shenanigans at broadband, she was well-versed in Andy's conflicts at LJM. But this was far more alarming. Even as she continued to gather information, Watkins raced to frightening conclusions. *This was the worst accounting fraud she'd ever seen!*

Determined not to go down with the ship, Watkins began interviewing for a job with Reliant, a rival Houston energy company. But she was determined to tell *someone* what she'd found. Watkins had no desire to take her fears outside Enron—to talk to the government or the media or even the board. As she saw it, nothing good could come of that. "When a company cooks the books," she later explained, "their only chance of survival is to come clean themselves." Her original plan was to meet with Skilling on her last day working there—to tell him that Enron had gone way over the line. But Skilling had quit before she had the chance. His startling exit redoubled Watkins's belief that Enron was in imminent peril.

So on the day after Skilling resigned, Watkins spent two hours in her office, tapping out an anonymous one-page letter to Ken Lay. The result read not as a classic whistle-blower screed about right and wrong, but as the product of a hash of motives: one part bitterness on missing out on the big score that so many of her colleagues had enjoyed, one part horror at Enron's manipulations, and one part fear that they'd be discovered. More than anything else, the letter served as a warning, a dead-on prophecy about what lay ahead.

> Dear Mr. Lay,
>
> Has Enron become a risky place to work? For those of us who didn't get rich over the last few years, can we afford to stay? Skilling's abrupt departure will raise suspicions of accounting improprieties and valuation issues.

"How do we fix the Raptor and Condor deals?" she asked. Enron had salvaged hundreds of millions in profits through the Raptor hedges, Watkins explained, but they'd have to be paid off with Enron shares, whose value was dropping. ". . . That won't go unnoticed," she wrote. "It sure looks to the layman on the street that we are hiding losses in a related company and will compensate that company with Enron stock in the future."

"I am incredibly nervous that we will implode in a wave of accounting scandals," Watkins wrote, in a line that would resonate powerfully. "My 8 years of

Enron work history will be worth nothing on my resume, the business world will consider the past success as nothing but an elaborate accounting hoax. Skilling is resigning now for 'personal reasons' but I think he wasn't having fun, looked down the road and knew this stuff was unfixable and would rather abandon ship now than resign in shame in 2 years."

"Is there a way our accounting guru's can unwind these deals now?" Watkins asked. "I have thought and thought about how to do this, but I keep bumping into one big problem—we booked the Condor and Raptor deals in 1999 and 2000, we enjoyed a wonderfully high stock price, many executives sold stock, we then try and reverse or fix the deals in 2001 and it's a bit like robbing the bank in one year and trying to pay it back 2 years later." Watkins fretted about the possibility of a whistle-blower dropping a dime on the company with the government—something she wasn't about to do. "We are under too much scrutiny and there are probably one or two disgruntled 'redeployed' employees who know enough about the 'funny' accounting to get us in trouble."

Watkins had her assistant drop the unsigned letter in a special box for questions to Lay at the upcoming employee meeting, to be held at the Hyatt. But she didn't have it in her to remain anonymous. She sent a copy of her letter to McMahon, then called to talk to him about it. When Lay didn't address her issues at the Hyatt, she went to human resources head Cindy Olson, identified herself as the letter writer, and agreed to speak to Lay face-to-face.

Before the August 22 meeting, Watkins expanded her warning to seven pages, offering fresh details, naming executives she said could back up her charges, and even offering Lay advice on how to manage the problem. She showed a draft to McMahon and sent a version to her mother. No true third party would have entered into the Raptor swaps with Enron, Watkins wrote. Sure, Andersen had blessed the accounting treatment. But "none of that will protect Enron if these transactions are ever disclosed in the bright light of day." If "the probability of discovery is low enough," Watkins advised, "we find a way to quietly and quickly reverse, unwind, write down these positions/transactions." But Watkins was skeptical that anything could be done quietly. "Too many people are looking for a smoking gun."

"There is a veil of secrecy around LJM and Raptor," she continued. "Employees question our accounting propriety consistently and constantly." Among those sharing her concerns, Watkins cited McMahon ("highly vexed over the inherent conflicts of LJM") and Cliff Baxter ("complained mightily to Skilling and all who would listen about the inappropriateness of our transactions with LJM"). Eager to grab Lay's attention, Watkins recounted hearing one midlevel employee say: "I know it would be devastating to all of us, but I wish we would get caught. We're such a crooked company." Watkins believed Lay should launch an investigation but steer clear of using Vinson & Elkins and Andersen because of their obvious conflicts. The best case scenario, Watkins advised: "Clean up quietly if possible." She also told Lay that he shouldn't name Fastow or Causey to replace Skilling.

When Watkins arrived at Lay's office on the fiftieth floor for her 1 P.M. appointment, the Enron chairman was winding up a private lunch with Greg Whalley, one of the candidates for Skilling's job. As Watkins made her case to Lay, he listened attentively. In truth, none of what Watkins told him should have come as much of a surprise. He had personally approved the waiver on Fastow's conflicts to let him run the LJMs; the Raptors had gone before both Lay and the entire board; their growing credit deficiencies were reported on daily position reports, distributed to scores of executives at Enron, and the restructuring had been disclosed in Enron's SEC filings. Still, Lay seemed concerned and surprised at what he was hearing. Watkins later recalled that he winced when reading the comment about Enron being "such a crooked company."

"Andy's a good CFO, right?" Lay interrupted at one point, according to Watkins' later account of the meeting. "He's doing a good job, right?" Lay also noted that Enron's accountants had reviewed the Raptors with their usual care. Perhaps so, said Watkins, but accounting rules generally barred a company from using its stock to boost its income statement, and Andersen had made mistakes in the past, as recent scandals at other Andersen clients showed. Lay asked one more question: "You haven't gone outside the company with this, have you?" Assured that she had not, Lay ended the meeting by telling Watkins he would deal with the matter and agreed to arrange her transfer away from Fastow, most likely to Cindy Olson's HR department.

Lay contacted Jim Derrick, Enron's general counsel, and they quickly made arrangements to have Watkins's allegations investigated by an outside law firm—namely, Vinson & Elkins. Watkins, of course, had explicitly offered the commonsense advice that another firm handle the matter; indeed, V&E had done legal work on the very transactions she was complaining about. But Lay later said he had concluded this conflict could be managed and that it made sense to hand the assignment to lawyers already familiar with the complexities of Enron. V&E certainly fit that bill: it was every bit as intimate with Enron as Arthur Andersen. Derrick himself was among the many Enron executives who were V&E alums.

One of the two lawyers retained to investigate Watkins' allegations was Joseph Dilg, a senior partner who had been responsible for the firm's relationship with Enron since 1991. Dilg had reason to be attuned to sensibilities at Enron: with annual billings running at $35 million a year, Enron was the giant firm's single largest client. Dilg also had reason to be especially attuned to V&E's interest; he was about to take over as managing partner of the 850-lawyer firm. Only one other V&E lawyer worked on the project: Max Hendrick III, head of the litigation department.

It was decided that Vinson & Elkins would conduct a very narrow inquiry.

The lawyers later noted in their written report that no outside accounting experts were to be hired. There would be no second-guessing of Arthur Andersen's work. And no one outside the walls of Enron or Arthur Andersen would be interviewed. This, the report would note, would serve merely as a preliminary probe, to determine whether Watkins had "raised new factual information that would warrant a broader investigation." Preliminary or not, a special board panel later concluded that this inquiry was essentially a whitewash, noting: "The result of the V&E review was largely predetermined by the scope and the nature of the investigation and the process employed."

Even before the investigation could begin, Enron asked another V&E lawyer—a specialist in labor law—for advice on a related matter: namely, what were the company's options in dealing with Sherron Watkins? The two-page memo from partner Carl Jordan to an in-house Enron lawyer arrived just two days after Watkins met with Lay. It outlined how Enron should manage the situation to minimize the risk of a lawsuit from Watkins as long as she remained at Enron. (Both her new supervisor and Fastow should be told not to treat her "adversely" because she'd spoken up, Jordan advised.)

But at Enron's request, Jordan also explored the possibility of firing her. "Texas law does not currently protect corporate whistle-blowers," he noted. Still, he concluded, getting rid of Watkins wouldn't be smart. It would invite the sort of ugly lawsuit that would be "very expensive and time consuming to litigate," and the company's books and records would then become "fair game during discovery." In addition, Jordan wrote, "there is the risk that the discharged employee will seek to convince some government oversight agency (e.g., IRS, SEC, etc.) that the corporation has engaged in materially misleading reporting or is otherwise non-compliant. As with wrongful discharge claims, this can create problems even though the allegations have no merit whatsoever."

Such niceties were lost on Fastow. After meeting with Lay, Watkins left town for a vacation to Mexico, she recalled in *Power Failure*, her account of life at Enron, coauthored with Mimi Swartz. In the meantime, the investigation had begun—and Fastow had found out who had fingered him. After receiving a copy of Watkins's letter from Derrick, he confronted McMahon, accusing him of conspiring with Watkins in hope of landing the CFO's job. Fastow also demanded that Watkins be fired immediately and her laptop confiscated. When Watkins returned from her trip, she later recalled in *Power Failure*, her new boss, Cindy Olson, advised her that "Andy is not behaving appropriately."

Sherron Watkins wasn't the only Enron employee writing a letter to her superiors warning about the company's accounting. On August 29, after she was laid off from her job at EES, Margaret Ceconi, who had previously e-mailed the SEC anonymously, wrote her own signed letter to the Enron board, addressing it to Cindy Olson and board secretary Rebecca Carter. It ran ten pages long and warned of huge woes at EES, including wasteful spending, customers threatening to sue over broken promises, and unprofitable contracts that had been booked for profits. But the most alarming part of the letter alleged "SEC violations" involving more than $500 million in losses that EES was "trying to hide in wholesale. Rumor on the 7th floor is that it is closer to $1 billion." Yet "somehow EES to everyone's amazement, reported earnings for the second quarter." She went on: "EES has knowingly misrepresented EES' earnings. This is common knowledge among all the EES employees, and is actually joked about. But it should be taken seriously."

"Some would say the house of cards are falling," Ceconi wrote. "You are potentially facing shareholder lawsuits, Employee lawsuits. . . . Heat from the analysts and newspapers. The market has lost all confidence and it's obvious why. You, the board, have a big task at hand. You have to decide the moral or ethical things to do, to right the wrongs of your various management teams. I wish you luck."

The letter was never shown to Lay or the Enron board. Ceconi spotlighted serious problems, but because she had been laid off, it was easier to dismiss her letter as the bitter rantings of a disgruntled former employee—which Enron did.

Ceconi, meanwhile, had also begun anonymously e-mailing, then calling, Prudential analyst Carol Coale. Using the e-mail name of enrontruth, she began feeding Coale tough questions to ask at analysts meetings and conference calls.

And then, on September 30, while out for drinks and dinner at a Houston tapas bar called Mia Luna's, Ceconi ran into a table full of high-ranking EES managers, including division CEO Dave Delainey, COO Jeremy Blachman, and star sales executive Angela Schwarz. Ceconi sauntered by their table on the way out. "What are y'all doing here?" she asked. "Trying to figure out how you're going to make up the numbers again this quarter?" The encounter turned into a shouting match. As Blachman tried to escort her out, Ceconi pulled away and told gawking bystanders: "He's from Enron—he thinks he owns everybody and everything!"

In the aftermath of the episode, Ceconi again reported her complaints to the SEC through its Web site, this time identifying Enron as engaging in the abusive accounting. But nothing happened.

In the wake of the Watkins letter, Fastow lost whatever chance he had to move up. Instead, on August 28—14 days after Skilling's resignation was made public—Lay announced that Greg Whalley, 39, would take over as president and COO while the 46-year old Mark Frevert would assume the senior-statesman role of vice chairman; both would join Lay in the "office of the chairman." Frevert was an old Enron hand; he'd started in origination, then helped launch Enron's trading operation in Europe before returning to Houston to serve as chairman and CEO of the wholesale business. But the key player was Whalley. The "union boss" was now the second-most powerful man at Enron.

Whalley strongly suspected that all wasn't well, and he wasted no time digging in. At 1:01 A.M. on the day after his promotion was announced, Whalley e-mailed investor-relations chief Mark Koenig about Lay's latest cheery pronouncement. "I guess Ken told someone today that we would make the numbers," Whalley wrote. "We need to be careful until we know what the numbers are."

In truth, Lay seemed preternaturally calm. In early September, he laid plans to assemble his newly appointed 25-member management committee for a two-day off-site meeting. It was to begin on a Thursday night with cocktails and a working dinner. Lay's proposed agenda for the next day began with two of his favorites, Cindy Olson and PR guru Beth Tilney (wife of Merrill banker Schuyler), tackling the topics of "culture" and "vision and values." Among the issues for discussion: "image and reputation" ("What is it? How do we communicate it?") and "How do we define Enron?" ("Not a trading company/More than a trading company/A trading company"). Next up: employee compensation and new businesses. The topics of risk management, electricity markets, concerns about the third quarter, and international asset sales were put off until the end of the day.

After looking over the schedule, Whalley fired off a blunt e-mail to Lay: "I'm sorry I haven't been more involved in setting this up, but I think the agenda looks kind of soft," he wrote. "At a minimum, I would like to turn the schedule around and hit the hard subjects like Q3, risk management, and asset sales first. I would also like to see a discussion on our funds flow, and our balance sheet. If we don't get these things right, none of the rest of it matters. . . . Also," Whalley went on, offering no deference to Lay's favorites (jokingly known as "Ken's harem"), "I notice that Cindy Olson and Beth Tilney are in attendance. This should only be for presentation, as they are not members of the management committee."

By the time of the management retreat, the issue of Fastow's partnerships had surfaced—just barely—in the *Wall Street Journal*. In an August 28 Heard on the Street column, headlined "Enron Prepares to Become Easier to Read," reporters Rebecca Smith and John Emshwiller had detailed Lay's promise of a "humbler," more open company. In a three-paragraph discussion buried deep in the story, they also noted that CFO Fastow "had quietly ended his ownership and management ties with certain limited partnerships" effective July 31. The story did not identify the partnerships as LJM.

At the off-site, nine days later, there was considerable grumbling about Fastow's passion for SPEs. The commercial executives complained that while they were making money for Enron, Fastow's finance people kept muddying the waters by stashing their assets in SPEs. Recounting the meeting, Lay later said he asked the two dozen top Enron managers how many of them had made use of Fastow's structured vehicles. The answer: pretty much everyone.

It took Joe Dilg and Max Hendrick about a month to make up their minds about Sherron Watkins's allegations. The Vinson & Elkins lawyers interviewed nine

Enron executives and two Arthur Andersen partners. Under the ground rules, Jeff Skilling, Cliff Baxter, and Michael Kopper were all off limits because they had left Enron.

While Jeff McMahon openly voiced his problems with Fastow's conflict, neither McMahon nor anyone else (except Watkins, of course) presumed to question Andersen's judgments about Enron's accounting. In fact, McMahon told the lawyers that a lot of the LJM transactions had been "highly beneficial" to Enron. Greg Whalley said flatly he didn't share Watkins's concerns. Causey and Buy insisted everything had been carefully reviewed—by management, lawyers, accountants, and the Enron board—and disclosed (if opaquely) in Enron's public filings. The view among Enron executives, the lawyers noted, was that the Raptors and Condor were "clever, useful vehicles."

Fastow himself had barely calmed down by the time of his own interview. Everything had been blessed, he pointed out to the V&E lawyers, not only by Andersen accountants but by lawyers from Vinson & Elkins. The letter writer, he said, was simply "second-guessing" Andersen's judgment. While he applauded the employee's "fortitude" for speaking up, he voiced suspicion about her motives, telling Dilg and Hendrick that the letter writer was "acting in conjunction with a person who wants his job," namely, McMahon. The LJM-Enron relationship, he said, was "good for LJM and great for Enron."

On September 19, while the investigation was still officially under way, Joe Dilg and his wife hosted a dinner for two Enron couples—including Andy and Lea Fastow—to introduce them to the new headmaster of the private school that all their children attended. Two days later, Dilg and Hendrick stopped by Lay's office at 4 P.M. Their written report wouldn't be ready for three more weeks, and they wouldn't officially inform the board's audit committee of the matter until early October. But they were ready to give Ken Lay an oral report on their conclusions: while Fastow's "apparent" conflict of interest presented "potential bad cosmetics" if subjected to a media exposé or a lawsuit, they had found nothing to warrant a full-fledged investigation.

Lay was delighted. In his opinion, Andy was a fine CFO, and Lay was bent on making sure he didn't join the recent exodus of top Enron executives. With the lawyers' finding and Fastow's sale of LJM, Lay considered the matter closed. He moved forward with his plans to tear up Andy's contract and reward him with a rich new pact.

Most of Enron's senior executives had multimillion-dollar contracts that ran for another year or more. Ken Lay had made it a top priority, after taking over as CEO, to negotiate more generous deals to lock them into the company for even longer.

Mark Frevert, for example, already had an existing deal, expected to total $6.7 million in 2001, that ran for two more years. But he'd received a promotion to the armchair job of vice chairman, a move that once would likely have produced a *cut* in pay. Lay extended his contract through 2004, boosting his base salary to $600,000, making him eligible for a seven-figure bonus, and awarding restricted stock grants valued at $2 million and options valued at another $5.5 million. Rick Causey was already bound to Enron through July 2002; Lay gave him a two-year extension, providing $600,000 in signing and retention bonuses plus restricted stock grants and options valued at another $1.5 million. Rick Buy, whose contract had expired, got a new deal through 2004 that included $800,000 in bonuses plus stock and options worth $1 million.

And Fastow? He'd always been the board's golden boy—the directors viewed him as one executive Enron couldn't afford to lose. Now, Lay negotiated an especially stunning deal for the CFO, even while he was still officially under investigation. Under Fastow's old contract, he was bound to Enron through February 2003. His new agreement ran through March 31, 2005, on far more generous terms. Fastow's base salary would rise from $400,000 to $600,000 a year, and he would get an annual "bonus target" of $1 million plus incentive compensation of $750,000 cash and Enron stock and options worth $3.45 million. Fastow's expected new annual take: $5.8 million.

Fastow also requested his own extraordinary version of a Kinder clause. He wanted to be considered "involuntarily terminated," with a payout of $5.7 million for each year that remained on his deal, if he wasn't awarded his targeted compensation, if he wasn't appointed to the office of the chairman within a year, or if the composition of Enron's board changed by more than 20 percent. Even the Enron directors wouldn't go for that. The agreement instead provided that involuntary termination would give Fastow a cash payment of $2.35 million for each remaining year of his contract.

Among the many people Sherron Watkins told about her concerns was her old boss at Arthur Andersen, a Houston audit partner named Jim Hecker. Hecker was the CPA who lampooned Enron's risky accounting with his satirical song, "Welcome to the Hotel Kenneth-Lay-a." After a lengthy conversation with Watkins, Hecker wrote a long note to the file about her complaints, which he then sent on to Enron audit partners David Duncan and Debra Cash with a message: "Here is my draft memo, for your review for 'smoking guns' that you can't extinguish."

In fact, though Watkins didn't know it, Arthur Andersen had already begun taking a closer look at the Raptors. The inevitable had already arrived: with Enron (and New Power) shares plunging and the value of the Raptor assets sinking, the springtime cross-collateralization fix couldn't hold any longer. After allowing Enron to avoid more than a billion dollars in losses in 2000 and 2001, the Raptors, even on a combined basis, were once again underwater by hundreds of millions of dollars—and Enron was again staring at the prospect of having to take the hit. The situation had gotten even worse after September 11, when the terrorist attacks on the World Trade Center towers and the Pentagon sent financial markets reeling, temporarily dropping Enron shares close to $25.

And the credit deficiency wasn't the only problem. In poring over the Raptor files, Andersen auditors realized they had made a huge accounting error on Enron's balance sheet. Several entries involving the funding and restructuring of the Raptors had been mistakenly booked as a boost in shareholder equity, which reflects a company's net worth. The screwup was missed for months. Now Enron needed to reverse the entries, cutting its shareholder's equity by $1.2 billion at the worst possible moment.

The wiser minds at both Andersen and Enron had long since been ignored. Carl Bass and John Stewart, partners in Andersen's PSG consulting group, discovered that David Duncan, head of the Enron team, had written memos that reported they'd signed off on virtually all aspects of the accounting for both the Raptors and LJM. In fact, both Bass and Stewart had been consulted on only limited issues and had strongly objected on some of those.

Likewise, Enron's Vince Kaminski, who'd earlier been cut out of discussions about the Raptors, had been consulted on questions about the vehicles' restructuring without being told what was really going on. He soon found out enough to conclude that Enron's accounting treatment was downright fraudulent and that he was being used as an accessory. Enron hedging with itself, he later noted tartly, was "an act of economic self-gratification." He informed Buy he wouldn't let his group do any more work on the Raptors, even if it meant his being fired. Well, he didn't have to worry about *that,* Buy replied; in the post-Skilling era, Enron's new mantra was: "We'll be honest."

With the Raptors sinking fast, that mantra was being put to the test. As the end of the third quarter neared, Fastow and Causey argued for shoring them up yet again with millions more shares of Enron stock, pushing the problem off to a future quarter. The alternative was terminating the Raptors immediately; that would mean taking a huge hit to earnings, perhaps as much as $700 million pretax. Under an agreement negotiated between Fastow (representing Enron) and Kopper (now representing LJM2), Enron would also wind up having to pay another $35 million as a termination fee to LJM2.

Whalley wanted to pull the plug. In his first quarter as COO, he was eager to clean up as much of Enron's dirty laundry as possible, just as Skilling had done in 1997 when he'd taken over the job. Enron was telling Wall Street it was simplifying its finances; it needed to come clean. The company could use the opportunity to toss in write-downs on other Enron disasters and get all the bad news out at once.

Lay agreed. The decision was a gamble, a bet that Enron's spin meisters could contain the damage, just as they'd always done before. Sure, it would be ugly for awhile, but the company could absorb the hit. After all, this was *Enron.*

Then they could all go about the happy business of watching the stock move back up.

Or so they thought.

On September 25, the day the Raptors were formally dissolved, Enron received a letter from John Emshwiller and Rebecca Smith, the two *Wall Street Journal* reporters who wrote the Heard on the Street story that briefly mentioned Fastow's partnerships. After that article appeared, Emshwiller and Smith got a tip from someone involved with LJM, telling them what they had stumbled onto. Now they were working on *another* story, and this time they were zeroing in.

The reporters submitted a list of 21 questions they wanted to cover with Lay and Fastow. The questions were devastating; there was no doubt that the two reporters had gotten their hands on the one thing no one at Enron had ever bothered to demand: partnership documents.

How much money has Mr. Fastow made from the LJM2 partnership? How does the amount compare to his compensation from Enron for his work as CFO?

How much money have Michael Kopper and Ben Glisan realized from their participation in LJM2?

Did Enron know that the general partner of LJM2 had a profit participation in the partnership that would produce millions of dollars?

Were LJM2 investors promised that they would receive special access to Enron investment opportunities, including the purchase of company assets?

Even after looking over the questions, Lay didn't seem worried. He met with Fastow and PR chief Mark Palmer the next day about the situation. He and Fastow decided they wouldn't grant interviews to the reporters. Palmer prepared a short, nondescript response: the partnerships had all been reviewed and disclosed. Fastow was out of them. This was old news.

But Fastow was nervous. Though the *Journal* still hadn't run a story a week after submitting its questions, he knew the problem wasn't going away. On October 2, he responded to a cheery e-mail from his brother, Peter, a Maryland lawyer, who wondered if Andy had gotten "any perks" from a recent EES deal between Enron and the Guinness Brewery.

"I may need to take advantage of that perk," Andy replied. "WSJ investigative reporter is doing an expose on LJM-Enron. Obviously, we've done everything we're supposed to, plus some, but they are going to do a character assassination on me based on hearsay from unnamed sources. Major hack job. I probably fired one too many people this year. You may not want to be seen at the pub with me."

Andy Fastow's family was well acquainted with some of his partnerships. He initially tried to arrange for his wife's wealthy family to serve as the Friend of Enron in the JEDI buyout. Skilling killed that idea, and Michael Kopper assumed that role by forming Chewco. According to the government, Fastow's father-in-law, Jack Weingarten, once received a breakup fee from Enron after a company lawyer re-

jected the Fastows' plans to have him serve as an equity investor in the RADR
wind-farm deal.

More recently, Fastow had installed two in-laws—Peter's wife, Jana Kaplan,
and Lillianne Weingarten, wife of Lea's brother Michael—as trustees of the Fastow Family Foundation. The foundation was the charitable entity Fastow created
and funded with the $4.5-million windfall from Andy's secret deal with the three
NatWest bankers.

In June, in fact, the three trustees—Andy, Jana, and Lillianne—traveled with
their spouses to the foundation's first "annual meeting," which Andy convened
at the Cheeca Lodge resort in the Florida Keys, a favorite of the Bush family.
The foundation picked up the tab for the four-day event, which—between mas-
sages, manicures, tennis lessons, and fly-fishing—included a single 30-minute
business meeting. The final item on the agenda: hiring Fastow's father as foundation administrator.

Although he'd reluctantly cut his official ties with LJM in selling out to Kopper in late July, Fastow was still spending time on the partnership, reassuring
nervous investors that LJM would remain "uniquely positioned" to benefit from
its relationship with Enron. Fastow even planned to attend the annual LJM2
partnership meeting in October, but Kopper canceled it, citing the tragedy of
September 11.

Through it all, Andy remained the picture of a devoted family man. He regularly left work for long lunches with his wife, whom he affectionately called the
"Shag Queen" in an e-mail. Every week, he penciled two hours into his busy
schedule for a special "Dad's night with the boys." Lea Fastow, meanwhile, was
busy with Enron's new art committee, which she chaired—it had been given a
$20 million budget to build a collection for display in the new Enron building. It
also gave her an opportunity to scout new cutting-edge acquisitions for the Fastows' own collection.

The Fastows were spending much time planning their River Oaks dream
home, then being built on a site they bought for $1.3 million. Their 11,493-
square-foot house would feature Italian blue flagstone flooring and museum-
quality lighting for artwork. (The Fastows also had two vacation homes, one in
Galveston on the Texas coast and another in Norwich, Vermont.)

With his new River Oaks estate, his vacation retreats, his Porsche, his
family's art collection, Lea's family connections, even his own charitable foundation, Andy Fastow, at the age of 39, had truly arrived. Although he'd never
been a commercial deal maker, his years at Enron had made him a very rich man.
In 2000 alone, he'd sold Enron shares worth more than $18 million—and even
after the big price drop, he still held shares that were worth another $10 million.
The Fastows' income had multiplied along with Andy's rise, from a reported
$1,287,543 on the joint tax return he filed with Lea for 1997 to more than $2 million in 1998, $9,129,602 in 1999, and an astonishing $48,583,318 in 2000.

(According to the government, the Fastows hadn't even reported all their taxable income.)

Of course, although no one at Enron knew it, the bulk of the Fastows' money hadn't come from Andy's work as CFO of Enron. It had come from his private partnerships' dealings *with* Enron. By the time he cashed out of the LJMs, his total take—including management fees, partnership distributions, and the buyout by Michael Kopper—had reached a grand total of more than $60.6 million.

When Enron's directors gathered in Houston for the October 8 board meeting, it was a little harder than usual to keep the spotlight on the good news. The company had finally found another buyer for Portland General, though the deal wasn't supposed to close until late 2002 on considerably less generous terms. And Enron's core businesses—now redefined to exclude broadband—were performing well, according to management reports.

But Dabhol remained a debacle. Elektro, the Brazilian utility company Enron bought in 1998, was really worth a billion dollars less than the amount reflected on Enron's books. Indeed, Enron's entire global assets division had earned a pathetic $12 million in the first nine months of 2001. And the broadband business was barely breathing. It closed the third quarter with a feeble $4 million in revenues and an $80 million loss.

For the first time, the board learned of the Sherron Watkins letter, identified only as having come from "an employee." But Joe Dilg assured the audit committee that it wasn't a problem; his preliminary investigation had already concluded there was no need to look any further. No Enron director asked to see Watkins's letter, with its provocative warning that Enron might "implode in a wave of accounting scandals," and there was no specific discussion of her concerns about the Raptors. Afterward, Jim Derrick asked if he could officially advise Andy Fastow that he was off the hook. He was told to go ahead.

The next morning, when the board reconvened in executive session, it learned about the giant charge Enron planned to take against third-quarter earnings. It was due to be announced the following week. There was discussion about the likely market reaction—Ben Glisan had already been making the rounds of the credit-rating agencies to give them a heads-up. Finance committee chairman Pug Winokur reported the rating agencies "were expected to afford the company time in executing its asset-sales program." Winokur also noted "the positive objectives of the Company to simplify its financings, produce quality earnings, and reduce debt." None of the directors were really worried. This would surely be just a bump in the road.

From the moment he took over as CEO, Ken Lay touted Enron's stock. He convened investor meetings. He gave media interviews. And he regularly preached to the most easily converted—Enron's own employees. In an August 27 e-mail, Lay declared that these efforts "should result in a significantly higher stock price." In an employee Internet chat on September 26, he reported that Enron's third quarter was "looking great." He added: "My personal belief is that Enron stock is an incredible bargain at current prices and we will look back a couple of years from now and see the great opportunity that we currently have." He urged employees to "talk up the stock." Enron is "fundamentally sound," he said. "The balance sheet is strong. Our financial liquidity has never been stronger." The flogging worked: in the week before Enron's earnings announcement, Enron's shares climbed back over $35.

Lay, of course, didn't reveal that in the previous two months, he had secretly cashed in $20 million of his own stock by drawing down his company credit line, then repaying it with Enron shares—part of the $78 million Lay had pocketed this way over the previous 12 months. While he later attributed this to his personal liquidity crisis, day-to-day life in the Lay household was continuing much as it always had.

Linda's son Beau worried about whether the impending sale of one of Lay's three multimillion-dollar Aspen homes would require the three couples he'd invited up for a long ski vacation to change their plans. No need, Linda Lay replied. Ken's daughter Liz checked in with her dad to ask whether she and her husband should make commercial reservations back from Aspen after the Christmas holidays. Lay's secretary e-mailed back: "Ken said to advise you that he'll plan to arrange a plane to bring you and others back on Jan 1." The traditional all-family dinner was planned for mid-October at the River Oaks Country Club. Dress would "remain casual to casual/chic, as usual," Linda advised. A photographer would be on hand "to help us take a few very special group photographs," with "very simple nonscary Halloween costumes for the wee ones to put on over their casual attire."

It was business as usual at Enron, too. After a board meeting, Ken and Linda Lay took a tour of the sleek new Enron building nearing completion. Enron was laying plans for a giant employee Christmas bash—a million-dollar extravaganza at Enron Field. The company donated $1 million to emergency relief efforts after September 11. Lay's calendar remained busy, not just with Enron executive meetings but with calls to governors, CEO forums, and charitable events. On October 10, he flew to Washington for dinner and a speech at the Library of Congress by former secretary of state Henry Kissinger, an Enron consultant.

While Lay was hobnobbing in Washington, Rick Causey was huddling with Enron's accountants in Houston, haggling over just how far the company could go in sugarcoating its bad third-quarter earnings news.

From the moment they decided to terminate the Raptors, Enron executives desperately wanted to avoid a restatement, which would mean the company was formally admitting mistakes, confessing to the world that its previous financial statements were wrong. Restatements triggered big stock declines, SEC inquiries, and shareholder lawsuits. It was far better instead to simply take a charge in the current quarter, something more akin to reporting that things hadn't gone quite the way they'd expected.

The balance-sheet error, of course, *was* a mistake. But Enron argued—incredibly—that this $1.2 billion balance-sheet error wasn't "material" under accounting rules, because it amounted to only about 8.5 percent of Enron's total net worth. David Duncan went along; Andersen didn't want to admit the screwup either. Enron reported the charge as a simple equity reduction.

The income-statement charges were harder to fudge. Enron was preparing to report a $544 million hit ($710 million pretax) for the Raptors' termination. There was another $287 million for write-downs of overvalued assets at Azurix and $180 million for restructuring charges at broadband, which included the cost of layoffs and belated acknowledgement that the much-hyped content business really wasn't worth much after all. The grand total was $1.01 billion after-tax, enough to throw Enron's quarterly earnings deeply into the loss column. Andersen had already agreed that this wouldn't require a restatement either, even though the Raptors, now being eliminated, had inflated Enron's reported earnings for four previous quarters.

The issue now was that Enron wanted to report these problems as nonrecurring charges, one-of-a-kind events that didn't really reflect on the underlying performance of the company's businesses. This too had big Wall Street implications. Analysts tended to discount nonrecurring charges and focus instead on operating earnings.

For precisely that reason, the accounting treatment on this front was rife with opportunity for abuse. And Enron was a habitual abuser: historically, it had treated routine business losses as nonrecurring charges, and booked onetime gains as operating profits. In the Braveheart deal, for example, Enron booked its dubious monetization of the Blockbuster contract as operating income; now, it wanted to call its write-down of the content business a nonrecurring loss. Similarly, while Enron wanted to treat the Raptors' termination as a nonrecurring event, it certainly hadn't hesitated to treat the $1 billion in income they contributed as operating profits.

Even for Arthur Andersen, this was going too far. David Duncan, uncharacteristically, was putting up a fight. With each new emerging problem, Duncan became more immersed in Enron than ever. He was so busy he even had to skip the big Arthur Andersen shindig in New Orleans, where his face was flashed on giant video screens in recognition of his status as one of the firm's stars. His sterling work on the huge Enron account had just earned him a partnership bonus worth about $150,000.

After seeing Causey's first draft of Enron's earnings release on Friday, October 12, Duncan alerted various Andersen partners and an in-house attorney named Nancy Temple. One partner quickly e-mailed back: "I agree with your comment about the nonrecurring wording which seems inappropriate given in one quarter they have multiple 'nonrecurring' items."

On Sunday, Duncan spoke to Causey, telling him that Andersen had "strong concerns that the presentation of the charges as nonrecurring could be misconstrued or misunderstood by investors" and that the SEC might well view it as "materially misleading." In a memo Duncan later wrote documenting the events, he also recalled advising Causey to "consider changing the presentation." Duncan's old friend was noncommittal. "Rick acknowledged my advice," Duncan wrote.

Causey spent half his workday Monday in meetings with Ken Lay and others, prepping for the critical conference call that would immediately follow the earnings release. When he saw Duncan again that night, Causey told him he had discussed his concerns internally and that the earnings release had gone through "normal legal review." Joined by other Andersen partners—some by conference call from Chicago—Duncan argued with Causey late into the night.

Ultimately, though, it was Enron's call, and the client wanted nonrecurring. The release didn't even make it to the PR department until 5:30 A.M.—not long before it was to go out on the newswires, ahead of the market's opening bell.

■   ■   ■

For those who didn't know any better, it would have been easy to conclude from Enron's third-quarter earnings release, issued Tuesday, October 16, that nothing was seriously amiss. The headline actually seemed reassuring: ENRON REPORTS RECURRING THIRD QUARTER EARNINGS OF $0.43 PER DILUTED SHARE; REPORTS NONRECURRING CHARGES OF $1.01 BILLION AFTER-TAX; REAFFIRMS RECURRING EARNINGS ESTIMATES OF $1.80 FOR 2001 AND $2.15 FOR 2002; AND EXPANDS FINANCIAL REPORTING.

What followed was classic Enron—an attempt to hide what was really going on by stretching the rules, twisting the language, and playing games. Instead of talking about quarterly earnings, as Enron's earnings releases usually did, this one focused on "recurring earnings." "Our 26 percent increase in recurring earnings per diluted share shows the very strong results of our core wholesale and retail energy business and our natural-gas pipelines," Lay was quoted as saying in the press release.

The billion-dollar nonrecurring charge was noted in the third paragraph, along with the $618 million net loss for the quarter. That was quickly explained away as a matter of housecleaning. The nonrecurring charges were described as "asset impairments" involving Azurix; "restructuring costs" at broadband; and $544 million "related to losses associated with certain investments, principally Enron's interest in the New Power Company, broadband and technology investments, and early termination during the third quarter of certain structured-finance arrangements with a previously disclosed entity." It was a massive obfuscation, calculated to hide the awkward fact that the now-terminated Raptors had hidden Enron losses. Even more astonishing, the release didn't even *mention* the separate $1.2 billion cut in shareholders' equity—which wouldn't show up on the accompanying financial statements since Enron never released its updated balance sheet until well after the quarterly-earnings statements.

In the 9 A.M. conference call, Ken Lay walked a carefully prepared line. First, he focused on the strong "recurring operating performance." When he turned to the "nonrecurring charges of slightly over $1 billion," Lay stuck to the script, again attributing most of the charge to "early termination" of "certain structured-finance arrangements with a previously disclosed entity." Then he noted, for the first time, the giant balance-sheet hit: "In connection with the early termination, shareholders' equity will be reduced by approximately $1.2 billion with a corresponding significant reduction in the number of diluted shares outstanding." In other words, Lay was tying the equity cut to the purported housecleaning decision to terminate the Raptors. In fact, they were unrelated.

Now, Lay insisted, all of Enron's problems were on the table. "If we thought we had any other impaired assets, it would be in this list today." Enron stock actually climbed a bit through the day, closing near $34.

But Fastow knew trouble was on the way. "Well, you probably saw the earnings release and some of the interviews already," he wrote in an e-mail to a family member. "Needless to say, things have been a little busy around here. I wouldn't be surprised to see the LJM article appear tomorrow as part of the earnings story."

Sure enough, Enron's financial dealings with Andy Fastow were finally placed on public display the next day in the long-awaited story in the *Wall Street Journal*. Using the billion-dollar charge as their peg, Emshwiller and Smith did two things Enron had long feared: they cited the big third-quarter loss as evidence that Enron's business was, in truth, perilous, and they showcased the sordid details of Enron's relationship with Fastow's partnerships, raising "vexing conflict-of-interest questions."

This time LJM was front and center. The page-one story quoted from the offering memo's discussion about how Fastow's involvement would help LJM2 cash in on its deals with Enron—and noted that the company had embraced an arrangement that could provide "potentially huge financial rewards for Mr. Fastow." Lay was described as having insisted in an interview that the arrangement didn't really present any conflicts. Equally damning, Charles LeMaistre, chairman of the board's compensation committee, told the *Journal* he viewed the arrangement as a supplemental form of compensation that helped keep Fastow, the valued CFO, at Enron. "We try to make sure that all executives at Enron are sufficiently well paid to meet what the market would offer."

After reading the *Journal*, Merrill banker Schuyler Tilney e-mailed a colleague: "Not a great article, but frankly could have been worse."

Fastow had a different reaction. Later that day, he e-mailed Ben Glisan with a simple message—"5:00 pm get drunk with Andy."

This story was just the beginning. The next day, Thursday, October 18, the *Journal* focused on the $1.2 billion hit to shareholder equity, highlighting *its* link to Fastow's partnership and Enron's failure to disclose "the big equity reduction" in its earnings release. Asked why Enron had hidden the cut, PR man Palmer was left to insist that it was "just a balance-sheet issue," immaterial for disclosure purposes.

Peter Fastow e-mailed his brother that morning. "Jana and I read the WSJ article with great revulsion," he wrote. "We know, without a doubt, that there was nothing inappropriate with your involvement in LJM while serving as an officer of Enron. We support you 100%. Anyway, we both found the content of the article to be extremely suspect. If you were really making millions from LJM, there is no way you'd let your brother continue to drive a 7 year old Toyota Camry. We both wish there was something we could do to help you combat this attempt at character assassination."

The third shot arrived on Friday, headlined: "Enron CFO's Partnership Had Millions in Profit." Noting that LJM2 reaped more than $7 million in management fees in 2000, this story drove home the central nature of the conflict. Though the reporters didn't know precisely how much Fastow had personally cleared, it was obvious that he'd pocketed millions doing business with Enron.

"There I go, making money again," Andy e-mailed his brother. "That is even allowed in Russia and China today. The saga continues."

As Fastow circled the wagons, some of his banker friends rushed to display their loyalty. CSFB's Osmar Abib sent Fastow the dismissive research note that Curt Launer, his firm's Enron-friendly analyst, wrote in response to the *Journal* stories. ("In our view, the so-called 'LJM Partnerships' were fully disclosed in ENE's financial statements and were subject to appropriate scrutiny by ENE's board, outside auditors and outside legal counsel ... we continue to rate it Strong Buy.") "Thought you would appreciate the support," Abib wrote. "Hang in there."

Enron's stock, meanwhile, had fallen more than 20 percent during the week, to $26, and was approaching levels not seen since 1997. On Tuesday, after the earnings call, Moody's announced it was placing the company's long-term debt on "review" for a possible ratings downgrade.

There was yet another ominous development that week: after reading the *Journal*'s first story on Wednesday, SEC officials began an informal inquiry into Enron's dealings with Fastow's partnerships. Strange as it might seem, it wasn't unusual for the agency to begin a securities probe on the basis of a media report. The SEC was short staffed and overwhelmed; its staff hadn't conducted a routine review of Enron's annual financial filings since 1997.

In a letter sent by the SEC's district office in Fort Worth, the agency informed the company that it wanted to "determine the nature and amount of the interests, profits, and losses of Enron and Mr. Fastow in the Related Party transactions." Among other items, it wanted "an accounting of Mr. Fastow's interests in each Related Party transaction, and showing his profits or losses with regard to the individual transaction."

Though the inquiry was short of a full-fledged investigation, it was still very bad news. On Monday, October 22, when Enron announced the informal probe—five days after getting the letter—its stock sank another 20 percent, to $20.65.

At this point, Lay believed he was the only one who could keep Enron together long enough to turn the ship around—and there were others telling him that as well. Lay responded to Enron's growing problems like a politician under fire: he began polling his constituents. First, he conducted his own in-house sampling—called the Lay It On the Line survey—which revealed the unsurprising news that Enron employees were very concerned about their stock. Then he hired a political consultant—a high-profile Republican pollster named Frank Luntz—to conduct focus groups at Enron.

Luntz's report, which landed on Lay's desk two days after the letter from the SEC, made brutally clear that the CEO's exalted notions of Enron's culture were a delusion. "Instability and chaos" were defining features at Enron, Luntz said. Far from reveling in their freedom, employees complained bitterly about senior management's "lack of corporate vision": "there appears to be no long-term thinking, strategy, or game plan." Enron's constant reorganizations—six in just the previous 18 months—were a running joke. The PRC was viewed not as a meritocracy but as "punishment." Only deal makers got ahead; "no one in the corporate leadership truly cares about those charged with executing the deals and making them actually produce profit." Enron's lack of discipline wasn't something noble that nurtured creativity; it was destructive and demoralizing. Commented one Enron employee: "We're a major corporation still acting like a dot-com start-up."

But what Lay seems to have taken away from the exercise was Luntz's belief that Lay alone had the "credibility, confidence, and trust" to deal with Enron's crisis. "Ken is your most powerful weapon. A personal commitment from Ken Lay will go further than [from] the entire executive team combined," Luntz wrote. "Employees want to see Ken Lay's face. They want to hear from him and be led by him."

So Lay tried to lead. On Monday, October 22, he convened a meeting at the Hyatt of Enron's best and brightest—not just members of the management committee but all the company's managing directors, about 80 people in all. Andy Fastow wasn't there; he'd been instructed not to attend.

The meeting was cast as part of Enron's new open communication in the post-Skilling era. The discussion quickly turned to Fastow's partnerships. The board and senior management were behind Andy, he said; the managing directors needed to be supportive too. Enron had done nothing wrong, Lay insisted, "but knowing what we do now, we would never do it again."

"I'm in the terrible position of having to disagree with you," said Vince Kaminski from the audience.

Lay encouraged the risk-management wizard to speak his mind, so Kaminski stepped up to the microphone. Enron should never have gotten involved in Fastow's private partnerships, Kaminski said. "The Raptors were not only improper," he declared. "They were terminally stupid." The company's murky dealings had caused a crisis, Kaminski said. "The only fighting chance Enron has is to come clean."

Lay looked stunned; this was getting out of hand. "Enough, Vince," Whalley interrupted, and he led Kaminski from the podium.

Later that same day, a few hours after the managing directors meeting, Enron's board met. Unsure whether he was officially persona non grata, Andy asked a board secretary to "double-check that Ken wants me to attend." He didn't.

Among the directors, there was much concern about the impending rating review by Moody's, which had advised the company that it would be focusing on three issues: negative cash flow from operations, slow progress in the promised asset sales, and the likelihood of more write-offs involving Dabhol, Azurix, broadband, and California.

The most pressing discussion was about Fastow. It was now painfully obvious that the media knew more about Andy's partnerships than the Enron board did. The directors struggled to recall just what they had been told about the money Fastow made from the partnerships. The minutes noted: "Mr. Lay asked for a discussion regarding if the members of the Board had any recollection of information regarding the financial returns by Mr. Andrew S. Fastow in conjunction with certain financial arrangements."

In fact, the board *had* requested that information earlier. Back in October 2000 in Palm Beach, when Fastow won approval for LJM3, the directors actually asked the compensation committee to check on the CFO's compensation from the partnerships. The committee chair, LeMaistre, even made a feeble attempt to carry out the request. Initially, he asked Mary Joyce, an Enron compensation executive, to give him information on the outside income for all of Enron's top management. LeMaistre later explained that to avoid spreading office gossip he didn't ask specifically about Fastow. When Joyce said she didn't have the information, he asked her to let him know when she did. Six months later, he asked again. When no information arrived, LeMaistre simply dropped the matter.

Now the board belatedly resolved to do the obvious: ask Fastow directly.

Andy Fastow was up early the next day, Tuesday, October 23. At 6:36 A.M., he e-mailed his office: "Mickey LeMaistre called and asked that I have a conference call today at 4 P.M. with him and John Duncan. I'm not sure who is supposed to arrange it. Could you coordinate?"

Fastow then headed into the office, for an 8:30 A.M. analysts conference call. Determined to reclaim the initiative, Lay scheduled the call to address "investor concerns." The executive team carefully prepared for the session with Enron's outside accountants and lawyers. Vinson & Elkins partner Ron Astin displayed a Q&A script he'd marked up to the group—Lay, Fastow, Koenig, Causey, and Buy were all in the room. Included in the talking points was that Fastow had come up with the idea for LJM and presented it to the Enron board. "This is wrong!" Fastow screamed; LJM was *Skilling's* idea.

Lay opened the call by telling the analysts he was eager to address their questions and expressing his dismay at Enron's stock price, then flirting with $20. "To say the least, we are very, even extremely, disappointed with our stock price, particularly since our businesses are performing very well and we are continuing to conduct business as usual," he said.

Before turning the call over to Fastow, who was supposed to reassure investors about the state of Enron's finances, Lay paused to make clear that he was standing by his man. "I and Enron's board of directors continue to have the highest faith and confidence in Andy and believe he is doing an outstanding job as CFO," Lay declared.

After Fastow gave his presentation, the questions came fast and furious. What would Enron's earnings for 2000 and 2001 look like without the LJMs?

Causey told the analysts the absence of the partnerships would have had a "minimal impact." Enron, he said, could have simply done the same deals with other "third parties."

Richard Grubman, the short seller Skilling had called an asshole, took his turn. He asked about Marlin, the Enron debt vehicle that financed Azurix. By Grubman's calculations, its assets were worth less than its debt; thus Enron was left holding the bag. Causey and Grubman argued over the analyst's numbers until Lay jumped in. "Now I know you want to drive the stock price down, and you've done a good job at doing that, but I think that's that," he scolded.

"That's pointless," Grubman shot back.

"Let's go to the next question, Richard," said Lay. "You're monopolizing the conference. We've got a lot of people out there with real serious questions."

"I would appreciate an answer to the question," Grubman responded. "That's fine if you move on. I think everybody understands why."

One analyst asked what would happen if Enron's debt fell below investment grade.

Lay dismissed the possibility: "First of all, we'd have to be downgraded three notches to go below investment grade. And there's—at least we don't think there's any chance of that."

The analyst pressed the ugly hypothetical, and Glisan finally acknowledged that such a downgrade would trigger other repayment obligations for Enron. The company's entangled financial structure was becoming a public issue.

"Let's take a stab at the worst-case scenario here," said another analyst. The worst-case scenario wouldn't happen, Lay protested.

Asked about Fastow's partnerships, Lay insisted that the board had put controls in place to make sure that the interests of Enron shareholders wouldn't be compromised. "And I will also say," added Lay, waxing indignant, "that having checked just in the last several days, these procedures have been rigorously followed. So we do not—we're very concerned the way Andy's character has been kind of loosely thrown about over the last few days in certain articles, as well as, of course, the integrity of the company."

"With all due respect," retorted Goldman Sachs analyst David Fleischer, usually a company supporter, Enron's credibility was now being "severely questioned." There was a need for "much more disclosure," Fleischer continued. "There is an appearance that you're hiding something . . . that maybe there's something beneath the surface going on that is less than—that may be questionable."

"We're trying to provide information," Lay insisted. "We're not trying to conceal anything. We're not hiding anything."

John Olson, Lay's old nemesis, told the Enron chief it would be "important in terms of credibility" for Fastow to describe his role in the LJMs and how "closely monitored" he had been.

But Lay wasn't about to be *that* open. The SEC investigation would reveal everything, he insisted. There were legal issues involved. "I would prefer that Andy not get in too much detail as far as LJM. And let me say," Lay rushed to add, "there was a Chinese wall between LJM and Enron."

After the disastrous conference call ended, the Enron brass rushed over to the Hyatt for another packed all-employee meeting—held in a distinctly different climate. With Enron's stock heading toward $19, Lay evoked the events of September 11. "Just like America is under attack by terrorism," he declared, "I think *we're* under attack."

Lay tried to tell his employees he shared their pain. "I am absolutely heartbroken about what has happened, both the last few months and, more importantly, the last several days." He'd taken a financial hit right along with them, he said. "I've lost a substantial portion of my net worth." Yet Enron had done everything appropriately, Lay insisted. What no one had properly appreciated "was how difficult it was to explain it—the perception of it."

Lay then launched into a history of all the near-death experiences Enron had survived. The nationalization of its Peruvian oil and gas interests in 1985. The drop in gas prices in 1986. The Enron Oil scandal in 1987. J-Block in 1997. Enron always came back stronger, "and that's exactly what I think is going to happen here."

"I also know that many of you who were a lot wealthier six to nine months ago are now concerned about the college education for your kids, maybe the mortgage on your house, maybe your retirement, and for that I am incredibly sorry. But we're going to get it back," he vowed.

Turning to LJM, Lay uttered words he soon regretted. "I and the board are also sure that Andy has operated in the most ethical and appropriate manner possible." Still, Lay was "very sorry that this incredibly complicated thing ever happened and the damage was done to our image."

Several minutes into the question period, Lay was handed a written query, which he read aloud:

"I would like to know if you are on crack. If so that would explain a lot. If not, you may want to start because it's going to be a long time before we trust you again."

LeMaistre prepared carefully for his conference call with Fastow late that Tuesday afternoon. Jim Derrick, Enron's general counsel, provided a script, including introductory remarks and specific questions, and faxed it to LeMaistre, who was in Colorado. John Duncan, the second board member on the call, was patched in from Houston.

When everyone was on, LeMaistre began reading: "We very much appreciate your willingness to meet with us. Andy, because of the current controversy surrounding LJM1 and LJM2, we believe it would be helpful for the board to have a general understanding of the amount of your investment and your return on investment in the LJM entities."

Then the first question: "What was your aggregate income attributable to LJM1 and LJM2, inclusive of salary, consulting fees, management fees, partnership distributions, and gain on the sale of your partnership interest?"

For more than a year, Fastow had bobbed and weaved, dodging bosses, lawyers, and security regulations to avoid addressing this very question. But now, backed into a corner, he gave the directors a startling answer: he had made $23 million on LJM1 and another $22 million on LJM2. Fastow was telling them he'd pocketed $45 million—on a partnership that was supposedly occupying him just three hours a week! And he'd made the money doing deals with *Enron*. "Incredible," LeMaistre scrawled on his script.

In fact, Fastow's true take was even larger: $60.6 million.

What was his rate of return? LeMaistre asked. Fastow said that he had invested $1 million in LJM1 and $3.9 million in LJM2 but couldn't immediately tell them his rate of return.

Did he know of any other Enron employees besides Kopper who had "any economic interest" in the LJMs or had received "any benefit" from them? Fastow told them he did not—saying nothing about Glisan, Mordaunt, and the others who were members of the Southampton partnership.

And, finally, did he know any other "potentially troublesome matter of which we should now be apprised in connection with the LJM relationship?"

"No."

At 8 A.M. the next day, Greg Whalley walked into a conference room on the fiftieth floor of the Enron Building where a handful of executives were already gathered. They included Ken Lay; treasurer Ben Glisan; former treasurer Jeff McMahon, now running Enron Industrial Markets; and Andy Fastow.

Whalley pointed to Fastow: "You're not the CFO anymore," he told him. Then he pointed to McMahon: "You are." As the meeting continued, the talk turned to a finance issue. When Fastow tried to chime in, Whalley instantly shot him down. "Didn't you hear me?" Whalley snapped. "You're *fired*."

Fastow and his wife were supposed to have lunch that day. He e-mailed her to cancel. "Sweetheart, I can't do lunch because I've got to be here to find out my final status (reassigned, leave of abs, gone), work out details with ENE, and help with press release. Love you." Lea Fastow e-mailed back with some advice. "Important," she wrote. "The press release needs to say that you voluntarily stepped down due to your reduced effectiveness as CFO as a result of the character assassination."

In fact, Fastow was officially placed on a leave of absence, but McMahon's appointment as his replacement was announced immediately. Just 24 hours after Lay publicly insisted that Fastow's character was being unfairly maligned, the CFO was gone.

By the close of the day's trading, Enron shares had fallen to $16.41.

Not long after word of his "leave" got out, Andy Fastow received a call from his old boss, Jeff Skilling. In the two months since leaving Enron, Skilling had closely monitored events at the company. Even now, he checked in regularly with the PR department, asking Mark Palmer, "What are you hearing?" and volunteering his advice for dealing with the company's growing problems.

As Skilling watched from the sidelines, his frustration had grown. "Somebody needs to say something," Skilling railed. "The stuff being written is just crazy! It's not the company I know."

"Andy, what is going on?" Skilling now asked Fastow.

"Jeff, I don't know," the deposed CFO responded. "They won't tell me. I don't think I did anything wrong."

While Fastow was trying to sound chipper, Skilling could tell that he was down in the dumps. Skilling told his old colleague he should get on antidepressants and start seeing a psychiatrist—just as Skilling had done.

CHAPTER 22

"We Have No Cash!"

Scott Gieselman, a Goldman Sachs energy banker in Houston, was still in his office when the phone rang. It was late Wednesday night, October 24. Jeff McMahon, who had replaced Andy Fastow as Enron CFO that morning, was on the other end of the phone. "What can you monetize for me in the next 24 hours?" asked McMahon. He sounded frantic.

By the time of Fastow's firing, Enron's "perception" problem had evolved into something far worse—a cash crisis. With Enron's stock continuing to sink, panic was taking hold. The immediate problem was that Enron had been unable to roll its commercial paper—the portfolio of unsecured short-term loans that all big companies use to fund their day-to-day needs. Renewing such debt was normally a routine matter. Though the amounts involved were huge (for Enron, about $2 billion), the exposure was so brief (as little as 24 hours) that, for lenders, it was really nothing to worry about—unless they had reason to wonder if the company would survive long enough to pay it back.

And in Enron's case, that's just what was happening. McMahon was shocked to hear this. "If we can't roll commercial paper, we can't pay the janitor," he told Whalley. "We have *no cash!*"

McMahon and Whalley quickly set up a special war room over in Enron's new Cesar Pelli–designed headquarters across the street, where the traders had just started moving in. They summoned a clutch of corporate finance executives, lawyers, and the heads of Enron's business units for quick briefings to get a fix on the situation.

Enron, McMahon quickly realized, needed a billion, maybe two to three billion, *fast*—before word trickled out and a rush of panicked creditors shut the company down. The new CFO launched a desperate phone-a-thon, dialing up the big banks, and asking them—on a moment's notice—to write checks for $500 million or more.

The banks were welcome to sell or lend against anything Enron owned, McMahon advised. If it would help persuade Goldman Sachs to open its coffers, he told Gieselman, Enron would even give the firm full access to its secret trading books. "Nothing is off limits," he said. "What do you want?"

But this time, the answer came back from everyone: nothing. No one would move that fast, not for Enron, not now.

When that failed, Enron had no choice but to immediately deploy its backup plan. On Thursday, the company drew down the $3 billion in backup credit lines to its commercial paper. To Wall Street, this was instant confirmation of Enron's desperate straits. Virtually all large companies have such backup credit as part of their financing structure, and they're technically entitled to tap it whenever they want. But no lender ever expects—or wants—it to be used, since the debt is totally unsecured.

Enron tried to cast this act of desperation as a strategic move, one intended "to dispel uncertainty in the financial community." It was supposed to offer proof that the banks (which actually had no choice in the matter) were standing squarely behind the company. In a late-afternoon press release, McMahon was quoted explaining the drawdown this way: "We are making it clear that Enron has the support of its banks and more than adequate liquidity to assure our customers that we can fulfill our commitments in the ordinary course of business. This is an important step in our plan to restore investor confidence in Enron."

The same release announced that Enron Online had completed an "above average" day, with more than 8,400 trading transactions involving 1,387 counterparties. "We are especially gratified by this strong vote of confidence from both our customers and banks because that, more than anything, should enable the financial community to look beyond today's headlines and focus on the inherent value of our company," said Lay. As ever, Enron was trying hard to deliver the message that everything was fine.

Incredibly enough, that's what Lay, at least, truly seemed to believe. As one Enron executive put it: "Ken thought there was nothing wrong with Enron that what was right with Enron couldn't fix." And what was right, above all, meant the trading business. After Skilling quit, Lay had hired Gieselman and his colleagues at Goldman Sachs to assess Enron's finances. Fastow quickly encouraged them to focus their attention on finding a buyer for the pipelines, the only steady cash generator Enron had left. The thought was that everything would be fine if Enron could simply unload the pipelines to lighten the company's debt and unburden the trading business.

In the middle of all this sat McMahon, who had finally gotten the job he'd wanted, though the circumstances couldn't have been worse. Of the people now leading the company, he was the only who really understood corporate finance. Whalley had no experience in these matters. Neither he nor Lay could be much help in managing the cash crisis.

McMahon was operating under several serious handicaps. He hadn't worked in corporate finance for a year, and he had no idea where Fastow had buried the bodies. Nor did he have any easy way of finding out. Under Fastow, Enron had operated quarter to quarter. The company lacked the kind of sophisticated cash-management systems that big companies required. McMahon couldn't even find a maturity schedule showing when all Enron's debt would need to be repaid—a basic tool in corporate finance. In fact, with all the tangled off-balance-sheet machinations—obscuring what obligations were truly Enron's, obscuring even what was truly debt—no one could immediately tell McMahon how much money Enron owed.

There were other perils. Many of Fastow's structured-finance vehicles, which seemed so clever—even elegant—not long before, now stood revealed as rickety contraptions, lashed to one another and rigged to explode. The problem was that several of the deals, including Marlin and Osprey, had triggers requiring the immediate payback of billions in debt if Enron's share price fell below certain floors and its credit rating dropped too low. The stock price had already crashed through the floors; the challenge was to keep the credit ratings from dropping as well. After learning that Enron was drawing down its credit lines, S&P changed Enron's "credit outlook"—an interim step toward a ratings change—from stable to negative. Fitch had already done the same. Moody's had Enron's rating under review.

There was another frightening problem that was already taking hold. By its nature, a giant trading operation depends on credit to survive—it is the oxygen for the business. This was especially true of Enron, because of the giant cash needs of Enron Online. Rating-agency downgrades—even just shattered confidence—would prompt trading partners to start demanding cash collateral, producing what would amount to a run on the bank. If that couldn't be stopped, a few billion dollars of cash wouldn't last long.

As things stood at the moment, $2 billion from the credit lines would be needed just to pay off the commercial paper loans. This meant that Enron was already down to its last billion, and that was disappearing fast. As one Enron executive later put it: "Trading companies fall quickly—like a helicopter running out of fuel."

In the aftermath of his departure from Enron, Andy Fastow assumed a pose of being at peace with the world. On the day Enron had tapped its backup credit lines, he received a supportive e-mail from Seth Vance, a London-based banker for Citigroup. "Hang in there," Vance wrote. "The news will subside and I'm sure when the facts are out, it will be clear that everything you did was approved by the board. Shareholders will sue over anything when they lose as much as they have—looks like they are grabbing for anything and everything. I guess Jeff S. and Cliff B. timing of leaving Enron could not have been better—?").

Fastow responded that afternoon. "Needless to say, this has been quite an experience," he wrote, "but the great thing is that today I had breakfast with my family, drove my kids to school, had coffee with my wife, and soon I'm going for a run. I'm sure I'll have moments of frustration, but right now this is OK. I wish I could be in there helping Enron, but they've got a lot of smart people that will figure this out."

At the same time, Fastow was playing hardball with Enron. His attorneys threatened legal action, insisting that Fastow—officially still on leave of absence—had been involuntarily terminated without cause, triggering the severance provision in his new contract, worth more than $9 million. (The board dithered over Fastow's status for weeks until concluding that it had grounds to fire him for cause.)

Fastow's friends at Merrill, meanwhile, prevailed on Michael Kopper to stop making new LJM2 investments. In fact, noted Rob Furst, in an e-mail to Schuyler Tilney and two other Merrill bankers, Kopper now said he would "orderly liquidate the partnership." With Fastow's departure from Enron, LJM2's critical edge—its knowledge advantage—was gone. Kopper had to recognize, Furst noted, that "the premise for which the money was raised . . . is valid no longer."

As the Enron mess mushroomed and the Houston auditors belatedly scrambled to get a handle on it, Andersen executives in Chicago finally realized that Enron's problems could imperil the entire firm. Even as David Duncan and others were generating a written record of what was going on, a 38-year-old in-house laywer named Nancy Temple had begun looking over their memos, advising them to edit out language, and even destroy documents that might look bad in court. As it turned out, this campaign to sanitize Andersen's files proved even more lethal than the firm's craven accounting.

Temple became involved in September, when it first became apparent that Enron's accounting might require restatement. On October 9, during a conference call with two top Andersen lawyers, she jotted a note: "Highly probable some SEC investig[ation]." This alone was cause for alarm. Andersen had just paid a $7 million fine in connection with the billion-dollar accounting fraud at Waste Management; it was operating under an SEC cease-and-desist order barring it from further misconduct. Thus for Andersen, as Temple noted, an Enron restatement posed a huge danger—"probability of charge of violating C+D in WM."

The next day, Andersen's practice director in Houston, Michael Odom, gave a videotaped talk to a conference room jammed with audit managers—including Duncan—on the touchy subject of destroying files. In the Waste Management case, Andersen's records had provided government regulators and plaintiffs' lawyers with all the ammunition they needed. Andersen didn't want that to happen again.

Under the firm's document-retention policy, everything that isn't an essential part of the audit file—drafts, notes, internal memos, and e-mails—should be promptly discarded, Odom said. Once a lawsuit was filed, nothing could be destroyed, he noted. But "if it's destroyed in the course of the normal policy and litigation is filed the next day, that's great, you know, because we've followed our own policy, and whatever there was that might have been of interest to somebody is gone and irretrievable."

Two days later, on Friday, October 12, Temple, fresh from sifting through the embarrassing internal memos revealing the audit team's rejection of the PSG's advice on the Raptors, offered her own prod, advising Odom in an e-mail: "It might be useful to consider reminding the engagement team of our documentation and retention policy. It will be helpful to make sure that we have complied with the policy."

Such helpful reminders about document retention were starting to produce results. When David Duncan's assistant, Shannon Adlong, arrived for work the following Monday, she noticed bags filled with paper ribbons in the office break room, where the shredder was located. "There was food everywhere," she later recalled, "like they had been there the whole weekend."

On October 16, Temple e-mailed Duncan on the subject of his memo documenting events surrounding Enron's third-quarter earnings release, the one that criticized Enron's characterization of its big write-off as a nonrecurring charge. Temple offered Duncan "a few suggested comments for consideration." She encouraged "deleting reference to consultation with the legal group and deleting my name on the memo. Reference to the legal group consultation arguably is a waiver of attorney-client privilege and if my name is mentioned it increases the chances that I might be a witness, which I prefer to avoid." She also advised "deleting some language that might suggest we have concluded the release is misleading"—even though that is *exactly* what Andersen had concluded.

Temple later explained her aim to an outside lawyer for Andersen, saying she was "trying to balance documenting our discussion with possible subsequent challenges that we somehow had a responsibility to follow up when we knew the client had issued a press release that was potentially misleading."

In the days to come, Temple continued to edit internal documents even as they were being generated; at one point, she suggested deleting senior Andersen partners from the circulation list for Enron e-mails because it "increases their likelihood of being a witness."

Duncan, of course, was forwarded Temple's reminder about document retention. Although he later said he took it as a coded message to start destroying Enron files, he was too busy dealing with the Enron crisis to do much about it for a week. By October 23, the matter had become more urgent. The SEC inquiry had been announced, Andersen was taking a closer look at more of its old accounting decisions involving Enron, the first lawsuits against the energy company had already been filed, and Enron, just that morning, had held its disastrous conference call with the analysts. Andersen's window of opportunity for cleaning up its Enron files might slam shut at any moment.

At 1:30 P.M. that day, Duncan presided over an all-hands meeting of the Enron team, where, among other matters, he noted that Andersen would invariably become involved in the SEC inquiry and reminded his team to comply with the firm's document policy. Immediately, Andersen's Houston office began working overtime shredding documents.

One day into it, Adlong, Duncan's assistant, dispatched an e-mail: "ARRR-GGHHH, send more shredding bags! (just kidding we have ordered some)." The machine at Andersen's Enron office was quickly overwhelmed; dozens of trunks and boxes filled with documents—more than a ton of paper—were shipped to the main downtown office, where files awaiting destruction spilled out into the hallways outside the shredding room. It was more than the entire Houston office typically shredded in an entire year. The load was so great that Andersen summoned a shredding truck from a local disposal company called Shred-It. (The company's motto: "Your secrets are safe with us.") Andersen's offices in London, Portland, and Chicago joined in, shredding their Enron documents. In addition to the paper, almost 30,000 e-mail messages and computer files were deleted.

On October 26, Andersen audit-practice director John Riley, in town to help sort out the Enron accounting, heard a high-pitched whine in the office. "What's that noise?" he asked Duncan. "You guys have a shredder up here?" Duncan told him the Enron team was merely destroying routine client documents. "Well," Riley responded, "this wouldn't be the best time in the world for you guys to be shredding a bunch of stuff." Four days later, David Stulb, an in-house Andersen investigator, arrived in Houston to discuss the Enron situation. Duncan pulled out the cover page on Jim Hecker's e-mail about his conversation with Sherron Watkins—with its remark about "smoking guns you can't extinguish"—and announced: "We need to get rid of this." Stulb instructed him to keep it, then notified his bosses in New York that "Dave Duncan needs some guidance on document retention."

Finally, the shredding stopped—but only after Andersen received a subpoena from the SEC. Adlong, Duncan's assistant, sent out a final e-mail on the subject: "Per Dave: no more shredding. If you are asked, tell them Dave said we can't. We've been officially served by the attorneys for our documents."

Even as Andersen was shredding documents, it was also stumbling across huge mistakes hidden in Enron's books. One after another, they were blowing up, like long-buried land mines.

The first involved Chewco, the Kopper-managed SPE that Fastow formed back in 1997 to buy out CalPERS's 50 percent interest in JEDI, its investment partnership with Enron. The deal had kept more than $600 million in debt off Enron's books. With Fastow and Kopper now gone, Enron accountants had finally shown an Andersen partner documents revealing that Enron, under a secret side deal, had put up cash collateral to help provide the 3 percent outside equity

Chewco required. This meant that Chewco didn't really qualify as a third-party SPE; both it and JEDI should have been consolidated on Enron's books.

Andersen also learned of another reason why Chewco's dealings probably didn't merit off-balance-sheet treatment: the outside partnership was really controlled (and partly funded) by Kopper, then an Enron employee; Kopper, in turn, had tried to disguise his role by transferring his controlling interest to Bill Dodson, who—unbeknownst to Andersen—was Kopper's domestic partner.

The second big revelation involved LJM1; this mistake dated back to 1999. After studying the documents, Andersen realized that LJM Swap Sub—the partnership subsidiary that helped generate the secret windfall for the NatWest bankers and their Enron counterparts—had never been properly capitalized with 3 percent outside equity. This meant that its transactions also had to go back on Enron's books.

This time, Andersen resolved: no more games. Enron would need to restate its earnings all the way back to 1997, adding debt to its teetering balance sheet and wiping out a big chunk of its reported profits. All this was horrible news—for both Arthur Andersen and Enron.

As each deal painfully unraveled, Whalley convened a meeting to brief a half-dozen senior executives, including Lay, about Enron's latest accounting disaster. Chewco proved especially challenging to explain, especially as the discussion turned to the related-party issue. "There's just one problem," someone said. "We're not sure whether the related party is Michael Kopper—or Michael Kopper's gay lover."

Ken Lay turned pale. "His *gay lover?* What the fuck is going on around here?"

"C'mon Ken," Whalley responded, after a moment of shocked silence. "Haven't you seen the way Michael Kopper dresses?"

As Enron's troubles continued to gather, like the ghosts of quarters past, Lay seemed almost paralyzed. "He was curled up in the fetal position the whole time," says an Enron executive in the thick of it all. Lay continued to believe that Enron would survive this crisis, just as it had survived those in the past. He also continued to believe it was still primarily a public-relations problem.

In late October, Lay received advice on how to manage the situation from an unlikely quarter—Sherron Watkins. The Enron whistle-blower met with Lay again, this time bearing a letter with her advice on spinning Enron's crisis. Offering herself as Lay's personal crisis-management adviser, Watkins urged him to blame his subordinates—to "admit that he trusted the wrong people" and announce that "the culprits are Skilling, Fastow, Glisan, and Causey as well as Arthur Andersen and V&E."

In Watkins's scenario, the party line would go like this: "Ken Lay and his board were duped by a COO who wanted the targets met no matter what the consequences, a CFO motivated by personal greed and 2 of the most respected firms, AA&CO and V&E, who had grown too wealthy off Enron's yearly business. . . ." Lay should exploit his personal goodwill to sell the story, Watkins wrote—after all, "nobody wants Ken Lay's head." (For her part, Watkins had sold off her own modest Enron stake, unloading a grant of shares for $31,000 in August after writing her letter to Lay and netting $17,000 from a sale of options in October. Watkins said she'd sold the first block for "tax reasons" and the second over concerns about the impact of September 11.)

Inevitably, Lay reacted to the crisis by seeking to cash in his political chips, looking to win help for Enron through his powerful Washington connections. He called Secretary of the Treasury Paul O'Neill, himself a former CEO; former Treasury secretary Robert Rubin, now at Citigroup; Secretary of Commerce Donald Evans, an old Texas hand; even Alan Greenspan.

Lay spoke darkly about the impact Enron's failure might have on global energy markets; he likened its plight to that of Long-Term Capital Management, the giant hedge fund that was rescued by a 1998 federal bailout; and he wondered aloud what a few well-placed calls might do to pry an extra billion or two loose from the banks and keep the rating agencies from downgrading Enron's debt.

Yet despite all of Lay's presumed clout, no one did anything meaningful to intervene. It seemed as though everyone was turning on Enron, even those that the company had always been able to manage—first Wall Street, then the media, now Washington.

Lay sought comfort from a few trusted Houston ministers. Dr. Steve Wende, the pastor at First United Methodist, a large downtown church, recalls that Lay would periodically interrupt his business day to call "because he felt like he needed God's help." Lay and the minister would then pray together over the phone. Lay spoke to Wende about the press's "unfair" treatment of Enron and how he'd made "a number of mistakes early in his life." Lay told Wende he believed he could save Enron, and he wanted to do it "God's way."

In the darkening days of October, Lay's family sought to offer the beleaguered CEO their own special form of solace. Earlier in the year, Lay's son Mark had left behind his troubled business career—including a string of ventures that did business with Enron—to enroll at Southwestern Baptist Theological Seminary in Houston. Now he began e-mailing biblical passages to his father. In one accompanying note, Mark likened his father to Solomon ("there is no doubt God has already given you great wisdom").

In another installment, which Mark titled "Take it to them," the younger Lay offered his father "bullet points" about the tale of King Hezekiah, "the most Godly man . . . after him there was none like him among all the kings of Judah." Hezekiah, too, had found himself under siege, Mark told his father: "The Assyrians surrounded his city with a great army. He went to God with great faith and honored God. God sent an angel."

> . . . And it came to pass that night, that the angel of Jehovah went forth and smote in the camp of the Assyrians a hundred fourscore and five thousand: and when men arose early in the morning, behold, these were all dead bodies.

A day later, Linda Lay received an e-mail from a friend named Phyllis Bronson, a Ph.D. "new medicine" expert in mood disorders, such as anxiety and depression. Bronson, a biochemical nutritionist, lived in Aspen, where the Lays vacationed.

"So much for your quieter time of life," Bronson wrote. "After seeing the NY Times article yesterday, I am glad for Enron that Ken is back at the helm; I trust he will persevere and be more than successful in whatever he does." She went on: "I am concerned about his level of stress, and would highly recommend that he keep up that anxiety control formula, taking two after meals 3x a day. I have stronger things in my arsenal if needed. Also, perhaps when he is here sometime, I could check his blood chemistry for stress factors and optimal brain function."

Linda responded on Tuesday, October 30:

> Dear Phyllis,
>   Bless you for your care and concern. I have forwarded on to Ken's office and will get him to Aspen as soon as the smoke clears. He is burning the candle day and night with very little sleep. I am praying hard for him and Enron and know that he has the strength, wisdom, skills and courage to persevere and succeed. I will stay in touch.
>
> Love, Linda.

Linda sent the e-mail on to Ken's office, with her own accompanying note:

> Dear Ken,
>   I am packaging up extra anxiety control pills to go down to your office. Please have Earl [Lay's driver] pick them up at the front door. I love you, Linda.

■   ■   ■

In the thick of Enron's crisis, there were some bankers who caught the scent of opportunity. With Fastow gone and the company in desperate straits, they were finally in the driver's seat. They'd consider lending Enron money, but now it would be on *their* terms.

At first, Enron didn't fully appreciate just how much things had changed. Immediately after drawing down its backup credit lines, the company informed the banks it needed an extra $2 billion cash, at least. Despite its predicament, Enron executives still thought they could borrow the money unsecured, as they always had. To head off a panic, they wanted to announce the deal the following Monday, October 29—just five days after Fastow was ousted. As one Wall Street analyst put it: "They were beggars long before they knew they were beggars." Enron quickly got a reality check. The banks flatly turned the company down.

J. P. Morgan Chase and Citi agreed to talk about lending an extra $1 billion, though Enron clearly needed much more. But now, they were demanding the only real collateral the company had left, the Transwestern and Northern Natural pipeline systems. For years, Enron's natural-gas pipelines had been an afterthought. Now they were the company's lifeline.

And the pipes weren't all the banks wanted. J. P. Morgan Chase and Citi extracted commitments that Enron would use them exclusively for all its investment-banking work for the next 18 months. "Due to the company's recent liquidity issues, J. P. Morgan is well-positioned to realize further business," a Morgan internal memo crowed. "In addition to our leadership role in the arrangement of $1.0 billion in financing . . . we have been mandated as a strategic advisor to Enron with an initial retainer provided of $15 million. Further, we anticipate additional restructuring and arrangement fees going forward."

Enron executives railed privately about the banks' "strong-arm tactics" and "extortion"—oblivious of the rich irony. Indeed, Enron tried to turn the tables on Goldman, demanding that it either lend the company money or make an equity investment if it wanted to keep earning advisory fees. When the Goldman executives kept asking sticky questions, the relationship ended with a major blowup. "Get out of our offices right now unless you're willing to cut a check," Whalley told Gieselman.

Still, by November 1, Enron was able to announce that it had secured another $1 billion in financing. But as it turned out, $250 million of the package was merely the refinancing of an existing loan from Citi that was expiring at year-end. It improved the bank's collateral position but gave Enron no new cash. Even after hocking its pipelines, Enron had generated only $750 million more, which wasn't going to last long.

One of the prices of becoming a supplicant is having to expose yourself to unfamiliar scrutiny. Before the crisis—still only a few weeks old—Enron had protected its darkest secrets, allowing the company to freely spin its tale of an untroubled, ever-brighter future. But Enron's need for money forced the company to open its books to the banks. As they burrowed in, Enron's lenders experienced their own revelations about the business they financed for so many years.

It was hardly news that the international assets had been a money pit, that Azurix had been a disaster, that Enron had spent far too much on broadband. But one of the company's fundamental premises was that all was well at the core trading operation—that Enron Wholesale, where trading was harbored, was not only hitting its lofty numbers but would generate bigger profits in the years to come. Indeed, saving the trading operation became the core premise of Enron's survival strategy, even though it would consume billions in precious cash. As the Whalley-led management team saw it, this was the company's crown jewel, its only path to salvation.

But for the banks, even trading had now become suspect. In one memo to an Enron finance employee, Deutsche Bank's Paul Cambridge openly wondered whether Enron was making up some of its trading profits. "With regard to the risk book, a constant concern for our derivatives and credit people is Enron's mark-to-market methodology," he noted. "There is a concern that as an unregulated trader, the mark to market is very much an Enron-driven internal process as opposed to seeking three quotes etc. etc. This is exacerbated by the belief that a significant component of the risk book is either illiquid long-term trades or exotics (weather derivatives paper etc)."

J. P. Morgan Chase dispatched a full due-diligence team to Houston to test Enron's claims that the core business was in good shape. The SWAT team soon reported back with fresh intelligence after a bank executive named Charles Freeman found, to his surprise, an Enron executive who was "a straight shooter, and seemed to know just what was going on, and where the money is or isn't."

"I was struck by the [cash flow] analysis shown to us," Freeman advised. "The key question in my mind is the reason ENE has had to continually raise very large sums through prepays and the other off-balance-sheet financing." One explanation, from Enron treasurer Glisan, was that "the rating agencies needed to see that there was cash flow to match MTM [mark-to-market] earnings." But Freeman was skeptical of this. "The real reason," he wrote, "must be their need to finance all the businesses that are soaking up cash."

The evidence was in Enron's cash-flow schedule—"an eye-opener," Freeman reported. It broke down the separate businesses inside Enron Wholesale, showing earnings and cash flow for the first nine months of 2001. "The core Enron North America is the cash producer—everything else is soaking up cash," Freeman reported. But the "key question"—which he couldn't yet answer—was whether the trading operation's cash flow had been "puffed up" by "hidden financing." From "a number of comments made by Enron people," he wrote, it was "clear," despite the company's assurances, that 2002 trading profits were going to drop. The only issue, he wrote, is "by how much."

Freeman also spotted the hidden stinkers. The trading division "is carrying a bunch of loss-making businesses," he reported. "This explains the need of ENE to close large prepay financings in Q4 (this year and in previous years) to get the cash needed to stay afloat." The "biggest culprit," he added, was EES. "There have been big losses in this retail book, carried on wholesale's books." The numbers he'd been given put EES's trading losses at $496 million for the first quarter and $230 million for the second. Enron's European operation too—long touted as a "barn-burner" and reporting profits—was barely scraping along.

• • •

After a few weeks of kicking back and watching Enron unravel without him, Jeff Skilling was getting his mojo back. Skilling had intended to ease back into the world of business. He was talking to Lou Pai about doing some deals, and he hoped to teach; he'd already agreed to offer a class at Rice University in Houston on Business Strategy and Microeconomics.

Three months earlier, when he quit Enron, Skilling felt certain that his presence had become a lead weight on the company's stock. But Enron's real collapse had begun only after he'd left. To Skilling, this sequence of events could only mean one thing: he hadn't been the problem after all! What's more, as Skilling saw it, there really wasn't anything wrong with Enron. Like Lay, he saw it primarily as a perception problem. Despite everything, the company was still promising profits of $2.10 a share in 2002—while the stock price was down to ten dollars. Sitting on the sidelines, Skilling became increasingly agitated. This was *nuts*!

Whalley was smart but green, in way over his head, with little experience. Wall Street viewed him as a bully. Lay was clueless. *Someone* had to take charge. Skilling decided it should be him. He built Enron; now he could save it. So Skilling called Lay, offering himself as savior.

"Ken, you've got to bring me back." Skilling told him. "As interim CEO, COO—*something*. You've got to get ahead of this thing!"

Skilling explained what had to be done and, as always, made it sound simple. They needed billions, he figured, and that meant they had to get on a plane to New York, right away. They needed to go see J. P. Morgan Chase vice chairman Jimmy Lee. They needed to sit down across the table and tell him face-to-face: *There's nothing wrong with Enron. You're going to get paid back!*

Never mind that the banks had already made it abundantly clear they weren't going to hand money over to Enron anymore. Skilling had always been able to work his magic before. No one was more convincing. Even now, just listening to him, it seemed that he might be able to pull it off. It could be the best chance Enron had. "I'm very interested," Lay told him. "*Very* interested."

The next day, Lay sent Whalley to Skilling's home. They talked about liquidity. "I'm just horseshoes-and-hand-grenades guessing," said Skilling, "but I think you need about $3 billion."

"Our guess is about $3.5 billion," Whalley told him. After 30 minutes of conversation, Whalley said he was ready to welcome Skilling back.

For a few hours, back at Enron, the idea of bringing back Skilling was seriously entertained. Lay summoned a handful of executives to a conference room on the fiftieth floor to talk about it. "I think it can work," he told the group. "What do you think?" Whalley agreed. "Jeff knows the business and can get everybody back on board," he said. "He can go up to New York, and explain the story and get the liquidity."

When McMahon arrived late for the meeting, he was shocked at what he was hearing. How could they even *think* about bringing Skilling back? Who did they think was responsible for this mess? Who was responsible for *Fastow*? What's more, Jeff had *walked out on them.* It was as though they'd fallen back under Skilling's spell, mesmerized by the thought of his return—like Jim Jones's followers in Guyana, ready to drink the poisoned Kool-Aid. "You guys are out of your minds!" McMahon told them.

Whalley told Skilling the deal was off. The consensus view was that his return would spook the market, Whalley explained. No one would understand.

Still, Skilling wasn't ready to give up on the idea that he could rescue Enron. He began trying to put private equity together on his own, calling friends with big money, like the Chicago billionaire Sam Zell, who might help recapitalize the company. Baxter and Pai agreed to go in on it with him. It would be just like the ECT days. The old gang would be back.

Skilling and Baxter starting spending four to five hours a day on the phone, cooking up plans until one in the morning. It *was* just like the old days. Right around that time, an SEC subpoena arrived. Skilling dropped the idea.

For Enron's directors, there was a new leading indicator of the company's deepening problems: the presence of a fresh team of lawyers at their frequent special meetings. On Sunday, October 26, it was William McLucas, former enforcement director for the SEC. After leaving the government, McLucas went into private practice with the Washington law firm of Wilmer, Cutler & Pickering. Now he was the go-to man for companies embroiled in accounting scandals.

McLucas had the process down to a drill: serving as the company's independent counsel, he'd conduct a detailed internal investigation, backed by a special team of forensic accountants, experts in dissecting complex transactions. The process would be overseen by a special board committee, which would issue a public report, aimed at reestablishing the company's credibility by airing out all the dirty laundry.

Lay had resisted hiring McLucas and his high-powered team, insisting to Enron subordinates, "They'll just find something wrong." But now, he had no choice. The SEC was about to announce that it was elevating its informal inquiry to a formal investigation; Enron's credibility on the propriety of its dealings with Fastow's partnerships—which Lay had so doggedly defended—had evaporated. A newly appointed director, University of Texas Law School dean William Powers, would chair the special investigative committee for the board. Deloitte & Touche would do the forensic accounting.

At another board meeting two days later, there was an even more sobering legal presence: Martin J. Bienenstock, corporate America's grim reaper. Bienenstock, with the New York firm of Weil Gotshal & Manges, was the nation's preeminent bankruptcy lawyer. No one at Enron was ready to throw in the towel, but his appearance was a signal that the situation was becoming dire. Bienenstock's mere presence, had it been leaked to the press, would have been suffi-cient to throw Enron's stock into a further tailspin.

Enron was running out of options. Even after the new $1 billion loan from the banks—which still hadn't closed—the big issue remained liquidity. No longer willing to trust Enron's credit, more and more of the company's trading counter-parties were demanding cash collateral. Money was rushing out the door faster than Enron could raise it.

By early November, with the banks balking at ponying up any more cash, En-ron was engaged in a wide-ranging search for capital. It was desperately trying to sell assets. It had contacted the big private equity firms. It had made inquiries to potential strategic partners, including Shell and British Petroleum, about buy-ing a stake in the business. It had put out feelers to Omaha billionaire Warren Buffett, Saudi Prince Al-Waleed, and—indirectly—even Rich Kinder. There was time for just one more desperate Hail Mary pass—a last-ditch deal, code-named Project Notre Dame.

The day after Andy Fastow was fired, Enron pipeline chief Stan Horton sat down in a private room at Houston's Plaza Club for his regular lunch with his old friend, Steve Bergstrom. Bergstrom, an Enron alum, was the number-two man at Dynegy. On this day, they weren't eating alone; Horton had brought along his bosses, Enron president Greg Whalley and vice chairman Mark Frevert. As the four broke bread, Whalley posed a question that would have seemed unimagin-able just a few days earlier:

Would Dynegy be interested in buying Enron?

Bergstrom was astounded. *They're in worse trouble than I thought!* When lunch was over, the Enron executives returned to headquarters and reported the Dynegy president's response to their overture. "They're horny," Whalley said.

For Dynegy's top executives, the thought of acquiring Enron was indeed alluring. CEO Chuck Watson and his company had operated in the shadow of Ken Lay and Enron for more than a decade. Since 1985, when Watson had taken over the business—then called the Natural Gas Clearinghouse—Dynegy had en-joyed a stellar run. The company had grown rapidly; its earnings and stock price had steadily climbed. It owned power plants and pipelines and traded gas and power too.

Yet Dynegy, whose headquarters was just a few blocks down the street, had always been perceived as an Enron wannabe. It was only one-third Enron's size. As Enron emerged as the industry superstar, Enron's executives—especially Skilling—always treated Dynegy with disdain. They regarded Watson's com-pany as an unimaginative pipsqueak—a stolid bunch of Enron castoffs and working stiffs, with hardly a Harvard MBA among them. Even Dynegy's slogan seemed pedestrian: "A leading global energy company respected for the manner in which we deliver extraordinary value to our stakeholders."

Like Lay, Chuck Watson was a pillar of the Houston community. An economics major at Oklahoma State, the 51-year-old CEO had chaired Houston's United Way campaign, owned Houston's minor-league hockey team, and held a minority stake in its new NFL franchise. Where Lay was cerebral and measured, Watson was blunt and folksy. A large, beefy man, he was a dead ringer for Chuck Connors with forty extra pounds. Watson also was tough and not just at the bargaining table. As he contemplated buying Enron, he'd just finished a course of radiation treatments for prostate cancer, which he'd scheduled for 4:30 A.M., so he wouldn't miss any time at work.

Personal motivation aside, Watson had sound business reasons to consider a deal. For years, Enron's high-flier status had lifted all energy companies' shares. As Watson put it, "they had drug everybody else up." Now, if Enron failed, they might well drag everybody else down. But the most obvious attraction was that Enron's stock was in the toilet—not much above ten dollars. The entire company, valued at close to $70 billion less than a year earlier, could be had for less than $10 billion. If the trading business was really operating as promised—if there really weren't any more surprises—Enron could be a steal.

Watson was in his office when Bergstrom raced in to tell him the news from lunch. A call from Lay soon followed, and the two CEOs—knowing they needed to keep any meeting secret—agreed to have breakfast at 8:30 Saturday, at the Lays' condo in River Oaks.

Over rolls and coffee, Lay played it cool. His company was in a pinch, to be sure, but he was exploring a number of options. Still, they needed to move fast. As Lay envisioned things, the deal would be a merger of equals. They could come up with a fresh name for the new company, just as he had when Enron was born. Lay even imagined himself holding an exalted title with the new enterprise, perhaps something like chairman emeritus.

Watson wasted no time shattering such illusions. This would be an *acquisition,* he told Lay. Dynegy would buy Enron—for market price, without a premium. The combined company would be called Dynegy, and Watson's team would be firmly in charge.

Lay wasn't in much of a position to argue. The two men talked through lunchtime, hashing out how a merger might work, and agreed to set it all in motion.

One week later, on November 2, Lay placed Project Notre Dame before his board. In a handout detailing the transaction, Enron was code-named Gipper, Dynegy was Rockne, and ChevronTexaco, which owned 26 percent of Dynegy, was Heisman. The sale to Dynegy was structured to give Enron what it most needed—a quick infusion of capital. ChevronTexaco had committed to providing $2.5 billion—$1.5 billion right away and another $1 billion when the merger closed.

In truth, even that amount was far less than Enron really needed. A board document prepared by Enron's bankers concluded it would take at least another $3 billion just to keep Enron alive through the end of 2002, about the time the deal was likely to close. A fundamental premise of their thinking was that the involvement by ChevronTexaco, the global oil giant, would be so reassuring to Enron's trading partners that it would bring an immediate halt to the ongoing run on the bank. All this meant that the deal was woefully undercapitalized from the start. The Enron team saw it as a way to buy a little time—they'd find the extra billions they needed later. None of this was shared with Dynegy.

For Enron, the prospect of a sale to Dynegy was humbling. But if all went according to plan, it would preserve the core energy-trading operation and give them all a chance of staying in business. Other alternatives Enron had explored wouldn't generate cash soon enough to keep the business alive. J. P. Morgan Chase vice chairman Jimmy Lee, sitting in with the Enron board (the bank, which was advising Enron, had agreed to help finance the deal), pointed out its crucial advantage: "Dynegy can move fast." Enron wanted to sign the merger agreement on Sunday, November 4, and announce it the following day.

Enron desperately needed some good news, especially since it was about to drop another bombshell on the markets: the huge accounting restatement. Andersen delivered the news to the board that same weekend: Chewco and LJM1 hadn't really qualified for off-balance-sheet treatment. And Andersen had concluded that the $1.2 billion equity write-down Enron had already disclosed—which it had previously deemed immaterial—would also require restatement.

Lay, Causey, and the board were furious. *Flip-flop, flip-flop*—how could Enron trust its auditors on *anything?* Why hadn't these problems been uncovered long ago? If Andersen had done its job properly, Lay complained, "we wouldn't be here today." True enough. In its accounting work for Enron, Andersen had been sloppy and weak. But that's how Enron had always wanted it. In truth, even as they angrily pointed fingers, the two deserved each other.

In the first full week of November, Enron's very survival seemed to hang on delicate issues of timing. The SEC was demanding that Enron make another painful disclosure—immediately. After launching its formal investigation and reviewing Lay's performance on the October 23 conference call with analysts, the agency fired off a private letter to McLucas, complaining of Enron's "apparent unwillingness to provide meaningful disclosure to the investing public" about the "nature" and "performance" of Fastow's partnerships. The letter demanded that Enron disclose such information "in a form that a reasonable investor would find helpful and would understand" and that it do so "in short order, certainly no later than Monday, November 5, 2001." At the same time, Arthur Andersen was insisting that Enron's restatement be issued as soon as possible lest they all get into *more* trouble for market manipulation.

Yet however fast everyone was moving, the Dynegy deal wouldn't be ready to announce until late in the week. If Enron couldn't break the good news first, the weight of the combined disclosures to the SEC would almost certainly sink the company.

Enron asked McLucas to "grovel" with the feds for an extension. He explained to the government regulators that the company was preparing a major restatement and the required disclosure and could announce both simultaneously but needed a little more time. The SEC gave the company until Thursday, November 8.

Meanwhile, Enron discovered even more bad news to disclose. Kristina Mordaunt had confessed her involvement in Fastow's lucrative Southampton partnership and revealed the names of other employees who'd been involved, too, including treasurer Ben Glisan, who'd remained silent about the matter through this entire period. Glisan and Mordaunt, the only ones who remained on Enron's payroll, were swiftly fired. An Enron executive named Ray Bowen replaced Glisan as corporate treasurer.

Enron spent the week riding a rollercoaster. On Monday, Fitch, citing "an erosion in investor confidence," cut Enron's debt to one notch above junk status; Moody's and Standard & Poor's had already downgraded a few days earlier. The stock tumbled below $10. On Wednesday, shares dropped 25 percent more on news that Enron was unable to line up $2 billion it was seeking from private investors. The stock recovered after a well-timed leak, released before the market closed, that Dynegy was in talks to buy Enron.

By Thursday, November 8, everything was ready to go. The boards of Enron, Dynegy, and ChevronTexaco had approved the merger. The rating agencies had been privately briefed. The press releases were prepared.

First, Enron announced its restatement, consolidating the troubled partnerships and rewriting more than four years of its accounting history. About $586 million in profits—20 percent of Enron's previously reported net income dating back to 1997—was simply erased. In a 21-page SEC filing, Enron told the truth about these issues for the first time. Partnerships were named, transactions described, and financial details disclosed. Fastow, Enron conceded, had made "more than $30 million" from the partnerships.

The merger was supposed to be announced Thursday, too. But at seven that morning, Moody's called with startling news: it planned to cut Enron's debt rating again, this time *below* investment grade. Moody's thought the combined company's balance sheet would be shaky, and it didn't like the terms of the merger—it gave Dynegy and the banks too many outs.

This couldn't be allowed to stand. A junk-bond rating would pull the triggers on billions of Enron debt. The game would be over—for the Dynegy deal *and* for Enron. McMahon begged Moody's to hold off. If the rating agency didn't like the deal, they could *change* it. Moody's was noncommittal but agreed to listen.

Everyone then went into mad-scramble mode. Moody's executives started getting calls from powerful people like New York Stock Exchange CEO Richard Grasso and ChevronTexaco's CEO. Former treasury secretary Rubin called a treasury official. A meeting was quickly arranged between the rating agency and bank heavyweights—J. P. Morgan Chase CEO William Harrison, vice chairman Jimmy Lee, and Citi investment-banking chief Michael Carpenter. By the end of the day, the deal had been changed. The easy outs were eliminated, and the two banks, which were also serving as Enron's financial advisers, tentatively agreed to commit $500 million in equity capital. Moody's was appeased; the deal could go forward.

The rating agency downgraded Enron the next day, Friday, when the merger was officially announced but did keep it a notch above junk status. S&P downgraded it one step too. Enron now barely clung to its investment-grade standing. After the previous day's earnings restatement, the Dynegy deal was now the only thing keeping Enron alive.

The terms of the company's sale made clear just how far Enron had fallen. Watson had agreed to pay about $9 billion in stock—0.2685 Dynegy share for each Enron share—and to assume Enron's outstanding debt. For its $1.5 billion capital infusion, Dynegy would get preferred stock in Enron's prized Northern Natural pipeline system; if the deal fell through, Dynegy would have to the right to buy it.

And there would be no danger of the predator's quickly being eaten by the prey—as had happened 16 years earlier when Omaha's InterNorth had bought Lay's Houston Natural Gas. Watson, Bergstrom, and Dynegy CFO Rob Doty would sit atop the combined company. Dynegy directors would dominate the board, with 11 of 14 seats. There would be no place for Ken Lay, except possibly a seat on the board. Of Enron's senior executives, only Whalley would have a major role, with the title of executive vice president. Watson, too, was eager to keep the traders happy.

On the day the company's sale was announced, Lay denied it was the product of desperation. "We had other alternatives," he told skeptical reporters. During the week, Enron publicly insisted that it had plenty of cash, that its trading business was doing fine, and that it was paying all its bills. In fact, none of these things was true.

Early on Thursday night, during the tense hours while Enron was waiting to hear whether Moody's would pull the plug, Jeff McMahon delivered a sobering report to the board. According to board minutes, the CFO "expressed concerns on the inadequate level of financial liquidity, noting that the Company had begun to defer certain trade payments currently due, noting that if the Moody's published debt rating was not maintained at investment-grade, significant obligations would become due immediately and the Company would be illiquid."

Wall Street seemed to like the deal—at first.

In the days following the announcement, Enron's shares rose 16 percent, to $10; Dynegy's were up 19 percent. The two CEOs said all the right things. Lay, though, seemed a bit desultory, shell-shocked that it had come to this. "This is a very reflective time for me," he told the press and analysts. "I did not expect to some day be involved in creating the next world-leading energy-merchant company by merging Enron into another company."

Watson insisted his team had been extraordinarily conservative in sizing up the deal. They were cautious in projecting Enron's future earnings; they made a big allowance for Enron litigation; and they weren't counting on a penny of the $400 million in savings they were expecting from combining the two companies' operations. Still, he said, the numbers came out great. Once the deal closed in late 2002, Enron would boost Dynegy's earnings per share by about 35 percent. "From a financial standpoint," Watson declared, "there's nothing but upside in this transaction."

At the same time, Watson realized, this was a huge, high-stakes gamble. If it worked, he'd end up running a powerhouse—the world's dominant energy trader, with prized power plants and pipeline systems, revenues of more than $200 billion, more than $90 billion in assets, and 25,000 employees. He'd have vaulted Dynegy from obscurity into the ranks of America's biggest companies. Even those in Dynegy's camp marveled at the turn of events. "That Enron, who had been the big bully, kicking sand at everyone, was in a position to be acquired by Dynegy—on Dynegy's terms—was amazing," says a key Watson adviser.

There were also mammoth risks. Enron had been generating bad news practically daily—any more might drag it under, and Dynegy could be caught in the undertow. Besides, everyone knew Enron was a snake pit. Was there anyone there Watson could really trust?

Wall Street started to wonder too. For all the deal's potential, powerful doubts lingered. Did Dynegy really know what it was getting into? How could Watson, after only two weeks of due diligence, really be sure there weren't more surprises lurking? And what about the problem of melding the two companies: how would Watson keep Enron's sharpies from eating his choirboys for lunch? *Could Chuck really pull it off?*

Publicly, Watson assured Wall Street that his team had considered all the angles. "We looked under the hood and—guess what? It's just as strong as we thought it was," he said. Dynegy had been doing business with Enron for 15 years, Watson noted. "We know the company well. It's not like we just started fresh." And: "Culturally, it's a good fit. There has been great mutual respect between us over the years."

Watson's plan was to shut down everything at Enron that wasn't making money. He'd keep the gas and power traders but get rid of all the exotic stuff. Metals trading? There were 200 guys on the payroll, but the business wasn't making a dime. Pulp and paper? Weather derivatives? Freight? He'd shut them all down, too, and unload all the overseas assets, what little was left of broadband, and maybe even EES. Then he'd pay down the debt and recapitalize the operation, unwinding the entire off-balance-sheet mess.

What Watson didn't fully appreciate is how Enron felt about Dynegy. He'd assumed that his company would be greeted as a savior, the only thing keeping the sheriff from locking the doors. But many Enron employees—especially the traders—weren't seeing things that way at all. In truth, many at Enron didn't expect to ever work for Dynegy, merger or no merger. Some thought of Watson's company as nothing more than a temporary refuge. They'd play out the deal for a few months until some really *smart* money came along and paid Dynegy to walk away. Others figured after the merger closed, they'd ultimately wrest control by dint of stronger will and superior brainpower. "They were going to save us," says one Enron executive, "but typical of the Enron swagger and arrogance, we all just thought we'd take over Dynegy."

On many floors at 1400 Smith Street, in fact, Dynegy was regarded as simply *unworthy* of buying Enron. The traders were in open revolt from the moment they got wind of the deal. In truth, they'd been in a rage for weeks, furious about the events that sent the stock into a tailspin. Much of their pay was in Enron shares, and the company's string of ugly accounting revelations confirmed all their longstanding suspicions. As they saw it, they were being cheated—*robbed*—by the same corporate incompetents their business had been carrying for years.

It was especially galling to contemplate working for Dynegy, a competitor they'd always held in contempt, where multimillion-dollar bonuses were rare and where they simply wouldn't have the freedom to make glorious, outsize bets. "They sold us short," said one trader, describing the mood.

On a weekend, the brethren gathered in one trader's backyard, and started plotting. They *were* like a union. Now they had leverage, and they intended to use it. All of Enron's old guard—Rice and Pai, Baxter and Mark—had walked away with fortunes. They wanted theirs, too—but not in Dynegy stock. They didn't want to scuttle the company's chance of survival, and some even worried about looking greedy. But in the end, they were resolved: if they were going to stick it out and go to work for Dynegy, they told Whalley, they wanted to get big bonuses for the year—and they wanted them in cash, up front, *now.* Or they'd blow up the entire deal!

Whalley moved quickly to put down the rebellion. He proposed a big retention package (officially termed performance bonuses), providing payments to 76 key gas and power traders and originators that averaged close to $1 million apiece. When Watson heard, he erupted. "These are *performance* bonuses? The company's on its *ass!*" The pool was cut by a third, to a more modest $50 million, and Dynegy signed off. Still, at least 12 employees got more than $1 million; John Arnold topped the list at $8 million. (Whalley himself didn't take a bonus.)

And that wasn't the only surprise. Watson soon learned that Lay, under the change in control provision of his new contract, was entitled to a huge cash payout when the sale closed—$60.6 million. When the news broke, four days after the merger was announced, the outrage was instantaneous—from the traders. Whalley's top deputies, John Lavorato and Louise Kitchen, marched into Lay's office. "This is killing morale," they told him. With the stock's collapse, people had lost their retirement money and college savings; with the sale to Dynegy, there'd be layoffs. There's blood in the streets, they said—*you can't take $60 million.*

Lay was taken aback. "Well, is it okay if I call my wife first?" he asked. Lavorato and Kitchen stepped outside Lay's office. What they didn't know was that Lay needed the $60 million, that he was struggling to pay off his debts. But Lay did realize that he simply couldn't keep the money, not now. After ten minutes, Lay stepped out and told the traders he was giving up the payout.

Afterward the traders joked about using the $60 million to launch a contest to boost sagging morale. Each week, they'd award one lucky Enron employee $1 million. "Win Ken's money," they'd call it.

On Tuesday, November 13, more than $2 billion arrived on Enron's doorstep— $1.5 billion from Dynegy and $550 million from the first installment of its bank pipeline loans, which had taken a long time to finalize. The bank loans and Dynegy's money "should easily provide Enron with adequate liquidity to conduct business," Dynegy CFO Rob Doty noted a day earlier. "This should put any fears surrounding Enron's liquidity immediately to rest."

Enron executives agreed. Greg Whalley said the Dynegy deal provided the company with "ample liquidity." On a November 14 conference call with analysts, CFO McMahon pointedly denied Enron was experiencing a "cash drain." That very day, John Arnold instructed a trading subordinate to take a harder line with a counterparty asking for cash collateral. "Since ENE is flush with liquidity," Arnold wrote in an e-mail, "he should be very comfortable that we can pay our bills."

But just four days later, McMahon reported a very different situation to the Enron board. "Mr. McMahon reported liquidity was very tight," noted the minutes from the Sunday, November 18, meeting. Management was still chasing after more capital; McMahon "noted the need to extend the debt maturities of the Company." Treasurer Ray Bowen added that if Enron couldn't postpone $1 billion in debt coming due, "the Company could end the year with inadequate liquidity for its operations."

Even after the Dynegy deal was announced, cash continued to rush out the door. Trading partners refused to take Enron's credit, insisting on more collateral. The number of transactions on Enron Online plummeted—50 percent below normal levels—as counterparties struggled to cut their Enron exposure. Many companies stopped trading with Enron altogether. The company's European operation was deteriorating too. And EES reported trouble closing new contracts. Enron's earthward spiral was accelerating.

Desperate for a way to shift the momentum, Enron executives pressed the special investigative committee of the board—the one that had started work just three weeks earlier, with the help of special counsel Bill McLucas and his forensic accountants—to complete its work and issue its report. "These guys actually thought that the big-picture problems were not going to yield anything fundamentally wrong," recalls one of the investigators in amazement. "Everyone wanted us to come out and say to the masses outside of the operating room, 'We've opened the patient up, and everything's fine.' "

On Monday, November 19, McMahon and Whalley led a two-hour presentation to more than 200 bankers from 75 lenders at the Waldorf-Astoria Hotel in New York. Security guards checked identification at the doors. Once inside, the bankers received copies of a 65-page presentation, marked privileged and confidential.

The meeting was billed as a detailed review of Enron's problems and how management was tackling them. The idea was to air everything out, then enlist the banks' help in restructuring the company's crushing debt so that Enron would survive long enough to complete the Dynegy merger. By Enron's calculation, the company would need to repay more than $9.1 billion in debt by the end of 2002.

Much of the meeting served as a remarkably blunt repudiation of the Skilling era. Lay, whose credibility was shot, was absent; Whalley and McMahon wanted to present themselves as the company's new guard that could lead Enron out of this mess.

This accounting was far more candid than any that had come before. Enron, the presentation noted, was suffering from "a complete loss of investor and creditor confidence," "no access to capital," maturing debt that exceeded its cash flow, and "too much leverage tied to stock price." Enron had borrowed too much and issued too little equity, blown the money on bad investments, and suffered from "possible control failure." The off-balance-sheet debt, structured-finance deals, and prepays were all detailed.

Part of the problem, the bankers were told, was that large strategic transactions—Azurix, broadband, Dabhol, and New Power—had been exempt from RAC scrutiny. Buy's role had merely been to "highlight the risk" for senior management. Now—belatedly—that would change. Beginning in December, all Enron deals would require RAC approval. Only the board would be able to override a RAC veto.

Whalley and McMahon summed it all up by contrasting the "Old Enron" and "New Enron." The old Enron was characterized by a "deal shop mentality," a "black box" approach, "constant development of new businesses," and related-party deals; and it was "earnings-driven." The new Enron would offer "open communication," "financial transparency," an emphasis on cash, and a focus on the core business and completing the Dynegy merger.

But as Chuck Watson saw it, when Enron filed its third-quarter report with the SEC that day, it was strictly the old Enron. The 10-Q filing, which the company delayed five days to better sort out its various problems, contained three pieces of terrible news.

First, Enron's earnings for the third quarter were actually worse than previously reported—a loss of $664 million—and things also looked bleaker than expected for the fourth quarter. Enron attributed its latest problems to "a reduced level of transaction activity by trading counterparties." In other words, the trading business was drying up.

Then there were fresh surprises on the SPE front. The assets inside Whitewing had dropped far below the amount of its obligations; this meant Enron might have to take a new $700 million charge to earnings. Enron also revealed that a ratings downgrade one week earlier had triggered an obligation to repay $690 million in debt in an off-balance-sheet vehicle called Rawhide. For some reasons, this SPE—the creation of Michael Kopper and Ben Glisan—had been rigged to explode if S&P cut Enron to one step *above* junk grade. No one appeared to have even known about the problem until the default notice arrived. Now Enron had eight days to come up with the money.

And cash, the company also revealed, was in desperately short supply. Despite the $2 billion that had arrived on November 13, Enron had only $1.2 billion left. Counting the money it had in hand before getting the $2 billion, that meant Enron had burned through at least a billion dollars *in six days* and $2 billion in less than a month. Clearly Enron no longer had ample liquidity.

Watson went ballistic. He fired off a letter to Lay: "We have not been consulted in a timely manner regarding developments since November 9. We were not briefed in advance on the issues in your 10-Q. Our team had to make repeated phone calls to your finance and accounting officials in an attempt to obtain information. Some of the most significant information in the Q was never shown to us at all." Watson added: "We believe that Enron is going to have to do a far better job of communicating with us and with the marketplace for this transaction to reach a successful conclusion."

Watson also gave Lay a call, telling him: "You and I need to go to lunch, buddy." The Dynegy CEO was now harboring serious doubts about the deal. With this latest revelation, Enron was back on the ropes. Where had the $2 billion gone? Incredibly, Enron didn't seem to know. Enron quickly negotiated some extra time on the $690 million Rawhide debt, but the company would now need billions more. Where would it come from?

Watson was also embarrassed by the Enron disclosure. To the reporters who called Dynegy for comment, it was obvious that his team hadn't known this news was coming—and that's how they would cast it in their stories. It wasn't just bad faith; the news made Dynegy look foolish. Watson's company was using its credibility to prop up Enron's; now Enron's behavior was damaging Dynegy.

"I'm not used to people lying to me," Watson told Lay during a two-hour lunch in a private room at the downtown Coronado Club. "You guys need to get your act together, or this deal's not going to close." Suddenly all of Dynegy's "conservative" assumptions didn't look so conservative after all. By week's end, Enron's shares had fallen to $4.71. Goldman Sachs had downgraded both merger partners, but Dynegy's stock was down only 7 percent; apparently Wall Street now assumed that Watson would find a way out of the deal.

In addition, Watson was discovering that the Enron culture wasn't such a good fit after all. After getting a peek at Lay's new G-5 jet, he told a colleague, "I nearly had a heart attack." He kept learning about Enron executives who made twice what their Dynegy counterparts made. And as Enron started planning for layoffs, he heard about the company's extravagant severance plan: two weeks' pay for each year of service—plus *another* two weeks for each $10,000 of base pay. It wasn't hard to see where *some* of Enron's money went.

In the week after the merger was announced, Watson went on an East Coast swing to pitch the deal to analysts and investors. He took Whalley and Horton along with him. Everywhere they went, the Enron executives came under attack. They finally left the road show early and went home. "These people are hated worse than I thought," Watson later said.

The list of those suing the company grew to include Enron's own employees, who had seen much of their retirement-plan savings disappear. They claimed Enron's top executives had misled them about the riskiness of Enron shares and locked them into their plummeting holdings for a month while the company changed plan administrators. Between the company's savings and stock-ownership plans—60 percent of the total assets in both consisted of Enron stock— 20,000 Enron employees lost about $2 billion in 2001.

Some, however, did manage to get some of their savings out. During November, as Enron was spiraling downward, scores of current and retired executives who had participated in the company's deferred-compensation program—which set aside earnings in exchange for tax breaks—clamored for their money. Formal requests for such accelerated distributions were submitted by 211 plan participants. Some 126—personally approved by Whalley—received $53 million in cash. The rest are likely to get virtually nothing.

In the chaos of late November, everyone was maneuvering for position, elbowing for money that Enron didn't have. Jordan Mintz, for instance, was working on Thanksgiving Day when a call came in from a Lehman Brothers lawyer who'd been threatening to go to court to force immediate repayment on a $120 million Enron debt. "I just faxed you a draft complaint," he said. "You might want to take a look at it." Back off, Mintz finally told him. "You want to be the one to throw Enron into bankruptcy?" He didn't—Lehman was also serving as Dynegy's financial adviser.

Dynegy's deal team had responded to the startling Enron 10-Q by intensifying its diligence, fueled by rage. "We were ripshit," recalls one Dynegy adviser. Watson's side began to suspect that this was yet another Enron scam. Says an executive involved in the deal: "They thought they could just get our money and keep their game going."

Given all the anger, it was hard to see how the deal could still work. But Watson agreed to try, on one condition: Ken Lay had to go—immediately. Watson had concluded he needed his own team running Enron, right away. This was an audacious proposal; an acquirer usually keeps its hands off the target until the acquisition closes. Any change would require the agreement of the Enron board, which had long been in Lay's pocket. But Watson felt he had no choice. Without a different team in place, he figured, Enron would be dead and buried long before the deal could close.

Watson wasn't just after Lay's head; he wanted to replace Jim Derrick, the general counsel, and appoint a new CFO, too. He planned to bring in a cash-management team to get a handle on the finances and a divestiture team to start selling assets.

To replace Lay, Watson tapped a respected Houston executive named Joe Foster. Foster was a true heavyweight; he had served as chairman of Tenneco, then started his own oil and gas company, called Newfield Exploration, where he remained board chairman. The two men knew each other partly from working together on the board at Baker Hughes, where Foster had served as interim chairman and CEO. As Watson envisioned it, Foster would hold the same posts at Enron until the sale closed.

With a new executive team as a starting demand, Watson dispatched his CFO and investment bankers over the Thanksgiving weekend to a resort in Westchester County, New York, where everyone met to see if the deal—and Enron—could be saved. Enron sent its top executives: Lay, Whalley, and McMahon. Watson remained at his new vacation home in Cabo San Lucas, Mexico, monitoring events by phone. His number two, Bergstrom, stayed away, too.

By Sunday, it looked as if the pieces might come together. A little after 10 P.M., Lay convened a conference-call meeting to update his board. Because of the severe drop in the price of Enron shares, it had been clear that the deal would need to be recut just two weeks after it was struck. This also was extraordinary. The new exchange ratio—0.12 Dynegy share for each Enron share—valued Lay's company at about $4 billion, less than half the previous price. The board unanimously approved the new terms.

But the deal wasn't yet done, not by a long shot. To maintain an investment-rade rating, Enron needed new capital. The idea was that J. P. Morgan Chase, Citi, and Dynegy would each put up a third of the money. And that would be enough only if the company could reschedule all of the debt that was supposed to be paid off by the end of 2002. The banks would also need to convert much of their debt to equity. But after initially talking about big dollars—"We're in for a billion," Chase's Jimmy Lee proclaimed at one point—the banks danced away from making giant commitments even though closing the deal was supposed to bring them a giant payday. In addition to the $15 million advisory fee each had already received, J. P. Morgan Chase and Citi were due to get an additional $45 million apiece from Enron.

Finally, there was the issue of replacing Lay. The Enron CEO had dutifully explained the demand to his board. It made no decision that Sunday night.

On Monday, talks continued in Houston. Lay told his board that he thought the deal could still be saved. Now the rating agencies started expressing doubts. They noticed that the banks, for all their talk, weren't putting up the big money. They were worried about the deterioration of the trading business, which had generated almost all of Enron's reported profits. With Enron's crushing debt load, they didn't see how the company could borrow any more on its own. And without a big infusion of extra cash, they didn't see how Enron could pay off the $9 billion in debt coming due. Still, reluctant to provide the death blow, the rating agencies agreed to hold off on an immediate downgrade.

Then came the clincher: Lay wasn't going to leave. Enron was prepared to take Joe Foster on but only as an interim *vice chairman.* Watson called Foster to apologize; he thought Enron had already committed to make the move. "I'm embarrassed," Watson told him. "You shouldn't be embarrassed," Foster responded. "But good luck, buddy, because you're going to *need* it."

Talks among Dynegy, the banks, and the credit agencies continued late into the night on Tuesday, even after Watson went to bed telling his board and advisers that he'd pretty much made up his mind. The banks weren't stepping up the way Enron needed, he reasoned, thus making the repayment of all the debt impossible. It just wasn't going to work. And he'd also had a bellyful of Enron. He didn't trust any of its numbers, and he didn't want anything to do with its culture. "At the end," he later told friends, "you couldn't *give* it to me."

The next morning, Wednesday, November 28, as Watson waited, the rating agencies made the first move. S&P downgraded Enron two notches, deep into junk-company territory, citing its "loss of confidence that the Dynegy merger will be consummated." Moody's and Fitch soon followed. The downgrades immediately triggered $3.9 billion in Enron debt.

Watson placed a call to Lay to tell him the Dynegy board was terminating the deal. "I'm disappointed this didn't work out; I wish you the best of luck," Watson said. "I'm disappointed, too," Lay responded. "I'll go on to our other alternatives."

Enron Online shut down that morning. Enron shares closed the day at 61 cents.

At six o'clock that evening in Houston, Ken Lay met with the Enron board. He announced the demise of the deal with Dynegy and explained that it was likely to produce a court battle over the ownership of Enron's Northern Natural Gas pipeline, to which Dynegy was laying claim. A financial consultant offered the board a discussion "on alternatives to bankruptcy." Even now, for all its problems, the trading business remained Enron's great hope—or at least that's how Enron's board saw it. The adviser noted that his firm had contacted a number of prospects who might be interested in "financing or purchasing an interest." Treasurer Ray Bowen, who had quickly moved to more closely monitor the company's liquidity, noted that Enron's cash stood at $514 million.

Then Charles LeMaistre moved for approval of a new Enron Corp. Bonus Plan. This special fund, board minutes noted, would set aside $55 million "for the purposes of retaining key people given the uncertainty surrounding the Company's business and the need to maximize the value of the Company." The funds, which required the recipients to remain with the company for just 90 days, would be distributed to more than 500 employees. The biggest payments, of course, went to trading executives: Lavorato got $5 million, Louise Kitchen $2 million, and Jim Fallon $1.5 million.

There was one other piece of business. With the end of the Dynegy deal and Enron's fate uncertain, Ken Lay offered to fall on his sword. He "advised the Board that they continued to have the right to choose another chief executive officer for the Company and indicated that the Board should take whatever action is determined to be in the best interest of the Company," according to the minutes. "He stated the importance of the Board and the chief executive being very aligned going forward and stated his willingness to serve in that capacity."

With that, Lay left the room so the board could talk in private. A few minutes later, the directors adjourned, without taking any further action.

For four days, Enron lingered painfully in the land of the undead, and Ken Lay remained in open denial. "As you have heard," Lay advised employees, "Dynegy is terminating the merger agreement today. Among other things, this means we are now free to pursue other alternatives—which we are actively doing."

In the meantime, there would be some layoffs "to establish a more solid footing for the rest of Enron," Lay advised. "Although there are no guarantees, you should know that we are still in this fight and remain absolutely committed to protecting the value of the ongoing businesses of Enron. . . . Even six or so weeks ago, none of us could have imagined that we would be where we are today. We will not recover in six weeks what we have lost, but we will work to stabilize and rebuild this great company. As always I appreciate the extraordinary contributions each of you make. Thank you, Ken."

But as Enron's cash rapidly dwindled, others harbored few illusions. Enron's debt—both on the balance sheet and off—totaled a staggering $38 billion. On December 1, retail chief Dave Delainey responded to a former Enron executive who had e-mailed him with suggestions for making improvements at EES. "Dick, thanks for your e-mail," Delainey wrote. "I don't think I disagree with any of the points you made. . . . Unfortunately, a lot of these changes in thinking, sales and cost structure are too little too late. It is highly unlikely at this point that EES will exist beyond next week."

As Enron spiraled toward bankruptcy, its banks labored to minimize their losses. Marc Shapiro, the J. P. Morgan Chase executive, e-mailed two bank colleagues about his efforts to recover money from Enron before it was too late: "On several occasions during the week of November 26, I called Ken Lay, CEO of Enron, to request the return of excess collateral that Enron was holding for our account. My first call was midday on Wednesday, November 28. I requested return of about $50 mm, representing collateral held by Enron in excess of what we owed them. I next called late in the day on 11/29 to inquire about the status, and I indicated that they now owed us about $100 mm. Ken said that they were reviewing their cash position, and he did not know if they would have sufficient cash to pay. I called again at midday on Friday, only to be told that a decision would not be made until the end of day. Ken called on Friday afternoon to say that they did not have sufficient cash to return our collateral or anyone else's."

Sunday, December 2, was the day it finally happened. Electronically, at 2 A. M., Enron's lawyers filed the largest bankruptcy case in U.S. history. The Chapter 11 papers had been rushed together. Just days before, everyone was focused on the Dynegy deal. Once that collapsed, bankruptcy was really Enron's only alternative.

After the papers were filed, a six-man contingent from Enron flew to New York on Sunday afternoon for a routine court hearing on "initial orders," which would allow the bankrupt company the ability to conduct ordinary business, like paying employees and vendors. But this bankruptcy was obviously anything but routine. The courthouse was jammed with lawyers and press. Ken Lay flew up with the group—he felt it was the right thing to do—but it was decided that his presence in the courtroom would only turn the occasion into more of a circus.

The Enron contingent included CFO Jeff McMahon, Enron Wholesale general counsel Mark Haedicke, and associate counsel Richard Sanders. An adviser from the Blackstone Group and a Weil Gotshal lawyer were there, too. Lay was still in denial, a posture he maintained indefinitely. "We were the quickest ones in," he told the group, "and we'll be the quickest ones out."

They traveled on the crown jewel of the Enron air fleet, the $45 million G-5 corporate jet, whose interior design was personally selected by Lay. After the jet reached cruising altitude, Lay rose from his leather chair to serve everyone sandwiches and fruit, as he had so many times before. They stayed in New York's plush Four Seasons Hotel. Heading back to Houston, Sanders was sickened by the opulence of it all, the money Enron still spent freely when the company had just gone broke.

"We should have flown up on Southwest Airlines," he said, "and stayed at the Ramada Inn."

Isn't Anybody Sorry?

"Today's verdict is wrong. . . . The reality here is that this verdict represents only a technical conviction."

This statement was issued by Arthur Andersen on June 15, 2002, six months after Enron filed for bankruptcy. The firm had just been found guilty in a Houston courtroom of destroying evidence—those thousands of pages of Enron-related material that had been shredded at the prodding of David Duncan and Nancy Temple. As a firm, Andersen was finished even before the trial, decimated by client defections once it became clear that this time the Justice Department was not going to look the other way. Yet from the beginning through the bitter end, Andersen took the position that virtually everyone involved in the Enron scandal to one degree or another would embrace. Arthur Andersen claimed it was a victim—a victim of an unjust, politically motivated prosecution and a victim of Enron itself.

It was an astonishing comment on the mores of American life at the dawn of a new century. In the aftermath of one of the largest corporate scandals in American history, precious few were willing to concede that they had done anything wrong. Wasn't anybody sorry?

The after-the-fact rationalizations were strikingly similar to the mind-set that brought about the Enron scandal in the first place. All the arguments were narrow and rules based, legalistic in the hairsplitting sense of the word. Some were even arguably true—in the way that Enron itself defined truth. The larger message was that the wealth and power enjoyed by those at the top of the heap in corporate America—accountants, bankers, executives, lawyers, and members of corporate boards—demand no sense of broader responsibility. To accept these arguments is to embrace the notion that ethical behavior requires nothing more than avoiding the explicitly illegal, that refusing to see the bad things happening in front of you makes you innocent, and that telling the truth is the same thing as making sure that no one can prove you lied.

Take Arthur Andersen. In the firm's view, it was taken down by a trumped-up obstruction-of-justice charge—that mere "technical conviction." Sure, David Duncan pled guilty to obstruction of justice, but, as Andersen saw it, he knuckled under only because of the brute force of the federal government. No one had found Andersen guilty of fraudulent accounting. Even though Duncan was a government witness, he defended Enron's accounting.

Andersen argued that some dubious Enron accounting moves were business decisions made by the company and as such simply outside the province of the auditors. Duncan said at trial that the firm viewed LJM as a bad idea, but "we believed that this was an area of corporate governance, and as long as it had been thoroughly vented [*sic*] through the corporation, that was a business determination by Enron." Andersen viewed its responsibility as limited to ensuring that the transactions complied with individual accounting principles. And except where Enron lied, Andersen argues, they *did* technically comply. Through clever use of the rules, Enron transformed dogs into ducks.

Of course, this argument utterly ignores the larger picture, which is that those transactions added up to a completely illusory picture of Enron's financial health, to which Andersen was also legally required to attest. Shortly after the Enron bankruptcy, Andersen CEO Joseph Berardino said on NBC's *Meet the Press* that Enron had failed "because the economics didn't work." He was absolutely right. But who knew that better than Enron's own accountants? Didn't they have a basic responsibility to make sure those sorry economics were clearly disclosed to the investing public?

And so it went. The securities analysts who covered Enron—many of whom had buy recommendations on the stock right up until the end—claimed that Enron lied to them. "It now appears that some critical information on which I relied for my analysis of Enron was inaccurate or incomplete," CSFB's Curt Launer told Congress. The analysts for Standard & Poor's and Moody's offered a similar lament, insisting that the information they were given justified Enron's investment-grade debt ratings. To be sure, Enron, with Andersen's assistance, did everything it could to camouflage the truth, but there was more than enough on the public record to raise the hackles of any self-respecting analyst. Analysts are supposed to dive into a company's financial documents, pore over the footnotes, get past management's assurances—and even get past accounting obfuscations. Their job, in short, is to *analyze*. If the analysts covering Enron had done that, how could they not have seen a very different story? The short sellers certainly did.

Then there were the banks and investment banks—the best supporting actors of the Enron scandal—without whose zealous participation Enron's financial shenanigans would simply not have been possible. Hauled before the Senate Permanent Subcommittee on Investigations in the summer of 2002, the bankers could only duck and weave, always denying responsibility. "We have been one of the parties substantially harmed by its [Enron's] failure," said a J. P. Morgan Chase banker. Citigroup said it believed "Enron was making good-faith accounting judgments that were reviewed by Arthur Andersen, which was then the world's premier auditing firm," and that the "Audit Committee of Enron's board exercised meaningful supervision over the company's accounting policies and procedures." In other words, it wasn't our responsibility.

By mid-2003, as the drumbeat of criticism—and a string of investigations—intensified, there were some hints of remorse. At its annual meeting in May, J. P. Morgan Chase issued a statement saying, "We have seen far more than the usual number of serious accidents at the intersection of Wall Street and Main. And our financial institutions, including J. P. Morgan Chase, must take their share of responsibility for that." Two months later, J. P. Morgan Chase and Citigroup agreed to pay a combined $286 million for "helping to commit a fraud" on Enron's shareholders, as SEC enforcement chief Stephen Cutler told reporters. The two banks also agreed to ensure that their clients who used complex financial structures account for them in ways that investors could readily understand. Investors will have to wait until the next bull market to gauge whether anything has really changed.

In 2003, the SEC charged Merrill Lynch and four executives, including Schuyler Tilney, with aiding and abetting securities fraud at Enron. All four executives left Merrill. Tilney was fired after refusing to testify to the SEC and Justice Department. Merrill agreed to pay $80 million in fines and penalties without acknowledging that it had done anything wrong.

Here's the most amazing denial of all: Even Enron's board of directors—the people formally responsible with serving as a check on management and guarding the interests of shareholders—disclaimed any responsibility. The board says it relied on the advice of Enron's accountants and lawyers—and *that's* where the blame really lies. In response to bitter criticism from Congress, the directors issued a report claiming that they "in good faith and prudently performed their fiduciary duties based on the information provided to them." As for all Enron's accounting contortions, the audit committee "knew that Arthur Andersen was paid specifically to ensure that the 'innovative structures' conformed to GAAP, and hence took comfort that Arthur Andersen 'was OK' with them."

Some board members point the finger at Enron's management. Longtime director John Duncan told investigators after the bankruptcy that he thought "Skilling was brilliant. He was extremely articulate and always seemed to have the right answer." But, the investigators continued, "Duncan has discovered many facts that make him believe that Skilling did not keep the Board fully informed. He cannot recall any discussions with Skilling that the company was encountering or was susceptible to any financial problems." Another director privately puts it this way: "The board was duped. I don't see any other answer. These things could not have happened without Skilling being a part of it." The board's lawyers have reread every presentation Enron executives gave to them, adds a director. "There was nothing there for the board to have reason to suspect something was wrong," he says. "A few bad apples spoiled the barrel."

Of course, there was plenty there to inspire the board to ask tougher questions, had it been so inclined. Was it really "prudent" for Enron, with its lack of cash flow, to have $38 billion of debt? Wasn't the directors' responsibility broader than merely listening to the "information provided to them?" According to that narrow, legalistic mind-set, the answer was simple: no.

No matter who you asked, it was always somebody else's fault.

■ ■ ■

For some, however, a reckoning loomed.

As we write this, in the summer of 2003, the Enron case is far from closed. Bill Lerach, the fearsome plaintiff's lawyer, is leading a huge lawsuit on behalf of Enron shareholders. Other civil suits seek to recover hundreds of millions of dollars on behalf of Enron employees who lost everything in their retirement accounts when the company went bankrupt. The fact that their accounts were frozen for weeks while the stock plummeted and top executives had walked off with fortunes became the focus of national outrage. Such cases usually settle for hefty sums, though individuals typically wind up with just pennies on the dollar.

The SEC, which already has filed several cases, continues to investigate. The Labor Department has filed suit against Enron, its former executives, and the board for failing to properly oversee employee retirement plans. Employees have filed claims to recover millions in bonuses paid to company executives. It appeared likely that the first suit to go to trial would be a separate state case filed by 12 residents of tiny Brenham, Texas, who bought shares of Enron after hearing Ken Lay tout the company in a speech before a local civic group.

But the biggest hammer belongs to the Justice Department, which has charged more than a dozen individuals, with promises of more to come. The first indictment was filed against the three NatWest bankers who had helped Fastow carry out his Southampton scheme. Then, on October 31, 2002, almost a year after the Enron board discovered his LJM earnings, Andy Fastow was indicted on 78 counts of fraudulent conduct. Six months later, the Justice Department indicted Ben Glisan for his involvement in Fastow's schemes and a midlevel Global Finance executive named Dan Boyle for his role in the Nigerian barge deal. The government charged Lea Fastow with conspiracy to commit wire fraud, money laundering, and filing a false income tax return in connection with the alleged kickbacks in her husband's partnership deals.

And it indicted seven former Enron Broadband executives. Ken Rice, Kevin Hannon, Joe Hirko, and two others were charged with fraud and insider trading, accused of lying to the investing public about broadband's technological capabilities to inflate market valuations of the business while collectively selling more than $150 million worth of stock. Kevin Howard and Michael Krautz were indicted for the Braveheart deal.

Most of the Enron executives charged by the government vowed to fight in court. Not all of them, though. Michael Kopper and Tim Belden both cut deals with prosecutors in which they pled guilty and promised to cooperate in return for leniency: this provided the feds with a critical window into the complex worlds of Global Finance and California energy trading. Both agreed to disgorge millions in ill-gotten gains—in Kopper's case, $12 million; in Belden's case, $2.1 million. When the former Portland trading chief appeared in court, he told the judge that "I did it because I was trying to maximize profits for Enron." His lawyer later said that his tactics were just the way Enron had trained Belden to do business. (Another Portland-based trader also pled guilty; a third, who maintains his innocence, has been indicted.)

Most former Enron employees voiced outrage upon learning how their company remained such a high-flyer for so long. Their faith in Enron—their pride in working for the coolest company in America—had been shattered. It was as though they were all now wearing a scarlet E. And it was far more than just a matter of wounded pride. Thousands had lost most or all of their retirement savings, which they'd invested in Enron stock at the urging of Lay and Skilling. Some were too old to start again.

But in some cases, the anger was mixed with rationalizations—rationalizations that, like those of Enron's enablers, surely contain shards of truth but ignore the larger unpleasant reality. Some took the view that the government was going after Enron executives because it needed scalps to show that it was serious about corporate crime. A more extreme version of this is that Enron's sins were not incompetence and fraud but rather innovation and free spiritedness. Just as Michael Milken's defenders in the 1980s claimed that he was being prosecuted because he was a threat to staid old corporate America, so now did Enron's defenders make the same claim. "You can always tell who the pioneers are, because they're the ones with arrows in their backs," became their refrain.

Still, it was hard for some to get beyond the Enron version of reality: if it looked good on paper, then it really was good. Sitting in the coffeeshop on the ground floor of Enron House in London just a few days before Enron filed for bankruptcy, a twentysomething accountant who had worked on the Raptors lamented that he and his colleagues had done exactly what they were supposed to do. Their clever creation had successfully protected Enron's earnings until that fateful October 16 write-off. Listening to the accountant, an older colleague could contain himself no longer: "We're going to go bankrupt!" he sputtered.

Even those who'd been indicted had defenders. For instance, many former Enron Broadband executives were appalled at the indictments of Rice, Hirko, and the others who were accused of hyping the business, then selling their stock before the truth came out. According to this view, what the Enron executives had done was nothing worse than what dozens of CEOs in Silicon Valley had done—where people who worked for companies with far less to offer than Enron fed Internet hype, cashed out, and walked away unscathed.

As for Andy Fastow, he has his own line of defense, which pointed the finger right back at Enron. The signals reporters got from his camp strongly suggest that he was embittered at being made the fall guy for the Enron fiasco. Like everyone else, he had his own rationalization. His went something like this: Skilling and the other Enron executives created businesses that were either huge cash drains or didn't make nearly as much money as Enron needed them to. Fastow was charged with the impossible task of raising the capital that allowed the company to appear successful and kept the stock price going up. He did precisely what he was asked to do.

What's more, Fastow was far from the only one who benefited from the convoluted financings he cooked up. *Everyone* at Enron benefited: the stock options worth millions, the excessive pay, the Enron lifestyle were all made possible by Fastow. In Fastow's view, every Enron millionaire owed him a debt of gratitude. And yet they were all now throwing him to the wolves.

Those who want to blame all of Enron's woes on the greedy former CFO claim that Enron was a good business brought down by Andy Fastow. But that was never true. Ultimately, Enron was a bad business that was, for a time, propped up by Andy Fastow.

Back in Houston, the immediate aftermath of Enron's bankruptcy was nothing short of surreal. Lawyers of all sizes and stripes descended on 1400 Smith Street, along with dozens of FBI agents who confiscated hard drives, hauled off boxes of documents, and excitedly pawed through Fastow's office in search of the smoking gun. The Reverend Jesse Jackson flew into the media circus to help console Enron employees and to pray with Ken Lay. One day when Lay was still ensconced in his fiftieth-floor office, Jackson paid him a visit. On his way out, he discovered more tortured souls, as an Enron lawyer named Rob Walls discovered when he walked out of his office to find Jackson in a prayer circle, holding hands with Enron general counsel Jim Derrick, several executive assistants, and a half-dozen FBI agents.

The lowest point of all surely came in late January, when word emerged of Cliff Baxter's suicide. His body was discovered less than two months after the bankruptcy filing and ten days after Sherron Watkins's letter, released by congressional investigators, threw the unwelcome media spotlight in his direction by saying he'd "complained mightily" about LJM. Baxter's handwritten suicide note, left on the dashboard of his wife's car, parked in the family garage, was ordered released over the protests of his widow. "I am so sorry for this," he wrote. "I feel I just can't go on. I have always tried to do the right thing but where there was once great pride now it's gone. I love you and the children so much. I just can't be any good to you or myself. The pain is overwhelming. Please try to forgive me. Cliff."

But in time, the furor quieted down, and Enron entered that weird land where bankrupt companies go. Thousands of people still showed up to work: someone had to sort out what little was left for creditors, and someone had to operate the pipelines and power plants around the globe. In mid-2002, Enron wrote down the value of its assets, which it had calculated at $62 billion at the time of the bankruptcy, by a stunning $14 billion. According to the company's new post-bankruptcy management, some $3 billion resulted from "possible accounting errors or irregularities," in part due to Mariner and Sithe. Overall, it appears that Enron's businesses lost well over $10 billion in cash over the course of their life.

In July 2003, Enron finally announced its reorganization plan. It planned to spin off two new companies to shareholders. One, dubbed CrossCountry Energy, would be built around the remaining North American gas pipelines. The other, named Prisma Energy, would hold 19 of the international assets, including much of the South American business but not including Dabhol. Enron had tried to find buyers for many of these assets, but there were no takers at an acceptable price. Still, in the end, hard assets were what Enron had left. To Rebecca Mark, this offered an odd sort of validation. "Enron International survived," she told friends. "We left something of value behind."

When the trading business was put up for sale, the traders thought there would be a fierce auction for their talents. As one trader put it in an e-mail to John Lavorato, "So many banks, so little game." The traders wanted their Enron salaries preserved and were agitiating for a bonus pool of at least 15 percent of pretax profits. Tim Belden, who had hired a lawyer even before Enron went bankrupt, wanted a buyer to indemnify up to $4 million of his 2001 compensation. As he wrote in an e-mail, "it is unlikely I would be here today if it weren't for the collective comp conveyed to me."

In mid-January 2002, UBS Warburg announced that it was buying the Enron trading business, though it wasn't exactly paying top dollar. The existing trading book stayed at Enron, and, in fact, UBS didn't pay anything at all for the 650 Enron traders. It simply gave Enron the right to a portion of the traders' profits—one third for the first five years—while assuming none of Enron's past, present, or future liabilities. Whalley resigned his post at Enron to join UBS.

As always, the traders cut a good deal for themselves. They were guaranteed $11 million in first-year bonuses, $6 million of which was paid by Enron. Enron itself hasn't done as well. Through the summer of 2003, UBS did not pay a penny to Enron. By August 2002, UBS was laying off traders. By early 2003, there were so few traders left—only about 70—that UBS shuttered the Houston operation and moved the trading desk to Stamford, Connecticut, where the firm's other commodity trading operations are based.

Part of the problem was that traders at other companies didn't want to do business with the former Enron traders. But the far larger problem was that there simply wasn't much business to be done anymore. The energy trading business, which only a few years earlier seemed so prosperous, largely evaporated amid a storm of revelations about inflated volumes and price manipulation. Partly because of the rampant abuse of mark-to-market accounting, it was an industry that had never been firmly grounded in economic reality. One by one, many of the energy traders announced they were cutting back on trading or abandoning the business entirely. The list included Dynegy. That company was already sinking under the weight of skepticism about its business when the *Wall Street Journal* revealed that it had set up its own special-purpose entity to create cash flow. Two months later, Chuck Watson resigned as CEO. Later, Dynegy paid a $5 million fine to settle charges that it had manipulated natural-gas prices.

"When a whole industry collapses in a brutally ugly way, you look back and wonder," says a former Enron managing director. "I'll always wonder how much of what we did there was real."

■   ■   ■

Ken Lay wasn't about to take the blame, either.

In the postbankruptcy Enron, he installed Beth Tilney—yes, that Beth Tilney—as the head of PR, above Mark Palmer; Tilney and Lay suggested that Palmer pitch stories to the media that would put Lay in a better light. An exasperated Palmer finally told them: "Forty billion dollars in obligations is a PR problem, but it wasn't caused by PR."

On January 23, 2002, Lay was forced to resign as Enron's chairman and CEO, though he clung to a board seat until early February, when the special board committee issued its report, noting that Lay, as Enron's CEO, was "in effect, the captain of the ship," with "ultimate responsibility" for what happened at the company. (In the wake of that report, Causey and Buy were both fired.) In the ensuing months, although Lay made virtually no public statements himself, he conveyed, through various surrogates, his continuing belief that he was being wronged by a vicious media and that he was a good man who'd been taken advantage of by corrupt underlings. He had trusted Arthur Andersen and Vinson & Elkins to tell him if there were problems, his surrogates insisted, but they never had. As for the Justice Department, Lay showed visitors a sign he kept in his private office: "Cowboy's logic: Getting up a lynch party is not group therapy."

In February 2002, Lay's wife, Linda, appeared on the *Today* show in defense of her husband. The Lay family had "gone down with the ship," had "lost everything," and was "battling for liquidity," she said tearfully. Her appearance was widely ridiculed, for good reason. The Lays still owned millions in real estate, much of it not even on the market. Ken and Linda also continued to live in their exclusive condominium, and Lay still enjoyed his private office on the top floor of a building in River Oaks, where he was attended to by a small personal staff. He still owes $7 million on his Enron line of credit.

Although he eventually began to emerge again in Houston society, it wasn't the way it used to be. How could it be? Houston had taken immense pride in Enron, and its fall hit the city hard. Lay remained under intense criminal investigation. While many Houstonians found it hard to see him as a crook, they also found it hard to reconcile his secret stock sales with his preachy morality. And of course, Lay's flaws as a businessman could no longer be hidden behind Enron's glossy facade.

Then there was Jeff Skilling. In the months following Enron's bankruptcy, Skilling's performance was one of the stranger parts of the whole affair. "I had no idea that the company was in anything but excellent shape," he told the *New York Times* in a December 2001 interview. "In the last two months, I've gone through everything in my mind that was done when I was there that could have been related to this. . . . After much soul searching, given the information at the time, I would not have done anything different."

In the months to come, Skilling denied knowledge of all sorts of things, from Fastow's scamming of Enron to issues as basic as the triggers in the Marlin and Osprey debt. He claimed that despite his Harvard MBA, he didn't know enough about accounting to answer detailed questions. He counted on those under him to make sure it was all right.

Skilling was the one Enron executive who did not take the Fifth Amendment before Congress, though his lawyer advised him to do so. Instead, he put forth his theory that Enron was brought down by a classic run on the bank. He has been making that case ever since. "There was a liquidity problem, and people got scared," he has said. "That's what caused the problem. All the rest of this is ridiculous."

Skilling has insisted that Enron's mark-to-market accounting was conservative, that those who claim otherwise are just disgruntled accounting clerks, and that the values in the trading book were "pure gold." It was natural for Enron to experience some failures, he has claimed. "How many business have *you* started?" he rhetorically asked his critics.

If Skilling has taken any lessons away from Enron's collapse, they are different lessons than others have come away with. He does not seem to have any remorse about his own actions, any sense that he hired the wrong people, got into the wrong businesses, or emphasized the wrong values. The fault, in his view, lies in a world that did not and will not appreciate the sheer newness of what Enron was trying to do.

As for the Justice Department, which was clearly gunning for him, he continued to rail to friends that it was a "witch hunt" and an "absolute travesty." It was inconceivable to him that the government could come up with a legitimate case against him. "Show me one fucking transaction that the accountants and the attorneys didn't sign off on," he told people. "If they concoct some bullshit, they're going to have a fight on their hands, because it—is—not—there!" He added: "Until the day I die, I'm going to fight this thing."

Above all else, Jeff Skilling believes this: "They killed a great company."

INDEX